A LIBRARY OF LITERARY CRITICISM

Leonard S. Klein
General Editor

A Library
of Literary Criticism

VOLUME I

American
British
Irish
German
Austrian
and Swiss
Dramatists

Frederick Ungar Publishing Co., New York

MAJOR
MODERN
DRAMATISTS

Compiled and edited by
RITA STEIN

FRIEDHELM RICKERT

PN
1861
.M27
1984
V I
150599
2 a. 1991

Library of Congress Cataloging in Publication Data
Main entry under title:

Major modern dramatists.

(A Library of literary criticism)
Contents: v. 1. American, British, Irish, German, Austrian, and Swiss
dramatists.
Includes index.
1. Drama—20th century—History and criticism—Hand-
books, manuals, etc.   I. Stein, Rita.   II. Rickert,
Friedhelm.   III. Series.
PN1861.M27   1983   809.2′04   78-4310
ISBN 0-8044-3267-8

CONTENTS

INTRODUCTION

The two volumes of *Major Modern Dramatists* are the first in the Library of Literary Criticism series to present writers from the point of view of genre rather than nationality or language. Because of the popularity of both graduate and undergraduate courses in modern drama, it was felt that such a presentation would serve a useful purpose. No one survey of modern drama in any university will cover all the playwrights included here, but almost all will come up at least as points of reference or suggestions for further reading or outside papers. The focus on major figures has permitted more extensive coverage for each writer than in other volumes in the series.

What does "major" mean? The criteria for inclusion here are, of course, quality and talent, but also an international reputation, translation and performance of plays outside the writer's own country, and the existence of a substantial body of serious criticism. In a few instances, the compilers of this reference work have chosen to cover an established playwright still not well enough known in the United States because of insufficient or inadequate English translations.

In the context of these volumes, and in terms of dramatic literature in general, "modern" applies to the drama that began with Ibsen's plays, including late-nineteenth-century realism and all the twentieth-century continuations of and reactions to it. Inevitably there will be objections about some omissions, both of older playwrights whose reputations were substantial in their day and of younger ones who seem to be establishing major reputations now. Space limitations and/or the lack of extensive writing about these authors are the reasons for their exclusion. Additionally, the volumes are limited to "Western" dramatists; the scope of coverage does not include Asian and African playwrights, although the editors acknowledge their growing importance.

The principal aim of this work is to give an overview of the critical reception of the dramatist from the beginning of his career up to the present time by presenting excerpts from reviews, articles, and books. The writers are grouped by region and arranged alphabetically within each section. The critical excerpts are arranged chronologically. A list of periodicals with an explanation of abbreviations is at the front of each volume. Excerpts translated into English expressly for this series are indicated by a dagger at the end of the credit line. In the case of plays written in a language other than English, a literal translation of the title or the title of the published English version closest to a literal translation is given. In the back of each volume is a list of Plays Mentioned giving full information about original titles, dates, and published translations.

The compilers wish to thank the many copyright holders who have granted permission to reprint the selections in these books. A list of acknowledgments will be found at the back of each volume, followed by an index to critics.

DRAMATISTS INCLUDED, VOLUME I

AMERICAN

Albee, Edward
Hellman, Lillian
Miller, Arthur
Odets, Clifford
O'Neill, Eugene
Wilder, Thornton
Williams, Tennessee

BRITISH AND IRISH

Behan, Brendan
Bond, Edward
Coward, Noel
Eliot, T. S.
Galsworthy, John
O'Casey, Sean
Osborne, John
Pinter, Harold
Shaw, Bernard
Stoppard, Tom

Storey, David
Synge, John Millington
Wesker, Arnold
Wilde, Oscar
Yeats, William Butler

GERMAN, AUSTRIAN, AND SWISS

Brecht, Bertolt
Dürrenmatt, Friedrich
Frisch, Max
Hacks, Peter
Handke, Peter
Hauptmann, Gerhart
Hochhuth, Rolf
Hofmannsthal, Hugo von
Kaiser, Georg
Schnitzler, Arthur
Wedekind, Frank
Weiss, Peter
Zuckmayer, Carl

PERIODICALS USED

Where no abbreviation is indicated, the periodical references are used in full.

Adelphi	The Adelphi (London)
AGR	American German Review (Philadelphia)
AHR	American Historical Review (Washington, D.C.)
AM	The American Mercury (New York)
AS	The American Scholar (Washington, D.C.)
Atlantic	The Atlantic Monthly (Boston)
	Berliner Börsen-Courier
BkmL	The Bookman (London)
BA	Books Abroad (Norman, Okla.)
BR	The British Review (London)
BuR	Bucknell Review (Lewisburg, Pa.)
ChiR	Chicago Review
CE	College English (Urbana, Ill.)
Cmty	Commentary (New York)
Com	Commonweal (New York)
CompD	Comparative Drama (Kalamazoo, Mich.)
CLS	Comparative Literature Studies (Urbana, Ill.)
CQ	The Critical Quarterly (Manchester)
	Deutsche Allgemeine Zeitung (Berlin)
DU	Der Deutschunterricht (Stuttgart)
	Drama (London)
DramaS	Drama Survey (Minneapolis)
	Edinburgh Review
ETJ	Educational Theatre Journal (Washington, D.C.)
	Encore (London)
Enc	Encounter (London)
EngR	The English Review (London)
	Esquire (New York)
EG	Études germaniques (Paris)
Fortnightly	The Fortnightly Review (London)
Forum	The Forum (New York)
FMLS	Forum for Modern Language Studies (St. Andrews, Scotland)
FH	Frankfurter Hefte (Frankfurt am Main)
	Frankfurter Zeitung (Frankfurt am Main)
	The Freeman (New York)
GL&L	German Life and Letters (Oxford)
GQ	German Quarterly (Cherry Hill, N.J.)
GerSR	German Studies Review (Tempe, Ariz.)
GR	Germanic Review (New York)

Guardian	The Guardian (Manchester, subsequently London)
	Hannoversches Tageblatt (Hannover)
Harper's	Harper's Magazine (New York)
	The Hound & Horn (Boston)
HudR	The Hudson Review (New York)
JEGP	Journal of English and Germanic Philology (Urbana, Ill.)
JML	Journal of Modern Literature (Philadelphia)
London	London Magazine
LM	The London Mercury
MR	The Massachusetts Review (Amherst)
MAL	Modern Austrian Literature (Pittsburgh)
MD	Modern Drama (Toronto)
MLN	Modern Language Notes (Baltimore)
MLQ	Modern Language Quarterly (Seattle)
MLR	Modern Language Review (London)
ML	Modern Languages (London)
Monat	Der Monat (Hamburg)
	Monatshefte (Madison, Wis.)
	Mosaic (Winnipeg, Man.)
Nation	The Nation (New York)
NRs	Neue Rundschau (West Berlin)
NewL	The New Leader (New York)
NR	The New Republic (Washington, D.C.)
NS	The New Statesman (London)
NSN	The New Statesman and Nation (London)
NYRB	New York Review of Books
NY	The New Yorker
NAR	North American Review (Boston)
Obs	The Observer (London)
	Pacific Spectator (Stanford, Cal.)
PR	Partisan Review (Boston)
	Players (DeKalb, Ill.)
PP	Plays and Players (London)
PMLA	Publications of the Modern Language Association of America (New York)
	Poet Lore (Boston)
	Poetry (Chicago)
PrS	Prairie Schooner (Lincoln, Neb.)
	Preuves (Paris)
QQ	Queen's Quarterly (Kingston, Ont.)
Reporter	The Reporter (New York)
SR	Saturday Review (New York)
SR (London)	The Saturday Review (London)

	Scrutiny (Cambridge, Eng.)
	Seminar (Vancouver, B.C.)
SewR	Sewanee Review (Sewanee, Tenn.)
SuF	Sinn und Form (East Berlin)
SAQ	South Atlantic Quarterly (Durham, N.C.)
SHR	Southern Humanities Review (Auburn, Ala.)
SoR	The Southern Review (Baton Rouge, La.)
SWR	Southwest Review (Dallas)
Spec	The Spectator (London)
SP	Studies in Philology (Chapel Hill, N.C.)
	Symposium (Syracuse, N.Y.)
TM	Les temps moderne (Paris)
TSLL	Texas Studies in Literature and Language (Austin)
ThA	Theatre Arts (New York)
TheatreQ	Theatre Quarterly (London)
TW	Theatre World (London)
	The Times (London)
TLS	The Times Literary Supplement (London)
TC	Twentieth Century (London)
TDR	Tulane Drama Review (New Orleans)/The Drama Review (New York)
UDR	University of Dayton Review (Dayton, Ohio)
VV	The Village Voice (New York)
VQR	Virginia Quarterly Review (Charlottesville, Va.)
WB	Weimarer Beiträge (East Berlin)
WSCL	Wisconsin Studies in Contemporary Literature (Madison, Wis.)
YFS	Yale French Studies (New Haven)
YR	The Yale Review (New Haven)
Zeit	Die Zeit (Hamburg)

A LIBRARY OF LITERARY CRITICISM

Leonard S. Klein
General Editor

AMERICAN DRAMATISTS

RITA STEIN, EDITOR

ALBEE, EDWARD (1928 –   )

Edward Albee . . . comes into the category of the Theatre of the Absurd precisely because his work attacks the very foundations of American optimism. His first play, *The Zoo Story,* which shared the bill at the Provincetown Playhouse with Beckett's *Krapp's Last Tape,* already showed the forcefulness and bitter irony of his approach. In the realism of its dialogue and in its subject matter—an outsider's inability to establish genuine contact with a dog, let alone any human being—*The Zoo Story* is closely akin to the work of Harold Pinter. But the effect of this brilliant one-act duologue between Jerry, the outcast, and Peter, the conformist bourgeois, is marred by its melodramatic climax; when Jerry provokes Peter into drawing a knife and then impales himself on it, the plight of the schizophrenic outcast is turned into an act of sentimentality, especially as the victim expires in touching solicitude and fellow feeling for his involuntary murder.

But after an excursion into grimly realistic social criticism [*The Death of Bessie Smith*] . . . Albee has produced a play that clearly takes up the style and subject matter of the Theatre of the Absurd and translates it into a genuine American idiom. *The American Dream* . . . fairly and squarely attacks the ideals of progress, optimism, and faith in the national mission, and pours scorn on the sentimental ideals of family life, togetherness, and physical fitness; the euphemistic language and unwillingness to face the ultimate facts of the human condition that in America, even more than in Europe, represent the essence of bourgeois assumptions and attitudes. . . . The language of *The American Dream* resembles that of Ionesco in its masterly combination of clichés. But these clichés, in their euphemistic, baby-talk tone, are as characteristically American as Ionesco's are French. The most disagreeable verities are hidden behind the corn-fed cheeriness of advertising jingles and family-magazine unctuousness. There are very revealing contrasts in national coloring of different versions of the absurd cliché—the mechanical hardness of Ionesco's French platitudes; the flat, repetitive obtuseness of Pinter's English nonsense dialogue; and the oily glibness and sentimentality of the American cliché in Albee's promising and brilliant first example of an American contribution to the Theatre of the Absurd.

Martin Esslin. *The Theatre of the Absurd* (Garden City, N.Y., Doubleday, 1961), pp. 225–27

Strangely enough, though there is no question of his sincerity, it is Albee's skill which at this point most troubles me. It is as if his already practiced hand had learned too soon to make an artful package of venom. For the overriding passion of the play [*Who's Afraid of Virginia Woolf?*] is venomous. There is no reason why anger should not be dramatized. I do not object to Albee's being "morbid," for as the conspicuously healthy William James once said, "morbid-mindedness ranges over a wider scale of experience than healthy-mindedness." What I do object to in his play is that its disease has become something of a brilliant formula, as slick and automatic as a happy entertainment for the trade. The right to pessimism has to be earned within the artistic terms one sets up; the pessimism and rage of *Who's Afraid of Virginia Woolf?* are immature. Immaturity coupled with a commanding deftness is dangerous.

What justifies this criticism? The characters have no life (or texture) apart from the immediate virulence of their confined action or speech. George is intended to represent the humanist principle in the play. But what does he concretely want? What traits, aside from his cursing the life he leads, does he have? Almost none. Martha and George, we are told, love each other after all. How? That she can't bear being loved is a psychological aside in the play, but how is her love for anything, except for her "father fixation," and some sexual dependence on George, actually embodied? What interests—even petty—do they have or share? Vividly as each personage is drawn, they all nevertheless remain flat—caricatures rather than people. Each stroke of dazzling color is superimposed on another, but no further substance accumulates. We do not actually identify with anyone except editorially. Even the non-naturalistic figures of Beckett's plays have more extension and therefore more stature and meaning. The characters in Albee's *The Zoo Story* and *The Death of Bessie Smith* are more particularized.

Harold Clurman. *Nation*. Oct. 27, 1962, p. 274

Sterility is our enlightenment, Albee's surprise. And in looking back upon [*Who's Afraid of Virginia Woolf?*], we find that the difference is all in ourselves. We feel something we didn't feel when the play was in the cruel fertile land: compassion. Every time the little bugger is mentioned, we hear "barrenness" instead. And Martha and George become less horrible. Anyway their blackness is less black, somewhat grayer. But our compassion comes only through our rewriting of the play—and evidently Albee did not want this or he would have done it himself. What he allows us, in fact, after the surprise, is pity, and the feeling of pity is always a kind of judgment. Our feelings tell us the truth. The playwright has walked out on stage with bench and gavel, full of self-righteousness, and has passed sentence on his characters: "Martha and George, for abominable behavior, for immoral actions, for being wicked parents and evil people, I hereby sentence you to sterility by retroaction." They become sterile by decree, not by virtue of dramatic reality. And no sooner do we feel this than we are aware that he has been imposing punishments on these people from the beginning—the chiefest of them being the length of time they must appear before us naked, deceitful, gruesome. It is only then, after the completion of their tortuous punishment, that the spectator is permitted some pity. And Martha and George go hobbling off alone, barren. No wonder the play is successful on Broadway; it provides the audience with a guided tour away from, and safely back at last into, the most repugnant kind of puritanical priggishness. The morality of *Virginia Woolf* is one which conceives that folly, desperation, frustration, hate, are not themselves their greatest penalties—as virtue is said to be its own reward—but must be judged and punished from above, beyond, without.

With our new knowledge, we look back upon Honey and Nick, and what do we see? The same unlovable pair. But now perhaps we see something we noticed earlier in a clearer light. In literature, as in life, unlovable people often get that way because they are unloved. And Mr. Albee does not love Honey and Nick; he hates them, maybe even more than he hates the other couple. He has pursued them through the play, tirelessly, relentlessly, whispering and shouting dark accusations, and although he has imposed upon them the same sentence given to Martha and George, he has done it so deviously that they can never come to Edward Albee's kind of grace—pity from the audience.

Alfred Chester. Cmty. April, 1963, pp. 300–301

Well, I felt privileged by the humor in [*Who's Afraid of Virginia Woolf?*] because it is the humor of my privileged intellectual class. But that considerable part of Mr. Albee's audience which is not of the professional intellectual class felt privileged, too, because it was assumed of these playgoers, no less than of myself, that they could enjoy Martha and George's sophisticated idiom. The play made them a gift of status. It permanently added to their sense of having successfully tuned in on a hitherto closed circuit.

And it is not only Mr. Albee's wit that offers a new inside track to his large public of outsiders. The content of his play represents a view of the world that, as I say, has for several years now been the informing view of advanced literature in the democracies, the "inside" view. Not only our own beats and hipsters or the angry young men, as they are called, of England or the New Left of America and England, but advanced writing in France, in Italy, even (we now learn) in Germany—all of these are committed to the idea that modern life is a pattern of meaningless violence alternated with emptiness and that the modern individual has been stripped of everything which once described his humanity, left with only his raw nerves and naked skin. To subscribe to this particular vision of our contemporary situation is to qualify for membership in the cultural elite. Thus Mr. Albee's play by its content no less than by its idiom confers a gift of cultural status. An audience which might otherwise be relegated to the outer darkness of a traditional optimism, of a traditional ongoing view of life, makes the acquaintance of Mr. Albee's four miserable characters and recognizes their kinship with the characters to whom it has been introduced by the most advanced of our contemporary playwrights and novelists, and instinctively it appreciates that it has been tuned in on the closed circuit of the best and newest that is being said by the art of our time. Whatever preconceptions it may have brought to this contemporary experience are understood to be old hat if not yet entirely fake or phony. *Who's Afraid of Virginia Woolf?* Mr. Albee calls his play, and even this title, which really has no perceptible relation to the story Mr. Albee is telling, suddenly reveals its purpose. Who indeed need be afraid of the lady-writer of Bloomsbury, that quintessential literary aristocrat whose cultural fortress could once be thought so impregnable to the assaults of a vulgar democracy? Certainly not Mr. Albee, or George and Martha, or Nick and Honey. And certainly not a public let in on Mr. Albee's cultural secret—that distinction, whether of birth or achievement, is merely a joke, that the values which once supported our society no longer prevail, and that modern man is on his desperate, ugly, and meaningless own.

Diana Trilling. Esquire. Dec., 1963, p. 83

Who's Afraid of Virginia Woolf? is successful because it uses the rich resources of Albee's language both to peel back the veil on the unacknowledged terrors of "normal" life and by denying their power to indulge its audience's sadism and flatter their ignorant hope. It removes the viewer from the action enough to protect his sense of life, but keeps him close enough to indulge his taste for blood. It both scores his world and flatters his confidence that he is not an inhabitant. It allows him the childish pleasure of throwing bricks at Mommy and Daddy without the burdensome need to ask how they got that way or why they can't be cured. It titillates his sentiments while leaving his emotions and his mind intact. It forces him to three and a half hours of discomfort he'd flee in the world outside (imagine really standing still for such an argument!) for the supreme pleasure of the final purgation which will release him with a sense of well being.

When you have allowed Albee his linguistic verve you have said everything good about him. But you must also note the debased and debasing uses to which he has put that talent. Language may be used both to elevate and to corrupt, and I'm not talking the naïve 19th century moralism which Albee, with his talent for hunting straw men, so rails against in his preface. A solidly pessimistic piece like [Beckett's] *Waiting for Godot* is as pure as *Rebecca of Sunny Brook Farm;* in the only relevant sense of the term: its language is the outward display of a coherent inner vision. In Albee the language debases by pretending a meaningful rage which the author cannot have, since he lacks a reasonable object, and by creating a despair which is pure indulgence, released as it is at the final curtain. Albee's language is all display: kicks for the carriage trade.

Charles Thomas Samuels. *MR*. Autumn–Winter,
1964–65, pp. 199–200

Edward Albee has called his new play [*Tiny Alice*] a "mystery story," a description which applies as well to its content as to its genre. The work is certainly very mystifying, full of dark hints and riddling allusions, but since it is also clumsy and contrived, and specious in the extreme, the mystery that interested me most was whether the author was kidding his audience or kidding himself. *Tiny Alice* may well turn out to be a huge joke on the American culture industry; then again, it may turn out to be a typical product of that industry. The hardest thing to determine about "camp" literature, movies, and painting is the extent of the author's sincerity. A hoax is being perpetrated, no doubt of that, but is this intentional or not? Is the contriver inside or outside his own fraudulent creation? Does Andy Warhol really believe in the artistic validity of his Brillo boxes? *Tiny Alice* is a much more ambitious work than the usual variety of "camp," but it shares the same ambiguity of motive. For while some of Albee's obscurity is pure playfulness, designed to con the spectator into looking for non-existent meanings, some is obviously there for the sake of a sham profundity in which the author apparently believes.

My complaint is that Albee has not created profundity, he has only borrowed the appearance of it. In *Tiny Alice,* he is once again dealing with impersonation—this time as a metaphor for religious faith—and once again is doing most of the impersonating himself. The central idea of the play—which treats religious ritual as a form of stagecraft and playacting—comes from Jean Genet's *The Balcony;* its initial device—which involves a wealthy woman handing over a fortune in return for the sacrifice of a man's life—comes from Duerrenmatt's *The Visit of the Old Lady;* its symbolism—revolving around mysterious castles, the union of sacred and profane, and the agony of modern Christ figures—is largely taken from Strindberg's *A Dream Play;* and its basic tone—a metaphysical rumble arising out of libations, litanies, and ceremonies created by a shadowy hieratic trio—is directly stolen from T. S. Eliot's *The Cocktail Party*. The play, in short, is virtually a theatrical echo chamber, with reverberations of Graham Greene, Enid Bagnold, and Tennessee Williams being heard as well; but Albee's manipulation of these sources owes more to literature than to life, while his metaphysical enigmas contribute less to thematic perception than to atmospheric fakery.

Robert Brustein. NR. Jan. 23, 1965, pp. 33–34

From the broadest perspective, Albee is a moralist, despite objections to the adultery, profanity and perversion in [*Who's Afraid of Virginia Woolf?*]. Lionel Trilling has pointed out that the artist who includes degradation, sin, and vile language in his work is attacking not goodness, but *specious* goodness by revealing the corruptions which are concealed by a puritanical moral code, an observation rooted in Freud's *Civilization and Its Discontents*. Because the release of our inhibitions in dreams is often unpleasant, or in action is unsettling or even subversive, our frustrated impulses often emerge in ugly, but disguised ways. By allowing the dramatic expression of these frustrated urges, the artist is purging or "exorcising" the impulses which otherwise strengthen our self-destructive urges. Although Albee makes almost no overt comment of the shortcomings of our society (we cannot assume that George is an author *persona*), he has had to select his absurdities, and this act of selection is a moral act.

Emil Roy. BuR. March, 1965, p. 36

Drama is the most socially rooted of the arts, and aestheticism as an affirmation has never been wholly comfortable on stage. Because Albee is so incapable of *historical* affirmations, he identifies too closely with his symbolic transcenders and loses aesthetic distance. These difficulties become audible [in *Who's Afraid of Virgina Woolf?*] in George's rhetoric when he is serious: the spark of slang goes and his speech becomes amazingly opaque. This is even more true in *Tiny Alice,* since all the characters' language is projected in Julian's mind and can be turned into dry cant. Tired, unfelt commonplaces about the Human Condition abound, ritually uttered substitutes for real human conditions enacted in history.

In *Tiny Alice* a final problem also comes to a head, caused by Albee's uncritical presentation of his heroes. Julian's imagination, which creates the action, is too homosexual for general application or comprehension. Most plays "compromise universality" in the other direction; they generalize and fantasize about existence with an implicit heterosexuality just as narrow, and just as blandly disregard the other side of sexuality. However, though a homosexual viewpoint may make some special contribution, it is less generally valid, balanced, and embracing than is the best pondered heterosexual outlook, given a world in which the homosexual still is despised and persecuted. It may be intensively and effectively expressed—Genet's *Our Lady of the Flowers,* as well as *Tiny Alice,* shows what remarkable art is thus engendered. But as a rule art gains when a writer pleads neither the homosexual nor the heterosexual vision, but maintains a nice understanding and irony for both. The homosexual vision is not in itself debilitating; what hurts is not to have it set in the broadest perspective.

Lee Baxandall. *TDR*. Summer, 1965, pp. 39–40

Since *The Zoo Story,* the steady target of Albee's satire has been modern woman. Today's women, he insists, are pernicious both in temperament and influence. Endowed with more energy and appetite than their male counterparts, they easily gain domestic power in spite of the men's nobler aims and more nimble minds. The easy fellowship that develops smoothly between Mommy and Mrs. Barker [in *The American Dream*] and between Martha and Honey [in *Who's Afraid of Virginia Woolf?*] hints of an unspoken conspiracy to wrest power from their mates. But this dramatic fact takes root in Strindberg rather than in contemporary life. Albee's claims about women must be perforce conjectural, residing as they do in interpretation and observation and not in empirically verifiable fact. His view of contemporary women as vessels of shrieking sadism is theatrically exciting. Arousing laughter and applause from an audience by savagely ridiculing their inherited values is an accomplishment beyond most dramatists. But it is also a gift that in a less vigilant artist could harden into a manner. Albee has tempered and modified his magnificent showmanship in *Tiny Alice*. Without sacrificing any of the raw, searing power of the earlier works, the new play incorporates what may prove to be a major revision of his basic premise. Through the character of Miss Alice, he advances the idea that today's women often find themselves compelled to act against their principles. Although Miss Alice is involved in a terrible calamity, her acts, like those of Miss Amelia in *The Ballad of the Sad Cafe,* are largely forced upon her. Her failure to rise above the monstrous task devised by her conspirators makes her, as well, much more pathetic than any of Albee's other women. It might even be argued that her role in the scheme revolving around Julian is, in the last analysis, more redemptive than destructive. He never relinquishes his quest for union with a spiritual ideal. And although his ideal is displaced, he does learn through his painful association with her that moral progress in our contingent world can only result from dense involvement with another person. Miss Alice, then, performs the metaphysical service of deepening the quality of his commitment without personal benefit. Her sacrificial act, which she performs in spite of the lawyer (secular law) and the Cardinal (God's law on earth), strongly suggests that Albee is working to refresh artistically his diatribes against modern women and their destructive role in American society.

Peter Wolfe. *PrS*. Fall, 1965, pp. 261–62

Just as the satire and inventiveness of an Albee play are inadequate to explain its power in the theatre, so is Albee's homosexual imagination inadequate to the characters and action of his work. Although the Tyrones are long on their journey into night before the curtain ever rises, there is at least in O'Neill the memory of a time when marriage or the family were more than monstrous conceptions. There is nothing inherently sacred about either family or heterosexual life, but Albee's criticism or attempted transcendence of them loses conviction in the face of his holding only a poor idea of what they *might have been like*. As a result, behind the lunging language of the plays there is more pathos than terror. An hysterical note keeps slipping through the words, and words prove as incomplete as Albee's perspectives. To argue that Albee has made whatever contacts he knows how addresses a consideration that ought never to have been raised. The plays are admittedly dramatic; the texts, impressive; Albee, intellectually honest. But in the end we must return to the plays, an art in which Albee expects language to accomplish too much and in which his confined vision of human relationships begs for alternatives. In *The American Dream* a hint of the family as other than nightmare might have prevented satire from turning into caricature. In *Who's Afraid of Virginia Woolf?* some notion of only the *possibility* of a creative marriage—something like that presented in John Updike's short story "Wife-Wooing"—might have been useful. And in *Tiny Alice* a clearer idea of the *real* life or "dimension" that Julian rejects might have resulted in less aesthetic confusion and in a more satisfying and major play.

Arthur K. Oberg. *PrS*. Summer, 1966, pp. 145–46

Historically considered, Albee falls directly in the long line of the French theater extending back as far as the *fin-de-siècle* Surrealism of Alfred Jarry's *Ubu Roi*. But, on the American scene, Albee's strangely fascinating experiments, his adaptation of what the French call "black humor" to American settings, are akin to the revolution in poetry that occurred in the early 1920's when Pound, Eliot, and others looked backward to the English metaphysical poets of the seventeenth century and saw in them a possibility for a new kind of modern poetry by shaping their methods to new subject matter.

One of the big questions, I suppose, in evaluating the place of Albee in the modern theater, is whether or not the phenomenon characterized as "theater of the absurd" will last. . . .

It will be interesting, therefore, to observe whether or not Albee, who is still relatively young, can continue his present leading position in the theater, one which some critics have accounted for by the dearth of good writers and good plays. Certainly Tennessee Williams' statement that "Edward Albee is the only great playwright we've had in America" seems like the gross exaggeration of an elder man in Madison Avenue advertising who is trying too hard to help a younger colleague make a quick ascent to fame and fortune.

Richard E. Amacher. Edward Albee (New York, Twayne,
1969), pp. 169–70

Albee has been moving away from political and social structures toward moral and religious illusion. Thus, the greedy, conformist American family of *The American Dream* differs markedly from the greedy, love-bound family of *A Delicate Balance,* as apocalyptic Jerry of *The Zoo Story* differs markedly from apocalyptic Julian of *Tiny Alice.* Common to several of Albee's plays is the existentialist view of an Outsider who suffers at the hands of the Establishment—social, moral, or religious—which announces itself in "peachy-keen" clichés that indict those who mouth them—Peter, Mommy, the Nurse, Nick. Albee has moved from this American anti-American idiom into the metaphysical suggestiveness of *Tiny Alice* and *A Delicate Balance,* and his language accommodates both colloquialism and convolution, both excruciating specificity and horrifying generality.

The shadow of death darkens all Albee's plays, growing into the night of *Tiny Alice* and *A Delicate Balance.* Man's mortality is the subject of both plays, and the drama arises from man's terror. Transitional, *Who's Afraid of Virginia Woolf?* touches on the fear in human love without illusion. *Tiny Alice* probes the heroism of a shrunken earth; the house appointed for all living is shaken by the living dead, but accident and brinkmanship salvage the equilibrium.

Like the Absurdists whom he defends, Albee is anguished because men die and they cannot make themselves happy with illusion. He absorbs this condition into art by counterpointing interrogation and repetition, familiar phrase and diversified resonance, repartee and monologue, minute gesture and cosmic sweep, comic wit and a sense of tragedy. The Albeegory is that distinctive allegorical drama in which ideas are so skillfully blended into people that we do not know how to divorce them or how to care about one without the other.

Ruby Cohn. Edward Albee (Minneapolis, University
of Minnesota Press, 1969), pp. 43–44

In his one-act plays Albee often reaches into the vitals of American attitudes to strike at what he thinks sham and superficiality. In *The Zoo Story* he reveals the complacent businessman to be a vegetable incapable of experiencing any kind of real feeling; in *The American Dream* he presents our idealization of physical beauty and sexual power in all its vacuity. The validity of the satire in these plays rests on the exposure of the veneer that disguises fear, ruthlessness, savagery and self-interest without any attempt to solve the problems. There is always an implicit recognition of the depth of the problem. It cannot be solved by any quick panacea. . . . The conclusion of *Who's Afraid of Virginia Woolf?*, however, advocates a simple standard: no salvation from without, a reliance on "truth" and the resources of the personality. Though Albee sounds the "maybe" of caution with regard to the final situation of George and Martha, he also holds out a "romantic" hope that "it will be better." But the ironist of the first two-and-a-half acts has left his imprint on the play. There seems no reason why the old cycle of games should not begin again.

Thomas E. Porter. *Myth and Modern American Drama* (Detroit, Wayne State University Press, 1969), pp. 246–47

In the theatre Edward Albee writes reformist plays of social protest which unflinchingly reveal the pustulous sores of a society plagued with social ills. His first decade of playwriting has consistently displayed an unyielding social commitment as he experimented with varying dramatic styles and playwriting techniques. Realism served admirably for the shocking events of *The Zoo Story, Who's Afraid of Virginia Woolf?*, and *A Delicate Balance;* surrealism provided the form for the socio-political didactics of *The Sandbox* and *The American Dream;* impressionism was the major style of social protest in *The Death of Bessie Smith;* symbolist mysticism permeated the theological metaphysics of *Tiny Alice;* and theatrical revolution prompted the polyphonic, non-narrative design of *Box-Mao-Box.*

Albee's early plays from *The Zoo Story* through *The American Dream,* though vastly different in theatrical form, are all protests in defense of those outcasts of society who have been victimized by the stupidity and bias of the successful elite. In *Who's Afraid of Virginia Woolf?* his sociological vantage point changes, and he attacks the hypocrisy and corruption in some circles of the intelligentsia of our society, stripping all comfortable illusion from the protagonists in an effort to make them face the truth of their barren lives. The later plays, *A Delicate Balance* and *Tiny Alice,* continue the destruction of individual illusion, but go further into an exploration of modern man's very real sense of isolation and estrangement from society and his God. The adaptations, *The Ballad of the Sad Cafe* and *Malcolm,* though certainly not up to the level of his indigenous works, support his defense of the misfit—society's outsider—while the last of these, *Everything in the Garden,* continues his assault on an affluent society gone amoral. His newest theatre piece is actually two short but highly original plays of The New Theatre. The first, *Box,* a post-holocaust requiem for the dead, performed in monodic fashion, is carefully interwoven into the second, *Quotations from Chairman*

Mao Tse-tung, a contrapuntal score for voices whose main theme is man's impending doom.

Michael E. Rutenberg. Edward Albee: Playwright in Protest
(New York, DBS, 1969), pp. 8–9

Albee . . . shares with most American playwrights an idea of the utility of art, the supposition not only that art should convey truth, but that it should do so to some purpose. There is a strong strain of didacticism in all his work, but it is balanced by a certain ambiguity about the nature of the instructive fable. In interviews, he harps on how much of the creative process is subconscious, how little he understands his own work, how a play is to be experienced rather than understood. Insofar as this is not sour grapes pressed to make an aesthetic (his reaction to the reviews of *Tiny Alice*), it may be his way of recognizing that there is a conflict between his attitude toward man's situation and his suspicion (or hope: certainly *conviction* is too strong a word) that something can, or ought, to be done about it; between his assumption that this is hell we live in and his longing to redecorate it.

Gerald Weales. The Jumping-Off Place (New York,
Macmillan, 1969), p. 35

Albee is the only playwright, after O'Neill, who shows real growth, the only one who has made a serious effort to break away from the "message" plays which have plagued our theater since O'Neill. Experimentation, for Albee, is a slow internal transformation of the dramatic medium, not an arbitrary exercise in expressionism, or Freudian symbolism, or stream of consciousness. His arrogance is not an empty gesture. He is the only one of our playwrights who seems to have accepted and committed himself to serious articulation of the existential questions of our time, recognizing the incongruity of insisting on pragmatic values in an age of relativity. Dramatic "statement," as Ibsen defined it, through realism, is no longer effective in such an age as ours. Albee has taken on the challenge as no one else in the American contemporary theater has. His work is a refreshing exception to John Gassner's judgment that our theater—with its message plays and its outgrown realism—is in a state of "protracted adolescence" which gives it a "provincial air."

"Happenings" are the extreme reaction to our fossilized theater and play an important role in trimming away the deadwood; Albee represents the first sober attempt to effect a transformation at the core. He has given arbitrary experimentation direction and purpose.

Anne Paolucci. From Tension to Tonic: The Plays
of Edward Albee (Carbondale, Ill., Southern Illinois
University Press, 1972), p. 3

All Over provides reason for being rather more sanguine about Albee's future than we have had the right to be for some years. His only two previous attempts at a fusion between his off-Broadway experimentalism and his Broadway naturalism were *Tiny Alice* and *A Delicate Balance:* the new play is a more honest piece of writing than the former and more original than the latter. He is still one of the most powerful influences in the American theatre, although he has not yet equalled the success of *Who's Afraid of Virginia Woolf?* and his three adaptations seriously damaged his reputation. The rival pulls of Beckett and Broadway have brought his talent dangerously near to disintegrating but there is still hope that it will recover.

Ronald Hayman. *Edward Albee* (New York, Frederick
Ungar, 1973), p. 138

Throughout his work, Edward Albee has always been concerned with the failure of love to neutralize the pain of an existence which he thinks finally absurd if not redeemed by the integrity of human values. He has constantly flirted with apocalypse and has revealed a puritan conviction that the path to redemption lies through suffering. But he has repeatedly drawn back from the brink, sustained by a vision of liberal concern, by a conviction that it remains possible for individuals and, perhaps, nations, to be shocked into an awareness of the true nature of their situation and thus of the paramount need for compassion and, in the last resort, love, however imperfect that love may be.

With *Box* and *Quotations from Chairman Mao Tse-tung,* that conviction seemed more attenuated and shrill. In his more recent play it genuinely seems *All Over*. For the basic process of human life appears to be structured on a slow withdrawal from the Other; a gradual plunge into the Self which must eventually result in spiritual collapse. Love itself seems nothing more than an expression of self-concern. As The Wife remarks, in what seems to be an accurate observation of the motives of those who surround her, "Selfless love? I don't think so; we love to *be* loved. . . . All we've *done* is think about ourselves. Ultimately." This is as long a step from the self-sacrificing love of Jerry, in *The Zoo Story,* as the essentially static quality of his recent plays is from the exuberant action of his early work. The play ends, significantly, too significantly, with the words, "All over."

The tone of his recent plays is, then, no longer that of a confident liberalism rehearsing the great verities of the nineteenth century—personal and public responsibility. As The Mistress remarks, the only way "we keep the nineteenth century going for ourselves" is to "pretend it exists." The tone now is elegiac. The rhythm is no longer the vibrant crescendo and diminuendo of *Who's Afraid of Virginia Woolf?* and *Tiny Alice*. It is the slow, measured, and finally faltering pulse beat of *Box* and *Quotations from Chairman Mao Tse-tung*.

Yet, Albee's concern in *All Over* is essentially that of his earlier work. He remains intent on penetrating the bland urbanities of social life in an attempt to identify the crucial failure of nerve which has brought individual men and whole societies to the point not merely of soulless anomie but even of apocalypse.

C. W. E. Bigsby. In C. W. E. Bigsby, ed., *Edward Albee: A Collection of Critical Essays* (Englewood Cliffs, N.J., Prentice-Hall, 1975), pp. 168–69

Counting the Ways, subtitled "A Vaudeville," is a series of brief monologues and dialogues separated by blackouts. The two characters are a soigné middle-aged couple, named in the program as "She" and "He." Among the subjects they allude to are love, death, and crème brûlée. "Here's a thought," says She, "I think it was my grandmother's. Love doesn't die; we pass through it." There are occasional presentational devices: "He: Where are you going? She: Off." *Counting the Ways* is so slight it's hardly there, but it is harmless and graceful enough. . . .

Listening is a dignified, elliptical piece, redolent of James and Eliot, of Beckett *(Krapp's Last Tape)* and Pinter *(Landscape* and *Silence).* Like *Counting the Ways,* it is very capably performed. It bored me very much.

As will now be apparent, I am not an admirer of Mr. Albee's recent plays. But I am not in sympathy with the rather hysterical critical attacks against him that have appeared in recent years. Some people do seem to like his late plays, and these people are not necessarily *non compos mentis*— only, I think, a little overrefined; but they could argue with equal cogency, perhaps, that I am underrefined, with no relish for delicate flavors. Mr. Albee is still a gifted, intelligent, scrupulous writer, doing the best he can; if, as I believe, he has fallen out of touch with his own talent, that is scarcely an indictable offense.

Julius Novick. *VV.* Feb. 21, 1977, p 99

Edward Albee's *Seascape* is obviously not a realistic play. When the two great lizards slide onto the stage behaving like ordinary married human beings and speaking perfect English, realism is immediately dispelled. Encounters between human beings and talking animals are the stuff of fairy tales. Bruno Bettelheim, in *The Uses of Enchantment,* describes a fairy tale as a work of art which teaches about inner problems through the language of symbols and, therefore, communicates various depths of meaning to various levels of the personality at various times. This is the method of *Seascape.*

The play's principal concern is the realization of the proximity of death that comes with the passing of middle age. Albee depicts the adjustments that this realization entails, adjustments made difficult in the twentieth century by a tendency to deny mortality. Sigmund Freud spoke of this denial as an inner struggle between Eros and Thanatos, which he viewed as the wellspring of all neuroses. Friedrich Nietzsche wrote about the need for a oneness that would embody the affirmation of death as well as life. More recently, Norman O. Brown has maintained that constructing "a human consciousness" capable of accepting death "is a task for the joint efforts of" psychoanalysis, philosophy, and art. *Seascape* takes up this cause and earns importance because of it.

Symbols are the play's basic medium. Through symbolism the title announces that death is a part of the flux of life. A seascape is a view of the sea whose ever-moving waters are the meeting place between air and ground, heaven and earth, life and death. The waters of the sea are both the source and the goal of life. Returning to the sea is equivalent to the birth waters of mother's womb; it is the symbolic equivalent of death. The seascape is also vast: its final shore is the product of continuous evolution— unstoppable in its insistent progress. The sea is also deep and dark; beneath its bright ripples are undercurrents, eddies, unseen life, and unplumbed depths. So is man's awareness merely the outer rim of an inner self that seethes with the buried life of the subconscious. Thus, the play intertwines three levels of meaning, ingeniously allowing each to add insight to the other. All three are condensed in the symbol of the lizards who come up from the sea. They concretize the evolution of mankind from water animals, the emergence of the individual embryo from its watery womb, and the return to consciousness of the repressed self.

Lucina P. Gabbard. *MD*. Sept., 1978, pp. 307–8

Obviously, Albee's themes [in *The Lady from Dubuque*] are not new, either for the modern theater or for Albee. The "Who am I?" question has its prototype in Sophocles' *Oedipus,* which makes that theme well over 2,000 years old. The despair which we have seen for decades as characteristic of the human condition has been the subject of modern drama at least since Beckett's *Waiting for Godot,* and Albee's earlier plays, including *The Sandbox, The Zoo Story, The American Dream, Tiny Alice,* and *A Delicate Balance,* all deal with the sterility of human relationships in death-within-life situations. In particular, his first play of the 1970's, *All Over,* dramatizes spiritual collapse in the presence of death, that relentless announcer of man's absurd existence. But literature invites the reworking of viable themes, and the fact that Albee has not said anything new in this play, nor offered any answers, should not in itself prevent the play from working. The problem with *The Lady from Dubuque* is not that Albee has said what has already been said—Beckett, after all, keeps repeating himself—but simply that, in dramatic terms, he has not said it effectively. The play offers nothing new structurally yet fails as a realistic play, and the dialogue, which has always been Albee's strength, is singularly undistinguished.

To Albee's credit, the relationship between music and drama which has always fascinated him and which is so apparent in *All Over* is reflected in this play as well, with the theme "Who am I?" stated and restated throughout, beginning with Sam's opening, "Who am I?" and ending with his cry to the Lady from Dubuque, "Who are you really?" The question punctuates the play and nicely balances the two acts by beginning the first with the question as part of a game and the second, posed by Sam when he first sees Elizabeth, as a question very much in earnest. The final notes of the play turn the inconclusiveness of the question into a satisfying cadence, with the Lady from Dubuque saying to Sam, "I thought you knew," and then, to the audience, "I thought he knew." But despite this counterpointing, the rest of Albee's dramatic sonata is undeveloped and sparse. In between each resounding of the "Who am I?"–"Who are you?" motif is the monotony of dialogue which neither responds to nor poses any dramatic questions.

June Schlueter. In Patricia De La Fuente, ed., *Edward Albee:*
Planned Wilderness (Edinburg, Texas, School of
Humanities, Pan American University, 1980), pp. 115–16

HELLMAN, LILLIAN (1905–   )

Here is a play to wring the heart and fire respect, an adult, steadfast play so conspicuously fine and intelligent that, beside it, much of the theater's present crop becomes shoddy and futile. This is the first play of this erratic season in which power, intellect, and a glowing sense for theater combine for a terrifying and ennobling experience. The new play is *The Children's Hour*, a first play by Miss Lillian Hellman, and overnight, by the force of its own stature, it has become the most important play in New York.

Here is a play that shines with integrity. It is, definitely, the first play of the season in which for two whole, consuming acts the First Audience sat completely silent, held taut by the richness and reality of the tragedy which it describes.

In *The Children's Hour* there is conspicuous and magic correlation between the author, the producer, and the cast. It is evident that each contributed a positive majesty of sincerity to it and that all three together determined to make this a play to command the appreciation of its audiences.

Literary Digest. Dec. 1, 1934, p. 20

Watch on the Rhine . . . binds the attention of the audience to the stage, and very often binds it tight. A great deal of this is due to the expert stage craft of the melodrama itself. But a great deal, also, come from the author's remarkable gift for character, the way in which she can lay out a group of characters that are not crudely differentiated one from another or hammered at in the writing or thrown at each other's heads for the sake of contrasts and variety. They are observed with much pains as to the exact kind of detail that will convince us of their actual existence and difference, relationships and mutual reactions to each other, and that will brighten our eyes and ears to note them pointedly with pleasure. . . .

As an indictment of Nazism, *Watch on the Rhine* will seem more or less pointed and forceful according to the spectator. You may say quite plausibly that the play would get pretty much the same results if the hero's enemy were almost any sort of men and things that he was at odds with, that he had fought bravely against and been persecuted by, and that make his return to save a friend highly dangerous, and his whole resolution heroic and appealing. In sum it is the story and characters that really carry us along with the play, however much or little the anti-Nazi connotations may stick in our minds. Any way you take it, *Watch on the Rhine* is infinitely better than the propaganda plays we are used to in the theatre.

Stark Young. *NR*. April 14, 1941, p. 499

That *The Searching Wind* is neither so appealing nor so wholly satisfactory as *The Little Foxes* or *Watch on the Rhine,* that its means of achieving revelation are somewhat awkward, and that its implications are not entirely convincing—this is not very important: the play relies to a remarkable extent on the characterization and not on the story, on the dialogue and not on the plot; it needs no violence other than the violence precipitated by the impact of person on person, idea upon idea. Most notable, however, is the author's own attitude toward the problem she wants to set forth. She is no longer the special pleader for this or that type of reform, and she is evidently not ridden by the notion that all you have to do to win the Good Life is to eradicate the evil men and substitute the good. "I love this place," says Sam, and Sam speaks for the author, "and I don't want any more fancy fooling around with it." This place is, of course, our country, or perhaps all those countries in which our way of life is held to be the best.

Lillian Hellman has been writing plays for only a little over a decade; she has pretty well mastered the tools that every dramatist must use in order to gain the attention of the public; she is conscious of the limitations of the drama medium, and she has found out at moments how to make the best of them. She is still unwilling to use her talent except directly in the service of humanity. It is possible, I am convinced, for her to speak just as eloquently on behalf of the oppressed and the blind if she is willing to forget the immediate good to be won by this reform or that and to concentrate on the far more difficult and rewarding task of illuminating the world she knows *as she sees it,* through the power of her imagination, without insisting too much on guiding and instructing it. It is questionable whether the preacher ever did anything as effectively as the poet.

Barrett H. Clark. CE. Dec., 1944, p. 133

In many ways *The Autumn Garden* is unlike any of Lillian Hellman's previous works. The same muscularity of mind, the same command of authentic dialogue, the same willingness to face unpleasant people as they are, and the same instinctive awareness of the theatre's needs which have always animated her writing are present. But the mood, the tone, the flavor, the point of view and hence the means employed are so different from those of *The Children's Hour, The Little Foxes, Watch on the Rhine,* and *Another Part of the Forest* that it is no overstatement to say a new Miss Hellman has emerged.

For the first time in her distinguished career she has, so to speak, turned her back on Ibsen and moved into the camp of Chekhov. To the casual reader such a shift in allegiance may seem unimportant. To the theatre-minded, however, it represents a change in attitude, method, and purpose of the utmost significance. . . .

Even in her most loyal Ibsenite days Miss Hellman was never a copyist. Far from it. She had found her own way of making her own comment upon the American scene. She was a progressive who was old-fashioned only in the sense that in a period of slovenly workmanship she continued to write "well-made plays." Her pride as a craftsman was clear. She excelled at contrivances, at big scenes, and sulphurous melodramatics. Although sometimes misled into overcomplicating her plots, she wrote with fervor as a person to whom ideas and causes came naturally. The protest in her voice was strong. It was as characteristic of her as the energy of her attack or the neatness of her planning.

John Mason Brown. SR. March 31, 1951, p. 27

The Autumn Garden is written in prose. By the very nature of the medium, the tragic intensity and, to a lesser degree, the tragic nobility of the characters and their situations are rendered less magnificent than if the play were phrased in poetry. In one sense, this is a purely mechanical problem. But prose can take on certain of the qualities of poetry, or, I should say, certain poetic devices are available to the prose writer, particularly to the dramatist. Perhaps the most significant of these is symbolism. In *Days to Come* (a play whose shortcomings Miss Hellman admits, but, as she says, "with all that is wrong, all the confusion, the jumble, the attempt to do too much, I stand on the side of *Days to Come*"), one of the characters says: "I don't like autumn anymore. The river is full of leaves and it was too cold to walk very far." This speech, as any clever sophomore could tell us, has symbolic overtones. In *The Autumn Garden,* aside from a few incidental references to roots and trees, there is no mention of a garden, but the title adds a necessary symbolic note to the whole play. Miss Hellman has used a number of such titles, particularly those which emphasize the organic, natural aspects of human existence: in both *The Searching Wind* and *Another Part of the Forest,* she has used the significant relationship between man and nature to extend the meaning of her dramas. So in *The Autumn Garden,* the symbolism inherent in the title adds a poetic dimension to the scope of the play.

In fact, this is my central point: that the kind of drama we have in *The Autumn Garden* is the only kind which makes for modern tragedy. It is not merely psychological (as in Tennessee Williams) nor sociological (as in Arthur Miller) but it is artistic (poetic) and moral—and all in the Chekhovian sense. And so Miss Hellman's movement in this direction is a movement toward seriousness. As one New York critic ironically put it, Miss Hellman is "our most promising playwright."

Marvin Felheim. MD. Sept., 1960, pp. 194–95

It is the measure of Lillian Hellman's superiority to most American playwrights that nine years after *The Autumn Garden* she could return to Broadway with an original play that gave no sign of diminished energy. *Toys in the Attic,* which opened on Broadway toward the close of the 1959–60 season, proved to be one of her most hard-driving plays. Among her earlier works only *The Little Foxes,* her masterpiece of the strenuous Thirties, had possessed as much penetration and dramatic vitality, and rarely before had Miss Hellman written dialogue with such vigor and virtuosity. It was possible to realize at the end of the decade that at least one American playwright had kept her sword of judgment—or rather her "knife of truth," as the neurotic child-wife of the play would have said—unblunted in the damp mental climate.

She had brought to the task of adapting Emmanuel Roblès' *Montserrat* earlier in the decade an existentialist concern with decisions that test men's stamina; and in adapting Anouilh's Joan of Arc drama, *The Lark,* she had invigorated the play by counteracting the French author's rather facile skepticism. If a loss of dramatic voltage was apparent in *The Autumn Garden* at the beginning of the decade it could be attributed to her experimentation with a relatively loose form of dramaturgy for the purpose of securing amplitude of characterization and giving a rueful account of enervation and failure in society.

In *Toys in the Attic* Miss Hellman picked up the sword of judgment many playwrights of the Fifties had laid aside and wielded it with renewed vigor. But this time, compassion guided her hand so that she performed surgery on her characters instead of summarily decapitating them.

John Gassner. Theatre at the Crossroads (New York,
Holt, Rinehart and Winston, 1960), p. 137

Since she is a playwright of the thirties, she has sometimes been taken simply as a social playwright. Although there is implicit anticapitalism in *The Little Foxes* and explicit antifascism in *Watch on the Rhine,* Miss Hellman has always been most concerned with personal morality, although, as both *The Little Foxes* and *Watch on the Rhine* indicate, personal action has public consequences. Any social content in the recent plays is far below the surface. One of General Griggs's speeches in *The Autumn Garden* suggests that the characters are failures because they belong to specific families, the decaying end of the post-Civil War money-makers, but the implication is not diagnostic; Miss Hellman makes quite clear that the problem is personal, not social, determinism. Something might be made once again of the Hubbards as budding capitalists, but in *Another Part of the Forest,* greed spreads to every character in the play (except perhaps Lavinia and Coralee) and the Hubbards have here become grotesques, their nastiness almost biological. If a character in any of these plays may be said to suggest social criticism it is the off-stage Cyrus Warkins in *Toys in the Attic,* the respectable businessman who uses thugs to beat up Julian Berniers and Mrs. Warkins, although even Cyrus' motivation may mix jealousy with outrage at being bested in a business deal. Despite her obvious concern with social evil, Miss Hellman more often seems preoccupied with abstract evil, even to the point of caricature, as in *Another Part of the Forest,* or she goes out of her way to provide acres of psychological motivation, as in *Toys in the Attic.* For Miss Hellman, however, psychological determinism, as *The Autumn Garden* shows, is never an excuse. Always the moralist, the playwright is usually intent on pointing a critical finger not only at the eaters of the earth, but at those who, in Addie's words from *The Little Foxes,* "stand and watch them do it."

> Gerald Weales. *American Drama since World War II*
> (New York, Harcourt, Brace & World, 1962), pp. 89–90

Lillian Hellman's strength lies in the dramatic power she can extract from the realistic form. *The Little Foxes,* like [Ibsen's] *Ghosts,* is almost flawless in economy and structure, realization of character, and pertinence of dialogue. Characters generate events and in turn are influenced by them. *Toys in the Attic* has a weak first act with too much preparation for what follows, but its final resolution is explosive. Hellman's mastery of technique has led to the accusation that her plays are too contrived, too adroitly arranged by the author. Such charges are valid, but it is a pleasure to watch the work of a skilled craftsman. All writers rearrange life and impose their own will on the chaos of reality. The test in the realistic theatre is whether the characters appear to be self-propelled, as they do in *The Little Foxes,* a masterpiece of the Ibsen-influenced theatre. *Toys in the Attic* shows bits of the machinery, perhaps because family plays of psychological insight have become too familiar, but is so artfully contrived that it becomes compelling drama. Hellman does not use her skill to exhibit technical prowess, but to expose the extent to which greed and avarice have corrupted the human soul. She strives for a Chekhovian complex of frustrated and unhappy people, but her use of violence and sexuality brings her close to Tennessee Williams. . . .

Hellman's bitter complaint is that greed and avarice have eroded love, and that the cause is a social system in which human relations are a product for sale. She is a moralist, and her major weakness, by her own confession, is the obvious addition of the moral, either by an all too obvious explanatory speech or through an arranged resolution that borders on the melodramatic.

Allan Lewis. *American Plays and Playwrights of the Contemporary Theatre* (New York, Crown, 1965), pp. 107–8

In many ways *The Autumn Garden* marks a new stage in Lillian Hellman's writing. For the first time she renounced the presentation of her favorite topic—social criticism in one form or another—and concerned herself with a human problem that is not bound to social conditions. The problem of facing old age, the summing up at the middle of one's life, is the main theme of this drama. The play closed after 102 performances. Critics have divided opinions on this drama, which in my view, suffers greatly from the fact that its main theme is presented in too many cases and thus tends toward a statistical account rather than toward the depiction of an individual tragic fate. Controversial as it may be, *The Autumn Garden* has similar importance for the artistic development of Lillian Hellman as had *Days to Come,* though in quite another respect. *The Autumn Garden* marks Chekhov's influence on Lillian Hellman at its closest, indicated by the play's title, which is reminiscent of the Russian dramatist's *The Cherry Orchard.* How intense Lillian Hellman's interest in Chekhov is can be judged in the introduction of the selected Chekhov letters which she edited.

Manfred Triesch. *The Lillian Hellman Collection at the University of Texas* (Austin, Tex., Humanities Research Center, University of Texas, 1966), pp. 51–52

What is the play [*The Little Foxes*] about? I don't think it would have occurred to us to ask that in 1939, when it was first presented. The answer was clear. *The Little Foxes* was about Tallulah Bankhead—a greedy bitch who, along with her coarse brothers, Ben and Oscar Hubbard, was the very spirit of ruthless Capitalism and ravening Big Business. This family preyed upon some pleasantly pastoral persons, who chattered aimlessly, drank too much, and were innocently, graciously impractical. The extremity of the pastoral weakness is embodied in the condition of Horace Giddens, Regina's husband, who is dying of heart disease. The play was a melodrama, mechanically put together, but redeemed as a composition by the energy of Regina and the brutal yet enjoyable piracy of the brothers, Ben and Oscar.

But what odd things time has done to the text—or to us. It appears to me now—perhaps because of a world around us begging for "development"—that the play is about a besieged Agrarianism, a lost Southern agricultural life, in which virtue and sweetness had a place, and, more strikingly, where social responsibility and justice could, on a personal level at least, be practiced. . . .

Behind Lillian Hellman's plays there is a torn spirit: the bright stuffs of expensive productions and the hair-shirt of didacticism. Between these two, her genuine talent for characterization is diminished. Regina and the brothers go too far. (Why the absurd idea of the marriage between Leo and Alexandra should be added to all the other treacheries one can't decide.) But they are alive and interesting. The little prostitute in *Another Part of the Forest* is a striking vignette. That these characters and others should be squeezed to death by the iron of an American version of Socialist Realism and the gold of a reigning commercialism is a problem of cultural history.

Elizabeth Hardwick. *NYRB.* Dec. 21, 1967, pp. 4–5

What sustains Miss Hellman is in part, of course, craftsmanship—in plot construction, in dialogue, in creation of vivid character, in the presentation through plot and character of a clear cut theme. This craftsmanship represents hard and humble labor through many months and many drafts. But craftsmanship is not the whole story. What sustains her, too, is a concentrated presentation of sheer, almost supernatural evil, to be matched in almost no other modern playwright anywhere: a concentration which comes close to transcending the limitations of realistic form. But evil brings with it its opposite, and it is recognized comparatively seldom that in such plays as *The Little Foxes* and *Watch on the Rhine,* Miss Hellman shows goodness as unmistakable and convincing as her more celebrated evil. Her range of evil is, moreover, wide: the conscious, gleeful, intelligent machinations of a Ben or a Regina; the complex, condescending, and almost witty sadism of their father; the snivelling amorality of Oscar; the repellent trickery of the count in *Watch on the Rhine,* who can still respect good and wish he could afford it; the infantile mischief of the self-pitying poseur Nick in *The Autumn Garden,* who would find an accusation of evil incredible; the psychosis of Mary Tilford, who craves superiority and who attains it through acts of cruelty; the pitiable state of Carrie in *Toys in the Attic,* driven helplessly to a wickedness she does not even recognize. For some of these people, moreover, Miss Hellman displays compassion. And frequently, in almost all the plays, she gives us wit and humor—to a degree, in fact, which critics have rarely noted. There is hope in Miss Hellman's world—hope, indeed, in the very act of presenting it. And her gallery of portraits, good, evil, mixed, is a gallery of memorable human beings in wide variety. She is perhaps best compared to some minor Jacobean playwright—no Shakespeare, no Jonson—who is too vivid ever to be allowed quite to die. Like the Jacobeans' methods in some periods, Miss Hellman's methods are these days considered out of date. We are suspicious of the well-made, the realistic, the clear-cut. But fashions in taste should not be allowed to mislead us. Miss Hellman's methods are viable methods, and of them she is a minor master.

Jacob H. Adler. Lillian Hellman (Austin, Tex.,
Steck-Vaughn, 1969), pp. 41–42

Ultimately *The Little Foxes* may be interpreted as a rational assessment of the historical forces it dramatizes. Given its dramatic premises, the play stringently adheres to causality and probability and thus reflects the spirit of objectivity which Émile Zola considered imperative to dramatic realism. The final scene prominently manifests this rational process by offering no facile resolution of the complex moral conflict which structures the play or of the democratic dilemma which that conflict represents. Hellman's rational process serves to strengthen the validity of the play's moral stance (i.e., the preoccupation with detrimental effects of economic expansion). By a synthesis of rational formulation and moral commitment, *The Little Foxes* gains particular authority in casting an image of American destiny— the continuing dialectic of the privileges versus the responsibilities of liberal democracy.

James Eatman. Players. Dec., 1972–Jan., 1973, p. 73

Lillian Hellman wrote eight original plays, four adaptations of plays or stories by others, and wrote or collaborated on more than seven screenplays. The original plays fall into two principal groups, based on Hellman's view of human action and motivation—a highly moral view, interpreting both action and the failure to act in terms of good and evil.

The first two plays became signposts, marking the directions to be taken by the later plays. *The Children's Hour* concerned active evil—here the ruin of two women by the spreading of a malicious lie. The drama pointed the way toward the three plays whose chief characters are despoilers—those who exploit or destroy others for their own purposes. Hellman's second play, *Days to Come,* was not so much about the despoilers—the evildoers themselves—as about those characters who, well-meaning or not, stand by and allow the despoilers to accomplish their destructive aims. Often these bystanders may be the victims of their own naïveté or lack of self-knowledge.

The despoiler plays are *The Little Foxes, Another Part of the Forest,* and *Watch on the Rhine.* Each is a tightly constructed drama, leading to a violent climax that is the result of evildoing. Most of the characters are clearly defined as evil or good, harmful or harmless. But the so-called by-stander plays—*The Searching Wind, The Autumn Garden,* and *Toys in the Attic*—are as different from the despoilers in structure as they are in theme. The action is slower, the plot more discursive and low-keyed, moving more within the characters and the events that befall them, than through their actions. For most of these people are unable to act positively or with con-viction. They let things happen and they become the passive victims of the despoilers and themselves. Despoilers and bystanders appear in some form in all the plays, but Hellman clearly differentiates between evil as a positive, rapacious force in the first group, and evil as the negative failure of good in the second.

Doris V. Falk. *Lillian Hellman* (New
York, Frederick Ungar, 1978), pp. 29–30

Any final judgment must include a perception of Hellman as ironist, with a way of seeing, and seeing again. This is not to say that such an aware-ness will necessarily cause a reader to prefer Hellman to other major American playwrights. But it should prevent one's judging her by inappli-cable criteria. To "rank" Hellman in a Williams-Miller-Odets-whoever list is, as she might put it, "a losing game." In the modern American theater Lillian Hellman is *sui generis,* and a careful reading of her plays reveals that those generally considered her best *(The Little Foxes, The Autumn Garden, Toys in the Attic*—to which might be added *Watch on the Rhine* and *Another Part of the Forest)* are the most fully ironic (and novelistic). By the same criteria, *Pentimento,* in which Hellman most completely employs fictional techniques and a controlling ironic voice, is the superior memoir.

   D. C. Muecke [in *The Compass of Irony,* 1969] has described irony as "intellectual rather than musical, nearer to the mind than to the senses, reflective and self-conscious rather than lyrical and self-absorbed," having the qualities of "fine prose rather than . . . lyric poetry." Readers and audiences with no predilection for irony will perhaps prefer Arthur Miller's pathos of the common man, or perhaps Tennessee Williams' poetry of the sensitive, bruised soul. There will always be those, however, who will turn to Lillian Hellman for a view of life trenchantly expressed, often moving, frequently funny, uncomfortably accurate in its ironic vision of the fools met in the forest—and the fools *those* fools meet. In judging Lillian Hell-man's work, critics might abandon the automatic genre labeling and ex-amine her way of seeing and her appraisal of things seen, remembering that there is more than one valid way of looking at a blackbird. And a writer.

Katherine Lederer. *Lillian Hellman*
(Boston, Twayne, 1979), pp. 138–39

MILLER, ARTHUR (1915–   )

In *Death of a Salesman* . . . Miller has managed to rise above the ordinary flatlands of moralization and thesis drama. His play is a consummation of virtually everything attempted by that part of the theatre which has specialized in awareness and criticism of social realities. It is a culmination of all efforts since the 1930's to observe the American scene and trace, as well as evaluate, its effect on character and personal life. Clifford Odets succeeded in this enterprise more than creditably in *Golden Boy* and movingly, if somewhat dimly, in *Awake and Sing* and *Rocket to the Moon*. Generally our "social" playwrights' efforts, however, stressed the scene rather than the character even when they transcended special pleading or political agitation. Miller's achievement lies in successfully bridging the gulf between a social situation and human drama. The two elements in *Death of a Salesman* are, indeed, so well fused that the one is the other.

   Death of a Salesman succeeds, in truth, as its author himself appears to have realized, as a character drama and an exceptionally good example of so-called "middle-class tragedy." It follows the fate and final reckoning of a commonplace man in a commonplace environment. It is the kind of play that usually falls decidedly short of tragedy and settles on the lower level of pathos, a drama ordinarily conducive to tear-shedding or sympathetic clucking rather than to exaltation of mind and spirit through impressive suffering. That this is not conspicuously the case in *Death of a Salesman* is perhaps the ultimate proof of its author's dramatic powers.

John Gassner. *Forum*. April, 1949, p. 219

Mr. Miller's steadfast, one might almost say selfless, refusal of complexity, the assured simplicity of his view of human behavior, may be the chief source of his ability to captivate the educated audience. He is an oddly depersonalized writer; one tries in vain to define his special quality, only to discover that it is perhaps not a quality at all, but something like a method, and even as a method strangely bare: his plays are as neatly put together and essentially as empty as that skeleton of a house which made *Death of a Salesman* so impressively confusing. He is the playwright of an audience that believes the frightening complexities of history and experience are to be met with a few ideas, and yet does not even possess these ideas any longer but can only point significantly at the place where they were last seen and where it is hoped they might still be found to exist. What this audience demands of its artists above all is an intelligent narrowness of mind and vision and a generalized tone of affirmation, offering not any particular insights or any particular truths, but simply the assurance that insight and truth as qualities, the things in themselves, reside somehow in the various signals by which the artist and the audience have learned to recognize each other.

For indeed very little remains except this recognition; the marriage of the liberal theater and the liberal audience has been for some time a marriage in name only, held together by habit and mutual interest, partly by sentimental memory, most of all by the fear of loneliness and the outside world; and yet the movements of love are still kept up—for the sake of the children, perhaps.

Robert S. Warshow. Cmty. March, 1953, p. 267

Although there is no fundamental "philosophical" view which can be derived from Miller's plays, there is nevertheless a persistent and continuing problem which gives him the raw material of his plays and the means of expressing his ideas. It is a problem which enables Miller to narrow down the situation of universal man to the concrete situation of a particular American man. The relationship of the American father and son and of both to the American family in the American "situation" provides him, not with his themes, but with the raw material of tensions and conflicts between human beings. (Note how uninteresting and undeveloped the women are in Miller's plays; they witness the drama but have little to contribute to it.) For Arthur Miller it is not just the salesman which is interesting and which he is discussing, but the salesman as a family man; Willy Loman's greatest and most immediate failure was not his failure to sell whatever it was he was selling, but as a man in relationship to his son, a failure of love. His significance comes from the *fact* of the American family—the fact of those awful chamois cloths—and its failure. Miller evidently has some need for such a factual basis for his drama for he records in his introduction [to *The Collected Plays*] how his earlier (unpublished) plays were diffuse for lack of "cause and effect, hard actions, facts, the geometry of relationships." . . .

The substance of Miller's plays is . . . bottomed on a particular American experience. In each of his plays (with the exception of *The Crucible,* which is explicitly political in intent) the central situation centres around a child-father relationship in which the child is at an age when it is about to break loose from the family; in each case the father is faced with the consequent breakdown of the family-world he had tried to create; in each case the conflict between the child and father takes place in terms of the wider world breaching the walls of protection the father had built around the family; in each case the father is corrupt and is revealed to be corrupt by his child; and in each case this corruption leads the father to choose death as the penalty for destroying his own ideal. The pattern is so strictly followed—even in the curtain raiser, *A Memory of Two Mondays,* where the warehouse gang acts as the family to Bert—that it is clear that the failure of these families has given the central focus of Miller's work so far.

William J. Newman. TC. Nov., 1958, pp. 492–94

The most important single fact about the plays of Arthur Millier is that he has brought back into the theatre, in an important way, the drama of social questions. It has been fashionable, certainly in England, to reject such drama as necessarily superficial. In part, this rejection is in itself social, for it has shown itself in the context of a particular phase of consciousness: that widespread withdrawal from social thinking which came to its peak in the late nineteen-forties, at just the time when we were first getting to know Arthur Miller as a dramatist. Yet the rejection can be seen, also, as critically necessary, for there is little doubt that the dramatic forms in which social questions were ordinarily raised had become, in general, inadequate: a declined, low-pressure naturalism, or else the angularity of the self-conscious problem play, the knowingness of the post-expressionistic social revue. To break out from this deadlock needed three things, in any order: a critical perception of why the forms were inadequate; effective particular experiment; a revival, at depth and with passion, of the social thinking itself. Arthur Miller is unquestionably the most important agent of this break-out, which as yet, however, is still scattered and uncertain. His five plays to date show a wide and fascinating range of experiment, and the introduction he has written to the collected edition of them shows an exceptionally involved and perceptive critical mind, both self-conscious and self-critical of the directions of his creative effort. Yet, while he could not have written his plays without these qualities, it is probably true that the decisive factor, in his whole achievement, is a particular kind and intensity of social thinking, which in his case seems both to underlie and to determine the critical scrutiny and the restless experimentation. . . .

The key to social realism . . . lies in a particular conception of the relationship of the individual to society, in which neither is the individual seen as a unit nor the society as an aggregate, but both are seen as belonging to a continuous and in real terms inseparable process. My interest in the work of Arthur Miller is that he seems to have come nearer than any other post-war writer (with the possible exceptions of Albert Camus and Albrecht Goes) to this substantial conception. . . .

Raymond Williams. *CQ*. Summer, 1959, pp. 140–41

Death of a Salesman, even with its discordance of tone, its verbal furies, the shrill scrapings of certain insistent glances *au rebours,* remains a lesson of style for the most recent European writers who put flowers into the mouths of masks bearing "problems."

The name of Chekhov has been mentioned in Miller's case and with good reasons. Yet this comparison has tended to minimize the quality of psychological research that appears in the work of the American playwright with the same exactness as that of the Russian writer. A quality revealing not so much a derived technique as a vantage point of the soul from which it is possible to define a man.

Consider Miller's slightest touches both in the memory of the protagonist and in the action: think, for example, of the stockings that Willy Loman gives the prostitute and his tormented distaste for letting his wife mend his own stockings. Here we must say again that Miller has not tried to revolutionize theatrical technique, nor (as though that were possible) to invent new sentiments in man. His style is extremely simple even if it seems to have a cinematographic nature because we are accustomed to seeing it frequently portrayed on the screen. His thought, the remembrance of the character, in a monologue or in visual form; these have been techniques of theatre and of fiction for centuries. Nor can they now so mislead us as to blind us to the gaps in the sustained rhythm of Miller's tragedy, even if the staging has restricted in space the confession of the soul, the deliriums of Loman's mind.

The defeat of Miller's man is true and universal. He is so monotonous that he will repeat himself, reverberating as an echo in his children. Willy Loman, an injured man and a servant through his daily exercises of obedience, will in vain recommend to his dear Biff not to collect papers and objects which could by chance fall from the desk of his hypothetical boss the day be asks for a job. He has made those gestures all his life, and he will make them again until his last hour. His pride is nothing but an "idea," a fiction which he would like to be a strength in the heart of his son. Even this is a "stratagem," and a most desolate one, that serves to individualize a writer sensitive to the most intimate emotional convictions. [1960]

Salvatore Quasimodo. *The Poet and the Politician*
(Carbondale, Ill., Southern Illinois University Press,
1964), pp. 149–50

Responding to the political climate, Miller's plays have moved steadily inward. Although each play has probed the impact of large, bewildering issues upon a simple man, the large issues have become increasingly dim. Some of the haziness is intrinsic, but some of it is induced by the simple man's mounting personal problems. In *All My Sons,* the issue is no less than the war itself. The play shares the weakness of its chief character, who finds it hard to make the war's values immediate and meaningful. *Death of a Salesman* strikes a balance between the social problem of the shattered myth of success and Willy Loman's sex and family problems. *The Crucible* shows us witch hunts, but the obvious contemporary reference is masked by the historical setting and by the very distinctive seventeenth-century speech; what remains is the tension between the incalculable malice of private individuals and the conscience of a guilt-ridden husband. With *A View from the Bridge,* Miller's focus moves still further within. Eddie Carbone is not only troubled and guilty; he is sick, and his symptoms resemble those that Tennessee Williams, the most typically "internal" of contemporary American dramatists, had made the common substance of Broadway drama—incestuous inclinations, psychotic sexual jealousy, frenzied hostility to homosexuality, and possibly incipient homosexuality. If these symptoms are present, it is less important that the immigration service also has its shortcomings; the play's main topic has become Eddie's troubles.

Henry Popkin. *SewR*. Winter, 1960, pp. 59–60

These, then, are the strengths of Arthur Miller: an acute awareness of the "public" nature of theatre, the desire to see and report life realistically, an unwillingness to settle for a merely positivist version of reality, and a desire to see a theatre of "heightened consciousness." By putting these concerns before the public, Arthur Miller has shown that his sights are higher than those of any of his competitors at the Broadway box-office. The fact that such concerns exist in a playwright of his prominence is proof that our theatre is still alive. It is perhaps unfair to judge Miller's work as a playwright by his own critical standard. To do so, however, will reveal not only the deficiencies of much American theatre but will also be a way of seeing certain weaknesses that lie in Miller's thought. . . .

Two weaknesses are fatal to Miller's attempt to write the kind of objective theatre he sees is needed. First, his view of man in society is too narrow. He is restricted, as many have pointed out, by a particular social theory which he seems not to have had the inclination to probe until it yielded him a fundamental ideal of human nature. Brecht, to take an opposite example, did such probing. Apparently Miller's Marxism changes as he goes along, and it would be going beyond the evidence to suggest that he adheres to any "line," whether political or ideological. Nevertheless, he bears a quasi-Marxist stamp and most of his plays tend to become mere partisan social critique. The momentary usefulness of that social critique, or the extent to which it actually is Marxist, is nothing to the point. The point is simply that his conception of the "reality" with which man must deal is limited. . . .

Miller deplores the loss of a "universal moral sanction," but he does nothing toward the discovery of a conceivable basis for one. In that respect he is, perhaps, no different from the majority of his contemporaries. It is not a surprising result, however, that he falls so easily into preaching and scolding his audience. . . . Miller's strident moralism is a good example of what happens when ideals must be maintained in an atmosphere of humanistic relativism. There being no objective good and evil, and no imperative other than conscience, man himself must be made to bear the full burden of creating his values and living up to them. The immensity of this task is beyond human capacity, even that of genius. To insist upon it without reference to ultimate truth is to create a situation productive of despair. This point has been seen by many writers of our day, but not by the liberal optimists, of which Miller is one. Here we have come to the second weakness which inevitably robs his work of stature.

Tom F. Driver. *TDR*. May, 1960, pp. 47–48, 50–51

The very considerable power of *The Crucible* derives from its revelation of a mounting tide of evil gaining, in an entire society, an ascendancy quite disproportionate to the evil of any individual member of that society. What is so horrifying is to watch the testimony of honest men bouncing like an indiarubber ball off the high wall of disbelief that other men have built around themselves, not from ingrained evil, but from over-zealousness and a purblind confidence in their own judgment. What meaning has proof when men will believe only what they want to believe, and will interpret evidence only in the light of their own prejudice? To watch *The Crucible* is to be overwhelmed by the simple impotence of honest common sense against fanaticism that is getting out of control, and to be painfully reminded that there are situations in which sheer goodness ("mere unaided virtue," in Melville's phrase about Starbuck) is just not enough to counter such deviousness.

In this respect, too, it will remain a more important document of McCarthy's America than would a more partisan piece. The ugliness of that affair, which caused so much perplexed anxiety to friends of the United States, was not the megalomanic aspirations of a cynical demagogue, but the appalling ease with which his methods achieved results. So fast and so wide did the infection spread that it could only be visualised as a force of evil of which ordinary men and women were the unintentional agents and the unrecognising victims. In many ways its moral damage was more serious to those who accepted it than to those who fought against or were victimised by it, and this is what *The Crucible* so splendidly communicates.

Dennis Welland. *Arthur Miller* (New York, Grove, 1961), pp. 84–85

Miller's view of man has been too simplified to finally convince us that his work is an adequate representation of reality. Each of Miller's central characters, the living embodiments of his point of view, has been engaged in an action which his creator clearly considers the most significant one which a man can undertake, the search for a sense of personal dignity and identity in a hostile world. It is in this search that Willy Loman resembles the cowboys of *The Misfits* and, in fact, all of Miller's central characters, for each of them, though he lives most explicitly amidst the problems of the modern world (Miller's one historical play is a thinly disguised presentation of the McCarthy era), is engaged in this essentially personal quest for his own self.

When he has found that self—and a Miller hero almost inevitably does so—he has, in the mind of his author, reached the point of rest at the end of his journey. This faith in the efficacy of self-knowledge, the one element that appears in all Miller's plays, is far more central to his view of life than any of his ideas, however serious, concerning the immediate problems of society. But as with many faiths the problems of achieving and retaining it are great.

Arthur Ganz. DramaS. Oct., 1963, p. 231

At the time we produced The Crucible, Miller was already the most powerful rational voice in the American theater. Questioning the play later, I wanted the company to understand that to criticize him was to take his ideas seriously, and to begin to give some shape to our own. The people we often had to question most were those with whom we seemed to agree. Because we were all vulnerable to easy judgments and that depth psychology of the surface which is so inherent in American drama (and acting), it was necessary to see why The Crucible was not really the "tough" play that Miller claimed; I mean dramatically tough, tough in soul, driving below its partisanship to a judgment of anti-social action from which, as in Dostoyevsky, none of us could feel exempt. I wouldn't have asked the questions if Miller didn't prompt them with his reflections on Social Drama and the tragic form. But compare the action of Proctor to that of the tragic figures of any age—Macbeth, or Britannicus, or Raskolnikov: can you approve or disapprove of their action? Can you make the choice of imitating them? Or avoid it? The Crucible may confirm what we like to think we believe, but it is not, as Miller says, intimidating to an "Anglo-Saxon audience" (or actors), nor does it really shock us into recognizing that we don't believe what we say we do. Beyond that, the profoundest dramas shake up our beliefs, rock our world; in The Crucible, our principles are neither jeopardized nor extended, however much we may fail to live by them anyhow.

As for the inquisitors, Miller wants us to see evil naked and unmitigated. I am prepared to believe it exists (I am certain it exists), and I won't even ask where it comes from. But—to be truer than tough—if you want absolute evil, you've got to think more about witches. Miller wants the Puritan community without Puritan premises or Puritan intuitions (which is one reason why, when he appropriates the language, his own suffers in comparison). His liberalism is the kind that, really believing we have outlived the past, thinks it is there to be used. The past just doesn't lie around like that. And one of these days the American theater is really going to have to come to terms with American history.

Axiom for liberals: no play is deeper than its witches.

Herbert Blau. The Impossible Theater (New York,
Macmillan, 1964), pp. 191–92

It is not easy to write a three-hour play, and even less easy if you are an Arthur Miller with a conscience prickly enough for six men. In his earlier plays (with the exception of the equivocal *A View from the Bridge*), Miller's writing took fire because he was on the attack—against the greed of private industry, against society's disposition to use up people as if they were products, against the hysteria bred by investigations. In *After the Fall* he mounts the attack against himself, and does not take the measure of the enemy. The cause, I think, is twofold.

First, Miller cannot create a flawed hero, possibly because he makes heroes out of himself. The sins of Quentin, like those of Willy Loman and John Proctor, amount to little more than a mischievous night or two out. Second, he has thickened his dialogue with "stage directions." This is a pity. Miller can place words in context with a vernacular precision and melody unequalled in American drama. But in this play [Jason] Robards often finds himself treading wet tar, especially during the soliloquies. In them Miller does not so much feel; he spends words, like a Jacobean melodramatist, to appease sentiment.

Yet, for all that it falters and maunders, this play commands one's attention and, intermittently, respect for three hours. Miller can strike drama even against himself, even against a cloaked image of himself. . . .

Albert Bermel. NewL. Feb. 3, 1964, p. 31

I am haunted by a pair of caricatures Max Beerbohm might have drawn: Williams, encircled by his characters, in a pool of tears, and more dejected than they; and Miller gazing calmly at his—"Don't come and tell me about all you can't do. Why can't you?" Where Williams sympathizes, Miller more restlessly looks for a cure. It is the difference between "How pitiful!" and "What can be done about it?" The nearest Miller can come to a "Tennessee Williams character" is Maggie in *After the Fall* and, lost as she is, Quentin's insight might have saved her had she been able to take it for her own. There is always this outside voice in Miller, an alternative truth that in no way lessens the character's subjective truth.

The affirmation in Miller's plays stems from his belief in man's freedom of will. For Miller, man's failure is "his failure to assert his sense of civilized life." In the plays his committed man tries to transcend his apparent powers and find his selfhood. Miller counterbalances acceptance by exploring the reasons behind a situation, socially and psychologically, with the energy of a bankrupt prospecting for gold. It is part of the passionate search for meaning and relatedness going on in his plays. A man's life must be meaningful, and if it is not, why? The struggle is never abandoned. Against a fully realized determinism, Miller's hero protests Miller's refusal to believe in man's helplessness and predestined defeat. His recognition that a situation is not ideal is coupled with the realization that it does not have to be accepted. Even Willy Loman does not have to accept the fact that there is nothing he can do for his son. Chris Keller does not have to live with his father's guilt; John Proctor need not compromise nor Eddie Carbone settle for half.

Sheila Huftel. *Arthur Miller: The Burning Glass*
(New York, Citadel, 1965), pp. 71–72

In his second play, *Incident at Vichy,* at the Repertory Theater of Lincoln Center, Arthur Miller recovers somewhat, even if only to a limited extent, from the disaster of *After the Fall,* a piece so pretentious and defensive that virtually nothing good can be said about it. In an openly subjective or confessional mood, bringing his own life behavior into question, Miller is more pitiable than ingratiating. In this new play, however, what is perceptible is not callow subjectivity but an overstrain of intellectual capacity. Still, its director, Harold Clurman, has very ably succeeded, in so far as it was at all within his power, in staving off some of the hazards of the author's ideological ambition and the frequent sententiousness of his language. . . .

What *au fond* I find objectionable, in a dramaturgical as well as in a plain logical sense, is the surprise ending of the play (welcomed by not a few reviewers as giving it "a jolt it badly needs," as one of them put it), in which at the very last moment the Austrian prince, a liberal of refined sensibilities, is released by the interrogators only to hand over his exit-permit to the doomed Jewish psychoanalyst. This Myshkin-like act of self-sacrifice seems to me to belie the entire portentous dialectic of guilt, responsibility, the horror of Nazism as the horror of human nature, etc., which Miller develops throughout the production. It is an ending dramatically unearned, so to speak, because on the symbolical plane at least it contradicts the entire emphasis of the ideas that preceded it. It is a melodramatic contrivance pure and simple, a sheer *coup de théâtre*. It may give the audience a lift, but it drops the play's intellectual baggage with a heavy thud. After all, liberalism, especially the aestheticized type of liberalism represented by the prince, has been belabored throughout, and here all of a sudden he gives his own life to save another man's, who is a stranger at that; nothing whatever in the play has prepared us for this exhibition of saintliness. Thus the author has it both ways: he condemns human nature ("We're all scum") at the same time that he appears to exonerate it in the way he brings his action to a close. Everything is indeed possible in life, but in dramatic art what is required is the seeming inevitability of an end, however tragic, which is truly a conclusion vindicating the organizing principle of the work as a whole.

Philip Rahv. *The Myth and the Powerhouse* (New York,
Farrar, Straus & Giroux, 1965), pp. 225–27

Arthur Miller and Eugene O'Neill have done more than other American dramatists to "relate the subjective to the objective truth": *Death of a Salesman* and O'Neill's *Long Day's Journey into Night* are two of the finest works in the American theater. Contrary to Miller's assertion, however, there *is* in his plays a contradiction between passion and awareness, between irrational impulse and rational concept. His best dialogue mirrors psychological conditions, yet he constantly returns to the formal generalization; he can skillfully manipulate emotional tension, yet he seeks esthetic detachment; his figures act most intelligibly in a family context, yet he feels obliged to make explicit their connection with a social "environment." Miller sees his principal subject—the drive for self-justification—primarily as an *internal* process activated by "mechanisms" that repress or involuntarily recall shameful memories and motives, that effect rapid transitions between taut and relaxed moods. When his characters fervently defend egocentric attitudes, their futility evokes a genuine sense of terror and pathos that indirectly but powerfully reinforces his thesis on the necessity for "meaningful" accommodation in society. When, on the other hand, his characters intelligently reform, their self-knowledge remains only a rhetorical promise. The mature new-men—Lawrence Newman, David Frieber, Chris Keller, Biff Loman, John Proctor, Gay Langland, Quentin, Leduc, and Von Berg—appear just long enough to predicate their liberating insights. A tendency to impose judgment upon action—the tendency Miller worried about after writing his first Broadway play, *The Man Who Had All the Luck*—has prevented him from achieving the harmony of styles he has long sought. His attempt to enlarge the "interior psychological question" with "codes and ideas of social and ethical importance" has distorted his subjective perspective and so compromised his exceptional talent.

Leonard Moss. Arthur Miller (New York, Twayne, 1967),
pp. 108–9

Although some of the stage sets for his plays may have suggested the contrary, Arthur Miller's theatre has never been experimentally avant-garde: from his beginnings he has aimed at a critical clarification of the already existent attitudes of liberal-minded American theatregoers. His plays are written for and largely from the point of view of a man whose attitudes are not radical and innovatory but puzzled, confused and absolutely resolved not to break with his fellow countrymen. He has maintained his theatre as nearly popular as an intellectual playwright may and still be tolerated on Broadway since the 1940's. Two of his plays were included in the opening season of the Lincoln Center repertory company, the New York approximation to an initiatory national theatre, where he functioned as the official contemporary dramatist. *After the Fall* and *Incident at Vichy* seemed to satisfy no one at the time, and yet in these plays once again Miller dealt with

his local themes of faith and meaning within the confused national and personal life of America, and dealt with them without abstractions which might
call for a re-thinking of the Great Society.

Miller once remarked: "I can't live apart from the world." Yet his
plays dramatize the ways in which a man alienates himself from his society
and fights to get back into it. Until his most recent play, the structure of
that society goes uncondemned and unanalysed, taken as if it were an unchangeable artifact. The weight of action falls cruelly on the individual
within the fixed, powerful society which fails to support him at his moment
of need and remains, as he falls, monolithically immovable. "Evil" is those
social pressures which conflict with an equally vaguely defined individual
integrity in the hero or heroine. But critical though he is of American, perhaps Western, values, Miller finally has come to believe that "evil" is
really the natural cruelty of human nature seen, not as a product of historical
social structures, but as inevitable data. The dilemma of his last two plays
lies here in a nagging circularity which makes his work typical of frustrated
American liberalism.

Eric Mottram. In John Russell Brown and Bernard
Harris, eds., *American Theatre*, Stratford-upon-Avon
Studies 10 (London, Edward Arnold, 1967), pp. 127–28

Thematically, and this is one measure of his achievement, Miller has created
a related body of work. Certain themes, such as "integrity" or "compromise," may be—and too often are—isolated for discussion; but this abstraction, perfectly valid on one level, tends to ignore other themes in Miller's
work. . . . And these themes are not easily given one-word tags. To say,
for instance, that Willy Loman, John Proctor, and Eddie Carbone are all
concerned with their "integrity" is true—but that observation scarcely does
justice to the thematic complexity of their respective plays. It may seem that
I am undercutting my previous assertion that Miller's plays are related.
What I am trying to say, however, is that there is both unity and diversity
in Miller's work, and that we oversimplify and distort his achievement by
focusing too narrowly and too insistently on one or two obvious and fashionable aspects of his work. One must beware, for example, of branding
Miller merely a "social" dramatist, for as analysis of the plays makes clear
he is equally a "psychological" playwright. At his best, Miller has avoided
the extremes of clinical psychiatric case studies on the one hand and mere
sociological reports on the other. Assimilating available technical devices to
his own unique aims, he has indicated, often in the face of incredible critical
stupidity, contradiction, and malice, how the dramatist might maintain in
delicate balance both personal and social motivation. Nor is it correct to say
that the main burden of guilt in his plays is borne by society. Miller's characters—Willy Loman, John Proctor, Eddie Carbone, Quentin, and Von

Berg—"take their life in their arms" (as Holga put it in *After the Fall*), with the result that the accusing finger of guilt is leveled at *both* the individual *and* society. If one rejects Miller because he is too "narrow," because he lacks a metaphysic or a theology of crisis, then one should be prepared, I think, to reject some of the most vital playwrights of the modern theater.

Edward Murray. Arthur Miller, Dramatist (New York,
Frederick Ungar, 1967), pp. 180–81

Arthur Miller, despite his reputation as a "social dramatist," has attained to something considerably more than a humanised social play. If his earlier work never finally breaks free of a standard railing against the pursuit of success, his consciousness that "a play which appears merely to exist to one side of 'ideas' is an aesthetic nullity" does something to explain the significance of his work to a theatre obsessed with emotion and escapism. Miller's triumph lies in his refusal to evade and his distrust of resolution. To him the core of action lies in integrity. This in turn depends upon a clear perception of the reality of a naked identity forged out of choices made and not moulded to fit the illusions of a dream world. In so far as this penetrates the theatrical weaknesses of his plays it can be seen as the main inheritance which he has passed onto those dramatists who have succeeded him. His commitment to a theatre of ideas lifted him above the norm of an enervated theatre. His concern with the establishment of a dialectic having its base in a real world anticipated Albee's . . . concern with the necessity of seizing the reality of the human condition as the one legitimate theme for a modern American drama free at last of the responsibility for justification or for the ritualistic destruction of social scape-goats. The line from *All My Sons* to *After the Fall* is a logical one. In successive plays Miller has probed deeper and deeper into the metaphysical life of man while simultaneously moving away from that distrust of "rectitudinal fever" demonstrated by Ibsen towards a faith in the necessity for confrontation. This faith is in essence that outlined by James Baldwin in an early essay published in *Notes of a Native Son* (1955), "People who shut their eyes to reality simply invite their own destruction, and anyone who insists on remaining in a state of innocence long after that innocence is dead turns himself into a monster." If the affirmation of *Death of a Salesman* is largely unconvincing and unjustified that of *After the Fall* is a genuine aspect of a dialectic which sees confrontation as the necessary prelude to a renewed faith in the "humanist heresy" of belief in man. While in his early plays Miller was clearly moving towards the position adopted by the drama of confrontation it is equally clear that it was not until his vision had been tempered by the cold pessimism of the absurd that his belief in affirmation through confrontation could offer any truly universal meaning. For it is only in his last plays that he attempted to define the full nature of the human situation which must be faced. He is no longer content with demonstrating that a man is limited to his own possibilities. He now demands an acceptance of the full implications of human nature and the human situation. For between *Death of a Salesman* and *After the Fall* the theatre of the absurd had defined with meticulous care the nature of a world beyond the immediate comprehension of a Willy Loman—a world more terrifying than that represented by the mechanised unconcern of success-society.

C. W. E. Bigsby. *Confrontation and Commitment*
(Columbia, Mo., University of Missouri Press,
1968), pp. 48–49

In a time when so many playwrights are dealing with modern man's isolation and loneliness, Miller, without denying either the loneliness or the isolation, is convinced that "the world is moving toward a unity, a unity won not alone by the necessities of the physical developments themselves, but by the painful and confused reassertion of man's inherited will to survive." His passionate concern that attention be paid to the aspirations, worries, and failures of all men—and, more especially, of the little man who is representative of the best and worst of an industrialized democratic society—has resulted in plays of great range and emotional impact. For the past quarter of a century a disturbingly large percentage of the plays written for the American theatre have tended to be case histories of all forms of social and psychological aberration. For Arthur Miller, who has been a major figure during the whole period, this has not been the case; he has insisted with a continually broadening range that courage, truth, trust, responsibility, and faith must be the central values of men who would (as they must) live together.

Though the dominant tone of the theatre in the mid-twentieth century is despair, Miller continually demands more; he seeks a "theatre in which an adult who wants to live can find plays that will heighten his awareness of what living in our times involves." Miller's own sense of involvement with modern man's struggle to be himself is revealed in his own growth as an artist and has made him one of the modern theatre's most compelling and important spokesmen.

Robert W. Corrigan. Introduction to Robert W. Corrigan,
ed., *Arthur Miller: A Collection of Critical Essays*
(Englewood Cliffs, N.J., Prentice-Hall, 1969), pp. 21–22

Although what Miller has to say in the new plays is philosophically suspect, it is not his theme but his commitment to it that has crippled his work. His new truth is not an impetus to creativity, but a doctrine that must be illustrated. . . . Miller's most recent play [*The Price*] is set in the same thematic country as *After the Fall* and *Incident at Vichy*. . . . If this were all there were to *The Price,* it would not be that welcome a change from *After the Fall* and *Incident at Vichy.* Its strength lies in the character of Gregory Solomon, who dominates the play when he is on stage and, through well-timed intrusions during the brothers' discussion, continues to be a formidable presence even when he has moved to the periphery of the central action. A man almost ninety years old, a retired appraiser, who finds in the furniture an opportunity to begin again, he is an embodiment of the idea that life is the product of belief beyond disbelief. More important, he is Arthur Miller's first real comic character, a creation that realizes some of the possibilities implicit in Willy Loman's happier scenes.

Gerald Weales. *The Jumping-Off Place* (New York,
Macmillan, 1969), pp. 19, 21–23

In all [Miller's] works, despite crushing obstacles, something is achieved, the possibility of responsibility and action is restored. Dignity is reaffirmed.

And because this possibility permeates his work, Arthur Miller is one of the most rebellious writers in the modern drama. His continuing exploration of the ramifications of determinism and free will, guilt and responsibility, drift and action, represents his revolt against a theater singing dirges of woe. Miller rebels against the fashionable complacency and chic lamentation that dominate so much of the contemporary stage, on, off, or below Broadway. His consideration of responsibility and free will is a challenge to the paralyzing morbidity of a drama which views man as trapped in a cosmic straitjacket, thrashing about in his pettiness and helplessness. His characters are not defined in terms of hysteria, but of history; they are not only affected by their world, they are able to affect it as well.

Miller does not invite his audience to luxuriate in a velvety cloak of universal despair and self-pity, nor does he subject us to sadomasochistic barrages under the shrill slogans of joy, freedom, and liberation. In a theater of angry young men, frustrated old men, and precocious adolescents of indeterminate age, Miller goes his own way, committed to a drama of communication based on the reasonable assumption that the stage may still be the place for an aesthetic and civilizing act.

Benjamin Nelson. *Arthur Miller: Portrait of
a Playwright* (New York, McKay, 1970), pp. 318–19

In spite of personal dedication and public optimism, Miller's plays are remarkably full of suicide. Larry Keller crashed his airplane, and Joe Keller shot himself. Willy Loman crashed his car and did not die his dream death of a salesman. John Proctor (and several lesser characters) of *The Crucible* went to death to assert their integrity, as Eddie Carbone met death in a vain effort to assert his integrity. Lou and Maggie killed themselves in despair in *After the Fall.* Prince Von Berg sacrificed his life to prove his faith in individual life, and Gregory Solomon lost his daughter by a suicide that is not particularized. For all these misfortunes, Miller seeks our pity, and pity is what he evokes when most adept. Though Miller is said to specialize in the inarticulate, all his victims are articulate; they talk. Incisive dialogue etches Miller's low men in our minds; Joe Keller, Willy Loman, Eddie Carbone, Gregory Solomon are vigorous with concrete colloquialisms, Jewish inflections, or rhythmic repetitions of everyday words. Often, however, Miller tries to convert his low man into Everyman, or—worse—into the Tragic Hero. Then Miller is betrayed by his weakness for sonorous abstraction or incongruous image. He finds it hard to accept that he is most true when most trivial.

Ruby Cohn. Dialogue in American Drama (Bloomington,
Ind., Indiana University Press, 1971), p. 95

Although a "surgeon" and a "policeman" may be much like a "salesman" in allegorical import, Miller does seem [in *The Price*] to be advancing toward a more open confrontation with the raw material from which he has fashioned these family works. At the same time, he has not abandoned his concern with "symbol" and the making of large philosophical statements, an impulse clearly reflected in his titles and in the underlying concerns these titles suggest: *All My Sons, Death of a Salesman, After the Fall, The Price,* each implying a dimension beyond the immediate and concrete.

Miller in *The Price* is still trying to understand the phenomenological particularity of contemporary American life through some large-focusing generalization. In his concern for such structuring, the small moment encapsulating a large "idea," he also suggests the point of the old-fashioned concern with the well-made play: there *is* order in the universe, and it can be represented in a careful control of event on stage. The good-natured whimsicality of the old furniture appraiser is divine in its patient benignity, in its gratuitousness, in its radiating and impersonal benevolence. There may be a price exacted for all bargains in this world, but the person setting this price is genial, amiable, kindly, forgiving, if ultimately hard-nosed about true worth. God is not only omniscient, knowing both the price of everything and its true value as well, and omnipotent, able to exact the right price finally in all situations, but, lest we tend to lacerate ourselves too mercilessly for our greed or stupidity, benevolent. We need, then, not be sensitive about being shortchanged: we will get the right price in the end. This meliorism accords with the American Jewish experience in its most obvious and in its coarsest aspects, and perhaps it is still too early to expect to find any subtler truths recorded in popular drama.

Morris Freedman. American Drama in Social
Context (Carbondale, Ill., Southern Illinois
University Press, 1971), pp. 57–58

Miller's drama now looks old-fashioned both in its assumption that the past does not undergo any chemical change in the memory and in the related assumption that it is possible to make meaningful statements about causal connections between one event and another. Avant-garde art, like quantum mechanics, has questioned the possibility of isolating anything as the cause of anything else. Robbe-Grillet has said that chronological time distorts our experience because it "forces events into a pattern of causality and imposes an unjustifiable logic on them." Like so much of what Robbe-Grillet has said, this has its roots in Sartre and Camus. In *L'étranger,* as Sartre pointed out, Camus deliberately suppressed all causal links between the sentences. It is this which so often gives an appearance of absurdity to a totally unexceptional series of incidents.

A strong case could be made for calling Miller the most Sartrean contemporary dramatist, and while it would be oversimplifying things to argue that his social commitment has forced him into an old-fashioned method of storytelling, it is obviously almost impossible for a playwright to make statements about society except in terms of cause and effect; Adamov and Arrabal, for example, have been pulled damagingly in different directions by social commitment on the one hand and formal experiment on the other.

Essentially a social playwright, Miller has always used his character to make statements about society, though he has done this in different ways. . . .

Ronald Hayman. *Arthur Miller* (New York,
Frederick Ungar, 1972), pp. 112–13

It is perhaps inevitable that *After the Fall* will continue to be seen and discussed as autobiography and not drama. Miller's strength as a playwright, however, lies in his ability to give dramatic life to the fundamental assumptions concerning the American experience, its values and inflated sense of self-importance, through an imaginative and coherent vision of its immense potential for the individual life and consciousness. Like Joseph Heller, following his success with *Catch-22,* Miller achieved prominence early in his career, and could have quite easily chosen to continue his recognition as the author of *Death of a Salesman* by writing alternate versions such as *Death of a Lawyer, Death of a Doctor,* or perhaps even *Death of a President*—the possibilities seem endless. That he has not chosen to retread the same ground is evidence that, like Heller, who could have continued with *Catch-23, Catch-24, 25, ad infinitum,* he is possessed of courage and insight exceptional for the artistic atmosphere of his time. His further explorations of the present in terms of the past in *Incident at Vichy, The Price,* and *The Creation of the World and Other Business* have demonstrated once again that he views the theater and his contribution to it as "a serious business, one that makes or should make man more human, which is to say, less alone."

And it is to the "aloneness" of contemporary society that Miller has increasingly directed his thought and plays. *Incident at Vichy* has as its resolution the embodiment of not being alone as an act of individual choice when Von Berg, an Austrian prince, hands his pass to freedom over to Leduc, a Jewish doctor. In *The Price,* Miller returned to his family theme to point out the psychological price they pay for their inability to resolve misunderstandings from the past. Two brothers who have been separated for sixteen years come together briefly, but leave singly and alone by the end of the play. *The Creation of the World* is also about aloneness, the kind that results from moments nearly existential when man stands on the brink between murder and forgiveness, innocence and guilt. And it may be worth pointing out that if Miller has relied less directly on the legal analogies and lawyer figures in his plays since *After the Fall, Incident at Vichy* takes place in a detention room for suspected Jews in Vichy, France, in 1942, and is structured around a police investigation complete with guards and detectives, while *The Price* has as one of its two central characters a policeman, Victor Franz, whose only comment, after spending twenty-five years of his life in the New York City Police Department, is "I've hated every minute of it." Although *The Creation of the World* is based on the Biblical account of Adam and Eve, Cain and Abel, it too is predicated on the consequences of a legal violation that occurred some time ago in the Garden of Eden, and which can be seen metaphorically or literally as a legal precedent of considerable significance to present-day society.

Robert A. Martin. Introduction to *The
Theatre Essays of Arthur Miller* (New
York, Viking, 1975), pp. xxxvi–xxxviii

Full of variety, and with a cast that seems as limitless as *42nd Street*'s, [*The American Clock*], subtitled "a mural for theatre," sets out to tell the story of a Jewish family in Brooklyn during the Depression, but digresses from one peripheral scene to another like an elderly uncle reminiscing at dinner.

Many of the scenes, as scenes, are enchanting: the grandpa who grieves because the new (smaller) house has no room for his walking sticks; the whore who gives her favors to dentists in return for root canal work; the menacing Southern sheriff who is actually in thrall to the black short-order cook—these people are a delightful change from the usual Miller characters, burdened with social and psychological meaning. The Depression having been so widespread, the pressure to symbolize its economics is lighter on each individual, and the psychological pressure on the three central figures is alleviated by the presence of so many other souls in misery. It is the first Miller play not driven by the need to become a tract.

At the same time, though, it does not become anything else; the reminiscer, misled by his digressions, has forgotten the point of his anecdote.

It's true that he wants to tell us his parents' marriage was embittered, his mother driven to the brink of insanity, by the Depression, but this is in itself not dramatic substance. Other marriages, including many worse off economically than the Baums' in this play, were lasting and happy; why did theirs crack? Just at the point where Miller might be able to tell us, the play stops short. The mural, thronging with subsidiary characters, is left unfinished, sketched in rapidly fading chalk. Only with one stroke—a scene between father and son in a relief office—does he hit off depth and surface at the same time, and this comes from nowhere and is not pursued.

Michael Feingold. VV. Nov. 16–Dec. 2, 1980, p. 83

ODETS, CLIFFORD (1906 – 1963)

Awake and Sing! shows great promise, especially in the field of melodrama. It begins, moves along and develops with real skill. The attention it exacts is definite and constant. The only boredom I felt was with the recurring ugliness, sometimes so prolonged that I was led to wonder why I should bother with such people as these characters seemed to be.

This effect of stridency and ugliness, however, diminished after the first act. The growing intensity of the play replaced that yapping quality which, if spread throughout the household of characters, passes endurance. It is practically impossible to feel either the tragedy or the comedy of such rowing, jawing, prideless and uninspired human beings. This sort of judgment of that type of Jewish life seems to me necessary and right; how otherwise are we to measure and evaluate the nobler and more beautiful forms of Jewish life that are to be found? Any general front rigidly preserved merely means that the lower Jewish forms of life gain, the higher lose. . . .

As a workaday drama *Awake and Sing!* seems to me far above the average. The author of it has talent, a sense of character drawing and a clear sense of emotional contrasts. The scene of the grandfather cutting the rich son's hair is genuine drama and is moving. What the play lacks is a deep basis in the dramatist's own conception. What life, beneath the incidental, has he in mind? What, for instance, does he think of their constant patter about getting on, in money, in advantages, when all the time there lie within his Jews' grasp their own marvelous inheritance? Are we to weep because this family that might have possessed one of the great racial traditions of the world, its poetry and prayer, are sour because they cannot have Packards? Where, for Mr. Odets, is the race's dream and shadow of divinity? From the dramatist's point of view we have a right to ask a more fundamental conception on his own part. On what, in his opinion, does this life that he portrays rest? The actual conveyance technically of the bases on which a play rests is a part of the dramatist's technical problem.

Stark Young. NR. March 13, 1935, p. 134

In all that has been written about the plays of Clifford Odets it is odd that little attention has been paid to the fact that first and foremost these plays are Jewish, and that Mr. Odets himself is a direct descendant of those playwrights such as [Jacob] Gordin and [Z.] Libin who once made the Yiddish theatre in America so extraordinarily vital. What has been impressive in Mr. Odets's plays has not been their ideas, which are usually pretty confused, or their structure, which has been pretty melodramatic, but the fact that the characterizations and the dialogue have a bite and an originality of turn which set them apart from the somewhat pallid characters and dialogue of most modern plays. It is true that Mr. Odets's people often shout at the top of their lungs, that their emotion is unrestrained, and at times they utter appalling banalities with an air of owlish wisdom. But all in all their vitality, both emotional and intellectual, is a welcome relief equally from chatterers or sophisticated nothings and from people who are all hard-boiled surface, with no intelligence underneath. Mr. Odets's people are at once primitive and intelligent, and it is this antinomy which imparts to them their color and variety. Neither of these qualities are hurt by the fact that their emotion is not strong enough to conquer their intelligence nor their intelligence deep or keen enough to kill their emotion. It is this struggle of emotion with intelligence which is the basis of much of the great drama of the world, and it is this struggle which is abundantly evident in the half-Americanized Jews of Mr. Odets.

A man familiar with the Yiddish drama told me recently that many of Odets's most pungent speeches are practically direct translations from the Yiddish, and it is this that makes the dialogue so alive and vital. It is dialogue, not created by the dramatist, but inherited by him from the speech of his people, which gives the feeling at once personal and universal which informs the talk in all his plays and notably in his latest success, *Rocket to the Moon*. Up to the present Mr. Odets has given no sign of understanding people other than his own type of Jewish-Americans, and for this reason it is not well to hope for the great American play from him; indeed it is unfair. It is unfortunate that at times, as in *Paradise Lost* and *Golden Boy,* he labels his characters as American or Italian, for they are always Jewish in mode of thought, in emotion, and in expression. But as a dramatist of the melting-pot he is unique and unapproached.

Grenville Vernon. Com. Dec. 16, 1938, p. 215

By a considerable margin, the most important achievement in the literature of the American Jews is that of Clifford Odets. No one else has been able to maintain that degree of confidence in the value of the exact truth which made his best work possible. His social understanding is limited, but he has been able to keep his eyes on reality and to set down his observations with great imagination and remarkable detachment. Jews are never commonplace to him—they are never commonplace to any Jew—but neither are they prodigies, either of absurdity or of pathos or of evil. He has perceived that they are human beings living the life which happens to be possible to them. . . .

In reading *Awake and Sing!*, one is likely to be struck by its crudity: there is an illegitimate pregnancy and a hasty marriage, a life insurance policy, a suicide; the final curtain is brought down on a puerile note of "affirmation" (Odets has said, "New art works should shoot bullets"). But in the last analysis these crudities are of no great importance. The special experience of reading or seeing the play has nothing to do with the dramatics used to make it progress through its three acts.

For the Jew in the audience, at least, the experience is recognition, a continuous series of familiar signposts, each suggesting with the immediate communication of poetry the whole complex of the life of the characters: what they are, what they want, how they stand with the world.

It is a matter of language more directly than anything else. The events of the play are of little consequence; what matters is the words of the characters—the way they talk as much as the things they say. Odets employs consistently and with particular skill what amounts to a special type of dramatic poetry. His characters do not speak in poetry—indeed, they usually become ridiculous when they are made to speak "poetically"—but the speeches put into their mouths have the effect of poetry, suggesting much more than is said and depending for the enrichment of the suggestion upon the sensibility and experience of the hearer. Many of the things said on the stage are startling for their irrelevance; they neither contribute to the progress of the plot nor offer any very specific light upon the character of the participants: the hearer supplies a meaning.

Robert S. Warshow. Cmty. May, 1946, pp. 17–18

[Odets'] virtues as a dramatist are great. No one has shown keener observation of the little people of the bourgeois world—the Berger family; the philosophical Mr. Carp; Siggie, the wisecracking taxi driver; Sam Feinschreiber, who runs to his mother-in-law for consolation after a marital dispute; Cleo Singer, dental secretary and eternal Eve. These and similar types are made to live on the stage with the aid of Odets' great gift for stage dialogue—crisp, dramatic, humorous. Odets' humor is rarely contrived or factitious but arises naturally out of character. The author's concern with love is unusual in proletarian drama. In his plays this passion is often shown as frustrated by social or personal restraints; only by the breaking of sentimental or conventional shackles does it find true fulfillment. This personal rebellion seems as prominent in Odets' work as his more Marxian protest against society. Be yourself, lead your own life—he seems to say—give in to love but don't allow it to interfere with your mission; protest against poverty and social evils, and unite with others in creating a better world. Through love, self-expression, and rebellion Odets' characters are driven to personal conversion—not unlike religious conversion in its intensity—which leads to full realization or to action. This is characteristic of the reforming movement of the thirties and rather than strict ideology accounts for much of the leftism in Odets' plays.

Edmond M. Gagey. *Revolution in American Drama*
(New York, Columbia University Press, 1947), p. 173

Although *The Country Girl* is not Mr. Odets's best play, it has some of his best writing in it. Moreover, it discloses a new and unexpected Odets. This in itself is reassuring and welcome. Mr. Odets has usually been associated with dramas of social significance if not of social protest. His favorite theme song, sung in anger or with enormous vitality, has been "Awake and sing, ye that dwell in the dust." His characters have shared "a fundamental activity: a struggle for life amidst petty conditions." His explanation of their personal frailties used to be the over-simple one that they were victims of The System.

It is interesting to see in *The Country Girl* that Mr. Odets can write from affection with the same intensity and insight with which he first wrote from indignation. This time he is making no plea, addressing no mass meeting, and leaving The System not only unblamed but unmentioned. The theatre, which he loves as warmly as he hates Hollywood, is his background, and its people are his concern. He is telling the story, a messageless one, of how a devoted wife struggles to keep her actor-husband sober so that he can make a comeback in the leading part a trusting producer is convinced he can play. The director falls in love with the wife after having at first misunderstood her. At the end, however, hers is Candida's choice of the man who has the greater need of her because he is the weaker.

Plainly such a theme in such a setting is neither new nor earth-shaking. As Sidney Howard pointed out long ago, the age and service-stripes of a story have little to do with eligibility. The point is that Mr. Odets makes the story his own. He gives it the benefit of his high-voltage feeling and phrasing. He allows us to see far beneath the surface of his characters into what is the mainspring of their frustrations or their actions. With skill and subtlety he misleads us at the outset into accepting as true the lies the actor has told about his wife in order to excuse his own weaknesses. Then, little by little, Mr. Odets enables us to see her as she is. His scenes race forward with the drive of his earliest works. His gift for deriving tension from small things is as effective as it used to be in developing large climaxes. [Dec. 9, 1950]

John Mason Brown. *As They Appear* (New York, McGraw-Hill, 1952), pp. 169–70

No more gifted playwright has appeared in the past fifteen years. I doubt whether any American playwright at all has a greater talent for living dramatic speech, for characterization, for intensity of feeling. Above all, Odets is a true theatre poet: he is never literal, and his power with words does not represent verbal proficiency but a blood tie with the sources from which sound literature and dramatic action spring.

Apart from a certain romantic afflatus, which is at times an easily discernible defect but more often a virtue, the strength of Odets' work lies in his main theme and the particular quality of its statement. The question Odets constantly asks is: What helps a man *live?* Since we are citizens of the twentieth century, we may translate this as: What today injures man's spirit? What enhances or diminishes the creatively human in him? "It's trying to be a man on the earth," a young boy confesses naïvely in *Waiting for Lefty*. All Odets is a variant on this theme, while the childlike pathos of its utterance reveals the Odetsian touch at its most naked.

Odets' art has an immediacy and an *intimacy* equaled by no other dramatist of our generation. His plays strike home; they touch us where we live. Though they often shout, they are powerful because, in fact, they speak quietly to our hearts. They are moving because beneath their occasional bluster they sigh and weep with our own unadvertised and non-literary anguish. Their tone sometimes has a slight aura of portentousness, but at bottom they are unabashedly homey.

Harold Clurman. *NR*. Dec. 11, 1950, pp. 29–30

Mr. Clifford Odets' new play [*The Flowering Peach*] is a work of secular piety, imperfect and somewhat arid, but nonetheless, luminously touched with the imagination of reverence. If—in this fastidious production—it curiously disappoints, we must, I should say, seek the cause in a rigid convention which the contemporary theater imposes on its craftsmen. That will be the inflexible assumption that only the large is important, that truth which may be art for an hour will be double-truth in two. No less than many another, Mr. Odets has been victimized by this straitening theatrical compulsion. He has been forced to amplify his work—essentially a meditative idyll of religious experience—with a web of extraneous detail; the threads, so richly woven at the outset, tangle and snarl. Nothing is won in range, much lost in concision, force, pressure. Ideally, *The Flowering Peach* would take a temporal form, somewhat like Christopher Fry's *A Sleep of*

Prisoners or Anouilh's *Antigone,* yet this is not a form to which our present theatrical temper is congenial.

But it is idle and even impertinent to conceive of possibilities: we must confront the play in its actuality. To his recasting of the Biblical tale of Noah, Mr. Odets brings a discreet humanism which shapes the experience beautifully, constantly points but never presses its contemporary reference. He was not, I think, wise to include among his dramatic baggage on the Ark so many rancorous family disputes: they do not illumine, rather they rasp and fatigue. They are, moreover, the remains of a moral intention exhausted in the more ''activist'' plays of Mr. Odets' youth, and as such have a somewhat gratuitous, calculated air. The same uncertainty of tone mars Mr. Odets' drawing of the important roles of Rachel and Japheth: these characters seem like intrusions from an alien world—their anguished self-regard is too conscious, too articulate, and dwarfed by the massive, obliterating humanity of Noah and Esther. Yet beyond these flaws, how vivifying it is to hear the Jewish idiom transmuted by tact and wit into art; how wonderful, above all, to find in this time of noisy commitments and harassing coercion a serious statement about human life which never says *must* or *should,* never imposes, sets up programs, announces, prescribes—only draws from the neglected well of our common pieties the small, permanent manifestations of tenderness and affection, of pleasure and reverence and a faith rich enough to nourish the seeds of the world.

Richard Hayes. *Com.* Feb. 11, 1955, p. 502

It was doubtless the attention attracted by *Waiting for Lefty* when it was first given before a special audience which led to the production of *Awake and Sing!,* a full length play by no means so perfect but much more ambitious, and also revealing dramatic talents of a kind which had not been demonstrated in the shorter piece. The conclusion of the play in which one of the principal characters announces his intention to devote the rest of his life to promoting the cause of the working class is obviously tacked on, but it was not only because most of the play was written before his conversion to Communism that the characterization is richer than that found in any other of our ''revolutionary'' plays. In his most recent work also Mr. Odets demonstrates his ability to create vivid and passionate individuals and he does not seem to have lost that interest in the study of human character which most radical playwrights, not unnaturally perhaps, lose as soon as they become convinced that what is traditionally called ''personality'' is only an epiphenomenon accompanying the true phenomena of the economic processes.

Joseph Wood Krutch. *The American Drama since 1918*
(New York, George Braziller, 1957), p. 267

It is important to note that Odets' social concern in the 1930's was timely and topical. In his plays after this period, his basic social concerns did not alter; however, he gave evidence of his artistic versatility by broadening his scope and dealing with situations relating to levels of society with which, in the 1930's, he was but meagerly acquainted. Because Odets has always written about issues and characters which he fully understands, his work has had about it a high degree of authenticity.

Odets has never lost interest in the lower and middle classes of society. It is because America's social scene has changed that this more recent writing has been about issues which are not uniquely lower- or middle-class. As the old problems became dated, he had no choice but to write of issues which were more timely.

Hollywood, contrary to much general opinion, appears not to have ruined Odets as a creative artist. Movie writing, if anything, has made him more adroit and polished in his writing than he was at the beginning of his career. His characterization in the later plays is most convincing and the characters are developed with great verbal economy. In the earlier plays one often comes to know the characters by being told about them; in the later plays, they are developed primarily through their actions, and the development is often swift and direct.

In his early plays, Clifford Odets suggested answers to the ills of a troubled society. There is often a call to action of some sort in the early plays, and the action suggested is usually affirmative in nature. However, in *Golden Boy, Rocket to the Moon, Clash by Night,* and *Night Music* there are strong overtones of negation, suggesting that Odets is struggling with himself, trying to find answers but unable to do so. *The Country Girl* and *The Big Knife* do not contain the affirmation of the early plays and it is obvious that in these plays Odets is still engaged in an ideological struggle on a scale much broader than the mere subject matter of his dramas. Only in *The Flowering Peach* does there appear to be a real mellowing in the author. This play is richly affirmative and, to a large degree, is similar to the social conflicts which Odets has witnessed. The play depicts the inevitability of human struggle and the necessity of acceptance of that which cannot be forestalled. But the play ends with the thought that continuance is inescapable. The earth has been almost totally depopulated; but a few have been saved and they will repopulate.

It is perhaps too early to indicate Odets' position in the history of American drama. It seems evident that he is not of the stature of Eugene O'Neill; however, he may well be called the most significant of the specifically proletarian playwrights of the 1930's. His poetic use of language, his accurate capturing and reproduction of the vernacular, as well as his keen understanding of human motivation, have led the way to such modern playwrights as Arthur Miller, Tennessee Williams, and Truman Capote. It would not seem extravagant to state that the name Clifford Odets is firmly fixed and importantly placed in the drama of twentieth-century America.

R. Baird Shuman. Clifford Odets (New
York, Twayne, 1962), pp. 147–48

Despite the effectiveness of realistic detail, it is apparent that *Awake and Sing!* still retains strong agit-prop roots. But instead of appealing directly for revolutionary action, it attempts to demonstrate the thesis of revolutionary awareness in the relationship between Jacob and Ralph against the family background of middle-class decay. Its success is dependent upon this conjunction of thesis and detail. Odets never was a genre painter; his strokes are broad, his dialogue heightened. What he succeeded in delineating were the specific images of social dislocation. The importance of the Marxist premise from a dramatic point of view does not lie in its specific truth or falsity; it serves rather as a dramatic metaphor which orders the disparate elements of the play, which relates the images of frustration and dislocation to a guiding thematic concept. The spine of the play is the conviction that the world of the Bergers must be changed if human potentiality is to be realized. For Odets at that time this faith was affirmed by Marxism; far from marring the play, the Marxist metaphor gathers the various dramatic strands and relates them to the basic theme of social resurrection.

Odets, then, was never primarily a realist. *Awake and Sing!* and his next play, *Paradise Lost,* are essentially allegories of middle-class decay. It was the inability to recognize this fact which was primarily responsible for the critical furor which attended the production of the latter play.

Gerald Rabkin. Drama and Commitment (Bloomington,
Indiana University Press, 1964), pp. 185–86

The principal problem for Odets was the difficulty of finding appropriate focal points for his abundant sympathies. Plots came easily, themes did not. As late as 1949 he continued to write the best American plays of the thirties, and nothing else. Much the most skilled of the radical playwrights of the Depression stage, he wrote his first plays of economic injustice with such flair that the political right and left alike acknowledged their theatrical viability. Nevertheless, he was capable of no greater judgment than may be credited to the less intelligent dramatists of his generation; in attempting to develop class-consciousness among the Depression's victims for an attack upon their presumed oppressors, he did not recognize that he was merely substituting one brand of materialism for another. More damaging to the growth of his talent was the inability to free himself completely, as the years passed along, from the materialist theme with which he began his career. His perception of the world around him dimmed with the beginning of the national economic recovery late in the prewar decade, and the mind that

should have taken cognizance of the new situation contented itself with af-
ter-images of the poverty of the Depression's worst years. It is true that
Odets took up other issues in certain works, particularly in his late plays;
but whether subsidiary or paramount, class-consciousness is never absent,
regardless of the year and the remoteness of his characters' concerns from
money worries. Having taken a stand with the destitute proletariat, he could
not recognize the fact of a rising employment index. After the first six plays,
handsomely brought together in an omnibus volume in 1939, Odets's work
dwindled in relevance to the age, until finally, after 1954, he could give the
stage nothing at all.

> Malcolm Goldstein. In Alan S. Downer, ed., *American*
> *Drama and Its Critics* (Chicago, University of
> Chicago Press, 1965), pp. 134–35

In [*Awake and Sing!*] there was a lyric uplifting of blunt Jewish speech,
boiling over and explosive, that did more to arouse the audience than the
political catchwords that brought the curtain down. Everybody on that stage
was furious, kicking, alive—the words, always real but never flat, brilliantly
authentic like no other theater speech on Broadway, aroused the audience to
such delight that one could feel it bounding back and uniting itself with the
mind of the writer. I wanted to write with that cunning anger and flowing
truth; the writer would forget his specialness, his long loneliness, and as he
spoke to that mass of faces turning on in the dark, the crowd would embrace
him, thank him over and over for bringing their lives out into the light. How
interesting we all were, how vivid and strong on the beat of that style!

> Alfred Kazin. *Starting Out in the Thirties*
> (Boston, Little, Brown, 1965), pp. 80–81

Clifford Odets was a complex man, nurtured in a complicated age, but out
of his intense struggles with self and society were born six plays of continuing importance. The stock picture of Odets as the radical author of *Waiting
for Lefty*, who later abased himself before the Un-American Activities Committee and sold out to the Establishment, makes classification easy for criticism at a gallop. Such a view fails to do justice, however, to the depth,
intensity and relevance of Odets' plays. It is simply untrue, for example,
that the later work of Odets is uniformly poor. *The Big Knife, The Country
Girl* and *The Flowering Peach* can stand comparison with *Awake and Sing!,
Golden Boy* and *Rocket to the Moon*. Indeed, the early *Golden Boy* and the
late *The Flowering Peach* are probably—all parts considered—the two best
plays Odets wrote in his twenty years as a major American dramatist.

Although *Waiting for Lefty* will continue, no doubt, to be required
reading in college survey courses (it fits so snugly into an anthology and it
is, moreover, so conveniently pigeonholed!), Odets was moving away from

"proletarian drama" by 1936. (Even *Awake and Sing!* has a rich personal, or psychological, dimension and a level of thematic concern which resists glib labels.) Like every play that has ever been written, *Golden Boy* bears the stamp of its decade. Nevertheless, this fine play also transcends the narrow interests of the thirties, for in Odets' depiction of a young man's struggle between self-realization and self-destruction, between idealism and materialism, *Golden Boy* persists in being meaningful. Similarly, the later plays project specific preoccupations of the post-Second World War period; yet *The Big Knife, The Country Girl*—and especially, *The Flowering Peach*—also reveal themes that have obsessed imaginative writers in every decade since, at least, the First World War. Odets, in other words, is very much in the mainstream of modern theater and literature.

Edward Murray. *Clifford Odets: The Thirties and After*
(New York, Frederick Ungar, 1968), pp. 219–20

It is evident that Odets always loved People, in that vague, abstract, idealistic way which makes the Thirties writers of the Left admirable and, at the same time, difficult to understand for the often more cynical and more individualistic succeeding generation. Undoubtedly Odets' contributions to American dramatic literature are, at least in part, the product of that love and of the sensitivity or social consciousness which compelled him to become a writer in the first place. There is little reason to believe that he would have written anything had he not been motivated by the inequities of American society that he observed. As a young playwright Odets once asserted in an article, "I see it every day all over the city, girls and boys were not getting a chance. . . . No special pleading is necessary in a play which says that people should have fuller and richer lives." Throughout his life he maintained the same position. His characters are obliged to burst the bonds that restrict them in their middle-class milieu, to avoid being tied down by family and tradition, to seek their own place in the sun. This concept was repeated often in Odets' works, but with ever-diminishing stridency. Early in his career Odets believed that he had a mission, and, like so many mission-inspired men, he occasionally allowed the cause to obscure the logic of his work.

Michael J. Mendelsohn. *Clifford Odets: Humane
Dramatist* (Deland, Fla., Everett/Edwards, 1969), p. 127

The artistic consequences of Odets' ideational approach to man are less conjectural than the personal ones. The plays are their own testimony. "I believe in the vast potentialities of mankind . . ." Odets wrote to John Mason Brown back in 1935. "I want to find out how mankind can be helped out of the animal kingdom into the clear sweet air." The rhetoric may be a little heady (Odets was only twenty-nine), but the line contains a statement of artistic intentions that can be tested in all of Odets's plays. The "how" is finally less important than that there be a way into the "clear sweet air." From the certainty of *Waiting for Lefty* to the uncertainty of *The Flowering Peach,* Odets has organized his plays to make a specific point about human possibility; he has manipulated his characters to let one or more of them reach the moment of change, or recognition that will allow the play to look into a better future. A propagandist, first and last, he has always held out hope of the happy land. It is this quality that makes Odets such a likable playwright, since a happy ending (even if it is a tragic one) is hard to resist. The same quality limits him as a playwright, threatens to reduce him to the simplicity of his ideas, his themes. Yet the observer in Odets never let the preacher run free, the pessimist hobbled the optimist, the realist partnered the idealist.

Gerald Weales. *Clifford Odets: Playwright*
(New York, Pegasus, 1971), p. 188

Odets' plays, even those that end sadly, are dramas of hopeful beginnings, in which men are brought to the threshold of wisdom by understanding themselves and their world. Nor are these plays facile in their optimism. For twenty years Odets looked hard and critically at the myths of American life—the bourgeois dreams of family respectability, the magical promise of overnight success, the fantasy that love could save us—and noted how the media mocked us and the past eluded us. Out of his own tangled, often contradictory responses to these myths, he created dramas that capitalize on this very ambivalence for artistically satisfying tension and rewarding insights.

Odets was a socially committed playwright who loved the middle class he wrote about, and stubbornly refused to desert it for a plunge into existentialist "nightmares of the self." Though he did not seem relevant to the New Critics of the Fifties and Sixties, time may be on his side, as a new generation—struggling with the alienating effects of affluence and technology—turns toward communal and nature-oriented environmentalist solutions. While no new generation can ever recapture the precise ideological set of an earlier one, Odets has much to say to us because our social dilemmas have not changed in kind. The middle class has moved into suburbia, but is still plagued by the disturbing thought that "life should not be printed on dollar bills." Odets speaks even more directly to the insurgent minority groups; the new black playwrights echo his plays and unconsciously reflect his influence. Odets has something universal to say to those who still believe that man, through group action, is capable of "changing the world." More important, he has a universal understanding of the kind of mind capable of such idealism, and of the environment which nurtures it and the corruptions that threaten to destroy it.

Harold Cantor. *Clifford Odets: Playwright-Poet*
(Metuchen, N.J., Scarecrow, 1978), pp. 203–4

O'NEILL, EUGENE (1888–1953)

The new volume of Eugene O'Neill's plays contains *The Hairy Ape, Anna Christie* and *The First Man*. The first of these seems to me almost the only thing that Mr. O'Neill has yet written that has very much value as literature apart from its effectiveness as drama. As a rule, the plays of O'Neill are singularly uninviting on the printed page. The dialogue is raw and prosaic, in texture quite undistinguished, and the author has made no attempt to appeal to the imagination by way of the stage directions, which are not lifted above the baldness of the prompt-book. These plays appear too often, in short, as rather second-rate naturalistic pieces that owe their eminence, not to their intrinsic greatness, but, as Marx said of John Stuart Mill, "to the flatness of the surrounding country." The dialogue of *The First Man,* which I have not seen on the stage, proves in the reading so tasteless and dreary that one does not see how one could sit through it.

But Eugene O'Neill has another vein in which he is a literary artist of genius. When he is writing the more or less grammatical dialogue of the middle-class characters of his plays, his prose is heavy and indigestible even beyond the needs of naturalism. People say the same things to one another over and over again and never succeed in saying them any more effectively than the first time; long speeches shuffle dragging feet, marking time without progressing, for pages. But as soon as Mr. O'Neill gets a character who can only talk some kind of vernacular, he begins to write like a poet. We had already had evidence of this in the Negro hero of *The Emperor Jones* and in the first act of *Anna Christie,* but when one saw *The Hairy Ape* produced by the Provincetown Players, one had the feeling that Mr. O'Neill had for the first time become fully articulate. As Walter Pritchard Eton said, he wrote slang like "a sort of wild organ music." The scenes in which the non-illiterate characters talk are as clumsy and dead as ever, but the greater part of the play, in which Yank, the stoker, discourses, has a mouth-filling rhythmical eloquence very rare in naturalistic drama.

When the speeches came to life in this way, the drama was always more moving. One felt that Mr. O'Neill, in his gift for drawing music from humble people, had a kinship with Sherwood Anderson. For *The Hairy Ape* is the tragedy not, as in the common formula, of the American pitted against his environment nor even of the proletarian pitted against capitalism, but of the universal human being pitted against himself. It is, as Mr. O'Neill has labelled it, a play "of ancient and modern life." I have heard this disputed by people who had got the impression from seeing the play that the hero of *The Hairy Ape* is thwarted by the forces of society instead of by his own limitations. But I believe that if anyone will read the last scenes in the printed text, he will see that though it is a consciousness of social inferiority that gives the first impetus to Yank's débâcle and though he himself at first supposes that it is society he has to fight, the Hairy Ape's ultimate struggle for freedom takes place within the man himself. I am not sure that Mr. O'Neill always gives enough dramatic emphasis to his most important ideas. The significance of these last scenes of *The Hairy Ape* was not thrown into relief on the stage. People seemed to understand the play better when they saw it a second time. This is a reason— aside from the fact that the *Ape* is good literature—that it is useful to have it in a book. [Nov., 1922]

Edmund Wilson. *The Shores of Light* (New York, Farrar, Straus and Young, 1952), pp. 99–101

The structural power and pre-eminent simplicity of these works [*Anna Christie, The First Man, The Emperor Jones,* and *The Hairy Ape*] are intensified by the use of certain technical expedients and processes which seem dear to the heart of this dramatist and, I may presume, to the heart of the American theatre-goer as well; for instance, the oft-used device of the repetition of a word, a situation, or a motive. In *The Hairy Ape,* the motive of repetition progresses uninterruptedly from scene to scene; the effect becomes more and more tense as the action hurries on to the end. Mr. O'Neill appears to have a decided predilection for striking contrasts, like that, for instance, between the life of the sea and the life of the land, in *Anna Christie,* or between the dull narrowness of middle-class existence and unhampered morality, in *The First Man*. The essential dramatic plot—the "fable," that is—is invariably linked to and revealed by that visual element which the theatre, and above all, I believe, the modern theatre, demands. The dialogue is powerful, often direct, and frequently endowed with a brutal though picturesque lyricism. . . .

The characters in Mr. O'Neill's plays seem to me a little too direct: they utter the precise words demanded of them by the logic of the situation; they seem to stand rooted in the situation where for the time being they happen to be placed; they are not sufficiently drenched in the atmosphere of their own individual past. Paradoxically, Mr. O'Neill's characters are not sufficiently fixed in the present because they are not sufficiently fixed in the past. Much of what they say seems too openly and frankly sincere, and consequently lacking in the element of wonder or suprise: for the ultimate sincerity that comes from the lips of man is always surprising. Their silence, too, does not always convince me; often it falls short of eloquence, and the way in which the characters go from one theme to another and return to the central theme is lacking in that seemingly inevitable abandon that creates vitality. Besides, they are too prodigal with their shouting and cursing, and the result is that they leave me a little cold towards the other things they have to say. The habit of repetition, which is given free rein in the plot itself as well as in the dialogue, becomes so insistent as to overstep the border of the dramatically effective and actually to become a dramatic weakness.

Hugo von Hofmannsthal. The Freeman.
March 21, 1923, pp. 39–40

O'Neill deals with men and women, not as conventions of the stage, not even as they should be, but exactly as he sees them, far too often creatures blindly, helplessly driven by forces they have not the character to withstand. It is a Greek view of tragedy, this of his, notably so in *Desire under the Elms*. The mistake the public often makes in judging O'Neill is to assume that what he says of individuals he means to have expanded into truth about the majority or even a class. He understands fully that the drama deals best with the individual. Doing that, it has for centuries found adequate forms and revelatory processes. Only very recently has it tried more and more to dramatize the emotions of groups, of the masses, to visualize by other means than soliloquy the inmost contents of the mind in emotional experiences. Even this O'Neill has attempted in his most recently produced play, *The Great God Brown*.

Naturally, the play has confused many people and consequently annoyed some. Here, after some ten years of work, is the most mature accomplishment of O'Neill. It does not treat merely individuals, but rather human relations, great forces in conduct rather than individual characteristics. It is concrete, but only against a background of mysticism. Naturally, if the subject is experimental, form and method must correspond. Hence the masks—not used in mere imitation of the Greeks, but freshly, imaginatively, as a real means to an attained artistic end.

George P. Baker. YR. July, 1926, pp. 791–92

One group of our playwrights may go on painting amusing pictures which the comic supplement throws upon the screen of American life. That our audiences should crown the theatres where such plays are produced is easily understood. But it is encouraging that when an artist like Eugene O'Neill resolutely sets his face against the picturing of the merely little things of life he should have won the wide recognition he already enjoys. He paints little souls and big souls, but he never consciously gives us the unimportant or the mean. We may not like all of his characters—we may even shudder at them—like the Emperor Jones himself, but O'Neill found in that thief and murderer a spark that distinguished him from all the natives of that imaginary island. We agree with the epitaph of Smithers: " 'E's a better man than the lot o' you put together."

O'Neill found that spark, of course, because he put it there. Even in the most degraded man, O'Neill recognizes the saving grace that comes from his divine origin. Nearly a century ago, Emerson called this universal brotherhood in us the creation of the Oversoul, the Life Force that animates everything, and founded on this conception his gospel of hope. O'Neill has dared to go further into the depths than Emerson or Hawthorne, for the Puritan had reactions of conservatism from which the Celt is free. But it is a pitiful stupidity of criticism that sees only the repellent in *All God's Chillun Got Wings* or *Desire under the Elms*. I confess frankly that on reading the first I could see little beauty in it, but in the theatre I recognized again the vision of the poet who saw more deeply than I. I felt, too, my academic objections to soliloquy on the stage go by the board, when I recognized that to these characters soliloquy was natural. But I have become accustomed to seeing theatrical rules broken with success by O'Neill because he practically never breaks dramatic laws. It is a great thing for art when academic definitions are shattered by creative genius, and it is to be hoped he will go on shattering them. For he has become the concrete expression of the greatest principle in art, that of freedom, freedom to choose one's subject anywhere, to treat it in any manner, provided always that the characters are great figures and the treatment is sincere.

Arthur Hobson Quinn. *A History of the American Drama
from the Civil War to the Present Day* (New York,
Appleton-Century-Crofts, 1927), Vol. II, pp. 205–6

The burden of [*Lazarus Laughed*] is carried by two elements: by Lazarus' philosophical arias, and by spectacular effects of crowd movements and colored lights. About the first of these, enough has been said. With regard to the element of spectacle, [Max] Reinhardt has shown us what can be achieved in this line, especially in his production of [Georg] Büchner's *Danton*. Gordon Craig has hailed these departures as first steps toward a new form, his hypothetical "pure art of the theatre." As a form, it is related to the 17th Century Masque, and the modern revue. It seems to mean a dissolution of the classical partnership of actor and author, to which we owe most great drama, in favor of a third figure, the regisseur. A good regisseur may of course get artistically satisfying effects with well-trained crowds and carefully calculated light and sound effects—too often at the author's expense. When an author resorts to it, it usually means that he has ceased to be interested in mastering the medium of the stage. This is certainly true in *Lazarus Laughed:* the stage becomes Mr. O'Neill's lifeless megaphone. Nothing stands between the audience and Mr. O'Neill, shouting his views. For his relation to his ideas, in these prophetic plays, is the same as his relation to his characters in his middle period: they are emotionally significant to him, they play a part in his equilibrium as a man. Attaining no vision outside himself, his plays remain attached to him by his external immaturity.

We are not surprised to find, therefore, that his audience is often more interested in the author than in his play . . . . The very imperfection which connects the author with his play also connects the author with his audience. The one quality which his admirers agree in stressing is his sincerity. We have seen that he believes in his own mood in his early plays, and in the personal reality of his characters in his middle period, while in his latest plays he is in earnest in asserting some Nietzschean war-cry. As a person, he is sincerely interested in figuring out his life, and perhaps in attaining a stable point of view—though unconsciously. He has in fact never attained it. He has managed to recognize his emotional demands, but he has not reached the further heroism of accepting what becomes of them: of describing them with reference to some independent reality. He has a sense of human needs, but none of human destiny. He offers us the act of seeking, but no disinterested contemplation; himself, therefore, rather than his work. Only the dead cease to change; but by discipline it is sometimes possible to produce a work complete and independent of the suffering individual. Mr. O'Neill's failings may all be ascribed to the fact that he has never found any such discipline.

Francis Fergusson. The Hound & Horn.
Jan.–March, 1930, pp. 154–56

The two gifts that Eugene O'Neill up to now has displayed are for feeling and for dramatic image. His plays have often conveyed a poignancy that is unique in the modern drama, you felt that whatever was put down was at the dramatist's own expense, he paid out of himself as he went. His great theatre gift has been in the creation of images that speak for themselves, such for instance as the tittering of the Great Khan's ladies-in-waiting at the western Marco Polo [in *Marco Millions*], the dynamo in the play by the same name, and many another, images so vivid that their mere repetition in people's talk makes the play sound better and more complete than it ever was. Sometimes this dramatic image spreads to the scope of a dramatic pattern that is the whole sum of the play. This happened not in more recent and elaborate plays, such as *Strange Interlude,* but in at least two of the earlier, *The Emperor Jones* and *The Hairy Ape,* where the whole plot was like an expanded sentence. In *Mourning Becomes Electra* Mr. O'Neill comes now into the full stretch of clear narrative design. He discovers that in expressive pattern lies the possibility of all that parallels life, a form on which fall infinite shadings and details, as the light with its inexhaustible nuances and elements appears on a wall. He has come to what is so rare in Northern art, an understanding of repetition and variation on the same design, as contrasted with matter that is less deep or subtle, though expressed with lively surprise, variety or novelty. It is a new and definite stage in his development.

Stark Young. NR. Nov. 11, 1931, pp. 354–55

No modern is capable of language really worthy of O'Neill's play [*Mourning Becomes Electra*], and the lack of that one thing is the penalty we must pay for living in an age which is not equal to more than prose. Nor is it to be supposed that I make this reservation merely for the purpose of saying that Mr. O'Neill's play is not so good as the best of Shakespeare; I make it, on the contrary, in order to indicate where one must go in order to find a worthy comparison.

True tragedy may be defined as a dramatic work in which the outward failure of the principal personage is compensated for by the dignity and greatness of his character. But if this definition be accepted, then it must be recognized that the art of tragic writing was lost for many generations. Neither the frigid rhetorical exercises of the Victorians nor the sociological treatises of Ibsen and his followers are tragic in the true sense. The former lack the power to seem real enough to stir us deeply; the latter are too thoroughly pervaded by a sense of human littleness to be other than melancholy and dispiriting. O'Neill is almost alone among modern dramatic writers in possessing what appears to be an instinctive perception of what a modern tragedy would have to be.

Unlike the plays of "literary" playwrights, his dramas have nothing archaic about them. They do not seek the support of a poetic faith in any of the conceptions which served the classical dramatists but are no longer valid for us. They are, on the contrary, almost cynically "modern" in their acceptance of a rationalistic view of man and the universe. Yet he has created his characters upon so large a scale that their downfall is made once more to seem not merely pathetic, but terrible. [1932]

> Joseph Wood Krutch. Introduction to *Nine Plays by Eugene O'Neill* (New York, Random House, 1952), pp. xxi–xxii

[O'Neill] is of course, despite his enormous talent, curiously handicapped. He has no felicity; he has not the sweetness that one would expect of his strength. Nor has he the rounded form which can perfectly be combined with an ethically indeterminate ending. Hence neither the spectator's nor the reader's catharsis at the end of any play by O'Neill is final or complete and that leads one to suspect that the creative self-catharsis of the dramatist has been equally imperfect, a circumstance that would go far to account for the rapid change of mood, of dramaturgic method and form, and for the almost fevered productivity already amounting to the equivalent of twenty full-length plays and about to be increased by a trilogy!

Whence comes this imperfection amid so much wealth and vigor, this emotional residuum of void and distaste that O'Neill's plays leave? My criticism may not, of course, be granted; it will certainly not be granted by his closer followers. Yet I have been impressed and stirred by the performances of very many of his plays; I have worked through the entire canon of his works in the study with careful passivity: with more than passivity, with good-will and admiration and the desire to be at once shaken and reconciled as I am, as everyone is, at the conclusion of the major works of the drama. The effect is never single and entire; the catharsis is never complete. What is lacking? An element that is akin to both love and joy—an element allied to zest and relish. There is a sense, a very deep sense, in which the creative artist loves all his characters in their quality of characters within the world of his creative cosmos. He may have loathed their prototypes in life. He relishes the character *qua* character. He devours people because he has an endless creative appetite and relish for them. The snake he has created is as dear to him in this sense as beauty or genius. Now I have the unescapable impression that O'Neill neither loves his kind as a man, a Swiftian indignation being of course only disappointed love, nor enjoys his characters as a creator. He has neither the brooding large love of Dreiser or Hauptmann nor the sharp joyous delight of Shaw, not the bitterness of love outraged of Strindberg, nor even the cold contempt under which a passion of hatred, but still a passion, is held in leash, of such a dramatist as Wedekind. O'Neill's heart is arid toward his creatures. Or, at least, he has not the means of projecting them in a spirit of creative love. Hence there is about all these many people in the plays and about their conflicts something hard and dry; power, in this world of the dramatist's imagination, always has something of violence, the fable always a touch of the coldly arbitrary and intensity at its height is somehow drained of passion.

Ludwig Lewisohn. Expression in America (New York,
Harper & Brothers, 1932), pp. 544–46

With the poet, our real concern is with the new forces of will, understanding and charity we can discover at work in the objective form of his characters. Suppose we were to say to ourselves, Robert Mayo, the Hairy Ape, and Bill Brown and Nina Leeds and Abbie Putnam and Brutus Jones and John Loving and young Richard Miller are all one person, one many-sided person trying to find a way through the maze of life's emotions, temptations, sins, victories over self, storms of false pride and moments of great peace. At first it would seem preposterous. Then, as we caught the feeling of a great poet, as we began to understand his strange inner union with the highest and lowest in human emotions, we might know in our hearts that it was not preposterous at all but the simple statement of a towering truth. We might begin to see his plays in an entirely new aspect as a progressive document of the immemorial experience of mankind. We might see about them the flickering shadow of our own day and times. We might also see something of the poet himself as an individual, living in our times, and inspired or distressed or angered by them, even limited and warped by them, but struggling constantly to rise above them to a life as broad and unlimited as the souls of men have ever known.

We would surely see something we had not seen as clearly before of good and evil in mortal conflict, of human will girding itself for the passage through the valley of tears, of the human soul crying aloud for help from a power greater than itself. Our charity might be stirred at the sight of repeated failures, and our admiration unleashed at the sight of renewed struggle and increasing courage. Certainly our own problems would become clearer from this better understanding of one who is part of our own life. Eugene O'Neill is neither prophet nor saint. As his characters tell us, he has often, even as a poet, been deeply confused. Many of his darkest doubts and many of his most tragic defeats have sprung from immature emotions. But so have most of our own temptations and failures, not only as individuals but also as a nation. We should accept O'Neill as a companion on our own pilgrimage rather than as a leader, but surely as a companion whose poetic insight is deep, whose consciousness of our moral problems is vibrant, whose experience of the soul's conflict is sharper through intuition than most men's, and whose willingness to seek a path even in the darkest shadows marks an extraordinary tenacity and the quality of a high romance. [1934]

Richard Dana Skinner. Eugene O'Neill: A Poet's
Quest (New York, Russell & Russell, 1964), pp. 35–36

Whatever is unclear about Eugene O'Neill, one thing is certainly clear—his genius. We do not like the word nowadays, feeling that it is one of the blurb words of criticism. We demand that literature be a guide to life, and when we do that we put genius into a second place, for genius assures us of nothing but itself. Yet when we stress the actionable conclusions of an artist's work, we are too likely to forget the power of genius itself, quite apart from its conclusions. The spectacle of the human mind in action is vivifying; the explorer need discover nothing so long as he has adventured. Energy, scope, courage—these may be admirable in themselves. And in the end these are often what endure best. The ideas expressed by works of the imagination may be built into the social fabric and taken for granted; or they may be rejected; or they may be outgrown. But the force of their utterance comes to us over millennia. We do not read Sophocles or Aeschylus for the right answer; we read them for the force with which they represent life and attack its moral complexity. In O'Neill, despite the many failures of his art and thought, this force is inescapable.

But a writer's contemporary audience is inevitably more interested in the truth of his content than in the force of its expression; and O'Neill himself has always been ready to declare his own ideological preoccupation. His early admirers—and their lack of seriousness is a reproach to American criticism—were inclined to insist that O'Neill's content was unimportant as compared to his purely literary interest and that he injured his art when he tried to think. But the appearance of *Days without End* has made perfectly clear the existence of an organic and progressive unity of thought in all O'Neill's work and has brought it into the critical range of the two groups whose own thought is most sharply formulated, the Catholic and the Communist. Both discovered what O'Neill had frequently announced, the religious nature of all his effort.

Lionel Trilling. *NR*. Sept. 23, 1936, p. 176

That [O'Neill] is the foremost dramatist in the American theatre is, as has been recorded, generally granted. His eminence is predicated on the fact that no other has anywhere nearly his ability to delve into and appraise character, his depth of knowledge of his fellow man, his sweep and pulse and high resolve, his command of a theatre stage and all its manifold workings, and his mastery of the intricacies of dramaturgy. His plays at their best have in them a real universality. His characters are not specific, individual and isolated types but active symbols of mankind in general, with mankind's virtues and faults, gropings and findings, momentary triumphs and doomed defeats. He writes not for a single theatre but for all theatres of the world.

It is argued by some against him that he is no poet, and that his drama hence misses true stature. Specifically and in the conventional sense, he may not be, but he is nevertheless, as must be evident to the close student of his work, driven ever by the poetic spirit. His weakness, where and when it exists, lies in his excesses—the excesses of overemphasis, over-embroidery and over-melodramatization of the psychological aspects of his drama and of that drama itself. At his worst, these qualities edge him close to brooding travesty.

He has worked expertly in the field of tragedy, nimbly in the field of comedy, and less happily in that of fantasy. His brutality in tragedy is a handmaiden of the truth as he sees it. He cannot compromise with himself, right or wrong. Uncommonly gifted in a knowledge of the theatre, it may seem to some that he resorts occasionally to critically invalid devices to further his dramatic ends. If he does so, he does so unconsciously, never with calculation and deliberately. He would be content, I am assured, to publish his plays and forgo the profits of production.

He has written muddled and poor plays along with the valid, some very muddled and very poor. But the great body of his work has a size and significance not remotely approached by any other American. In a broader sense, he is plainly not the mind that Shaw is, not by a thousand leagues— his is an emotional rather than an intellectual; he is not the poet that O'Casey is, for in O'Casey there is the true music of great wonder and beauty. But he has plumbed depths deeper than either; he is greatly the superior of both in dramaturgy; and he remains his nation's one important contribution to the art of the drama.

George Jean Nathan. *AM*. Dec., 1946, pp. 718–19

[*Mourning Becomes Electra*] is no stunt. O'Neill does not trifle with the theater; even in his most obviously experimental plays the form he uses is always the result of a conscious effort to dramatize clearly some aspect of human activity. His worst mistakes are the result not of trying to see what he could do with his gifts but of his efforts to rephrase or reinterpret something he thought it worth his while to express. *Mourning Becomes Electra* is the logical outgrowth of O'Neill's other work, and closely related to it. To judge it properly, it should be looked at as part of his entire output. If you think of it this way you will see in it much more of O'Neill than of Aeschylus; in spite of his deliberate use of the trilogy form and the basic similarity of the two stories, *Mourning Becomes Electra* remains a contemporary work. It presents, quite aside from its external form, another aspect of O'Neill's development not only as a writer but as a man of our day and civilization searching for a rational explanation of life and death, and what used to be called sin and evil. Directly in *Lazarus Laughed* and indirectly in *The Great God Brown, Strange Interlude, Dynamo* and *Days without End*, O'Neill has done a lot of thinking in public, and I mean this in no derogatory sense, convinced though I am that his best plays are those that have to do not so much with expounding a philosophy as with presenting dramatically the less reflective sorts of men and women. I am here tracing his ideas rather than his development as an artist. In giving us such characters as Reuben and Dion and Nina, he is dramatizing not so much the people of our day as the abstract questions that make life an unhappy matter for so many of us. Such persons would have little reason for living if we were to accept them as human beings and not as abstractions; like their creator, they are in search of some kind of philosophy to which they can cling.

Barrett H. Clark. *Eugene O'Neill: The Man and His
Plays*, rev. ed. (New York, Dover, 1947), pp. 125–26

No matter what our opinion may have been of this or that of O'Neill's dramas; no matter how small the biggest of them may have proved compared to the masterpieces of Shakespeare and the Greeks; no matter how tarnished most of them have become by 1949, it was excitingly clear twenty-five years ago when *Desire under the Elms* was produced that in America, of all surprised and surprising places, a dramatist had emerged who was tormented and inspired by the truest sensing of the tragic which the modern world has known.

Few dramatists of his importance have written more unevenly than O'Neill. Few capable of rising as near to the heights as he has soared have sunk into the mire of more pretentious or deplorable mediocrity. Yet even the poorest of his dramas have been enriched by the courage of the man and by that fierce willingness to grapple with the imponderables which has made his best works memorable. What has enlarged the most unsatisfactory of his scripts, and made his career at once heartening and unique, has been the largeness of his concerns. No one, may I quickly add, has attested to this fact with greater warmth or discernment than did Mr. Krutch himself when, in a more cheerful mood, a short four years after his requiem for tragedy [in *The Modern Temper*, 1929], he wrote a preface to a collection of O'Neill's plays welcoming their author to the select company of tragic dramatists.

Like Yank in *The Hairy Ape*, O'Neill's central characters have wanted to "belong." They have been visible cogs in the invisible machinery of the universe. Whatever the crimes into which their passions may have led them, they have cared passionately about the forces controlling their being and their undoing. Not only that, these forces have not been indifferent to them.

This high concern in play after play, regardless of its individual merits, has given to the body of O'Neill's work a significance at once solitary and touched with grandeur. Most dramatists in America and elsewhere during this past quarter of a century have at their moments of greatest seriousness gone no further than to oppose their characters to their neighbors or the social systems under which they have lived. Not so Mr. O'Neill. The barricades his people have assailed have been of a kind unfound in city streets. The altitude of his reach has been the measure of his magnitude and more outstanding than any of his plays. It has set him apart, granted him a deserved pre-eminence, left him lonely but a rallying point. [Aug. 6, 1949]

John Mason Brown. *Still Seeing Things*
(New York, McGraw-Hill, 1950), pp. 186–88

The recurrent critical complaint about Eugene O'Neill is the failure of his language to equal the intensity or excitement of his action or situations. Even Professor Krutch, in a friendly comment, calls *Mourning Becomes Electra* a "scenario" and declares that no modern writer is "capable of language really worthy of O'Neill's play." Yet, are there not compensations? Was not a 1934 audience enwrapped in the five-hours' traffic of the trilogy, sharing the experience of the contemporary audiences of *Othello* or *Antigone*?

Other men have conceived tragic situations, and other men have made full use of the resources of the modern stage. Few, however, have achieved a balanced combination of the two with the consistency of Eugene O'Neill. O'Neill has a unique combination of skill and vision: born and raised in the theatre he was well-versed in the secrets of stage effect; years of travel and experience gave him a sense of the mystery of life which prevented him from using his skill for effect alone.

His earliest vignettes of the sailor's life suggest how his skill is to serve the purposes of his vision. His father, James O'Neill, who destroyed his own artistic career by yielding to his audience's thirst for sensation, would have been baffled by such a play as *Bound East for Cardiff,* although the violent action of *'Ile* would have comforted him. *Cardiff,* however, is a more direct statement of O'Neill's vision; the sailor, dying against a background of his quarreling, disinterested mates, is an image of the loneliness and frustration of man. The playwright's early choice of the sea or the farm as his setting is a recognition of their symbolic, as well as their realistic, value: life on shipboard as the world in miniature, the farm juxtaposing the order of nature and the disorder of man.

Alan S. Downer. *ThA.* Feb., 1951, pp. 22–23

We are told that myth is useful because the audience knows the plot already and can turn its attention to the how and why. To this I would not protest that all adapters, including O'Neill, change the mythic plots, though this is true; what I have in mind is, rather, that they do not always change them enough. Events in their works have often no organic place there, they are fossilized vestiges of the older version. We ask: why does this character do that? And the answer is: because his Greek prototype did it. In *Mourning Becomes Electra* the myth makes it hard for O'Neill to let his people have their own identity at all, yet to the extent that they do have one, it is, naturally, a modern and American identity, and this in turn makes their ancient and Greek actions seem wildly improbable. Heaven knows that murders take place today as in ancient times; but the murders in O'Neill are not given today's reality.

Instead, the characters are blown up with psychological gas. O'Neill has boasted his ignorance of Freud, but such ignorance is not enough. He should be ignorant also of the watered-down Freudianism of Sardi's and the Algonquin, the Freudianism of all those who are ignorant of Freud, the Freudianism of the subintelligentsia. It is through this Freudianism, and through it alone, that O'Neill has made the effort, though a vain one, to assimilate the myth to modern life. Now, what is it that your subintellectual knows about Freud? That he "put everything down to sex." Precisely; and that is what O'Neill does with the myth. Instead of reverent family feeling to unite an Orestes and an Electra we have incest. *Mourning Becomes Electra* is all sex talk. Sex *talk*—not sex lived and embodied, but sex talked of and fingered. The sex talk of the subintelligentsia. It is the only means by which some sort of eloquence and urgency gets into the play, the source of what is meant to be its poetry. The Civil War never gains the importance it might have had in this telling of the story, it is flooded out by sex. "New

England," surely a cultural conception with wider reference than this, stands only, in O'Neill, for the puritanic (that is, sexually repressive) attitude. [1952]

Eric Bentley. *In Search of Theater*
(New York, Vintage, 1953), pp. 232–33

In critical retrospect the unpretentious earlier pieces are more striking than the bigger works: three of the four Glencairn plays [the four plays later published under the title *S.S. Glencairn* are *Bound East for Cardiff, In the Zone, The Moon of the Caribees,* and *The Long Voyage Home*], *The Dreamy Kid, The Emperor Jones, Desire under the Elms.* These, not only expertly but effortlessly written, clear in their conception, firm and powerful in their effect, displayed more beauty and truth than their ponderous successors. Both *The Emperor Jones* and *Desire under the Elms* remain unsurpassed in the entire range of American drama and deserve to be ranked with the finest anywhere since Ibsen. Here was the "sweep and size" which [George Jean] Nathan thought he saw in *Mourning Becomes Electra;* and no *Weltschmerz,* no personal writing, no obfuscation. What is more, the monolithic figures, Brutus Jones and Ephraim—not Eben—Cabot, in their crude grandeur appear more likely than any other of O'Neill's characters to withstand the erosions of time. Bigger than life, they gave the illusion of life—before both life and illusion had come to be regarded as lies. They typified that aspect of their creator the development of which was numbed by circumstances—internal and external—and were frozen eventually into mere statues of eminent dead men. The Mannons, Larry Slade and company, Tyrone Jr. may more accurately have embodied the spirit of the death-ridden world of the past quarter century; they surely reflected faithfully O'Neill's forlorn outlook. Perhaps as much as the rest of us he would have liked to continue with life as it seemed in the days of *The Emperor Jones* and *Desire under the Elms.* But O'Neill would have been the last person in the world to falsify reality as he saw it—even at the expense of the theatre, through which his life blood had flowed long before he was born.

Edwin A. Engel. *The Haunted Heroes of Eugene O'Neill*
(Cambridge, Mass., Harvard University Press, 1953), p. 303

O'Neill's conception of process as the unity in which opposites are reconciled has numberless philosophical parallels and sources—in the works of Heraclitus, Plato, Aristotle, Lao-tse, Nietzsche, Emerson, to suggest only a few. The greatest heroes and heroines of O'Neill's plays belong to the literary tradition of the Fall through Pride—the tradition of Prometheus, Oedipus, Tamburlaine, Macbeth, Satan—and Adam, Faust, Ahab. From its very origin in ritual, the drama has always drawn together the elements of process and pride; the same god who was slain and reborn in the primitive rite

representing the cycle of seasons is destroyed in later tragedy by his arrogance—*hubris*.

But O'Neill was after all not a Greek, nor an Elizabethan, nor a nineteenth-century Romantic. As a twentieth-century man, he had to interpret
the ancient idea in twentieth-century terms and symbols. He found those in
the conditions of modern living and in the language of psychoanalysis.
O'Neill knew, of course, the general outlines of Freudian theory, but his
imagination was stimulated most by the work of Jung, and especially by
those Jungian concepts formulated by analogy to the universal human problems expressed in art, literature, and philosophy.

Jung sees man's primary need not in the desire to satisfy physical
drives or to fulfill any single emotional necessity such as power, security,
or love, but in a longing for a life of meaning and purpose—for a sense of
order in the universe to which man can belong and in which he can trust.
Jung is a mystic in the same sense that O'Neill is mystical: He recognizes
what he calls "psychological truth" as existing independently of objectively
provable fact. The constant, eternal longing of the human mind for a universal order and the expression of the longing in archetypal symbols constitute what Jung accepts as the "psychological" truth of the existence of such
an order. To O'Neill also, the order of existence which he refers to as
"Fate," "Mystery," "the biological past" is to be sought in the forces at
work in the human psyche. O'Neill assumes, with Jung, that one's problems
and actions spring not only from his personal unconscious mind, but from a
"collective unconscious" shared by the race as a whole, manifesting itself
in archetypal symbols and patterns latent in the minds of all men.

> Doris V. Falk. *Eugene O'Neill and the Tragic
> Tension* (New Brunswick, N.J., Rutgers University
> Press, 1958), pp. 5–6

[O'Neill's] vocation of writing plays was not followed for the purpose of
achieving the best possible plays, the right forms incarnating the right conceptions, but rather for the purpose of using the writing to wrestle with life
itself. This accounts for the strength and weakness of his work. It is weak
at almost every point where we care to ask an aesthetic question, and therefore, by implication, where we care to ask the question of what is being
affirmed outside of man. It is strong wherever we care to look at man coming to terms with himself in a world of total darkness.

O'Neill thus affords us a clear example of the close, if usually unacknowledged, connection between art and religious or philosophical assertion. To be concerned about the creation of a work of art is to be able to
back off far enough from the existential battles to adopt a standing place,
on the basis of which the form of the work of art may be established. Those
who say, therefore, that O'Neill lacked only the ability to write well miss

the point. To be concerned about writing well would have been to deny the very obsession which impelled him to write in the first place. It would have assumed a stasis, a sense of completion or wholeness which his radical pessimism had completely overthrown. In a situation in which the only reality is death and the only question how to meet it, necessarily a tormented question, there are no values, proportions, relationships, traditions, or ultimates according to which the artistic work might be fashioned and judged. The particular existential power of O'Neill's work and its aesthetic raggedness go hand in hand.

Tom F. Driver. TDR. Dec., 1958, p. 17

Everything is to be found in Eugene O'Neill's plays: naturalism, symbolism, expressionism, *intimisme,* decadence, pessimism, spiritualism, Freudianism, and all the rest of the *isms,* all singularly confused and singularly un-worked-out. It has often been said that the founder of American drama lacks any positive faith: and in particular that he was tormented all his life by the problem of God and of the *raison d'être,* a problem that he never succeeded even in stating, let alone in solving. It would be easier to say that he was unable to see it in theatrical terms, to make it the material for dramatic action.

But, in spite of all his weaknesses and exaggerations, his oppressive wordiness and the irrepressible bombast of his style, O'Neill remains the most original playwright after Pirandello. Tormented in mind and troubled by physical disabilities as he was, it cannot be said that he was unsuccessful as a writer. In the first place the circumstances in which he began to write for the theatre, in the America of the years immediately after the first world war, were particularly favorable for the expression of his talent: there was a readiness for theatrical experiment and for the fight against commercial theatre. Then, as happens in America, O'Neill had no sooner thrown down his challenge than fame clamorously befriended him. And his success brought a new freedom to the American stage (to playwrights, actors, and producers). He was followed by disciples and imitators: Clifford Odets, Tennessee Williams, and Arthur Miller owe to O'Neill the road along which they so rapidly sped towards success.

Everything can be found in O'Neill, but his main characteristic is an honesty, sincerity and integrity which can only be defined as "romantic." The use he makes of the stage is romantic, displaying, declaiming and proclaiming there his problems, or I should rather say dreams and nightmares of problems, including the most romantic of all, the dream he never fulfilled, of reaching the heights of tragedy. But romantic above all, romantic in an American way, is the stand he takes both as prosecution and defense, his deliberate pessimism, his malcontented and sullen pose as *poète maudit.* For, in the end, O'Neill's accusation against American morality, and life in general, is not in social terms. Soviet critics were right, after applauding him at first, to turn against him: he is not concerned with capitalism and the redemption of the oppressed. O'Neill is concerned with the fact that no individual can live his life in accordance with those rare and fleeting moments in which each man is aware that he contains the absolute: moments which can only be expressed in poetry, after which (as Edmund says in *Long Day's Journey into Night*) "God is dead," and the Catholic religion (Irish rather than Roman, in O'Neill's case) can no longer help him.

Nicola Chiaromonte. *SewR*. Summer, 1960, pp. 494–95

There are two points in Aristotle on which modern drama departs from the classic definition, or at least from the traditional interpretation of that definition. Pertinent to the study of an O'Neill tragedy are character and *hamartia*, the fall from high station due to some "flaw," human error, or failure in sound judgment. Aristotle's conception of the tragic character holds that he is a man of high station, a king or a leader of his people in some great cause. General Mannon *(Mourning Becomes Electra)* is the only one in O'Neill's world who in any sense at all measures up to the specific requirements of Aristotle, if he is to be taken in a literal sense. *Hamartia* is a different problem, but even here Aristotle could not conceive of the fall from greatness as being tragic unless the leading character was victim of some slight flaw, because to have a perfectly good man fall from prosperity into adversity would be "impious" or "merely shocking"; it would in fact, question the goodness of the Gods. This, in its traditional interpretation by critics found expression in the assumption that at the end of a tragedy there was a *katharsis,* which in turn was interpreted to mean that man was "brought face to face with universal law" and "the divine plan of the world."

Neither the traditional Aristotelian character, nor the pious belief in a divine order of things has validity in the best of modern tragedy from Ibsen and Strindberg to O'Neill, and of these, it applies least of all to O'Neill. His tragedy, if it has universal appeal, must deal with the fall of man from prosperity into adversity in a manner that is "shocking" and through causes that lie within man himself in relation to the outward forces of his world. He is brought to disaster by forces that are stronger than he is. This attitude toward man has been apparent in O'Neill's plays from the first to the last. The men and women of his world are victims of a cosmic trap, cold and impersonal as steel.

Sophus Keith Winther. *Eugene O'Neill: A Critical Study,* 2nd enlarged ed. (New York, Russell & Russell, 1961), pp. 297–98

Dramatic inventiveness is O'Neill's surest claim to fame. I include in this term both the feeling for theatre which enabled him to hit upon highly effective devices for the staging of his plays, and another kind of imagination which enabled him to find situations corresponding to his various concepts of the human dilemma. The attempt to find answers to all the big questions in life produced some exquisitely painful prose in such plays as *Lazarus Laughed* and *The Fountain,* but it also determined the characteristic form of an O'Neill play. The answers themselves, unsatisfactory as they are, contribute importantly to the success of the best characterizations. . . .

Masks were used in several O'Neill plays staged in the twenties: in *The Hairy Ape, The Ancient Mariner, All God's Chillun Got Wings, The Fountain, The Great God Brown, Marco Millions* and *Lazarus Laughed.* In 1932, two years before resuscitating the device in *Days without End,* O'Neill published his "Memoranda on Masks" in *The American Spectator.* Here he expressed his conviction that masks would be found to be the "freest solution" of the problem of expressing in drama "those profound hidden conflicts of the mind which the probings of psychology continue to disclose to us." In an oracular style, probably influenced by *Thus Spake Zarathustra,* he gave his "Dogma for the new masked drama.—One's outer life passes in a solitude haunted by the masks of others; one's inner life passes in a solitude hounded by the masks of oneself." But the most significant of the "Memoranda" for the understanding of O'Neill's technique was the question, "For what, at bottom, is the new psychological insight into human cause and effects but a study in masks, an exercise in unmasking?" The mask was a way of getting at the inner reality of character. In fact, it may be said that for O'Neill it was *the* way, for even in the many plays where actual masks are not used, we find the same preoccupation with concealment and discovery. These plays too are studies in masks.

Eugene M. Waith. *ETJ.* Oct., 1961, pp. 182–83

In *Ah Wilderness!,* romanticized sex and half-baked philosophy, finally, are the enthusiasms of a character who is an adolescent himself; and as a result, the play marks a turning point in O'Neill's relation to his material. If *Days without End* suggests a new detachment towards his religious questing, *Ah Wilderness!* prefigures his transformation into an objective dramatic artist. As his self-awareness grows, O'Neill is beginning to distance himself from dogma and opinions. In the mouth of the seventeen-year-old Romantic, Richard Miller, the author's familiar paeans to Beauty, Love, and Life seem perfectly acceptable, since O'Neill is treating these affirmations with gentle satire and indulgent whimsey. It is the character, not the author, who is now identified with *fin de siècle* pessimism, culled from Swinburne, Nietzsche, and Omar Khayyam, just as it is the character, not the author, who is inclined to sentimentalize prostitutes. The play, in short, has finally become more important than the theme—ideas are effectively subordinated to "the experience in which they are implied." By projecting his literary self-consciousness onto an earlier Self, O'Neill is beginning to free himself from it. And in *Ah Wilderness!*, he exposes previously suppressed talents for depicting the habitual and commonplace side of existence, along with unsuspected gifts for portraying the humorous side of Irish family life. . . .

Ah Wilderness! is like all the plays which are to follow in being a work of recollection—nostalgic and retrospective. And significantly, it does not contain a trace of Expressionism, being surprisingly conventional in technique and structure. Later, O'Neill is to develop a different kind of realism all his own, built on a centripetal pattern in which a series of repetitions bring us closer and closer to the explosion in the center; but *Ah Wilderness!* is typical of O'Neill's late plays in its avoidance of conspicuous formal experimentation. Masks, split characters, and choruses are gone forever. As a result, O'Neill abandons those ponderous abstractions and inflated generalizations which Expressionism invariably dragged into his plays. If the author once complained, about *The Hairy Ape,* that "the public saw just the stoker, not the symbol, and the symbol makes the play either important or just another play," then he is now able to subordinate symbolism, and sometimes suppress it entirely for the sake of penetrating studies of character.

Robert Brustein. *The Theatre of Revolt*
(Boston, Little, Brown, 1964), pp. 336–38

The reasons both for O'Neill's greatness and for his limitations lie implicit in his theory of tragedy. Although he never proclaimed this formally, or developed it in detail, he suggested the outlines of it in early letters and interviews. Moreover, this theory guided his dramatic practice throughout his career, and it was realized progressively in the composition of his plays. But he was so little the philosopher that its fundamental importance has often been overlooked. The earlier chapters of this book have suggested the literary origins of his theory and the pattern which he realized in his plays. But there were certain underlying principles.

O'Neill's theory of tragedy consisted of two positive principles and of a negative one. First, he asserted that our emotions are of primary importance, both in theory and in practice. Second, that the expression of our emotions, through the medium of tragic drama, is a "life-giving" process, leading to a "deeper spiritual understanding." But third, because our emotions are primary, and the expression and understanding of them is of first importance, it follows that our thoughts and even our actions are of secondary importance. . . .

The peculiar nature of O'Neill's theory and practice of tragedy is defined by the extreme nature of his belief in the value of emotion and by his corresponding disbelief in the value of practical action. His early plays had concerned themselves more with the external realities of setting and action, and it is significant that critics who dislike O'Neill have usually preferred the early *The Emperor Jones* and *Anna Christie*. But beginning with *The Hairy Ape,* O'Neill's tragic heroes progressively insisted that action is relatively unimportant because: "Dis ting's in your inside." And O'Neill's tragedies progressively dramatized conflicts of inner emotion rather than of external action.

Frederic I. Carpenter. *Eugene O'Neill* (New York,
Twayne, 1964), pp. 174–75, 177

O'Neill's deepest affinities are back in the first flowering of American literary culture, the so-called American Renaissance; in fact O'Neill represents the belated explosion in the American drama of themes and concerns that had first appeared in other literary genres in the nineteenth century. In her introduction to *Six Plays of Strindberg,* Elizabeth Sprigge remarks that the "drama had, as usual, lagged behind the times," asserting as a fact of literary history that new ideas and concerns that first appear in the other genres, in the novel, for instance, have a tendency to show up last in the drama. Thus Shaw injected into the English drama preoccupations and concerns that had been agitating Victorian culture in the novel and poetry for decades: feminism, the nature of the relation between the sexes, marriage, the "new morality," social injustice, the workings of modern capital, socialism, the implications of modern science, the consequences of "the death of God," the meaning of history, the nature of the great man, teleology, and so on.

The analogy holds for O'Neill, but with the important difference that while there are many ideas, and discussions of ideas, in his plays, the ideas keep changing from play to play, and there is not, as in Shaw's plays, a consistent ideological pattern, nor is there the implication that ideas finally are of great or determining importance in human affairs. Rather, in considering O'Neill's plays in their totality and attempting to ascertain what they mean or signify, one feels that they contain an over-all quality, indefinable but unmistakable, that is not ideological at all. Profound, obscure, dark, tortuous, and powerful emotions are brooded over; no conclusions are reached; and we are finally presented with an ambiguity. In short, the O'Neill corpus suggests nothing so much as the complex tortuousness of classical American literature of the nineteenth century. Almost everything is there in O'Neill: Henry Adams' dynamo; Hawthorne's scenes in the spiritualizing moonlight and his New England family, ancestrally cursed and inhabiting a gloomy mansion from whose walls glare down the grim visages of the Puritan, witch-burning ancestors; Dana's folk material of sea life; Melville's "melting pot" crews and mystique of the sea; Whitman's "roughs"; Henry James, Sr.'s "Mother God"; and Poe's tubercular heroines, dope addiction, incest, alcoholism, icebergs, fog, and orangoutans, all presided over by "the imp of the perverse." . . . That O'Neill himself was aware of his tradition is evidenced by the fact that one of his favorite quotations was Whitman's "Do I contradict myself? Very well, I contradict myself."

John Henry Raleigh. *The Plays of Eugene O'Neill* (Carbondale, Ill., Southern Illinois University Press, 1965), pp. 242–43

The focal themes of division and alienation are carried by O'Neill's scenic means of expression. An effort to see the typical position of his scenic images as functional parts of his plays leads us to the word "massive." . . . There are certainly paradoxes in the psyche of a man who writes a farce about his attempted suicide; among the paradoxes of Eugene O'Neill the artist there is the fact that he is a combination of clumsiness and explosive energy. From the jerky dialogue of *Thirst* to the awkward exposition of *A Touch of the Poet* there are indications of overgrowth; on the other hand, the plays are full of incommensurate energy. One of O'Neill's scenic units is an automaton, moving mechanically; on the other hand, it cannot be said that his late dialogue was void of subtlety. We can object to O'Neill's stiffness, we can remark upon it; yet we cannot deny that this vice is a result of his virtues. Without the repetitions, without constant interaction, the central scenic images would not work; there would not be any play at all. It is as if both O'Neill and his Yank in *The Hairy Ape* had been compelled to give their clumsiness its say before they were able to explode.

And the basic paradox in Eugene O'Neill: he was a divided monomaniac. He experienced and expressed, with all of his furious energy, a sense of being out of harmony. This is the point where his matter and manner meet. It can be seen from his scenic units and images; both are essential parts of a playwright's world.

Timo Tiusanen. *O'Neill's Scenic Images* (Princeton, N.J., Princeton University Press, 1968), pp. 342–43

Although he did not use the term until 1924, O'Neill was always in spirit a super-naturalistic playwright, a playwright who, due to his keen religious and psychological concerns, was constantly striving to express profound inner experiences. At the same time, however, he always attempted to retain a realistic surface layer in order to make his plays dramatic in an immediate, elementary way and to enable the reader and spectator to empathize with the characters. This is true even of *The Great God Brown* and *Lazarus Laughed*, his least illusionistic dramas.

Because of this amalgam technique, O'Neill's work is open to interpretation on different levels. Much of the controversy regarding its meaning and quality—and opinions have been, and are still, very divided on these issues—is clearly due to completely different ideas of what the author is trying to communicate. Some commentators have limited themselves to a consideration of the realistic surface layer or have read into the plays a topical meaning never intended by the dramatist. Others have been sensitive to the universal implications and super-naturalistic overtones of the drama. Literary interpreters often tend to regard the stage directions as extraneous parts of little significance. Directors, similarly, are frequently inclined to subscribe to the widespread view that a first-rate dramatist—and, as ever, Shakespeare is used as a paragon—needs no or few stage directions. O'Neill, in accordance with this view, is considered a major dramatist despite rather than because of his extensive stage directions. Even those directors who take a more positive view of O'Neill's efforts and make a serious attempt to realize the author's ideas on the stage, often find that it cannot be done, simply because their resources do not meet the playwright's demands. Hence the problem arises: if both the literary and the theatrical experts neglect a substantial and integral part of the plays, who is going to be concerned with the dramas as the playwright conceived of them, when he wrote them for his "dream theatre"?

> Egil Törnqvist. *A Drama of Souls: Studies in O'Neill's Super-naturalistic Technique* (New Haven, Conn., Yale University Press, 1969), p. 253

One characteristic is consistently evident throughout O'Neill's career: an unusual technical flexibility, a readiness to experiment and take risks, which he never lost even in his later years. His plays explore the full range of dramatic expression, which continued to fascinate him as long as he lived. Parallel to this runs his experimentation with ideas. Many writers have left their mark, stylistic or philosophical, on his work; they include Spengler, Nietzsche, Marx, Freud, Aeschylus, Shakespeare, Ibsen, Strindberg, Gerhart Hauptmann, and Georg Kaiser. While O'Neill's work in its totality indicates chaos and helplessness, the individual plays show a tentative reaching out, quickly overcome, toward nihilism and Catholicism, determinism and the triumph of human freedom. This is what St. John Ervine meant when he said that O'Neill does not develop, he just expands. But it was precisely this infinite reluctance to declare or commit himself that constituted the artistic as well as the philosophical and religious freedom so indispensable to O'Neill. This predilection for epic completeness—or rather "all-embracingness"—is just as evident in the total *oeuvre* as in the individual later plays and dramatic cycles, which can no longer be contained within conventional limits. . . .

To look for O'Neill's enduring value in his flexibility and his adroit acrobatic (often superficial) handling of ideas—the sort of relative value that Joyce enjoys—may seem questionable. Nevertheless his great works are best approached, not by way of his technical experiments or his "ideas," but by insight into an experience of life almost untouched by ideas and mastered only through the imposition of artistic form. The quality of a play like *Long Day's Journey into Night* stemmed from personal suffering rather than from a dramatic idea. O'Neill's often unique experiments may prove to be dated, but his best plays, with their spontaneity and confessional intensity, are genuine and powerful expressions of the spiritual anguish, helplessness, lies, and mutual human destruction, which O'Neill knew only too well. They give us a glimpse of the man behind the experimenter, suffering and sacrificing himself to art. This is what distinguishes O'Neill from any fashions, trends, or movements to which he may have subscribed or with which he may have been identified.

Horst Frenz. *Eugene O'Neill* (New York,
Frederick Ungar, 1971), pp. 104–6

O'Neill's influence as a man of the theatre can best be measured in general, rather than in specific terms. As he began to write, the theatre was dominated by a superficial realism which barely concealed a tawdry artifice. In 1918, efforts to move the American theatre toward the province of art were spasmodic attempts, lacking as visible proof plays that would attest to the truth of theory. In cooperation, first, with the Provincetown Players, then with an experimental theatre in association with Kenneth Macgowan and Robert Edmond Jones and finally with the Theatre Guild, O'Neill demonstrated decisively that drama could be an art. In very literal terms, his work between 1920 and 1928 proved the theories of "Theatre Art" to be valid. Admittedly, he was not alone in this. As the decade passed, serious theatregoers in the United States increasingly were able to see important demonstrations of the new theatre aesthetics from sources both European and American. Among innovative dramatists in this country, however, O'Neill was clearly the leader, insisting in both his successes and his failures that his work be considered as an art.

In small ways and in large he pushed at the practical and theoretical limitations of the American stage, and, in doing so, he taught others to do the same. *Lazarus Laughed* is subtitled "A Play for an Imaginative Theatre." O'Neill, struggling to find someone capable of producing the play, said sourly that by the phrase he did not mean an "Imaginary Theatre." A theatre to produce not only that play but all of his works had to be forced into being. By his imagination and boldness and by his uncompromising sense of the value of his writing, he played a major role in bringing that theatre into existence. Much of what he did is now contemporary routine; many of the new theories he championed have become commonplace in the course of time. By the same token, the wheel, once it was invented, became obvious.

Travis Bogard. *Contour in Time: The Plays of Eugene
O'Neill* (New York, Oxford University Press,
1972), pp. xiv–xv

O'Neill's successful nonrealistic plays, *The Emperor Jones, The Hairy Ape,* and *The Great God Brown,* were effective on the stage primarily because of their portrayal of subjective soul states. These plays possess a dynamism that catapulted American drama into world prominence. For O'Neill enriched native drama with his masterful use of poetry of aural and visual effects which, as Jean Cocteau pointed out in defining his *poésie de théâtre,* the modern playwright offers as a substitute for verbal poetry in the theatre. O'Neill's skillful projection of his characters' inner states through distorted settings and masks suggests a much closer affinity with the German expressionists than with Strindberg, in whose dream plays the consciousness of not the protagonist but the author holds sway over the surreal action. Unquestionably, O'Neill derived much inspiration from Strindberg, but he also absorbed the basic principles of the contemporary avant-garde theatre of Germany and selected from these the devices that best suited his purposes in dramatic construction. It is with considerable justification, then, that a German critic has referred to him as "the American Georg Kaiser." For Eugene O'Neill was above all a sensitive artist of the theatre. His plays, like those of Kaiser and the expressionists in general, have more power on the stage than in the library.

Mardi Valgemae. *Accelerated Grimace: Expressionism in the American Drama of the 1920s* (Carbondale, Ill., Southern Illinois University Press, 1972), p. 40

All the fury and anguish, all the vital agony of living, which had been dissipated in his earlier plays by undigested bits of philosophy and unearned attempts at lyricism, had this time [in *Long Day's Journey into Night*] been given clear, hard outlines. Perhaps because the Tyrones had been constructed around personal remembrance, they were freed from the tendentiousness that fettered so many O'Neill characters, and the terrible truths they told to each other were not statements about life but embodiments of it. They were released also from the need to speak to each other in the fustian vernacular of a Hairy Ape or, like Lazarus, in cloudbursts of grandiloquence. When they argued, teased, cajoled, confessed, and complained, they did so in precise, rich human speech that was colored just enough by the dramatist's art so that it remained both unobtrusive and remarkable. Having overcome the need to prove himself a thinker and poet, a fuzzy combination of Shaw and O'Casey spiced with a bit of Nietzschean suffering, O'Neill was free to be what he superbly was: a dramatist of courage and force who understood very well how to construct the tensions and rhythms of a play so that it becomes infused with crude theatrical life and capable of sustaining the needs of the singular vision that give it birth.

Jack Richardson. *Cmty.* Jan., 1974, pp. 52–53

Perhaps a better slogan for O'Neill than art for art's sake would be art for life's sake. He tried to convert the theater back into a church because he had a deep psychological need to do so. Only art could turn doubt into will and despair into acceptance. Only art could release his pain of spirit and allow him to transcend himself. O'Neill was driven by personal demons in all his work, demons that had to be exorcised over and over. The inward turn of his mind away from political or social preoccupations toward its own workings was the turn of his plays. The tension of his inner conflicts was his plays' tension. And this tension, this pain of spirit, could only be released if shared by an audience, by a body of fellow sufferers who in the sharing became father confessors. The exorcising could only take place through the performance of rituals that were communal in nature.

Yet O'Neill's plays amount to more than elaborate confessions or disguised autobiography. For his attempt to make of the theater a place where rituals were acted out had broad cultural significance. It was an attempt to restore to the theater the function it had possessed in ancient Athens and, in more sublimated form, in Elizabethan England—the function of life celebration. The attempt was shared in by others, some of whom considerably influenced O'Neill. In fact, the theater avant-garde in America was then dedicated to just this ideal. While the emotional wellspring of O'Neill's work was wholly personal, he was constantly reminded of the need to keep his plays objective enough to have a wide appeal. The shapes they assumed were even derived from the outer currents of other people's thoughts and the theater itself. So the secret of O'Neill's achievement lies as much outside the realm of his demons as inside. He manifested his genius not merely in dramatizing his conflicts but in making them into a religious experience. Indeed, to properly evaluate his work one must first understand his conception of religious theater.

Leonard Chabrowe. *Ritual and Pathos: The Theater of O'Neill* (Lewisburg, Pa., Bucknell University Press, 1976), pp. xii–xiii

I do not wish to present an argument that O'Neill is an absurdist dramatist, but would suggest that in his insistence that his realistic manner must also be expressive, must be "real realism," he did play a part in extending the limits and did assimilate into his form means of exploring areas of human experience which continue to be of pressing interest to us today. Retention of the realistic framework seems to have been essential to the functioning of his creative imagination. He did experiment with expressionist and symbolist techniques but . . . even within such experiments he constantly veered towards sets and situations in which the familiar and human, as opposed to the remote and metaphysical, could be recreated and explored.

And yet. Whilst O'Neill never does break the illusion he does go to the edge, does threaten it. Within the conventional performing of the play itself, his characters perform for each other and adopt a succession of different roles. The characters in *Long Day's Journey into Night* introduce their quotations or passages of heightened prose with a self-conscious gesture, they praise each other's performance and comment on the quality of each recitation; Con Melody [in *A Touch of the Poet*] strikes poses before a mirror, into which he also performs his recitations of Byron's poetry; Don Parritt's final exit in *The Iceman Cometh* is accompanied by a consciously histrionic "curtain line," whilst in *A Moon for the Misbegotten*, Jamie gestures to the sunrise with the words "Rise of Curtain, Act Four stuff." Such speeches contribute to the ongoing action. They are "in character," notably so in the case of the Tyrones, who are presented as being professional actors. And yet, they also bring consciousness of performance and playing into the audience's minds, in much the same way as does the reiterated play metaphor in Shakespeare's drama.

Similarly, although in the late plays O'Neill does appear to keep to a sequential time span, there is, co-existent with the realistic rhythm of linear time, a different temporal rhythm: a strange recurrence and circularity of the kind that would be explicit in the drama of the post-war period. . . . In his fully achieved "real realism," O'Neill gains the capacity to speak with a voice that is at once familiar and original, of the paradoxes that beset our human existence.

> Jean Chothia. *Forging a Language: A Study of the Plays of Eugene O'Neill* (Cambridge, Cambridge University Press, 1979), pp. 188–89

Only two of the [projected] cycle [*A Tale of Possessors, Self-Dispossessed*] plays survived: *A Touch of the Poet* and *More Stately Mansions*. It can be argued that O'Neill perhaps unconsciously did achieve his goal, combining elements of both proposed cycles [the other one autobiographical]. These two surviving works when combined with *Long Day's Journey into Night* and *A Moon for the Misbegotten* do form what can be termed a "New England Cycle." Comprised of semi- and totally autobiographical plays, they are unified by the theme of the attempt of the Irish immigrant and his descendants to survive in a hostile, alien land—a struggle the dramatist knew well from his heritage, environment, and own tormented soul. One of the recurring themes in these last plays, the struggle for place here in this world, is demonstrated in the conflict between the New England Yankees and the Irish, symbolically for land—whether it be a lowly tenant farmer's shack or the more stately mansions. In a sense, the struggle is futile, for the possessors will ever be self-dispossessed. In a historical sense, both the Puritan descendants and the Irish are foreigners. O'Neill's comment, "There is hardly one thing that our government has done that isn't some treachery—

against the Indians, against the people of the Northwest, against the small farmers,'' reveals his attitude about who has first claim to the land.

A *Touch of the Poet,* set in 1828, depicts the rise of the Irish immigrant Melody family; in *More Stately Mansions,* set in 1832, Sara Melody defeats the Yankee New England Harfords. *Long Day's Journey into Night* and *A Moon for the Misbegotten* reveal the moral dissolution of the Irish Tyrones nearly a century later. The two surviving cycle plays are crucial for an understanding of the picture of America that O'Neill was trying to draw, the key to his social statement and coda to the early plays. Con Melody represents every immigrant who tried to take root in a Yankee-Puritan stronghold. Suspended between two worlds, he reflects in his character a dual nature: the idealistic poet-hero of the Old World, the realistic Irish misfit in the new. At the end of the play, when Con kills the mare, he kills forever the former noble dreamer and with him his pride and the illusions that made his life bearable. America had destroyed the best that was in him. Sara Melody symbolizes America coming of age and the price the Irish immigrant paid for a more stately mansion. In her ruthless schemes to prosper, she crushes the last vestiges of the poet in her Yankee husband, Simon Harford, and in herself.

Virginia Floyd. Introduction to Virginia Floyd, ed.,
Eugene O'Neill: A World View (New York,
Frederick Ungar, 1979), pp. 8–9

O'Neill's *The Iceman Cometh* abandons the effort to transcend the paradoxes and oppositions of existence. The playwright no longer ''exultantly'' affirms life as he does in his earlier works. But he does not cease to believe in living. Rather, he explores man's possibilities within the context of the absurd. He anticipated Camus, who was to write, ''In this unintelligible and limited universe, man's fate henceforth assumes its meaning.'' O'Neill, like Camus, ''wants to find out if it is possible to live *without appeal.*''

O'Neill's sense of the absurd condition led him, as he wrote *The Iceman Cometh,* to express the difficulty of existing in a situation marked by the absence of guiding absolutes. In the lives of the characters in his play, he studied different responses to confusing and uncertain existence. Harry Hope and his regulars cope with ambiguous reality by evasion; Hickey and Parritt face it with denial and despair; and Larry, after great struggle, comes to terms with it. In the end, only denial appears untenable. As the various attempts at survival are enacted on the stage, the characters are seen sympathetically, and yet tragically. Each of the characters is exposed fully, but this is done with understanding and compassion. O'Neill wrote that as the lives of his characters unfold, there are moments ''that suddenly strip the secret soul of a man stark naked, not in cruelty or moral superiority, but with an understanding compassion which sees him as a victim of the ironies of life and of himself.'' To the problem of living, O'Neill offers no answers. The drama reveals, as [Robert] Brustein observes, ''the impossibility of salvation in a world without God.''

The Iceman Cometh is a tragic study of existence in the absurd situation; Hughie is a comic coda in which illusion is affirmed. In The Iceman Cometh, illusion separates men from death, but it also separates them from life. Those who survive by the pipe dream exist in stasis, detached from vitality. In Hughie, the constructed image of self not only sustains life, it makes dynamic living possible. . . .

In Long Day's Journey into Night, The Iceman Cometh, and Hughie, the problem of existence is depicted both comically and tragically. The characters include survivors, such as Edmund Tyrone, Larry Slade, and Erie Smith, and casualties such as Hickey, Don Parritt, and Jamie Tyrone. In each of the plays, man is alone; he seeks his reason for being without God. In the face of nothingness, O'Neill's final characters exist in isolation and in pain. Courageous or resigned, they attempt to live. Deprived of any organizing principle, cast into an ambiguous world and uncertain of themselves, these men represent O'Neill's final response to the difficulty of existence. Uneasy in the absurd condition, they show us exile without remedy, but not the defeat of man.

J. Dennis Rich. In Virginia Floyd, ed.,
Eugene O'Neill: A World View (New York,
Frederick Ungar, 1979), pp. 271, 274–75

WILDER, THORNTON (1897–1975)

Our Town, Thornton Wilder's new play . . . is not easy to describe. On the surface it is only a few typical days in the life of some typical New England citizens as those days were lived in a typical village of a generation ago. As such it sounds commonplace enough, and so far as action goes that is what it is intended to be. But Mr. Wilder—who seemed to me so precious and so thin in The Bridge of San Luis Rey—has brooded over his subject and at last succeeded in communicating a mood as rich and tranquil and satisfying as it is hard to define.

Two attitudes toward the recent past are so familiar that one or the other seems almost inevitable, but the mood of Our Town is neither sentimental nor satiric. Here is no easy fun poked at the age of buggies and innocence, but here also is no sentimental overvaluation. Indeed, it is amazing how little Mr. Wilder claims for his villagers, how readily the local editor admits with a shake of the head that there is no ''culture'' in his town, and how calmly the commentator remarks at the wedding of his chief personages that the result of such unions is interesting "once in a thousand times." There is no tendency to claim for the homely virtues more than their due, no effort to hide the fact that such simple lives are led in ignorance of the heights as well as of the depths of possible human experience.

And if one asks what remains, what is left to feel when one feels neither condescension nor partisan warmth, the answer is simply that the mood of quiet contemplation which Mr. Wilder generates is one which would be hopelessly submerged by any suggestion of either satire or sentimentality. The spectacle of these undistinguished men and women living out their endlessly retold tale fascinates him, I think, not because undistinguished men and women are more admirable than others but because even they are men and women, because even undistinguished lives tease the imagination with a riddle not to be solved and stir it with an emotion not to be analyzed. Satire and sentiment alike are efforts to dispose of the problem by passing a judgment. The still sad music of humanity is most clearly audible when both are rejected.

Joseph Wood Krutch. Nation. Feb. 19, 1938, p. 224

The Skin of Our Teeth, with the usual serious emphasis on human values, is the funniest of Mr. Wilder's plays. Our more venial sins—those of appetite—are embodied in Sabina, a character whose blend of selfishness and good-heartedness creates sheer mirth. The technique, which Mr. Wilder here perfects, of treating time as relative, and jumping back and forth in it with gay abandon, is used for both serious and comic purposes. He used it in his earliest book, *The Cabala,* where, under another name, the dying poet Keats is introduced briefly into the story. *The Long Christmas Dinner* takes a family through several generations. But nowhere is Mr. Wilder so successful with the device as in *The Skin of Our Teeth,* where it becomes an integral part of the play, and no mere trick caught from the expressionists. It suggests the eternity of Mr. Wilder's themes, and it startles us to laughter; this dual effect of the serious and the comic is a most valuable asset to the theater. The technique of breaking down the barriers between actors and audience, between the play and reality, has a similar dual function: it provokes laughter, and it supplies that actual integration of art with life which John Dewey might theoretically approve. At the same time it emphasizes Mr. Wilder's constant theme: the eternity of human values.

In style there is more development than in thought. The early style is rather on the precious side, and includes such sentences as "Triumph had passed from Greece and wisdom from Egypt, but with the coming on of night they seemed to regain their lost honor, and the land that was soon to be called Holy prepared in the dark its wonderful burden." True, his early style does not cloy; but it is mannered and it does call attention to itself. Not until *The Long Christmas Dinner* and *The Happy Journey from Trenton to Camden* did Mr. Wilder's excellent grasp of colloquial speech become fully apparent, and with it his respect for ordinary people—mothers and wives, boys and girls, husbands and sons, living ordinary lives. It is present in all his plays. . . .

Joseph J. Firebaugh. Pacific Spectator. Autumn, 1950, pp. 436–37

The whole tone of *Our Town* is understatement. The colloquial run of the talk, its occasional dry wit, the unheroic folk, all contribute to this tone. So does the important admission that this *is* a play: we are not bid to suspend our disbelief in the usual way; and so does the bareboard, undecorated presentation. All is simple, modest, easy, plain. And so, in tone, the Stage Manager's revelation is utterly casual. But with it Wilder sets in countermotion to the little wheel a big wheel; and as the little one spins the little doings, the big one begins slowly—slowly—for it is time itself, weighted with birth and marriage and death, with aging and with change. This is the great thing that *Our Town* accomplishes; simultaneously we are made aware of what is momentary and what is eternal. We are involved by the Stage Manager in these presented actions and yet like him we are also apart; we are doubly spectators, having a double vision. We are not asked, as in the presentation of some philosophical concept, to perceive an abstract intellectualism. This is a play—this is art. So we are involved sensually and emotionally. Out of shirt-sleeved methods that would seem to defy all magic, and because of them not in spite of them, Wilder's play soon throttles us with its pathos; convinces and moves us so that we cannot imagine its being done in any other way; assumes a radiant beauty. And indeed we are not taken out of ourselves, we are driven deeper into ourselves. This, we say, is life: apparently monotonous, interminable, safe; really all mutable, brief, and in danger. "My," sighs the dead Mrs. Soames in Act III, "wasn't life awful—and wonderful." For what Wilder's art has reminded us is that beauty is recognizable because of change and life is meaningful because of death.

Winfield Townley Scott. VQR. Winter, 1953, pp. 108–9

After a good dinner, and a better bottle of wine, Mr. Thornton Wilder's farce about marrying and being taken in marriage, *The Matchmaker*, seems the quintessence of high-spirited wit. I might suggest, however, a hardy vintage to sustain you through the somewhat desperate *longueurs* of the second act: but this is a graceless kind of carping, and on the whole, Mr. Wilder has bagged that most exotic of game, a comedy for serious people: *The Matchmaker* is, to borrow the Anouilh term, a *pièce rose:* a delicate lustre of sentiment warms and softens its blunt texture of reality: no great weight here, no burden, no statement about mortality or human endurance—

only freshness of feeling, animation, a current of lyricism fashioned exquisitely to the small proportions of the play. Much has been made of Mr. Wilder's resumption of the great trumpery of farce—masquerades and disguises, mixed identities, etc.—but it is not this which gives *The Matchmaker* its interest or its charm: as I sought to illustrate some months ago in my notice of the revival of *The Skin of Our Teeth,* Mr. Wilder as theatrical innovator is most obvious, but not always most satisfying. Rather, it is again the dramatist's nostalgic sunniness of spirit—suffusing the shopworn debris of farce—which seems to me to give *The Matchmaker* its quick, bright, small, secure vitality. Mr. Wilder is ever concerned with life lived intensely, on however homely or domestic a scale, and never more so than in this comedy which ends by wishing for its audience openness and joy, the right proportions of action and contemplation, or as one of the characters so lightly puts it, of adventure and of staying-at-home.

Richard Hayes. Com. Jan. 13, 1956, p. 379

Every form, every style, pays its price for its special advantages. The price paid by *Our Town* is psychological characterization forfeited in the cause of the symbol. I do not believe, as I have said, that the characters are identifiable in a psychological way, but only as figures in the family and social constellation, and this is not meant in criticism, but as a statement of the limits of this form. I would go further and say that it is not *necessary* for every kind of play to do every kind of thing. But if we are after ultimate reality we must make ultimate demands.

I think that had Wilder drawn his characters with a deeper configuration of detail and with a more remorseless quest for private motive and self-interest, for instance, the story as it stands now would have appeared over-sentimental and even sweet. I think that if the play tested its own theme more remorselessly, the world it creates of a timeless family and a rhythm of existence beyond the disturbance of social wracks would not remain unshaken. The fact is that the juvenile delinquent is quite directly traced to the breakup of family life and, indeed, to the break in that ongoing, steady rhythm of community life which the play celebrates as indestructible.

I think, further, that the close contact which the play established with its audience was the result of its coincidence with the deep longing of the audience for such stability, a stability which in daylight out on the street does not truly exist. The great plays pursue the idea of loss and deprivation of an earlier state of bliss which the characters feel compelled to return to or to re-create. I think this play forgoes the loss and suffers thereby in its quest for reality, but that the audience supplies the sense of deprivation in its own life experience as it faces what in effect is an idyl of the past. To me, therefore, the play falls short of a form that will press into reality to the limits of reality, if only because it could not plumb the psychological interior lives of its characters and still keep its present form. It is a triumph in that it does open a way toward the dramatization of the larger truths of existence while using the common materials of life. It is a truly poetic play.

Arthur Miller. *Atlantic*. April, 1956, p. 39

A reading of *Our Town* and *The Skin of Our Teeth* suggests that Wilder's extraordinary freedom and virtuosity in the theatre is gained through eluding rather than solving the problem which most playwrights feel as basic: that of embodying form and meaning in character and language. If he had addressed himself to that problem in *The Skin of Our Teeth,* Antrobus, as the father-pilot of the race, would have had to sound a little more like Spinoza and a little less like George F. Babbitt. But Wilder has seen how it is possible to leave the "greater number" in peace with the material understandable to it, and Plato in peace in the super-temporal realm of the Mind of God. He is thus able to be "for" Plato (as politicians of every persuasion are for Peace, Freedom, and Prosperity), and at the same time devote his great gifts to entertaining the crowd.

This type of allegory is perfectly in accord with the Platonic kind of philosophy which it is designed to teach. The great Ideas are timeless, above the history of the race and the history of actual individuals. Any bit of individual or racial history will do, therefore, to "illustrate" them; but history and individual lives lack all real being: they are only shadows on the cave wall. It may be part of Wilder's consciously intended meaning that the material understandable to the greater number—comic-supplement jokes, popular tunes—*is* junky and illusory. That would be one explanation of the bodiless and powerless effect of his theatre, as compared, for instance, with Brecht's. Brecht's vision is narrow and myopic, but a sense of the reality (at however brutal a level) of individual experience is truly in it. Brecht's philosophy is, of course, a philosophy of history, and leads him naturally to sharpest embodiments of the temporal struggle. But Wilder's philosophy lacks the historic dimension, and its intellectual freedom is therefore in danger of irrelevancy, pretentiousness and sentimentality.

Francis Fergusson. *SewR*. Autumn, 1956, pp. 561–62

Certain of [Wilder's] one-act plays are preparatory studies for the major dramatic works. They test the essential "round" pattern that characterizes *Our Town* and *The Skin of Our Teeth,* the spirit of which might be vulgarized as "here we go again." Thus the short plays are a valuable study in the development of technique and idea, as a set of variations in music may be seen sometimes as part of the growth of a work.

The Long Christmas Dinner telescopes ninety years into a single meal, as *The Skin of Our Teeth* traverses all the ages of man in three acts. The latter play's procession of planets and hours has a trial run in *Pullman Car*

Hiawatha. And in this, and in *The Happy Journey to Trenton and Camden,* plain chairs are made to serve whatever setting is needed. *Pullman Car Hiawatha* also has a versatile, chatty Stage Manager, all in anticipation of *Our Town.* The pullman car stops at "Grover's Corners," but the long later play relocates this from Ohio to New Hampshire. The emotional final sequence of *The Happy Journey* resembles in tone the intimate home scenes of *Our Town.* Finally, in *Pullman Car,* a dead young woman makes an itemized good-bye speech to persons and places anticipating Emily's tender good-bye to the world and Grover's Corners.

In speaking of these experiments in time and space Wilder defined the purpose that informs all of his work in all media—the attempt "to capture not verisimilitude but reality." This is pregnant with counsel for an over-literal age of letters, bogged down often in the narrowest naturalism, or worse still and even more prevalent, pseudo naturalism. Wilder's is that truer realism, unconfined in its means, seeking, as he said of *Our Town,* to "find a value above all price for the smallest events in our daily life." He achieved this aim uniquely in that play.

Edmund Fuller. AS. Spring, 1959, pp. 215–16

Thornton Wilder's plays in one way or another break down the barrier of the proscenium arch. They involve the spectator directly by frankly making him once more a participant in a theatrical experience. These plays have been and continue to be highly successful. They point the way the living theatre should go, for if it is to survive as anything but a luxury for the few, it must discard the conventions of "illusion" and revive the older conventions of "make-believe." It should leave the creation of "illusion" to the moving picture and to television, both of which are infinitely better equipped for it. The theatre should reaffirm itself as an art of "pretense" not of "illusion," of living actors not real people, and of an active not a passive audience.

Thornton Wilder is important in today's American theatre because he is a believer, a yea-sayer. He says "yes" to the life of the theatre, still struggling to escape the strangling embrace of realism and illusion. And through the theatre he says "yes" to human life. In what sometimes seems an unbroken chorus of aggression and rejection by contemporary American playwrights, his is one strong, affirmative voice.

Barnard Hewitt. TDR. Dec., 1959, pp. 119–20

In *The Skin of Our Teeth,* Thornton Wilder has let loose all of his secular and Protestant fantasy in an allegorical "human comedy." Western culture (by now a great deal of restraint is necessary in defining this word) through Moses and the Tablets, Homer and the reality of poetry, Plato and the government of the *res publica,* Spinoza and the goodness within man, etc., has become in Wilder's mind a terrible problem of fusion and contamination. But, while in *Our Town* and in part in *The Long Christmas Dinner,* the balanced correspondences between life and death had been conceived within the center of the Anglo-Saxon poetic tradition (it is sufficient to mention here Edgar Lee Masters), here the American writer has recourse to a technique which we could call "divisionary," analytical and demonstrative, putting his work on the plane of an irritating and meticulous cinematographic staging. I say irritating in order to bring out one aspect of the immediate and noncritical reaction of the European spectator before this confused and at the same time elementary situation of man of earth. Man is then safe by *The Skin of Our Teeth,* that is to say by the thinnest of surfaces, by the margin of a *physical nothing,* by chance? A European could translate the American sentence also "by a miracle" and, remaining quite close to the exact interpretation, without really so intending, give a precise explanation of his own civilization. Chance and faith: there is the strongest motive of the unconscious reaction (Wilder's play is quite ironical, swift and compact) that some may even call insult, the will to destroy a poetic unity upheld for centuries by Western civilization. But without attempting to resolve here the spiritual position of the author of *The Bridge of San Luis Rey,* we may recognize that Wilder has faith in man's destiny, which exists in that he "must" do something which up to now has escaped his perception. [1960]

Salvatore Quasimodo. *The Poet and the Politician*
(Carbondale, Ill., Southern Illinois University Press,
1964), p. 151

Wilder has not been interested in psychology and has never used psychological techniques to solve the "modernists' " problems in the theatre. This accounts, I think, for his great influence on the continental avant-garde dramatists who are rebelling against our psychologically oriented theatre. Wilder sought to achieve the sense of an ultimate perspective by immaterializing the sense of dramatic place on stage. The bare stage of *Our Town* with its chairs, tables, and ladders, together with the Stage Manager's bald exposition, are all that he uses to create the town. The same is true of *The Skin of Our Teeth;* you never really know where the Antrobuses live—nor when. This is his second dominant technique; by destroying the illusion of time, Wilder achieves the effect of any time, all time, each time. But this is risky business, for without the backdrop of an ultimate perspective to inform a play's action, it can very easily become sentimental or satirical, or even pretentious. Wilder at his best keeps this from happening, but his only weapons are wit and irony. And a production which does not succeed in capturing these qualities (as alas most college and school productions do not) is bound to turn out bathetic and sentimental; when technique is used as a compensation for the ultimate perspective, the resultant work of art always lies precariously under a Damoclean sword.

It is important that we see the dangers in Wilder's methods, but that a tragic sense of life informs his plays is best illustrated by his sense of destiny. . . . Wilder is aware, like Eliot, that "human kind cannot bear very much reality," but his plays fall short of tragedy because he takes the Platonic escape, he moves into a world that denies the reality and the nemesis of destiny. Nor does he have the solution of an Eliot. For in denying, finally, the reality of destiny he shuts out the possibility of ever providing the means to perfect our fragmentary and imperfect vision. He fails, to use Karl Jaspers' phrase, to go "Beyond Tragedy." That Wilder lacks this dimension is not to discredit him, however, for no other American dramatist more fully affirms that miracle of life which so much modern drama would deny.

Robert W. Corrigan. ETJ. Oct., 1961, pp. 172–73

Wilder's choice of New England for the setting [of *Our Town*] strengthens the play to the extent, as we have observed, that a depiction of fundamental passions may be especially moving to an American audience if the scene itself is fundamentally and simply American. In this regard, no region qualifies so well as does the birthplace of the nation. On the other hand, nothing vital would be lost if the setting were changed to any other uncomplicated community. . . . For Wilder's purposes in the play, the uniquely indispensable characteristic of the community's populace is its colloquial speech. Familiar everywhere in the nation, it possesses the quality which Wilder admired in Gertrude Stein's *Narration*. In his preface to the book he described it as coming from the "daily life." Before Wilder, writers had refrained from using it in tragedy out of fear of lowering the tone, or, like O'Neill in *Desire under the Elms,* had buttressed it with regional idioms.

That the play is a tragedy, despite the simplicity of the dialogue, is beyond dispute, for we see the death of Emily cutting short the happiness which the young protagonists had earned by the conduct of their lives. Their distress brings the reminder that no amount of effort to achieve honor and dignity such as theirs will confer immortality. The only mitigating notion lies in Emily's urgent lament for the lost opportunity to enjoy simple pleasures. The wisest onlookers will respond to the implicit warning of her last speeches and make what use of it they can. Possibly it will function in their lives to increase their own awareness. Yet it is true that the theme is equally suitable for comedy, as Wilder had demonstrated with *The Cabala* and *Heaven's My Destination*.

Malcolm Goldstein. The Art of Thornton Wilder
(Lincoln, University of Nebraska Press, 1965),
pp. 106–7

In *The Merchant of Yonkers,* Wilder employed the machinery of farce to effect the ground of timelessness and the absence of a particularized place. Farce is necessarily artificial, and no one need believe in its actuality. Only the truth it presents is important. The characters are stock characters and are not limited by any time. By definition the action of farce is based on an absurd premise, which is, however, developed logically. Having its bases in the imagination, or Human Mind, which ranges with complete freedom, the comic imagination shows us the vast human possibilities that can be ours if only we have the mind and strength to make them so. To be sure, the possibilities are not always pleasant, as for example the plays of Molière. Both the writer and the audience of comedy are in the position of God, for it is they who manipulate, who laugh at, who contain all the actions of the characters moving before them. Jokes and references may be topical, and they may stale with the passage of time; but the action of comedy is timeless because it, like the American, is insubmissive to anything outside it. The comic spirit of *The Merchant of Yonkers* presents the individual existing, related to totality, and freed from obedience to destiny.

Wilder's accomplishment in the willful manipulation of time and space largely went unperceived. Most critics saw *Our Town* as a nostalgic tribute to the good years before World War I in America, carefully limiting its time and place. *The Merchant of Yonkers* was regarded as a failure, having as its only redeeming feature the setting and costumes designed by Boris Aronson. *The Skin of Our Teeth* might have corrected the false view of Wilder's skill, but a large part of its audience felt, or at least proclaimed, that the play was mad and incomprehensible. People by no means ill educated or stupid who saw the original production will claim still, whenever the play is mentioned, that they did not understand a single word of it. Amazingly enough, this attitude is contradicted by those who almost immediately found it simple-minded. In fact, neither attitude is reasonable.

Donald Haberman. *The Plays of Thornton Wilder*
(Middletown, Conn., Wesleyan University Press,
1967), pp. 68–69

The literary problem of *The Skin of Our Teeth* was defined in a continuance of the dissolution of form, already suggested in *Our Town,* and now greatly radicalized with the introduction of anachronism, though not to the point of complete dissolution. At the end of the thirties Wilder had been intensely occupied with James Joyce, whose influence was to appear clearly in the multiple symbolism of *The Skin of Our Teeth,* and which led to not always gratifying disputes in American literary magazines.

Viewed in relation to previous drama, the Wilder play differs in the manner of its division into three acts, and in a way also in the kind of plot as given by the title. The title implies that man once again escapes from his current plight and that his personal behavior approximates that of characters in comedy—a comedy, to be sure, with metaphysical overtones rather than a straight comedy of definite time and place.

The play's three acts do not represent one continuous action. Each culminates in a great world catastrophe: the Ice Age, the Deluge, and the World War. Out of each catastrophe man finds his way by dint of his enthusiasm for a new beginning, without fundamentally changing his ways, for the evil which drove him into the catastrophe remains immanent in him.

Thus man is seen under two aspects: as a creature who is delivered up to these catastrophes, and as a creature who lives in the self-contained unit of the family. [1965]

Helmut Papajewski. *Thornton Wilder* (New York, Frederick Ungar, 1968), p. 110

Whereas Wilder's novels (with the exception of *Heaven's My Destination*) owed so much to the spirit of Greece and Rome, with a Christian background, that superficially one might conclude they were written by a European, this is not true of the plays. These could have been written only by an American. In the drama, Wilder seems to have found his own form to express the ideas that basically mattered to him.

The Skin of Our Teeth, which appeared in 1942, seems to confirm this. The play has been criticized for being an historico-philosophical book drama containing a bloodless theory of history. From the formal point of view, *The Skin of Our Teeth* represents something positively revolutionary. But with it, Wilder—who raises such basic questions as: What shall we eat? What shall we drink?—was able to grasp the reality of the present. It became a hit throughout a world in which the very existence of man is at stake, and later it made an especially deep impression on the defeated of World War II, for whom the announcement that there is a recipe for grass soup that does not give one diarrhea was met with a good deal of understanding.

Hermann Stresau. *Thornton Wilder* (New York, Frederick Ungar, 1971), p. 62

If *The Trumpet Shall Sound* was not theatrically effective—and one of its weaknesses was its excessive length—his next collection, *The Angel That Troubled the Waters,* was composed of pieces that were much too short. Several of them were written in college; all were deliberately conceived as three-minute plays. Although published later, in 1928, most of them were marred by a youthful preciousness of language and an insubstantiality of structure. Yet again, they contained the same themes that continue to preoccupy Wilder today, and all of them were concerned with a moral conflict. In his preface, after pointing out that almost all the plays were religious in tone, Wilder indicated that they might serve a useful instructive purpose in an age of literature when religious writing was not too well understood or too welcome. For his part, he felt that to write this kind of drama well would be to write the best kind of drama that existed.

The most arresting quality in this collection of plays is the scope of the subject matter. Characters like the Virgin Mary and St. Joseph, Christ, Satan, Judas, Mozart, Gabriel, Shelley, Ibsen, and a talking donkey named Hepzibah people the various plays; the periods range from Biblical times to Renaissance Paris to eighteenth-century Vienna to nineteenth-century Wales (typically, twentieth-century America is not represented); the settings move from Heaven to the prow of a ship to a goldsmith's shop to a peasant's cottage; and the themes concern themselves with the relationship of the artist to the universe, the meaning of morality, the nature of salvation, the necessity for recognizing beauty in the world, and the importance of living life to the full. When one considers the type of play that Wilder was writing at almost the same moment Eugene O'Neill was producing dramas like *Before Breakfast,* in which a shrewish wife drives her husband to offstage suicide while she is preparing their meal in a shabby, run-down kitchen, one begins to appreciate the individuality of Wilder's vision; before long a large number of aspiring American playwrights would model their dramas first after those of O'Neill, then after those of Clifford Odets, and, in succeeding years, after those of Arthur Miller, Tennessee Williams, and Edward Albee, all of whom owed a heavy debt to realism. Only Wilder remained apart from this vogue. . . .

In one way or another, these plays contain the seeds of almost all Wilder's future subjects. They reveal his impatience with the confining aspects of realism and his need to move freely in space and time. They mix myth with parable, classical tradition with religious orthodoxy. They stress his interest in abstracts rather than concretes, in philosophical rather than purely human considerations. And therefore they lack characterization, suggesting the technique of the early artists of the Middle Ages, flat and one-dimensional. (Even at the height of his skill, Wilder never produced more than two memorable characters in his novels and perhaps two in his plays—and only then because of very special circumstances.) But they show the stamp of an original, or, at the very least, an individual talent.

M. C. Kuner. *Thornton Wilder: The Bright
and the Dark* (New York, Thomas Y.
Crowell, 1972), pp. 41–42, 50

As we might expect, where the inclusiveness of a fully developed conflict is absent, Wilder achieves his moral and religious affirmations too easily. Antrobus in *The Skin of Our Teeth* survives the disasters that beset mankind, but most of mankind is destroyed by them; and we see no real suffering during his times of crisis. Granting that moral courage and a sense of humor can help minimize the tyranny of circumstance, we do not see Antrobus' courage tested in serious conflict on the stage, and the comedy—sometimes slapstick—largely negates the serious themes. Again, in *The Alcestiad* it is no real struggle for Alcestis to conquer the plague. Acting as if by impulse, she sends her son and his companion for some sulphur with which to purify the drinking water and thereby saves her people from disease. The serious problems of life, we feel while observing Alcestis solve this one, are likely to be more formidable. This is not to say that the problems of modern man cannot be dealt with in an ancient setting. Sartre's *The Flies,* for example, pictures man at odds with powerful social forces that deny his freedom. But whereas Sartre draws clearly and powerfully the antagonists to Orestes— Zeus, Aegistheus, and finally Electra—Wilder fails to provide a well-defined human antagonist to Alcestis; and, with the absence of a visible struggle such as Orestes undergoes, her victory seems too easy. These are Wilder's greatest weaknesses.

The best qualities of his art appear where he wrests his affirmations from a fully developed moral conflict and when they are gained through irony—through a conflict in which moral or religious skepticism appears to gain justification but is undermined by a portrayal of great human spiritual depth and nobility. His best works from this standpoint of conflict are *The Bridge of San Luis Rey, Heaven's My Destination, The Ides of March, Our Town,* and *The Eighth Day,* where death or apparent defeat place the moral affirmation in bold relief. Less satisfactory are *The Woman of Andros, The Skin of Our Teeth,* and *The Alcestiad,* in which themes are stated directly and arbitrarily either by dialogue or, particularly in *The Alcestiad,* through nonrealistic action that leaves no moral option for those who cannot accept the mystical nature of the affirmation.

When irony enriches the affirmations through qualification and understatement, Wilder's vision is most compelling. Much of the dramatic impact of *Our Town,* for example, consists in the fact that life in Grover's Corners is at once beautiful and banal. The simple life as lived by the archetypal George and Emily is priceless, but Wilder offers the village drunk—a frustrated musician—as evidence that it can be deadly to talented and sensitive people.

Rex Burbank. *Thornton Wilder,* 2nd ed.
(Boston, Twayne, 1978), pp. 128–29

WILLIAMS, TENNESSEE (1911–1983)

[*The Glass Menagerie*] gives every one of the four characters that it presents a glowing, rich opportunity, genuine emotional motivations, a rhythm of situations that are alive, and speech that is fresh, living, abundant and free of stale theatre diction. The author is not awed by the usual sterilities of our play-writing patterns. On the other hand he is too imaginative, genuine, or has too much good taste, to be coy about the free devices on which his play is built, a true, rich talent, unpredictable like all true talents, an astute stage sense, an intense, quivering clarity, all light and feeling once the intelligence of it is well anchored—a talent, too, I should say, that New York will buy tickets for in later plays, especially if enough of the sexy is added to things, but will never quite understand. . . .

To say, as Mr. Nichols does in his review in the New York *Times,* that there are such unconnected things with the story as "snatches of talk about the war, bits of psychology, occasional moments of rather florid writing" is mistaken indeed. The part Miss [Laurette] Taylor plays [Amanda] is, quite aside from her rendering of it, the best written role that I have seen in a play for years. All the language and all the motifs are free and true; I recognized them inch by inch, and I should know, for I came from the same part of the country, the same locality and life, in fact, that Mr. Williams does. Such a response and attitude as that Mr. Nichols expresses is the kind of thing that helps to tie our theatre down. It is the application of Times Square practical knowledge, the kind of thing that makes, to take one instance, the writing, the talk, in *The Late George Apley* so sterile and so little like the Boston it assumes to be. One of the things most needed in the theatre is a sense of language, a sense of texture in speech, vibration and impulse in speech. Behind the Southern speech in the mother's part is the echo of great literature, or at least a respect for it. There is the sense in it of her having been born out of a tradition, not out of a box. It has echo and the music of it. The mother's characterization is both appalling and human, both cold and loving. No role could be more realistically written than this, but it has the variety, suddenness, passion and freedom, almost unconscious freedom perhaps, of true realism. [1945]

Stark Young. *Immortal Shadows* (New York,
Charles Scribner's Sons, 1948), pp. 251, 252

A *thought*—directing finally consists of turning Psychology into Behavior.

Theme—this is a message from the dark interior. This little twisted, pathetic, confused bit of light and culture puts out a cry. It is snuffed out by the crude forces of violence, insensibility, and vulgarity which exist in our South—and this cry is the play [*A Streetcar Named Desire*].

Style—one reason a "style," a stylized production is necessary is that a subjective factor—Blanche's memories, inner life, emotions, are a real factor. We cannot really understand her behavior unless we see the effect of her past on her present behavior.

This play is a poetic tragedy. We are shown the final dissolution of a person of worth, who once had great potential, and who, even as she goes down, has worth exceeding that of the "healthy," coarse-grained figures who kill her.

Blanche is a social type, an emblem of a dying civilization, making its last curlicued and romantic exit. All her behavior patterns are those of the dying civilization she represents. In other words her behavior is *social*. Therefore find social modes! This is the source of the play's stylization and the production's style and color. Likewise Stanley's behavior is *social* too. It is the basic animal cynicism of today. "Get what's coming to you! Don't waste a day! Eat, drink, get yours!" This is the basis of his stylization, of the choice of his props. All props should be stylized: they should have a color, shape and weight that spell: style. [1947]

Elia Kazan. Notebook for A Streetcar Named Desire.
In Toby Cole and Helen Krich Chinoy,
eds., Directors on Directing (Indianapolis,
Bobbs-Merrill, 1963), pp. 364–65

[*A Streetcar Named Desire*] is better than Williams' other success, *The Glass Menagerie,* because, while it has all of the tenderness, poetry, observation and wit of the earlier piece, it adds the element of true tragedy to its other merits.

It is a despairing and lovely play, in which the author, in oblique parable form, says that beauty is shipwrecked on the rock of the world's vulgarity; that the most sensitive seekers after beauty are earliest and most bitterly broken and perverted. It is an answer, however unintended, to [Mary Chase's] *Harvey* and [O'Neill's] *The Iceman Cometh,* which said that Illusion provides the necessary armor behind which life can survive. *A Streetcar Named Desire* (and what a haunting, musically dissonant title it is) tells us that Illusion is an armor, but one which is always pierced, and in the most mortal spots.

But the parable is hidden artfully in the body of the play. While you are exposed to the magic on the Barrymore stage, you see only the suffering, doomed struggles of a lying, posing, half-demented, pathetic, fully drawn woman, whose dreams are all lace and magnolia, and whose life, given cheaply to whisky and men, has been unbelievably raw and sordid. You may think, as I do, that Williams' generalization is too easily defeatist, that he himself has dipped into the most squalid depths and come up with a steadily beautiful work of art; but, particularly, there is an awesome credibility about the character of his main creation, Blanche DuBois. She is as real to us as if she were a living woman put to the torture and done to death in our own front parlor.

The play is written with a triumphantly heightened naturalism, in which the rhythms and images of ordinary life are subtly combined and contrasted with a verselike elegance of phrase. It falls on the ear like fresh rain after the businesslike tracts of manufactured dialogue which have too long done duty for human speech on the American stage. It finally has the surprising effect of seeming infinitely more real, more like life itself, than all the clipped banalities lesser playwrights put together in the dreary name of realism.

Irwin Shaw. *NR*. Dec. 22, 1947, p. 34

The strange experience of seeing *Camino Real* divides itself into three: things you like, things you dislike, and things you are held by without knowing whether you like them or not. The script, when I read it some time ago, I disliked—partly because it belongs to the current deliquescent-rococo type of theatre and even more because it seemed far from a brilliant example of the type. The genuine element in Tennessee Williams had always seemed to me to reside in his realism: his ability to make eloquent and expressive dialogue out of the real speech of men and his gift for portraiture, especially the portraiture of unhappy women. There is also a spurious element. Sometimes it's his style that is spurious, for when he is poetic he is often luscious and high-falutin'. Sometimes it's his thought; one day a critic will explain what Mr. Williams has made of D. H. Lawrence. Nor are Mr. Williams' reflections on art more convincing than his pseudo-Lawrentian hymns to life; and when he tells you his theory of the Awful, he is awful. Sometimes the trouble is with Mr. Williams' material: surely it would take more than a theory to justify the subject-matter of his novel or of, say, the short story of the man who likes being beaten and is finally *eaten* by a negro masseur. . . . The spurious element seemed to me notably large in the script of *Camino Real*. [1953]

Eric Bentley. *What Is Theatre?*
(New York, Atheneum, 1968), pp. 74–75

[*A Streetcar Named Desire*] is perhaps the most misunderstood of his plays: the English and French productions were both so blatantly sensationalised that Williams' underlying lyric fibre passed unnoticed. If [Arthur Miller's] Willy Loman is the desperate average man, Blanche DuBois is the desperate exceptional woman. Willy's collapse began when his son walked into a hotel apartment and found him with a whore; Blanche's when she entered "a room that I thought was empty" and found her young husband embracing an older man. In each instance the play builds up to a climax involving guilt and concomitant disgust. Blanche, nervously boastful, lives in the leisured past; her defence against actuality is a sort of aristocratic *Bovarysme*, at which her brutish brother-in-law Stanley repeatedly sneers. Characteristically, Williams keeps his detachment and does not take sides: he never denies that Stanley's wife, in spite of her sexual enslavement, is happy and well-adjusted, nor does he exaggerate the cruelty with which Stanley reveals to Blanche's new suitor the secrets of her nymphomaniac past. The play's weakness lies in the fact that the leading role lends itself to grandiose over-playing by unintelligent actresses, who forget that when Blanche complains to her sister about Stanley's animalism, she is expressing, however faintly, an ideal. . . .

When, finally, she is removed to the mental home, we should feel that a part of civilisation is going with her. Where ancient drama teaches us to reach nobility by contemplation of what is noble, modern American drama conjures us to contemplate what might have been noble, but is now humilitated, ignoble in the sight of all but the compassionate. [1954]

Kenneth Tynan. Curtains (New York, Atheneum, 1961), p. 263

The team of Tennessee Williams, playwright, Elia Kazan, director, and Jo Mielziner, designer, is as potent an artistic force as Broadway can boast today. Their newest collaboration, the Playwrights Company production of *Cat on a Hot Tin Roof . . . ,* is a really remarkable piece of work. It is also the season's most solid dramatic success. One should perhaps take spe-cial note of the fact that the *kind* of theatre produced by this particular team is a strictly American creation and has as yet no European counterpart: it is, in fact, *the* singular dramatic achievement of the postwar decade on Broad-way (the only other new achievements of any artistic kind being in the field of the musical). One senses it as an important creation, and one that is now arrived and may be ready for an interesting future. The technique of it is based on a curious dialectic of intense realism and rather eloquent fantasy, a dialectic which is present in every part of the final creation—it is there in the writing, in the open half-abstracted settings, in the play of the lights, in the postures and delivery of the actors. It is an intensification of life posed against abstractions from it, artifice breaking down into nature, nature build-ing up into artifice. Specifically, it is real speech with unnatural inflections, solid furniture in rooms with no walls, naturalistic acting that assembles itself into highly posed and static images, normal realistic light that gives way to follow-spots and chiaroscuro, talk that develops special rhythms and elevates itself into speech.

Nor is this phenomenon, even fundamentally, a playwright's creation, nor a director's, nor a designer's. One senses it as thoroughly eclectic, col-laborative, fluid, and the final product as one in which the individual contri-butions are so harmoniously blended as to create a fully synthetic piece of theatre—a sort of *Gesamtkunstwerk* minus the music. The production pro-cess is more than just an achievement of the play; it is actually its comple-tion, with the result that the design of the set and the basic elements of the staging get built into the script—quite literally, as anyone who has had the opportunity to compare an original Williams text with the final published version will know. No future production of the play can ever depart very successfully from the basic scheme that emerges.

William Becker. *HudR*. Summer, 1955, p. 268

Is there a basic flaw in Williams that blights his work? I don't know. There are flaws, of course. He is not much at constructing a plot, and plot elements in his plays tend to stick out and suggest conclusions that were not intended. He has a compulsion to dredge up bits of human degradation that are not always essential to the play. And lastly, because he is a sensitive romantic, Williams has an insecurity which sometimes leads him into giving in to inferior suggestions from stronger people rather than to do nerve-shattering battle for his own judgment.

His relationship with director Elia Kazan is a case in point. Williams recognizes the dangers of submitting to Kazan's strong personality, but he simultaneously cherishes its qualities in a show-biz world he feels incapable of coping with by himself. Kazan, on the other hand, works on the theory that it is part of the director's function to produce a play in such a way as to make the playwright's attitudes and personality come over the footlights with greater intensity than is explicit in the script. In *Cat on a Hot Tin Roof* he persuaded Williams to do extensive rewriting. He also used a poetic setting rather than the realistic one Williams had intended. Probably much of the stylization that is attributed to the Williams of *A Streetcar Named Desire, Camino Real,* and *Cat on a Hot Tin Roof* is really the influence of Kazan, who believes that this stylization is bringing out the playwright's personality. Kazan and Williams both make the strongest possible effort to remain great friends. When together they joke about and exaggerate the phony aspects of living. Thus, one feels that Kazan encourages Williams to laugh at the world's falsities without the discipline Williams might normally apply. But, while encouraging excesses of uninhibitedness, the director also tends to remove a certain antisocial flavor by persuading Williams to make his antagonists more likable, and by getting him to come up with softening after-thoughts like the suspense ending of *Baby Doll,* which negates the hardboiled ending of "Twenty-Seven Wagons Full of Cotton."

Henry Hewes. *SR*. Dec. 29, 1956, pp. 23–24

Every age offers hemlock to its greatest moralists—perhaps persecution is the proof of a man's opinions. Nobody could accuse Tennessee Williams of being unaware of the world he lives in; his image of it goes so deep that it disturbs and discomforts his hearers. In spite of our crowded cities and increasing gregariousness, the desire to belong, to be loved, to enter into the hearts and minds of our fellows is more and more frustrated. This loneliness is Williams' concern. Through particular studies of the lonely human heart, he finds universals. Lack of communication, an inability to "reach" each other is the great modern agony whether in personal, national or international matters. In *Cat on a Hot Tin Roof,* a suffering family forces communication with each other, and in the process, dispels many of the lies they are each living. By the end, two lonely people—Brick, an alcoholic with a secret who has given up the struggle, and Maggie his wife locked in a prison of desire for her unreachable husband—are forced together by the insistence of life. This is not, as some critics have found, a play of decadence and death.

Williams has said that he has never met a human being that he could not in some way like, and this spirit of understanding and compassion for his fellows is strong in all his work. We live in a violent age which is constantly on the brink of a cataclysm more formidable than all the plagues, pestilences and wars of the past. Williams does nothing to disguise this violence and unrest. He studies perversion, nymphomania and all the strange manifestations of frustration, not because they are sensational dramatic material, but because they are symptoms of the stresses and strains of modern living. He believes in happiness and the peace which we can give each other. (The tragedy of *Summer and Smoke* lies in two people missing this understanding of each other by a hair's breadth.) And in this sense Williams is a religious man: he believes in life. But it is a life which he must scrutinise closely and in all its forms; he refuses the blinkers of conventional religion, and in doing so he finds his own faith. The central quotation of *Camino Real* is expanded into "The violets in the mountains *can* break the rocks if you believe in them and allow them to grow." Given enough strength, tenderness can indeed move mountains.

Peter Hall. *Encore.* Sept.–Oct., 1957, p. 17

Williams has a long reach and a genuinely dramatic imagination. To me, however, his greatest value, his aesthetic valor, so to speak, lies in his very evident determination to unveil and engage the widest range of causation conceivable to him. He is constantly pressing his own limit. He creates shows, as all of us must, but he possesses the restless inconsolability with his solutions which is inevitable in a genuine writer. In my opinion, he is properly discontented with the total image some of his plays have created. And it is better that way, for when the image is complete and self-contained it is usually arbitrary and false.

It is no profound thing to say that a genuine work of art creates not completion, but a sustained image of things in tentative balance. What I say now is not to describe that balance as a false or illusory one, but one whose weighing containers, so to speak, are larger and greater than what has been put into them. I think, in fact, that in *Cat on a Hot Tin Roof,* Williams in one vital respect made an assault upon his own viewpoint in an attempt to break it up and reform it on a wider circumference.

Essentially it is a play seen from the viewpoint of Brick, the son. He is a lonely young man sensitized to injustice. Around him is a world whose human figures partake in various ways of grossness, Philistinism, greed, money-lust, power-lust. And—with his mean spirited brother as an example—it is a world senselessly reproducing itself through ugly children conceived without the grace of genuine affection, and delivered not so much as children but as inheritors of great wealth and power, the new perpetuators of inequity.

Arthur Miller. *Harper's*. Aug., 1958, p. 41

After seeing the plays, one is left with the feeling that Williams is basically a sentimentalist who fluctuates like a thermometer in uncertain weather between bathos and poetic rhetoric, between the precious and the bawdy, and between adolescent admirations and histrionic displays of violence. He sobs over failures, the aimless, weak, frustrated seekers; envies vicariously his own characters, male and female, radiantly happy in their physical love; idolizes those men who inherited the virility of a prize bull; and lacerates those human beings, mostly women, driven by an unsatisfied sexual hunger. Perhaps he *is* a dramatist who feels rather than thinks, because he seems to be more interested in emotional crises involving a few character types than in developing an idea, or character, or action, as is habitual with the Greeks he professes to admire. Like so many modern writers who are afraid that they will be uttering the obvious, he indulges in the kind of obvious symbolism that has been called "ladies' club mystifications," in fancy names and fancy settings, in mood music, in tableaus—affected Madonna poses and settings in della Robbia blues. There is so much posturing in the plays, so much of the same thing over and over again, one has the feeling that Williams writes like a man who has spent hours before the mirror, playing a limited number of roles in a variety of exotic costumes.

This Pulitzer prize-winning dramatist has confessed, "The more I go on, the more difficult it becomes not to repeat myself," perhaps one of the truest statements he has made to date about his work. If one considers the types that keep reappearing in his plays, and what they represent, he will find that the world of Tennessee Williams is a very limited one, where people are characters created by a writer who is sometimes perceptive and honest, sometimes sentimental and cruel, and sometimes merely vulgar.

Signi Falk. *MD*. Dec., 1958, pp. 173–74

In *Sweet Bird of Youth*, Tennessee Williams seems less concerned with dramatic verisimilitude than with communicating some hazy notions about such disparate items as Sex, Youth, Time, Corruption, Purity, Castration, Politics and The South. As a result, the action of the play is patently untrue, the language is flat and circumlocutory, the form disjointed and rambling, and the characters—possessing little coherence of their own—function only as a thin dressing for these bare thematic bones. Cavorting through the forest of his own unconscious, Williams has taken to playing hide-and-go-seek with reality in a manner which he does not always control. *Sweet Bird of Youth,* in consequence, contains the author's most disappointing writing since *Battle of Angels,* and frequently looks less like art than like some kind of confession and apology.

Even so, the confession might have assumed the dimensions of art if it were not so clearly that of a solipsist. About to be castrated, the play's hero, Chance Wayne, turns to the audience to ask for "the recognition of me in you, and the enemy, time, in us all!" Since Chance has had about as much universality as a character in an animated cartoon, to regard his experience as an illuminating reflection of the human condition is a notion which borders on the grotesque. For *Sweet Bird of Youth* is a highly private neurotic fantasy which takes place in a Terra Incognita quite remote from the terrain of the waking world. There all events have a mechanically sexual construction, everyone is caught up in extravagant depravity, success and failure alternate with astonishing swiftness, letters are sent but never delivered, and people not only get threatened with castration but have this threat executed and do nothing to avoid it when it actually comes. That this world is to be regarded as real or meaningful is a surprise sprung too often to promote much confidence in the author's vision.

Robert Brustein. HudR. Summer, 1959, p. 255

In *Orpheus Descending,* Williams tried to present two of his major themes conjointly: the tragic isolation of the artist in the hell of modern society and the crucifixion of the pure male on the cross of sexuality. He also wrestles with the worthy but extremely difficult experiment of amalgamating realism and imagination, and of transforming literal reality into poetic reality.

The fact that *Orpheus* was a failure on Broadway does not lessen its superiority to most new plays on view in New York and London. Williams was straining to make a refractory medium express the visions of reality that he shares with other negativistic modernists. He can be roughly compared, for example, with Samuel Beckett, but what distinguishes him from the author of *Waiting for Godot* is the romantic expansiveness of his dialogue, characterization, and plot-making. On these and other grounds we cannot relate Williams to Ionesco, either. In our time only Jean Genet, whose grueling and perversely absorbing plays, *The Maids, Deathwatch,* and *The Balcony,* which were briefly displayed at tiny off-Broadway theatres, has displayed the same melodramatic imagination and partiality for naturalistic effluvia.

Orpheus Descending was apparently a necessary recapitulation for Williams. An important venture even in failure, it did credit to both the author and his director. Evidently they disagreed on which aspect of the work needed stressing—the realistic or the symbolic—and on where the concentration of the play should come. But though I would have preferred a fuller development of Val as an individual rather than as an Orpheus symbol the important fact is that a theme very close to a greatly gifted playwright's heart continued to resist his dramatic talent while continuing to fire his imagination.

John Gassner. *Theatre at the Crossroads* (New York, Holt, Rinehart and Winston, 1960), pp. 225–26

Summer and Smoke, as in the case of the better known plays of Tennessee Williams, *A Streetcar Named Desire* and *The Glass Menagerie,* moves among crepuscular tones (and this refers to language and the faint images deriving from it) in which idyll alternates with tragedy through overtly cinematographic technique. This lack of unity manifests itself not so much in the internal temporal flow of the characters as in the writer's complacently fragmentary manner of sketching figures and events in a style more appropriate to a long narrative than to a play. In *Summer and Smoke* there is only one character, Alma, the daughter of the evangelist Winemiller, since John Buchanan is barely the necessary interlocutor of a convulsed and desperate monologue of the ''soul.'' The idyll is born in the gray atmosphere of the American South, in a place close to the slow flowing Mississippi River, during Alma's and John's infancy, among the trees which divide their houses and under the glance of an angel of eternity who from his pedestal symbolizes the absence of time. John is cruel and unstable like the changing seasons (Tennessee Williams's seasons are decorative, musical), and Alma is a sensitive spirit, firm in her affections. They will grow up, one following the studies of his father, Dr. Buchanan, with the certainty of a scientific truth, the other close to her demented mother, convinced of a celestial truth but with a feverish soul which gives to her body recurrent tremors and perpetual instability. Alma's neurosis, for Williams, comes certainly from her mother's confusion complicated by religious humours, and John's crude sexual power comes from his father's clarity. The contrast between flesh and spirit is set in peremptory terms with a presumed distinction of a physiological order. [1960]

Salvatore Quasimodo. *The Poet and the Politician* (Carbondale, Ill., Southern Illinois University Press, 1964), pp. 153–54

In the plays of Tennessee Williams, as in the works of other able and prolific American dramatists, a pattern emerges that continues to appear, with minor variations, over and over again. Williams is remarkably loyal to his favorite archetypal pattern, and, for that reason, it seems to provide an indispensable key to the nature and meaning of his plays. The typical event is the meeting of a healthy, handsome man and a nervous older woman who is losing her looks. I call this couple Adonis and the Gargoyle—Adonis after the classical ideal of male beauty and the Gargoyle after the grotesque by-products of medieval architecture. The contrast between them is alone enough to enforce one major point: it is better to be a carefree man than to be a worried, married woman. A second thought occurs: freedom is better than dependence, but, first, any examination of these plays must begin with a close scrutiny of their protagonists.

Adonis is young and extraordinarily virile and muscular. His magnificent physical endowments make him unusually self-confident. He is cool and tough, so sufficient and so self-contained that he does not say much for himself. This is fortunate because he has no great skill in speech. No eloquence is needed: his physical beauty and his powerful spirit are more eloquent than any words. He can talk in Stanley Kowalski's city slang or Val Xavier's rustic language, but what he conveys is, most of all, coolness. He is sure of himself, basically unruffled on all occasions. Even his rages are strangely controlled; when Stanley Kowalski of *A Streetcar Named Desire* throws crockery on the floor, he makes a deliberate object-lesson out of what he does. Angry as he is, the sullen Brick, of *Cat on a Hot Tin Roof,* is the coolest of all. He has "detachment"; in the sexual act, he is like a gentleman "opening a door for a lady." His wife tells him: "You look so cool, so cool, so enviably cool." Since she is the nervous cat of the title, she has good cause to envy him.

Henry Popkin. TDR. March, 1960, p. 45

On the face of it, *Summer and Smoke* need not have been set in the South at all. The situation that it develops, of the oversensual boy and the over-spiritual girl, could have spun itself out almost anywhere. Williams does not even provide, as he does in the other plays—notably for Amanda in *The Glass Menagerie*—an appropriate accent or rhythm of speech. No Negroes appear, and the only visible class differences are based on morality (patently loose women are outcast), as they might be in any small Midwestern town. The minister is a minister from anywhere, the doctor a doctor from anywhere, the Fourth of July celebration—itself a surprise; most writers might have used a Southern Memorial Day—has much the same flavor, and occurs in about the same year, as the one in the Connecticut of O'Neill's *Ah, Wilderness!*

Nor is Alma's predicament, on the face of it, related closely to the South, as that of Blanche DuBois in *A Streetcar Named Desire* so unmistakably is. One thing that Alma represents, the soul which must find its body, is of universal application—as much so, and in the same way, as the New England village of Thornton Wilder's *Our Town*. That majority of Broadway critics who dismissed Alma as just another neurotic Southern female were wrong. Neither her plight, that of the repressed small-town minister's daughter, nor her story is obviously Southern; and in one sense the play's locale is Mississippi only because that is the region Williams knows.

Yet Alma Winemiller is beyond question Southern. Even today there are Southern women (though only a few) so like her as to make a Southerner's hackles rise in recognition as he reads her lines: the overelaborate vocabulary, the overgreat expectations from others, the living of life as though it were a work of fiction, the insulation from the world. The genteel code was stronger in the South, and lasted longer, and caused perhaps more pain.

> Jacob H. Adler. In Louis D. Rubin, Jr., and Robert
> D. Jacobs, eds., *South: Modern Southern Literature*
> *in Its Cultural Setting* (Garden City, N.Y., Doubleday,
> 1961), pp. 352–53

Tennessee Williams is the protagonist of the romantic quest, and yet it is precisely his inability to carry this quest through to fruition which gives his work its particular defining characteristic.

No one in Williams' universe can triumph because there is nothing to which the individual can appeal. The sins of the earth are its incompletions, Williams tells us; the universe is fragmented and man born into it is born into incompletion. Everything that governs human action emanates from the broken condition which is the root condition of the universe. Man's life is a constant attempt to compensate for this lack of wholeness which he feels in himself. In the work of Tennessee Williams, human action is defined by universal incompletion. Not only can the individual not appeal to forces beyond himself, but because his life is defined in terms of his universe and is thus marked by guilt and atonement, he cannot rely even upon personal responsibility. There is no sense of individual responsibility in this deterministic view of existence, and without this responsibility no one can attain tragic fulfillment. If there is tragedy in Williams' work it is the tragedy of circumstance rather than character: Blanche trapped by her past and her dreams and fighting heroically for survival; Amanda struggling to hold a disintegrating family together; and Big Daddy Pollitt desperately attempting to save his son. With the exception of Big Daddy the characters are not large enough spiritually or morally to triumph even in their destruction. Their universe will not allow for tragic exaltation. Only Big Daddy possesses this possibility, but characteristically Williams is unable to sustain him.

> Benjamin Nelson. *Tennessee Williams: The Man and*
> *His Work* (New York, Ivan Obolensky, 1961), p. 290

Since the function of art should be communication, the artist can easily justify reaching for popularity. However, when he has a vision of pure art, he is haunted by a fear of cheapening the object of his worship. He also finds that his vision of the world makes him look like a lunatic to the more prosaic and practical. As Williams expresses this relationship between insanity and art: "If artists are snobs, it is much in the humble way that lunatics are: not because they wish to be different, and hope and believe that they are, but because they are forever painfully struck in the face with the inescapable fact of their differences which makes them hurt and lonely enough to want to undertake the vocation of artists." Therefore he believes that men are sentenced to solitary confinement within their own skins. In his forays into a cold-eyed, rational world, he feels like Jack in the Beanstalk Country.

The genius of Tennessee Williams is his ability to transform this fearful world into living and universal art. He says that he has spent his entire life trying to master the trick of "rising above the singular to the plural concern." He can't always do it; when out-of-character lyricism and disembodied fantasy take over, he fails; and he also trips frequently over his symbolic regalia. But at his best, he shows a genius for realism, an ear perfectly attuned to conversational speech and an eye keenly perceptive to human idiosyncrasies. He is then unsurpassed in achieving living characters and expressing deep emotional realities.

Nancy M. Tischler. *Tennessee Williams: Rebellious Puritan* (New York, Citadel Press, 1961), pp. 303–4

By now it should be clear that Tennessee Williams' real subject is the painfulness (not the tragedy) of existence, and the fate of human dignity (not of the soul) in the face of suffering. It should also be clear that however neurotic Williams himself may be and however widely neurosis enters into and affects his work, there is little point in looking for the roots of his art, and less in searching out the meaning of any particular play, on one or another categorical Freudian plot of ground; because to Williams *everything* is painful—sexuality, touch, communication, time, the bruteness of fact, the necessity to lie, the loss of innocence. And finally it should be clear that toward his material Williams has alternately been elegist, soothsayer, mythmaker, immolator, exorcist or consoler—none of the incarnations final and no one incarnation carried through to finality. . . .

In the general eagerness to rediscover a humane or optimistic or elegiac or nonapocalyptic Williams, the Williams of *A Streetcar Named Desire* and *The Glass Menagerie,* two things have mostly been ignored. The first is that *The Night of the Iguana* perpetuates nearly all of Williams' failings as a dramatist; the other is that the renewal, the moving up from the depths of *Sweet Bird of Youth* and *Period of Adjustment,* is precisely of a kind to throw light on what those weaknesses are.

Essentially, it is the never-settled dilemma of what kind of playwright to be. The problem divides here into three. The decor: a detailed, exact reproduction of a seedy Mexican hotel near Acapulco, circa 1940; realism at the zenith (flakiness of walls, lushness of vegetation, *real* rain), yet also attempts at ''poetic'' atmosphere, suggestions of symbolic values. The text: an amalgam of hard realism, expert and winning, and sloppy lyricism; the dialogue used conflictingly to advance the plot or create character or establish vision or as abstract self-sufficiency. The structure: two nearly separate plays, a first act of tedious naturalism filled with supererogation and subsidiary characters of strictly commercial lineage (a Nazi family, a lesbian, Mexican boys lounging darkly); and a second wherein much is stripped away and a long central anecdote with its attendant effects rests securely on a base of true feeling and dramatic rightness.

Richard Gilman. *Com*. Jan. 26, 1962, p. 460

''Moralist,'' desperate or not, may seem a perverse appellation for a playwright whose works concern rape, castration, cannibalism and other bizarre activities, but in examining the work of Tennessee Williams it is exactly this point—that he is a moralist, not a psychologist—that should be borne in mind. Williams' powers of characterization are real, but they are not his central gifts: witness *Cat on a Hot Tin Roof*, which contains Big Daddy, one of Williams' most striking characterizations, but which fails none the less because in this play Williams' moral vision becomes blurred, and it is in the clarity and force of that moral vision that his strength as a playwright lies.

Admittedly, Williams' morality is not the morality of most men, but it is a consistent ethic, giving him a point of view from which he can judge the actions of people. Yet to say that Williams rewards those who, by his standards, are virtuous and punishes those who are evil is to oversimplify, for in the world of Williams' plays, good often has a curious affinity with evil. Beneath the skin of the Christlike martyr destroyed by the cruel forces of death and sterility lies the disease, the sin that has made his creator destroy him. The character who is most fiercely condemned may at the same time be the one for whom pardon is most passionately demanded. From the self-lacerating desire simultaneously to praise and to punish stems the violence that disfigures so many of Williams' plays.

To understand this violence in Williams' work we must first look at his gentlest plays, those in which the virtuous are rewarded, for here is most directly revealed the morality by which the guilty are later so terribly condemned. Surprisingly, one of Williams' most significant plays is an indifferent and undramatic one-acter about the death of D. H. Lawrence, only slightly redeemed by the audacious and successful title, *I Rise in Flame, Cried the Phoenix*. The play is significant because it gives us the central fact we must have to understand Williams' work, the nature of his literary parentage. In art, a son must seek out a father who will give him what he needs. Williams needed a rationale for the sexual obsessions that dominate his work, and it was this that Lawrence seemed to give him.

Arthur Ganz. *AS*. Spring, 1962, p. 278

Tennessee Williams is not our best, but our only American playwright since O'Neill. His imagination, magnetized though it is by the outlandish and the outré, is a kind of fever chart of our national ailments. There is, for instance, an image which runs obsessively through Williams' plays—the beautiful young man at bay, the quarry ringed by his pursuers. The mind, the sensibilities, the stomach, all recoil from this image when it is served up with obvious relish in a darkened theater, snakily choreographed by Kazan or distended on wide screen in all the glory of MGM technicolor. Yet that image is frighteningly akin to the one emblazoned not so long ago on all the front pages of the land: Meredith ringed by the Mississippi National Guard on the campus at Ole Miss; and in the background, blurred figures with clenched fists. Who knows what goes on behind those flat faces with steel-rimmed eyeglasses and slits for mouths? One has a sense that Williams dwells closer to that knowledge than other dramatists writing about us, for us, today. Though Williams has not, so far as I know, delivered himself of a single pronouncement on the question of integration, though his signature is never to be found on a petition or a full-page ad in the New York *Times*, he seems to have located the trouble spots more precisely than Arthur Miller, for instance, who deals so conscientiously with "social" questions. Williams is American in his passion for absolutes, in his longing for purity, in his absence of ideas, in the extreme discomfort with which he inhabits his own body and soul, in his apocalyptic vision of sex, which like all apocalyptic visions sacrifices mere accuracy for the sake of intensity. Intensity is the crucial quality of Williams' art, and he is perhaps most an American artist in his reliance upon and mastery of surface techniques for achieving this effect.

Marion Magid. *Cmty*. Jan., 1963, pp. 34–35

The drama of the American playwright Tennessee Williams represents a significant level of achievement in the total movement of Western theatre toward a distinctively contemporary form. There has developed around this playwright a highly articulate dramaturgy. A whole art of writing, staging, acting, and design has resulted which has synthesized elements drawn from European drama with pure native forms. Williams' form retains characteristic aspects of American cinema, dance, painting, and sculpture, as well as features drawn from the tradition of American poetry and fiction. Williams describes his theatric form as "plastic," as a kind of drama in which he has rewoven the complete fabric of the performing arts. Despite its debt to the theories and practices of earlier epochs, the theatre of Williams may be described as the image of a "new sensibility"; that is, its idea of form represents a major adjustment in the concept of dramatic imitation. Like other contemporary playwrights, Williams has transposed into the fabric of his drama a new perception of reality. The image of experience which appears in works such as *A Streetcar Named Desire* is not, however, entirely the creation of the dramatist. On the contrary, it is a symbol that owes its existence, in part, to the cultural history of the late nineteenth and twentieth centuries, especially to those explorations in thought which are given explication in the work of Hegel, Nietzsche, Darwin, Jung, Freud, Bergson, and others. Williams, like these thinkers, seeks to engage modern man in a search for new dimensions of truth, to develop within our time a "will-to-meaning."

> Esther Merle Jackson. *The Broken World of*
> *Tennessee Williams* (Madison, Wisc., University
> of Wisconsin Press, 1965), pp. 156–57

In general, we might reasonably think of Williams as experiencing a tension between fantasies of catastrophe and fantasies of salvation. Fantasies of catastrophe produce dramas of disaster; those of salvation may lead him to the basic structure of melodrama—twice, we note, with a dea ex machina. In *The Milk Train Doesn't Stop Here Anymore,* of course, Williams works in another manner, that of the allegory; here his interest is not in catastrophe or in the success or failure of the savior type, but in the complex attitudes of the affluent society toward the equivocal figure who is both pensioner and alleviator. If the dramatic focus is on the sick or disintegrating character who simply follows his sad downward course, or whose strongest act is to be the beneficiary of someone else's supporting clasp or cool hand on fevered brow, then the direction is not a tragic one. Nevertheless Williams shows himself also able to imagine the relatively well or strong person or that in-between figure who has had to struggle for wellness or strength. The last of these, Hannah Jelkes in *The Night of the Iguana,* is moving toward dramatic centrality. If such a character gains the center of the stage, it will be a move away from dramas of disaster (without drifting into drama of easy triumph). So far, the occasional moves have been toward comedy. They could also be toward tragedy.

> Robert B. Heilman. *SoR*. Oct., 1965, p. 790

The life of Williams' plays, like the life of Shakespeare's, Strindberg's, or even Beckett's plays, is meant, of course, to look like life as we think we know it. But this is no more than to say that plays are not paintings, buildings, or symphonies; that the element in them corresponding most directly to the paint in a painting, the mortar in a building, or the instruments in an orchestra, is something that looks alive, acts as if it is alive, and is, in fact, very much alive: the actor taking the *role* of a human being. The illusion, such as it is, depends finally upon the persuasive union of the actor and the character *invented* by the author. Which means quite plainly that nothing in the end is ever really real on stage. The illusion is real enough, but the medium used—a person—is no more real aesthetically (which is to say animate and alive) than an oboe, a pigment, or a stone. Whatever he may say, if a dramatist had no ambition beyond the literal presentation of reality, he would not then be writing plays. He would be making personal appearances.

Williams reveals, for better and sometimes worse, areas of thought, feeling, and imagination that extend above, below, and frequently beyond the literal details of any man's daily life. He is not always strictly modern in his technique, though with *Camino Real* he tried to build—not always successfully—a romantic abstraction into a sustained drama; and in his latest work, *Slapstick Tragedy* (two short plays), he aims for what he calls "vaudeville, burlesque and slapstick, with a dash of pop art thrown in." But whether he is "current" with any given play, whether he succeeds or fails with technical experiment, he is surely modern in temperament, though never making a sound quite like anyone else's.

Gordon Rogoff. TDR. Summer, 1966, p. 85

Everything Tennessee Williams has written springs from his continuing preoccupations with the extremes of human aspiration and frustration. His plays deal with the war perpetually waged within the hearts of men between death and desire, the public and the private, the real and the ideal, the need for faith and the inevitability of inconstancy, the love of life and the overpowering urge towards self-destruction. But underneath these dualities we discover that each of his tormented characters is trying to touch someone in a meaningful way. Whenever people accuse Williams of being morbidly obsessed with violence and perverted sexuality, I recall a remark he made shortly after *Sweet Bird of Youth* had opened. He said then: "Desire is rooted in a longing for companionship, a release from the loneliness which haunts every individual." Williams has always been primarily interested in dramatizing the anguish of solitude, a solitude which is made increasingly unbearable as the individual feels cut off from all the old securities, as he becomes conscious of the disparity between the outer life of one way of living and the inner life of a different way of dreaming; but it was not until *The Night of the Iguana* that we find him confronting directly the anguished condition of man's spiritual life with the result that in this play the continuing theme of all his work has an added dimension of depth.

All of the well-known Williams trademarks are still present, but they have been recast. The sexuality and violence so characteristic of his earlier plays have been softened and moved to the play's outer edges; and the sense of human fragility has taken on a new and steely strength. The central action of *The Night of the Iguana* takes place in the world of inner disturbance and the dominant force in that world turns out to be the fantastic, that mysterious chemistry in human encounters which, to use theological terms, has the transforming power of grace. Both Shannon and Hannah, the play's central characters, have been brought to the last outpost of human possibility and in their different ways they discover and earn a moment of peace.

Robert W. Corrigan. The Theatre in Search of a Fix
(New York, Delacorte, 1973), pp. 277–78

Critics point out that when Williams was not in sufficient control of his craft, his attempts to broaden his plays' meanings resulted in stereotyped characterizations *(Camino Real, Sweet Bird of Youth, Orpheus Descending, The Rose Tattoo, The Seven Descents of Myrtle)*, heavy-handed symbolism *(Summer and Smoke, Camino Real, Orpheus Descending, The Milk Train Doesn't Stop Here Anymore, Slapstick Tragedy, In the Bar of a Tokyo Hotel, Small Craft Warnings)*, and unsuccessful experimentation *(Slapstick Tragedy, Small Craft Warnings, Out Cry)*. But in his best plays, *Cat on a Hot Tin Roof, Suddenly Last Summer* and *The Night of the Iguana*, as well as *The Glass Menagerie* and *A Streetcar Named Desire*, his unique sense of the theater's enormous flexibility is usually combined with the necessary artistic control.

Another of Williams' dramatic gifts that critics praise is his command of dialogue. While functioning organically to further plot line, Williams' poetic dialogue fulfills esthetic purposes as well. In his finest dramas *(Menagerie, Streetcar, Cat, Suddenly,* and *Iguana)*, the playwright's dialogue simultaneously serves the functions of plot progression, revelation of character, and thematic and symbolic patterns. Although they are functional, the lines of Williams' dialogue sound natural and appropriate to the characters who deliver them—a fact which testifies to the playwright's careful attention to nuances of speech.

Williams' attempts by means of symbolic and nonrealistic dramatic techniques to shock people into recognition and understanding has often been mistakenly criticized by those critics who view his plays as traditional realistic dramas. However, the passing of time has already abated the shock value of Williams' sexual and violent symbolism so that during the past fifteen years several critics and scholars have begun to reassess with greater objectivity and insight such once shocking works as *Cat on a Hot Tin Roof* and *Suddenly Last Summer*.

Williams made another contribution to the American theater by dealing with subjects that had before his time been carefully avoided. Through his handling of sexuality and violence, Williams served as a harbinger for the new generation of playwrights who followed him—writers like William Inge, Edward Albee, Jack Richardson, and LeRoi Jones. The general favorable critical and popular reception of their bold treatment of sex and their hard-hitting dialogue is doubtless to some degree the result of Williams' having broken ground for them in these areas.

Critics agree that Williams' creation of a new poetic drama in the United States is the foundation upon which his permanent literary reputation is most likely to rest. Nevertheless, since Williams is still writing plays and since critics continue to revaluate his dramatic works, his position in American theater history will doubtlessly be modified with time. At present, the increasing respect accorded to *Cat on a Hot Tin Roof, The Night of the Iguana,* and *Suddenly Last Summer* during the past fifteen years, along with the fact that *The Glass Menagerie* and *A Streetcar Named Desire* have not diminished in stature during the twenty-five years since they were first produced, indicates that Williams, his failures notwithstanding, has already established himself not only as a crucial figure in the history of the American theater but also as a playwright of the first rank.

S. Alan Chesler. In Jac Tharpe, ed., *Tennessee Williams: A Tribute* (Jackson, Miss., University Press of Mississippi, 1977), pp. 879–80

[In *The Red Devil Battery Sign*] . . . certain themes clearly emerge, and with real, if uneven, power. These themes will be familiar to readers of Williams' plays of the 1940s and 1950s who remember those characters so often victimized by both natural and human malevolence. Common calamity, or impersonal victimization by disease, for example, or the natural cannibalism of nature are intimidating enough in themselves in Williams' world, but there is a special viciousness in human actions intentionally cruel, mendacious, and vengeful. Often the events of the calamitous natural world become the large symbols for the depravities of the human heart. Whether victims of irrational nature or man, Williams' sympathetic characters respond with courage and dignity, and are defeated with grace. To a great extent, the two leading characters in *Red Devil* are cast from this old Williams mold. Presented on the whole realistically, the heroine, called the "Woman Downtown," reminds one, in her distraught, pressed condition of the famous Blanche DuBois of *A Streetcar Named Desire;* her lover, the Mexican band leader called King, dying of a brain tumor as a result of a car accident, reminds one of other sympathetic male characters, such as Kilroy in *Camino Real,* brought down from heights of personal vigor. . . .

Williams offers us in *Red Devil* a grim parable of the contemporary world divided into two sets of menacing images: the slick and powerful conspiracies, with the red devil sign as cosmic symbol of hex and hell, and the alternate savagery of fugitive and warring street gangs. King, a temporary savior, dies, as does the Woman's guardian; the brutalized Woman and a ravaging Wolf stand triumphant over slag heaps. Between these alternatives there is no cervice of escape for the individual. In earlier plays, and even as late as *Kingdom of Earth,* psychologically uncomplicated sex offers some defense against, or recompense for, the natural terrors of the world, as well as a basis for love; in *Red Devil* sex is debased and love doomed. Violence and revolution are the final response to a civilization beyond redemption. Always given to a rather paranoiac and pessimistic view of the world, Williams in this play gives full expression to his feelings of oppression, alienation and inevitable defeat, even though King maintains a certain dignity until his death. Without him, the "Woman Downtown" becomes the Woman Underground in a darkening, cataclysmic landscape, but with the seed of revolution quickened within her.

> Sy M. Kahn. In Stephen S. Stanton, ed.,
> *Tennessee Williams: A Collection of*
> *Critical Essays* (Englewood Cliffs, N.J.,
> Prentice-Hall, 1977), pp. 175–78

The last time I reviewed a Tennessee Williams play (it was an early incarnation of the creature now called *Out Cry*), I said that I wished one could easily dismiss Tennessee Williams. This provoked a little outcry of its own, from Williamsites who thought I *was* dismissing the Great Man before he was gone, and so forth. Now I will probably infuriate the Tennesseeans more by saying I wish I *had* written Williams off when they thought I did, since I then would not have had to sit through *Vieux Carré.*

Not all of late Williams is dreadful, and not all the dreadfulness of *Vieux Carré* is Williams's fault. Most of it, in fact, is Arthur Allan Seidelman's clumsy directing and vices attendant thereon. But there is very little in the output of Williams's last decade or so that one would want to see onstage again. The Ionescan brashness of *The Gnädiges Fräulein* makes it revivable, and I always felt the eerie, eye-dropper use of language in *In the Bar of a Tokyo Hotel,* coupled with the intensity of its attempt to make a serious statement about art, entitled it to a second hearing. Then there are some playably wistful and comic monologues in *Kingdom of Earth* and *Small Craft Warnings.* But that is really about it.

The plain fact is that Williams is a writer in whose work an enormous emotive power and magical gift for juggling poetry out of Southern gutter speech are the depths of a decidedly narrow and strictly circumscribed field. You can see his limitations dramatized perfectly in the atmosphere- and feeling-less flatness of Seidelman's staging for the opening scene: The characters march on, one two three four, like automata on a Swiss clock, each bearing the scars of use in earlier Williams plays: the bossy padrona of a rooming house; the sensitive young writer of no fortune and dubious sexual identity; the old queen in the kimono—a painter this time—who drinks too much and talks with grandiloquent sadness about Art and Loneliness; the neurasthenic young woman—also an artist this time—busily fighting off her sexual drive; the brainless, beautiful young stud to whose cock she is a loving prisoner; and the daffy spinsters and the crass, gaping tourist women. The gang's all there.

Michael Feingold. *VV*. May 30, 1977, p. 87

BRITISH AND IRISH DRAMATISTS

RITA STEIN, EDITOR

BEHAN, BRENDAN (1923–1964)

"Bloddy sparklin' dialogue," said a pensive Irishman during the first inter-val of *The Quare Fellow*—and sparkle, by any standards, it amazingly did. The English hoard words like misers; the Irish spend them like sailors; and in Brendan Behan's tremendous new play language is out on a spree, ribald, dauntless, and spoiling for a fight. In itself, of course, this is scarcely amaz-ing. It is Ireland's sacred duty to send over, every few years, a playwright to save the English theatre from inarticulate glumness. And Irish dialogue almost invariably sparkles. . . .

In adversity the Irish always sparkle. "If this is how Her Majesty treats her prisoners," said one of them, handcuffed in the rain *en route* for gaol, "she doesn't deserve to have any." With this remark of Oscar Wilde's Mr. Behan, who has spent eight years of his life in prison for sundry acts of I.R.A. mischief, entirely agrees; and his protest is lodged in the same spirit of laconic detachment. The Irish are often sentimental about human beings. So far from trying to gain sympathy for the condemned man, an axe-mur-derer known as "the quare fellow," Mr. Behan keeps him off-stage throughout the action. All he shows us is the effect on the prison population of the knowledge that one of their number is about to be ritually strangled.

There are no tears in the story, no complaints, no visible agonies; nor is there even suspense, since we know from the outset that there will be no reprieve. Mr. Behan's only weapon is a gay, fatalistic gallows-humour, and he wields it with the mastery of Ned Kelly, the Australian bandit, whose last words, as the noose encircled his neck, were: "Such is life." Mr. Be-han's convicts behave with hair-raising jocularity, exchanging obscene in-sults even while they are digging the murderer's grave. An old lag feigns a bad leg in order to steal a swig of methylated spirits; a newcomer anxious to raise bail is blithely advised to "get a bucket and bail yourself out."

Even the hangman is presented serio-comically as a bowler-hatted publican with a marked addition to the wares he sells. The tension is intolerable, but it is we who feel it, not the people in the play. We are moved precisely in the degree that they are not. With superb dramatic tact, the tragedy is concealed beneath layer after layer of rough comedy. [May 27, 1956]

Kenneth Tynan. *Curtains* (New York,
Atheneum, 1961), pp. 136–37

The Hostage is constantly swivelling into the reflexive, knowing itself, mocking itself, and occasionally washing its hands of itself. It is less coherent and less cohesive than *The Quare Fellow,* but the plea is clear. No follow-my-leader games. Innocence is no excuse. Apart from its shape, which keeps on throwing out a thrashing new limb in spite of Joan Littlewood's strong-willed production, *The Hostage* is Dublin's *Dreigroschenoper*. It is abrasive, obstreperous, funny, and serious. Instead of Kurt Weill there is a fiddler who plays any tunes he can lay his hands on—a hymn, *Auld Lang Syne*—as a setting for the impudent lyrics. . . .

Language hasn't had an outing like this since *The Quare Fellow*. The English habitually write as though they were alone and cold at ten in the morning; the Irish write in a state of flushed gregariousness at an eternal opening time. "There are two kinds of good men," says the caretaker. . . . "There's the earnest religious kind and there's the laughing boys." *The Hostage* is a huge belly-laugh that secretes enough morality for a satire. It puts politics where they belong: in the midst of life, where they seldom appear in English theatre. [Nov., 1958]

Penelope Gilliatt. In Charles Marowitz, Tom
Milne, and Owen Hale, eds., *The Encore
Reader* (London, Methuen, 1965), pp. 94–95

We come out of jail in *The Hostage*—but only just so, since the central character, the young English soldier held in a Dublin house by the IRA, is again a prisoner. Despite its fateful ending, this is the gayest of Brenden Behan's works and the most overtly political. The Irish resentments of England, and their human sympathies for an Englishman, are beautifully conveyed by a houseful of comicals all sharply individual, not stereotypes. And for Behan, a man who has sacrificed so much for his political ideas, and who holds them so absolutely, it is brave not to hesitate to mock the sterile elements in Irish nationalism that he finds repellent. I think the fact is Behan is much more than an Irish nationalist merely—though he certainly is that: he is a revolutionary humanist, and his heroes belong to one nation of the socially oppressed in every country. . . .

There remain two key elements in Behan's writing I must refer to, since I am sure of their importance, though with diffidence because of ignorance. The first is that he is an accomplished writer in Gaelic; and as I believe any writer who possesses two mother tongues is able to effect happy transmutations from the one speech to the other, this gift may help to account for the rich flexibility of his English prose. (Some of the African writers—for instance Chinua Achebe—can thus write impeccable English which is clearly enriched by the familiar possession of another tongue. And conversely, the "picturesqueness" that afflicts Synge's Anglicized Gaelic may be due to his not knowing the native language.) The other element is the saturation of Behan's thought and speech by the spiritual inheritance of the Roman Catholic Church into which he was baptized. It is hard to tell from Behan's writings—which praise and castigate the Church with equal vehemence—how far he is what is known as a "believer." But that he has a religious instinct in the profoundest sense there can be no doubt; nor that his familiarity with Roman Catholic history, ritual and doctrine have contributed to his style and artistic temperament.

In the fickle "literary world" it is customary to deplore that Brendan Behan has not written more than he has. I shall not join in this impertinence if only because his life has been harder than most of his critics can imagine and, even more, because of the magnificence of what he has in fact achieved. All I feel I have a right to say is that I esteem his talent so highly, and admire so much what it has produced, that I hope with all my heart that we shall hear from him again.

Colin MacInnes. *London*. Aug., 1962, p. 61.

[Behan] was an astonishing man of the theater. Whatever the willful excesses or woolly inspirations that overtook him, Mr. Behan could make the actors on stage blur into the folk out front with an intimacy and a dour communion that was infectious. The ribald evening was blatantly, boastfully, unself-consciously alive.

Why? The energy that stirred so mysteriously at the center of the stage [in a performance of *The Hostage*], tumbling over all the usual conventions of the theater as though they were so many unimportant ninepins, came, I think, from two definable sources. One of them was the plain certainty that Mr. Behan, for all his celebrated tosspot habits, does possess the single-minded, self-generating, intuitive power of the natural-born artist. He may have neither discipline nor taste; but he has a gift that speaks, in however irresponsible and unmodulated a voice, for itself.

Nothing here should have been cohesive, and everything was. Simply, it seems never to have entered the author's head that his lapses of invention or his headlong determination to make hash of the proprieties should in any way compromise the truly lyrical or observant or just plain funny things that represented him at his individualistic best. And, somehow, they did not get in the way of our hearing "He couldn't knock the skin off a rice pudding" or of our exploding into laughter as a Negro boxer marched into a melee carrying an enormous placard, "Keep Ireland black!" The borrowed, the blue, and the Behan seemed all the same man: a gregarious and all-devouring personality shouting its own name from the Dublin chimney pots. Everything on the menu was malicious.

Walter Kerr. *The Theater in Spite of Itself* (New York, Simon and Schuster, 1963), pp. 110–11

The writer in Behan was continually in danger of being shouted down by the talker, the playwright upstaged by the vaudevillian, the artist elbowed aside by the anecdotist. But at his best—in *Borstal Boy, The Quare Fellow* and *The Hostage*—he had his clowns and leprechauns, imps and improvisations, so under control that when they did appear, as they constantly threatened to do, it was at a writer's command. The trick, as Behan said, was that of the music hall, where, if things got dull, you livened them up with a song and a dance "and while the audience were laughing their heads off you could be up to any bloody thing behind their backs."

It was, he said, what you were up to then that made your stuff great. Behan was up to a number of things.

Not surprisingly, the best things he did are all three concerned in one way or another with men in prison. Or, put more portentously, man the criminal. *The Quare Fellow* is a savagely hilarious commentary on the idiocy, the moral hypocrisy of capital punishment in a society which prides itself, as in Ireland and elsewhere, on its moral refinement. But the tone of this commentary never betrays the underlying seriousness.

This is through a play which, though it has no discernible plot, creates a suspense, at once relentless and uproarious, from the emotional interplay—jocular, obscene, derisive or sardonic—among prisoners and their wardens, who, it is clear, are no less prisoners than the men they keep watch over.

At the very end of the play, Behan for all his cleverness at concealment almost gives the game away. "The Quare Fellow" (who never appears on stage) has been hanged, his grave dug, and the prisoners who dug it are set to quarrel over the last mortal possessions of the dead man—final letters to his family "worth money to the Sunday papers"—which are supposed to be flung into the grave after him. Instead, they divided the spoils among themselves, tossing the last letter up in a play of chance. The identity of the Quare Fellow—and his relation to prisoners, wardens, and audience—is intimated, but no more insistently than this.

And so the game is not quite given away, the tragic mask is not displayed, and the dramatic surfaces of the play are preserved intact and unspoiled. The tragedy remains as invisible as the Quare Fellow himself, in an almost pure state, so to speak, so perfectly is it encapsulated in the coarse rinds of comedy.

Kevin Sullivan. In Sean McCann, ed.,
The World of Brendan Behan (New York,
Twayne, 1966), pp. 93–94

Behan creates a unique world in *The Hostage,* better in ways than the prison world of *The Quare Fellow*. Some critics have pointed out that certain characters and incidents are unrealistic, but I think that they are deliberately so and that the play has about the same connection with reality as do O'Casey's later satires, fantasies, and pastorals. It comments on reality by heightening it and seeing it through a unique, sometimes bleary, often humorous, and finally sad imagination. No matter how much help he had in refashioning the play, this point of view is indisputably Behan's own.

Although this is both an angrier and a happier play than *The Quare Fellow,* its characters are not unfeeling Jonsonian monsters. They detest both the inhumanity of established society and that of the rebel army. And, amazingly enough, Behan makes us believe, at least momentarily, in their view. He has worked his trick again and worked it more startlingly than in *The Quare Fellow,* for he hurls his accusation of inhumanity pointblank at his audience. That moment at the end of *The Hostage* is one of Behan's triumphs and a great moment of the modern theatre.

Robert Hogan. *After the Irish Renaissance* (Minneapolis,
University of Minnesota Press, 1967), p. 205

Behan can not be ranked among the great writers, for he did not produce a sufficient volume of work, and even what he did produce is not without flaw. . . . Nevertheless, Behan was much more than a gifted leprechaun. He was a conscious artist, and the charge that his work is slapdash is not altogether justified. He took the same liberties with traditional notions of language, plot construction, and character development as have many other contemporary writers. He realized, with such writers as Beckett, Ionesco, Osborne, and Pinter, that nineteenth-century standards would not serve twentieth-century artists. Unfortunately, a good many critics who admire the unorthodox structure of the plays of Beckett or those of Pinter decry the same structure in Behan's plays. . . .

Behan possessed a marvelous comic talent. That he wasted a good deal of it cannot diminish his solid achievements. He wrote two of the best plays of the contemporary theater, and one of the best autobiographies of this century. He wrote with an exuberance and a humanity which will remain unexcelled. To a confused and self-destructive world, Behan gave a simple and cogent reminder: human existence, though painful, is worthwhile. Or, as Behan stated it in *The Quare Fellow,* life is "a bloody sight better than death any day of the week."

Ted E. Boyle. *Brendan Behan* (New York, Twayne, 1969), p. 134

Brendan Behan's *The Hostage* is a popular play just now—popular with producing companies and audiences alike. Its mode and energy are especially appealing to those interested in the new, freer, not-so-literary theatre of the moment. The evolution of the play from the original Gaelic conception, to the English version for Dublin's Abbey, to its fuller development under the direction of Joan Littlewood at her London theatre at Stratford-East is widely known. That the play grew to its present shape out of improvisations by Littlewood's actors, that it still contains open-ended dramatic structures, and has no definitive text demanding respect are features that invite directors to mount original, even eccentric productions for the immediate purposes of particular theatres and audiences. In fact, it is probably impossible to produce *The Hostage* without expanding the scenario to define and clarify certain characters and actions that the text leaves obscure. But this obscurity is only apparent; while Behan leaves the surface data of his dramatic ideas open to invention and improvisation, he is careful enough with his essential drama.

In order to see this drama clearly, we must look past the language, an uncertain element here, and, as though looking through the wrong end of a telescope, watch the action in broadest outline, the diverting detail of its "concatenated events" no longer visible. Paradoxically, the characters, miniaturized by the inverted optics, take on a larger meaning: they now suggest their archetypes and put us on the proper track toward understanding the structure that they represent. *The Hostage* invites us to look for a rhythm and shape built into the spectacle's scenario and residing on the far side of literature where a poetry unique to the theatre lies deeper than the words. This poetry arises from the kind of discoveries that Jerzy Grotowski's actors make as action bombards action, actor confronts character and himself to reveal new elements of myth and emotion in dramatic concert. Ludwik Flaszen writing on Grotowski says, "Theatre starts where the word is not sufficient." Behan's theatre springs from such beginnings, and in *The Hostage* the playwright develops a heroic rhythm not very different from the *tragic rhythm* that Francis Fergusson describes in his *The Idea of a Theater* as the essential of tragic action.

Gordon M. Wickstrom. *ETJ.* Dec., 1970, p. 406

Although there is a great deal said about hanging and although the play is strongly opposed to legalized execution, *The Quare Fellow* is not merely a diatribe against capital punishment. It is a study of human nature which irreverently but compassionately confronts man with a reflection of himself, his society, and the facile distinctions he makes about his own behavior and that of his fellow creatures. Not only are the penal system and government-sanctioned executions subjected to close scrutiny, but so are public attitudes toward such matters as sex, politics, and religion.

Although it deals with a number of serious themes, *The Quare Fellow* is filled with humor, much of it hilarious. However, within almost every humorous line and scene there is a bite. Spontaneously one laughs at the deftly delivered witticisms, only to sense, in the midst of laughing, the presence of pain. This occurs time after time, and the viewer, while enjoying the gaiety of the proceedings, sees his prejudices, pretensions, and preconceptions, and those of his society, exposed for what they are. Viewing the play is a bittersweet experience out of which emerges an energetic affirmation of life.

Raymond J. Porter. Brendan Behan (New York, Columbia
University Press, 1973), p. 21

Richard's Cork Leg had been the turning-point. As in the case of *the catacombs*, it is unfair to treat it as a finished work. A happier Behan would have worked on it, gradually discovering his theme and structure. At the time, he felt otherwise. For all his talk about music hall and the problems of the contemporary playwright, he knew little of dramatic theory and cared less, preferring to leave such speculations to the critics. *The Hostage* had succeeded despite the general feeling that "its line of action is not vital and its scenes, with a few obvious exceptions, are almost interchangeable"; why should he bother with plot or structure? It was the atmosphere and energy of the play which had won people over; surely the same spirit in a different form would conquer them again? He had done it all before, almost casually; how could he possibly fail now if he put his mind to it? Choose a setting which is visually striking, bring on a few colourful characters, introduce sex, religion and politics, and baste well with song-and-dance, stand-up jokes, slapstick business and some references to himself.

Richard's Cork Leg was obviously written to such a formula. As a piece of pure entertainment its major fault is that it is no longer new. Various lumps of raw material were thrown into the cauldron and spoiled. The story of Honor Bright, a prostitute with whose ugly murder a police officer and a doctor were charged and whose grave is a place of annual pilgrimage for the united prostitutes of disunited Ireland, had unlimited potential in the hands of the man who had written *The Quare Fellow*. The principal male character, The Leper Cronin, is a witty critic of left, right and centre, cheerful despite his disenchantment with all that organised society had to offer, a selfish philanthropist. It is tantalising to wonder what the author of *Borstal Boy* would have made of him if Cronin were given *his* novel or *his* play.

But the ore of the draft, which would have been refined in the process of rewriting, is wasted. The sparkle of the two whores is dulled by some appallingly decrepit jokes and the Honor Bright motif is allowed to fizzle out. Cronin competes for our attention with a black aristocrat who plans to transform the Irish graveyard into another Forest Lawn, and with a shortsighted dramatist who neglects him time after time in search of cheap laughs. The title of the play is apt even though it is totally irrelevant to the action. The story goes that Joyce, having had a play rejected as too gloomy, remarked that he might have fared better had he given Richard, one of the characters, a cork leg. Unlike Joyce, Behan was willing to "jolly things up" to suit the public.

Colbert Kearney. The Writings of Brendan Behan
(New York, St. Martin's Press, 1977), pp. 140–41

BOND, EDWARD (1934–   )

What the majority has refused to see in this case (the majority of critics, that is—the second-night audience, with whom weeklies were invited, listened intently and applauded vehemently) is that *Saved* is a play about poverty in Britain now. True, it's difficult for most newspapers to recognize such poverty. Haven't they established that the poor are no longer with us, except for the "new poor," ground by taxes to the point where they must skimp to educate their children privately, deprived now even of their expense-account lunches? . . . Mr. Bond is out to rub noses in the fact that the real new poor are the old poor plus television, sinking deeper in a form of poverty we do not yet recognize—poverty of culture. . . .

It is also, of course, the notorious scene in which five tittering South London youths torment Pam's baby to death in its pram. This runs slightly over five minutes out of some 160: it is not the reason for the play; the play is the reason for the scene. "Sooner murder an infant in its cradle," the programme quotes Blake, "than nurse unacted desires." The rest of *Saved* is about all the frustrations which explode in that act of savagery, the slow strangling of lives for which it is an inarticulate revenge. They are strangled literally in a lack of concepts, a lack of words: these people communicate only in blunt, concrete monosyllables. . . .

Ronald Bryden. NS. Nov. 12, 1965, p. 759

In his play of marvellously observed dialogue and first-rate dramatic form [*Saved*], Edward Bond places his act of violence in the first half, as is done in *Macbeth, Julius Caesar,* etc. Unfortunately the extreme horror of this scene, though no more lurid than many an accustomed fact to which English railway toilets can give testimony, has run away with most dramatic criticism and blinded it to the rare qualities shown in the rest of the play, which from time to time achieves astonishing heights of dramatic prowess and containing a last scene of which Chekhov himself would have purred his approval, a scene lasting how many minutes (time stood still for me) with its one singular utterance of three words? . . .

The first time a school-master ordered me to take my trousers down I knew it was not from any doubt that he could punish me efficiently enough with them up. The theatre is concerned, whether in the deepest tragedy or the lightest comedy, with the teaching of the human heart the knowledge of itself, and sometimes, when it is necessary—and we are obviously going through such a time with the study, understanding and recognition of that most dreaded and dangerous eccentricity in the human design, the tripartite conspiracy between the sexual, the excretory and the cruel.

As I have said, *Saved* is not for children but it is for grown-ups, and the grown-ups of this country should have the courage to look at it; and if we do not find precisely the mirror held up to nature in which we can see ourselves, then at least we can experience the sacramental catharsis of a very chastening look at the sort of ground we have prepared for the next lot.

Laurence Olivier. *Obs.* Nov. 21, 1965, p. 11

[Bond], I take it, is not a collectively-minded Left-Winger . . . but chiefly an anarchistic individualist in a state of almost complete despair about the modern world in all its aspects: politics, education, industrialism, commercial entertainment, etc. . . . In view of this, it is a little surprising that Mr. Bond should have chosen to give aesthetic expression to his concern by ''reworking'' Shakespeare's *Lear*. . . . The Shakespearian play deals with the eternal evil of human nature in an elemental, relatively primitive society, not corrupted at all by education, industrialism, or commercial entertainment. I heard Mr. Bond being condescending about Shakespeare on television, because, he said, Shakespeare is reconciled to things in the end. This is like Shaw maintaining that Shakespeare ''onions the handkerchief.'' . . . Mr. Bond, I suspect, objects to [Shakespeare] because behind the anarchistic individualist is a half-revolutionary who would like to think that evil is produced by society and could be eliminated from the world by rearrangement. The difference between Shaw and Mr. Bond is that Shaw recoils from evil and will not contemplate it honestly (this is one of the factors that limit him, in spite of his exhilarating intelligence), whereas Mr. Bond is fascinated with evil in some of its forms, and indeed seems to me to have a strong sadistic streak. . . .

If the incidental sadism is removed, Mr. Bond's *Lear* is just a simplistic fable, set in some indefinite modern period. . . . The message is that successive regimes behave mistakenly in similar ways in order to preserve their authority, and that improvement can only come through a change of heart. We have heard this a thousand times in connection with the replacement of dynastic or class autocracies by totalitarian regimes, but the fable is too abstract to have much relevance to our problems in the confused and relatively tolerant world of the Western democracies. We are not bothered much at the moment by Lears, Bodices and Cordelias, at least in internal policies, but rather by the complexities of industrial society. The horror that Mr. Bond presents us with—mangling, gouging out of eyes, goring of a ghost by pigs, etc.—is not symbolically representative of the evils of our society; it is a projection of individual cruelty, of which Mr. Bond is genuinely conscious. . . . Mr. Bond has a black vision of a humanity of ferocious beasts, far less redeemable than the characters in Shakespeare's *Lear*, and scarcely leavened at all by the presence of one or two decent people.

John Weightman. *Enc*. Dec., 1971, pp. 30–31

Tenderness and weakness are things that the inhabitants of the *Saved* desert have been conditioned to abhor. Status is gained through sexual and physical prowess. Even though he has been exonerated by the coroner, Pete pretends he deliberately ran down a child in a motor accident. It is the very weakness of the baby that triggers off the worst violence—"Look at its little legs goin'."—"Couldn't yer break them little fingers easy though?"—together with its incontinence and its refusal in its aspirin-drugged state to respond to their menaces as they think it should. (Fontanelle shows remarkably similar motives in her mutilation of Warrington in *Lear*—"O Christ, why did I cut his tongue out? I want to hear him scream!" and "Look at his hands! Look at them going! . . . Smash his hands!") It is Fred who throws the first stone in an attempt to negate his suspected parenthood.

The difficulty with *Saved* is too much realism, too well done. Audiences were affronted not only by the impact of the murder scene, but by the total lack of any overt condemnation. Edward Bond has questionably asserted that "Compared to the 'strategic' bombing of German towns it is a negligible atrocity" (it is questionable, surely, whether *any* atrocity can be negligible), and has rightly followed this with "compared to the cultural and emotional deprivation of most of our children its consequences are negligible." This is the point of the play, but when it goes on to sketch in, somewhat vaguely, the processes of law and punishment, implying that only one of the youths is charged and that he is released after what seems to be a pretty short sentence, it may seem to condone a "negligible" atrocity. To follow this argument would lead to irrelevant discussion about the value of prison sentences and so on, whereas the purpose of the play is to lay the corpse of the child on the doorstep of society. That this is where it belongs is confirmed by the vigour with which society tried to sweep it (and the play with it) off its doorstep into the gutter. It is regrettable that the uncertain treatment of realism in the play allowed its critics an excuse for doing so.

Arthur Arnold. TheatreQ. Jan.–March, 1972, p. 17

Bond has wanted to change society through his plays, for he is convinced that society today is in no way capable of driving out the animal in man; rather, it cultivates it. He welcomes every effect, however shocking, that will make man come to his senses. In *Early Morning* the regression to primitive life is even more marked [than in *Saved*]. The monster man takes the greatest pleasure in feeding on his own kind. His limbs continue to grow without stopping so that murder and death can go on for all eternity—a horrifying picture. *Narrow Road to the Deep North,* called a comedy by Bond, takes place in an imaginary Japan of the past. As in his previous plays, the main character is caught in a trap; he does not struggle to escape and instead commits suicide. Bond has used almost exclusively the lowest possible form of language in his dialogue. The directness and obscenity of this idiom is part of the shock effect that is his goal. . . .

Bond considers existing society primitive, dangerous, and corrupt. He calls himself an anarchist, because government is anticreative and only oriented toward law and order, and he, as artist, is searching for personal justice. The time has come to stop telling people that the few shall lead the many. Bond considers man's gravest danger the fact that he lives in a social order for which he is not biologically equipped. The human organism, for instance, is not suited for work in factories. This has led to the development of an aggressive society, in which things like hydrogen bombs exist. This situation is aggravated by the educational system. Bond equates schools with prisons: both serve, according to Bond, to create slaves, or at least people who have so adapted themselves to the prevailing forms of society that they will conform to it. He does not object to knowledge itself, only to the force-feeding of knowledge. By nature man is not violent; on the contrary, love is the natural condition in which man is born—the ability to love and be loved. Bond feels that this ability is being beaten out of man so that he can conform more willingly.

Horst W. Drescher. In Ivar Ivask and
Gero van Wilpert, eds., World Literature since 1945
(New York, Frederick Ungar, 1973), pp. 117–18

Edward Bond's latest play was called *Bingo: Scenes of Money and Death;* and no one would have guessed from the title or the subtitle that its hero was William Shakespeare. This is entirely appropriate because in an important sense it is not about Shakespeare at all. When it opened at the Royal Court just over a year ago most of its critics discussed it by comparing it with Bond's earlier play *Lear.* . . . There are, of course, points of similar-

ity between *Bingo* and *Lear,* of which more in a moment. But essentially
the later play is the continuation of an argument Bond had begun earlier
still, in *Narrow Road to the Deep North,* his bitter parable about the seventeenth-century Japanese poet Basho. In the play, you will recollect, Basho
helped to bring terrible suffering to his country by ignoring individual suffering as he travelled north in search of personal enlightenment.

The subject of *Bingo* is the same: the utter inadequacy, indeed the
harmfulness, of the artist as a social animal. Bond's point is that writing is
not enough: the artist is a man among men and must be a functioning part
of the moral structure of society. This of course is refreshingly different
from the hazy Romantic belief in what amounted to the helplessness and
therefore the amorality of art—a view which lingers happily about to this
day. . . .

Bingo . . . is best in its first two scenes where Shakespeare hardly
speaks: a picture of mute moral degradation. His state, as I have said, is not
properly accounted for; but in the theatre it makes a powerful dramatic impact. The play fails in the end not only because of the improbability of
Shakespeare's death; not only because Bond never explains, cannot explain,
why Shakespeare had got into a state of moral checkmate in the first place;
but also because of the formal, over-written language of his disintegration
in the snow. The phrases are ponderous, turgid and hollow: they present the
idea but not the suffering of human failure. This climactic scene carries
intellectual force but no real feeling and conviction whatever. Bond the puritan moralist executes Shakespeare; Bond the poet, who wrote *The Sea* and
the last scene of *Saved,* seems to co-operate without conviction. It is as if,
in killing the other poet, he were killing a part of himself.

John Peter. Drama. Autumn, 1975, pp. 28, 31–32

If there is to be a criticism to be made of *Bingo,* it should not be of Bond's
use of history or of his use of the Welcombe enclosure affair; he has been
scrupulous and, given the need for compression, exact. The most common
recent criticism of him has been that his apocalyptic messages outstrip his
dramatic performances, but I am not particularly conscious of that, either.
It is not the intellectual substance of *Bingo* that is worrying, but the staging
of people whose lives are symbolic beyond the realities of their world.
Bingo offers us something very unusual in Bond: a very narrow range of
human experience. Combe is a simpler and less interesting figure than
Basho, or Shogo [in *Narrow Road to the Deep North*], or Cordelia and the
Carpenter in *Lear*—characters whose toughness and practical politics were
offered as representative of the kind of society to which we are accustomed.
Combe is almost wholly functional. He isn't cardboard, because his language is vivid and convincing, but his function seems more important than
his dramatic presence. The same is true of the Young Woman; it is signifi-

cant that four of the play's central characters are called Old Man, Old Woman, Son, and Young Woman. Their roles and functions are most of the time more important than their individuality; and though it is doubtless part of Bond's point that only the gentry in this society have much individuality, that is a dramatist's point, not a dramatic reality. Even the briefly named and occasional characters of *The Pope's Wedding,* like Bill, Ron, Len, Lorry, and Joe, are more themselves than these central characters. It is as if Bond found himself having to write a modern morality play. His subtitle suggests that he himself was conscious of that: "Scenes of Money and Death." It sounds a little like [Chaucer's] *Pardoner's Tale,* told by someone other than the Pardoner. Shakespeare himself is the character most affected by this; we are, anyway, less prepared to grant him individuality since history has refused to give it to him; and he isn't here the creator of Falstaff or Hamlet, but the man who wrote the scenes on the heath in *King Lear*— almost exclusively those—because Bond is worried by the contradiction between *that* and his role as a secure member of the gentry.

John Worthen. ETJ. Dec., 1975, p. 477

The Sea, a comedy performed in a relatively realistic setting—an English coastal village about the year 1907—is the first Bond play with a recognizable, if not immediate, locale since *Saved.* Although none of his plays lack moments of incisive satire, *The Sea* also maintains a comic tone over a longer period than any previous work. Bond's two shorter plays, *Black Mass* and *Passion,* are also comedies, but they were first seen in the context of two highly serious events—the Commemoration of the Tenth Anniversary of the Sharpesville Massacre and the Committee for Nuclear Disarmament Festival of Life, respectively. Therefore, the audience presumed serious intent. Moreover, both plays were brief and neither imposed a realistic plot between idea and audience. *The Sea,* on the other hand, stands alone. It is Bond's most conventionally plotted play and the first to have a conventionally happy ending.

The Sea represents a refinement in Bond's structural style. Bond has always insisted, and his plays have amply proved, that his writing is not loosely episodic but rather is very tightly constructed along intellectual lines. The problem has been throughout, especially in *Early Morning,* that if one failed to grasp Bond's idea, he was left with a number of marvelous scenes that didn't add up to a play. *The Sea,* on the other hand, poses no such problem. While the full richness of the play can in no way be tapped by following only the "boy-meets-girl" plot, it does provide a highly visible lifeline in relation to which the significance of other scenes and characters can be more readily understood.

Bond has also developed in his control of mood. One of his strengths has always been the evocation of atmosphere and many of his best effects have been the result of contrasting the tones of consecutive scenes—effects that have sometimes been dissipated by the change of scene itself. For example, *Narrow Road to the Deep North*, Bond's shortest "full-length" play, contains eleven scenes. *Early Morning* contains twenty-one. *The Sea*, however, manages with only eight scenes because Bond is able to sharply change moods within the scene.

Richard Scharine. *The Plays of Edward Bond*
(Lewisburg, Pa., Bucknell University Press,
1976), pp. 251–52

The relatively few published studies of Edward Bond show that he is a skillful and self-conscious artist well aware of his own aims, ideas, and methods, and suggest that many aspects of his work remain to be explored. One of these, central both to his ideas and his dramatic method, is his use of the child and the old man as recurring figures. Through their many shifting roles in Bond's five major plays, the child and the old man are keys to his depiction of a society after the fall, but one for which there is still an almost irresponsible hope. Bond has described the stoning of the baby in the pram in *Saved* as a "dramatic metaphor" for the way in which we "batter" children with "the weight of aggression in our society." The destruction and corruption of the young is a major theme in Bond's work. The old man may be a victim like the child, the oppressor who helps to victimize the child, or both; the youth may become figuratively identified with the old man. The children in Bond's plays almost always lose their lives or are psychologically injured; those children who become old men usually contribute to the injustice of a fallen society, but sometimes they point the way toward escape or salvation.

Bond probably has formulated a social philosophy more systematically than any dramatist since Shaw. In his prefaces and plays he interprets the formation of our present unjust and corrupted society in scientific, chiefly biological, terms. Bond sometimes seems to make contradictory or insufficiently precise statements on the thorny subjects of evolution and human liberty, but the main sweep of his thought is clear. The fall, the background of all of Bond's plays, occurs when humans or other animals are forced to live unnaturally, to behave in ways for which they are not designed. They become destructive and neurotic and make bad parents.

Joseph E. Duncan. *MD*. March, 1976, pp. 1–2

Already in *Bingo*, the passivity and relative silence of Shakespeare was a striking feature. In *The Fool*, Clare at first hardly emerges from the crowd as an individual. We are hardly shown any of his poetic achievement, and only see it, indirectly, in the admiration accorded him by the literary enthusiasts who take him up. If, as I assume, Bond is dealing with the artist's experience in society from the artist's (that is, his own very personal) point of view, this technique seems to me wholly justified. A young ploughboy who writes verses would probably see this activity as a personal eccentricity without any wider significance; and he, like the audience of the play, would receive evidence of his own genius (which to him is as natural as the air he breathes) merely through the reaction of his readers and admirers.

The Fool dramatizes the life story—and the bewilderment—of an individual of great talent who lacks the self-awareness which would enable him to master his personal destiny, just as he also lacks the historical and political consciousness that would allow him to make rational political decisions. The passive central character is designed to draw the spectator into the position of such a person, who sees the world revolve around him without fully understanding what is happening. It is this lack of understanding which makes Bond's Clare a fool.

Now it is true that it is an axiom of handbooks of dramatic technique that a passive central character does not work. Only a playwright of exceptional ability and genius could bring off such a tour de force. And that, precisely, is what Bond has done, both in Bingo and The Fool.

Martin Esslin. TheatreQ. No. 21, 1976, p. 44

Having so thoroughly anatomised religious belief in Narrow Road to the Deep North, Black Mass and Passion, in the plays that follow Bond allows priests and religion to take their place in a wider social pattern as one of several elements in authoritarian societies. Bond's criticism of religion is thorough and yet curiously yielding. His achievement has been to create theatre which is Marxist in that his characters are the products of social processes, whose motivations and actions find their energy in social relationships. This doesn't imply a simplistic or determinist idea of human nature. On the contrary, Bond is a playwright who reconstitutes the idea of Free Will for human beings, and his fundamental objection to religious belief is that it takes responsibility away from human beings. It is, in its way, an ecstatic conviction. Bond is so impressed by the unrealised potential in human nature that idea-systems like religion which devalue Man before God serve only to smother alarming and beautiful energies. The Parson in The Fool turns his thoughts to death when events round on him, but Bond's plays urge us to resist despair, to take responsibility for our own lives, and to create the societies that will make that possible. . . .

If, in Bond's human-centred vision, religion is a fantasy or an evasion or a tool of power politics, then the world into which we are born must be above all a material one. People's lives are not, in Bond's work, divorced from their natural environments, like actors in the Georgian theatre walking about in front of painted trees and avenues. Much of the suffering and misery that his characters undergo occurs precisely because their social lives have somehow lost contact with their existence as elements of the natural world. "We evolved in a biosphere," writes Bond, in the *Lear* preface, "but we live in what is more and more becoming a technosphere." . . .

Few modern dramatists create landscape quite as vividly as Edward Bond. Most dramatists who criticise and analyse society usually prefer to concentrate on a world dominated by technology and man-made objects. Pinter or Wesker, for example, will lavish great care on interiors, detailing props, costume and furniture, but Bond, who *can* do these things, will more often be creating precise outdoor settings. He is, perhaps more than any of his contemporaries, an outdoor playwright, making of the English landscape, even in cities, something individual and powerful, possessed of its own life. Nature is important not as decoration for the action but because Bond sees there the objective evidence for his own moral sense.

Tony Coult. *The Plays of Edward Bond*
(London, Eyre Methuen, 1977), pp. 30–31

The Woman contains a number of major characters who are as fully drawn as any in Bond's previous plays, but it is important that the audience doesn't interpret the play as a conventional tragedy played out between the characters of Hecuba, Ismene and Heros. One guarantee against this is the weight which any production gives to the minor roles, particularly the Trojan poor and the Islanders—the term minor roles is in itself a misnomer, when the significance and the authenticity of what Bond shows is so strongly dependent on the conviction that the actors bring to these parts. In any of Bond's plays, the minor characters have an important function in that they represent contrasting elements in the society Bond shows us. In *The Fool* and *The Woman* Bond tries to reconcile his primary intention—which is to examine a diseased culture and to suggest what is needed to effect a cure—with the use of a main character, a theatrical device which, as Bond recognises, carries with it the attendant danger of seeming to place too much weight on the historical and social role of distinct and favoured individuals: "I think it's natural to provide the audience with certain figures, just as people in their daily life want to know one or two people and not everyone they see in the street. There are advantages in the theatre in concentrating a lot of the experience in one or two characters. But I don't want to resort to the idea of a central *heroic* character. . . ." With *The Woman,* there will always be a danger that an audience will respond to the main characters but fail to see, or ignore, the social analysis which Bond is presenting. In the next play, there is no room for doubt or evasion; *The Bundle* can only be understood as a study of a whole community. . . .

What distinguishes *The Bundle* from any of the plays in the two earlier series is its last scene. In scene ten we see the peasant community after the revolution, living and working in a new, rational society, free of repressive and coercive structures. Where in earlier plays, such as *Early Morning* or *Lear* or *The Woman,* Bond had shown characters who couldn't accept an irrational and unjustly ordered society and so attempted to bring about change, he now shows change not just as a possibility to be striven after but as a practical reality.

Malcolm Hay and Philip Roberts. *Bond: A Study of His Plays* (London, Eyre Methuen, 1980), pp. 264–65, 267

[A] major offering with elements of the musical embedded in it was Edward Bond's new piece *Restoration.* Be it said at once that it was a very decided advance on his not-quite-so-new *The Worlds,* playing simultaneously on the Eastern fringe and quite the most arid and inhuman play he has yet written. Those terms could never be used of *Restoration.* Setting out with the improbable aim of pastiching Restoration comedy with a serious purpose—to show the brutal underside of the aristocratic society so wittily conjured up by Congreve, Wycherley and Vanbrugh—Bond has produced an amazingly accurate piece of character creation in his Lord Are, magisterially played by Simon Callow. Here one cannot help wondering if the creation has not run away with the creator, since Lord Are is so charming and witty while doing the most awful things (like getting his idiotically loyal servant to go to the gallows for murdering Lady Are, which in fact Lord Are did in a moment of forgivable misunderstanding) that we are likely to extend all the grace in the world to a witty sinner. The servants thus mistreated are either so stupid and servile that one can have little sympathy with their plight, or incapably rebellious and surly in small things while letting the big issues pass them by. Or, in one case, they are black. This seems, for Bond, to bestow instant sainthood, and we are constantly told that were it not for white man's evil the blacks would still be living in perfect prelapsarian harmony and health. How, you may wonder, is this improbably and irrelevant information conveyed? Why, through the songs, of course. Every now and then (but far too often) the working-class characters step out of the action to deliver ditties of no tone, again put to music by Nick Bicat, about the revolution that is coming, the evils of capitalism and the like. Nearly all these ideas are clearly implicit in the main body of the text, but I suppose Mr. Bond does not trust us to get his drift unless he spells it out, which he does tiresomely in the first half and interminably in the second. Whether this should be accounted lack of confidence on the playwright's part or an ungovernable desire to preach to an audience in his own person, I am not quite sure. But I do know I shall long remember Simon Callow's dissolute rake, and marvel at the ability here shown by

Bond, never exactly the lightest-touched of our playwrights, to come up with something so triumphantly out of character.

John Russell Taylor. *Drama*. Winter, 1981, p. 33

"Ripplingly funny," "Highly effective scenes of wit and comedy" proclaim the newspaper advertisements. "Yes," says the Royal Court box-office clerk unhesitatingly when asked by a doubtful customer, "Is it a comedy?"

Well, all true in a way, but how much it leaves out, not least the ending of Bond's new play . . . , which is on a high and sombre note. If, as Bond once said, *The Sea* dealt with tragedy but was a comedy, then *Restoration* deals with comedy but is a tragedy. More precisely, it begins as an extremely funny parody of a familiar comic mode and, without ever quite parting company with the comic, moves inexorably closer to melodrama— the pure, primitive melodrama of the early nineteenth century to which Bond gives another dimension by the force of his wit.

Wit is the word throughout. Bond ingeniously plays one convention off against another, juggling with the audience's expectations, sometimes gratifying, sometimes undermining and thwarting them. He effects unexpected and disturbing emotional shifts, and must surely leave any audience in a state of mind which they would find hard to describe without taking time for some close analysis. The play was no doubt written to bring such analysis about . . . .

Restoration seems to open up all sorts of new possibilities for Bond's future writing, especially in its innovatory use of music and its witty play with a theatrical convention which he has not used before. It will be hard to see Wycherley or Farquhar in quite the same light after *Restoration;* some shadow must surely fall from Bond's darker and yet still so witty version of that comedy. There are some signs in the play that it was rushed in preparation; Bond has said that time for teaching and rehearsing the songs was rather limited. One or two motifs tend to fade away or are not quite established: [Lord] Arc's venomous references to his enemy Lord Lester, for instance, do not quite get over; one or two of the songs were rather flat in the first performance; and the length of the second part risks losing the exciting momentum built up in the first part. The text, however, is still provisional, and Bond has indicated his intention of shortening it somewhat before publication.

These minor matters apart, the play is a thrilling event, both in itself and as an augury for a continuingly rich and varied contribution to the English theatre by this, the most strikingly talented and profoundly moving of its contemporary practitioners. Always something new out of Africa, it was said. From Bond too; the fertility of his invention is a thoroughly invigorating element in modern theatre.

Katharine Worth. *MD*. Dec., 1981, pp. 479, 493

COWARD, NOEL (1899–1973)

Coward must have been born with a sense of the stage, though I think it is more obvious in some other of his plays, but it is there in *The Young Idea*. None of his plays that I have read reads half as well as it acts. His script is merely a shorthand note of action in three dimensions. How he does it I don't know; the thing escapes my analysis. Probably it escapes his.

You will imagine that his stage sense and his gift for smart yet natural dialogue are one and the same, since a script is surely nothing but dialogue and stage directions. And certainly there is nothing more in the play—*except the play*. The play only happens when dialogue and stage directions become one on the stage—*before an audience*.

But of course the naturalness of the dialogue counts, and, what is more extraordinary, in the case of Coward so does the smartness. Usually verbal cleverness holds up the action, but in *The Young Idea*, as in *The Importance of Being Earnest*, the sparkle is a lamp to the actors' feet.

But *The Young Idea* derives far more from Shaw than from Wilde. It is not a question of imitation, Coward is original enough—if originality counts for anything. But, like Shakespeare, whom he does not otherwise closely resemble, he is content to take material where he finds it and make it his own. He took the twins from *You Never Can Tell*, put them into *The Young Idea*, and then started working on them. He has been working on them ever since. They are the Adam and Eve of his creation.

W. R. Titterton. *TW*. Dec., 1927, p. 24

If Mr. Coward is really going to turn his attention from his everlasting attack upon Respectability and his everlasting satire against Modernity (it is odd, by the way, how Modern Youth should hail as their leader and representative a man who was old at twenty and who never stops withering them with irony), the next phases of his development may be of the utmost importance to the theatre. The knowledge and the experience of the stage are his already; his also a nimble mind and an inexhaustible energy and industry. If he turns his mind and his energy and his industry a little more to thought and study, and a good deal less to producing and lyric-writing and song-composing, he may yet live down his colossal success.

Mr. Coward is a strange figure in this post-war England. He belongs to no "school," he has no "master" whom he copies, he writes no newspaper articles, he is seldom interviewed or photographed. His name hardly ever appears in "Social Jottings." The Lido knows him not, nor Deauville, nor Le Touquet, nor North Berwick. He has not written his reminiscences. He has not pulverized America in a book of travel. For all his immense notoriety he is an aloof and retiring individual. And, for all the wealth that he has garnered, he is an indefatigable worker. In the last hundred years only Disraeli and Wilde and Shaw have started from nothing and conquered England as Mr. Coward has conquered. It is curious that he is the first Englishman to do so.

A. G. Macdonell. *LM*. Nov., 1931, p. 76

[Coward's plays] are all the more valuable because their author's attitude is sometimes so discontented, not to say agonized. Almost from the beginning Noel Coward, chief patentee of the dramatic possibilities of his times, hated what he was dealing in. Not all the time, of course; he is occasionally subject to a natural clannish admiration for the insouciant glitter of jazz-age high jinks. He can be almost dazzled by the smarter aspects of post-war "sophistication," as if he had borrowed the romanticizing spectacles of Michael Arlen. It is the presence of this element of admiration which bewilders the spectator when *Design for Living* is labelled satire. However its characters malign themselves, they are the standard Coward types of *Private Lives,* rather more sentimentalized, and their creator is very fond of them. Yet this comradely enjoyment of his contemporaries' flippancies often carries over into a frenetic horror of the galvanic, tinselled recklessness of the world that succeeded the war. It was his vibration between these two points of view and his competence in expressing both which made him versatile in spirit as well as in technique.

So that the author of *Hay Fever*, that classic among modern farces, and *Private Lives,* that fond study of hilarious impropriety, is also the author of *The Vortex,* the most neurotic of all the plays about the morning after the world war. Beneath his occasional mask of gaiety he is obsessed with the spectacle of post-operative shock as it affects both the elder and the younger generations. Being a birthright member of the society of lost souls, he could not help liking some of its aspects and gaily comprehending what excellent raw material they were for the stage. Yet, being both in and out of sympathy with the 'twenties, he could never avoid nausea when he really looked at what went on round him.

J. C. Furnas. *Fortnightly.* Dec., 1933, pp. 710–11

Mr. Coward, who has often been held up as himself the prototype of the post-war young man, does not fulfil the popular conception of an irritable and irritating person, dispirited and boneless, who drifts about asking people what he shall do to be saved. If anybody has worked in the past sixteen years, Mr. Coward indisputably has. In spite, however, of the profound dissimilarity between him and the young men whose prototype he is said to be, there is, I think, ample warrant for regarding him as their prototype. More clearly than any of his contemporaries he expressed the harsh and impatient cynicism of the young who grew to early manhood in the War. A world was wrecked, and in it they, weakened by malnutrition and unnerved by strain, had to make a living. They looked at the earth, but, unlike God, did not find it good. An immense flippancy pervaded their generation, and they asserted, with a singular lack of happiness and spirit, that they believed in a good time. But their good time would have been any other generation's bad time. They despaired of life. All standards were dropped. Self-indulgence was the only virtue, and not too much of a virtue. Effort was thought to be boring. Objects must be attained, if they were to be attained at all, easily, thoughtlessly, and were not to be sought if their achievement involved any labour. A heart-breaking Brightness animated young minds, and the bright remark was always made, even if, or perhaps because, it wounded or humiliated the person about whom it was made. There was a great deal of noise.

It was this world which Mr. Coward, with uncanny skill and exactness, portrayed in his early plays. His characters were divided into the clever young and the stupid old, the former being free of conventions, the latter being imprisoned in them. These characters, whether they were old or young, skimmed over the surface of life, sneering at it, the young scoffing at the old, the old snarling at the young. Any person in these plays who tried to see under the surface was said to be stuffy, solemn, a prig. One ate, drank, but was not merry, and to-morrow one died.

St. John Ervine. QQ. Spring, 1935, pp. 2–3

The real question about Mr. Coward is whether some one of his numerous talents will finally seduce and betray him. A few years ago he seemed in some danger of becoming a mere writer of sentimental operettas and revues. At present his facility in handling farcical dialogue seems more likely to lead him astray. As Gilda in *Design for Living* says of Leo's play, "He flips along with easy swift dialogue, but doesn't go deep enough." His weakness has always been in the creation of character; but in *The Vortex, This Was a Man,* and *Cavalcade* he proved that he has powers of characterization which he has never fully developed. He ought not to be content with writing the most amusing sex farces of our time; his best talent is for realistic and satiric drama. *Tonight at 8:30* gives some hope, at least, that his mind is turning to his real job.

It must be admitted, however, that the self-portrait Mr. Coward has recently given us in *Present Indicative* throws doubt on hopeful prophecies. It is hard to say how deliberately the book is designed as an autobiographical vaudeville; but essentially it is not much more than that. The figure that emerges is frank, likable, engagingly impudent, but utterly self-centered, and almost completely theatrical. One thinks, as so often in connection with Mr. Coward, of that earlier versatile and volatile entertainer, Colley Cibber; but Cibber's *Apology for His Life* shows a far firmer grip on reality, and a better understanding not only of others but of himself and his own powers.

If the Noel Coward of *Present Indicative* is the real Noel Coward, it would seem safe to predict that he will never write better plays than he has written. But if, as seems more likely in view of Mr. Coward's stronger plays, the book is a sort of self-caricature, written to exploit the "Noel Coward" who is adored by undergraduates, it can be discounted along with *Private Lives* and *Design for Living*. The hero of the book reminds us too often of Otto and Leo: did he sit for their portraits, or did they sit for his? Evidently he put something of himself into them; I suspect that he put even more of them into his picture of himself.

Homer E. Woodbridge. *SAQ*. July, 1938, pp. 250–51

All comedies of manners are games played against nature in a drawing room or its equivalent. The real point of their joke, as John Palmer once noted, is that man is pretending to be civilized. "The elaborate ritual of society is a mask through which the natural man is comically seen to look." From Wilde's time to Coward's this joke, like everything else, has altered. It has altered if for no other reason than that so many of Coward's characters make no pretense of being civilized, in the Wildean sense. They are hilarious rebels from society's elaborate rituals. That is one of the sources of the pleasure they usually give. They remain comic characters, but they have misplaced their manners. Oddly enough, though their gifts have increased, their minds seem less sharp. Perhaps one of the surest manifestations of their "nerves" is that they substitute nonsense—delectable as it can be—for the wit of Wilde and the glittering precision of Maugham's mind.

At their best, however inferior that best may be to Wilde's and Maugham's, the comedies of Coward can be taken seriously as social histories. My complaint against *Present Laughter* is that, though it makes every panting effort to be gay, I found it difficult not to be serious in its presence. [1946]

John Mason Brown. *Dramatis Personae* (New York, Viking, 1965), pp. 189–90

"An improbable farce," the redundant subtitle of *Blithe Spirit*, is suggestive, for whereas there is considerable farce in Coward's other comedies, in this one improbability has been carried to an extreme that the playwright had not reached before and that no other playwright could effect more successfully. Coward has a genius for making the slightest of substance highly entertaining. In *Blithe Spirit* he dares to move his comedy over into the realm of the supernatural. And he is successful there too. One of the characters is a ghost, and another becomes a ghost before the play is over. Madame Arcati, the medium with the school-girl enthusiasm and the bromidic jargon, represents Noel Coward's satire at its best. But except for this character and the startling innovation of the supernatural, *Blithe Spirit* is cut according to the typical Coward pattern. Even some of the lines are borrowed almost verbatim from his other plays. Its comedy turns on domestic quarrels, violently farcical action, and general invective. It is marked, too, by the familiar Cowardian wit, particularly in lines depending for effect on situation.

Most comedies act better than they read, and this is particularly true of *Blithe Spirit*. In the first place, the dialogue is extremely real rather than literary. Like [Arthur Wing] Pinero, Coward writes for the actors, his experience on the stage having given him a sense of sound and rhythm that enables him, as he composes the lines, to hear them as they will be spoken in the theatre. Then, too, much in this play depends on stage business, gestures, facial expression, the mere lifting of an eyebrow or the slightest movement of the hand, all of which requires considerable imagination to obtain in the reading. Furthermore, since much of the effect in *Blithe Spirit* depends on situation entrances and exits, and the groupings of actors on the stage, the acting must not only be minutely timed but be expertly pointed up by appeals to the eye as much as to the ear. In comparison to the considerable stage movement and stage business the play demands, there are few stage directions. Noel Coward expects the actors to know what to do without being told. Finally, *Blithe Spirit* is singularly lacking in epigrams, those pithy observations which, even apart from their context, provoke laughter and which characterize *Private Lives* and *Design for Living*. Much of the laughter in *Blithe Spirit* is provoked instead by comments which if detached from the circumstances under which they are uttered would be only commonplace. Thus to appreciate the play through the printed page is a test of one's feeling for sheer theatre.

A. R. Fulton. In A. R. Fulton, ed., *Drama and Theatre* (New York, Henry Holt and Company, 1946), pp. 462–63

To many playgoers [Coward] must remain always the *enfant terrible* of the nineteen-twenties, the writer whose clipped dialogue started a fashion, who set the young generation "talking like typewriters," as Mrs. Patrick Campbell put it, and whose quick, brittle, tap-tapping wit sounded the note of an uneasy decade. That was a long time ago. Coward is middle-aged, and yet he has not grown up. It is odd to find that young people, fresh to the theatre and ready to smile tolerantly at the odd stuff written in the dark ages before the war, usually treat Noel Coward as one of themselves. The name seems still to have a ring of youth. When Coward is in his sixties he will stay, in some queer fashion, as a symbol of youthful defiance, tapping out that defiance in the same witty Morse. And yet—here is one of his paradoxes—he has never been really young: from his early days in the theatre he has been a sophisticated veteran. Hot ice and wondrous strange snow! How are we to resolve the concord of this discord?

The truth, maybe, is that in spirit Coward has stayed round about the same age since he began to write. (You can choose the age.) But few dramatists have made less progress than he has done between *I'll Leave It to You* and *Quadrille*. Once he had thrown off his early comedies, of which *The Young Idea* (with its pair of fizzing twins, Gerda and Sholto) is still cunning and actable, he settled down to flick a dart at every type of play on the board except the Verse Drama; to become a flashing technician; and yet to preserve an unvaried cast of mind and outlook. A Coward play has always been highly theatrical and glossily professional. We know that the dramatist feels the spot-light full upon him as he lifts his pen—as he flourishes it in a manner familiar only on the stage where any actor can write a long letter in twenty seconds and sign his name with a single dab.

J. C. Trewin. *Dramatists of Today* (London, Staples Press, 1953), pp. 151–52

How, then, do we explain Coward's longevity? Not, plainly, by mere luck. Luck certainly plays a large part in the theatre, but no man's luck lasts for thirty-five years.

Logic seems to provide us with a choice between two answers. The secret of Coward's continuing popularity lies either in the fact that he writes the sort of play that is as entertaining to an audience of the 'fifties as to one of the 'twenties—i.e., the sort of play that does not "date"—or the critics are wrong and he *has* in fact developed as a playwright.

I believe the truth to be a combination of the two. His plays, in general, do not "date." Admittedly the idiom is personal and he often writes much as, in real life, he speaks; but that is merely to say that he writes with wit; and wit is a quality that does not date. The things that do date, in the theatre, are attitudes of mind inspired by purely contemporary factors—political opinions, for instance, or moral judgments, or messages on How To Save The World. All such paraphernalia are happily mainly absent from Coward's work. He is interested only in humanity, its quirks and foibles, its vanities and idiocies, its prejudices and pomposities, and these things, as Congreve and Sheridan have taught us, are changeless. What is more, he expresses that interest with a verbal dexterity unmatched in our time. It is not a difficult idiom to imitate—and many have done so—but it is impossible to reproduce. In fact, it is the imitators who now sound dated, not Coward.

Terence Rattigan. In Raymond Mander and Joe Mitchenson, *Theatrical Companion to Coward* (London, Rockliff, 1957), p. 3

A dramatist selects his material, his method and his audience, in that order. Mr. Coward's mistake is that he is doing this, but backward. It cannot but lead to the gravest errors of taste. And these Mr. Coward commits in abundance. He is against the playwright as social realist, but nothing could be more unreal than Mr. Coward's view of present-day society as exemplified in a work such as *Sail Away*.

To stay sane under such an assault as this musical makes it is as well to remember that *Hay Fever* and *Private Lives* are the two best comedies written in English since *The Importance of Being Earnest*. Also that *Bitter Sweet* and *Conversation Piece* rank with the best Johann Strauss operettas. Keeping this in mind, and remembering that Mr. Coward is a very young man, let us look to the future.

Could we not have next a court play? Hush, I don't mean a Royal Court play. I mean a play designed to be performed before the very best people, such as myself and my friends, not more than two hundred of us in all. It should be given one performance, and published in a limited edition of fifteen copies. The loudest sound in any of its three acts should be the shutting of a door. The characters should be enormously rich, appallingly idle, and titled to a man. The setting should be a garden or a deserted ballroom. If Mr. Coward thinks such material for a comedy no longer exists, then let him get into a motor car and drive slowly about Europe for a little while.

Must we wait for the day when the aristocracy rises before we get this play? I hope not. Mr. Coward adores excitement, that's obvious. Well, nothing would give him a greater kick than an outright bid for unpopularity. God knows, he might succeed. Many of us do. But what is very important is that it might restore him to his position as a major artist of the theatre. Hell! more than that. It might put him back in the unique position he held twenty years ago.

John Whiting. *London*. Aug., 1962, p. 66

Mr. Coward writes dialogue as well as any man going; it is seemingly effortless, surprising in the most wonderfully surprising places, and "true"— very, very true. He is, as well, a dramatic mountain goat; his plays are better made than most—but not in the sense of the superimposed paste job of form, but from within: order more than form. And Mr. Coward's subjects—the ways we kid ourselves that we do and do not exist with each other and with ourselves—have not, unless my mind has been turned inward too long, gone out of date.

Notwithstanding it all, Noel Coward can be a bore. He bores his admirers every time he gets within earshot of a reporter by announcing how old-fashioned a writer he is, how the theatre has left him behind, how he does not understand the—to use an expression vague and confusing enough to have become meaningless and therefore dangerous—"avant-garde" playwrights of today, feels no sympathy with them.

It is difficult to imagine him wringing his hands and seeking reassurance when he says these things, and it is equally difficult to think that there is a smug tone to the voice, so I don't really know what Mr. Coward's problem is. . . . But let me stop being churlish. A man I know and like and whose opinion I respect, a man involved with the theatre, a man who has produced the work of such playwrights as Beckett, Ionesco, Pinter, Arrabal and Ugo Betti, said to me not long ago that he greatly admired Noel Coward's plays, that he thought Coward a better playwright than Bernard Shaw and that Coward's plays would be on the boards long after most of the men writing today had been forgotten.

Edward Albee. Introduction to *Three Plays
by Noel Coward* (New York, Dell, 1965), pp. 4–5

Noel Coward . . . made his first stage appearance in 1911. During the fifty-five years since then, he has been prodigiously active; and the range of his output has been astonishing. Even now, when he has as much fame as any man could desire, he is returning [with *Suite in Three Keys*] to Shaftesbury Avenue in the dual role of actor and playwright. Laurels, he manifestly feels, were made for wearing, not for resting on.

As a dramatist, Mr. Coward did not merely start young: he succeeded young. *The Vortex* won him, at the age of 25, golden opinions from all sorts of people. It also brought him attendant publicity. One particular photograph, he claims in his autobiography, that showed him looking "like a heavily-doped Chinese illusionist," caused him to be unfairly identified for many years after with a life of dressing-gowned degeneracy. The play itself, as a revival at Guildford last year showed, has a bitterness unusual in Coward and remains a scathing indictment of the vain, self-absorbed and neglectful mother. Yet a year later, in *Hay Fever,* Mr. Coward used exactly the same character traits to make up the endearing comic figure of Judith Bliss.

The ease with which Mr. Coward switched from anger to approbation illustrates perfectly his most essential quality: sheer professionalism. If he were asked to dramatise the Book of Job, one feels that he would bring to it the same professional zeal that shines through his countless plays, his musicals and revues, his film-scripts, novels and autobiographies. Always dexterous, he is sometimes inspired: Think but of *Hay Fever, Private Lives, Blithe Spirit* and *Present Laughter*. Three of this luminous quartet have been revived in London recently with heartening success. Immaculate in their conception, they contain the sort of unfailingly funny situations that ensure them a long life in the theatre.

In recent years, Mr. Coward has added one more to his many roles— that of embattled controversialist. With downright zest, he has attacked the younger playwrights, the "scratch-and-mumble" school of acting and the incivility of certain critics. This, allied to the uneven standard of his later plays, has made him an obvious target of abuse for theatrical progressives. But even his detractors will have to admit that the arrival of a full-length play and a double-bill by Mr. Coward in the West End remains a major event.

Michael Billington. PP. April, 1966, p. 9

A Song at Twilight . . . marks the closing of a circle. For what we tend to forget today is that Coward, now the old master of the classical tradition in English drama, has not always been, or been taken to be, the obvious logical successor of the well-made-play tradition. On the contrary: in his early days he was regarded as a young revolutionary, all too ready and eager to throw out of the window everything which Pinero, say, would have thought most important in drama. If *The Vortex* now seems to us in most ways—and especially in technique—a thoroughly conservative play, in 1924 it looked very different. (It is interesting to remember that another, comparable play considered revolutionary in its time, [Osborne's] *Look Back in Anger,* also seemed to its author a few years after the event to be ''a formal, rather old-fashioned play.'')

And the revolutionary quality critics and audience detected in the early works of Noël Coward were by no means entirely a matter of the subjects he treated (an unhealthy relationship between mother and son, gleeful and shameless adultery indulged in by nice middle-class wives, etc.). His technique too was considered revolutionary, precisely because it went right against the canons of the well-made play in one particular. Well-madeness was originally—as viewed by Sardou for instance—not so much having a neat plot as having a lot of plot and telling it in such a way that the audience's interest was never allowed to flag. The French farce-writers refined this in many ways, by harnessing the mass of plot material to a rigid symmetrical frame, but still the amount of plot, the proliferation of incident, was vital. The decisive step Noël Coward took here, whether in comedy or drama, was a drastic lightening of the plot-load.

John Russell Taylor. The Rise and Fall of the Well-Made
Play (New York, Hill and Wang, 1967), pp. 126–27

The entertainer's job is to make time pass pleasantly, enjoyably, while making the audience forget about the time that is passing, to remove the present moment from the flux of time and erase, for a moment, both past and future. The purest entertainment is the perfect escapism, and Coward's high farces are his closest equivalent to the magician's suspension of gravity and logic. His aptest title is *Present Laughter,* and the chief device on his coat of arms should be a circle; for not only do almost all his plays end by returning to their beginnings, but their circularity, even when the play covers a good deal of time, is a denial of organic development and change and decay and time itself. The surest sign that Coward is really the craftsman that he wants the audience to recognize is the vividness and variety he has given to this view and the thoroughness with which he has confounded all those who predicted that—without his presence as performer, and as soon as theatrical fashions shifted a bit—even the best plays would simply evaporate. Yet there they are on the printed page, as brittle, as shallow, as mindless as ever; but they are still sealed within an envelope of special stage air, still breathing—still, astonishingly, alive.

Milton Levin. Noel Coward (New York, Twayne, 1968), p. 143

Baudelaire, Huysmans, Wilde, Yeats, James, even Chekhov, whose melancholy crew daydream in the provinces—the beginnings of modern art are the beginnings of artifice. The repertory has different accents, different programs, but throughout the underlying disgust or disenchantment with the common world is the same. With Coward, with the age of the entertainer, artifice became another aspect of the world, became, in many respects, *the* world: deluxe gossip, journalistic "profundity," scandal. Coward created his mark, his style, but it was also a creation of the day. His was a talent which could only have worked in a seller's market. What it had was the fortunate moment, the decisive conjunction between performer and audience. Looking at life as fabulous and heartbreaking, creating always without real reference to himself, without vulgar experience, Coward gave us characters who are not so much worldly wise as "world weary," who have about them something so sleek as to be a little inhuman, an inhumanity that became best expressed with the cult of "personalities" in public life and the press.

In Coward, of course, what you observe is the growth of a "personality," rather than that of a writer, a sort of glittering stasis. That the career, nevertheless, has been unique and exhilarating, that more than one generation of playwrights (including Osborne and Albee) have taken its lessons to heart, that an "evening's entertainment" by Noel Coward will be on the boards twenty years from now—who can doubt that?

Robert Mazzocco. NYRB. March 14, 1968, p. 31

In March 1966, against the advice of his Swiss doctors, Noel flew to London and started rehearsals with Irene Worth and Lilli Palmer for *Suite in Three Keys*. Of these three latest Coward plays, *A Song at Twilight* is the most important and also far and away the best; it is an earnestly moral drama about an aging, distinguished, petulant, bitchy and truculent writer who manages to conceal his homosexuality from the world at the cost of warping his talent and cutting off his human sympathies. Yet curiously enough *A Song at Twilight* started out in Coward's mind as a comedy; he had recently read David Cecil's biography of Max Beerbohm, which describes Constance

Collier's visit to Max when they were both in their seventies and long after
their friendship had ended. . . .

But gradually, as the play developed in Coward's mind, he realized that
there could be more to it than just the meeting of a couple of Elyot and
Amanda figures in their old age. What if the writer, unlike Max Beerbohm,
had been homosexual for most of his life; and what if the woman brought
with her letters that could incriminate him in the eyes of posterity? Slowly but
surely this became the theme of *A Song at Twilight:* an old, queer author
fighting off a threat to his "good name." Given that plot, it is not altogether
surprising that many critics took the play to be firmly based on Somerset
Maugham, an illusion which Coward fostered by making up to look curiously
like him on the stage. But if Beerbohm and Maugham were the direct influences on the creation of Sir Hugo Latymer, there was also a certain amount of
Coward himself in the character he had written and was about to play.

Sheridan Morley. *A Talent to Amuse: A
Biography of Noel Coward* (Garden City,
N.Y., Doubleday, 1969), p. 402

ELIOT, T. S. (1888–1965)

In *Sweeney Agonistes* Mr. Eliot comes to us as the men of the neighboring
tribes came to Joshua under a camouflage of frayed garments, with mouldy
bread in the wallet. But the point is not camouflaged. Mortal and sardonic
victims though we are in this conflict called experience, we may regard our
victimage with calmness, the book says; not because we don't know that
our limitations of correctness are tedious to a society which has its funny
side to us, as we have our slightly morbid side to it, but because there is a
moment for Orestes, for Ophelia, for Everyman, when the ego and the figure it cuts, the favors you get from it, the good cheer and customary enco-
mium, are as the insulting wigwaggery of the music-halls. . . .

Mr. Eliot is not showy nor hard, and is capable at times of too much
patience; but here the truculent commonplace of the vernacular obscures
care of arrangement, and the deliberate concise rhythm that is characteristic
of him seems less intentional than it is. Upon scrutiny, however, the effect
of an unhoodwinked self-control is apparent. The high time half a dozen
people of unfastidious personality can seem to be having together is juxtaposed with the successful flight of the pursued son of Agamemnon, and it
is implied, perhaps, that "he who wonders shall reign, he who reigns shall
have rest." One is obliged to say "perhaps"—since Sweeney in conflict is
not synonymous with Sweeney victorious.

Marianne Moore. *Poetry*. May, 1933, pp. 106–7, 109

The prose dialogue [in *The Rock*] which maintains the action of the pageant is distressing. It is difficult to believe that the spinsterish Cockney of the builders was written by the author of the public house scene in *The Waste Land*, and the speeches of the Agitator and the fashionable visitors to the Church are just the usual middle-class caricatures of a reality that has never been accurately observed. They are the caricatures of a class by a class, and well-worn and blurred they are, inevitably. The reach-me-down character of the dialogue is partly responsible for and partly derived from—in fact is one with—the banal and sentimental treatment of a scene like The Crusaders' Farewell, which offers so painful a contrast to the dignity of the liturgical Latin that comes next. Only in some of the ingenious pastiches of archaic styles which Mr. Eliot introduces from time to time is the prose readable with even mild pleasure.

The verse is altogether more interesting. Naturally in a work written to order and presumably in a limited time there is included some which is not as fine as most of what Mr. Eliot has published. Necessarily, too, this verse cannot have the concentration and subtlety of a short poem intended for many attentive readings. Its interest lies rather in its experimentation with a tone of address. Innovations of "tone" (in [I. A.] Richards' sense) are at least as significant as innovations of "technique" in the restricted sense, and in the addresses of the Chorus and The Rock to the decent heathen and the ineffectual devout, who are taken as forming the audience, Mr. Eliot achieves a tone that is new to contemporary verse.

D. W. Harding. Scrutiny. Sept., 1934, pp. 181–82

In *The Family Reunion* Mr. Eliot has attempted for the first time to dramatize the issues which concern him without the support of the visible forms of his faith. His task in the theater has been the extraordinarily difficult one of presenting the action of redemption to audiences for the most part unconvinced that such an action exists. In *The Rock* and *Murder in the Cathedral*, he sought to mitigate the gap between himself and his audiences by staying within the church, writing about church issues for church audiences. This procedure permitted him to "assume some moral attitude in common with his audience" and so avoid in a measure the didacticism of imposing his assumptions. But the effect of staying within the church was also to make his productions special, as the precincts of the church are special for the general modern public. The public at large beat a path, it is true, to *Murder in the Cathedral*. But most of them went as sightseers, ready to forget their own standards when these were burlesqued in the murderers' Erastian apologies, but in a spirit which regarded as historical not only the events, but also the Christian values and standards of the play. In *The Family Reunion* Eliot has deliberately made impossible any such facile acceptance of the reality of the supernatural. He has sought to confront the modern world with the necessity of redemption at its starkest, without benefit of clergy. Christian terms are virtually excluded from both action and verse; the intention is to have the Christian view of man's condition emerge from a commonplace setting of secular modern life. The difference between a natural and supernatural view of man's destiny is put squarely in the middle of the action—not, as before, on the periphery, where it could be left by the audience in abeyance, outside their experience of the play.

C. L. Barber. SoR. Autumn, 1940, pp. 387–88

Although its choruses give voice to some of the same profound kind of meditative poetry that he was to develop in his *Quartets, The Rock* hardly meets Eliot's test for a religious play, "that it should be able to hold the interest, to arouse the excitement, of people who are not religious." Nor, through the very nature of its inception, could it possibly rise to his far more exacting demand of creating an indisseverable double pattern of poetry and drama. Such a set-piece could not possess the wholeness of vision and movement of a *Polyeucte* or an *Athalie*. But the case was very different with the play which Eliot wrote for the Canterbury Festival the following year.

Murder in the Cathedral, like many of the morality plays, is a drama of temptation, but Becket as the great archbishop proves superior to his tempters. One of the most conspicuous technical triumphs in all Eliot's poetry is in the choruses that were designed to be spoken by the working women of Canterbury. Here he carried further his experiments in finding verse forms suitable for ritualistic drama. He had no living stage tradition upon which to draw, but he believed that a chorus could still perform something of the same fundamental function that it had for the Greeks. It could "mediate between the action and the audience"; it could "intensify the action by projecting its emotional consequences, so that we as audience see it doubly, by seeing its effect on other people." [1947]

F. O. Matthiessen. The Achievement of T. S. Eliot
(New York, Oxford University Press, 1958), p. 162

Whatever one may think of its theology and its epistemology, [*Murder in the Cathedral*] cannot be dismissed as simply "unreal." It almost completely eschews photographic or modern realism; but the sense of human action which it conveys is very much like that which we get from other first-rate modern drama with a strong intellectual and ethical motivation, Ibsen's and Pirandello's for example. If one learns to understand the extremely consistent conventions of *Murder in the Cathedral,* one may read it as an imitation of that human action which we know from a thousand other sources: human life divided by the machinery of the mind, and confined by the greedy idolatries of the sensibility. The theological "basis in reality" which Eliot accepts may be regarded as an interpretation reached inductively through this common experience, even though Eliot presents it as the truth from which all is deduced.

The second observation follows from the first: in spite of its absolute finality and its ideal perfection, *Murder in the Cathedral* should be regarded as employing only one of many possible strategies for making modern poetic drama—which is as much as to say that the problem has not been solved in the sense of Sophoclean or Shakespearean drama. Mr. Eliot himself has explored other modes of action and awareness, other, less idealized relationships between poet and audience, both in his verse and in his other plays.

Francis Fergusson. *The Idea of a Theater* (Princeton, N.J., Princeton University Press, 1949), p. 221

Though the play seems very much closer to *Sejanus* than to *Every Man in His Humour* one cannot feel that it was strange of Jonson to call *Volpone* a comedy. Some such description was usual on the title-pages of his times and of the two chief he chose the least misleading. But when Mr. Eliot calls his new play [*The Cocktail Party*] a comedy he seems to me to be closer to the position of a Shakespeare calling *Macbeth* a comedy on the strength of the Porter Scene. Only the incidentals in the play are, in fact, comic and, though on the stage they should be much more effective, on paper they barely deserve the adjective. I suppose that the more perspicacious readers will think of Dante and accept the description in the very limited sense in which it seems intended; the rest are likely, however, to yield to the general chorus of the dramatic critics, to accept the play as "witty" and "delightful," and to get little further into it than the title might seem to tempt them to get. If they find it unsatisfactory it will be on the grounds that parts of it are dull and not because—what is surely the real criterion for judgment—it is unsuccessful on the terms that it prescribes for itself.

A good deal of the play, and particularly that part of it that relates to Celia Coplestone, is a development of the ideas handled in *The Family Reunion,* and the reader will be well advised to discard any presuppositions which the use of the term "Comedy" may raise and to treat the play with the same sobriety that he would bring to its predecessor. Like *The Family Reunion* it is an attempt to discuss religious topics in theatrical terms and, again like that play, it essays this discussion by using situations from modern life.

John Peter. *Scrutiny.* Spring, 1950, p. 61

A play is not fully "out"—Bernard Shaw and Henry James agreed on this point—until we have both seen the stage production and had the text in our hands. By this test . . . Mr. Eliot's play [*The Cocktail Party*] is only half produced—except for those who saw it in Edinburgh and Brighton, or for the Americans. . . . It is difficult to judge how the text will strike those who have not seen the production. But I who have can vouch for its being highly effective with the kind of audience which probably does not read (and would not necessarily enjoy if it did read) Mr. Eliot's poetry. . . . But this success is achieved at a price. The text makes it clear that we lose in depth and richness what we gain in ease and speed.

Of course Mr. Eliot does not take the drawing-room comedy conventions perfectly seriously. There is a touch of slyness in his use of interruptions, telephone calls, door bells, not dissimilar to that which Bernard Shaw displayed in his early plays towards the current melodramatic conventions. But Mr. Eliot uses these conventions and devices so effectively that the play, together with whatever larger implications it tries to carry, slips down the ordinary theatregoer's throat as smoothly as an oyster. In this sense at least he may be said, with this play, to have achieved a more direct contact with ordinary human beings than he has ever achieved before. If the texture of the verse here is much less dense than it was in *The Family Reunion*—carries less overtones and richness of associations—it is yet remarkably lively and witty, pointed and shapely, and achieves a kind of Wildean elegance while retaining Mr. Eliot's very personal rhythm, idiom and irony. . . . Behind the easy comedy façade flicker all the time the disturbing shadows of a world behind the world. He creates two layers of living and keeps them moving in the same ambit, and he keeps our expectation alive all the way through to know how they will finally fit.

T. C. Worsley. *NSN*. March 18, 1950, p. 322

[Celia's] sufferings are dwelt on, are indeed gloated over, and no doubt this is consonant with Mr. Eliot's religious outlook and with his "comedy." But aesthetically, the sufferings disturb the reader and distract him. The Christian ethic of atonement, which has been impending over his head since the end of the second act, comes down with too sudden a bump. He hears the doctor-priests analysing the successful martyrdom as they sip their drinks, and he wonders.

The difficulties of *The Cocktail Party* do not extend to its diction. It is most beautifully and lucidly written. Mr. Eliot can do whatever he likes with the English language. This time he has selected a demure chatty verse-form which seems to be like prose, but it is full of turns and subtle echoes, and always open for the emotional intensity he occasionally needs. On the stage, such diction may well carry all before it, and, reinforced by the sound stagecraft, may place affairs in a less puzzling perspective.

E. M. Forster. *List*. March 23, 1950, p. 533

In criticism of a play of this kind [*The Cocktail Party*], I think we are involved in a larger number of judgments than is normal. Not only do we have to estimate the play which most people saw—the rather amusing and bewildering secular comedy with Christian overtones—but we also have to come to terms with the total play—the Christian play *and* its secular mask. Judging a Christian play means, I think, judging the Christianity of the play as well as the way that Christianity gets into the drama. If Eliot is dramatically creating a Christian society, you will have to criticize that society when you criticize the play, for the play happens to be inseparable from the society and the Christian experience it creates. Finally, you have to judge the way in which the exterior is related to the interior: how well has it been made possible for a perceptive reader to make his way from the outside in? I am not sure that all these judgments are yet possible in our present ignorance of the play, but I should like to put forward several points.

There is something imprudent about asking whether the popularity of a popular play is deserved. Given Eliot's purpose—a profound play in popular disguise—it is perhaps enough that the play was popular. But it seems to me a miscarriage of the artist's job if his reputation does his work for him, and I think Eliot's reputation is very much at the root of the play's popularity. I doubt that this was intentional: Eliot could not have foreseen that his audiences were as anxious to move about on his level as he was to operate on theirs. But this fact has made it difficult to estimate whether or not *The Cocktail Party* is viable as a popular play. On the whole, I doubt that it is. True, it is amusing, it is polished, well-constructed, even "different," and it has a readily accessible moral intent. But as a secular comedy it will not bear comparison to Coward or to Shaw, and it is difficult to see, on the interpretation of the popular reviews, that the play has been more than an interesting *tour de force*. Quite simply, it was not written in the dramatic mode demanded of a popular play, and that demand has to be met, more or less, if the purpose of the play is to succeed. It is, of course, a difficult thing to write one play which has two different surfaces. But I suspect Eliot's failure is due to his not having understood just *how much* of some things a popular play demands from the dramatist; this, I think, is a part of his judgment, as a Christian, upon the world of "a thousand lost golf balls." It impoverishes the play.

William Arrowsmith. HudR. Autumn, 1950, pp. 424–25

Mr. Eliot's creative work in the drama is small in quantity: it is also, one hopes, unfinished. As yet, there are the three major plays—*Murder in the Cathedral, The Family Reunion,* and *The Cocktail Party*; the important fragments of *Sweeney Agonistes*; and, though it cannot really be said to count, *The Rock*. On these few works a radical innovation in the European drama has been based, and recognition of their quality and influence is general. Assertion of the importance of Eliot's dramatic experiments, which for some people and in several places and not so long ago was a minor crusade, is now an established and metalled road of pilgrimage. The change is partly due to a recognition of the achievement itself; it is perhaps even more due to "the *susurrus* of popular repetition," and to the perhaps final act of contemporary literary faith, commercial success. In any case, strict critical assessment of the achievement, in the context of modern dramatic development as a whole, is particularly necessary. The plays are no longer isolated successes, but the beginning of a movement; we must try to see where Eliot's influence is taking the drama. Moreover, even the small body of the work contains a wide variety, both of method and of success; the time for proclamation of the work as a manifesto is past; we must be concerned now with precise distinctions and discriminations.

Raymond Williams. *Drama from Ibsen to Eliot* (London,
Chatto & Windus, 1952), p. 223

It is not one of the motives of *The Rock* to suggest to the audience a negative way of sanctity through contemplation or martyrdom. The effort of the saint to transcend time by union with God differs from this affirmative law of service to the Church, and to Christ through the Church, by labors of body and mind which sanctify time "under the aspect of eternity." *The Rock* contains, in other words, a philosophy of using time rather than of escaping from it, of focusing upon the life of the wheel as the means to attain the point rather than of neglecting the wheel—nature and time and man's active life—for the sake of a more immediate communion. Yet ultimately both ways are the same if every moment under the aspect of eternity is synchronous with the moment of the Incarnation, which has redeemed all the moments of time that meet and become eternal in it; the saint's absorption in the moment of Incarnation brings him no closer to God than does the worker's absorption in the moment of his toil. But it is doubtful whether these themes, as handled by Eliot, furnish anything to the average public listener's understanding. They are hard to trace and compare even on close reading. One suspects that much of the choric verse could convey little meaning when recited; it would merely punctuate the shifts of action. These facts are regrettable, for this verse admirably fulfills the ambition of Eliot not only to make poetry have an auditory force but to put it where it is ideally heard— in the theater. Obviously the choruses, referring in their themes to serious and potentially very dramatic situations, contain also a comedy of time and eternity that latently unifies an irregular, episodic train of incidents.

Grover Smith, Jr. *T. S. Eliot's Poetry and Plays*
(Chicago, University of Chicago Press, 1956), pp. 178–79

Murder in the Cathedral is a remarkable evocation of Christian fears; remarkable for the strength of these fears and the horrible beauty in which they are dressed; remarkable, too, for the religious convictions from which they spring. The year in which it was published was 1935. If this was a godless and frivolous period, frivolity masking the guilt and uncertainty of our western behaviour, and if there was once a better behaviour, running in the churchly times of Mr. Eliot's choice, then this play comes like Hamlet's portrait of his father which he shows to Gertrude. Look on this, it says, and reform yourself. The author's purpose is as serious as Hamlet's and as violent. But Hamlet was violent because he was going off his head for worry lest the ghost prove false; Mr. Eliot's violence does not always seem so straightforward as this, but rather to be used as a cover for some thoughts that are equivocal, as in the speeches the knights make to justify their murder. In these speeches may be seen all that Mr. Eliot believes, and thinks we should believe, about the sickness of states and the lies of statesmen, and the shared guilt of the public, "living and partly living," who allow smooth-speaking fools and villains to lead them astray. But this does not seem a constructive political opinion, it seems rather childish, as if he thought men did not sometimes have to govern, as if he thought that by the act of governing they became at once not men but monsters. It is a disingenuous and not uncommon thought, it is one aspect of the arrogance of art and the arrogance of highmindedness divorced from power, it is something one should not put up with. But just as Shakespeare's poor Gertrude, who has all the same more spirit than Mr. Eliot's people of Canterbury, was struck with swords to the heart when Hamlet showed her the Royal Dane's picture, so audiences and readers of this play are meant to be struck. But what, in fact, is the effect? Uneasiness, I think—to begin with. And not because we are drawn into the guilt of the two sorts of sinners who are depicted here, the sinners who are powerful in action and the sinners who are feeble and small and too frightened to act at all. No, it is the uneasiness of dubiety.

Stevie Smith. In Neville Braybrooke, ed., *T. S. Eliot:*
A Symposium for His Seventieth Birthday (New York,
Farrar, Straus & Cudahy, 1958), pp. 170–71

The Confidential Clerk is a much more successful play than *The Cocktail Party*. Think of the integrity of tone in *The Confidential Clerk,* which the earlier play lacked. It will be recalled that the most serious flaw in *The Cocktail Party* was the failure to bring into harmonious relation the two actions and the two worlds represented. This defect has been completely eliminated in *The Confidential Clerk.* In this play the two worlds impinge: although different, they are presented as being not completely discontinuous; they acknowledge the reality of a common, circumstantial world. It is important to emphasise this consideration because at least one critic of repute, William Arrowsmith, has argued that the play shows "a gnostic denial of the reality of the world." He maintains that Colby is an inadequate presentation of the incipiently perfect Christian life. It is just because the positive

Christian in Colby has been negatively defined as the denial of the world, he argues, that Colby is interesting neither as a Christian nor a man. All that his Christianity comes to is renunciation of worldly love, father, and vocation. He maintains, finally, that it is this doctrine of negative transcendence, steadily denying dignity or reality to the illusions of the world which the play is intended to transfigure, that impoverishes its human characters and makes their conversion a hollow ritual. These comments on *The Confidential Clerk* are probably remnants of the critic's distaste for *The Cocktail Party;* the philosophical case against Eliot had far more cogency in the case of the earlier play. The clue to *The Confidential Clerk* is indeed *The Cocktail Party,* both in its similarities and, no less, in its differences.

Indeed, pausing to consider the two plays again in association, one realises that *The Confidential Clerk* is in fact a *critique* of the moral rhetoric of *The Cocktail Party*. The theme of *The Cocktail Party* is restated, but with a difference which not only redeems it as doctrine but strengthens it as drama. It is unnecessary to present the doctrine as either prior or secondary to the drama; one is happy to find that a more humane presentation of existence and a more harmonious dramatic unity are now available in the same play.

> Denis Donoghue. *The Third Voice* (Princeton, N.J., Princeton University Press, 1959), pp. 153–54

The growth of *Sweeney Agonistes* into a completed play appears to have been inhibited by Eliot's two interrelated difficulties with the drama, his reluctance to conceive drama as primarily an orchestrated action, and his bias toward a poetry that exteriorizes but does not explicate the locked world of the self. The former is not even partially solved until, in *The Confidential Clerk,* the dénouement readjusts the values of five people: the first real modification of Eliot's generic Lazarus plot in which the man who returns from the dead, Prufrock or some other, passes across the stage possessed by his own doom and merely sets surfaces rippling. The second difficulty inheres in the Lazarus plot itself, for this plot turns on the fact that Lazarus, however he may ache for communion, cannot "tell you all" (though if a lady, "settling a pillow by her head, should say: 'That is not what I meant at all,' " he can always adopt Sweeney's solution and drown her). It comes to be solved only in appearance, by making the verse so light that we seem to see through it. The characters of the later, finished plays remain inviolable monads, and (making a virtue of this necessity) the theme of the plays, like that of *Sweeney,* depends on the fact that they are inviolate. If some of them change, it is they who will that change. Eliot becomes very resourceful in giving them means of making conversation, one reason why he prefers a drawingroom milieu and a convention of urbane chit-chat more varied, though no less confining, than the *Sweeney* jazz-matrix.

Subduing these two inherent contradictions between his poetic method and the nature of the acted drama afforded Eliot a program for thirty years' intermittent work with the stage. He conceived in addition another outstanding obligation, which was to finish the unfinished *Sweeney Agonistes* itself. It was ultimately finished after some fifteen years, rewritten from beginning to end and entitled *The Family Reunion*.

Hugh Kenner. *The Invisible Poet: T. S. Eliot* (New York, Harcourt, Brace & World, 1959), pp. 234–35

Considered as a literary problem, the revival of poetic drama is feasible, for as Eliot has said: "A literature is different from a human life, in that it can return upon its own past, and develop some capacity which has been abandoned." But the problem is not a purely literary problem. Eliot has perceived this more clearly than anyone, and has perceived also that the requisite wholeness of outlook can only come from religion, for nothing else comprehends all aspects of human life. And, from one point of view, his plays have been a subtle demonstration of the relevance of religion to all spheres of human activity. They throw light on aspects of modern life normally thought of as removed from the "sphere" of religion as well as on areas of experience that modern psychology and sociology fail to take account of. Because they are implicitly and not explicitly Christian, they surprise people into an awareness of the meaning and implications of Christianity. In *The Idea of a Christian Society,* Eliot says: "A Christian education would primarily train people to be able to think in Christian categories." This is, in a sense, what his later plays have been unobtrusively doing. Eliot has therefore been contributing to the creation of the kind of wholeness of outlook without which poetic drama cannot be accepted as the normal mode of drama.

David E. Jones. *The Plays of T. S. Eliot* (Toronto, University of Toronto Press, 1960), pp. 214–15

Like Coleridge's, Eliot's range of work is notably of a kind. Therefore it may be appropriate to call upon evidence of his thinking from a different context. In his seminal book *Notes towards a Definition of Culture* we may read this: "Neither a classless society, nor a society of strict and impenetrable social barriers is good; each class should have constant additions and defections; the classes, while remaining distinct, should be able to mix freely; and they should all have a community of culture with each other which will give them something in common." The people of Eliot's drama have in a sense been moving towards another community of culture, one which seems to have thrown over the very additions and defections which he declared were essential to a vital society. Acknowledged distinctions between tones and attitudes were a source or real dramatic vigour in his earlier writing, which was then dramatically capable of bringing both tragic and comic life to his stage. Now the ironic pincer of contrasting planes of sensibility has relaxed its grip, and his tragicomic interest has finally slipped away. As we watch his latest play, *The Elder Statesman*, we are distinctly not involved. We sit like a smug audience of psychiatrists listening as their patient, Lord Claverton, strips himself of his illusions for purely clinical purposes.

J. L. Styan. *The Dark Comedy* (Cambridge, Cambridge University Press, 1962), pp. 186–87

The Elder Statesman is a fitting play with which to close a study of Eliot's drama for it stresses the quality of divine resolution and reconciliation to God's will through human love which are the keynotes of Eliot's thought in his most recent writings. Both the relationship between Lord Claverton and his daughter and the playwright's use of *Oedipus at Colonus* as his Greek source are important elements in establishing the play's tone.

The poet's attitude of conciliation and resolution of differences is also evident in the fact that he has removed the last interference between himself and his audience by changing his dramatic tone of voice from that of farce to that of romantic comedy in order to make the mood of the surface compatible with the play's religious theme of the relationship between human and divine love. Indeed, so well has the author matched his surface action to his deeper meanings that *The Elder Statesman*, at first, seems to conceal no further undercurrents of meaning than those present in the relationship between Lord Claverton and his children and their mutual search for personal happiness.

Carol H. Smith. *T. S. Eliot's Dramatic Theory and Practice* (Princeton, N.J., Princeton University Press, 1963), pp. 214–15

A decade has passed since the end of Eliot's playwriting life. As I have reviewed the rich experience of twenty-five years' work with him, certain features of that work stand out in my mind. Eliot was always determined to go on growing. It was not merely that he did not want to repeat himself: it was that he always saw deficiencies to overcome, problems to solve, possibilities to explore. Having staked a convincing claim to be the foremost English poetic dramatist of our century, he proceeded to challenge his own position by trying to do the most difficult thing—to write verse plays of contemporary life. He achieved a verse form perfectly suited to this purpose. He advanced with each experiment his mastery of the playwright's craft; and the themes which remained central in his thinking were given a great variety of expression. His gift for the precise delineation of character, already seen as early as Prufrock and Sweeney, was effectively developed in the comedies written after the Second World War.

I am sure that these plays, as well as the earlier ones, will be found to have a permanent place in the repertory of English drama. Yet I feel that, by adopting this pattern of ironic social comedy, Eliot placed upon his genius a regrettable limitation. He tied himself to social, and still more to theatrical, conventions which were already outworn when the plays were written. Perhaps they reflect an unconscious reversion to the drama that Eliot must have seen as a young theatregoer before 1914. At any rate, the result was that, while he was working successfully to free his dramatic verse from the exhausted post-Shakespearean forms, he was submitting his dramatic form to the same kind of constriction.

And to do so, he put his poetry, as he says, "on a thin diet." We have seen the progressive diminution of poetry in these plays, quite deliberately achieved. The poet's skill is still supremely evident in the choice of language, and his inspiration often peeps through it; but too much of his energy is devoted to the correct expression of unimportant social niceties. The comedy is often delightful, but one pays too great a price for it in prolixity; the comedy of *Sweeney* is more concise, and its comic form is an evident reflection of the depths beneath. Of *The Cocktail Party* this is still true, and in a more extended work. But even here, the rationing of the poetry has begun.

E. Martin Browne. *The Making of T. S. Eliot's Plays*
(Cambridge, Cambridge University Press, 1969), pp. 342–43

What makes *The Cocktail Party* finally unsatisfactory is not of course the unpleasantness of its characters, nor the blackness of its jokes, but the insistence that all this is not so, that it is a play about heaven as well as about hell. Here, of course, the Coward formula works against Eliot's intention, rather as do the Wilde mannerisms against the pious conclusions of *The Confidential Clerk*. For though the formula allows for a good deal of oddity—it can accommodate an unprofessional psychiatrist, a son choosing his parents from a plethora of candidates, even a "suburban Pallas Athene," granting wishes all round—what it does not allow are situations of domestic snugness and sweetness, such as *The Cocktail Party* offers. Ideas of conversion and reform are alien to it; when Eggerson predicts a future for Colby as chapel organist reading for orders the effect is as grotesque as though *Design for Living* were to end with Gilda taking up welfare work.

In selecting a form giving splendid opportunities for exploring conditions of alienation but none at all for solutions in terms of "ordinary, social morality," Eliot followed his theatrical instinct, though only by making things difficult for himself as a moralist.

Katharine Worth. In Graham Martin, ed., *Eliot in
Perspective* (New York, Humanities Press, 1970), pp. 164–65

Eliot's dramatic efforts can be seen as attempts to objectify, in what he later called the "third voice" of poetry, certain pressing if obscure personal preoccupations. The exceptional individual who is separated from those around him by a fatal burden of consciousness and insight is recurrent, and can be expressed in a criminal, like Sweeney, or a saint, like Becket, or a character who has elements of both, like Harry Monchensey. The distinction between those who are elected to a peculiar destiny—whether salvation or damnation is immaterial—and the decent but imperceptive multitude was fundamental to Eliot's apprehension of experience, and can be seen as a highly personal variation on a major Romantic theme.

Bernard Bergonzi. *T. S. Eliot* (New York,
Macmillan, 1972), p. 149

Eliot was an extremely conscious artist who knew what he wanted to do, and who had the genius and the patience to pursue his aim to what he considered a satisfactory end. His aim was to win for poetic drama the place which it no longer held with the average theatre public. He did not attempt, like Giraudoux or Anouilh, to modernize myths through the use of topical language, situations and characters, and neither was he laboriously Freudian in the style of O'Neill in *Mourning Becomes Electra*. What he did was to weave modern, everyday situations into the framework of an ancient myth and then to deepen these situations down to the point where, through the transparency of the naturalistic surface, shines the immanent perennial reality of affective truths which are valid for all men at all times. Being a religious writer in the sense that he was constantly concerned with the interplay of immanence and transcendence, whether he disguised his pursuits under secular terminologies and analogies or used straightforward Christian symbolism and references, Eliot was always in search of the kind of truth which relates his dramatic characters to the society to which they belong, and, beyond that, to a God-made creation.

He used Greek myths in his last four plays, and in some instances he has so well covered up his tracks that, had he not declared his debt to the Greek dramatists, probably no one would have discovered it. Whether it is a comedy like *The Confidential Clerk* or a serious drama which, though it ends with death, as in the case of *The Cocktail Party,* is also a kind of comedy, the naturalistic surface of the situations and of the characters always casts out long shadows which plunge deep into the perenniality of human life. Eliot is in this respect both Ibsenian and Strindbergian. His "naturalism" is a complex structure of essential traits and elements acting as a façade to hold the attention of the audience, which, more often than not, finds itself unexpectedly out of its depth, and which, once it has regained the shore, spends its time trying to discover, with the help of very ingenious critics, how it was lured away towards the open sea and the depths, where it caught a frightening glimpse of the hidden reality that is a reflection of "le Dieu caché."

Joseph Chiari. *T. S. Eliot: Poet and Dramatist*
(London, Vision, 1972), pp. 118–19

"Nothing is more dramatic than a ghost," says Eliot, and his remark offers an illuminating technical insight into every play he wrote. It also has the virtue of forcing us to think specifically about drama, rather than, say, prosody or moral philosophy. Eliot's own practice as a critic and reputation as a poet have tended to concentrate discussion on either the versification and language of his plays or their Christian implications, and this, while leading to much excellent and valuable criticism, has helped promote a serious misunderstanding of his achievement as a dramatist—as a writer, that is, whose texts are designed to allow a group of actors to shape an audience's experience in a theater over a finite interval of time. The possum-like tone Eliot reverts to in discussing most aspects of his dramaturgy other than verse and idiom has encouraged the notion that in matters of dramatic design, particularly the shaping of the action and the use of dramatic convention, Eliot was content to follow the techniques of the commercial theater, and not always the most up-to-date techniques at that. The picture that emerges seems to be of an Eliot laboring to do indifferently what Noel Coward did well, in the hope that verse meditations on the Christian life might somehow be smuggled to an audience while it was being diverted by boulevard entertainment. But if we allow Eliot the benefit of the doubt and approach his plays as the work of a serious dramatist, we can form quite a different impression of their design and of the originality and value of their achievement.

Michael Goldman. In A. Walton Litz, ed., *Eliot in
His Time* (Princeton, N.J., Princeton University Press,
1973), pp. 155–56

Eliot's plays gradually develop from the heroic to the ironic mode, and, so deeply has the ironic mode taken root in our sensibilities that we can say that, for all practical purposes, this means they gradually become more human. *The Elder Statesman* is Eliot's most human play, the one in which he is least concerned with improbable adventures of the spirit which fail to convince because they depend upon ideal longings of a kind which can no longer be effectively realized in a dramatic action. It is in one sense Eliot's most personal play, in another sense his most impersonal, if his remarks in the essay "Ben Jonson" are to be taken as a description of true impersonality:

> The creation of a work of art, we will say the creation of a character in a
> drama, consists in the process of transfusion of the personality, or, in a deeper

sense, the life, of the author into the character. This is a very different matter from the orthodox creation in one's own image.

In all the other plays there is an element of wilful insistence in dealing with matters which Eliot all too clearly didn't understand well enough to convey them in dramatically effective ways. The exception is, perhaps, *Murder in the Cathedral:* the dramatization of a saint and martyr's career can more easily succeed in cases where the dramatic form approaches so close to ritual that the assent of the audience is won almost before the play begins. To dramatize an extraordinary religious sensibility without such a specially prepared audience was a task beyond Eliot's dramatic skills. He did not possess the immediate instinctive understanding which enables the great dramatist to seek and find the way in which assent for the extraordinary can be *won* from his audience. And it took him all his life to move towards the understanding that the ordinary is extraordinary enough; that the painful difficulties of understanding self and understanding others are as fit subjects for the most serious kind of drama as martyrdom or total renunciation of the world.

David Ward. T. S. Eliot between Two Worlds (London,
Routledge & Kegan Paul, 1973), pp. 218–19

The action of T. S. Eliot's comedies takes its origin, as everyone now knows, in Greek theatre: the *Eumenides* in *The Family Reunion,* the *Alcestis* in *The Cocktail Party,* and the *Ion* in *The Confidential Clerk.* The Christian transformation which Eliot effects on themes in these originals enables his plays to possess a mythological framework which gives them an unusual kind of depth, and an explicitly Christian emphasis, indicating a sharply defined view of existence. But the most telling aspect of the plays is that however much is known about Greek drama, Christianity (or even Jungian archetypes) none of these explains their effect, whether being read or seen. If the dramatic experience *could* be explained by a knowledge of the ingredients which had gone into its making, there would of course be no reason to return to these plays because the heart of their mystery would have been plucked out. But renewed acquaintance does not dull the response they produce; and this, I think, is due to the nature of Eliot's success in modifying the tradition of high comedy. . . .

Eliot's extension of the tradition of high comedy remains a qualified success. But his plays do provide that combination of pleasure and interest which belong to a literary and dramatic kind rarely achieved: laughter at human folly, delight in comic situation, seriousness of viewpoint—and a restraint of feeling that enables us to enjoy the comedy without losing sight of its more sombre implications. But the manner in which he adapted the discarded image of a religious world to create, through his verse, a theatre of enlightenment also remains a unique achievement. It was not to be expected that any high comedy in the twentieth century could have the completeness of its great forebears. The religious image was lacking, the social situation too confused and indistinct. It remains astonishing that Eliot achieved high comedy at all; and there can be no doubt that especially in *The Cocktail Party* he did.

P. G. Mudford. *CQ*. Summer, 1974, pp. 132, 140

Trying to see Eliot's dramatic work as a whole is like looking at one of those optical diagrams where, according to the way we look, we see first one then another figure stand out in relief. There is Eliot the ceaseless experimenter, moving from one "possibility" to another, learning from each, and refusing easy solutions. And there is Eliot the preserver, who refused extreme solutions—such as Yeats' withdrawal from the public theatre, and Beckett's struggle to re-create language from its ruins. The experimenter started with a radical modernist approach to dramatic language; the preserver went back, ironically, to the "tradition" of naturalism, elements of which served his desire to "humanise" dramatic language. Whichever way we look, we find much of that "sustained, heroic and indefatigably resourceful quest" which Dr. Leavis finds in the poetry alone. If there is less resourcefulness—or more fatigue—in the growth of Eliot's dramatic language, it is because Eliot withheld from it much of the pressure that went into his poetry. In part this springs from his quest for a "social usefulness" for poetry in the theatre—something increasingly conceived as the need to come to terms with the established conventions of the theatre: even at the cost of taking over a certain load of conventionality, which went against the grain of his creativity (the pull of an inward language).

The conservative impulse in Eliot's dramatic language is, clearly, inseparable from his increasingly conservative conception of the viable theatre and, beyond it, of the Christian-Classical culture under extreme attack. The language itself had to be preserved. We may apply to his dramatic language what he said of poetry: "it should help not only to refine the language of the time, but to prevent it from changing too rapidly: a development of the language at too great a speed would be a development in the sense of progressive deterioration, and that is our danger today." Eliot recognised that the stuff of dramatic language, human speech, was unique—it was not for him, after *Sweeney Agonistes,* to speed up its development (or subject it to abstract pattern-making) on the moving platform of modern art, as though it were music, or only human noise.

Andrew K. Kennedy. *Six Dramatists in Search of a Language* (Cambridge, Cambridge University Press, 1975), pp. 128–29

With the completion of *Four Quartets* Eliot ceased to be a poet, and became in his art simply a dramatist. His pre-war drama had worked on both levels, the human and the transcendental; but in the three plays produced in the last twenty years of his life the metaphysical poet disappears in the writer of well-made drawing-room comedies. Regrettable as this may be, it was not simply a consequence of failing powers. For one thing, the poet could only have repeated himself, having said all that he had to say in the perfected Quartets. For another, it is just by their not being poetry that the late plays add something to his *oeuvre*. It is not a new vision that they offer, but a progressive revision of that of the poet who would be a saint. *The Cocktail Party* transposes *The Family Reunion* and *Four Quartets* into the audience's own terms, and in doing so significantly alters the emphasis towards the occupations of "most of us." In *The Confidential Clerk* the dramatist develops a point of view distinct from that of the poet, and for the first time in Eliot's work the poet is observed in a light other than his own. Then *The Elder Statesman,* which is in certain respects a summing up of the whole of the poet's life-work, brings us at the end to a radical revaluation of it.

This last play gives us something genuinely new and shocking to reckon with. In it the poet, that ideal, elected self, fashioned throughout a lifetime's death in love, who had already turned back to be the dramatist of his world, assumes an ordinary personality and declares himself a human lover like any other. By way of the dedicatory verses with their obvious connection with certain passages in the play, Eliot as good as made a personal appearance on the stage, affirming his need to be loved by a woman and his joy in the liberating experience of sexual love. This was to come back out of the refining fire and through the looking-glass into the secret rose-garden—to go back on the poetry, and to give the last word to the human being whom the poet had all his life been struggling to transform and to transcend.

A. D. Moody. Thomas Stearns Eliot, Poet (Cambridge, Cambridge University Press, 1979), p. 267

GALSWORTHY, JOHN (1867–1933)

I think that in *Justice* as in *Strife,* it is because Mr. Galsworthy so carefully eschews any show of sympathy with one character, or of antipathy against another, that the charge of cinematography is preferred against him. . . . Mr. Galsworthy never takes an unfair advantage. He dispenses with many quite fair advantages. Is this because he is merely a detached and dispassionate observer of life? The reason is the very contrary. It is because he is filled with pity for the victims of a thing he vehemently hates, and because he is consumed with an anxiety to infect his fellowmen with this hatred and this pity, that he strives so unremittingly to be quite impartial. He knows that a suspicion of special pleading would jeopardise his case. . . .

In some of his works he does certainly lay himself open to a (very superficial) charge of inhumanity. In *Strife* he showed us a conflict, and in *Fraternity* a contrast between the poor and the rich; and the implicit moral of the play was that this conflict would be for ever. If things are irremediable, why, it might be asked, harrow us about them? To which, I take it, Mr. Galsworthy's answer would be that to recognize the sadness of things is a duty we owe to honesty, and is good for our souls. In *Justice,* however, there is no fundamental pessimism. . . . No one, nowadays, has a word in defense of solitary confinement. And I shall be surprised if Mr. Galsworthy has not delivered its death-blow. [1910]

Max Beerbohm. Around Theatres (New York,
Simon and Schuster, 1954), pp. 566–68

It should be the tritest commonplace to say that no playwright can make great drama out of little people. The naturalistic drama has had opportunities enough in Europe during the past thirty years, and it has justified itself only in proportion as it has created exceptional figures and splashed the grey background of actuality with living colours; in proportion, that is to say, as it has become unnaturalistic. Its naturalism is then only external. Mr. Galsworthy's is internal. The characters of *Justice* are grey at heart. The play has many extraordinarily moving passages. It is a fine destructive attack upon solitary confinement as a part of the prison system, but it is not a tragedy, and it is not great drama. Mr. Galsworthy has a place of his own upon the modern stage. Every play of his has a strongly marked individual atmosphere; his characters are distinctive without being distinguished. He understands the limitations of the theatre as well as its advantages, and he has never sacrificed drama to dialectics. At the beginning of the new movement the English theatre was out of touch alike with art, with ideas and with actual life. The latter two are only accessories—but let that pass. Bernard Shaw and Mr. [Harley Granville] Barker brought the ideas; in a measure, too, the art. Mr. Galsworthy's preoccupation is with actuality. A gulf still remains.

Ashley Dukes. Modern Dramatists (London, Frank Palmer,
1911), pp. 149–50

Mr. Galsworthy's plot-workmanship is excellent. He realizes every step of the action, uses detail in incident with most telling effect, and never fails in probability. All necessary facts, including those preceding the action of the play, he brings into the framework of his plot with perfect ease, without using the clumsy mechanism of the inset narrative: the necessary facts about Mrs. Gwyn's marriage, in *Joy*; Robert's invention and its insufficient reward by the company, in *Strife*; the sordid tragedy of Ruth Honeywill's marriage, in *Justice*; the earlier trouble of Jones and Mrs. Jones, and the parallel earlier fault of Jack Barthwick, in *The Silver Box*. He uses contrast and comparison admirably, especially in *The Silver Box*. Dramatic suspense, when at an important point the action hangs in the balance for a moment, occurs less often than we should expect; the finest examples are in *Strife,* in the parallel scenes of Roberts's appeal to the men and John Anthony's to the directors, and in the last act of *The Eldest Son*. Similarly, though he is too good a playwright to forget the value of the tense dramatic moment, Mr. Galsworthy never strains his material to this end; and here he stands in striking contrast to Shaw, Pinero, [Otto Erich] Hartleben, [Hermann] Sudermann—indeed to most modern dramatists. His method is to reveal meaning in every moment, rather than to lead up to a few great moments. He combines intellectual with emotional appeal, not only making the spectator feel, but also stimulating him to inquire the significance of the situation which moves him.

A. R. Skemp. In *Essays and Studies by Members of the English Association,* Vol. IV (Oxford, Clarendon, 1913), pp. 167–68

One of the remarkable points about Mr. Galsworthy's work is that he does not care or is unable to characterise his *personae,* except in the most formal fashion. Mr. Galsworthy is something of a poet, and his drama is at its best when it is most spiritual and imaginative. Characterisation is the work of the writer of comedy. Character itself is always more or less comic, being a deviation from the norm, a subtle caricature of some general ideal. Yet through Mr. Galsworthy's genius has not much of the comic spirit in it, he uses the figures of comedy for his plays. He takes traditionally comic figures, such as Sir William Cheshire in *The Eldest Son* or John Barthwick in *The Silver Box,* and moves these figures about in the rarefied monochrome of his social plays.

His outlook is broad and spacious. It is the outlook of a highly imaginative man. But this sensitive imagination seems to satisfy itself by creating only atmospheres and environments peopled by stock figures. It expresses itself in the drama of social and economic rather than personal crises, though it spiritualises and makes them fine in the same way that the writer of more human drama uplifts us by evoking ecstasy from the clash of temperaments. Here is at once the success and the failure of Mr. Galsworthy's art. He humanises social contradictions—and drama is the spirit of contradiction—till they become real and poignant, and he dehumanises his own characters by making them the servants of a theory, or a condition, or a social anomaly. In *Justice,* for instance, not one of the characters can breathe freely. They are all in prison, the police, the lawyers, the chaplain, the prison doctor, as much as poor Falder himself. Yet, on the other hand, to have extracted so poignant a piece of dramatic art from the difficult medium of a civic institution like imprisonment is a triumph of a high order. The scene in the prison, when from the tortured souls of the prisoners there escapes— more dramatic than a cry—the sudden madness which passes from cell to cell, and makes them beat their hands on the doors, is one of the highest moments that the modern English drama has known.

Edward Storer. BR. Nov., 1913, pp. 255–56

Mr. Galsworthy has all the thoughtfulness and earnestness of [Eugène] Brieux, and he is an incomparably finer artist. Brieux has never written anything equal to *The Silver Box* or *Strife,* while the subtlety and fantasy displayed in *The Pigeon* are wholly beyond the grasp of the Frenchman. The two men are most nearly alike in *Justice* and *La robe rouge.* But *Justice,* with all its stirring scenes, is quite inferior to the three other plays (just mentioned) by its author, and is inferior for precisely the same reason that makes Brieux inferior to Galsworthy.

Brieux is primarily an advocate, Galsworthy is primarily an artist. Many playwrights whose works are devoid of cerebration and who succeed merely by "action" and excitement and suspense, and the familiar bag of tricks, could take lessons in technique from Mr. Galsworthy. Omitting the content (if one could) *The Silver Box* is a magnificent play. Not even Clyde Fitch, that master of beginnings, ever captured an audience more suddenly or more completely than they are caught at the first rise of the curtain in this drama. It is a perfect opening, and from the start every speech and every gesture push the action along to the triumphant conclusion. It is extraordinary that an author's first piece should be so weighty in thought and so brilliant in action.

William Lyon Phelps. Essays on Modern Dramatists (New York,
Macmillan, 1921), pp. 112–13

Mr. John Galsworthy belongs to the modern school of dramatists, that is to say, he believes that drama should treat of the actual conditions of life without reserve; it must be conducted, however, in a frank and open spirit which shall not take sides in any controversy, but attempt to keep the balance of opinions even. If there is one characteristic more than another which belongs to his work it is his impartiality. It is a question whether this is an attribute which improves the range and value of the dramatist's work. Sometimes it is almost an annoying feature. We find ourselves wishing that in the play of forces which Mr. Galsworthy has set in motion before us in vivid fashion there was also some hint, or indication, as to which side the author himself took in the controversy. We might even pardon, possibly we might welcome, a burst of indignant rhetoric which should give us Mr. Galsworthy's real estimate as to the final truth of things. We might have to discount such rhetoric on the ground that it is avowedly the utterance of a partisan, but, at all events, we should leave the theatre with some definite issue in our minds, with which we might or might not agree, but which would represent an approach to a dramatic *dénouement*. This, however, is not Mr. Galsworthy's way. If we take a play like *Strife,* we find that the two sides are carefully contrasted in their aims and methods—the capitalists with their views, the workmen with their passionate revolt against the conditions of their existence—and we are not invited to take merely superficial aspects of such antagonisms, but to observe the intimate tendencies and motives of the personages, and the differences of atmosphere to be found in the two camps. David Roberts speaks for the men at the tin works, John Anthony for the proprietors. Both of these represent extreme views which finally are allowed to cancel each other. Both Anthony and Roberts are sacrificed by the parties to which they belong, and the final conclusion reached is precisely that compromise which had originally been suggested before the strike began. When one leaves the theatre after listening to a play like this, it is not unnatural for the spectator to ask on which side his sympathies are supposed to be enlisted; and if the answer comes that the dramatist does not want us to take sides, but to keep a clear and open mind and recognise the amount of justice which exists in the one camp and in the other, it is impossible to avoid a feeling of dissatisfaction with a play which is intended to excite the keenest interest, but which finally resolves itself into a drawn battle.

W. L. Courtney. *Fortnightly.* March, 1922, pp. 441–42

The dominant quality of Mr. Galsworthy's work is realism of detail. In the minutiae of local colour and in accuracy of setting he is one of the cleverest and most careful dramatic craftsmen of the day. His anxiety to achieve realistic effect leads him to an abhorrence of the unrealistic theatricality which characterizes so many modern plays. Anxious to show us a slice of life he avoids the conventional situation of the theatre and the device of working up to a striking episode at the fall of the curtain. His dialogue is very natural. Although it is crisp and pointed, it does not scintillate with the unnatural theatrical brilliancy of Wilde and Pinero.

The greatest menace to Mr. Galsworthy's realism is his didactic tendency; but his skill enables him to cope with the demon of didacticism, and with the utmost subtlety he succeeds in giving it ample scope and yet in keeping it within the bounds of realism. This he achieves by the device of creating occasions for speech-making—the same trick as is found in some of Mr. [Harley Granville] Barker's plays. Mr. Galsworthy uses this means in *Strife* to give Anthony, Edgar, Roberts and Thomas an opportunity for commenting at length, each from his own point of view, on the central problem of the play. In *Justice* Frome, the barrister, has a chance in the trial scene of making a long speech in which he can propound, on Mr. Galsworthy's behalf, much that the dramatist is anxious to plead on the subject of the treatment of criminals. Again, Stephen More, in *The Mob* is made to talk at length, but quite appropriately, on political questions on which Mr. Galsworthy obviously has strong views. [1923]

A. E. Morgan. *Tendencies of Modern English Drama*
(Freeport, N.Y., Books for Libraries Press,
1969), pp. 121–22

What must chiefly impress the reader of [Galsworthy's] plays . . . is the prevailing restlessness and complexity of Galsworthy's world. Here the sunny tracts and smiling landscape are few or none. All is strife, tumult, agitation, beneath a lowering sky. The individual is distracted between the claims of his ideal, it may be, and the claims of kith and kin. The family is divided against itself, so that a man's worst foes are often those of his own household. The ties that bind wife to husband, children to parents, are strained to the utmost, if not broken. Loyalty to one's class involves one in ruinous complications with the members of other classes. Society falls apart into hostile camps. Privacy fights for its life against the impertinent invasion of a curiously prying public. Fraudulent finance casts its dark shadow over half the world.

In general it may be said that the tension, friction, and injustice here revealed spring from a principle of insufficiently checked self-interest. Galsworthy's world, indeed, is the world naturally produced by a century of individualism and economic freedom. We have an aggregate of warring persons, and groups of persons, which has not yet become in the proper sense of the word a social organism, with a sufficiently developed communal consciousness and ethic.

Hence the protecting sanction and encouragement given to the possessive, rather than to the creative, tendencies and dispositions of human nature. Under a system of materialistic determinism, and free, economic, competitive individualism, such as prevailed throughout the nineteenth century, extreme wealth tends to gravitate to one end of the social scale and extreme poverty to the other. This state of things has disastrous ethical and legal, as well as economic results. The power of wealth determines the difference between right and wrong, and even weighs down the scales of justice. In Galsworthy's plays the poor, who have precisely the same instincts as their wealthier fellow-citizens, and would exercise these harmlessly if they possessed economic freedom, are heavily penalized because of their poverty. The petty thief or forger is punished: the large-scale swindler is rewarded. Moral judgments largely reflect social judgments, and social judgments in their turn are mainly determined by financial considerations. The social institutions which are the expression of social judgment, such as the Law and even the Church itself, tend to uphold tradition and give their sanction only to the already existing order, punishing remorselessly any who venture to depart from it.

R. H. Coats. *John Galsworthy as a Dramatic Artist*
(London, Duckworth, 1926), pp. 200–202

Galsworthy draws the neatest pattern of any contemporary dramatist. His plays are studies in parallelism, not in perpendicularity. They are specimens of social contrast, not of individual conflict. Galsworthy, so far as I know, is the first man in the history of the theatre who refuses to mark the cards, is strictly, almost painfully, impartial, and insists on letting the play's meaning rest implicit in the situation and the characters. "Matters change and morals change," he once observed; "men remain, and to set men and the facts about them, down faithfully, so that they draw for us the moral of their natural actions, may also possibly be of benefit to the community. It is, at all events, harder than to set men and facts down, as they ought or ought not to be." Shaw and Galsworthy are poles apart in this respect. Shaw shouts the moral through every convenient mouthpiece, whether appropriately or not; and also writes a lengthy preface to explain the meaning and moral of the play. Galsworthy ruthlessly excises every epigram, witticism, joke which is not in character; and dams back the emotional flood and moralizing impulse of his characters almost at the expense of their humanity. As he himself once wittily observed: "It might be said of Shaw's plays that he creates characters who express feelings which they have not got. It might be said of mine that I create characters who have feelings which they cannot express." It should be added that the inarticulateness of Galsworthy's characters is deliberately imposed on them by their author; Galsworthy insists that by the actions and the circumstances, and not out of the mouths of the characters, shall the story be told and the moral drawn.

Archibald Henderson. *European Dramatists*
(New York, D. Appleton, 1926), pp. 476–77

Mr. Galsworthy's eminence? To what, looking back upon his long and honorable career as a dramatist, has that eminence been due? It is the custom to answer that it is and has been due to certain qualities of mind, an intelligence at once calm and discerning, and one expert in surveying both sides of a question and meditating more or less profoundly the tilting of the scales now this way and now that. But I doubt it. The eminence of Mr. Galsworthy in the field of drama is and has been due to the dignity not of his thought, but to the dignity of his emotions. One can name a number of dramatists with minds on a level with Galsworthy's who have not achieved anything like his eminence, for they have not, like him, possessed synchronously the emotions of scholars and gentlemen. The true mark of an artist is to be found not in his head, but in his heart, or at least in what passes for the seat and capital of his emotions. Many a playwright with a clear head has had muddy emotions, and many a playwright with a soundly reasoning mind has found it corrupted, in dramatic paractice, by cheap feeling. Galsworthy's emotions are those of a civilized gentleman. The emotions of so many of the younger British playwrights of the day are those of wise and sophisticated, and very clever, bounders. [1928]

George Jean Nathan. *The Magic Mirror* (New York, Alfred A. Knopf, 1960), p. 195

Galsworthy is as relentlessly realistic in almost all his plays, as in his novels, and short stories. He shows us things visualised through his temperament, not as many people would prefer to see them. An incorruptible lover of truth, he attempts to shape all his plots and problems, with the greatest impartiality, allowing both sides to air their opinions and throwing light on their ideas in all possible ways.

For him the task lies in the unrolling of the problem, not in its solution. The unrolling of the problem should serve to make us think and reflect, to make us realise, to awaken our interest in what is hitherto unknown to us, or viewed in a wrong light. We ought to understand, not to condemn, to try to approach one another, and be conciliatory.

Drama means strife and contrast, and through the characters in most of his plays contrasts are worked out sharply, yet plasticly. His conflicts are nearly always of a social nature, based on social confrontations. Strange to say, Galsworthy is sometimes reproached for being too theatrical. He certainly flings the spectator at once into the centre of the plot, to ensure his interest in the idea, but the conflicts always arise from the characters themselves, never from abstract ideas. His characters are direct in action, never far-fetched or self-stultifying; they are mostly drawn from the average man and woman of our immediate surroundings. From the very outset he surrounds his play with a peculiar atmosphere of its own, and maintains it throughout, and this, in each case, has something fateful, something inevitable about it. He does not invent a plot for its own sake, but builds it of the varying human attitudes, towards incident, or even, revealing the characters by argument and contest, from which the central idea emerges sharply defined.

Leon Schalit. *John Galsworthy: A Survey* (New York, Charles Scribner's Sons, 1929), pp. 219–20

Unlike Shaw, Galsworthy has no doctrine to preach, although he is as well aware as Shaw of the harshness and absurdities of conventions that no longer correspond to realities. His aim is essentially expository. As he has written: "Every grouping of life and character has its inherent moral; and the business of the dramatist is so to pose the group as to bring the moral poignantly to the light of day." This conception is one to which he has been more faithful than most writers whose theories so often bear only the slightest relation to their own practice. He balances his groups, each composed of various types who, while differing slightly amongst themselves, combine in giving collective expression to the viewpoint of the group as a whole. From the contrasted situation of the groups the public can draw its own moral. Galsworthy pities but he never preaches.

Notwithstanding the essential humanity of the situations and the questions with which he deals, despite an external realism, there is some quality of abstractness in Galsworthy which detracts from his power as a dramatist. Miss Sheila Kaye-Smith, one of the few critics who have rated him more highly as a dramatist than as a novelist, has argued that the very fact that his characters are abstract, that is, types rather than individuals, is an advantage. "Types," she says, "are always more convincing on the stage than individuals, the necessary personal touch being given by the actor." To an age as fiercely interested as the present in problems of personality, of the individual, as skeptical of the value of wasting time upon the consideration of abstractions, Galsworthy's humanitarianism cannot make any lasting appeal. If he were not so skilled in the mechanics of playmaking, his aloofness would be even more deadly than the didacticism of Shaw, for humor is not exactly his strong point. His interests, if not his illusions, are those of his particular period, which never seemed so far off as it does today.

Ernest Boyd. *ThA*. May, 1929, p. 341

Galsworthy's occasional attempts at writing symbolical drama, such as *The Little Dream*—a purely poetic fantasy—and *Windows*—a combination of an inner symbolism with external realism—are scarcely adapted to a writer whose talents so obviously lie in the exploitation of concrete social phenomena. The most successful attempt at symbolical drama is probably to be found in the small play, *The Little Man,* where the central figure emerges as a modern altruistic Christ-like type amid a group of self-centered personalities. And in this play, as in two earlier ones, *The Pigeon* and *Joy,* the author gives us a glimpse of a world that is less inherently tragic than his usual milieu, though in all of them potential tragedy is implicit. It looks as if Galsworthy has been reaching out in various directions in his later plays, but has never discovered a medium better adapted to his special gifts than the early sociological dramas. It is undoubtedly in this group that he has made his greatest contribution to modern dramatic literature.

Henry Alexander. *QQ*. May, 1933, p. 188

Broadly speaking, it is not the curtain-raisers or the experimental plays, not the comedies or the poetical symbolical dramas, not even *The Pigeon,* original and valuable as it is, that we have in mind when we think of Galsworthy as a playwright, but his naturalistic dramas, such works as *The Silver Box, Strife, The Eldest Son, Loyalties,* etc. In number they hardly make up one half of their author's dramatic output; but they are most representative of what may be called the Galsworthian atmosphere, which is no other than the phantasm of Galsworthy's personality.

A general attitude towards life and its problems, the recurrence of a definite set of qualities and defects repeatedly manifested in many guises, and uncompromising faithfulness to an ideal of philosophical sincerity and artistic conscientiousness are the permanent, outstanding features of this work. Throughout it all, we hear an unmistakable note of profound humanity, sometimes of ironical pity for the tragedy of man's condition. There is revealed to us the author's keen perception of some vices of the social structure, above all in what concerns the treatment meted out by the collective body to its component individuals, and with peculiar sensitiveness to the situation of the unhappily married woman, born of an unconscious idealization of womanhood. Flashes of noble indignation are to be observed at every spectacle of hard-heartedness and deliberate cruelty. And a plea rises from the whole for the liberation of the human unit from the burden of persecution and constraint exercised by society and aggravated by the tyranny of caste and tradition, class prejudices and class interests.

The presence of a social subject and philosophical theme in Galsworthy's plays invests these with a certain interest beyond that imparted to them by their artistic quality. At the same time, the nature of the author's creed, his sentimental approach to the problems that force themselves upon his attention, his perception of the distressing irony of things, enable him to make excellent dramatic use of his questions and suggestions and to write serious plays that are not lifeless demonstrations, such as we usually label "plays with a purpose"—that is, with a purpose distinct from the artist's.

V. Dupont. John Galsworthy: The Dramatic
Artist (Cahors, France, Imprimerie Typographique
A. Coueslant, 1942), pp. 195–96

In essence all drama is symbolic; every act and every actor is a refinement of life off-stage, and no object or setting can receive attention from the audience without gaining symbolic value. This offers great freedom to the moralist playwright, who can thereby avoid the fallacy of the specific by creating a general conceptual structure in which his audience can roam freely. Realism, on the other hand, relies for its force on immediacy and particularity—it carries itself to the life of the audience rather than waiting for the audience to make use of it. To use realism to carry a weighty moral argument is thus to bring both into danger. The audience which saw Galsworthy's plays as intensely realistic *was* right, in that it shared his way of looking at life. But we too are right, who see them at best as presenting a special point of view and at worst as unreal, biased, and propagandistic.

In Galsworthy then we may have the case of a potentially great artist who saw the real world and the moral world as coextensive and who neither destroyed his art to make a point (like the propagandists) nor falsified life to suit his audiences' tastes (like the melodramatists). But he was ruined by his desire for realism, reduced to impermanence by the strength of his desire to communicate his great truths with both vivid passion and complete immediacy. There is a strong element of irony in the lasting success of his greatest single scene, that of Falder's isolation in *Justice,* which is the only scene he wrote for a definite propagandist purpose and which was thought to have produced its astonishing effect because it was so intensely realistic. Perhaps the truth is that it made its first impression, and continues to be moving, not because it is a detailed picture of contemporary life. As a burning metaphor of any man in any confinement in any era, it brought the strength of a universal symbol to bear on a contemporary issue.

Gary J. Scrimgeour. *MD*. May, 1964, pp. 74–75

Taking Galsworthy's writings for the theatre as a whole, it can be seen that it was his misfortune to come on the scene with an initial delusion that a play was something less serious, or less important, than a novel at a time when the English stage was in the opening phase of a rebellion against the stagey, and against the exhausted conventions of the "well-made play." When Galsworthy offered *The Silver Box* to the Vedrenne-Barker management at the Court Theatre and launched himself on the world as a dramatist, his offering was snapped up precisely because it was a structureless and antidramatic animation of the thesis that there is one law for the rich and another for the poor. Received by Harley Granville Barker on a Saturday, it was accepted by him on the following Monday. This instant collapse of the walls of Jericho apparently gave Galsworthy the wholly mistaken idea that he had no need to learn more than he already knew about the theatre, and that there was no important distinction to be made between the novelistic and the dramatic. He consequently never developed a feeling for the necessities of dramatic construction, and never reached the level of professional competence as a playwright. *Justice* and *The Silver Box* were his two happiest hits, and they are essentially amateurish. His most successful play from the commercial point of view. *The Skin Game,* now reads like a parody, and the majority of his plays are never far from it in their stagey extravagance of language and plotting.

It would, of course, be altogether unjust to deny the entire corpus of

Galsworthy's work any merit apart from its value as inadvertent self-reve-
lation. He set out to hold a reducing glass up to the world of middle class
custom and aspiration that he knew, and attempted to capture its essences
in his miniature. He did this so successfully that many people can still recognize themselves, their relatives, and the matter of their own lives in his
stories. But Galsworthy was able to do more than to persuade his readers to
identify themselves with his characters, he engaged their interest in what
was to happen next. In the context of his time, he was, for his class, a
master storyteller.

Anthony West. Introduction to *The Galsworthy Reader*
(New York, Charles Scribner's Sons, 1967), pp. xx–xxi

O'CASEY, SEAN (1880–1964)

O'Casey has never written for popularity. Rather the opposite. There is
probably no man more surprised—yes, and even a little embarrassed—by
the meteoric success of *Juno and the Paycock* than its unsophisticated author. And, as the reception of *The Plough and the Stars* now shows, he is
becoming even more fearless in his disregard for the approval or disapproval
of the crowd than ever he was. It is encouraging, too, to note that though
his house may hiss and shout and to some extent pretend to be shocked, yet
they come again, and will continue to do so, in spite of everything. And
strange also as it may seem, the main opposition to his work comes not
from the men whom he debases but from the women whom he glorifies. It
was a women's row in Dublin, and a women's row almost entirely. It appears to be the romantic female, and not the sentimental male, who is
goaded to fury at the state of nakedness in which O'Casey leaves his townspeople.

And yet Dublin as a whole does not seem to be ashamed of her nakedness or of her latest contribution to the international world of letters. Possibly it is because she knows that the only malady from which she suffers is
not an Irish but a world disease. Or possibly because with the originality of
the Celt, she would rather be violent than smug.

As for her new prophet, it is becoming more and more clear that as
a realist he is an impostor. He will tell you the name and address of the
person who made each individual speech in any of his plays, but we are
not deceived by his protestations. His dialogue is becoming a series of
word-poems in dialect; his plots are disappearing and giving place to a
form of undisguised expressionism under the stress of a genius that is
much too insistent and far too pregnant with meaning to be bound by the
four dismal walls of orthodox realism. It will be interesting to see how

long in the future he will try to keep up so outrageous a pretence. [March 11, 1926]

Denis Johnston. In Ronald Ayling, ed.,
Sean O'Casey: Modern Judgements (London,
Macmillan, 1969), p. 85

[*The Plough and the Stars*] takes place immediately before and during the Easter Rebellion instead of during the post-war disturbances in which *Juno and the Paycock* was set. Nevertheless, it would seem to be increasingly obvious that Mr. O'Casey's dramatic inspiration comes almost entirely from the misfortunes of his countrymen during the last decade. Apparently he sees the sequence of revolutionary episodes as one vast drama, and from it selects for his own purposes dramatic episodes which he places against a shrewdly observed background of Irish proletarian life. This would seem to explain the very real lack of structure to be noticed in both these plays, since he conceives the frame of them to be outside of both of them, and many other plays which he has written and, it is to be hoped, will write. He himself sees so clearly a beginning, an end, and a middle in recent Irish history, that he conceives it unnecessary to stress these dramatic props in the segments of that history which he chooses to dramatise.

The Plough and the Stars is a better play than *Juno,* because there are not three distinct strings of plot to unravel—more poignant in the characters selected from Dublin's underworld as mediums for alternate passages of humour and terror. No one of the characters, perhaps, suggests the potential greatness of Captain Boyle, but none of them cheat their promise as did he. . . .

It is my guess that, although Mr. O'Casey will never *construct* a play so as to attain the maximum effect out of its rhythm and movement, he will in his succeeding plays increasingly eliminate such devices and other breaches of dramatic taste, with the result that we shall have greater power with no less of the entertainment which he undoubtedly affords.

Milton Waldman. *LM*. July, 1926, p. 299

Whatever may be the future of Sean O'Casey there is now no doubt that he is a considerable dramatic artist, and a man who is so intimate with the people of his plays that he could not fail to portray them justly. That his work since *Juno* has shown no advance, and that he is disposed to change his locale to London, is disquieting. His success is attributable entirely to his intimate knowledge of his native city, and it is there that his future must be decided. He is a realist of the most uncompromising kind, an ironist, and a traditionalist, much to the disappointment of some critics who expected him to write "proletarian" plays in the new German manner. He has accepted the realist tradition of the Abbey Theatre, and no Irish dra-

matist since the death of Synge is more likely to influence the Irish playwrights of the immediate future. Already it is plain that the methods of
O'Casey are being imitated, even by dramatists whose reputations were
high before the name of O'Casey had been known. The disillusionment of
Ireland has aided O'Casey to popularity, and the success of his plays
makes it certain that Irish drama will remain realistic for a considerable
time to come.

Andrew E. Malone. The Irish Drama (New York,
Charles Scribner's Sons, 1929), pp. 218–19

Life has changed greatly in Ireland since 1914. Not only has the "stage
Irishman" completely disappeared, but his offspring the political playboy
type has become rarer and rarer. The seriousness of the modern revolutionary Irishman contributes to produce a grotesque humour which acts
like Pirandello's little demon and destroys every image created by the
emotions. Sean O'Casey is the dramatist of Ireland who has reflected
these tendencies most unmistakably in modern Ireland. He is the comple-
test expression of the drama of the post-war moment—the drama of the
city, in contrast to the drama of the rural districts. Though Ireland is essentially an agricultural country and her destiny must always rest with the
farmer, she cannot escape the influence of modern mechanical civilisation, which tends to gather all people into cities and hold them together
in serried masses. Even in the golden age of Augustus it was necessary
to call up a Virgil to sing of simple joys of the country, to arrest the city
invasions. In Sean O'Casey the problem of the city becomes paramount,
because he does not set out to describe life in the gilded salons of the
rich, but rather the garrets of the poor. A workman and son of workers,
he was born and bred in the most squalid quarter of Dublin. All through
his life he has lived a life of privations and has gazed at sights of physical and moral degradation. His dramas one by one become the chronicles
of his life in days that were full of despair for his country. He is no idealist to raise up an unsubstantial pageant: he never alters the truth. He
possesses not only the normal gaze of Bernard Shaw, but also a lens to
magnify the details around him. What Goethe said of himself might also
be said of O'Casey: "The organ which enabled me to understand the
world was my eye." Every one of his earlier plays was the result of mature observation: the dramatist remained rigidly objective and became the
sensitive receiver of impressions. He watched his characters work upon
the stage without ever giving his own thoughts. We must not consider
Sean O'Casey a social dramatist like many of his contemporaries, who are
eager to preach against this or that vice by means of thesis-drama; he simply
looks around him and determines to omit none of the details that appear to
him. His spirit of observation is totally different from that of English au-

thors: Sean O'Casey is not Anglo-Saxon in spirit; he is like a man of the Mediterranean, for whom the most important element is not the essence of anything, but rather its presence.

Walter Starkie. In Lennox Robinson, ed., *The Irish Theatre* (London, Macmillan, 1939), pp. 149–51

Mr. O'Casey tells his part of the story in *Inishfallen Fare Thee Well* and *Rose and Crown* (the fourth and fifth volumes of his autobiography). His three plays of the mid-twenties made enemies but they made powerful and numerous friends. They gave O'Casey an identity; and this proved precisely to be the problem when, a little later, he proceeded to write a little differently. . . .

Mr. O'Casey rightly implies that there is a sense in which even his early plays are not realistic. Conversely there is a sense in which it was the realism of the later plays that offended an influential section of the public. *The Silver Tassie* gave offence for not being [R. C. Sherriff's] *Journey's End*—that is, for exposing wounds instead of filming them over with gentility. *Within the Gates* gave offence for giving a close-up of a bishop instead of hiding him in a cloud of incense. *The Star Turns Red* gave offense for turning red—when the palette of a Cecil Beaton or an Oliver Messel had so many other colors to offer. It was opposed in England not for its brand of politics but for being political at all. The point of view is familiar to readers of Mr. O'Casey's arch-antagonist, James Agate, who, for example, complaining of J. B. Priestley, not that he wrote badly, but that he wrote politically, had clearly no means of distinguishing the Yorkshireman's defects from the Irishman's qualities. . . .

One cannot study this man's career without convicting the world around him of jealous meanness. First, they shelved his early works as "classics"; second, they took a stand which explained and dismissed his later works before they appeared. Between these two phases, there was one crucial and receptive moment, a moment when the O'Casey story, as Hollywood would call it, could have been given another turn, and by a single man. This was the moment when W. B. Yeats was reading *The Silver Tassie* for the Abbey Theatre. Not understanding the crucial nature of this moment, we are likely to misread large portions of the autobiography as megalomania. Actually, we should be less surprised at Mr. O'Casey's continual return to the crisis of *The Silver Tassie* than at the fact that his attitude to Yeats even after it was one of filial love. [Oct. 13, 1952]

Eric Bentley. *What Is Theatre?* (New York, Atheneum, 1968), pp. 26–27

Where O'Casey proves himself a dramatist by instinct is in his violent mixing and effortless handling of passions and characters. Given the conditions of "chassis," the playwright does not bother to contrive what all the critics would be sure to call a powerful play. Instead, he scatters poets, bombs, love-making, cowards, gaudy uniforms, blatherers, random shots, drunkards, ideologies and prostitutes with a free hand, taking as much time to get his story started as if all his creatures were not hastening to their inglorious ends, and relying not so much on last-minute inspiration as on well-worn tricks to wind up for the evening what cannot be wound up this side of eternity.

Moreover—and this is what makes them repeatedly readable—these plays are mostly talk. It is O'Casey, not Shaw, who among modern playwrights forgets action in a rush of words. This does not mean that there is any lack of that apprehensive hostility among characters which a play needs to keep us going. This domestic strife matches the violence of O'Casey's public world and its supply is inexhaustible; for besides having the gift of gab the characters are, with a few exceptions, moral imbeciles. Products of a triply mismanaged country, they have no strong attachment except to momentary feeling or old superstition. In short they are ruled by their real sensations and imaginary fears.

This is what makes it impossible for O'Casey to write a drama of ideas, while it saves him from writing a drama of near-ideas, or thesis play. Try to find out from the body of his work whether he is for or against the Church, for or against the workingman, for or against poets, for or against social revolution—you cannot. Whenever he emits what he believes is an idea it is so put that we hardly notice it save through a pang of boredom; and whenever he embroiders that same idea, he crystallizes feeling, which infallibly recaptures our attention.

To say that a man is not a man of ideas is not to say he has no convictions. O'Casey is obviously full of them. His strong preference is for order, intellect, decency, courage, and justice. But this is seriously endangered by what becomes a main theme of the later plays, the love of love at whatever cost, the cost, being usually disorder, indecency, and injustice. He may think *Purple Dust* a high intellectual farce which gives the victory to youth and love, but it is as a whole a sadistic persecution of bungling philistinism. That it makes its point none the less is a sign of O'Casey's mastery in weaving, not in cutting, his cloth.

Jacques Barzun. *TDR*. Feb., 1958, p. 59

What are the later plays? What are O'Casey's intentions? Briefly, his intentions would seem to be the destruction of dramatic realism. It is something of a paradox that the reigning convention of the modern theatre should be realism although the greatest modern dramatists in their greatest plays are not realists. Perhaps the subtle influence of the film is responsible, and perhaps it is easier to understand the Ibsen of *The Pillars of Society* than the

Ibsen of *The Master Builder*. . . . Today's theatrical growth is from *Murder in the Cathedral* to *The Cocktail Party,* from poetry to prose. O'Casey, who has never attempted to come to terms with theatrical convention, has progressed from prose to poetry.· . . .

O'Casey's work, however, has tended in the direction of freedom, of breaking down the forms and conventions of dramatic realism. He cries with Shaw that there are no rules, but this statement should be taken probably as one of narrow polemic against realism, rather than as a broad statement of dramatic theory. In his early plays O'Casey was thought to be a realist of erratic and primitive genius, a dramatist of great original talent who, if he learned to harness and control his structure, would produce quite overpowering plays. *The Silver Tassie* and the subsequent plays, however, indicated the dramatist was getting too big for his britches, was setting himself up as an intellectual and a member of the avant garde, was throwing discipline out the window, whimsically dissipating his meager power in the slough of Expressionism and perversely biting the pale and poetic hand that fed him from the door (back door probably) of the Abbey Theatre.

Actually the early plays, like the later ones of Chekhov, seemed slovenly in form and slipshod in structure only because they were not based on the four-point traditional structure of *Protasis, Epitasis, Catastasis,* and *Catastrophe* which, under various pseudonyms, have been chewed over by critics from Donatus to Scaliger to Dryden to the latest composer of a "How to Write a Play" textbook. The early plays are far from structureless, but have a structure akin to [Ben Jonson's] *Bartholomew Fair* and *The Alchemist*. From the beginning, then, O'Casey was straining against the confines of realism and by the poorly understood success of *The Plough and the Stars* reasserting the vitality of this second structure with its unique utilization of tragic irony and its broadness of scope that the conventional, four-point, single-action plays of his contemporaries denied.

Robert Hogan. *The Experiments of Sean O'Casey*
(New York, St. Martin's, 1960), pp. 10–11

O'Casey's world is chaotic and tragic but his vision of it is ironically comic. It is in this war-torn world of horrors and potential tragedy that he finds the rowdy humour which paradoxically satirizes and sustains his earthy characters: they are the victims of their foibles yet they revel in their voluble absurdities. And it is clear that O'Casey himself enjoys his people no less for their follies, as he intends his audience to enjoy them. There is a sharp tone of outrage in his Daumier-like portraits of life in the slums of a beleaguered city, and this tone becomes even stronger in his later plays, but he was not dramatizing case histories. His plays do not follow the documentary principles of Naturalism—of Hauptmann's *Weavers* or Galsworthy's *Strife.* Low comedy is not one of the handmaidens of Naturalism. Even when he is in a serious mood O'Casey is likely to be satiric not solemn, poignant not pathetic. And when the tragic events or consequences of war and poverty become most crucial he will open up the action and counterbalance the incipient tragedy with a music-hall turn or a randy ballad or a mock-battle. While everyone awaits a terrifying raid by the Black and Tans in *The Shadow of a Gunman* the well-oiled Dolphie Grigson parades into the house spouting songs and biblical rhetoric in drunken bravado. Just when Mrs. Tancred is on her way to bury her ambushed son in *Juno and the Paycock* the Boyles have launched their wild drinking and singing party. While the streets ring with patriotic speeches about heroic bloodshed in *The Plough and the Stars* the women of the tenements have a free-for-all fight about respectability in a Pub.

This pattern of ironic counterpoint is maintained as a tragicomic rhythm throughout the plays. For each tragic character there are comic foils who constantly bring the action round from the tragic to the comic mood. . . . It is this attitude which keeps his plays from becoming melancholy or pessimistic. His humour saves him and his characters from despair.

David Krause. *Sean O'Casey: The Man and His Work*
(New York, Macmillan, 1960), pp. 71–72

The . . . group [of plays] comprising *Purple Dust, Cock-a-Doodle Dandy, The Bishop's Bonfire, The Drums of Father Ned,* and *Behind the Green Curtain* (the title-play in a volume including two other short plays) are entertainments propounding a moral view. They are all set in "imaginary" Irish villages, and, among the other things they have in common, what stands out prominently is O'Casey's attack on the Irish clergy and Catholicism, and the state to which Ireland has been reduced. The Irish, especially the clergy, have protested vehemently against O'Casey's "vilifying" Ireland and have argued that he was quite out of touch with the country as it is today. O'Casey, who left Dublin in 1926 and did not go back except for two brief visits, insisted that his portrayal was factual and that he had kept himself fully informed of life and events in Ireland through Irish newspapers and through visitors from across the Irish Sea. Barring for the moment the question of who is right and who is wrong, at least two things are obvious: first, that these plays, in spite of the occasional rancour and bitterness that runs through them, are the work of a man profoundly in love with Ireland; second, that the Irish clergy have successfully kept most of the later O'Casey plays from reaching the Dublin stage.

Saros Cowasjee. *Sean O'Casey* (New York, Barnes
and Noble, 1966), p. 85

Cock-a-Doodle Dandy is a song. "Enough, no more," one is compelled to add. "'Tis not so sweet now as it was before." Still, an excess of melody is much better than too little, or none at all. The spirit and language of O'Casey's comedy are lovely. They voice a celebration of life, a lilting and laughing hymn, as well as its converse crow of mockery, rich curses at O'Casey's two *bêtes noires,* bigotry and money meanness. He harps to the point of shrillness against the enemy, but poetry, laughter and love finally triumph.

The weakness of the play is an insufficiency of dramatic content; there is almost no "story." O'Casey wrote it after he had left Ireland, injured and insulted by its hermetic religiosity, its unfrangible mythmaking. . . . As a result, plays of that period, though never without moments of beauty and scenes of both power and hilarity, are more or less veiled preachments, with rumblings of rancor in the shadows. Therefore, the best work of O'Casey's last years is to be found in his multi-volumed autobiography, where his life struggle supplies a structure firm enough to sustain the rest.

What *Cock-a-Doodle Dandy* does have, and what saves it, is a striking image and captivating speech. The image is that of the indomitably rebellious Cock, symbol of nature in its gloriously telluric force and in its capacity to demolish the constructions of reason. Nature is not all divine harmony; it is also demonic anarchy. O'Casey understands that this is part of its grandeur, to be embraced with a mighty whoop of brave affirmation.

Harold Clurman. Nation. Feb. 10, 1969, p. 187

In the twentieth century, as a reaction to the extreme transparency of natural activity, with its loss of theatrical excitement as well as generalized significance, playwrights and performers have experimented with a wide variety of techniques for achieving a viable "artificiality." . . . Sean O'Casey develops a mixed method of "naturalism" and "expressionism." These writers also utilize song and dance to considerable effect, but it is in O'Casey's work that one can see the growth of artifice most easily. In his early plays, O'Casey employed song as natural activity, but with his turn to expressionism, commencing with *The Silver Tassie,* O'Casey employs song, dance, and scenic display as a direct expression of the action he wishes to convey. His most ambitious effort is found in *Red Roses for Me.* . . .

O'Casey tries to establish a new convention, shifting from the photographic to the apocalyptic. He foreshadows the vision [of a society of beauty and spiritual exaltation] through the introduction of songs early in the play and through Ayamonn's yearning for joyful beauty. In Act III he makes that yearning palpable. The colors of the city and the sky change, ostensibly because of sunset, yet the changes go beyond sunset's changes. Ayamonn and the women sing and dance, yet the singing and dancing are more than natural joy. All changes partake of a symbolic celebration of the future. In these ways O'Casey endeavors to fashion a mode of action that, through its beauty and ebullience, can be simultaneously opaque and transparent.

Bernard Beckerman. *Dynamics of Drama*
(New York, Alfred A. Knopf, 1970), pp. 126–28

It is a commonplace assumption that the self-taught playwright underwent several distinct stages. [O'Casey's] least friendly critics would classify these as first, that period of hit-and-miss dramaturgy which remained very close to traditional lines but somehow accidentally produced those early master-pieces; second, the attainment of an overenthusiastic bravado which allowed him to experiment with expressionistic techniques rather imitatively and clumsily; third, the time of his most naïve immersion in ideology which produced dull and wooden propaganda plays; and, fourth, a "sunset" stage in which he lost complete touch with the basic Irish sources for his material, but retained or regained his Irish sense of the wildly comic, adding an element of fantasy at times gay and at times obtrusive. No single critic actually rates O'Casey exactly in this way, but this is a composite of the general aspect of disapproval and the most frequent touches of begrudging praise.

The common denominator of all denigration of O'Casey's technique as a dramatist is the assumption that he never actually refined a fully conscious skill in *controlling* the important elements of his craft: that although he often created excellent pieces of drama and sketched some fine characterizations, O'Casey was never a play*wright*. Even those who insist upon O'Casey's "genius" use that term of exaggerated approbation to offset an insistence on his frequent gaffes. Yet these advocates perform an unnecessary disservice: Sean O'Casey is at his best precisely in what he had *wrought*.

Stagecraft at its most basic involves the necessity of setting a scene, and it is with this essential (often passed on instead to a designer) that O'Casey demonstrates his individual touch. The early naturalistic plays provided no difficulty for him; he was well versed in describing the basics of a tenement room, and if "photographic realism" means anything in regard to these plays, it is in such specific renderings as: "Between the window and the dresser is a picture of the Virgin; below the picture, on a bracket, is a crimson bowl in which a floating votive light is burning. Farther to the right is a small bed partly concealed by cretonne hangings strung on a twine." O'Casey would have been a poor choice indeed for an Abbey production had he not been able to pinpoint that facet of his known world, but it is in his later non-naturalistic works that his powers of evocative description are significant.

Bernard Benstock. *Sean O'Casey* (Lewisburg,
Pa., Bucknell University Press, 1970), pp. 89–90

To some extent the unique form that [O'Casey's] theatre took is a reflection of his own struggle from squalid obscurity to international recognition as a great playwright. At the same time it was determined by the direction that his own reading took.

As a young man he had little experience of the modern movement of Realism. Almost the only theatre where he could have seen representative examples was the Abbey which, according to his own testimony, he had visited "but twice." The dramatist he knew and admired most was Shakespeare whose influence was obviously profound and lifelong. Of modern dramatists the one he admired most was Shaw, not only for his ideology but because Shaw, to some degree, belonged to the tradition of the drama as literature.

As he came to write plays rather later in life than most other successful playwrights, after some disenchantment with the aims and actions of Irish politicians, the drama became a unique forum in which he, the artist, could refashion the world neglected or misunderstood by the politician. The outward, expansive form that it took was an expression of what he had seen and what he had read.

J. A. Snowden. In *Essays and Studies* [English Association]
(London, John Murray, 1971), p. 68

In chronological order of the subject-matter, *The Plough and the Stars* (1915–1916), *The Shadow of a Gunman* (1920), and *Juno and the Paycock* (1922) cover the most momentous events in recent Irish history, not from the point of view of the political or military leaders, but from that of the ordinary people unwillingly caught up in the indiscriminate savagery and recrimination of civil war and revolution. It is as though Ralph Mouldy, Peter Bullcalf, Francis Feeble and their families were at the centre of the dramatic action (with Bardolph, Nym, and Doll Tearsheet as minor characters) instead of Prince Hal and Hotspur. In this respect, of course, O'Casey is being realistic in writing about Irish history from the point of view of his own experience and realising (in however heightened a manner) people with whom he was intimately familiar. At the same time we can, with some advantage, think of his Dublin dramas in terms somewhat similar to Bernard Shaw's rebellion against the absurdly romanticised approach to history characteristic of the nineteenth-century theatre.

In O'Casey, as in Shakespeare's history plays, certain recurrent themes are uppermost: the inter-action of public and private drama, the horror of civil strife and anarchy in the state, and, likewise in both, a continuing debate on the ambiguous demands of justice and order in society. The Elizabethan playwright, conveniently distanced in time (but not relevance) from the events he chronicled, was provided with a firm moral as well as political pattern by the Tudor historians whose writings provided his main sources. The Irish author, writing in close proximity to the events he chronicled, naturally lacked so elaborate or consistent a narrative framework and the consequent opportunities for cross-reference within plays and from one play to another, yet even so he does succeed in imposing a sense of unity on the Dublin trilogy. This cohesion is maintained by a grim ironic vision of the destructive forces in society, a compassionate concern for the resultant human suffering, a highly idiosyncratic comic technique, and purposeful thematic patterning common to each of these dramas.

Ronald Ayling. JML. Nov., 1972, pp. 492–93

O'Casey's mind moves most fruitfully between two poles: the personal, sacred cycle of birth, copulation, and death, and the (for O'Casey) predominantly absurd structures of human commerce, institutions, and creeds. There is a simple honesty about his preference for the former that is attractive, but its very simplicity accounts in part for the incoherence in some of the plays, for the passionate opinions—instead of persuasiveness—that one frequently stumbles on in the occasional writings. Where there is appalling violence, the opposition of the private and the public is naked. The gulf between feeling and action, individual sentiment and the mass slogan, domestic sanctuary and the arena of war or riot speaks for itself in *The Shadow of a Gunman, The Plough and the Stars, Juno and the Paycock, The Silver Tassie,* and *Red Roses for Me.* These plays are all the better for that. It is when O'Casey involves himself in social satire against obscurantism, hypocrisy, religious mania, and the like, that a certain factitiousness enters his work. Then, to achieve a moral contrast between private and public forces, he is obliged to distort the size of his private figures, in itself an ancient theatrical device but valid only when the form of the play can contain it. It seems to me that it works in *Cock-a-Doodle Dandy,* a play radically conceived in one idiom, but does not, or not always, in *The Bishop's Bonfire* with its ill-assorted blend of styles.

Thomas Kilroy. Introduction to Thomas Kilroy, ed., Sean
O'Casey: A Collection of Critical Essays (Englewood
Cliffs, N.J., Prentice-Hall, 1975), pp. 4–5

Now if the cultural basis of O'Casey's work is, as I have suggested, a combination of mediaeval morality-play, Shakespeare, Bunyan, and Victorian popular melodrama, it cannot be said that he shares the normal literary equipment of the modern bourgeois intellectual. The latter will no doubt be familiar with all of these writings, but it would be surprising if three-fourths of them at least (which three-fourths would depend upon which intellectual) were not purely marginal to his personal preoccupations. Add to the amalgam the jokes and word-play of the building-site, the street-ballad (as understood in the street rather than the college library), the pictures and phraseology of popular religion, and the heroic tales of bronze-age Ireland: and one ends with a creative imagination which is so out-of-the-ordinary as to be positively crank. "Workerism" is an inappropriate label for it: but certainly it would not fit into any recognizable Marxist-bureaucratic pigeon-hole. O'Casey as an orthodox socialist-realist would never have been *reliable,* and it would have been hard to see how anyone in leftist circles in England in the thirties could have been any more adaptable to his inspirations than the managers of the West End. The Abbey Theatre as well, of course, never had a clue.

O'Casey's plays as social documents have not yet become out-of-date: as poetic creations they have not even begun to be realized. The theatre has changed a lot since his heyday—we have had the example of Brecht (who did have a theatre of his own, under a Stalinist government, and subjected by that government to continual niggling) to show us that the kind of emblematic precision that O'Casey required can in fact be attained on a stage, but only as a result of the coming-together of a series of fortuitous conditions in post-war Germany which no-one could have predicted. Brecht brought into the drama an apparently new vocabulary which was in fact a very old vocabulary revitalized: he took up at a different point the same tradition that O'Casey adopted: his discoveries are now part of every producer's stock-in-trade. If it has been done once it can surely be done again?

John Arden. In Thomas Kilroy, ed., *Sean O'Casey:*
A Collection of Critical Essays (Englewood Cliffs,
N.J., Prentice-Hall, 1975), p. 76

If we were to try to describe O'Casey's dramatic writing in general, one might say it is distinguished by melodious epithets, extended metaphors, and recondite symbols; by exclamatory statements, rhetorical questions, and inverted word order; by puns, limericks, and songs; by political, historical, and mythological allusions; by catalogs, linguistic fancies, and mock logic; by Gaelic overtones, biblical phraseology, and fractured Latin; by straight-away statement and oblique remark.

O'Casey's mastery was not confined to his use of language, however; his control and innovation in dramatic form was also impressive. From the beginning of his career, O'Casey employed certain techniques such as multiple plots, detailed stage directions, antiheroic irony and antirealistic symbolism, the mingling of realistic, fantastic, and poetic modes, the fusion of the tragic with the comic temper, the use of melodrama, satire, burlesque, and farce, the concentration on theatricality in settings, the incorporation of music and dance. And he utilized these techniques within the concept of drama as a parable that is both entertainment and an illustration of the conflict between man's will and society's strictures. Although O'Casey was very often criticized for having broken with his earlier realism (of, for ex-

ample, *Juno and the Paycock*) for totally different forms such as expressionism *(Within the Gates)* or fantasy *(Cock-a-Doodle Dandy),* no such dramatic
break ever occurred—the emphasis changed.

In addition to the full-length plays . . . , O'Casey wrote several
shorter dramas . . . . Many of them are delightful little pieces, also innovative in form, with gems of characterization and splendid dialogue. . . .

No one . . . can deny O'Casey's deep commitment to the ideals of
energy, youth, faith, beauty, joy, and art. His habitual patterns of feeling
might be described as sentimental, lyric, rhapsodic, comic, ironic, and even
bitter. He was a secular humanist who demanded a decent life for every
human being on earth, and defeat for those who would deny man that heritage. O'Casey saw the world as it is, and he projected the world as he felt
it could be.

Doris daRin. *Sean O'Casey* (New York,
Frederick Ungar, 1976), pp. 180–82

We have seen O'Casey's plays shift from the more naturalistic Irish-Elizabethan early plays to the experimental, expressionistic plays of his middle
period . . . and then to the later comic-imaginative plays. . . . This shift
(Irish critics notwithstanding) was not caused by O'Casey's leaving Ireland
to live in England. The primary reasons for this shift, we believe, are: (1)
the essential nature of Sean O'Casey's unique, restless, creative imagination
and (2) the Abbey Theatre's rejection of *The Silver Tassie.* The rejection of
The Silver Tassie appears especially important since O'Casey deliberately
(perversely, perhaps) restrained himself from writing any play to which
Yeats could point and say, "I told you so." And it is this restraint (as
evidenced by his refusal to create consistently drawn Irish-Elizabethan characters and his refusal to give his plays unity of action) rather than his departure from Ireland which perhaps accounts for much of the weakness inherent in the expressionistic middle plays. Although his colorful, creative
imagination and his sympathy for the exploited peoples of the world are
clearly present in these middle plays, they cannot save them; for neither his
imagination nor his sympathy appears (to us, at least) to be under artistic
control.

Finally, in the comic-imaginative phase of O'Casey's playwriting career, he achieves this control over his imagination and his politics. In the
last plays, as in *The Plough and the Stars* and in the best stories of the
Autobiographies, there is unity of action. Here . . . O'Casey's comic,
imaginative genius is directed to specific ends. If we, for example, compare
Cock-a-Doodle Dandy (the best of the comic-imaginative plays) to *The
Plough and the Stars* (the best of the early plays) these two dramas appear
approximately equal in terms of overall effectiveness. Both plays reveal
tight artistic control and consistent characterization, and the sheer imagina-

tive vitality of the later play balances off with the greater depth of characterization of the earlier one.

James R. Scrimgeour. *Sean O'Casey* (Boston,
Twayne, 1978), pp. 167–68

O'Casey's final period lasts from the composition of *Oak Leaves and Lavender* in the early 1940s until his death in September of 1964. During this
period, he continued to experiment with expressionism, fantasy, and morality plays. He continued, also, to harangue his enemies and to put didactic,
informative speeches in the mouths of his favorites. His basic themes—that
the old must give way to the new, that habitual servitude must give way to
joyful abandon, that lethargy must give way to action—are further developed and modified in plays that tend to focus on Ireland as microcosm. It is
essentially true that O'Casey sacrificed character to theme in this period, but
O'Casey would not admit the sacrifice as a weakness: for him, repetition of
a legitimate theme is but a way of instruction; for him, as his prefaces and
his essays clearly show, the plays themselves are best viewed as moralities
and their worlds as microcosms. Virtually every play from *The Silver Tassie*
on is, in many ways, a morality play; consequently, his specific attacks on
specific individuals and situations in Ireland are at the same time topical and
universal.

A legitimate argument might be made for discussing *Oak Leaves and
Lavender* in conjunction with *The Star Turns Red:* both are hate-filled and
splenetic attacks, both depict the essential strength and wisdom of the communist doctrine, and both trace a steady progression from despair to hope
and awareness of inevitable victory. *Oak Leaves* is better drama than *The
Star Turns Red,* but not as effective as *Purple Dust,* which portrays the old
house that is the microcosm of England in steady disintegration and decay,
augmented by the foolishness and stupidity of Stoke and Poges—the living
embodiments of a graveyard. The contrast between *Purple Dust* and *Oak
Leaves and Lavender* is an informative one. In the earlier play, the house
was a monument to the past at whose shrine the owners and perpetuators
worshipped. O'Casey's flood, not unlike Noah's, swept away the idols and
the idolators, leaving the world for the people of the present who had the
good sense to escape to higher ground. In the later play, the oak gives way
to steel and the shades give way to the living; then, victory is possible.

B. L. Smith. *O'Casey's Satiric Vision*
(Kent, Ohio, Kent State University Press,
1978), pp. 116–17

O'Casey was Yeats's first heir. He took over the idea of total theatre, carried
it from Dublin to London and turned himself into the flying wasp whose
task was to sting the English theatre into modernity. The history of his later

drama is a history of his struggle to naturalise techniques derived from Yeats in the realism-bound theatre of his adopted country. He had continually to explain or defend his experimental methods to the uncomprehending critics of the day. When James Agate berated him for causing confusion by mixing fantasy and realism he replied: "I do so, Sir, because, first, a change is needed in the theatre, and, secondly, because life is like that—a blend of fantasy and realism." On another occasion he said still more militantly: "I am out to destroy the accepted naturalistic presentation of character; to get back to the poetic significance of drama."

He was the coloniser of the Yeatsian theatre and in a way the popular-iser too, for although his experimental drama did not achieve popularity in his own time, being too far ahead of it, he gave a massive demonstration in the thirties and forties of how the Yeatsian dance drama could be opened up into popular forms and serve many purposes, including social satire, without necessarily losing the "interior" dimension. He suffered from a sense of neglect and his later plays were not generally understood, often, no doubt, because they were badly performed. But he did, after all, break into the West End theatre with two audaciously innovative plays, *The Silver Tassie* . . . and *Within the Gates* . . . and the other plays, even the most fantastic, did usually find some enterprising company like the People's Theatre, Newcastle, to perform them: his influence seeped into the English theatre in this way and helped to create the climate in which a whole crop of later plays in musical/balletic mode could flourish.

Katharine Worth. *The Irish Drama of Europe
from Yeats to Beckett* (Atlantic Highlands,
N.J., Humanities Press, 1978), p. 220

O'Casey delineates and denigrates two puritanical, proselyting priests who boo and bluster against the joy of life and their small regiments of obedient followers—bourgeois bigots, religious radicals, and lewd-minded lackeys in *Cock-a-Doodle Dandy* and *The Drums of Father Ned*, two Aristophanic allegories designed to diagnose Ireland's major malignancy as excessive and repressive clerical authoritarianism—a clerical control that breeds a pathological obsession with the pleasures of the flesh and a cultural stagnation.

The caped and cruel crusader, Father Domineer, and his followers are victorious in the first play, shouting down imaginative but dangerous writers, chasing vital and hopeful people out of the village, and instilling visions of woe and worship in the minds of those who remain behind in the depopulated, desolate village. Yet the reverse is true in the second play, in which Father Fillifogue and his middle-aged supporters are dazed and defeated by an enlightened and resourceful legion of young people. The latter are inspired by Father Ned, a priest who symbolizes (like the cock in the earlier play) the prime mover, the invisible agent of conviviality and creativeness that gives rise to the Tostal, a national festival embracing many aspects of international life. Indeed, the young people are, like Ayamonn Breydon in *The Star Turns Red,* committed to a liberated Ireland free of censorship, clerical tyranny, and economic and political bondage; and their program for future action synthesizes the heroic idealism of Ireland's past, Gaelic myth and legend, with certain aspects of Christian socialism. They dream, to be sure, of a brave new Ireland.

It is not, however, this focus on Ireland's future or on Ireland's problems with some of her priests that explains the extraordinary appeal of these plays for many students of drama. Rather, it is the montage of methods—the dazzling display of dramatic strategies and styles—that imparts to these extravagant fantasies their unique charm, vividness, and verve. Indeed, O'Casey is a virtuoso seemingly bent on experimenting with—juxtaposing and joining—all the paraphernalia and patterns in his large arsenal of theatrical techniques and tableaux in these late plays, which are distinguished, as are many of the poetic, modified Nō plays of William Butler Yeats, by a conscious and clever commingling of the mundane and the mysterious, the feasible and the fantastic. Ritualistic processions, music and dance, special lighting, offstage sounds, flashbacks, dream sequences, sudden disappearances, strange metamorphoses of people, birds, and objects, recurring symbols, choral voices, and emblematic or symbolic figures (all moving against evocative, colorful, and constantly changing landscapes) combine to give these plays a range and a resonance—a medley of moods and mannerisms—not to be found in any of the earlier works. Indeed, the verisimilitude and vision are, at intervals, almost indistinguishable in these comic-sad chiaroscuros.

Ronald Gene Rollins. *Sean O'Casey's Drama:
Verisimilitude and Vision* (University, Ala.,
University of Alabama Press, 1979), pp. 78–80

OSBORNE, JOHN (1929–   )

"They are scum" was Mr. [Somerset] Maugham's famous verdict on the class of State-aided university students to which Kingsley Amis's Lucky Jim belongs; and since Mr. Maugham seldom says anything controversial or uncertain of wide acceptance, his opinion must clearly be that of many. Those who share it had better stay well away from John Osborne's *Look Back in Anger,* which is all scum and a mile wide. . . .

Look Back in Anger presents post-war youth as it really is, with special emphasis on the non-U intelligentsia who live in bed-sitters and divide the Sunday papers into two groups, "posh" and "wet." To have done this at all would be a signal achievement; to have done it in a first play is a minor miracle. All the qualities are there, qualities one had despaired of ever seeing on the stage—the drift towards anarchy, the instinctive leftishness, the automatic rejection of "official" attitudes, the surrealist sense of humour (Jimmy describes a pansy friend as "a female Emily Brontë"), the casual promiscuity, the sense of lacking a crusade worth fighting for, and, underlying all these, the determination that no one who dies shall go unmourned. . . .

That the play needs changes I do not deny; it is twenty minutes too long. . . . I agree that *Look Back in Anger* is likely to remain a minority taste. What matters, however, is the size of the minority. I estimate it at roughly 6,733,000, which is the number of people in this country [England] between the ages of twenty and thirty. And this figure will doubtless be swelled by refugees from other age-groups who are curious to know precisely what the contemporary young pup is thinking and feeling. I doubt if I could love anyone who did not wish to see *Look Back in Anger*. It is the best young play of its decade. [1956]

> Kenneth Tynan. *Curtains* (New York, Atheneum,
> 1961), pp. 130–31

Of *The Entertainer* especially it can be said that it is toward some moment in which the hero must confront himself that the whole play properly tends. Underlying all Archie's fussing, and all Hamm's [in Beckett's *Endgame*], is the nervous dread of being left, finally, to himself—no murmur from a responsive audience rising any longer to give him reassurance. *Endgame* does move doggedly toward that moment. Hamm's parents die, Clov finally manages to leave him, and Hamm is alone. "Discard"—he throws away various comforting objects—among them the whistle with which he used to summon Clov—and, stoically, faces the silence. *The Entertainer* almost ends in a comparable scene. We see Archie for the last time up in front of the curtain, going through one of his numbers. He falters; his wife appears out of the shadows, holding his hat and coat, and we see that the drop curtain has vanished, the darkened stage is behind him; they walk off together. The moment is filled with a kind of terror; but the nature of the terror eludes one. What is Archie's sense of himself finally? How much, for example, have Jean's accusations bothered him? We cannot tell. All we really know is that he prefers himself, Archie Rice, to his brother. He has made that very clear. And it is clear enough that we are supposed to, too. (After describing the brother, in the playscript, Mr. Osborne taunts: "If you can't recognise him, it's for one reason only.") Archie does not remain, here at the end, to confront the silence. Instead, he returns for a moment to tease the audience: "Let me know where you're working tomorrow night, and I'll come and see *you*!"

No, it is a disservice to John Osborne, I believe, to congratulate him upon his war with the Philistines. Behind the smoke of this, he is actually taking cover. Instead of submitting his heroes to a final clear scrutiny, he turns to taunt: Oh, aren't all of you out there glad you're normal? Mr. Beckett puts in Clov's mouth the observation, "Nobody ever thought so crooked as we"; but neither Jimmy Porter nor Archie Rice makes any such admission; and Mr. Osborne seems unable, even to himself, to make it about them. He would paint a modern Hell. But he would if he could, damn only those who supposedly "don't know what it's like" for his heroes. If he could find the courage to examine the human heart without distraction—putting aside an anger that is really a complacent snobbery of his own—then his plays might indeed awaken us.

"The man," says Albert Camus, "who, as often happens, chose the path of art because he was aware of his difference, soon learns that he can nourish his art, and his difference, solely by admitting his resemblance to all." These are words for John Osborne to ponder.

Barbara Deming. *HudR*. Autumn, 1958, p. 419

Although I maintain that *The World of Paul Slickey* was a failure, I believe in failures. I think they are necessary. Among the most corrupting effects of the cult of the bitch-goddess success is the inability to make room for failures, to learn with them and live on them, to accept their possibility and importance. In the chaos of the entertainment industry, to score four "successes" in a run is rare—and not altogether desirable. What worries me about the failure of *Paul Slickey* is that its champions still insist that it is a success, killed by a Plot, too good for the sinful, reactionary theatre into which it was born. If the author went on thinking that too, after his wounds had healed, it would be a pity. For if Osborne is to play the vital role in British cinema and theatre that his rare talents indicate, if he is to write the show that *Paul Slickey* OUGHT to be, then he will admit the possibility that sometimes it is not other people's prejudice but his own incapacity that may be the trouble. He will get his ideas and feelings straight about The Audience—on first and last nights, in the stalls and the gallery, from Wimbledon or Wapping. He will learn to accept failure, and grow out of it.

This was, of course, an exceptional failure. A worthwhile failure. What Osborne meant to do, I took it, was to create a kind of *Threepenny Opera* of post-war England; to give teeth to the poor old English musical; to extend both its form and context; to break down, still further, the barrier between musical and non-musical theatre; to challenge the old audience and bring in the new; to say something loud and clear—in theatrical terms—about the shams of a dying social order under the shadow of the H-bomb. I admire the intention. But I deplore the result.

Richard Findlater. *TC*. Jan., 1960, pp. 31–32

If one looks closely at the crotchety, constipated, hypercritical figure of Martin Luther in John Osborne's newest play [*Luther*], one is forcibly reminded of that fuming British malcontent, Jimmy Porter; a protestant who bitched against the Welfare State as vehemently as the theologian wrangled with the Pope. The similarities do not end there.

Despite the jump in time, the clerical context and the change of venue, the play is not (as has been charged here) a *departure* for Osborne. There is a clear link-up between Luther's sixteenth-century Germany and our time. In both, the sense of cosmic imminence is very strong. "The Last Judgement isn't to come. It's here and now," says Luther, and the doomsday-mountain-squatters and the nuclear-psychotics echo his words. The church-sale of indulgences is put forward as if it were a commercial advertisement, and the suggestion here is that the Catholic Church at its lowest moral ebb is an appropriate symbol for modern ad-mass culture. And who is the cleric Tetzel but a kind of bloated Arthur Godfrey pushing piety with the same unctuousness used to boost Lipton's Tea?

The Osborne of *Look Back in Anger* and *The Entertainer* gave us the *temperature* of social protest. And it was blisteringly hot. In *The World of Paul Slickey*, no longer content with the charged implication and the social inference, Osborne issued indictments. One of these was made out for the church. There was something compulsive in the way that Osborne humiliated his churchmen in *Slickey*. I have a stark image of an obscenely capering clergyman shedding all the moral restraints one usually associates with the cloth. Osborne seemed to be taking it out on the church because of some fundamental failing, and it was tinged with a personal bitterness—as if Osborne himself had been let down.

Charles Marowitz, *TDR*. Winter, 1962, pp. 175–76

Of John Osborne's two new plays [*Plays for England*] one is overtly and the other covertly about England. *The Blood of the Bambergs* is set in a nation which has a constitutional monarchy and a socialist government. Could be anywhere, could be Ruritania, but I do not think Mr. Osborne wants us to be in any doubt in our inner hearts. The other one, *Under Plain Cover*, is placed four square in a suburb of Leicester.

The first is a satirical fantasy, impudent, rude, disrespectful, but not impertinent. The pertinence of some passages could cause pain to persons who thought it possible they were being represented on the stage—in particular a television commentator. To those who still attach a degree of divine right to Kings or Princesses the fantasy will seem distasteful, insulting and probably treasonable. To those who take a more relaxed view of royal symbolatry, it will seem more like a lighthearted crucifixion of excessive venerators.

There is a combination of cattiness and bitchiness, a blend of *The Pris-*

oner of Zenda with *The Apple Cart* which might almost make you think the play a product of collaboration rather than of a single mind. . . .

The play hangs together, hits its targets square, though not always fair, and provides a succession of laughs, some of them rather uncomfortable ones. It is one of Osborne's best works.

Gerard Fay. *Guardian*. July 20, 1962, p. 7

Look Back in Anger does not come into the category of "didactic, realistic" plays, Shaw's own description of *Widowers' Houses*. Osborne is not concerned with social theories and panaceas. Social questions loom large in his plays only as they are imaginatively apprehended by his characters: they do not form the action. In his essay of 1895, Shaw had envisaged some such process coming about: the sheer size of modern societies and the pressure exerted by modern methods of communication would, he conjectured, produce "a steady intensification in the hold of social questions on the larger poetic imagination." The "larger poetic imagination" is not to be confined by the topical: in Osborne's plays so far there can in fact be seen a significant movement away from such confinement. The result of this is not a decreased relevance to the life of our time: *Luther* has as much light to cast on characteristically modern problems of belief as *The Cocktail Party*, despite the surface modernity of Eliot's play.

It may well be asked what evidence of the "larger poetic imagination" there is in Osborne's plays. The evidence in *Look Back in Anger* is certainly incomplete, but there are already indications in the striking rhetorical power of the play that here is an imaginative vitality going beyond that commonly associated with the realistic prose drama. In re-experiencing the plays of Galsworthy, for example, one is often reminded of Synge's description of writers who deal "with the reality of life in joyless and pallid words." Osborne's play is by no means free of the slang and topical minutiae which have caused Galsworthy's dialogue to wear so badly, and his wit is often the brittle, theatrical kind which has still less chance of standing up to time. But these flaws do not conceal the genuine rhetorical force which sustains Jimmy Porter's long speeches: they are at the same time violent and controlled, sardonically humorous and in deadly earnest, evoking occasional echoes of both Shaw and Strindberg.

Katharine J. Worth. In William A. Armstrong, ed.,
Experimental Drama (London, G. Bell and Sons,
1963), pp. 150–51

If anyone still doubts that art knows better than censorship, John Osborne's new play at the Royal Court should provide clinching evidence. With the excision of this scene for which it will clearly go down in theatrical history, the Lord Chamberlain apparently might have considered licensing *A Patriot for Me* for public performance. Apart from the fact that it is one of the best things Osborne has written, the deletion would have been ludicrously self-defeating—as well urge that, to raise its moral tone, Nabokov should have erased from his novel all physical contact between Humbert Humbert and Lolita. Without its climactic evocation of high Hapsburg queerdom at its annual drag ball, *A Patriot for Me* would be, more or less, a sentimental, high-flown piece of propaganda for the rights of a noble and oppressed minority. Osborne's ball scene is not only magnificently theatrical, the best thing in his play, but its centre, its validation, the image from which all else takes perspective and completeness. It is funny, compassionate, grotesque, humane and defiant. . . .

Ever since *Look Back in Anger,* people have been comparing him with Noel Coward; between personal statements he's been no more afraid than Coward of beguiling his audiences with bits of pure, picturesque theatre, big with ironic romanticism and slapstick spectacle—*The World of Paul Slickey,* the *Plays for England,* his film-script for *Tom Jones.* They aren't his major work, but I'd rather have most of them than *Bitter Sweet, Conversation Piece* or *Operette.* Like *Luther, A Patriot for Me* comes from this side of his talent and then goes beyond it. Evidently he picked up the book about Alfred Redl which appeared two or three years ago, and seized on it simply as a marvellous story, crying for amplification into a full-blown Cinemascope spectacular-with-a-kink. Cooler reflection must have shown it to be too kinky for the commercial cinema but there's plenty of evidence still, in the play's huge cast, ambitious range and multiplicity of short, cross-cutting scenes, of fairly advanced early development as a film-scenario. Jocelyn Herbert has done wonders, with enormous back-projections and evocative bits of mobile decor, to give its 84 characters elbow-room on the little Court stage. But ideally it should have unfurled like *Cavalcade,* all gaslights, open carriages and chancellery staircases, over the stage-machines of Drury Lane.

Ronald Bryden. *NS.* July 9, 1965, p. 58

The past emerges in Osborne's writing in two ways: affectionately evoked as he imagines it; or presented with a sneer as a modern cliché. Thus, in his program note to the American production of *The Entertainer* he talks about the "admirable emotional securities" of national pride and craftsmanship. But when such concepts appear in *The World of Paul Slickey* or from the television commentator in *The Blood of the Bambergs,* they are presented as a bad joke. His attitude seems to be that in the England of the past there existed a sense of community and human contact which the pressures of modern life are now rapidly obliterating. Jimmy Porter is vocal about the lack of brave causes; but he feels equally starved of quiet human security.

There is nothing abstract about this. Osborne is one of the very few living dramatists with a real sense of community life: the warmth of the family scenes in *The Entertainer* is unparalleled in the postwar theater. Among other things, *A Patriot for Me* is an attempt to recreate such a community: an army society holding its members together with a "real bond" stronger than slogans that "all men are brothers."

The fact that he chose a setting out of the past to make this point is symptomatic of the way his talent works. In historical situations he shows a coolly articulate control of his material which tends to desert him when he is writing of the present. He has never made any secret of being conditioned by his surroundings. "If you are surrounded by inertia at home, it's not so easy to get steamed up about what's going on in Central Europe." This appears in a *London Magazine* essay in which he goes on to describe modern Britain as an "ashcan" whose inhabitants are made inert by a constant deluge of consumer goods and mass communication rubbish.

His thinking, as usual on these occasions, is hysterically imprecise, and the enemy is simply "the big boys." But the experience behind it is real enough, especially when translated into action by Bill Maitland: a man fighting to preserve his own mind in a society drugged with pseudo-events and technological conveniences. "Technology," says Max Frisch, is "the knack of so arranging the world that we don't have to experience it." That is what Osborne means by the ashcan; and Maitland, striking out indiscriminately against his country and himself (which is which?), is trying to rescue himself from being engulfed in it and, with whatever energy he has to spare, to save the audience from the same fate.

Gabriel Gersh. *MD*. Sept., 1967, pp. 142–43

Osborne's first plays were structurally conventional: *Look Back in Anger* and *Epitaph for George Dillon* are three-act plays set within realistic walls like most of their immediate predecessors. Exposition, development, and conclusion, clear character presentation and progressive building of conflict and tension are all duly there. What was new was the kind of life these plays mirrored in detail: Osborne's own world—young, uneasily married and loving—and its thwarted idealistic pretensions. All the conventional discretion, polish, and good manners of the English drama had gone; and there was no condescension—indeed there was a great show of sympathy—towards what his predecessors would have called "low" characters. Also, the central character in each was a misplaced artist, reduced to anger, double-talk and, temporarily, compliance. From this center, Osborne's later plays were to develop: the best of them are largely monologues, while the others use plot and situation to present an occasion for understanding and revaluation.

In *Luther,* the hero driven by his moral, sexual, and physical tensions brings terror and pain to himself and others; and this is viewed over against the misery and defiance of the Peasants' Revolt. For Osborne this was a

Brechtian experiment in historical drama, but his was a play of display rather than a parable or exercise in dialectics. The frankly apologetic presentation of Maitland, the central character of *Inadmissible Evidence,* shows the same emphasis on the hero as in *Luther* and the earlier plays; but now the other characters and the setting itself have become more mobile and less conventionally secure in presentation. Maitland's world is shown as *he* experiences it in his mind: one actress plays three parts—without disguise other than dress and manner of speaking—to show that Maitland is struggling with the same adversary all the time, that his dilemma is always in part his own, not that brought to him from the "real" world outside. So, too, his clerk becomes his client and his assistant his accuser; his daughter is held still and tantalizing before him, and what he sees in her can seduce his thoughts. Tempo and sequence of time are both fiercely irregular. Osborne has broken convention to center attention on his hero. But the continued interest in monologue is not all; to think that is to miss the most significant development. Osborne is no longer angry and defiant; he is asking for compassion and understanding and, more surprisingly to judge from his early work has found a way of recreating in physically realizable language, the inner, half-conscious pressures within his hero. The nightmare of a defeated idealist is not easily admissible in the theatre; even more rarely is it presented in palpable and challenging form, rather than in soliloquy.

John Russell Brown. In John Russell Brown,
ed., *Modern British Dramatists: A Collection
of Critical Essays* (Englewood Cliffs, N.J.,
Prentice-Hall, 1968), pp. 9–10

It is this innate ability of Osborne's to match language to character which marks his plays so indelibly as his own. This language is simple yet lyrical, contrived yet real. It is theatrically thrilling, and if the dialogue of the minor characters appears to be weak, might that not have been effected with the deliberate purpose of focusing our attention upon the central character. Had the "minor language" contained more substance, more argument, more invective, then our interest might have been diverted from the all-consuming heroes. What Osborne needed was to create plots of reasonable verisimilitude, but which permitted the central character to legitimately express his view within the action of that plot. Whilst these heroes are unable to alter society, for the odds against them are too great, they dominate those around them, and this is only natural. They themselves prevent any substantial minor dialogue developing, for they are always interrupting, questioning, rebuking, and inexorably giving their own opinion. It is the strength of their feelings which charges the plays with "electricity" and gives them so much impact. Jimmy's incredulity at Alison's departure, Archie's breakdown during his nun's story, Bill's panic when legal contacts refuse to speak to him,

Pamela's avoidance of an emotional scene with Murray and Constance; in each, the private fear becomes at the same time a public warning.

Osborne is not a didactic writer in the sense that he tries to turn his characters into socialist lecturers, although in fact one of them, Holyoake, is. He makes them believable human beings, and puts them in credible situations. If we choose to ignore the social or political implications of a play, we still have an effective drama. Osborne, knowing that his characters can never win their battle against society, spins a protective web around them, making a moral implicit rather than explicit, a hero human rather than symbolic. The heroes' failing is that they maintain idealistic purposes which are impossible to achieve, but their refusal to surrender to the social forces which threaten them is always plausible. Unless conditions are suitable (and they are not yet) ideals like theirs are meaningless in the practical sense. Such a high moral purpose endangers life, and ensures conflict and ultimate defeat. By witnessing the defeat of Osborne's heroes, we begin to question the means and ends of a society which ensures their failure. The playwright tries to impress his beliefs upon us within the action of his plays. If we recognised his principle as being substantially correct then he might well stir us to significant action; if on the other hand, we have rejected those principles, then he is more likely to arouse in us that hostility which his own characters seem to enjoy so much. In the sympathies and antipathies of a play we are able to make further refinements and definitions about ourselves, and about the playwright. We may feel ourselves into a play, or we may not. This accord will depend not only upon plot and character but upon thought and experience. The thought of a play will acquaint the spectator with what the playwright perceives as the forces which motivate men, and his view of the place of man in society and in the universe. Experience will condition whether we accept his view or reject it.

Alan Carter. *John Osborne* (Edinburgh,
Oliver and Boyd, 1969), pp. 172–73

Looking back on *Look Back in Anger,* it is a difficult but necessary exercise to try and see it through the eyes of its first audience. . . . Osborne himself later characterized it as "a formal, rather old-fashioned play," and the description is not unfair, though it should, of course, be read in the light of his accompanying statement that he dare not pick up a copy of the play nowadays, as it embarrasses him. Certainly there is nothing much in the form of the piece to justify so much excitement: it is a well-made play, with all its climaxes, its tightenings and slackenings of tension in the right places, and in general layout it belongs clearly enough to the solid realistic tradition represented by say, [Terence Rattigan's] *The Deep Blue Sea.*

No, what distinguished it as a decisive break with Rattigan and the older drama was not so much its form as its content: the characters who took part in the drama and the language in which they expressed themselves. Though Jimmy Porter and his milieu seem, even at this short distance of time, as inescapably "period" as the characters in [Noel Coward's] *The Vortex,* quintessentially "mid-fifties," it was precisely the quality of immediacy and topicality which makes them so now that had the electrifying effect in 1956: Jimmy was taken to be speaking for a whole generation, of which he and his creator were among the most precocious representatives, since it was essentially the post-war generation they represented, those who had, like Lindsay Anderson, "nailed a red flag to the roof of the mess at the fort of Annan Parbat" to celebrate the return of a Labour government in 1945 and then gradually became disillusioned when a brave new world failed to materialize. Most of the people who felt this way were inevitably in their middle to late thirties in 1956, but with Osborne as a figurehead they were all cheerfully labelled "angry young men" and Jimmy Porter was linked in a rather improbable twosome with Amis's Lucky Jim as the cult-figure of the younger generation.

John Russell Taylor. *The Angry Theatre* (New York,
Hill and Wang, 1969), pp. 40–41

Only in *The Hotel in Amsterdam*—and with unexpected abruptness after the archetypicality of *Time Present*—was Osborne able at last to render a balanced, mutually-adjusted group of characters. Simultaneously, he was also able to strip away most of the overlay of plot with which he had previously felt impelled to fill out—and sometimes to overburden—his plays. I think that *The Hotel in Amsterdam,* in these senses, marks the end of a phase in Osborne's creative development. His early preoccupation with the atrophying effects of rationalised nostalgia—with which Jimmy Porter and Archie Rice were both stricken—had persisted even in *Time Present.* But by this time Osborne's interest had already shifted to alienation of another sort—the existential alienation of the loss of one's sense of objective identity. This was Bill Maitland's estrangement, and the theme of *Inadmissible Evidence*—a theme expressed in a more appropriate *form* than in any of Osborne's previous plays. This same theme was latent, though buried beneath a debris of renaissance leftovers, in *A Bond Honoured.* And then, in *A Patriot for Me,* it was as if Osborne were trying to make out with a telescope what he had put beneath a microscope in *Inadmissible Evidence:* for instead of compressing a world into Bill Maitland's mind, he set Alfred Redl against a broader social tapestry than he had ever before tried to weave—reassembling its military, social and sexual patterns into all kinds of permutations, but permitting Redl himself to pick up threads in none. In that play, however, it was the society rather than the stranger lost in its midst which came to life: but in *Time Present* Osborne again chose to depict a solitary figure in an almost suspended environment, so that Pamela found herself alone against a hazily hostile background of family and friends, and of actors and affluent agents.

Simon Trussler. *The Plays of John Osborne: An Assessment* (London, Gollancz, 1969), p. 221

I have always hoped that some day I would wholeheartedly like and admire a play by John Osborne and, during the opening scene of *West of Suez,* I thought the time had come at last. . . . The dialogue is sharp, elliptical and up-to-date; the outspokenness, which Mr. Osborne helped to introduce with *Look Back in Anger,* has been carried much further since then, so that he himself is now able to profit from the example of his successors. The scene also has a philosophical dimension, because the husband is a scientist, a pathologist, who is keen enough on his work but is aware that science is only something he has found to do to while away the time. . . .

Mr. Osborne has been credited by the reviewers with Chekhovian ambitions, and indeed this opening part of *West of Suez* has about it something of the expectant symbolic air of *The Cherry Orchard* or, to mention an early Chekhovian imitation, Shaw's *Heartbreak House.* There is the bringing together of a group of people under the same roof or in the same garden to express a collective mood at a given moment in time. There is the same feeling that the family microcosm is meant to convey a larger truth; just as Ranyevskaya and her cherry orchard represent the beautiful fecklessness of the doomed Russia, or Captain Shotover's ship-like house is the vessel of England about to face the storms and explosions of a European war, so these people assembled west of Suez are clearly intended to be saying something about the present state of English civilisation. Perhaps Mr. Osborne has written the representative play of his maturity, as *Look Back in Anger* was the representative play of his youth; perhaps he has progressed from individual resentment and emotional confusion to a more general and objective statement.

Well, in a sense he has, but the statement remains so muddled, and the play is so poorly constructed that, after the opening scene, I suffered a tremendous sense of let-down. If one did not know that this was the umpteenth play of a practised playwright, one might suspect that it was another promising piece by a relative beginner who had managed his first act but did not quite know how to go on from there. . . .

After a while it becomes clear that *West of Suez* is basically the usual Osborne piece, with a big self-loving, self-hating character rampaging at the centre, and still not quite sure what he is rampaging about.

John Weightman. *Enc.* Nov., 1971, p. 56

Luther is just as much a one-man play as *Look Back in Anger,* with the difference that the one man doesn't emerge as clearly. In some places, the writing of the central part rises to energetic bursts of vivid identification with Luther, but it's still left very much to the leading actor to make him emerge as a rounded personality. Part of the trouble is that the writing doesn't give him an individual voice. . . .

[Osborne] was in love, as always, with the idea of defiance of authority, and the main attraction of Luther as a subject must have been his success in flouting the authority of the Establishment—one man who divided the world into two camps. But Osborne's Luther is a man whose motivations have very little to do with exterior reality. The characters in the play who are meant to stand for the various authorities against which Luther rebelled are mere papier-mâché figures. Except of course the working-class father, who is the only one of the other characters in the play who is developed into anything more than a feed or a foil or a one-scene cameo. Weinand and Staupitz are both like good television interviewers: they ask the right questions to cue in the best possible display of personality and they show the right sympathy. Tetzel certainly makes an impact, but only in his monologue and only in a revue-sketch kind of way. The subtlest writing comes in the scene with Cajetan, but this is made up more of interlocking monologues than of dialogue, while many of Cajetan's speeches are explanations of Luther to Luther, an extra interpretative gloss on his personality, thinly disguised as a scene between two characters. The Pope and von Eck are typical Osborne caricatures, and Katherine, Luther's wife, is extremely shadowy.

Ronald Hayman. *John Osborne* (New York, Frederick Ungar, 1972), pp. 58, 70–71

Looking over Osborne's sixteen plays and remembering that he probably has more playwriting years ahead of him than behind, what evaluation is useful? He has written no unflawed play and a cluster of bad ones—at least five. They are just *there,* and no amount of critical dodging ("if he hadn't gotten these out of his system, he wouldn't have had the inspiration for those") or authorial rationalization ("artists should have the right to relax . . . to indulge themselves") can disguise them. Nor would he rank high on the list of contemporary writers one would turn to for intellectual stimulation. Osborne is no playwright of ideas; his thought is easily compressible into a simple statement of experience-oriented humanist existentialism. All of his work, good or bad, is urgent, passionate, and deliberately anti-intellectual. Philosophy is embedded in behavior and affect usually organized into an action of increasing isolation of a main character. And he has had no lasting effect on dramatic form.

I must admit to frequent bafflement in trying to mobilize the tools of my trade—an exhaustive training in structural methodology—to deal with Osborne. He offers nearly none of the mythical density or intricate poetic patterning of a Beckett, Pinter, or Genet to test analytic ingenuity. His demands, rather, are almost solely on the store of our human sympathy. He always works in terms of immediate feeling and response, willing to risk a fall into sentimentality in order to gain a fierce truthfulness to "the burden of living" and "the texture of ordinary despair." This is another way of saying that he is essentially a man of the theater, particularly of an actor's theater. Undiminished is his amazing gift for creating magnificent roles that have been graced by some of the great performances of our time. And, although he has not written at the top of his talent for eight years, he remains the *exciting* dramatist he so brilliantly began as. Exciting because three times—in *Look Back in Anger, The Entertainer,* and *Inadmissible Evidence*—he has articulated as fully as any writer the central experience of his age. We look forward to his doing this again, anticipating that each next play might gather masses of the unclear feeling of these complicated times and help us to a harrowing revelation of the way we are living.

Harold Ferrar. *John Osborne* (New York, Columbia
University Press, 1973), pp. 46–47

A new attempt to break away from picture-frame illusion began in earnest on the English stage shortly after *Look Back in Anger,* and this is reflected in much of Osborne's work from *The Entertainer* onwards, until in many of his mature works he returns like a prodigal after a misspent youth to the naturalism he could never entirely reject. *Inadmissible Evidence* occupies a kind of half-way house. The hectoring tone of the opening stage direction, and some subsequent passages, insist that we should look on the action not as reality so much as some kind of hallucinatory reconstruction of events inside the hero's increasingly muddled and desperate head; we have only to listen to a few snatches of dialogue, as convincing as an overheard conversation, to realize that the quality of the play exists quite independently of its structural devices. . . .

Osborne is a dramatist who seems to catch character in a tone of voice. More than with any other dramatist I know, reading the text is like hearing the performance over again, so closely has Osborne linked language to the volatile personalities of his dramatic characters to produce superb, indelibly memorable performances from his actors; no one who saw Nicol Williamson in the part of Maitland is likely to forget the experience. It would indeed be possible to write a great deal about the "character" of Bill Maitland, both in psychological terms and as an acting role full of challenge and opportunity. His hypochondria, his womanizing, the barrage of sarcasm and invective that hides a burning need for the assurance of human contact, and above all the passionate egotism that forces us, willy-nilly, to see the world from his point of view—all these elements are far more compelling than the rather shadowy interviews he conducts with his clients or indeed the collapsing relationships with his wife, his daughter, his lover and mistresses which form the main thread of the plot. Indeed, if these elements were not compelling, there would be little to say about the play, since by far the largest part of it consists of dialogue delivered by Maitland to one captive auditor after another.

Michael Anderson. *Anger and Detachment: A Study of Arden, Osborne and Pinter* (London, Pitman, 1976), pp. 14–15

Seeing or reading *Look Back in Anger* today is rather like visiting the British Museum: we can see how we got from then to now. I suppose this is faint praise. One hopes to create a play that will speak not only to its time but out of it, and Osborne didn't. *Look Back in Anger* is already an anachronism. But it is also a landmark. And what it marks, namely that anger is a viable dramatic alternative to repression, is worth celebrating. *Look Back in Anger*'s greatest achievement is its emancipation of drama from the restrictions of past generations. Just when we expected emotional outbursts in the theatre to be forever off stage or in impeccably good taste, this play crept upon us, leaving us stunned, drained, almost disbelieving. Jimmy Porter is not an "Eminent Victorian," nor was he "born out of his time." One honors him more, and the play he dominates, by calling him an angry young man.

E. G. Bierhaus, Jr. *MD*. March, 1976, p. 55

If John Osborne [in *Watch It Come Down*] is aiming for "lacerating realism" (to quote the Faber blurb) can we not expect a rough-and-ready attempt to make one character speak in a different style from another? Instead, Sally and Ben, and Glen and even Jo, all are addicted to staccato lists, after the fashion of a Cole Porter lyric, which could even be set out as in song sheets . . . . Maybe if John Osborne had written it as a bitter-sweet operetta (called *Jeers of a Summer Night* or *A Little Night Cacophony?*) then *Watch It Come Down* might not have seemed such an artificial exercise in bilious ventriloquism.

But no, a libretto too needs to move towards some kind of statement, or anyway to move, to show some interpenetration of opposites, some clash of values. Despite the melodramatic bursts of physical action (as well as the dead dog, dead biographer, dead hippy girl and wounded film director, we have a bout of fisticuffs between Ben and Sally which she claims has broken her back, or at least her jaw) Osborne insists on telling us everything and showing us almost nothing. . . .

Watch It Come Down is simply an un-play, a wordy storm in a whisky tumbler, a circular tour around the shrinking world of Paul Slickey, conducted by a dramatist who once could reach across the footlights and drag us onto the boards, but now appears increasingly lost and adrift inside his own skull.

Alan Brien. *PP*. April, 1976, pp. 25–26

PINTER, HAROLD (1930–   )

When the play [*The Birthday Party*] flared up briefly at the Lyric Opera House in May it provoked such anarchy of opinions, all very dogmatically held, that you have to look towards French government before finding a fit comparison. Nowadays there are two ways of saying you don't understand a play: the first is to bowl it out with that word "obscurity," once so popular in poetry reviews; the second way is to say that the seminal influence of Ionesco can be detected.

Mr. Pinter received the full treatment. As well as standing for *x* in the formulae outlined above, he was described as inferior N. F. Simpson, a lagging surrealist, and as the equal of Henry James. Remembering James's melancholy affair with the theatre this last one carries a nasty sting; and within a couple of days of receiving it, the *Birthday Party* was over.

The comparison with James is quite baffling. Far from being a cautious verbal artist struggling to "throw away cargo to save the ship," Mr. Pinter has no difficulty in putting theatrical requirements first. No matter what you may think of the contents, the ship is afloat. And it is his very instinct for what will work in the theatre that has prompted hostility. One character in *The Birthday Party,* for instance, is given to tearing up newspapers: we are not told why. But the spectacle of John Stratton . . . holding his breath while rapt in the task of tearing each strip of paper to the same width, took on a malevolent power perfectly in key with the play and requiring no explanation. The device is an extreme example of the playwright's habit of introducing an intrinsically theatrical idea and letting it find its own road back towards common sense. Mr. Pinter's way is the opposite of setting out deliberately to embody a theme in action.

All the same a theme does emerge, closely resembling that of [Eugene O'Neill's] *The Iceman Cometh:* the play demonstrates that a man who has withdrawn to protect his illusions is not going to be helped by being propelled into the outer world.

Irving Wardle. *Encore*. July, 1958, p. 39

Mr. Harold Pinter is technically the most adroit and accomplished of the young playwrights. His work is never fumbling in the sense that both Osborne's and Wesker's often is. He knows exactly what effects he wants to get and exactly how to get them. But whereas in their different ways both

Osborne and Wesker are very conscious of their audience—Osborne deliberately trying to shake them out of their complacency, Wesker trying to guide them towards his vision of the good society—Pinter is quite indifferent to the problem of communication. Indeed he himself asserts that it is not a problem for him, since he writes his plays entirely for himself and is surprised to find that anyone else is interested in them at all. And indeed it is, on the face of it, surprising—and particularly surprising that the television companies have opened their screens to him so freely—for he is far the most obscure of all the young writers.

What is baffling and unnerving about Pinter's plays is that he absolutely refuses to give us what we are accustomed to getting in most plays: a neat little explanation of the events that take place, an explicit motivation for the characters together with some small potted history of their pasts. We come in on a play of his as we might come in on a street accident or a street fight in which we are not involved. We stay to watch, fascinated by the event itself and the reactions of the participants. But we know nothing about them—where they came from, or how they came to be involved in these particular circumstances, or what happens to them afterwards. When the incident, whatever it is, is finished, we pass on. But what has happened has happened with a dazzling clarity and vividness.

The vividness and clarity come from two things. First, Pinter has an amazingly vivid apprehension of the insecurity that lurks behind the lives of most people today. If I had to define his theatre in a word, I'd call it the Theatre of Insecurity. Very often it is symbolized by characters who are the flotsam and jetsam of life, but it infects everyone around them. And this insecurity is caught remarkably exactly in his dialogue. The realism of his dialogue is often praised, but the exciting thing about it is that it is not just the documentary realism of the surface realists based on good observation. The dialogue, simple as it seems, very exactly catches the habits of mind behind it. He reveals to us that the inarticulate use speech not so much to communicate as to reassure themselves. Those reiterations and those platitudes and commonplaces they utter are a defense against others, a reassurance to themselves, a form almost of propitiation.

T. C. Worsley. *ThA*. Oct., 1961, p. 19

Pinter's plays are frequently funny. They are also frequently frightening. Their meaning usually seems obscure. They are realistic plays, after a fashion, but not realistic in the sense that [Wesker's] *Roots* or [Osborne's] *Look Back in Anger* is realistic. The characters behave in a "believable" manner, but they are shrouded in a twilight of mystery. We are never precisely sure who they are, why they are there, or what they have come to do. Their motives and backgrounds are vague or unknown. We recognize that there is motivation, but we are unsure what it is. We recognize that there is a background, but that background is clouded. Each piece of knowledge is a half-knowledge, each answer a springboard to new questions. In *The Room* it is never completely explained why a blind Negro named Riley comes to visit Rose Hudd, what his message to her means, or even why Bert Hudd, Rose's husband, kills him. In *The Birthday Party,* we never really know why the strange visitors, Goldberg and McCann, intimidate Stanley or why they take him away with them. In *The Caretaker,* we do not know the precise relationship of the brothers or even the reasons for the younger brother's changing attitudes toward their visitor, Davies. In *The Dumb Waiter,* we do not know the reasons Gus and Ben have been hired to do their job. Yet at the same time we accept Riley's need to deliver his message and Bert Hudd's need to kill him; we accept the fact that Goldberg and McCann must do something to Stanley; we accept as logical the younger brother's treatment of Davies; and we accept the fact that Gus and Ben have been hired to do a job. Pinter's plays are not constructed in the familiar Ibsenite fashion, and yet they have a recognizable beginning, middle, and end. His characters are recognizable human beings who seem to behave according to valid psychological and sociological motives, and yet there is something bizarre about their very reality. They seem to be "real" people, for their speech, their concerns, their behavioral patterns, and their rhythms of daily living have the ring of truth to them. But it is the details of living and the individual sections of dialogue which have this ring of truth, not the overall pattern itself. They exist within the given framework of the play, and their overall pattern of reality is the bizarre world of the play. Pinter seems to be making a statement about life and the world we live in, but at the same time he seems to be saying something merely about a grotesque world of his own creation.

Bernard Dukore. TDR. March, 1962, pp. 43–44

The thing hardly anybody seems to have noticed about the plays of Harold Pinter is that what is so effective about them is also the source of much that is unsatisfying. At his best, Pinter is a dramatist of high urgency, clear color and unimpeachable intentions. He has the right kind of dissatisfactions and impenitences, the accurate chimeras, the anxieties, hungers and vertigos proper to our time. And he has a high degree of freedom from the expectations of audiences, an aloofness from the theatre conceived of as a place of mutual congratulation, a toughness, or blessed innocence, to resist most of the pressures to make his plays serve other purposes than their own—to prevent them from "commenting" on our condition, or offering explanations or providing us with solace. . . .

Yet in Pinter the action is not in fact much more than an introduction, the beginning of recognition and affect and change. The shapes he creates are skeletal and unfinished, as though they have known what not to be but do not yet know what to become. Having stripped away much of what is exhausted in conventional drama, having made a psychology that confirms or explains yield to a metaphysics that invokes, and having made the logic of narrative continuity yield to the terrifying arbitrariness of the way we really experience the world, Pinter hovers still on the threshold of the theatre of new events and new portrayals. Unlike Ionesco and Beckett, in whose light, especially the latter's, he has so clearly worked, he has been unable to do more than present the *reverse* side of existence, the underskin of emptiness that sheathes our habitual gestures and spent meanings.

Richard Gilman. *Com.* Dec. 28, 1962, p. 366.

Harold Pinter's people are generally at cross-purposes with each other and sometimes tangled in a world of disconcerting objectivity. Mental discontinuities balance objective absurdities to arouse suspense and a sense of threat, bordering on insanity, as when in *The Dumb Waiter* mysterious orders for elaborate meals come down the lift from what had once been a restaurant to the basement kitchen where the two ambiguous ruffians are at their simultaneously flaccid and ominous talk; wherein perhaps a lucid symbolism may be felt flowering from a superficial absurdity. Pinter's conversation is usually that of lower middle-class normality, and the disconcerting objects those of town life and human fabrication. In *The Caretaker* Mick reels off a speech about London districts and its various bus-routes and then one about the legal and financial conditions of letting his property, in such a way as to make one dizzy. Questions may be left unanswered: who is the negro in *The Room,* who comes up from the basement of the tenement house, striking terror? Much of this is in the manner of Eugène Ionesco. What is so strange is that we are nowadays given the experience of nightmare, almost of the supernatural, in terms not of devils or ghosts, but of ordinary, material objects and affairs; and of people at cross-purposes with each other and with the audience in a paradoxical and dangerous world.

G. Wilson Knight. *Enc.* Dec., 1963, p. 49

Pinter's new play, *The Homecoming,* itself a welcome return of a gifted dramatist to his native habitats—the full-length play, the stage (in spite of his forays in film and television, his true *métier*), his major themes. It is a play which, in its complexity, its achieved style, its mastery over certain limited but characteristic linguistic rhythms, deserves to stand beside *The Caretaker;* though it may not in fact mark an advance into new territory. . . .

The Homecoming is a play about the family—or rather, a Pinter family, in this case "new" working class, and, as in *The Caretaker,* deprived of the sympathetic influences of Mum. This takes the sentimental prop from under the situation and provides, in effect, the pivot of the play. Mum is never defined retrospectively, except in the most ambiguous terms. . . . But she is a "felt absence" in so far as it is her withdrawal from the scene which has liberated the men and set them free to roam and prey upon one another. In this primitive male world, according to Pinter's rigid dialectic, some have been raised as winners and desperadoes—Max, the father, ex-butcher and bully-royal, and Lenny, the sharp Greek Street pimp and casual denizen of the house: while others are cast in the "feminine" role—Sam, Max's brother, unmarried, a car-hire chauffeur, whose domain in the household is the kitchen sink and the washing up; Teddy, the Camden Town scholarship boy, intellectual, whose "homecoming" (together with sleek wife) the play "celebrates," and Joey, the loutish would-be boxer, who winds up on his knees in Pinter's own very special version of "mother's boy.". . .

The brutally "present" quality of family life—if it can be called that— is established in the opening scene: first between Lenny and his father, and then between the father and Sam. Pinter sets this up with such enormous economy that it almost escapes our notice how it is done: but this is central to the whole play. Like all of Pinter's characters, the men—Max, Sam, Lenny, Joey—are all granted that extraordinary racy way with language, an idiom all Pinter's own, which has its roots in the rituals and repetitions of working class speech, but with an extra charge of articulateness and a high literalness, a grip on detail, behind it: a common idiom, which is specially *inflected* for each character.

Stuart Hall. *Encore*. July–Aug., 1965, pp. 30–31

I am not much interested in seeking the "meaning" of Pinter's plays. However, I do want to disagree with those who see in Pinter a protest against the dehumanization of contemporary man. They take the pursuer-victim pattern and the automatic (or "already said") quality of many Pinter dialogues as indications of this protest. What I see in Pinter is a fine contemporary example of the "disinterested" artist. His attention is turned inward on the mechanics of his art. He is meticulous in scenic structure and dialogue for their own sake. He seems to me further from social protest than Ionesco or Genet, both of whom negatively point a "better world." Nor do I see in Pinter's work an analogue to Beckett's, except from a purely technical point of view.

In his plays Pinter asks "what can the theatre do?" much in the way that contemporary painters ask "what can pigments and form do?" His plays are often riddles because the insoluble puzzle is paradigmatically theatrical. Only within an art form which exists in time and which creates "reality" can one pose real questions without suggesting real answers. The audience is led to believe in the reality of both characters and situations. But the theatre is, finally, an illusion. Once we bring realistic attention to focus on an illusionistic presentation, we have set the stage for insoluble riddles. It remains only for the playwright to pose the questions. But Pinter is different from that other great riddler, Pirandello. Pirandello built his plays around contradictions, Pinter around conceptual incompletion. We cannot know in Pirandello; we shall not know in Pinter.

If there is a "meaning" in Pinter, it seems to me closely related to both Henry James and Franz Kafka. James was most interested in probing the human psyche to its depths of confusion and fragmentary bases. Kafka was always telling stories in which his heroes had no sense of what was happening to them. Combine these two, and I think you have what Pinter seeks.

Richard Schechner. TDR. Winter, 1966, pp. 183–84

[*The Homecoming*] parodies all those wet stories about sentimental home-comings. Like much postwar drama it will be—already has been—explained away as Absurdity, Anti-logic, The Impossibility of Communication, the Theaters of Cruelty, Menace and Metaphysical Mystery.

Since it is both farcical and melodramatic, a more rewarding guide is the chapters on melodrama and farce in Eric Bentley's *The Life of the Drama*. Bentley talks about the irrational fears that can be presented to us from a stage; we may thrill vicariously to the fears from a safe distance (melodrama), or laugh at them because they are somebody else's (farce). He writes, ". . . 'We have nothing to fear but fear itself' is not a cheering slogan because fear itself is the most indestructible of obstacles." . . .

Dreams articulated are the soul of Pinter's writing. Not dreams like Strindberg's *To Damascus, The Ghost Sonata* and *A Dream Play*, which are torn whole and quivering out of the unconscious, but portraits of fears that casually surface and take on an uncanny semblance of reality. In place of the commercial daydream-plays of affluence and ease, popularity and sexual go, Pinter (following Beckett, Adamov, Genet and Ionesco) dramatizes nightmares, the dread of death or of life in a dead world, a morgue in movement, the snatching away of somebody precious or of a characteristic (sanity, satisfaction, reputation) that is essential if one is really to live.

The playwright's dreads come forth to challenge his "hero," an incarnation of himself. The operative figures in the nightmare are relatives, supposed friends of relatives, rivals—takers all. They rob him; they humiliate him. But the injuries have no obvious motive. He may seek and find a motive, out of his torment: an accidental crossing of another person's wishes, an unmeant infraction of another's property. He may even bow to that motive and so justify in a fashion what is being done to him. But the motive is inadvertent, trivial, ridiculous.

Albert Bermel. NewL. Jan. 30, 1967, p. 30

In spite of the clever dislocation of common sense, Pinter's plays affect us because they are about the middle-class family, both as sheltering home longed for and dreamed of, and as many-tentacled monster strangling its victim. It does not, after all, surprise us that there is more menace and irrationality in this dramatic material than in any other. The London stage since 1945 (to look no further) has been very much occupied with the family as a trap-door to the underworld. Whether the angle of descent has been religious, as in Graham Greene, or social class, as in Osborne and Wesker, the game of Happy Families has provided the entertainment. Pinter, however, is by far the most radical in breaking with the naturalistic conventions of *drame bourgeois*. For he burrows into dark places where it is of little consequence whether a family is working-class or professional. If he is obsessed by the peculiar horrors of middle-class families, this is not within the larger view of social class, but simply because they epitomize everything that is horrifying in any family situation today. He makes us see that class distinctions are curiously out of date for today's theatre, and that a kitchen sink is no more enlightening than a coffee table. When such paraphernalia are made into class-symbols, they merely hide what Pinter knows to be the real drama. We cling to kitchen sinks in the belief that at last we have reached something solid and honest; but Pinter will have none of that. He destroys the predictable place of things, deliberately confuses and contradicts. As soon as a situation looks as if it were attaining a recognizable meaning, he introduces some nonsense, wild improbability or verbal play, and we fall once more through the trap-door. His plays consist largely of his dogged attempts to destroy consistency and any clue to a rational pattern. The act of writing becomes, then, the work of the repressive censor as much as what is usually thought of as the creative imagination. This would seem to account for the taste of ashes, the sterility which pervades not only Pinter's plays but the whole Theatre of the Absurd in spite of its wildly fantastic ingredients. But the interesting point about this censorship is that it in fact underlines, or at any rate circumscribes, the very clues it destroys. As a result the audience is insidiously attacked at a level where it hurts most.

R. F. Storch. *MR*. Autumn, 1967, pp. 703–4

If, as it is sometimes suggested, the ambiguity and uncertainty of Pinter's plays really was no more than the outcome of a deliberate manipulation of his audience by a clever craftsman of theatrical trickery, his use of repetition and absurdly inconsequential conversation no more than mechanical mannerisms, his work would be highly ephemeral and have no chance of making an impact on future generations of playgoers who would no longer be taken in or shocked by such superficially effective devices. If, on the other hand, as I believe it to be the case, the uncertainties, ambivalences and ambiguities of plot and language in these plays are the expression of a genuine perplexity about the nature of our experience of the world, the distillation of a deeply felt, painfully sifted and conscientiously recorded creative process, then they will surely endure as works not only of brilliant craftsmanship (which is already beyond doubt) but as considerable artistic achievements.

What speaks for the latter view is the undoubted evidence of a steady development in Pinter's style, his consistent refusal merely to reproduce the mannerisms and technical achievements of his early successes. *Landscape* and *Silence,* in particular, are so radically different from the formula of what is commonly regarded as Pinteresque, so uncompromisingly remote from cheap seeking after success, that the view of Pinter as a mere manipulator of mechanical formulae surely must break down. In these plays the *poet* following his own inner law and discipline is again to the fore. "My last two plays," said Pinter in an interview before the first night of *Landscape* and *Silence,* "are really rather different. They had to be from my point of view: I felt that after *The Homecoming,* which was the last full-length play I wrote, I couldn't any longer stay in the room with this bunch of people who opened doors and came in and went out. . . ." . . .

Pinter's ability to transcend the merely autobiographical subject-matter puts him, in my opinion, into a different class from most of the other, social-realist, playwrights of his generation in Britain. Moreover, and surprisingly, since so much of his effect in his own country derives from his witty use of local speech patterns, Pinter's plays have been as successful in America and in Europe across the Channel as they were in England. . . .

The three longer plays have, in my opinion, proved themselves beyond a doubt: *The Birthday Party* and *The Caretaker* have stood the test of repeated survival; *The Homecoming* also seemed to me, after a considerable number of encounters with the play, fresher and more durable each time, and able to preserve its impact and essence even in bad translations and abominable performances. These three plays are classics of our time, even though only future generations will be able to judge whether they can become classics for all time.

Martin Esslin. *The Peopled Wound: The Plays
of Harold Pinter* (Garden City, N.Y.,
Doubleday, 1970), pp. 249–50, 253

Pinter's particular achievement has been to sustain linguistically the sort of tensions which seem to drive his characters from within. The fragmentary sentence, the phrase left hanging, the awkward pause, become outer manifestations of the inner anxiety, the deeper uncertainty. The discordant clash of language in, say, *The Caretaker,* is indicative of the discord that arises not only between character and character but within each of the characters. The fumbling efforts at conversation which ensue indicate the desperate need the characters have to make themselves known. Paraphrasing von Clausewitz's definition of "war," language becomes *a continuation of tension by other means*. On such occasions, Heidegger reminds us, language seems not so much a faculty that man possesses as that which possesses man.

But the "continuation of tension" may not always have the exchange of information as its goal. Many of Pinter's characters, on the contrary, go to some length to evade being known by others. The sounds these characters exchange are a holding action, a skirmish designed to avoid the larger confrontation. Pinter describes such a strategy: "communication itself between people is so frightening that rather than do that there is continual cross-talk, a continual talking about other things rather than what is at the root of their relationship." One source of this circumvention of communication may derive from opposing levels of knowledge or intelligence. In *The Birthday Party*, for example, Goldberg and McCann can badger Stanley to distraction because of their continued reference to unknown forces or significant but hidden events. Or, as in *The Caretaker*, Mick can keep ahead of Davies because of his superior intelligence and wit. But the more important source of evasion arises out of the character's fear that if he reveals himself, if he comes clean, he will be at the mercy of those who know him. Davies, for example, will never admit much about Sidcup and expose his illusion. Everything he says then, however insignificant it seems, remains a part of his larger attempt to learn vital details about others and keep his own secrets to himself.

James R. Hollis. *Harold Pinter: The Poetics of Silence* (Carbondale, Ill., Southern Illinois University Press, 1970), pp. 123–24

Ritual functions in Pinter's dramatic world much as Jane Ellen Harrison suggests it functions in religion to keep the individual fenced-in soul open—"to other souls, other separate lives, and to the apprehension of other forms of life." The daily rituals that protect man from such openness and awareness are constantly undermined in Pinter's dramas by those sacrificial rites that impinge upon them and force contact. Goldberg and McCann disturb the breakfast rituals of *The Birthday Party* to conduct their own ritual party at which Stanley is sacrificed; and Petey can no longer hide behind his paper when the strips of it which McCann has torn during the party fall out to remind him of Stanley's victimization. In *The Room* Rose can no longer hide behind her ritual breakfasts with her husband when Riley appears from the basement and involves her in his fate as *pharmakos*. As much as his characters evade communication, Pinter involves them in an eventual confrontation. The structure is Aristotelian, the imitation of an action, and the impact of the characters upon one another, even in their silent exchanges, is as final and irrevocable as the impact of character on character in Greek tragedy.

The Golden Bough kings have served in this exploration of Pinter's dramatic world as a metaphorical clue to the ritual patterns that form the basis of it. The contests for dominance which are at the center of the dramatic action of each play invariably have been fought with the tenacity of those priests who defended the Golden Bough with their lives. The battles have also taken on the symbolic significance of seasonal change and renewal attached to the Golden Bough ritual by Frazer and the Cambridge school of anthropology. In the seasonal ritual the old king-priest-god invariably must suffer death or banishment (Davies, Teddy, Edward—all must be sacrificed), either to be reborn as the new spirit of spring and life (Edward becomes the match-seller, Stanley becomes the new creation of Monty and Co.) or to be replaced by a new god (Teddy is replaced by Lenny and Joey, Law is replaced by Stott, Davies loses the battle to the young gods already in possession, Mick and Aston). The role played by Pinter's women is also clearer if their place as fertility goddess in the ritual is understood: Flora's welcome of the match-seller as her new mate and Ruth's adoption of her new household both make ritual sense of what on the surface seem sluttish and irrational choices. The new god must receive a welcome and be joined with mother earth if life is to continue.

Katherine H. Burkman. *The Dramatic World
of Harold Pinter: Its Basis in Ritual* (Columbus,
Ohio State University Press, 1971), pp. 133–34

Harold Pinter is the finest playwright to emerge in our technological society; and it is ironic that the humanity of his vision is achieved by bringing audiences back to an awareness of the inherent mystery of people and objects. This is his obsession; and he pursues it with ruthless dedication. The act of writing is as much a process of discovery for him as following the protean moods and motives of his characters is for the audience. . . .

While Pinter dramatizes the ambiguity of language and man's penchant for evasion, his plays are never vague or murky. The realism of his work has the weight of such meticulous observation and control that this precision elevates it to the abstract. The audience is conscious of entering a world in which every prop and plot point exists in an electric, precarious balance. Pinter is creating a world as mercurial as the imagination itself. His moral "statement" is not in the mouths of his characters, but in his refusal to "cheat" an audience by limiting the theatrical experience to false simplicity or easy sentiment. . . .

The Homecoming is Pinter's major full-length work, a triumph of craftsmanship and artistic intention. Here, in the cavernous main room of Max's house, Pinter compresses the masks of language, the terror of identity, the instability of our notion of the past which are his main concerns. Visually, the room is cleaner, more spare than Aston's cluttered bed-sitter in *The Caretaker,* or the chintzy cosiness of Meg's seaside boarding house in *The Birthday Party.* The language, also, has been honed down; its resonance opened up with a much more daring, rigorous use of the pause and the silence. *The Homecoming* is a brilliantly sculpted stage event. The audience is forced to focus on the impact of the *moment.* In such a minimal environment, every gesture and word counts for something. The drama and terror Pinter feels in the world need not be the bravura shock tactics of Stanley's blindman's buff in *The Birthday Party* nor Mick's overt role-playing in *The Caretaker.* In *The Homecoming,* Pinter has refined his stage image. The fusion between word-gesture-environment is startling; the tension becomes volcanic. In this climate, simple actions have a tantalizing suggestiveness.

John Lahr. Introduction to John Lahr, ed., *A Casebook on Harold Pinter's "The Homecoming"* (New York, Grove Press, 1971), pp. xi–xii

It's relatively easy to "decipher" a plot and theme in *Old Times,* which I mean to do and then move on from it. It has only three characters. An English couple in their 40s are visited in their country home by a former girlfriend of the wife's whom she hasn't seen in 20 years. As single girls, they shared an apartment in London. It's easy to demonstrate that the two used to have a lesbian relation in atmosphere if not in fact; that the husband knew them at the time, although he and they now pretend he didn't; that there's a threat that the lesbian relation will be resumed, and that the husband breaks down and cries for pity at the end. I put all this more clearly than the play does. Pinter uses overlaid "exposures" as in photography. Details do not quite jibe. Time is constantly past *and* present, as in cubist painting that shows us simultaneous views which would be impossible simultaneously in life. But my précis is supportable.

Construed from this story, the theme can be seen as the power of the female—to create a realm in which the male is trapped, a kind of golden moist web woven by women laterally through time; within which men can strut for a bit but are finally subordinated. In short, the world as the realm of Astarte-Lilith-Erda, with men allowed to delude themselves about mastery. It's not a new Pinter theme. At the end of *The Homecoming,* the one woman is seated with two of the play's toughest men kneeling next to her, begging for affection. At the end of *Old Times,* the one man has wept, then kneeled with his head on his wife's lap, while the other woman waits prone on a bed.

I don't contend that this theme was carefully selected by Pinter. He himself has said that the play began for him with a flash of "two people talking about someone else," and his statement fits what we know of his methods: that he's largely an intuitive "automatic" writer, whose real work of design begins only as the words begin on paper. What lies behind this process is the esthetic history of this century. . . .

Pinter's playwriting can be seen as classic surrealism, dealing with well-defined objects arranged in such a way that the point is not in their detail—the fine details are in a way a deliberate deception—but in the trajectory outlined by the way they are deployed, in the space they enclose, in the surprise and shock and laughter that the succession of these details arouses in us.

Stanley Kauffmann. *NR*. Dec. 18, 1971, p. 20

As a Romantic artist, Pinter has known as much as any modern playwright the appeal of the liberated self. He has sensed, and embodied in the plays, that impulse toward the unlimited expansion of the ego, toward dominance, luxury, action, possession, sensual gratification. But as a late and disillusioned Romantic, Pinter has also known from the first that such an impulse was not to be trusted, that such qualities were as destructive as gratifying. Davies of *The Caretaker* is as near as Pinter has come to drawing a portrait of archetypal man; and though we pity Davies because he is, like all of us, weak, ignorant, lost on an endless journey, subject to age and death, nevertheless, we know that the endless self-aggrandizement of so vain and dangerous a creature cannot go unchecked. Yet so pressed are Pinter's characters by the demands of the self that the only way they can escape them is through total retreat into some state of withdrawal—some room—where they will be sheltered. Persons such as Stanley, Aston, Teddy, and Kate are not hiding from the I.R.A., or the trauma of a mental home, or a coarse family, or a lesbian past but from the demands of the inner self.

Pinter has often spoken of his admiration for Samuel Beckett, and his stylistic debt to the great symbolist playwright is easily enough perceived. Yet, though he shares Beckett's recognition of human vanity and fallibility, Pinter lacks the Irish writer's sense of the metaphysical on the one hand and his humane whimsy on the other. Of all the major modern playwrights, Pinter seems in certain essentials most closely allied to one comparatively distant in time and very different in style, Henrik Ibsen. Pinter shares with Ibsen a kind of grim humor, but more significantly, an essentially ambiguous view of the human condition. Both have given us figures possessed by a desire for self-aggrandizement, dominance, fulfillment, yet forever held back in a state of psychic paralysis. If he were not still trailing some clouds of Faustian glory, the Master Builder might find a place in a Pinter play; Hilda Wangel, the embodiment of feminine power, would probably not object to making certain contractual arrangements with Lenny and his family in *The Homecoming*. For the creators of Solness and Davies, of Hilda and

Ruth, are both attracted by the power of the vital inner self and repelled by its ruthlessness.

That there should be so marked a similarity between the first great modern playwright and the writer who has most recently assumed a place in the line of descent from him suggests not only a coincidence in personality but the extent to which the modern drama is a body of Romantic art. And as the Romantic writer has characteristically turned to the past as a source of fulfillment, so Pinter, in *Landscape, Silence,* and *Old Times,* has sought there for the resolution to the contradictions with which he has been concerned. If his search has not brought us answers, it has brought us his plays, which are significant records of his quest.

Arthur Ganz. In Arthur Ganz, ed., *Pinter: A Collection of Critical Essays* (Englewood Cliffs, N.J., Prentice-Hall, 1972), pp. 177–78

All attempts to explain [*Old Times*] involve an attempt to summarize something unsummarizable, and most of them enter too ingenuously into the game of finding different degrees of truthfulness in different speeches. "Yes I believed him when he said that but she wasn't telling the truth when she said that." No one in a play is telling the truth. None of the events happened in reality. But though we all know this very well, we still look for factual consistency in the fictional artifice that every play is, and Pinter is the first playwright fully to explore the theatrical potential of frustrating us.

The question of whether Anna really saw a man lying across Kate's lap is a meaningless question. What matters is the relationship between the words in which she speaks about it and the image we see at the end of the play when Deeley lies across Kate's lap. The question of whether Anna is alive or dead, an aspect of Kate, a separate person, or a set of memories in the minds of the other two is a question which deserves only a minimum of attention. It may not be wholly avoidable, but it does not need to be in the foreground of our minds; the criticism which sets out to bring it into the foreground is bad criticism. We go to the theater with our responses preconditioned by what we have heard and what we have read.

Old Times is not a puzzle to be solved; it is an elaborate construction of words, echoing silences and images which ought to be enjoyed as such. If it makes a statement—as every play, in some sense, must—it is a statement which could not have been made by Pinter in any other way, and which remains unparaphrasable. Murder plays are usually badly written and our interest in them exhausted as soon as the mystery is solved. *Old Times* is extremely well written, and the critic can best help us to relish the writing by weaning us away from trying to solve the mysteries.

Ronald Hayman. *Harold Pinter* (New York, Frederick Ungar, 1973), pp. 147–48

I am, in the last analysis, not quite so confident that Pinter's work will survive to "classic" status as Osborne's or Arden's—and he himself declares that "it's of no moment to me." For, so like yet so unlike his fellow Jewish writer Arnold Wesker, he is very much a man of his times, and writes for them—and for the actors who act in them. In another half a century there is the danger that performers may have lost the capacity to play Pinter as irrecoverably as we have today grown out of sympathy with the style of a [Henry] Irving or a [Herbert Beerbohm] Tree, or even of a [Donald] Wolfit.

Pinter is, then, an actor's playwright, with all the virtues and limitations that implies. He will, of course, continue to write—and, I suspect, continue to move disconcertingly from the master work of each period of his stylistic development to a formulaic *reductio ad absurdum* of the same manner. But he will remain, I think, a lyrical writer, choosing to ignore the possibilities of the narrative element in drama, continuing to write strong curtains—and continuing, above all, to write a play around a hard kernel of situation, enwrapping this in arbitrary layers of ambiguity at his worst, but at his best showing us the kaleidoscopic multiplicity of attitude, ambivalence, distortion and doubt that is the individual's attempt to bring reality within the bounds of personality, and so to make it bearable.

Simon Trussler. The Plays of Harold Pinter: An
Assessment (London, Victor Gollancz, 1973), pp. 187–88

I actually believe that Beckett and Pinter are poetic dramatists, in the proper sense of the word: they have a linear structure and a formal structure which you'd better just observe—don't learn it wrong, don't speak it wrong, you can't, you mustn't. But there are various things that you can exercise. One of the greatest influences on Pinter, obviously, is the early Eliot—particularly in the repeated phrase, the catching up of a phrase and repeating it over three sentences, keeping it up in the air, like a ball. Now, that is often written in three separate sentences: but it has to make a unit, and you don't find that unit till about the third week [of rehearsal]. So at the beginning it is better just to observe absolutely accurately what he's written.

I also know that the intensity of the feeling underlying Pinter's text is so very extreme, so very brutal, that you have to explore this melodramatic area that I was speaking about. And this of course raises the question of where the actors live in relation to each other, physically, because until you start letting loose the naked feeling, you don't know the answers to very basic questions, such as, are eyes necessary, or are they not? Are they part of the weaponry?

My vocabulary is all the time about hostility and battles and weaponry, but that is the way Pinter's characters operate, as if they were all stalking round a jungle, trying to kill each other, but trying to disguise from one another the fact that they are bent on murder. And whether you can see a character's face or whether you can't, whether you hold his eyes or not, is absolutely critical—and that to a very large extent comes out of the actor's psyche, once the feelings are being generated. So I wouldn't have anything to say about the physical life of a Pinter play until the emotions had been released, because I wouldn't know what they should be. Equally, Pinter deals in stillness, in confrontations which are unbroken, and I believe it mandatory to do as few moves in a Pinter play as possible. You don't want moves up to the drinks cabinet, or across to the table, in order to "break it up," or to make it seem naturalistic. It isn't naturalistic.

Peter Hall. *TheatreQ*. Nov., 1974–Jan., 1975, p. 7

In 1957, when *The Room* was first produced at the Hampstead Theatre Club, and again in the following year when Pinter arrived (for a rather brief stay) in the West End with *The Birthday Party,* two things about his work stood out and attracted much critical comment: one was the atmosphere of half-hidden violence and indefinable menace; the other was the accuracy with which he had caught the exact cadence and texture of local London speech, several layers down into the sub-culture. The latter of these two qualities—though certainly real and considerable—proved to be a stumbling-block to critics, more especially, perhaps, to *theatre* critics (as distinct from literary critics whose task is easier, since they have a text before them and are not called upon for instant decision and opinion). The difficulty about that uncannily-well-observed naturalistic dialogue was that it tended to direct attention to the idea of the plays as direct, surface portraiture of the East End of London, more especially since it was by then known that Pinter himself had grown up there. That photograph, on the dust jacket of the first edition of his early plays, of Pinter leaning on the counter of an all-night coffee stall and listening attentively to the old man who served the coffee, represented a popular misconception of what the main thrust of his early work was to be. The fact that almost all of Pinter's early characters speak the most accurate Cockney that has even been written for the English stage (compare it, for example, with Shaw's vaudeville-Cockney) was in one way misleading, for it was not the uneducated Cockneyness of his people that was their significant feature. On the other hand, that same Cockneyness provides us with one of the best examples we have of that curiously twentieth-century theatrical problem of establishing the right relationship between the surface-portraiture of naturalistic verisimilitude on the one hand and the inner sense of life (for the revelation of which all art exists) on the other. Clearly, some form of imagistic and ritual language and action are needed to fix and hold this relationship, but the inventing of such a language and action, with the capacity to capture authoritatively the imagination of the audience and at the same time keep alive the fictive entities of the characters, has proved in the present century extremely difficult.

Eric Salmon. MD. Dec., 1974, pp. 363–64

Attempts to categorize Pinter's plays have given rise to two descriptive terms: "comedy of menace" and "Pinteresque." . . . The great danger with such terms is that they tend to become institutionalized when they are not transcended. And as they interact only minimally with the details of the plays, they tend to obscure the subtlety and variety of P.'s work and contribute to the impression that his experimentation reduces to the mere repetition of consistent formula. At a certain level of abstraction, Pinter's work does deal with recurring problems: the problem of interrelational adjustment being a major one. But to give stress to less central generalizations at the expense of an acknowledgment of the great variety of his work is to promote . . . circularity of thought. . . .

The point which is basic to this approach to Pinter is that which should be basic to any approach to language. Far from being a monolithic unity, language is an essentially pluralistic activity. Even within a certain general function, such as its interrelational use, language is characterized by variety and adaptability as well as by recurring patterns. . . .

If one approaches the plays with a belief that truth, reality and communication ought to conform to certain norms, then the plays will remain tantalizingly enigmatic. But once it is realized that all of these concepts are, like any others, moves in language games, the barrier to an understanding of Pinter is removed.

In striving to adjust to one another, Pinter's characters are negotiating not only truth and reality but their very freedom to engage their preferred identities in the environments that surround them. Their linguistic battles are not the product of an arbitrary desire for dominance but crucial battles for control of the means by which personality is created in the social systems to which they belong. As they struggle to cope, their misunderstandings and miscalculations provide a great deal of amusement for any audience, but invariably desperation and terror are eventually revealed as the linguistic warfare becomes increasingly crucial.

Austin E. Quigley. The Pinter Problem
(Princeton, N.J., Princeton University
Press, 1975), pp. 274–77

No Man's Land . . . is very much a piece for Pinter devotees. The title is misleading. The scene is not laid in no man's land; we are in Pinterland once again, with most of those old familiar features that the author may have culled eclectically from various areas of the Absurdist universe or that he may, on the other hand, have largely invented for himself.

They have often been listed by the critics: the Closed Room (as in Sartre's *No Exit*) where the characters confront each other in their subject/object tensions, and which is at once home and hell, womb and battleground, a collective area or an image of the splintered individual mind; the Menace (as in Ionesco, Albee, Kafka) which is the subject/object conflict left in suspension, as it were, like a haze of paranoia; Time, Memory, and Identity (as in Ionesco, Beckett, Genet), the uncertainties of which lead to endless fluctuation of personae; and the Inexplicable Oneiric Detail (as in Ionesco, Beckett, Robbe-Grillet) which the mind can only chew on unsuccessfully, since it has no means of telling whether the detail is genuinely random, or significantly phenomenological, or symbolic within some given system—Christian, Freudian, Jungian, Marxist, etc. We can also mention the general paradox that, as in Robbe-Grillet, the language is always meticulously rhythmic and clear, while the overall effect is opaque.

The spectator can no more be clear about what is happening in Pinterland than the reader can be about the action in Robbe-Grillet's novels; and both authors have shown themselves quite expert at warding off interpretations. This is the Absurd, we might say, at one or more removes. The artist's response to the fundamental unintelligibility of the Absurd world is to create an artificially Absurd microcosm, in which our thirst for an explanation is at once stimulated and frustrated. Pinter, like Robbe-Grillet, sets up to be as inscrutable as God; or as God would be, were He not, by definition, absent from the Absurd universe.

John Weightman. Enc. July, 1975, p. 24

Tea Party is the picture of a man who is only superficially threatened by outside forces; it is the menace from within which destroys him, just as surely as it destroyed Edward in *A Slight Ache*. Pinter depicts Robert Disson as a man successful in all fields of endeavor: he is a good businessman, friend, husband, father, and son. And it is his very success which defeats him, somewhat like an Aristotelian tragic hero, though perhaps he is more akin to Joe in Arthur Miller's *All My Sons* because he does not have sufficient stature to make his fall meaningful in Aristotelian terms. . . .

Tea Party has a more pervasive surrealistic quality to it than many of Pinter's earlier plays, and it is fitting that in a tale of mental disintegration Theatre of the Absurd effects are employed to such a great extent (the two Ping-Pong balls, the chiffon scarf, the party, the two women lying on the desk). The blindfold applied at Disson's own insistence compounds the ambiguity of the drama because he cannot confirm his fears and suspicions visually, fears which may have at least some basis in reality, as suggested by the periods of blindness and Willy's actions with the two women, fears which have driven him to the point of suspecting everyone as being ranged against him ("playing at brother and sister").

In an extension of the reality/appearance theme (verification) Disson can no longer trust his senses to make sense out of the world which surrounds him. He cannot coordinate the sum of his many reflections, the kind that in *The Basement* became part of the physical environment. . . . The play starts out with Disson's perspective, but unlike *The Dwarfs,* in which the audience shares Len's mind and view of the universe, there is a separation as the audience is dissociated from Disson's point of view and the stream of consciousness disappears. At the beginning of the play the audience is with Disson; at the conclusion it is watching him from the outside. . . .

Although *The Basement* and *Tea Party* both seem to be out of place in terms of Pinter's thematic development, it must be remembered that the dates of composition, the early sixties, link them with his earlier works. The subject matter which the dramatist is considering (flux, verification) shows not thematic evolution, but the dramas come from a period during which he was still considering the potentialities of these themes, which means that he was interested in experimenting with the form of his expression rather than with new content. *The Basement* and *Tea Party,* then, are additional indicators of the playwright's thinking around the time he was working on *The Lover.*

Steven H. Gale. *Butter's Going Up: A Critical*
Analysis of Harold Pinter's Work (Durham, N.C.,
Duke University Press, 1977), pp. 171–73

[*The Collection*] was Pinter's second play written for television. The characters are not tramps or even ex-convicts but dress designers who have elegant rooms. There is still the comedy of menace (though it is very muted) but it is mainly a comedy of manners. . . .

The title, presumably, refers to the Chinese vases (an excellent symbol for the fragile sexual relationship as we can see in Wycherley's *The Country Wife* or Pope's *The Rape of the Lock*), [to] the collection of clothes shown at Leeds, but principally to the collection of "truths" the play displays. It is clearly not important whether or not Bill and Stella *did* sleep together in Leeds; what matters is the potential the idea of that act contains for liberating a large number of illusions which either strengthen or destroy the lives of four people. And the situation is given an extra twist because the quartet is not two couples but one woman and three men. In the action of the play Bill and Stella, who never meet (for such a meeting would be fatal), swap partners and then return to the status quo. So *The Collection* is not just a comedy of manners kept deliberately slight. . . . It is full of questions, it involves class warfare (which all good comedy of manners must), and it pushes the themes of menace, verification, and the sexual potential of a woman a stage further. . . .

Here, then, is a bedroom farce in which Pinter traces an ordinary story about getting at the truth. . . . This play recalls the [Noel] Coward of *Private Lives* in which the partners are restored at the end. And if it is an autumn play the collection shown will surely be for spring or summer.

Arnold P. Hinchliffe. *Harold Pinter*, rev. ed.
(Boston, Twayne, 1981), pp. 97, 99–101

In *Betrayal* . . . it is the arrangement of the scenes that makes ironies accumulate and the drama as a whole possible. It is not so much *what we know* but *when we know it* that is responsible for the real tension that bristles so ferociously beneath the contained surface of this work. . . . And when things happen in *Betrayal,* they happen visually rather than verbally. Props are made "to talk," time is allowed to speak for itself between the scenes and through costumes (were miniskirts really that short back in 1968?), and actors communicate to us in gesture, silence, and pause, all those characteristic Pinter "words" they never get to recite on stage.

With its emphasis on visual statement, and especially in its concise arrangement of nine short scenes which move so uninhibitedly back and forth in time, *Betrayal* shows more clearly than any previous Pinter play the profound effect his work in the movies has had on his dramatic technique. And although *Betrayal* reads at times like a filmscript, its real originality lies in the way it adapts certain cinematic strategies and makes them functional in terms of theater. *Betrayal* makes us concerned with the unities and disunities of time, with deception and self-deception, with the past in the present and the present in the past. In order to make these themes work on stage, the play must abandon realism's literal conformity to chronological time for the more representative patterning of temporality normally associated with cinematography and film-editing. . . .

In *Betrayal* Pinter has selected images for us by translating cinematic capabilities into what is for him a new theatrical idiom. His nine scenes of people talking allow the past to speak for itself. These may not be images for eternity, but they are without question concise momentary images of theatrical presentness. Pinter's characters are still "taking the mickey out of each other," to use [the director] Peter Hall's phrase, but his dramatic style now shows them doing it in a decidely cinematic way. The facts of this betrayal may remain forever ambiguous, but the form in which it takes place on stage could not be more precise. Pinter has gone to the movies, but in a work like *Betrayal* he comes back, invigorated by his experience, to the theater.

Enoch Brater. *MD*. Dec., 1981, pp. 506–7, 512–13

SHAW, BERNARD (1856–1950)

The promptest notice of *Mrs. Warren's Profession* would have been too late to guide anyone as to whether he should or should not go to see the play. And the belatedness of my notice matters the less because the play, though performed only twice, lives lustily in book-form, and will assuredly live so for many years. Not that it seems to me "a masterpiece—yes! with all reservations, a masterpiece," as Mr. Archer hastily acclaimed it. Indeed, having seen it acted, I am confirmed in my heresy that it is, as a work of art, a failure. But the failure of such a man as "G. B. S." is of more value than a score of ordinary men's neat and cheap successes, even as the "failure" of a Brummell is worthier than a score of made-up bows in the gleaming window of the hosier. *Mrs. Warren* is a powerful and stimulating, even an ennobling, piece of work—a great failure, if you like, but also a failure with elements of greatness in it. It is decried as unpleasant by those who cannot bear to be told publicly about things which in private they can discuss, and even tolerate, without a qualm. Such people are the majority. For me, I confess, a play with an unpleasant subject, written sincerely and fearlessly by a man who has a keenly active brain and a keenly active interest in the life around him, is much less unpleasant than that milk-and-water romance (brewed of skimmed milk and stale water) which is the fare commonly provided for me in the theatre. It seems to me not only less unpleasant, but also less unwholesome. I am thankful for it.

Gratitude, however, does not benumb my other faculties. With all due deference to Mr. Archer, "Not a masterpiece, no! with all reservations, not a masterpiece" is my cry. The play is in Mr. Shaw's earlier manner—his 'prentice manner. It was written in the period when he had not yet found the proper form for expressing himself in drama. He has found that form now. He has come through experiment to the loose form of *Caesar and Cleopatra*, of *The Devil's Disciple*—that large and variegated form wherein there is elbow-room for all his irresponsible complexities. In *Mrs. Warren* he was still making tentative steps along the strait and narrow way of Ibsen. To exhaust a theme in four single acts requires tremendous artistic concentration. When the acts are split up loosely in scenes the author may divagate with impunity. But in four single acts there is no room for anything that is not strictly to the point. Any irrelevancy offends us. And irrelevancy is of the essence of Mr. Shaw's genius.

Max Beerbohm. SR (London). Feb. 1, 1902, pp. 139–40

An intelligent critic of George Bernard Shaw's *Man and Superman*—without doubt the author's most notable and mature book—entitled his article "The New St. Bernard." There was a certain felicity in this emphasis of the resemblance between Shaw's attitude and that of the great saint with whom he is so closely connected. The famous Christian ascetics of mediae-val times, and very notably St. Bernard, delighted to disrobe beauty of its garment of illusion; with cold hands and ironical smile they undertook the task of analysing its skin-deep fascination, and presented, for the salutary contemplation of those affected by the lust of the eyes, the vision of what seemed to them the real Woman, deprived of her skin. In the same spirit Shaw—developing certain utterances in Nietzsche's *Zarathustra*—has sought to analyse the fascination of women as an illusion of which the real-ity is the future mother's search of a husband for her child; and hell for Shaw is a place where people talk about beauty and the ideal.

While, however, it may be admitted that there is a very real affinity between Shaw's point of view in this matter and that of the old ascetics— who, it may be remarked, were often men of keen analytic intelligence and a passionately ironic view of life—it seems doubtful whether on the whole he is most accurately classified among the saints. It is probable that he is more fittingly placed among the prophets, an allied but still distinct species. The prophet, as we may study him in his numerous manifestations during several thousand years, is usually something of an artist and something of a scientist, but he is altogether a moralist. He foresees the future, it is true— and so far the vulgar definition of the prophet is correct—but he does not necessarily foresee it accurately. [1904]

Havelock Ellis. *From Marlowe to Shaw*
(London, Williams and Norgate, 1950), p. 291

The announcement that Bernard Shaw, moralist, Fabianite, vegetarian, play-wright, critic, Wagnerite, Ibsenite, jester to the cosmos, and the most serious man on the planet, had written a play on the subject of Don Juan did not sur-prise his admirers. As Nietzsche philosophized with a hammer, so G.B.S. hammers popular myths. If you have read his *Caesar and Cleopatra* you will know what I mean. This witty, sarcastic piece is the most daring he has at-tempted. Some years ago I described the Shaw literary pedigree as—W. S. Gilbert out of Ibsen. His plays are full of modern odds-and-ends, and in form are anything from the Robertsonian comedy to the Gilbertian extravaganza. They may be called physical farce, an intellectual *comédie rosse*—for his people are mostly a blackguard crew of lively marionettes all talking pure Shaw-ese. Mr. Shaw has invented a new individual in literature who for want of a better name could be called the *Super-Cad;* he is Nietzsche's Superman turned ''bounder''—and sometimes the sex is feminine.

James Huneker. *Iconoclasts* (New York,
Charles Scribner's Sons, 1905), pp. 233–34

That Shaw will ever become a popular dramatist, in the sense that Sardou and Pinero are popular, seems to be beyond all probability. The vogue that his plays have had of late in the United States is to be ascribed, in the main, to the yearning to appear "advanced" and "intellectual" which afflicts Americans of a certain class. The very fact that they do not understand him makes him seem worthy of admiration to these virtuously ambitious folks. Were his aims and methods obvious, they would probably vote him tiresome. As it is, a performance of *Candida* delights them as much as an entertainment by Henry Kellar, the magician, and for the same reason.

But even among those who approach Shaw more honestly, there is little likelihood that he will ever grow more popular, in the current sense, than he is at present. In the first place, some of his plays are wellnigh impossible of performance in a paying manner without elaborate revision and expurgation. *Man and Superman,* for instance, would require five hours if presented as it was written. And *Mrs. Warren's Profession,* because of its subject-matter, will be unsuitable for a good many years to come. In the second place, Shaw's extraordinary dexterity as a wit, which got him his first hearing and keeps him before the public almost constantly to-day, is a handicap of crushing weight. As long as he exercises it, the great majority will continue to think of him as a sort of glorified and magnificent buffoon. As soon as he abandons it, he will cease to be Shaw.

Henry L. Mencken. *George Bernard Shaw: His Plays* (Boston, John W. Luce, 1905), pp. xxiv–xxv

[Shaw] is an artist with a difference. He is as free of the conventional artistic scruples as he is of the popular artistic follies. He is an artist without being artistic, and one is forced into the belief that he would drop art without the least compunction if it did not aid him in his preaching. Shaw is a preacher of philosophy first, an artist afterwards. But although he has no scruples about the use he would make of art, he does not confuse this personal matter with its real nature. Because he uses art to disseminate a philosophy, he does not commit the error of the moralist who announces that the end of art is to teach. Neither does he yield comfort to the aesthetically afflicted people who are under the equally prevalent illusion that art is the pursuit of beauty. Beauty is no more likely to occur in art because it is sought than happiness would occur in life for a like reason. Both beauty and happiness are the incidentals of true action. They are the very will-o'-the-wisps of any definite search.

Art, for Shaw, is something closely related to good workmanship. It is the craftsmanship of emotional and imaginative conceptions, having, in so far as its expression is worthy and thorough, a tendency to impel those that come in contact with it towards a similar thoroughness and worthiness of the faculties it affects. It is this power of profoundly moving people which revealed to Shaw the immense propaganda value of art. And he has deliberately used art for philosophical and political ends, just as the Church, perhaps less consciously, used art for religious ends. What art there is in his work stands in the same perspective to the vital thought of to-day as the Madonnas and holy men in the canvases of the old masters stood in relation to what was vital in the thought of their day. Or to take a more obvious parallel, the Problem Plays of Bernard Shaw, and for the matter of that of Ibsen, Tolstoy, and all who have made problem the life of their drama, are the modern substitutes for the Morality and Mystery Plays of the past.

Holbrook Jackson. Bernard Shaw (London,
E. Grant Richards, 1907), pp. 143–45

The brain of Bernard Shaw was like a wedge in the literal sense. Its sharpest end was always in front; and it split our society from end to end the moment it had entrance at all. As I have said he was long unheard of; but he had not the tragedy of many authors, who were heard of long before they were heard. When you had read any Shaw you read all Shaw. When you had seen one of his plays you waited for more. And when he brought them out in volume form, you did what is repugnant to any literary man—you bought a book.

The dramatic volume with which Shaw dazzled the public was called, *Plays, Pleasant and Unpleasant.* I think the most striking and typical thing about it was that he did not know very clearly which plays were unpleasant and which were pleasant. "Pleasant" is a word which is almost unmeaning to Bernard Shaw. Except, as I suppose, in music (where I cannot follow him), relish and receptivity are things that simply do not appear. He has the best of tongues and the worst of palates. With the possible exception of *Mrs. Warren's Profession* (which was at least unpleasant in the sense of being forbidden) I can see no particular reason why any of the seven plays should be held specially to please or displease. First in fame and contemporary importance came the reprint of *Arms and the Man,* of which I have already spoken. Over all the rest towered unquestionably the two figures of Mrs. Warren and of Candida. They were neither of them really unpleasant except as all truth is unpleasant. But they did represent the author's normal preference and his principal fear; and those two sculptured giantesses largely upheld his fame.

G. K. Chesterton. George Bernard Shaw
(London, Bodley Head, 1909), pp. 115–16

Dear Mr. Shaw, life is a great and serious affair, and all of us in the short interval of time granted us must try to find our appointed task and fulfil it as well as possible. This applies to everybody, and to you especially with your great gift of original thought and your penetration into the essence of all questions. And therefore, confidently trusting that I shall not offend you, I will tell you what seem to me to be the defects in your book [*Man and Superman*].

The first defect in it is that you are not sufficiently serious. One should not speak jestingly of such a subject as the purpose of human life, the causes of its perversion, and the evil that fills the life of humanity to-day. I should like the speeches of Don Juan to be not the speeches of a vision, but the speeches of Shaw, and also that "The Revolutionist's Handbook" should be attributed not to the nonexistent Tanner but to a living Bernard Shaw who is responsible for his words. The second reproach is that the questions you deal with are of such enormous importance that, for men with such profound comprehension of the evils of our life and such brilliant capacity for exposition as yourself, to make them the subject of satire may easily do harm rather than help the solution of these grave questions.

In your book I detect a desire to surprise and astonish the readers by your great erudition, talent, and cleverness. Yet all this is not merely unnecessary for the solution of the questions you deal with, but often distracts the readers' attention from the essence of the matter by attracting it to the brilliance of the exposition. In any case I think this book of yours expresses your views not in their full and clear development, but only in an embryonic state. I think that these views, developing more and more, will arrive at the one truth we all seek and toward which we all gradually approach. I hope you will forgive me if there is anything that displeases you in what I have said. I have said it only because I recognize your very great gifts, and for you personally have a most friendly feeling. . . . [1909?]

Leo Tolstoy. Undated letter quoted in Aylmer Maude,
The Life of Tolstoy, Vol. II: The Later Years, rev. ed.
(London, Oxford University Press, 1930), pp. 461–62

In the last act [of *Candida*] Mr. Shaw, with any amount of alertness and audacity, makes a feint at extricating himself from the odd hole into which his plot has led him, but the play does not really complete itself, it merely apologizes for not going on, and the apology has a touch of the sentimentality which is Mr. Shaw's dread, or one of his dreads. Still, the play, though broken off short as a play, is a finished masterpiece of satiric observation, not through books, newspapers, and other plays, as is commonest in our theatre, but at first hand.

The only trouble for the spectator, apart from the weak ending, is that Mr. Shaw cannot make Marchbanks talk up to his part. Marchbanks is to be a young Shelley; his talk is to be Shelleyan, at any rate poetic, and Mr. Shaw sees this and does his best to write non-metrical poetry for Marchbanks to speak. But Mr. Shaw's writing, while it has no stupidities, has no beauties: the fairies seem to have made a very strict arrangement, before his birth, that the ones with force, lucidity and mordacity to give away to newborn infants should all be there, and that all the ones with sensuous loveliness of any kind in their gift should stay away. . . . It is as if a master of positive clearness and directness like Huxley had attempted, with that equipment, to do Keats's work, or as if Comte had tried to write a Song of Solomon. When Mr. Shaw, the rationalist, the determinist, the literalist, the man who thinks, as Tybalt fenced, "by the book of arithmetic," essays the description of golden dreams, the result is a chill or a bewilderment.

C. E. Montague. Dramatic Values, 2nd ed.
(London, Methuen, 1911), pp. 78–79

In all Mr. Shaw's work in the arts, critical and creative, a part is . . . played by the irrelevant motive. Never very far from the centre of his mind are "all the detestable fruits of inequality of condition." In this life there are secular hardships and anomalies enough for correction, God knows; but the artist, qua artist, does not find, I suppose, the fruits of inequality of condition detestable. For him they rather add to the fun of the human spectacle. But Mr. Shaw is out to alter all that. What Mr. Shaw wants, more than anything else, is to change our ideas; and art is a weapon in the chambardement général. He condescends to the fun of the human spectacle, not for its own sake, but to point a moral. Just as the persons of his drama are logical abstractions to whom, to aid in their acceptance, a surface humanity is added, so is his drama itself a secondary image of his picture of the world. He sees men as ideas walking. He sees art as a conflict of ideas. A thousand lovable, intimate, humorous, ridiculous, recognizable traits he sees, and he makes a pastiche of them for his purposes. They do not result in the comic vision. (Impossible, when the whole stretch of his work is remembered, to say that they result in that!) They do not result in the tragic vision. "The very same thing, don't you see," says Tolstoy in Anna Karenina, "may be looked at tragically, and turned into misery, or it may be looked at simply and even humorously." Impossible to assert that Mr. Shaw has turned things into misery. All the time one remembers Trefusis, that hero of his early novel [An Unsocial Socialist], whose "sympathies were kept awake and his indignation maintained at an exhilarating pitch by the sufferings of the poor." Mr. Shaw's vision is so composed of mind and heart that it has maintained his indignation "at an exhilarating pitch." It is the publicist's vision.

P. P. Howe. Bernard Shaw: A Critical Study
(London, Martin Secker, 1915), pp. 160–62

With characterization and dialogue to his credit, we may add that he has a gift, over and above all that industry can do to develop it, for the dramatic nexus of a story blossoming in scene and situation: and we might define a situation as a scene at its tensest moment of interest. All the reiterated careless talk about Shaw's having no theatre sense for curtains and climaxes is comically erroneous . . . it overlooks his constant and brilliant control and manipulation of the raw material of the theatre in such wise as to give us scenes of all but unexampled power. Even in a play like *Getting Married,* which might be named as the least dramatic of his repertory, when we have listened straight through to the vivid battledore and shuttlecock of an argument which curiously neither tires nor bores, is not the scene when the mayoress turns mystic one that has very great stage value—allowing, of course, for the genre of the piece, namely, satiric high comedy?

Richard Burton. *Bernard Shaw* (New York,
Henry Holt, 1916), pp. 285–86

Bernard Shaw has confessed that he prefers Englishmen to Irishmen, "no doubt because they make more of me," yet he cannot refrain from adding that he never thinks of the English as fellow-countrymen. This is the quintessence of what Ireland knows as "West Britonism." Our West Britons are so enamoured of England that they desire above all things to mix with Englishmen, their children are educated, if possible, in English schools, and everything is done to eliminate the "vulgar Irish" element from their lives. These people are, for the most part, rewarded like Shaw, by finding West Britonism more profitable than Nationalism. Yet nobody who has lived among them can have failed to get an occasional glimpse of this underlying sense of alienism to which Shaw alludes. Sometimes the feeling comes out in the form of violent Irish patriotism, when in England, on the part of men whose contempt for Ireland, when at home, never lacks an excuse for its expression. At other times more discretion is shown, the outwardly staunch loyalist admitting, in private, that whenever he goes to England he feels himself a foreigner. . . .

English people have been disconcerted by Shaw's ability to view them from the outside, as it were. They should remember that he is merely exercising the privilege of the expatriate. Denationalised Irishmen are all capable of similarly disinterested criticism, and do not refrain from it, even in Ireland, where their position imposes obligations of caution. Shaw has no such obligations, and is, therefore, in a position to say more freely and more generally, what the others have whispered or felt, at least in some particular connection. . . .

Shaw is never more faithful to Irish Protestant tradition than when he exhibits scepticism towards the virtues of England, without, however, turning definitely against her. He is sufficiently aloof to be critical, but his instincts draw him so inevitably to the English people that he cannot be really inimical. In short, he is that perfect type of *sans patrie* which the anglicisation of Ireland has produced; men who cannot understand their own compatriots, and must necessarily take refuge among a people with whom they are condemned to be aliens.

Many critics of Bernard Shaw, struggling with the postulate that he is a puritan, have pointed out flaws in the theory. The contradictions can be resolved by reference to his Protestantism. Irish Protestantism differs considerably from English puritanism, although their lines coincide at certain points. The former has the advantage of presenting an undivided religious front, whereas the latter, by the exclusion of the Anglican Church, loses its homogeneity. Shaw himself has explained this solidarity of Episcopalian and Dissenter in Ireland, which enabled him to be educated at a Methodist College, where the minority of pupils belonged to that sect. Social and political circumstances make cohesion possible amongst Irish Protestants. The negative virtue of being non-Catholic dispenses with those dogmatic *nuances* which render intercourse between Anglican and Nonconformist a different problem in England. Shaw had the typical school life of his class, and justly boasts that, in consequence, his is the true Protestantism.

Ernest A. Boyd. Appreciations and Depreciations
(London, T. Fisher Unwin, 1917), pp. 111–13

Four hours of persistent button-holing at the Court Theatre convinced the dramatic critics that as a simple entertainment *Heartbreak House* was a failure. But what else it might be they did not try to find out. They hurled at the author the quite meaningless epithet of "Shavian"—as though it were his business to be Tchekovian or Dickensian or anybody-elsian except himself—and then ran away like children playing a game of "tick." What is there about Mr. Shaw that he should break so many heads as well as hearts? In and out of season, from his preface-tops, he has proclaimed that he is no leisurely horticulturist, pottering about Nature's garden and pruning it into trim shapes. The tragedy and comedy of life, he has shouted, come from founding our institutions—and in these he certainly includes our plays—on half-satisfied passions instead of on a genuinely scientific natural history. Well, here is natural history preached with all the fury of the Salvationist. With Shaw fanaticism means the blind espousal of reason, a marriage which, in the theatre, turns out to be rather a joyless one. . . .

When Whitman writes: "I have said that the soul is not more than the body, And I have said that the body is not more than the soul, And nothing, not God, is greater to one than oneself is," we must either assent or dissent. Simply to cry out "Whitmanesque!" is no way out of the difficulty. When Ibsen writes a play to prove that building happy homes for happy human beings is not the highest peak of human endeavour, leaving us to find out what higher summit there may be, he intends us to use our brains. It is beside the point to cry out "How like Ibsen!" *Heartbreak House* is a restatement of these two themes. You have to get Ibsen thoroughly in mind if you are not to find the Zeppelin at the end of Shaw's play merely monstrous. It has already destroyed the people who achieve; it is to come again to lighten the talkers' darkness, and at the peril of all the happy homes in the neighbourhood. You will do well to keep Whitman in mind when you hear the old sea-captain bellowing with a thousand different intonations and qualities of emphasis: Be yourself, do not sleep. I do not mean, of course, that Shaw had these two themes actually in mind when he set about this rather maundering, Tchekovian rhapsody. But they have long been part of his mental make-up, and he cannot escape them or their implications. The difficulty seems to be in the implications. Is a man to persist in being himself if that self run counter to God or the interests of parish, nation, the community at large? The characters in this play are nearer to apes and goats than to men and women. Shall they nevertheless persist in being themselves, or shall they pray to be Zeppelin-destroyed and born again?

James Agate, Alarums and Excursions
(New York, George H. Doran, 1922), pp. 187–89

Shaw himself has experienced and subsequently suggested that any person, in order to express frankly an opinion on anything, has to overcome a certain congenital fear—that of being presumptuous. He has taken care early in his career to prevent people from molesting him with insincere incense burning. (But he has done it without shrinking from being considered famous. He knows that the tools of an honest man must always include boisterous self-advertising. He proudly declines to hide his light under a bushel.)

Shaw has used a large part of his ingenuity to inhibit people to such a degree that they would need to have extreme insensitivity to prostrate themselves in admiration before him.

It should be clear by now that Shaw is a terrorist. The Shavian terror is an unusual one, and he employs an unusual weapon—that of humor. This unusual man seems to be of the opinion that there is nothing fearful in the world except the calm and incorruptible eye of the common man. But this eye must be feared, always and unconditionally. This theory endows him with a remarkable natural superiority; and by his unfaltering practice in accordance with it, he has made it impossible for anyone who ever comes into contact with him—be it in person, through his books, or through his theater—to assume that he ever committed a deed or uttered a sentence without fearful respect for this incorruptible eye. In fact, young people, whose main qualification is often their love of mettle, are often held to a minimum of aggressiveness by their premonition that any attack on Shaw's habits, even if it were his insistence on wearing peculiar underwear, would inevitably result in a terrible defeat of their own thoughtlessly selected apparel. If one adds to this his exploding of the thoughtless, habitual assumption that anything that might possibly be considered venerable should be treated in a subdued manner instead of energetically and joyously; if one adds to this his successful proof that in the face of truly significant ideas a relaxed (even snotty) attitude is the only proper one, since it alone facilitates true concentration, it becomes evident what measure of personal freedom he has achieved.

The Shavian terror consists of Shaw's insistence on the prerogative of every man to act decently, logically, and with a sense of humor, and on the obligation to act in this manner even in the face of opposition. He knows very well how much courage it takes to laugh about the ridiculous and how much seriousness it takes to discover the amusing. And, like all purposeful people, he knows, on the other hand, that the most time-consuming and distracting pursuit is a certain kind of seriousness which pervades literature but does not exist anywhere else. (Like us, the young generation, he considers it naïve to write for the theater, and he does not show the slightest inclination to pretend that he is not aware of this: he makes far-reaching use of his naïveté. He furnishes the theater with as much fun as it can take. And it can take a lot. What draws people to the theater is, strictly speaking, so much nonsense, which constitutes a tremendous buoyancy for those problems which really interest the progressive dramatic writer and which are the real value of his pieces. It follows that his problems must be so pertinent that he can be as buoyant about them as he wishes to be, for the buoyancy is what people want.) [July 25, 1926]

Bertolt Brecht. MD. Sept., 1959, pp. 184–85

I get the keenest pleasure watching Shaw squirm through a tattooed subject. He confesses he couldn't write words Joyce uses: "My prudish hand would refuse to form the letters; and I can find no interest in his infantile clinical incontinences, or in the flatulations which he thinks worth mentioning. But if they were worth mentioning I should not object to mentioning them, though, as you see, I should dress up his popular locutions in a little Latinity. For all we know, they may be peppered freely over the pages of the lady novelists of ten years hence; and Frank Harris's autobiography may be on all the bookstalls."

You will observe that he can find no interest in these matters, yet he appears to have read them all and remembers them pretty well; which would seem to belie his lack of interest in them. When I find no interest in a thing I simply drop it and forget it, but Shaw is made of sterner stuff. Like reformers and censors and smut-hounds generally, he wallows in what he likes to call dirt, not from pleasure, but as duty. This completely contradicts his simile that pornographic novels are like offering a hungry man a description of dinner, and that, even if the description was very lifelike, it could not satisfy his hunger. All I can reply is that these descriptions seem to have satisfied Shaw's hunger, for he seems to have read them all and gone without his dinner.

Frank Harris. On Bernard Shaw
(London, Victor Gollancz, 1931), pp. 229–30

Shaw identifies the modern drama with the type of play in which he excels. His first business is the exposure of current morality, with the implication that it would be wise and sensible to scrap it and resort to another kind. "People have told me that my plays have made them alter their whole view of life. This is probably an exaggeration; possibly an illusion. They do not say this of Shakespear and Molière. But with every disposition to do so, I do not on that account think myself greater than Shakespear or Molière.

Shaw . . . declares with delightful dogmatism that people do not go to the theatre to be amused. A great proportion, I contend, go to the theatre for no other purpose. It is quite true that they want to have a new light thrown upon their own lives and the lives of those around them; but they could often dispense with argument and discussion in favor of action: things actually happening. Shaw writes plays in which people argue things out, vehemently and boisterously; and then act or remain immobile as the result of their conclusions. Shaw's plays are not always sound, psychologically, since people's deeper motives are often not guided by reason at all, but by impulses which arise from the depths of the subconscious.

Shaw is one of those strange beings for whom the working of the intellect is a theme of passionate interest. In *Back to Methuselah* intellect figures as a passion capable of giving a more lasting enjoyment than any other passion. Shaw's plays show the excited cerebration of a number of people in combination; and the particular sort of mental stimulus which comes from the cut and thrust of dialectic and discussion fortifies and deepens the emotive appeal of the classic drama.

Archibald Henderson. Bernard Shaw: Playboy and Prophet
(New York, D. Appleton, 1932), pp. 602–3

What are the real themes of Bernard Shaw's plays?

He has not been a socialist dramatist in the sense that, say, Upton Sinclair has been a socialist novelist. His economics have served him, it is true, as anatomy served Michael Angelo; but to say that is to give as little idea of what kind of characters he creates and what his plays are about as it would of the figures of the sculptor to say that they were produced by an artist who understood the skeleton and the muscles. It is quite wrong to assume, as has sometimes been done, that the possession of the social-economic intelligence must imply that the writer who has it writes tracts for social reform. . . .

The principal pattern which recurs in Bernard Shaw—aside from the duel between male and female, which seems to me of much less importance—is the polar opposition between the type of the saint and the type of the successful practical man. This conflict, when it is present in his other writing, has a blurring, a demoralizing effect . . . but it is the principle of life of his plays. We find it in its clearest presentation in the opposition between Father Keegan and Tom Broadbent in *John Bull's Other Island* and between Major Barbara and Undershaft—where the moral scales are pretty evenly weighted and where the actual predominance of the practical man, far from carrying ominous implications, produces a certain effect of reassurance: this was apparently the period—when Bernard Shaw had outgrown his early battles and struggles and before the war had come to disturb him—of his most comfortable and self-confident exercise of powers which had fully matured. But these opposites have also a tendency to dissociate themselves from one another and to feature themselves sometimes, not correlatively, but alternatively in successive plays. In *The Devil's Disciple* and *The Shewing-up of Blanco Posnet,* the heroes are dashing fellows who have melodramatic flashes of saintliness; their opponents are made comic or base. *Caesar and Cleopatra* is a play that glorifies the practical man; *Androcles and the Lion* is a play that glorifies the saint. So is *Saint Joan,* with the difference that here the worldly antagonists of the saint are presented as intelligent and effective.

Certainly it is this theme of the saint and the world which has inspired those scenes of Shaw's plays which are most moving and most real on the stage—which are able to shock us for the moment, as even the "Life Force" passages hardly do, out of the amiable and objective attention which has been induced by the bright play of the intelligence. [1938]

Edmund Wilson. The Triple Thinkers, rev. ed. (New
York, Oxford University Press, 1948), pp. 184–86

One feels, indeed, that Shaw was always at his happiest when he left his own period and lived for a while with the people of another age; that although *Heartbreak House, John Bull's Other Island* and *The Doctor's Dilemma* may be revived as "period pieces" quite as often as *The School for Scandal, She Stoops to Conquer* and *The Importance of Being Earnest,* yet the most natural, most convincing, most imaginative, least self-conscious of his works are *Caesar and Cleopatra, Androcles and the Lion,* and *Saint Joan.* These will live as long as there is an English stage devoted to anything better than the sort of play from which he redeemed it. For reasons we have seen, most of his characters do not get far enough away from himself to attain a life of their own, and the really vital ones, the religious and self-conscious types, come straight from their creator. But in the three plays just mentioned the subsidiary characters catch some of the radiance spread by the protagonists and the strings of the puppet-master are fainter. Shaw must have felt where his real weakness lay as a dramatist of contemporary life; for he confessed that he had always been a sojourner on this planet rather than a native of it; that his kingdom was not of this world; that he was at home only in the realm of his imagination, and at ease only with the mighty dead: with Bunyan, with Blake and with Shelley; with Bee-thoven, Bach and Mozart.

Hesketh Pearson. *G. B. S.: A Full-Length Portrait*
(New York, Harper and Brothers, 1942), pp. 357–58

I am myself a Victorian, and am conscious in my bones of what he has done to me: for better or worse I am not the man I should have been had Shaw not tackled me, before I made his personal acquaintance, while I was still in my twenties. Let me own frankly that I began by disliking him; he was constantly offending my taste; and taste is often a protective extra skin which we have acquired from our parents, or have put on, to keep us from disturbing thought about things which are unpleasant. Sometimes he offends me still by his gratuitous exaggerations—not of facts, but of phrases; using, for instance, that worn-out cliché about grown-up lack of intelligence over things which "the mind of any child of ten could master." But I can still remember the characteristic Victorian statement which came out of my mouth in his hearing (the first time we ever met) at a small social debate, that, if the working class were paid better wages, they wouldn't know how to spend them properly, and how jovially he felled me to earth for it, and made it impossible for me ever again to defend an unjust wage system by that sort of argument.

It is worth noting, I think, that in his fight for the recovery of right values, in a social order which had become so mentally and morally defec-tive under its veneer of Christianity, Shaw (though much more a Christian in principle than most of us) was entirely secular in his method of attack on the social conscience; and it was not until he wrote his preface to *Androcles and the Lion* that he openly championed Christianity against the charge that it had become a proved failure, and declared that it had not failed because it had never yet been tried, and that it was about time that it *was* tried. It was a case of the Humanist once again (as has happened before) coming to the rescue of Christian realism from the cold formalism of other-worldliness.

Laurence Housman. In Stephen Winsten, ed., *G. B. S. 90*
(London, Hutchinson, 1946), pp. 48–49

If Shaw's plays are in the first place the meeting-ground of vitality and artificial system and in the second of male and female they are in the third place an arena for the problem of human ideals and their relation to practice. His characters may be ranged on a scale of mind, ideas, aspirations, beliefs and on a scale of action, practicality, effectiveness. At one extreme there are men of mind who make as little contact with the world of action as possible. Such are most of Shaw's artists. At the other extreme are men of action who lack all speculative interests and ideal impulses. Such are Shaw's professional men: soldiers, politicians, doctors. At a little distance from the one extreme are the men of mind who are interested in this world even if they can do nothing about it. Such, in their different ways, are Tanner, Cusins, Keegan, Shotover, and Magnus. At a little distance from the other extreme are certain practical men with a deep intellectual interest in the meaning of action. Such are the businessmen Undershaft and Tarleton, the soldiers Napoleon and Caesar.

The conversations which all these men, of mind or of action, have with each other have, perhaps, more nervous energy, a more galvanic rhythm, than any other disquisitory passages in all Shaw. For they are all pushing, probing towards the solution of the problem of morals in action. They are all part of the search for the philosopher-king. Keegan talks with the politician Broadbent, Shotover with the businessman Mangan, Magnus with his cabinet. Most strikingly, perhaps, Undershaft talks with his Professor Cusins. They are agreed that there is no hope until the millionaires are professors of Greek and the professors of Greek are millionaires.

Although the problem enters in all Shaw's plays there is one special repository for it: the history play. We have seen that *Caesar and Cleopatra* is a melodrama and one of the *Three Plays for Puritans*. It is also the second of three history plays—*The Man of Destiny*, and *Saint Joan* are the other two—in which Shaw worked at his problem by connecting it with great historical figures. One must however be very clear about the fact that Shaw never tried to do the job of the historical figures. As his way is, he informs everybody that his plays are utterly historical and defends their most whimsical anachronisms in notes that are not uniformly funny. However, there were scholars who fell for it and earnestly corrected Shaw's facts in solemn articles. A whole book was written to "refute" *Saint Joan*.

Shaw's claim was that he knew history intuitively! He writes his plays, reads the history books afterwards, and finds—so he says—that he was right all along, for "given Caesar and a certain set of circumstances I know what would happen." Those who think this a naïve confession are themselves naïve. . . . He retains his right to be absurd in everything but psychology. And he recognizes a limitation in all historical writing which our historians would be wise to grant: that our understanding of an historical character is a highly subjective affair.

Shaw differs from a sound historian not in being more subjective but in not being a historian at all. Shaw was not interested in the peculiar character of each period—Napoleonic, ancient, or medieval—but in indicating what has not changed. Seeing and hearing people much like ourselves (or better) the audience learns that no progress has been made during historical time.

Eric Bentley. Bernard Shaw (Norfolk,
Conn., New Directions, 1947), pp. 158–60

Shaw postulates a universe containing or consisting of two factors, life and matter. Admittedly, he sometimes speaks of life as creating matter as when, by willing to use our arms in a certain way, we bring into existence a roll of muscle, but the general rule is that matter is, as it were, there to begin with. Thus, matter is spoken of as life's "enemy." "I brought life into the whirlpool of force, and compelled my enemy, Matter, to obey a living soul," says Lilith at the end of *Back to Methuselah*. Regarding matter in the light of an enemy, life seeks to dominate and subdue it. Partly to this end, partly because of its innate drive to self-expression, life enters into and animates matter. The result of this animation of matter by life is a living organism. A living organism, then, derives from and bears witness to the presence of both the fundamental constituents of which the universe is composed; it is life expressed in matter. Shaw suggests rather than explicitly states that life cannot evolve or develop *unless* it enters into matter to create organisms; these are, in fact, the indispensable instruments wherewith it promotes its own development.

C. E. M. Joad. Shaw (London,
Victor Gollancz, 1949), pp. 177–78

Certainly whatever impact Shaw has made upon any of the numerous generations who have been exposed to his work has been in his role as dramatist. Though he no doubt would scream in denial, I contend that the prose polemics in his body of work are footnotes, even if some of the notes seem longer than the text. With the plays, however, I include the prefaces. They stand distinctly apart from the rest of his polemical writing, taking a life and spark from their juxtaposition to the plays.

But the Fabian essays and addresses, *The Intelligent Woman's Guide to Socialism and Capitalism, Everybody's Political What's What* and so forth, are more important to Shaw than to his public. They have their place in an exhaustive study and they may be cited, from time to time, in our discussion. Beyond this they would obscure, rather than clarify, our attempt to see Shaw, as thinker, in the whole. Essentially these other works repeat what is said in the plays and prefaces and repeat it weakly.

This decision takes some justification from Shaw's own insistence that truthtelling is better done by the creative imagination than by literal account. "You may read the Annual Register from end to end and be no wiser. But read *Pilgrim's Progress* and *Gulliver's Travels* and you will know as much human history as you need, if not more."

The novels, which in general I think are better than they are commonly supposed to be, nevertheless are not of great importance to his matured thought which found its natural vehicle in drama. *The Adventures of the Black Girl in Her Search for God,* a fable of great charm, does not go, in content, beyond the discussions of religion in *Androcles and the Lion, Back to Methuselah,* and *Saint Joan.*

I have divided the plays into First, Second and Third periods, which prove to be remarkably balanced as to volume of output, although this did not enter into consideration.

The plays of what I call the first period begin with *Widowers' Houses* and end with *Captain Brassbound's Conversion.* They mark the establishment of Shaw's success and the development of most of his characteristics. Had he written nothing more he would have been, on the strength of these plays, still the leading English-speaking dramatist of his time, though in the light of what was to come, it is almost impossible to conceive of such a termination.

I mark a second period with *Man and Superman,* for it seems to me that this play makes a forward leap in stature out of all ordinary relation to his previous rate of growth. This immense surge of creative power is sustained phenomenally through such master works as *Heartbreak House, Back to Methuselah,* and *Saint Joan.*

After *Saint Joan,* however, in the third period which begins with *The Apple Cart,* there is a steady diminution of power, though scarcely one of production.

Edmund Fuller. *George Bernard Shaw* (New York,
Charles Scribner's Sons, 1950), pp. 16–17

Though Bernard Shaw claimed that there was behind his plays a thought-out sociology, and said that for art's sake alone he would not have faced the toil of writing so much as a single sentence, his place in literature will in the long run be determined by his quality as an imaginative artist, not by his stature as a political thinker and social reformer. Posterity has always appeared to be singularly unimpressed by either political or religious zeal, except when it is distilled in a form which offers aesthetic satisfaction.

Yet whatever ground there may be for arguing that the after-fame of Shaw will depend on the literary quality of his writings, the argument can only be sustained if it is recognized that their aesthetic merit is the outcome of Shaw's fervent belief in the righteousness of his multiple crusade for a better and saner world. While a conviction of righteousness does not of itself produce art, it is nevertheless true that art is rarely generated in a moral vacuum. So although posterity is unlikely to concern itself greatly with the contemporary political, sociological, and religious background of Shaw's work, some brief account of it must be given, since that background provided his material, however thoroughly the material was changed in the creative process. Shaw's great gifts of eloquence and humour and wit could only be exercised upon important human issues. He mocked solemnity, even his own; but he never mocked seriousness, and never turned his eyes away from the present world in his desire to bring a new world to birth.

A. C. Ward. *Bernard Shaw* (London, Longmans, Green, 1951), pp. 1–2

Next to his optimism and his energy, the most striking thing about Shaw was his furious eclecticism. He felt no necessity to choose between the various modern prophets. He would take something from them all, and moreover he would reconcile the most disparate. He was an Ibsenite of course. But he was also, or was soon to become, a disciple of Marx, of Nietzsche, of Bergson, of Wagner, of Samuel Butler, and of John Bunyan. Besides becoming a socialist, he was also a nonsmoker, a teetotaler, a vegetarian, an antivaccinationist, an antivivisectionist and an advocate of reformed spelling.

All this would have been more than enough to give a serious case of intellectual indigestion to anyone else, but for him it was merely very stimulating and very nourishing. Sooner or later the teaching of all his masters was synthesized, one furnishing an economic system, another a moral system, a third a metaphysic, and a fourth a religion. Though he never wrote it all down in systematic form, Shaw has at one time or another propounded the parts of what is probably the most inclusive body of doctrine since Thomas Aquinas.

One thing which made this possible was a sort of cheerful optimism enabling him to temper the more intransigent doctrines of his various masters and to fall back upon the formula "What this really means is . . . " Moreover, what it really meant was usually something less intransigent as well as frequently gentler and more kindly than the doctrine of his masters is generally assumed to be.

In the plays of the first decade especially, this cheerful determination to tame the wild men and to draw the fangs of revolution seems particularly striking. Nietzsche's doctrine of the superman—which might seem to others to foreshadow a blond beast, amoral and ruthless—tends to become no more than a rather extravagant method of recommending self-help and improvement. *The Revolutionist's Handbook,* supposed to have been written by the rebellious John Tanner, hero of *Man and Superman,* begins by breathing fire and then carefully explains that in democratic England there is all the revolution necessary every time the voters have recourse to the ballot box. In the same book a shocking section ridiculing sexual morality and especially the sentimental word "purity" ends by demonstrating that, since the number of men and women in England is approximately equal, monogamy is the only sensible system. In that same play even Strindberg's battle of the sexes, described by Tanner in the first scene as a remorseless struggle where the only question is which party shall destroy the other, turns out to be but a sort of sham battle in the course of which the Life Force makes the hero and heroine temporarily irrational in order that it may benevolently trick them into sacrificing what they believe to be their desires in favor of their deepest impulse—which is to try to create better offspring.

Joseph Wood Krutch. *"Modernism" in Modern Drama*
(Ithaca, N.Y., Cornell University Press, 1953), pp. 50–51

You might say that he made up his mind too early, which gave him an immense advantage in debate, arming him at all points, but cost him something in wisdom. Bertrand Russell, who had known him a long time, said that G. B. S. was an immensely clever man but not a wise man. He seemed to me to have a sort of natural wisdom in his ordinary dealings with life (he must have given people in private more really good advice than any other man of his time), but to be perverse, obstinate, cranky, wrong-headed, in his positive philosophy. He was, in fact—and came at just the right moment—a great destroyer, head of the Victorian rubbish disposal squad. He hid any doubts he might have about his positive wisdom in quick mocking laughter, just as he hid so much of his face behind a beard, red and white at the proper seasons. But because he was an iconoclast, this does not mean, as many people imagine, that all his work will "date" itself into obscurity. I suspect that all the "dating" that can happen has already happened. His best pieces, those comedies unique in style and spirit, have the vitality that defies time and all social changes. Their character, their appeal, may be different—for notice how early plays like *Arms and the Man* and *You Never Can Tell,* once thought to be grimly shocking, now seem to bubble and sparkle with wit and delicious nonsense—but they will be alive. And existing still behind the work will be the memory and the legend of the man, half saint and half clown, preposterous in his Jaeger outfit and assorted fads, glorious in his long stride towards some kingdom worthy of the spirit—the wittiest of all pilgrims, humming an air by Mozart.

J. B. Priestley. *Thoughts in the Wilderness*
(London, Heinemann, 1957), pp. 186–87

The "significant action," in a dramatic sense, of Shaw's playwriting career can be given brief statement: he converted a rhetorical drama of the passions into a rhetorical drama of impassioned ideas, using as his vehicle the most popular and "theatrical" modes of the nineteenth-century theater. Such a synopsis leaves much to be inferred. But Shaw's exploitation of stock-company stereotypes; his deliberate attempts to embarrass, if not destroy, certain romantic conventions and genres; his exploitation of the rhetorical aspects of opera and music; his campaigns as a critic for and against certain kinds of drama and action; even his use of "comedic paradox," and of the wit and irony, the flirtation with logic and illogic, which are the weapons of intellect however impassioned, are all implicit in the central, governing action of Shaw's playwriting career. . . .

In a study of Shaw's relations with the nineteenth-century theater, it becomes notably apparent that stage conventions, critical debates, and indeed whole genres which went into the shaping and the substance of Shaw's drama of ideas have altogether dropped out of view without damaging his vitality. Revivals of Shaw are frequent, and they are not yet made in an antiquarian spirit. However, where a theater is literarily self-conscious, plays survive their initial productions by virtue of qualities which, after they charm in the theater, can capture an audience outside it. Consequently, however much Shaw was indebted to the dead conventions and genres, they are much more indebted to him. The nineteenth-century theater had a most awesome vitality which rose from other than literary greatness. Therefore, in its proper self, it was a perishable theater, and its literary remains, which were then most warm, are now most cold. Nevertheless, Shaw brought it into our time in his own plays, in a form not only literary, but theatrically viable and theatrically fertile. He saves the uses and the energies of the mortal nineteenth-century popular theater for a future classical repertory and for the living tradition.

Martin Meisel. *Shaw and the Nineteenth-Century Theater* (Princeton, N.J., Princeton University Press, 1963), pp. 446–47

[Shaw] has been a great fighting pamphleteer and journalist, who has left a deep imprint upon his time. This is the consciously thinking Shaw, who is very definitely "of an age"; the Shaw of the future, and perhaps "for all time," is the imaginative and intuitive creator of ten or a dozen great plays and of scores of unforgettable characters. As we have seen, the "division and estrangement" between the crusading philosopher-reformer and the dramatic prose-poet has extended into the plays, some of which are scarcely more than dramatized pamphlets, while others in which the poet has had a larger share are more or less crippled by his struggle with the pamphleteer. But the division is not complete. When the poet is in full command, as in *Caesar and Cleopatra* and *Saint Joan*, he has triumphantly fused the intellectual material with the imaginative into superb dramatic form. Something like this happened in *Mrs. Warren's Profession*, in all the *Pleasant Plays* and the *Plays for Puritans*, in *Man and Superman*, *Androcles and the Lion*, *Pygmalion*, *Heartbreak House*, *Good King Charles*, and in the best of the one-act pieces. In another group of plays, including the early prentice efforts, the series from *John Bull's Other Island* through *Misalliance*, and *The Apple Cart*, the dramatic poet is at work in uneasy partnership with the philosopher-reformer; here the result is a sequence of interesting and distinguished plays marred by more or less serious flaws and imperfections. In

Back to Methuselah and most of the plays since *The Apple Cart,* the didactic purpose operates with much less than the old intellectual vigor, and the imagination only flickers rather palely here and there. But Shaw's genius must not be judged by these. It is useless to speculate on what he might have accomplished if he had been content to be a dramatist only, but it is certain that he could not have been the author of some of the plays by which he will be remembered. His success in revitalizing English drama is due in part to the invigorating current of ideas which he brought into it. In far larger part, of course, it is due to his mastery of character, of dramatic situation, and of brilliant and flexible dialogue.

Homer E. Woodbridge. *George Bernard Shaw: Creative Artist*
(Carbondale, Ill., Southern Illinois University Press, 1963),
pp. 163–64

Shaw's belief in the slight superiority of women would be highly suspect had he not first made another kind of statement, more basic, more valid and far more needed. Shaw said early and often, in various ways, that woman is merely man in petticoats; in other words, that the apparent difference between men and women has been greatly exaggerated by costume, education, occupation and habit. The soul, he points out, is very largely androgynous. In this sense, Shaw also minimizes the role of sex in human life, though not in evolution, pointing out that we spend the larger part of our lives in activities in which the difference between the sexes is irrelevant. There is no contradiction between this view and Shaw's belief that the best contribution women can make is that of the distinctively feminine viewpoint: none, that is, unless one considers masculinity as a human standard and femininity as a deviation. The androgynous nature to which Shaw refers is by no means a masculine nature.

It is fair to say, then, that Shaw advocates all the equality between the sexes that nature will allow. He even goes so far as to favor a greater similarity between the sexes than has ever existed before. In the face of the irreducible differences which remain, however, he places the second sex first, but with a most important qualification. Woman may well be first in the sense that she has a closer connection with the evolutionary work of the Life Force; first in the sense that equal consideration will always dictate certain special privileges for her; first in the sense that her inspired practicality may be the salvation of a society that is heading for the rocks under masculine leadership. On the other hand, woman is never first for her own sake. Her evolutionary instinct, her reproductive labors and her place in the councils of state, all benefit her whole society. Shaw's inclusive spirit easily reconciles the good of society with the good of the individual woman, just as it reconciles a new appreciation of our common humanity with an unspoiled delight in sexual love. These are the fruits of an imagination which puts human qualities above all abstractions, and a spirit in which criticism and the joy of life are inseparable.

Barbara Bellow Watson. *A Shavian Guide to the Intelligent Woman* (London, Chatto & Windus, 1964), pp. 213–14

What essentially distinguishes *Candida* and the great plays that follow it from these four [*Plays Pleasant and Unpleasant*] is not simply the perfecting of technique or the clarification of themes. It is that in the earlier plays the socialism, anti-romanticism, Ibsenism, and so on exist for themselves alone, are disparate and in a sense constricting. In *Candida* and after, these themes have come under the control of a vision that is large enough to contain them, and can see them from without even when it is presenting them from within. That vision is Shaw's intuition of reality, felt by him as co-extensive with his experience, fully coherent within the framework of a hypothesis by which he is entirely resolved to stand or fall. In *Candida,* in short, we have entered the world of the mature artist, as distinctive and coherent as the artist's self, with a degree of communicability that is commensurate with his mastery of the medium.

What then are the characteristics of this Shavian world? I suggest that the most important fact about it is that it is a world not of being but of becoming. Its people are not called into existence for the sake of what they are and what they do, but for what they may and ought to be and do. Their actions raise questions of morality, but those actions are not contained within an unchanging moral order that commends the poisoned chalice to the poisoner's own lips and causes rebellion ever to find rebuke. . . . They are often creatures of laughter, but what makes them comical is not their extravagant departure from some conventional norm, as in the plays of Molière or Jonson. Shaw's comic figures themselves contain the criteria by which we judge them; indeed, they judge themselves. His world is not permeated by divine unalterable order to which all must return, but by living change in which all must participate.

He is thus, surely, one of the first writers to exemplify fully the plight of modern man, for whom every fact turns out to be a question, and especially of the modern artist, facing the problem of imposing a meaningful permanence on what is constantly shifting.

J. Percy Smith. *The Unrepentant Pilgrim* (Boston, Houghton Mifflin, 1965), pp. 253–55

"Learn everything," Shaw once advised novelists in a lecture on fiction, "and when you know it, stick to naturalism, and write every word as if you were on your oath in a witness box." It is not generally realized how seriously Shaw took his own advice as far as naturalism was concerned. Most training in literary tradition is in fact a positive impediment in understanding

Shaw. When Shaw introduces literary conventions into his plays, it is most often to demonstrate how absurdly they misrepresent human behavior, or how silly the moral assumptions behind them are. The effect of boldly introducing what he had observed in life onto the stage fell so far short of theatrical expectations that audiences frequently mistook Shaw's realism for perverse farce.

Sometimes the character types Shaw copied were common everywhere but in the playhouse. Sometimes his characters were the highly individualistic men and women who formed part of the same radical circles Shaw moved in at the turn of the century. To free Shaw from the charge of arbitrarily fantasticating, I have regularly related the characters in the plays to their real-life prototypes where they were identified by Shaw himself or where I felt I could make a reasonably safe guess at Shaw's models. If this leaves me open to the charge of counting Lady Macbeth's children, I can only reply that, in the long run, such efforts are less debilitating to literature than making it an autonomous activity sealed off from the rest of our existence.

Is Shaw dated? The answer is yes, as every classic is dated. The specific personalities and political crises that moved him to write are now part of history, as Plato's and Aristophanes' debaters and statesmen are. The images of his plays belong to an eternal world, as his ideas on government, economics, sex, psychology, logic, and art, now seen apart from the novel and amusing expression he gave them, form part of a perennial philosophy which we can call "Shavian." But there is still a third aspect of the question. One might perhaps hope that the particular social outrages Shaw wrote about in his "problem" plays might by now be things of the past. Nothing could be more gratifying than to pronounce Shaw hopelessly out of date in such matters. Unfortunately, I cannot see that this is so. To take two clearcut examples: the demoralization of men by poverty is still the world's first problem, and our national system of criminology is still outrageously perverse in its intentions and pernicious in its results.

Louis Crompton. Shaw the Dramatist (Lincoln,
Neb., University of Nebraska Press, 1969), pp. vi–vii

Dramatically speaking, *Back to Methuselah* is less than a masterpiece, and this is simply because it fails to conform to the basic Shaw formula: the clash of egos. When Shaw has a hero to write about he also portrays his other characters with conviction, particularly the people who counterbalance the hero—Mrs. Dudgeon, Roebuck Ramsden, Lady Britomart. When there is no hero his treatment of the other characters tends to degenerate into rather clumsy satire. The politicians of *Back to Methuselah* are absurd caricatures. Shaw would counter by replying that real politicians are caricatures. . . .

The truth is that Shaw, at sixty-five, was no longer very interested in people as such. His early novels are full of quite ordinary people, fairly well observed and portrayed; this is also true of *Widowers' Houses* and *Mrs. Warren's Profession*. These plays have a certain feeling of weight that comes from real life. Cokane and Sartorius, Mrs. Warren and Sir George Crofts may be "Shaw characters," but they are also recognisable as living types. As his skill as a dramatist increases, Shaw becomes less and less concerned about living types, and *John Bull's Other Island* and *Major Barbara* display Shaw at the height of his powers, delighting in his power of creating convincing caricatures. But the scene in Barbara's Salvation Army shelter already shows a falling-off in his ability to sketch real people; Bill Walker, Rummy Mitchens and Snobby Price are not well-observed cockneys, any more than the cowboys of *The Shewing-up of Blanco Posnet* are well-observed Westerners. The characters of *The Doctor's Dilemma*, *Getting Married* and *Misalliance* are simply amiable Shaw caricatures. *Pygmalion* shows an improvement, simply because Higgins provides it with a centre of gravity; and when there is a major Shaw character "coruscating" in the middle of the stage, the caricatures become perfectly acceptable. But when there is no central character, it is impossible not to notice that Shaw has lost sympathy with his creations as individuals; they are there merely to represent something that he wants to dramatise.

I have pointed out that one must make a clear distinction between Shaw as an artist and Shaw as a thinker. Shaw as an artist deteriorated after *The Doctor's Dilemma;* Shaw as a thinker showed no signs of flagging right to the end. His powers as a thinker increased as his power as an artist decreased. The preface to *Man and Superman* is unimportant compared to the play, but *Androcles and the Lion* and *Back to Methuselah* are well below the standard of their prefaces. The exception here is the last play of *Back to Methuselah*, which is, in effect, a dramatised preface.

It must be accepted that from now—1921—until the end of his life thirty years later Shaw has ceased to be a creative force as a dramatist. He has lost interest in people to an extent that makes it difficult for him to produce a recognisably real person. But he can still dramatise ideas so vividly that the audience fails to recognise the unreality of the characters. Unfortunately, this is only true when he *is* dramatising ideas, as in *The Apple Cart* and *In Good King Charles's Golden Days*. When he is not, the result can be almost painful.

Colin Wilson. *Bernard Shaw: A Reassessment*
(New York, Atheneum, 1969), pp. 255–57

The difficulty in finally assessing Shaw's relationship to the aesthetes is that he took pains to dissociate himself from the "art for art's sake faction" but was closer to it than he admitted, perhaps closer than he realized. Like

Whistler, who also denounced aestheticism, Shaw has many of the characteristics of the fin-de-siècle aesthetes; he consciously employs masks as a manner of coping with the world; he feels alienated from the world; he is aesthetically sensitive, at times hypersensitive; he defends immorality and the value of shocking conventional people; and he respects artifice, the craft of art.

His theory of art is the result of a curious ambivalence; he denounced art for art's sake but argued, as an aesthete would, that a work of art exists independent of conventional morality and expresses the artist's individual vision. Art for art's sake he associates with academicism and a decorative impulse arising from following rules of art instead of the writer's inner convictions. The passage repudiating art for art's sake in the Epistle Dedicatory to *Man and Superman* is really an attack on academic art which arises out of a knowledge of art rather than a vision of man; Shaw denies that style is possible without opinions, but he recognizes the fact that, long after the ideas are dated, "the style remains." His defense of didacticism is really on aesthetic grounds: the artist's convictions produce art; without them, art is impossible; hence he has "contempt for *belles lettres,* and for amateurs who become the heroes of the fanciers of literary virtuosity" because, having no convictions, they cannot produce great art. . . .

Though his final faith in the power of thought to transcend all sensory appeals, including the sensory appeal of art, keeps him from aestheticism, no aesthete could have placed more emphasis on the place of art in man's life than Shaw did. He believed that the artist's role is "to catch a glint of the unrisen sun," to "shew it to you as a vision in the magic glass of his artwork," or, as the She-Ancient who was once an artist says in *Back to Methuselah,* to provide a "magic mirror . . . to reflect your invisible dreams in visible pictures." Shaw saw himself in this role, and his plays are a testament to the poet-prophet who created them.

Elsie B. Adams. *Bernard Shaw and the Aesthetes* (Columbus, Ohio State University Press, 1971), pp. 157–58

Although Bernard Shaw called his *Heartbreak House* (written in 1916–17) a fantasia in the Russian manner upon English themes, and echoes of *The Cherry Orchard* unquestionably reverberate through it, the play might be profitably viewed as a fantasia in the Shakespearean manner upon Shavian themes. Whether or not Shaw recalled Swinburne's curious remark that *King Lear* was the work of Shakespeare the socialist, *Heartbreak House* seems clearly to have been designed, at least in part, as Shaw's *Lear.* Earlier he had tauntingly titled part of a preface to his *Caesar and Cleopatra* (1898) "Better than Shakespeare?"—suggesting a parallel with the Bard's *Antony and Cleopatra;* yet by presenting a kittenish young queen and an aging Caesar, rather than an aging but still sultry Cleopatra and a younger admirer, he had evaded any direct comparison. Like his Cleopatra play, Shaw's *Lear* was offered not in competition but as commentary.

G. B. S. waited until his nineties to point publicly to *Heartbreak House* as his *Lear*. Even then he did so guardedly through the disarming medium of a puppet play, perhaps to prevent the comparison from being taken as seriously as he inwardly still meant it to be, for in his lifetime the play's now very considerable reputation had never measured up to his expectation for it. "If the critics had the brains of a mad Tom," he grumbled, using a suggestive association with *Lear*, "they would realize it is my greatest play. But they don't. They all go following after the Maid of Orleans." Privately Shaw had hinted at the *Lear* connection almost as soon as he had completed the play. In 1917 actress Lillah McCarthy had asked him for details of the work, hoping to convince him to let her produce it or at least acquire a starring part in it. Shaw put her off. It was wartime, he pointed out, and the play was unpleasant, unsuitable fare for war conditions. The hero was an old man of eighty-eight, and there were no young males in the cast at all (its implicit recognition of the wartime dearth of leading men). The women were either too young or too old—an ingenue and two sisters in their middle forties. The sisters, Shaw confided—"I don't find them much more popular than Goneril or Regan"—were the old man's daughters. Disgusted with the dragged-out war and its effect on theatre as well as much else, he confessed that his heart was not in a London production of a new play. And Miss McCarthy—creator of some of Shaw's greatest roles, beginning with her Ann Whitefield in *Man and Superman*—appeared neither then nor afterward in a performance of *Heartbreak House*.

Stanley Weintraub. *Journey to Heartbreak:*
The Crucible Years of Bernard Shaw, 1914–1918
(New York, Weybright and Talley, 1971), pp. 333–34

Shaw has been more underestimated since his death than he was overestimated in his lifetime. His long-continuing artistic fertility and the variety and inventiveness still evident in the plays of his last period are impressive in themselves and contribute to the character of his eminence in the European theatre. If we are looking for signs of decline in his last plays, it may be granted that they are more simply and directly conceived and constructed, that the powerful control is less impressive as the vision is less complex, and fewer interrelated conflicts are held suspended in the artistic pattern than in some of the plays of twenty years before.

Yet, *The Millionairess* is enough to challenge any generalization that dynamism has been lost, as clarity and poise prevail. And none of his plays is stronger testimony to his penetration of the nature of his own genius. The bright light it sheds retrospectively on his whole career as a political dramatist may serve in guiding the present study to its conclusions. Epifania Orgisanti di Parerga is the Shavian muse unveiled and magnificently named. The power in Eppy has burnt up the ambiguousness that clung to Ann Whitefield, or to Candida, as a vessel of the Life Force. In the line of Shaw's women characters, she is the ultimate successor to Julia Craven of *The Philanderer,* not now condemned and rejected, but purified and apotheosized. The unhappy passion of Mrs. Jenny Patterson was not wasted after all: the young man she seduced and pursued grew to be an old man whose art acknowledged the glamour and potency of the life he had feared and fled. An essentially poetic manifestation took place in a context of economic thinking.

Margery Morgan. *The Shavian Playground*
(London, Methuen, 1972), p. 326

Most simply stated, Shaw's best plays have a classical quality as they achieve the depth, complexity, economy, and coherence of fine dramatic poetry. In each there is a coalescence of many aesthetic factors which are not only individually evocative, but which, as they interact and fuse, give the particular work an impressively rich, vitally reverberating aesthetic soundness. Such factors, possessing the intrinsic power lying within most great art, expand as they are scrutinized and gain clarity and force as they are defined in specific contexts. It is important to study the plays individually, therefore, for many of the same obvious reasons that it is important to study poems individually. A considerable diversity in matter and method separate them. Each develops in a distinctive context and idiom, from domestic comedy and romance to social drama and epic tragicomedy, from farce and parody to irony and allegory. As there is a great range of subject matter, there is a great artistic flexibility responding to and projecting that matter, and in the interrelation of matter and manner lie the subtlest dimensions of Shaw's achievement. This can be defined in many ways; for convenience, one may approach it in terms of dramatic action, characterization, and a pervasive, cohesive poetic spirit.

Charles A. Berst. *Bernard Shaw and the Art of Drama*
(Urbana, Ill., University of Illinois Press, 1973), p. 294

Bernard Shaw's sole aim in life was to make the world a better dwelling place for his fellow human beings. From *Widowers' Houses* to *Farfetched Fables* a genuine desire for the eventual perfection of the human race transcends all of his bitterness and devastating criticism of institutions which, to his way of thinking, were deterring mankind from achieving so lofty a goal. Even his last unfinished play, *Why She Would Not,* written three months before he died, shows evidence of his life-long purpose. Although it is far too fragmentary to suggest a clear-cut theme, there is a suggestion that the harnessing of atomic energy and rapid advances in American technical improvements may eventually offer man the needed leisure to cooperate fully with the Life Force in evolving a perfect state. Perhaps, had he lived, this method would have replaced his always reluctant acceptance of revolution as the most efficient means of achieving a society wherein such leisure could be realized.

Be that as it may, it is hoped that this study will help to perpetuate an image of one of the greatest humanists of all time and that its readers will regard his Marxian romance, successfully culminated in the reconciliation of Fabianism with Marxism, as further evidence of Shaw's intense search for a better world. Perhaps it was inevitable that the graphs and formulas of one of the most influential economic and political theorists of the nineteenth century should help to unleash and direct the comic genius of one of the most influential English dramatists whose life bridged the nineteenth and twentieth centuries.

Paul A. Hummert. *Bernard Shaw's Marxian Romance*
(Lincoln, Neb., University of Nebraska Press,
1973), pp. 216–17

Dramatic art consists, according to Shaw, in the truthful representation of reality and results in a picture of ourselves as we really are. This is not a very useful definition, but, in the light of his plays, it serves to indicate what Shaw meant in calling himself a realist.

Aristotle seems to have thought that the chief concern of the dramatist is drama. Shaw considered that the principal business of the dramatist is truth. The dramatist, in his opinion, is a philosopher. He does not create illusions; he dispels them. He is an observer and a thinker, concerned primarily with reality, and reality is what is perceived when the essential design of things becomes visible. A work of art based on such premises will be, above all, meaningful, and result in an aesthetic experience founded on comprehension. His pleasure of the theater is the pleasure of understanding.

But, in spite of Shaw's convictions and his manifest intent, what we miss in his comedies is precisely that sense of reality on which he prided himself. His characters are memorable, but they are partial, they cast no shadow. In his plays there are no bad people. There are stupid people, mistaken people, romantic people comically contrasted with the enlightened, the skeptical, and the wise. Shaw's characters, even the least admirable, are rational beings. They are moved, it is true, by varying degrees of intelligence, but they are all explicable and subject to analysis, motivated by their own ideas of self-interest toward goals which they consider desirable. The remedy against their shortsightedness, when they are shortsighted, is enlightenment, and enlightenment is the result of education. Thus, all Shaw's comedies are in some sort pedagogical exercises.

The dark side of human nature, which has increasingly absorbed the attention of the dramatists of our time, did not interest Shaw. What impressed him was not the madness of mankind, but its stupidity. Shaw's plays exhibit, accordingly, a view of life which is so far from reality that one thinks of them as fables. It is evident that in presenting them as authentic "natural history," Shaw was thinking of the underlying motives rather than the realism of the demonstration. These motives are rooted in a purely philosophic conception, for Shaw made no effort to sound the depths of the soul below the rational threshold. His comedies therefore go only a little way beyond common sense; but on this level, they have their truth; and in comparison with what ordinarily passes for truth in the theater, it is at first sight dazzling.

Maurice Valency. *The Cart and the Trumpet*
(New York, Oxford University Press, 1973), pp. 396–97

Characterization in his plays was too important for Shaw to leave to chance. For the key to Shavian drama is that the audience must become involved and want to watch the characters change, learn, become. No matter what the theme or the type of play, character is, in fact, one of the most important aspects of any Shaw play. And Shaw, with a typical bending of the truth, once said, "I avoid plots like the plague. . . . My procedure is to imagine characters and let them rip."

To achieve the necessary audience involvement Shaw was determined that his plays have the verisimilitude of actual events happening to actual people. But his concept of this reality was very different from the realism of the cup-and-saucer school. He knew that more than English tea in china cups is necessary for the illusion of reality. In an 1894 interview in *Today,* asked if he advocated stage realism, he answered, "I am an advocate for stage illusion; stage realism is a contradiction in terms."

In accordance with this stage illusion, Shaw scorned a production in which an actor gave anything away. He wrote to Mrs. Patrick Campbell that Eliza's explosive line in *Pygmalion,* "not bloody likely," must be delivered completely seriously without any awareness that the line might get a laugh. He also deplored a production in which the ending could be foreseen ten minutes before the final curtain. He blamed the director rather than the playwright and insisted that the audience should never be able to anticipate the end of any play, that the actors should deliver the last line of a play as if the audience still had the whole evening before them.

Shaw wrote dramas that could utilize the new realistic styles of ensemble acting that had been emerging with the little theater movement. And since he directed nineteen productions of his plays between 1894 and 1924 and co-directed four more, he was able to get rid of artificial acting in favor of realistic gesture and diction. But at the same time, whenever he felt that the part called for it, he also used classical bombast that could do justice to his own long, rhetorical speeches. He never limited himself or his actors to any one style, and while acting might be subdued and realistic, the dialogue might be shaped into operatic duets, overtures, arias, and quartets.

In the production of his plays, Shaw illustrated what Eric Bentley has called his "Both/And" attitude. He utilized anything that would lead to a "willing suspension of disbelief" and would educate an audience, "let them take something home," as Shaw put it. With calm eclecticism, he used what worked to stage his new discussion plays.

Pat M. Carr. Bernard Shaw (New York,
Frederick Ungar, 1976), pp. 41–43

In his plays [Shaw] created perhaps the most fascinating gallery of women in modern drama, female characters who usually prove more interesting and more vital than his male characters. His impatience with female stereotypes, although he used them where dramatically valid—and sometimes subconsciously in spite of himself—is everywhere in his writings. In *The Apple Cart,* Orinthia as royal mistress is no longer a sexual vessel but, in effect, a government employee whose "relationship" to the king satisfies the vestigial and vicarious machismo of the populace. In *Heartbreak House,* the husband, not the wife, is kept. In *Pygmalion,* the cockney flower girl is a human being clever enough to rise by her ability, and, if she chooses, to support a husband rather than fulfill her stereotypic destiny of seeking social and financial security through the prudent bartering of herself in marriage, as her male sponsors Pickering and Higgins recommend. As for romance between Eliza and Higgins, Shaw rejected, from *Pygmalion*'s original performance to its being made into a film, any suggestion that there could be a romantic attachment between the "middle-aged bully" and the now beautiful, young flower girl. In *Getting Married,* "Leo" Hotchkiss is not the victim of a mistress-seeking husband; she herself desires a legal, everyday husband and a "Sunday husband" for variety. (As far as marital relations were concerned, Shaw suggested that the public needed "a dose of castor oil" in the form of his plays, and pointed out that his Orinthia-Magnus relationship—a development of "Leo" Hotchkiss's dreams—is an idea Shakespeare had suggested when Beatrice says, in reply to Don Pedro's proposal, "No, my lord, unless I might have another for workingdays: your grace is too costly to wear every day.")

Other plays evoke even more outrageous reversals of tradition female subservience. In the fantasy *The Simpleton of the Unexpected Isles,* a communal—yet matriarchal—group of six persons of mixed races and sexes produces four futuristic offspring. Earlier Shavian women are less unconventional in their rejection of marriage. Lavinia in *Androcles and the Lion* spurns a husband because she has more important work to do, while the former Major Barbara of the Salvation Army embraces marriage and a husband because only in marriage can she inherit the power to do her work. Cleopatra in *Caesar and Cleopatra* is no seductive sex-kitten. Rather she is an innocent child whom Caesar regards as a future ruler to be trained in politics and governing. Saint Joan leads an army not because she is a woman, or even in spite of that womanhood, but because she has the instincts and the capacity for leadership.

Rodelle Weintraub. Introduction to Rodelle
Weintraub, ed., *Fabian Feminist: Bernard Shaw and
Women* (University Park, Pa., Pennsylvania State
University Press, 1977), pp. 8–9

What is significant about Shaw's plays is perhaps not so much the specific content of his theories, in terms of particular and social and economic programs he espoused, as the fact that the ideas are there, and that there are certain basic philosophical assumptions underlying and tying together the specific articles of his faith. Most importantly, these ideas have an organic relationship to the intellectual structure of the plays. Not only must a play have ideas, but the ideas will inevitably create their own necessary form: "New ideas make their technique as water makes its channel; and the technician without ideas is as useless as the canal constructor without water, though he may do very skillfully what the Mississippi does very rudely" [Preface to *Three Plays for Puritans*].

Looking at his plays to find broad basic patterns of ideas, rather than simply to identify and evaluate specific economic and metabiological doctrines, would not have disturbed Shaw himself, even though he basically distrusted abstraction and generalization. . . . He accepted the fact that particular ideas would, in the slow evolution of human thought, become outmoded and be superseded by new ones. What was important to him was that the act of bringing ideas into the theater—and even more, bringing them into collision with one another, hence making the conflict essential to drama a conflict of *ideas*—was itself contributing to the intellectual, and therefore the spiritual, development of his audience. Although Shaw distrusted rationalists as a species, he had a profound conviction that the future of man rested heavily on his use of his intellectual tools—his self-awareness, his wisdom, above all his drive to know more about himself and his world. By demanding that his audience bring "mind and conscience into the theatre," by stimulating thought and self-criticism, he was furthering that self-knowledge. It is safe to say, I think, that Shaw was more interested in provoking self-analysis and skepticism, in disturbing the complacency of all those who took their values and beliefs for granted, than in promulgating any well-defined philosophical system. At the same time, he did not conceive his function to be primarily negative or destructive, and the essential elements of a positive and creative system of thought can be found in his writing.

Robert F. Whitman. *Shaw and the Play of Ideas* (Ithaca, N.Y., Cornell University Press, 1977), pp. 26–28

Early in his career, Shaw proclaimed himself an old-fashioned playwright, and modern scholarship has seized gratefully on this admission and computed his debts to Scribe, Brieux, romantic comedy, the problem play, extravaganza and other contents of the Victorian property basket. No one, so far as I know, has followed up his equal acknowledgement to opera and Mozart as his supreme dramatic teachers; though modern directors like Clifford Williams have paid close attention to the musical expression marks with which Shaw decorated his prompt copies. Obviously the example of the past was of immense importance to him, and nobody is in any danger of missing it.

What repeatedly takes you by surprise are the occasions when he anticipates the styles of the future. The weird nursery rhyme ritual between Shotover and his daughters in the first act of *Heartbreak House* leads straight into the world of T. S. Eliot's riddling guardians in *The Cocktail Party*. "How much did the clock strike, Phyllis?" enquires the Lady in [*Passion, Poison and Petrifaction; or,*] *The Fatal Gazogene*. "Sixteen, my lady," replies the menial, and we are off into Ionesco territory, complete with a character eating the ceiling. There are Beckett images, like the Preacher in the howling wilderness in *Too True to Be Good*, and the "silenced" priest Keegan [in *John Bull's Other Island*] conversing with a grasshopper. Shaw is probably the last influence any of these writers would recognize, and all I am suggesting is that his genius pushed him into areas of feeling generally considered to be outside his range. In particular, his extension of Victorian burlesque yielded an effect indistinguishable from surrealism. Consider Shaw's stage pictures rather than his dialogue: a Magritte-like terrain dotted with bourgeois manikins, unperturbed by the dynamite in the gravel pit, visitors from the sky, bombardment by passing airships, giant microbes, and the sight of the local mayoress going off into a Delphic trance. It is customary to explain away all such effects, down to the lady in *Buoyant Billions* who stills alligators with a saxophone, as a throwback to extravaganza; but you could equally well cite them as early stirrings of the theatre of the absurd.

Turn up the dialogue, of course, and reason resumes control: events and images fall into place as a supporting pretext for the dance of ideas. . . . But under the words something can be heard echoing with the desolate resonance that E. M. Forster heard from the Marabar caves.

Irving Wardle. In Michael Holroyd, ed., *The Genius of Shaw: A Symposium* (London, Hodder and Stoughton, 1979), p. 145

Pygmalion's enduring popularity has somewhat embarrassed Shaw's critics. Its fairy-tale atmosphere, traditional form, and romantic undertones, as well as its apparent absence of philosophic weight and social significance, have made it seem rather an anomaly in the dramatist's output, and its very fame in several stage and screen versions has further encouraged the critics to dismiss it as merely a superior piece of commercial theater. Shaw himself abetted this snobbery by calling the play a "shameless potboiler" and by allowing it only a scanty preface, which reduced its meaning to little more than a plea for alphabetical reform. Yet despite the opinion of Shaw the critic and his more deferential followers, the public has been right to esteem this work, which is in fact one of his richest creations not only in its obvious charms but precisely in the depth of its psychological insights, the range of its philosophical implications, and the wit of its many literary allusions; and its apparent lack of the Big Issues in the other major plays only indicates Shaw's achievement here in weaving those issues so finely into the fabric of characterization and structure that one can scarcely talk about the ideas without talking about the people, who happily transcend anything that can be said about them. Moreover, like other true works of art, the play affects us in hidden ways and came from hidden recesses in the writer's own being. It was drawn from depths Shaw had never before reached and was incubated longer than any other play he wrote. His later belittling of the play arose in part from a desire to deflect attention from the ways it incorporated essential aspects of himself. In short, *Pygmalion* is neither the "lucky" hit that one critic has called it, nor yet again the oddly atypical work that others have considered it to be, but rather the one play of them all that Shaw was born to write.

.   Arnold Silver. *Bernard Shaw: The Darker
Side* (Stanford, Cal., Stanford University
Press, 1982), p. 179

STOPPARD, TOM (1937–   )

Tom Stoppard's *Rosencrantz and Guildenstern Are Dead* is obviously giving considerable pleasure to large numbers of people, so I advance my own reservations feeling like a spoilsport and a churl: the play strikes me as a noble conception which has not been endowed with any real weight or texture. The author is clearly an intelligent man with a good instinct for the stage, and his premise is one that should suggest an endless series of possibilities. But he manipulates this premise instead of exploring it, and what results is merely an immensely shrewd exercise enlivened more by cunning than by conviction.

As is now generally known, *Rosencrantz and Guildenstern Are Dead* is a theatrical parasite, feeding off *Hamlet, Waiting for Godot,* and *Six Characters in Search of an Author*—Shakespeare provides the characters, Pirandello the technique, and Beckett the tone with which the Stoppard play proceeds. Like Pirandello, Stoppard tries to give extradramatic life to a group of already written characters, introducing elements of chance and spontaneity into a scene previously determined by an author. His object is to discover what happens to people whose lives are completely fixed and formalized when they are allowed to meditate, self-consciously, upon their own predestination. . . .

It is, in fact, the characters of Rosencrantz and Guildenstern that account for a good deal of my queasiness about the play. In Shakespeare, these characters are time servers—cold, calculating opportunists who betray a friendship for the sake of a preferment—whose deaths, therefore, leave Hamlet without a pang of remorse. In Stoppard, they are garrulous, child-like, ingratiating simpletons, bewildered by the parts they must play—indeed, by the very notion of an evil action. It is for this reason, I think, that Stoppard omits their most crucial scene—the famous recorder scene where they are exposed as spies for Claudius—for it is here that their characterological inconsistency would be most quickly revealed. Since the author is presumably anxious to demonstrate the awful inevitability of a literary destiny ("We follow directions—there is no *choice* involved. The bad end unhappily, the good unluckily. That is what tragedy means"), it hardly serves his purpose to violate the integrity of Shakespeare's original conception. But I suspect the author has another purpose here—that of amusing the audience with winning heroes—and the necessity to be charming is not always easily reconciled with the demands of art. [Nov. 4, 1967]

Robert Brustein. The Third Theatre (New York,
Alfred A. Knopf, 1969), pp. 149, 151–52

Tom Stoppard's *Rosencrantz and Guildenstern Are Dead* . . . is *Waiting for Godot* rewritten by a university wit. Based on a nice conceit, it is epigrammatically literate, intelligent, theatrically clever. It marks a scintillating debut for its author.

An English drama critic was skeptical of its success in America because to appreciate it one had to be familiar with *Hamlet*! We may now reassure that critic as to our familiarity with *Hamlet* since Stoppard's play is a Broadway hit and our reviewers, to judge by the ads, have called it "a superb play," "very brilliant, very chilling," etc., etc.

Rosencrantz and Guildenstern are two ordinary youths called to the court of Elsinore to detect what it is that troubles the young Prince. They haven't the faintest idea of the tragedy into the midst of which they have been thrust. They do as they are bid and for their pains meet with sudden death.

This is a parable of little Everyman. We are thrown into a world in which events of great moment apparently take place, have only an inkling of our role in them and in one way or another we are their victims.

As bits of *Hamlet* are enacted in swift and dim outline, the dilemma of poor Rosencrantz and Guildenstern—confused even as to their own names or identities, though one is supposed to be smarter than the other—is immediately clear, and the intellectual pattern of the play is firmly set. . . .

There are jokes about the theatre and amusing cracks about Hamlet himself, who is described as being "stark raving sane." The best of these occurs when Rosencrantz decides what he ought to say to Hamlet. "To sum up: your father whom you love dies, you are his heir, you come back to find that hardly was the corpse cold before his young brother popped on to his throne and under his sheets. . . . Now why are you behaving in this extraordinary manner?"

All this entertaining stuff leads on to the play's profounder purpose, which is to declare that with life, "Wheels have been set in motion, and they have their own pace to which we are condemned." There is no true answer. "Uncertainty is the normal state." "But what are we supposed to *do*?" The answer is "Relax. Respond. We only know what we're told. And for all we know it isn't even true." The only certainty is death. "The bad end unhappily, the good unluckily."

The quips sparkle, the portentous reflections are neatly phrased. The play is civilized pastime, which is certainly as unusual as it is agreeable, and we are duly grateful. But we need not take the play's "deeper significance" too seriously; it is not thought but student chatter on a brightly dignified level.

Harold Clurman. *Nation*. Nov. 6, 1967, p. 476

Critical jargon—highbrow and philistine—is one of the things parodied in Tom Stoppard's new one-act comedy, *The Real Inspector Hound,* and it would require some courage to parrot, even approximately, Moon, the second-string critic, who makes this pronouncement about the Agatha Christie-type thriller he has just been watching (from the far side of the stage where another "audience" confronts the audience):

> If we examine this more closely, and I think close examination is the best tribute that the play deserves, I think we will find that within the austere framework of what is seen to be on one level a country-house weekend, and what a useful symbol it is, the author has given us—yes, I will go so far—he has given us the human condition.

We need not then go so far as to see in the two-level action of the play "the human condition." On the contrary, the play's interest may well lie in the cheerful and seemingly amoral way in which it makes the theatre feed on the theatre without urging us to perceive the old analogies between the world and the stage. When, towards the end of the play, the two parodied critics one after another step on the stage, get sucked into the mad logic of a theatrical thriller and assume parts that lead to a quick death by revolver shot, nobody is likely to experience the "felt life" that is always there in Pirandello's theatricality; nor is one invited to recognize some social nightmare as in the somewhat over-obvious metamorphosis of logical-political man into Ionesco's rhinoceros.

No-one, not even a critic, needs to feel involved beyond the level of a fine cerebral farce. It is comfortingly classical, as though Sheridan's *The Critic* were performed in Alice's Looking Glass; and the element of absurdity in the play rests in the comfortingly witty dream where everything is topsy-turvy—the Inspector turns critic, the Critic inspector, and so on—and the words of a card-game are jumbled up into the familiar stage rhubarb. The point is that Stoppard is not only using absurd elements that pre-date the so-called theatre of the absurd, but he plays with the latter—parodistically.

Andrew K. Kennedy. MD. Feb., 1969, p. 437

It would be tempting to label Tom Stoppard as the intellectual among our young playwrights, if "intellectual" did not always tend, in the British theatre anyway, to have the ring of a dirty word. Also, he does deny very firmly that it's true: however precisely calculated his plays look, he insists that when he starts writing them he has no clearer idea of exactly where they are going, or exactly how they will get there, than the most innocent, uninformed member of a first-night audience. Nevertheless, the most striking, and most strikingly individual, effect Stoppard's plays make comes from their evident concern with structure, with overall pattern. Where other dramatists produce big, untidy effects, spilling out their materials generously, and often too generously, with little apparent concern for economy, concentration and scrupulous adaptation of means to ends, Stoppard works by neatness, precision, a meticulous tying-in of loose ends. He professes to mistrust most of all the arbitrary in art, the play which works as linear experience from moment to moment; he likes and works towards the feeling of completeness as one piece after another falls into place, and finds it very important for him that the structure of his plays should lock finally into a clear pattern with a "clunk" at the end.

John Russell Taylor. The Second Wave
(New York, Hill and Wang, 1971), p. 94

Tom Stoppard's world is like Camus's telephone booth, except that there are many occupants and none has the proper change. And Camus can conceive of heroes flourishing inside: Don Juans, adventurers, actors pounding the walls in healthy revolt. But Stoppard's characters suffer. Most of those who survive become desensitized and unquestioning; the rest are overcome by madness or death.

Despite these distinctions, the world views of the two writers are basically alike. Both belong to what Camus terms the "tradition of . . . humiliated thought," born of the struggle to make reasonable and human a universe which is neither. Both are concerned with the nature and effects of absurdity. It is the expression of their concern and of their questions that differs. Almost immediately, Stoppard's plays and fiction abandon the conventional rhetoric that characterizes the work of Camus, Sartre, and many others who explore the absurd through art. Logical arguments and the devices they demand are replaced by features peculiar to the Theatre of the Absurd as Martin Esslin has described it. Stoppard's characters are rarely three-dimensional, his plots rarely linear. Though his settings generally are localized, the random action and dialogue they compass dramatize a confusion that has no bounds.

Stoppard's debt to the Theatre of the Absurd, particularly to Beckett, is often acknowledged without being analyzed. The connection with Beckett is especially important, a means of refuting the general notion that Stoppard is a clever prodigy whose productions do little more than glitter at the surface. For correspondences exist that are far more profound than casual parallels in situation and technique. They have to do primarily with characterization.

Jill Levenson. QQ. Autumn, 1971, p. 431

[*Jumpers* is] a delightfully Absurdist play, more successful in some respects than *Rosencrantz and Guildenstern,* although still a bit too scrappy and incoherent for my taste. I laughed almost continually and came out of the theatre feeling cheered up; but quite a bit of the action did not seem necessary and I have failed to understand a number of points, even after reading the text. Why, for instance, has Dorothy gone off sex with her husband, after the shock of the de-poeticisation of the moon? She is still fond of him, and she is not totally traumatised since she is having some sort of affair with the Vice-Chancellor. I suspect that it is simply because Mr. Stoppard wants to make a pun about a consummate artist refusing consummation. And why is the play weighted down at the end with the rather tedious coda? It could have stopped five minutes before it does. Is it because Mr. Stoppard cannot quite control his flow of language and gimmicks?

To judge by the extremely silly programme interview, it is almost as if he were afraid to think commonsensically, in case his demon should be castrated. In my opinion, this is an error which has weakened the work of some other Absurdists, such as Ionesco. But then my contention is that the conquests of the irrational should always be explicable eventually in terms of the rational, and that one should feel them to be rational even before one can discover why they are so. According to my antennae, quite a few bits of this play have not been brought fully into intellectual or aesthetic focus.

John Weightman. *Enc*. April, 1972, p. 45

In *Rosencrantz and Guildenstern Are Dead* we do not have the kind of theater characterized by such phrases as direct involvement, emotional, pre-critical theater of the heart, but rather a theater of criticism, intellectual, distanced, of the mind. In a very real sense, Stoppard is an artist-critic writing drama for audience-critics, a dramatist least effective when he points his finger directly at the existential dilemma—"What does it all add up to?"—and most effective when he confronts the play *Hamlet* and Elizabethan drama and theatrical art, thereby going roundabout to get to the important issues. Stoppard's play, because it feeds on both an Elizabethan tragedy and a modern tragicomedy, gives us the opportunity to consider the larger context of modern drama, especially Joseph Wood Krutch's well-known and ominous observations on the death of tragedy and his prediction of the devolution of tragedy from Religion to Art to Document. Krutch finds an interesting answer, I believe, in *Rosencrantz and Guildenstern Are Dead*. Using Krutch's words, but not in the way he uses them, we can say that *Rosencrantz and Guildenstern Are Dead* is art that studies art, and therefore serving as a document, dramatic criticism as play presenting ideas on Hamlet, on Elizabethan drama, on theatrical art, and by so doing commenting on the life that art reveals. That is, Stoppard's play is holding the mirror of art up to the art that holds the mirror up to nature.

This double image causes the modern audience to take the kind of stance often associated with satire. And yet, Stoppard's play cannot be called satirical, for it makes no attempt to encourage the audience into any kind of action, as do Brecht's plays, or to cause the audience to change the way things are. The play examines the way things are, or, more precisely stated, it intellectually confronts and theatricalizes the condition of man the player and the world as theater. By the pressure of its *critical* energy, the play awakens in the audience a recognition of man's condition, not in order to change that condition, but to see it clearly. In short, by presenting a theatrical, artistic document, Stoppard makes us think—the words "document" and "think" pointing to the modernity, the impoverishment, and the particular value of *Rosencrantz and Guildenstern Are Dead*. The play presents not revelation but criticism, not passionate art—Hamlet in the graveyard—but cool, critical, intellectual art—Hamlet playing with the recorders. *Rosencrantz and Guildenstern Are Dead,* in its successful moments, brilliantly displays the virtues of theater of criticism, and perhaps shows the direction in which some modern drama will be going—"times being what they are."

Norman Berlin. *MD*. Dec., 1973, pp. 276–77

In spite of all its merits, the first act of *Jumpers* left me unsatisfied. Mr. Stoppard's basic joke is the old one about the absent-minded professor: George's preposterous lecture is really a set of variations on this joke, and as George bombinates on and on, the joke begins to wear thin. (This parody-lecture, by the way, owes a good deal to a Jonathan Miller sketch from *Beyond the Fringe,* in which the Cambridge philosopher G. E. Moore figured very prominently. Mr. Stoppard's George, of course, is also a G. Moore. And while we're at it, Inspector Bones of the Yard bears a distinct resemblance to Inspector Truscott in Joe Orton's play *Loot*.) The bickerings between George and Dorothy verge at times on the tiresome. Worse, the play seems to be about nothing in particular at all; it appears to be a self-indulgent, wayward excuse for Mr. Stoppard to be too clever by at least three-quarters.

But in the second act, the various threads begin to weave together. Slowly it becomes clear that George, fatuous as he is, is the last of the civilized humanists (like that other George in [Albee's] *Who's Afraid of Virginia Woolf?*), doomed to go down before the soulless, crass "rationality" of the future that is represented by Sir Archibald Jumper. . . . The moon's violation by astronauts—Dorothy's obsession—is another symbol of the inexorable pollution of old purities by the Faustian mechanistic juggernaut that arrogantly proclaims, "No problem is insoluble given a big enough plastic bag."

George has two beloved pets, a tortoise and a hare that have been specially trained to refute Zeno's paradox. Their unhappy fate makes George keenly aware of his own weakness, caught between the egregious Archie and his jumper on the one hand, and the malevolence of chance on the other. . . . This second act, for me, tips the balance in the play's favor. Just in time, it becomes clear that Mr. Stoppard's cleverness is not just cleverness in a vacuum. My point is not that pathos is more satisfying than comedy, but that coherence is more satisfying than sprawl; coherence is what *Jumpers* attains, just in time.

Julius Novick. *VV*. May 2, 1974, pp. 83–84

Tom Stoppard's new play *Travesties* is the most startling of his startling comedies. Poised between history and farce, it demands a good deal of the actors. . . . Although the play bows repeatedly to Oscar Wilde and glances less deferentially at Gilbert and Sullivan, there has been nothing in the theatre quite like this. What connexions it has are with certain techniques in Joyce's later novels and, not incongruously, with vaudeville routines such as ''Mr. Gallagher and Mr. Sheen.'' If we don't easily get our bearings, we can at least see that Mr. Stoppard means it that way; he offers a continual displacement of perspective as if Argus eyes would make up for the defects of individual vision. At the same time, whatever the surface that is offered for inspection, the words dart and tingle. . . .

At the play's end Carr has to bear his wife's reproaches for having telescoped time, for having claimed to know people he didn't, and for having got it all wrong generally. But he defends himself against this subservience to the unimaginably real: ''What of it? I was here. They were here. They went on. I went on. We all went on.'' The great issues of twentieth-century art and politics have been sounded; instead of being debated directly, they have been debated in their travestied versions. The travesties do not quite cancel each other out. Art is to be allowed, like Carr, to go on. Comic irreverence conveys as much as solemnity. And does so with bravura. Not the least of Mr. Stoppard's inventions is what might be called a stoppardism or tomism, as when Tzara is accused of being ''Kant-struck,'' and Wilde disparaged as ''coxcomb and bugbear of the Home Rule sodality.'' Those laundered obscenities perhaps convey some sense of the flagrant high spirits of this admirable play.

Richard Ellmann. TLS. July 12, 1974, p. 744

Some five years ago I witnessed a production of Tom Stoppard's *Rosencrantz and Guildenstern Are Dead* at the Alvin Theatre in New York City. I left the theatre with the sense that I had just attended a production which had ''worked.'' To say this of a theatre production (or perhaps any work of art) is to express a feeling that the event was satisfying in ways which escape immediate or concrete explanation. Even when I reexamined the script of *Rosencrantz and Guildenstern Are Dead* the reasons for the effectiveness of Stoppard's play seemed elusive. The script is, after all, blatantly derivative, not only in its reliance for frame on *Hamlet*, but in its collage of themes and theatrical devices so clearly drawn from an assortment of major modern playwrights. Even a first reading of the play reveals its concern with such issues as the absurdity of human existence, alienation, the reality and illusion of theatre, the significance of history, and these concerns and their modes of expression readily call forth Pirandello, Brecht, Beckett and many others.

Many plays, of course, succeed despite the absence of any claims to originality or innovation. Broadway has been filled for decades with Xerox-copied productions. My troubling over the response to *Rosencrantz and Guildenstern Are Dead* is both a concern with the effectiveness of this particular play and with how and why one makes judgments about one's responses to any drama. The term ''worked'' is helpful to these explorations because it emphasizes the activity of the play as opposed to a perception of a play as a static object whose meaning or theme we search out. The term, however, can be too limited if we do not augment it with a preposition; that is, I am not as much concerned in my criticism with how the internal parts of a play fit or work in relation to each other, but with how the play works at, towards, or on an audience. Although I believe it crucial to consider every artifact in terms of its workings on an audience, in drama (and certainly in music and dance as well) the physical movement through time and space before an audience whose physical presence asserts itself pressures us constantly away from synthetic statements about *the* nature or *the* idea of the piece.

I believe that what we mean when we say that *Rosencrantz and Guildenstern Are Dead* "works" is that it has a potent and appropriate dramatic strategy, a lucid and meaningful grasp on the relationship of every moment of the play to an audience. I borrow the term strategy from Kenneth Burke, who speaks of focusing on the strategy of a work as the center of criticism and demonstrates this vividly in the brief essay, "Antony in Behalf of the Play." Burke's crucial insight is his perception of the script as manipulator of both actors and audience. The playscript not only thus has a discernible meaning, but a distinct task or set of tasks.

Helene Keyssar-Franke. *ETJ*. March, 1975, pp. 85–86

From *Enter a Free Man* to *Travesties* is a long way. Stoppard's habit of cannibalising old situations to make new ones tends to suggest repetitiveness but really he has been expanding his scope all the time. Take the meticulously extended preparation for the gag about the Rule Britannia clock in *Enter a Free Man*. In that apprentice work such devices are at first sight tangential enough to seem merely cosmetic. But hindsight reveals that they constitute the play's real originality. Otherwise the plot is like one of Ibsen's turned on its head, with the daughter continually telling her father the truth about himself, instead of the saving lie. The eccentric atmosphere suggests Saroyan's *The Time of Your Life,* which in turn was more solidly in the Broadway tradition than people thought at the time. If Stoppard had never written anything subsequently, we might think of Riley's indoor rain as being a nod to N. F. Simpson, and the concern with Time to be like J. B. Priestley's, or Christopher Fry's, or, at best, T. S. Eliot's. But in retrospect the architecture looks like decoration and the decoration looks like architecture.

In all the subsequent plays the texture is composed entirely of interweaving preparation. By the time of *Jumpers* it takes the whole play for the separate stories of the tortoise and the hare to catch up with each other— Zeno's paradox resolved at the intersection of long lines of coincidence. And in *Travesties* we find the long lines turning into curves, the planes curving into spheres, and the spheres making music.

And if the music of the spheres sounds cold, would it be more convincing if it sounded warm? There is abundant evidence in Stoppard's plays to show that he is as capable of emotion as anybody. In *Enter a Free Man* Linda is a finely tuned moral invention whose equivalents we might well miss in the later plays, if we really thought they should be there. The mainspring of *Rosencrantz and Guildenstern Are Dead* is the perception—surely a compassionate one—that the fact of their deaths mattering so little to Hamlet was something which ought to have mattered to Shakespeare. . . .

There is plenty to indicate that if Stoppard had done no more than employ the drama as a vehicle for moral messages he would still have been a force in the theatre. The playwrights who grapple with those issues supposedly too weighty for Stoppard's frivolous talent are likely to have been inspired by a view of their task which is not only less comprehensive than Stoppard's but less penetrating. Stoppard leaves them behind not because he can't do what they can do, but because he can do what they can do so easily. ("What's wrong with bad art," he told Ronald Hayman, "is that the artist knows exactly what he's doing.")

Clive James. *Enc.* Nov., 1975, p. 74

Is Stoppard, then, an absurdist? Like most arbitrary categories this is frequently more misleading than helpful, as has proved the case with writers such as Pinter and Albee. Yet the iconography of *Rosencrantz and Guildenstern Are Dead* is familiar to audiences who cut their critical teeth on Beckett and Ionesco. The absurdists captured a deracinated world—a world in which the potential for action and communication has been irrevocably eroded. The setting is timeless, the landscape an expressionistic desert reminiscent of Dali's lapidary wilderness or the claustrophobic living room of modern, uncommunal living. The capacity for action is minimal and ironic. Language itself is simply an elaborate papering over of cracks, which constantly threaten to open up beneath those who remain either blithely unaware of their plight or numbed with despair. That anguish obviously exists in Stoppard's play—a work in which two men are seen "passing the time in a place without any visible character," clinging fiercely to the conviction that they "have not been picked out . . . simply to be abandoned," that they are "entitled to some direction," only to confess at the end of their "play" that "it is not enough. To be told so little—to such an end—and still, finally, to be denied an explanation." The only resources available to these abandoned characters are the compassion with which they respond to one another and the humour which they deploy as a means of neutralizing their fear. [Reinhold] Niebuhr's comment that laughter is a kind of no man's land between faith and despair is clearly applicable to *Rosencrantz and Guildenstern Are Dead*. For Rosencrantz and Guildenstern themselves, humour is a means of preserving sanity; for Stoppard it is a natural product of disjunction—of the gulf between cause and effect, aspiration and fulfilment, word and meaning, which is the root alike of pain, absurdity, and laughter, and clue to the relativity of truth, itself a subject to which Stoppard has repeatedly returned.

Stoppard has said that, "What I try to do is to end up by contriving the perfect marriage between the play of ideas and farce, or perhaps, even high comedy. . . . To that end I have been writing plays which are farcical and without an idea in their funny heads, and I have also written plays which are all mouth . . . and don't bring off the comedy. And occasionally, I think *Jumpers* would be an example, I've got fairly close to a play which works as a funny play and which makes coherent, in terms of theatre, a fairly complicated intellectual argument." While it is true that the argument behind *Rosencrantz and Guildenstern Are Dead* is not complex, its strength lies precisely in the skill with which he has blended humour with metaphysical enquiry, the success with which he has made the play's theatricality an essential element of its thematic concern. It is, indeed, a kind of *Waiting for Godot,* in which Vladimir and Estragon become university wits.

Yet, as he indicates above, not all of his plays have such serious aspirations, and Stoppard followed *Rosencrantz and Guildenstern Are Dead* and *Enter a Free Man* with two adroit and well-constructed works (*The Real Inspector Hound* and *After Magritte*), whose chief fascination resides in the skill with which he unravels his own aesthetic conundrums.

C. W. E. Bigsby. *Tom Stoppard* (Harlow,
British Council/Longman Group, 1976), pp. 15–16

The idiom which has had the greatest impact on Stoppard's writing is "the absurd," a movement which shattered traditions of staging, character, dialogue, and plot. Theatrical order can never be the same.

But Stoppard has not been content to leave man in the absurdist void. True, his works always have elements of absurdity, manifested generally in his protagonists, who are nonentities swept into the action of a world they cannot understand. And Stoppard almost always displays their predicaments comically. However, he also develops undertones of seriousness, emphasizing the need for some action other than surrender to counteract absurdity. He explores man coping with the artistic world in such plays as *Rosencrantz and Guildenstern Are Dead, Artist Descending a Staircase, The Real Inspector Hound,* and *Travesties.* He explores man coping with political systems in *If You're Glad I'll Be Frank, Travesties,* and *Every Good Boy Deserves Favour.* He explores man coping in society in such plays as *Enter a Free Man, Albert's Bridge, Where Are They Now?* and *Professional Foul.* He explores man and his faith, both religious and secular, in such plays as

Jumpers and *Travesties*. Of course, in none of these works does any single theme long dominate, and the four areas are usually interlocked.

If one may single out any unifying element in Stoppard's works, it is his faith in man's mind. He rejects the irrational, the reliance on emotion instead of intellect, the retreat from independent thought. And this commitment is the foundation for his theatrical techniques.

First, he makes free use of form: linear movement, flashbacks, plots within plots, and innumerable references to other literary works. Yet amid all the clutter and episodic action, a structure emerges, a tribute to the organizing powers of the playwright's rationality and his expectations of the audience's ability to grasp that structure.

Second, his emphasis on variety of language, in terms of brisk pace, literary allusions, and double and triple meanings, reaffirms his own belief in man's ability to communicate. He manages at the same time to make his language amusing, yet richly woven with ideas.

Third, he maintains a concern for people, demonstrated more than ever in his latest plays. Even though his characters may be isolated, lost figures, they are never turned into the one-dimensional figures of standard absurd drama. Always Stoppard insists on their dealing with ideas, questions, and their own responsibilities as human beings. Ultimately, his plays may be understood as an affirmation of man's humanity in the face of all obstacles.

Victor L. Cahn. Beyond Absurdity: The Plays of Tom
Stoppard (Rutherford, N.J., Fairleigh Dickinson
University Press, 1979), pp. 156–57

The first thing we ever noticed about [Stoppard] was his wit: a man of his word who did not find it necessary to be modishly glum in order to assure us of his seriousness. And the second thing, as John Russell Taylor remarked in *The Second Wave*, was his passion for structure. Both features were there in *Rosencrantz and Guildenstern Are Dead*, combining together in a dazzling display of virtuosity that made one slightly uneasy: was this merely a *tour de force*? With only the slight weight of *Enter a Free Man* behind it—and even that in an earlier television version called *A Walk on the Water*—it could well have been. The brilliance was confirmed in *The Real Inspector Hound* and *After Magritte;* and so was the bright intellectual inquisitiveness, and the Autolycus-syndrome, for Stoppard showed himself to be a snapper-up of unconsidered trifles from the literary and theatrical debris of half-a-dozen centuries. And not always trifles—Stoppard's sense of the way cultural elements feed each other is very strong; he sees the present as founded on the past; what is there is there for all to use, is subtly modified by that use and is then passed on to others to add to the universal and ever-developing pattern.

But weight, authority, stature? Were they there in the small spate of plays after *R & G*? Not, I think, until *Jumpers* and *Travesties*. Then they are. And the two plays need to be considered together, as complementary pieces. They are conjointly an asseveration of faith in life, and in art as the true preserver and protector and purveyor of life. They assert the primacy of the intuitive sense of the world, the accuracy of the instinctive. Like that other theatrical arch-intellectual, Shaw, Stoppard turns out to be a mystic who is fascinated by the way in which our mystical sense of what *is,* our metaphysical understanding of the world, comes within reach of our comprehension through the probing of that sharp instrument, the human mind. Both of them delight in the intellectual process. Both celebrate it in their plays. But beyond it they celebrate that mystery which the intellect can apprehend but not explain, the inexplicable fact of life before which the intellect bows and acknowledges its fiefdom.

It is especially interesting and valuable to note this metaphysical bias in these two plays now that Stoppard seems, temporarily at least, to have turned his attention in his more recent works to more immediate social and political concerns—with a consequent diminution in the stature of the resultant plays. *Night and Day* . . . is about the capacity of a free press to defend all the other freedoms; *Every Good Boy Deserves Favour,* the 1977 play written for performance in the Royal Festival Hall by a cast that included, as well as sundry actors, the entire London Symphony Orchestra conducted by André Previn, is about the misuse of psychiatry in the Soviet Union; and *Professional Foul*, the best of these three, is—significantly— about the denial of the right of individual expression and the compulsion towards expediency in Stoppard's native Czechoslovakia.

Eric Salmon. QQ. Summer, 1979, pp. 215–16

The most striking characteristic of Stoppard's work is his unremitting self-consciousness. On the first level, this introspective quality manifests itself in his deliberate mining of theatrical resources. Along with other postwar dramatists, he has reclaimed and revamped the vehicles for direct address to the audience, notably the music-hall chairman and the Renaissance soliloquy, which violate the fourth wall of representational dramaturgy. Stoppard's experience as a reviewer taught him not only the formulas of drama but also what works well on stage. His borrowings from Wilde and Shakespeare, as well as his parodies, are indicative of his consciousness of writing in a dramatic tradition.

On the second level, this self-consciousness gives rise to the play metaphor that draws the analogy between all men and actors and between life and the stage. In *Rosencrantz and Guildenstern Are Dead,* the play metaphor is implicit in the relationship between the title characters and the Tragedians; in *The Real Inspector Hound,* it appears when the drama critics change places with the actors.

Third, Stoppard's self-consciousness directs him to question the artist, his responsibilities, and his place in society. In *Artist Descending a Staircase* and *Travesties,* he provides a forum for representatives of various aesthetic theories to voice their opinions. In *Night and Day,* journalists rather than artists must face the question of their responsibility to society.

Finally, the self-consciousness of Tom Stoppard leads him to challenge the validity and meaning of art. Underlying Stoppard's self-consciousness is a self-criticism that takes as its point of departure Auden's statement that art never saved anyone from death in a concentration camp, a comment Stoppard is fond of quoting. Stoppard's carefully cultivated refusal to moralize in his early works later yields at least to a concern with specific political issues, yet he never envisions a political purpose to his art. His aim, surprisingly, is much higher—toward morality not just politics. Stoppard is quoted as saying that "when, because, art takes notice of something important, it's claimed that the art is important. It's not"; rather, the issue that art notices, he implies, retains its importance. Elsewhere, Stoppard indicates that art itself is indeed important not merely as entertainment or spectacle, but because "it provides the moral matrix, the moral sensibility, from which we make our judgments about the world." From his apprenticeship in naturalistic dramaturgy through his reconsideration of the themes as well as characters of *Hamlet* to his concentration on particular political injustices, Stoppard's plays do indeed suggest such a moral matrix with increasing clarity and insight.

Joan Fitzpatrick Dean. *Tom Stoppard: Comedy as
Moral Matrix* (Columbia, Mo., University of
Missouri Press, 1981), pp. 14–15

Like *After Magritte, Dirty Linen* is a bit of fluff. Its flimsy structure exists only to support jokes—puns, double entendres, sight gags—all on a single subject: sex in high places. Since much of the verbal humor depends upon timing and inflection, *Dirty Linen* can be a far better play when seen in production than the text would suggest. This play and *New-Found-Land,* the companion piece it contains, were directed with great verve and inventiveness in both their London and New York premieres by Ed Berman, for whom the plays were written. . . .

It was also for Berman that Stoppard wrote three other equally insubstantial playlets: *Dogg's Our Pet, The (15 Minute) Dogg's Troupe Hamlet,* and *Dogg's Hamlet.* Although written during an eight-year period, these very short pieces have certain overlapping characteristics. The most recent of these one-act plays is the first half of a full-length bill called *Dogg's Hamlet, Cahoot's Macbeth,* which uses truncated versions of the two Shakespearean plays as points of departure. . . . *Dogg's Hamlet* is itself composed of two parts: the first section repeats a linguistic experiment Stoppard had conducted in *Dogg's Our Pet,* uses the same characters, and even incorporates some speeches verbatim from the earlier play; the second half of *Dogg's Hamlet* is, with only minute revisions, *The (15 Minute) Dogg's Troupe Hamlet.*

Stoppard acknowledges Wittgenstein's *Philosophical Investigation* as the source of his idea for *Dogg's Our Pet.* A more accessible influence is René Magritte, who is quoted in the catalogue of the 1969 Tate Gallery exhibition of his works: "No object is so attached to its name that another cannot be found which suits it better." Two languages are used in *Dogg's Our Pet.* One is English, the other is composed mostly of English words that mean something other than the meaning assigned by English-speakers. . . .

Shakespeare was also a resource for *Cahoot's Macbeth.* . . . Stoppard has pointed out that *Dogg's Hamlet* can be produced without *Cahoot's Macbeth,* but that the latter "cannot be done unless you've seen the first one first." This is a pity, because the wit, thought, and entertainment values of *Cahoot's Macbeth* far outshine the tedious foolishness of the frame story in *Dogg's Hamlet.*

[At the end of *Cahoot's Macbeth* the Inspector] . . . begins raising a wall. The metaphor is brilliant: artists under a totalitarian regime are physically walled in, but their thoughts and creative imaginations find their own form of expression—if necessary, a whole new language. As an ending to a play, the metaphor sums up what is best in Stoppard's sense of theatricality—the neatness of the packaging, the mutual reinforcement of visual and verbal cues, and the provocation to thought that seems like entertainment. As a statement, the ending of *Cahoot's Macbeth* is both an admission of horrors that exist in the human condition and a paean to the irrepressible human spirit.

Felicia Hardison Londré. *Tom Stoppard* (New York, Frederick Ungar, 1981), pp. 122, 128, 161, 164

STOREY, DAVID (1933–   )

David Storey (like David Mercer and David H. Lawrence before him) is concerned with the beast beneath the skin of civilised man. Sometimes his beasts rampage, terrorising the neighbourhood, as in *This Sporting Life.* At others they lurk neglected until such time as they can no longer be evaded, then rise up and tear a man to pieces—as in *The Restoration of Arnold Middleton.* . . .

Arnold himself is a schoolmaster, in a classical schizophrenic family situation. Being somewhat mother-obsessed, and having married his wife for maternal qualities which she refuses to display, he finds everything he needs in his mother-in-law, who is young enough to be still sexually viable, but old enough to be, as it were, his mother. As the three of them live together in one small house, the structure of Interpersonal Perceptions (and deceptions) becomes complex and frightening. He refuses to allow his wife to send her mother away (on grounds of human kindness—oh charity, your depths are murky!) until, at the climax of the piece, in chagrin at his own mother not turning up to see him, goaded on by the inanities of the schoolmasterly world around him, he gets moody, drunk, and sleeps with his mother-in-law. From this point onwards, temporary insanity sets in to express his inability to cope: it is only when the whole situation is destroyed by the removal of mother-in-law to a flatlet that normality beckons and his wife takes him back to her bed.

It is unfortunate that the last part of this story is such a schematic affair, because in principle it explores a resolution—a restoration—comparatively new to the theatre: I suspect that if it had been handled at the same pace (in the writing) as the first two acts—had, in fact, been two acts instead of one, David Storey would have had time to tease it out, give it that air of truth and humour which makes the first part of this play so memorable. Perhaps it is over-schematic because it owes too much to psychological theory: intellectual abstracts, however truthful, play havoc when allowed to creep in and dominate first-hand perception in a personal play. . . .

All in all, *The Restoration of Arnold Middleton* is worth seeing and worth following up by those concerned. The beasts that lurk in Arnold are ashamed to show their heads for the same reasons that the British bulldog is ashamed to bite: guilt, and lack of direction. The results in Arnold's life: bad faith, ignoble gestures, deceit, rash acts of aggression followed by temporary insanity, have their parallels in our public life. Arnold's constant reference to Robin Hood, heraldry and the many other myths of the late great Britain indicate that Storey is not altogether unaware of the connections. Arnold Middleton has meaning on several levels, and remains a brilliant portrayal of a person: a considerable creation in a considerable play.

John McGrath. *NS*. Sept. 8, 1967, pp. 298–99

In Celebration . . . is another study of the mind at the end of its tether, or nearly—for as Storey seems to have decided in his revisions of *Arnold Middleton*, the extraordinary thing about the human animal is his ability to keep going, even when everything seems impossible. The occasion is the fortieth wedding anniversary of the Shaws, an old coal-miner and his wife, which brings their three surviving sons, Andrew, Colin and Steven, home together again for one night. Gradually we see that all three of them, despite their varying degrees of success in the outside world, have all been psychologically crippled by their background and upbringing, and particularly it seems by the legacy of guilt from the death in childhood of an earlier-born brother, a brother conceived out of wedlock whose imminent arrival compelled their mother to marry beneath her and set up obscure chain reactions which are still reverberating in the adult lives of the whole family.

At least, this is the interpretation put upon things by Andrew, the most dynamic and, in worldly terms, the least successful of them. He still hugs to him his capacity for suffering, and his role in the family reunion turns out to be largely that of *agent provocateur,* forcing the others to look at themselves and one another again in the light of his own bitter logic, to feel something, if they still can, instead of atrophying because of their unwillingness to face any kind of emotional reality, accept any kind of emotional challenge, any more. . . .

The play is seemingly loose and discursive, but essentially it is very tightly knit, with no word or gesture left which could be taken away without damaging the delicate organization of the whole, the gradual stripping of layer after layer from the characters until they all seem to be stripped spiritually naked.

John Russell Taylor. *The Second Wave* (New York,
Hill and Wang, 1971), pp. 148–49

Now that David Storey has taken on shape and substance for me, I would like to take another look at *This Sporting Life*. When I saw Lindsay Anderson's 1963 film, for which Storey did the screenplay based on his own novel, it came as just another of those English movies about sad, grimy life in provincial industrial towns—*Saturday Night and Sunday Morning, The Loneliness of the Long-Distance Runner*—in which the toughness and realism were tinged with sentimentality and soap opera. Since the film was made, Storey, the novelist, has become a playwright, the most impressive one to turn up in the English theater since those early angry days when John Osborne, John Arden and Harold Pinter emerged. When I was in England in May, I saw two of his plays—*The Contractor*, in the best production I saw in London, and *In Celebration,* in a less happy production in Salisbury. The potential for sentimentality is still there, but these two plays, again in provincial settings, do not cluck over their characters as *This Sporting Life* seemed to do. What Storey has done in both instances is to establish a revelatory occasion, gather the characters and set them talking, uncovering in the course of the play the emptiness and pain in the characters and, at the same time, positing their solidarity, the force that sustains them. The means to these two ends are the words the characters speak, apparently random, often funny talk which establishes a stage reality that gives the plays their strength.

Storey is now making his American debut with *Home,* his most recent play. For the press, it is an occasion not so much for Storey's sake but because those two redoubtable English knights, John Gielgud and Ralph Richardson, are back on the American stage together for the first time since that lamentable *The School for Scandal* they brought over in 1962. This time they are superb, but since I like to think of the arrival of *Home* as the Storey hour, I want to look first at the play. On the face of it, *Home* appears to be a departure for Storey, for in this play he is very much in the Beckett-Pinter tradition. Yet, the jump from the working-class living room of *In Celebration* to the almost bare stage of *Home* is not so great as it seems. The action is minimal in the earlier plays—in *In Celebration,* an offstage anniversary dinner, in *The Contractor,* the raising and striking of a tent for a wedding that takes place between the acts—and the drama lives in the lines. The occasional rhetoric of the earlier plays gives way in *Home* to simple sentences—more often fragments—but there is still a family resemblance between this play and the ones that preceded it.

Gerald Weales. Com. Jan. 15, 1971, p. 373

The essential quality of [Storey's] work comes, above all, from the characteristic balance he achieves between the literary and the visual. Structure is particularly important in his plays: their overall shape is almost sculptured. *The Contractor* takes its form from the erection and dismantling of the tent. After starting with an empty stage, we see the tent being put up and then being prepared for the wedding breakfast. This takes place in the interval between Act II and Act III, and the lights next go up on the chaos of empty bottles, dirty glasses and plates, damaged decorations and overturned furniture that the wedding guests have left. This is cleared up, the tent is taken down and we end, as we began, with an empty stage. *In Celebration* also centres on a celebration meal, which again takes place in the interval. The play is about a family reunion occasioned by the fortieth wedding anniversary of a coal-miner and his wife. As the play begins, one of their three sons is arriving in the heavily furnished living room of their home. The other two arrive, the conversation between sons, parents and neighbours produces a series of insights into the lives they are all leading, and we see that those of the parents and neighbours have changed very little since the sons, now all in their thirties, were children. They stay overnight but leave in the morning. The excitement is over, the parents resume their lives.

In *The Contractor* a great deal of cutting was done but in *The Changing Room* the focus is wider, taking in all thirteen members of a professional rugby team, the cleaner of the changing room, the trainers, the referee and the club manager and chairman. Again, though the play is about the people, its shape—like that of Wesker's *The Kitchen*—is determined by the place, and though the place (unlike the tent in *The Contractor*) has a continuing existence both before and after the action, it comes to life only at the time of the game, and what we see is constructed around two busy climaxes, with the players changing first into their rugby clothes and, later, out of them. Again the main climax of action—the game itself—is excluded from the play, and again we begin and end very quietly, this time with the old cleaner, who never watches the game but whose life centres on the changing room. The wooden benches, the clothes-pegs, the towels, the rugby boots, socks, singlets and shorts, and the physical actions, including massage and the referee's inspection, contribute to the life of the play on almost exactly the same level as the words.

Ronald Hayman. Playback (London,
Davis-Poynter, 1973), pp. 12–13

I am not really sure what makes David Storey's *The Changing Room* so fascinating to me as a woman. It has no plot, no clearly individualized characters, no real dramatic conflict. It is about a group of working-class men in the north of England who play a game I am totally unfamiliar with, except that I know (mainly from the film *This Sporting Life,* based on a novel by Storey) that it is horribly brutal. If the play were about Tibetan monks it could not be more foreign to me. Even the language is half incomprehensible to me: Rugby jargon spoken in Yorkshire accent. It is as though I had been allowed to see the exotic activities of a men's room for the first time in my life, and perhaps that is one reason the play held me, good or bad as that reason may be. . . .

The play calls for meticulously directed ensemble acting and gets it from an American cast who handle their North country accents deftly. Equally believable are the actors who play the club owner and the club secretary, and if there is any direct social comment, it comes from the appearance of these two, for the players are very deferential to their titled owner; class barriers hold sway to a certain extent even under the stadium. Sir Frederic, the owner, loves his lads, but he also loves the brutality, vicarious as it may be for him. Perhaps what this play is really about is that love among males that flourishes especially in the world of sports, a love embarrassed at tenderness, which finds its outlet instead in the communion of organized violent contact and its bittersweet aftermath.

It is not really a homosexual love (Storey has wisely avoided this obvious and faddish possibility) but rather a comradeship that enables male athletes to retain, or recapture, the irresponsibility of boyhood, to touch one another physically with impunity and without arousing suspicion. In a world dominated by the cult of machismo, competitive team sports would seem to satisfy distinctly opposite urges. Male ego is bolstered by the toughness of play and the drive to win. On the other hand, nothing is more sentimental than the male sports world; and the locker room scene, the part the public, and especially women, do not get to see, is a place where conventionally ''masculine'' men can be less masculine, truer in themselves, perhaps, than their super-male image demands. It is this revelation that is at the center of *The Changing Room*.

Rita Stein. *ETJ*. Oct., 1973, pp. 370–71

David Storey came to the theatre in his middle thirties after careers as a painter, professional Rugby player, teacher, and successful novelist. His four published plays to date display a remarkable consistency of craftsmanship, and in spite of occasional lapses of structure and a few weak moments, all manage to achieve a degree of dramatic excitement and intensity which establishes him as one of the more talented playwrights of the contemporary British theatre.

American reviewers have compared Storey to Pinter, I think unfairly His two most recent plays, *The Contractor* and *Home,* have moved from an earlier conventional realism to a Pinteresque subtlety of dialogue and structure, but his themes and tone have remained uniquely his. A second comparison could be drawn with John Osborne, whose influence has been so pervasive on British theatre since 1956. But Storey's sense of outrage is more restrained and his sense of irony more biting than Osborne's. His themes touch those of Arnold Wesker; but he avoids the evangelical tone and epic sweep which tend to make Wesker's plays somewhat pompous. His ironic view of life somewhat resembles that of John Arden; but he does not indulge in the open theatricality that has alienated Arden from popular audiences. In short, Storey typifies the British theatrical revival of the sixties while retaining the stamp of an individual style.

Of all the arts, the theatre is perhaps the most completely situated in time and space. Certainly Storey is thematically a member of England's angry generation of now-not-so-young men. More specifically, he is a Royal Court dramatist, almost archetypically so. Born in 1933, the son of a Welsh coal miner, he rose into an intellectual bourgeois society which he clearly dislikes. His roots and his intellectual sympathies reach back into the working class; his various careers span the interests of the sensitive men of his class and time—the arts, education, athletics. He is part of the vanguard of that class of overeducated and disaffected men and women who rose from the working class and who were outraged and stimulated by the failure of the Labour Party to achieve the Camelot they had been led to expect. Educated for a way of life denied them, they created the cultural revolution which we identify with England in the sixties.

Storey addresses himself to the issue of the disaffected generation, particularly in *In Celebration* and *The Contractor,* both of which played at the Royal Court in 1969. But the thing which sets him apart from the other angry dramatists is a sense of irony which mitigates his anger. His comedy is not so dark as theirs. There are traces of *Look Back in Anger* in both plays, particularly in *In Celebration,* but in both—and particularly in *The*

Contractor, which achieves a use of dramatic space and expression new for Storey—the dignity of man's efforts and the humor of his ironic situation in life overshadow his frustrations and absurdity.

William J. Free. *MD*. Dec., 1973, pp. 307–8

I don't think [David Storey is] as interested in assessing his characters' attitudes as in showing us how diverse and irreconcilable those attitudes are. His plays are all about disintegration, fragmentation: of society, of belief, of the family, of the individual psyche. From *The Restoration of Arnold Middleton* to *Home* to *The Changing Room,* they tell us how difficult it is for man to cooperate with man, or even to achieve much coherence and unity within himself. In artistic endeavour, if anywhere, the mind, emotions and hands should function as one: they patently don't do so in *Life Class*. In fact, Allott is more thoroughly alienated from his work than any of those sad and self-doubting young men who have populated Storey's previous plays. . . .

Some people, I should warn you, left the theatre noisily announcing they'd seen nothing but some painfully literal cinema-verité about a dreary provincial art-school. But others, including myself, found the thing at least as rich as *The Changing Room.* As often with Storey's plays, much is asked of the audience: it's up to you and me to speculate about character and ideas on the basis of far less direct evidence than modern playwrights customarily offer. But the evidence exists, and the rewards are there to be grabbed. Those who are prepared to do a little homework in the stalls, instead of slumping back and passively absorbing, will leave the theatre feeling that a good deal more has occurred than they can remember having actually seen and heard on the stage.

Benedict Nightingale. *NS*. April 19, 1974, pp. 558–59

Storey's persistent exploration of the need for, nature of, and consequences of social commitment finally jell in the oddly structured play *Cromwell* (1973). Once more, the ostensibly dominant figure suggested by the title fails to appear onstage. Like the motifs that have preceded it in other plays, this one, too, serves primarily to catalyse needs and desires within the limited framework of options it makes available. Cromwell never appears; he is described only from afar as a big man passing between trees and shrouded in mist. The battle itself is fragmentary, complex, and mysterious, emerging only intermittently from the confusing confines of the forest. But this image of war caused by issues remote from the combatants and fought with tactics and strategies visible only fragmentarily to the participants provides yet another powerful structural image. Here the play is episodic because the social structures that prevail in times of peace have broken down. There are no reliable commitments to call upon except those that grow out of particular occasions. Here, the occasionality of social contracts is taken to its ultimate extreme. Characters have only what they can obtain in a momentary situation, and with that moment goes whatever has been built upon it. What this play explores is the conflict between the need for provisional social contracts and the need for total commitment to social contracts in a world in which all prior social contracts have suddenly been suspended. . . .

If the Irishmen's philosophy of "nothing ventured, nothing lost" has seemed the best of several unattractive options in *Cromwell*, its virtues are completely undermined in Storey's next play, *The Farm*, in which that characterisation of their position appears. The philosophy of acquiescence is given the same searching scrutiny in this play that was given to Proctor's philosophy of commitment in the preceding play. The governing image of war, which so clearly registered the dangers of ultimate commitment, gives way to the controlling image of a farm, which equally clearly registers the dangers of avoiding commitment. As *The Farm* demonstrates in a variety of ways, where nothing is ventured, things can indeed be lost—and not just the things that might concern an idealist like Proctor, but also the things that might concern those . . . who seem most ready to accept and make do.

Austin E. Quigley. MD. Sept., 1979, pp. 269, 271–72

David Storey's *Early Days* [was] written as a vehicle for Ralph Richardson. Richardson plays a retired politician, now extremely ancient, who laments his failed career, repeatedly recalls a stray incident in his childhood, and cunningly torments his warders in the prison of old age in which he is incarcerated. "People have no regard for age," Storey has him say. "They see their own destiny much too clearly." Richardson sent a shiver or two down my middle-aged spine but for most of the time I was too busy marvelling at his performance or appreciating the rich texture of Storey's writing, and the intellectual and emotional precision of Lindsay Anderson's direction, to allow myself to be carried away.

Early Days is the theatrical equivalent of a long short story: within its brief confines it is expansive, digressive and varying in pace. We are interested only in the central character and the other parts were, I thought, all underwritten except for the rich son-in-law . . . . Richardson was spell-binding not least for the perpetual fear that he would fall from the tightrope of his lines but he always managed to recover and to incorporate every fluff or mispronunciation within his characteristically impressionistic and highly individual act. Was this old age? I cannot say but it was ripe, vintage Richardson—utterly memorable and on no account to be missed by connoisseurs.

Peter Jenkins. Spec. May 3, 1980, p. 28

SYNGE, JOHN MILLINGTON (1871–1909)

Mr. Synge has in common with the great theatre of the world, with that of Greece and that of India, with the creator of Falstaff, with Racine, a delight in language, a preoccupation with individual life. He resembles them also by a preoccupation with what is lasting and noble, that came to him, not as I think from books, but while he listened to old stories in the cottages, and contrasted what they remembered with reality. The only literature of the Irish country-people is their songs, full often of extravagant love, and their stories of kings and of kings' children. "I will cry my fill, but not for God, but because Finn and the Fianna are not living," says Oisin in the story. Every writer, even every small writer, who has belonged to the great tradition, has had his dream of an impossibly noble life, and the greater he is, the more does it seem to plunge him into some beautiful or bitter reverie. Some, and of these are all the earliest poets of the world, gave it direct expression; others mingle it so subtly with reality, that it is a day's work to disentangle it; others bring it near by showing us whatever is most its contrary. Mr. Synge, indeed, sets before us ugly, deformed or sinful people, but his people, moved by no practical ambition, are driven by a dream of that impossible life. That we may feel how intensely his woman of the glen dreams of days that shall be entirely alive, she that is "a hard woman to please" must spend her days between a sour-faced old husband, a man who goes mad upon the hills, a craven lad and a drunken tramp; and those two blind people of *The Well of the Saints* are so transformed by the dream, that they choose blindness rather than reality. He tells us of realities, but he knows that art has never taken more than its symbols from anything that the eye can see or the hand measure.

It is the preoccupation of his characters with their dream that gives his plays their drifting movement, their emotional subtlety. In most of the dramatic writing of our time, and this is one of the reasons why our dramatists do not find the need for a better speech, one finds a simple motive lifted, as it were, into the full light of the stage. The ordinary student of drama will not find anywhere in *The Well of the Saints* that excitement of the will in the presence of attainable advantages, which he is accustomed to think the natural stuff of drama, and if he see it played he will wonder why Act is knitted to Act so loosely, why it is all like a decoration on a flat surface, why there is so much leisure in the dialogue, even in the midst of passion. [1905]

W. B. Yeats. *Essays* (London, Macmillan, 1924), pp. 375–77

At the time of his first visit to Coole he had written some poems, not very good for the most part, and a play which was not good at all. I read it again after his death . . . and again it seemed but of slight merit. But a year later he brought us his two plays *In the Shadow of the Glen* and *Riders to the Sea,* both masterpieces, both perfect in their way. He had gathered emotion, the driving force he needed, from his life among the people, and it was the working in dialect that had set free his style. . . .

I remember his bringing the play [*The Playboy of the Western World*] to us in Dublin, but he was too hoarse to read it, and it was read by Mr. Fay. We were almost bewildered by its abundance and fantasy, but we felt—and Mr. Yeats said very plainly—that there was far too much "bad language," there were too many violent oaths, and the play itself was marred by this. I did not think it was fit to be put on the stage without cutting. It was agreed that it should be cut in rehearsal.

Lady Gregory. *EngR*. March, 1910, pp. 559, 563

Mr. [P. P.] Howe, who wrote a sincere and able book on Synge, may be taken as a representative apostle of the Synge cult. He sets before us a god, not a man—a creator of absolute beauty—and he asks us to accept the common view that *The Playboy of the Western World* is his masterpiece. There can never be any true criticism of Synge till we have got rid of all these obsessions and idolatries. Synge was an extraordinary man of genius, but he was not an extraordinarily great man of genius. He is not the peer of Shakespeare; he is not the peer of Shelley: he is the peer, say, of Stevenson. His was a byway, not a high-road, of genius. That is why he has an immensely more enthusiastic following among clever people than among simple people.

Once and only once Synge achieved a piece of art that was universal in its appeal, satisfying equally the artistic formula of Pater and the artistic formula of Tolstoi. This was *Riders to the Sea. Riders to the Sea,* a lyrical pageant of pity made out of the destinies of fisher-folk, is a play that would have been understood in ancient Athens or in Elizabethan London, as well as by an audience of Irish peasants today.

Robert Lynd. *Old and New Masters* (New York, Charles Scribner's Sons, 1919), pp. 94–95

Whatever may be the unreality of Synge's Anglo-Irish, it remains that his dialect possesses a literary value which it is difficult to over-estimate. Leaving aside its strange aloofness and the sense of distance which it lends to the mind, its principal quality in this connection is its rhythm. The concept of rhythm, which holds so important a place in latter-day philosophy and aesthetics, underlies Synge's whole view of the drama, his technical execution, the antithetic design of all his plays, and, more especially, his literary use of the Irish *patois*. He was bent on reproducing the suave and subtle "synge-song" of peasant speech, and his vernacular has in it that happy coalescence of harmony and meaning which only a born musician can obtain. Doubtless he had read the wonderful essay in which Walter Pater shows that all arts have a tendency to verge towards, and finally merge in, music. We already know the importance he attached to this element of cadence, and how he trained the Abbey actors to recite the words in his plays with the right intonation and lilt, which are as essential to an Irish pronunciation as the brogue itself. In a day when the speech of the stage has a tendency to become mere stenography, Synge wrote in a prose that sets him high among the poets. His dialect reads as well as Mr. Yeats's blank verse. If he did not write his plays in verse, it is simply because he felt that peasant prose had that flavour of reality and raciness which was so dear to him. Yet his prose, without ever being sustainedly iambic, contains occasional lines of blank verse—about eighty in *The Playboy of the Western World* and ten at least in *Deirdre of the Sorrows*; and it should be remembered that towards the end of his life Synge tried to invent a new blank-verse form in dialect.

It now becomes evident that the Irishness of Synge's plays has its limitation. One must not treat them as absolute social documents; or if one does so, one must bear in mind that they require very careful handling. One must allow for the obvious exaggeration in the situations and language, which has its reason and excuse in the necessity for all drama to produce startling combinations. Above all, one must take into account the "personal equation" in the plays: Synge strove to express himself first, and his drama, if it is, in a way, true to Ireland, is primarily true to the individual vision of the playwright.

> Maurice Bourgeois. *John Millington Synge and the Irish Theatre* (London, Constable, 1913), pp. 229–30

The fact that Synge is dead is only an accident which should not prohibit his inclusion from the category of dramatists of to-day. His work is of to-day, and will surely be of to-morrow also, for it can hardly be doubted that of all the playwrights who have written for the English stage in the last twenty years Synge is the most important. There is a roundness, a universality about his work, in comparison with which the plays of his contemporaries seem mechanical and limited.

Synge was in the fortunate position of being a man who gave expression to his time without being affected by the illnesses which troubled it. His dramas are contemporary dramas, and at the same time so little harassed by the technicalities of the age which have pushed themselves into a braggart importance, that he must be as simple and comprehensible to his audiences of a hundred years hence as he is to those of to-day.

His early literary culture was French, and the irony, the clarity that is part of the beautiful tradition of Montaigne and Molière persists through all the work of the Irish dramatist. Synge, writing nearly always of peasants and of lowly men and women who cling to the soil, treating of crude and simple things in his plays, is never himself coarse, never brutal.

All is just and in keeping. We expect the loves of peasants to be rude and primitive, their language to be strong and unclarified, each word of their limited vocabulary to be as full of meaning and natural force as the simple events of the village where they live. When this is so, peasant plays may be as fine and gracious as the symbolic ecstasies of classical tragedy, just as a labourer roughly clad and with muddy feet tramping through a wood is as good a sight as an elegant in a drawing-room.

Edward Storer. BR. Jan., 1914, pp. 73–74

It is easy to see what a future Synge might have enjoyed had he lived to extend to other aspects of our national life the methods he employed to such perfections. The material of legend revivified in the theatre after the manner of *Deirdre* might have given us a more varied dramatic literature than we possess. The absence of any followers of Yeats in his treatment of legendary lore, and the prestige of Synge, suggest that the latter could have led the way to the dramatisation of the Heroic cycles which he desired. As it is, his prestige has tended to effect quite contrary results. It was not his isolated essay in heroic drama that influenced his contemporaries, but his so-called "realistic" folk-plays. The ceaseless flow of peasant comedy and melodrama, in which the National Theatre has been almost submerged, is the penalty exacted by the success of Synge. But the query suggests itself: was Synge really a writer of realistic peasant plays? Is not the influence in question attributable to a misunderstanding of his work? Nobody has asserted that *Deirdre* belonged to that category. In fact regret has been expressed that Synge should, at the end, have forsaken his early manner. But, at bottom, *Deirdre of the Sorrows* and *The Playboy of the Western World* have more points of resemblance than of dissimilarity, so far as their peasant or legendary character is concerned. Reference has already been made to Synge's habit of treating realistically subjects which his compatriots invariably approach from a different angle, the conflict of imagination and reality, for example, in *The Well of the Saints,* and in *The Playboy of the Western World* itself. The naturalness and actuality of the setting in the latter case are particularly misleading, but reflection would seem to confirm the belief that the adventures of Christy Mahon take place in the same world as did those of [Ibsen's] Peer Gynt. [1916]

Ernest Boyd. Ireland's Literary Renaissance
(New York, Barnes & Noble, 1968), pp. 332–33

Synge, then, as a tragedian, has only the philosophy of nature. His characters reflect nature even in their imaginative creativeness. They have no human detachment, and for lack of critical perspective are as cruelly crushed by nature's destructive forces as they are inspired by her creative. In *The Shadow of the Glen* he may hint at a metaphysical truth: "I'm thinking by the mercy of God it's few sees anything but them is blind for a space," but such philosophy is absolutely unsophisticated. It is the unconscious wisdom of the simple. These men in the West, blind or seeing, turn naturally from the desolate aspect of life to the bright country of their imagination, and, like Martin Doul, they often discover that the rapture of dreams is paid for by the disdain of a world that christens dreams deceptions. If, too, we wish to generalise, we might see in Martin Doul's defiance of the gift of sight something of the willing darkness of Ireland to the false light of much modern instruction. Nowhere has imagination, which concentrates on essences, preserved itself so inviolate against the assaults of knowledge, logic and opinion.

In *Riders to the Sea,* perhaps the most relentlessly melancholy and yet the least tragic of his plays, destiny is neither a deity nor the flaws in human character, but simple natural forces, and what drama exists in it is that of undisputing weakness, whose only heroism is to hold out despairingly against the challenge of the elements, and to accept defeat when it comes. Such a one-sided conflict is pitiful beyond words, but humanity is too dwarfed a participater in the contest, the ideal is too slenderly opposed to the natural for tragedy of a high significance.

Nor did Synge, as others, seek to suggest through tragedy any final reconciliation between man's aspirations and a callous universe. But while his plays deal with humble persons and what might seem trivial situations, their characterisation is so real and their language so intense as to universalise what are petty, personal, and often absurdly pretentious claims and conceits, and to reveal to us even behind apparent farce what a profound drama may exist in the life of tramps and tinkers, if they are dowered with imagination.

Hugh I'A. Fausset. *Fortnightly*. Feb., 1924, pp. 268–69

I think I know of people who could create plays penetrated with an inner harmony. The artificiality in such plays is not discernible—it is replaced by art. I consider the comedy of J. M. Synge, the Irishman, entitled *The Playboy of the Western World,* to be such a play. In it the comical side passes quite naturally into the terrible, while the terrible becomes comical just as easily. J. M. Synge, like a truly wise artist, does not inject his own point of view; he just exhibits the people: they are half gods and half beasts, and are possessed of the childish desire to find a "hero" among themselves. (This is, to my mind, an absurd desire, for every one of us is a hero, if he happens to remember all the victories and defeats he has met with in the struggle for life.)

The characters of Synge act in exactly the same way as people usually act and as we shall probably all act for a long time to come; they create heroes in order to ridicule them afterwards. In Synge's play I feel a subtle irony on the cult of the hero. That irony is not very remote from sadness over the stupidity of mankind, but there is in it, I repeat, nothing artificial; it is merely a pure and lawful irony of facts.

Maxim Gorki. *EngR*. April, 1924, p. 495

[Synge's] theory of what was serious drama had in it the narrowness of protest. It was a theory that prevented him from looking as comprehensively at life as one so gifted might have done. It made him overvalue the high-coloured gewgaws both of life and language. Yet, fortunately, that other article in his creed which held him fast to the profound and common interests of life saved him from becoming such a *fantaisiste* as his bent towards the imaginative would have urged him: he might have become a Lord Dunsany. His conversion to nationalism taught him the value of collaboration; also by giving him a *patria* it gave him material on which the profound depths of emotion natively in him could work. Whatever is of value in his writings arises from the genuine affection he bestowed upon the land and the people he had made his own. That emotion would have functioned more purely as an element in his creative processes were it not that certain inherited prejudices as well as an inherent lack of spiritual delicacy held him back from reading as deeply in life as he might have done. Greatly moved on one occasion, he achieved the shedding of these prejudices, and wrote his masterpiece: *Riders to the Sea*. It is the unique example where an Ascendancy writer entered with any effective intimacy into the life of the Catholic Gaelic people. [1931]

Daniel Corkery. *Synge and Anglo-Irish Literature*
(New York, Russell & Russell, 1965), p. 109

The exotic appeal of Synge's work can scarcely be exaggerated; and it is another aspect of his romantic and lyrical character. I think there can be no doubt that Synge himself experienced the language and life he found in the Aran Islands as something rare and strange, beautiful because it was unsophisticated, remote, elemental. It awoke the artist in him, as Paris had not been able to do, because he was a romantic. And in this Synge is the pure artist, without any admixture of the political intentions that have always to be reckoned with in Yeats and other adherents of the Celtic renaissance. Yeats it was who sent Synge out to the West, helping a genius to find his line, but also making a démarche in the political cause of Irish nationalism. It is clear that Synge was independent of causes; an unpolitical artist, whatever use others made of his work once it was done. His pleasure in observing his primitives and in savouring their musical and picturesque language was from any point of view but the artistic irresponsible and non-committal.

The storm about *The Playboy of the Western World* arose because there were many Irishmen who could not emulate such detachment.

As far as the Anglo-Saxons are concerned, I think Max Beerbohm came nearest to the truth when he stressed the exotic as the source of our greatest pleasure in Synge. It is, however, a judgement that has been obscured by more frequent tributes to his pure dramatic genius. No one would deny his natural sense of drama and theatre, his powers in comedy and tragedy. If he were without them his more personal charms would be thin and vapid perhaps. But he did not possess those powers in an astonishing degree, and they alone certainly do not make the Synge to whom we are endeared. They are the excellent soil above which the rare bloom raises its head. Synge's greatest distinction, the thing that gives our acquaintance with him its particular flavour, is his wonderful language, which pleases us not as a heightened form of the language we ourselves use, but as a picturesque deviation from it. Two things support each other; the setting of Irish character, atmosphere and speech is itself exotically attractive, and it is made more so, pointedly so, by Synge's exquisite and subtle handling of the imaginative peasant language he discovered in the West.

Ronald Peacock. *The Poet in the Theatre*
(New York, Harcourt, Brace, 1946), pp. 110–11

A few remarks are necessary . . . to clarify Synge's attitude towards society and the Hero [in *The Playboy of the Western World*]. The charm with which he invests the people of Mayo, and the fact that he is constantly critical of Christy, are enough to dissociate Synge from the currently fashionable school of "alienationists"—he is not defending the frail artistic sensibility from the onslaughts of a morality that stunts the artist's growth. The Hero and society are incompatible in the sense that they pursue different objectives, but the relation between them must be understood as one of reciprocal benefit no less than of antogonism. Christy develops into a Hero only when the superior instinct of society approves what he had done in ignorance and bewilderment, and the Mayoites, on the other hand, move from a primitive state of consciousness to a sense of civilization and its values through their contact with him. The West is a lonesome place, Synge tells us early in the play, but Christy has made his choice: "If it's a poor thing to be lonesome, it's worse, maybe, go mixing with the fools of earth." What he has to do, Christy must do alone. Synge, then, is alive both to the possibilities of the Shawns and the Michael Jameses, and to the worth of the Christies, and his sympathy is patently divided between those two extremes. His pity, however, Synge reserves for Pegeen, who—to paraphrase Eliot—has been visited by the vision of greatness for a few days and will for ever after be a haunted woman. The tragic implications of *The Playboy of the Western World* are that the type represented by Pegeen—those who can perceive greatness but cannot rise to it, who are weighed down by the "society" within them—can neither live in the lonesome West playing out their days, nor be happy in the little world of daily preoccupations. The Christies are somehow taken care of, and so are the Shawns; it is the Pegeens who suffer most from the radical incompatibility of Hero and society.

Norman Podhoretz. *Essays in Criticism.* July, 1953, pp. 343–44

Synge is the only great poetic dramatist of the [Irish dramatic] movement; the only one, that is, for whom poetry and drama were inseparable, in whose work dramatic intensity invariably finds poetic expression and the poetic mood its only full expression in dramatic form. All the other playwrights of the movement seem, in the last analysis, to have been either dramatists in whom the instinct for dramatic expression sometimes brought with it the poetry of diction, imagery or cadence, or poets who turned for a time to the dramatic form, returning, sooner or later, again to other forms. But it is hard to imagine this separation in Synge: poetic and dramatic expression in him are one and simultaneous, as they appear to have been with Shakespeare and with Webster, in whom the presence of a high degree of one mood meant the presence of a high degree of the other, whether the form were prose or verse, the matter comedy or tragedy.

Yet there is a paradox in Synge's genius, a dualism of a different and a rarer kind. For while he is essentially a dramatic poet, one of the roots of his poetry is mysticism, such as he recognized in the mountain and seafaring Irish peasants living far enough out of reach of civilization to respond to and reflect the nature about them. And mystical experience, particularly the extreme form of nature-mysticism that we find in Synge, is in itself as nearly as possible incompatible with dramatic expression. Yet the presence of nature is as strongly felt in the plays as in *The Aran Islands* and *In Wicklow and West Kerry* and it is not there as a digression, irrelevant or undramatic. Nature is a protagonist in *In the Shadow of the Glen* and *Riders to the Sea,* so filling the minds of the characters as to shape their actions, moods and fates; it is the ever-present setting, genially familiar, of *The Well of the Saints* and *The Tinker's Wedding*; it remains as a continual and surprising source of imagery and incidental reference throughout *The Playboy of the Western World* and becomes again a poetic protagonist in *Deirdre of the Sorrows.* When Synge began to draw his material from the Aran Islands he had found, by one of those accidents of fortune which sometimes save genius from extinction, the people who alone could stimulate his imagination and offer him something on which this strange combination of dramatist and nature-mystic could work. They were the human theme which drama must have and yet they were in part at least nature itself.

Una Ellis-Fermor. *The Irish Dramatic Movement,* 2nd ed.
(London, Methuen, 1954), pp. 163–64

It is worth noting how closely bound into one main theme are the three elements of tension between dream and actuality, interaction between Man and the natural world, and awareness of mutability. All the sympathetic figures in Synge's plays are driven by an impossible dream; each, with a single-minded, intense, almost child-like longing to become "a wonder" is continually reaching out for a finer and fuller life. Imagination is creative in each of them, and it gives them a vision of some good beyond the poverty or drabness or terror which surround them; towards that vision, that dream, they strive. Yet they are nearly always frustrated. Only in *The Playboy of the Western World* does the power of the imagination make dream and actuality one, and accordingly this play is the richest and most joyous that Synge wrote. *The Tinker's Wedding* too is largely happy, because Sarah's dream is of something worse than her normal life and she gets rid of it in the end and returns thankfully to her proper station. But in *In the Shadow of the Glen,* although it is clearly implied that Nora's choice was the right one, it is not asserted that she and the Tramp attain what they seek, and in the other plays and in the prose works and the poetry the dream is invariably overcome by actuality. Hence the tragic undertones, the sombreness and the awareness of mutability pervading Synge's work.

The reason for the defeat of dream and spirit by the inhumanity of the universe and time is that all Synge's figures are very closely linked to the world around them. There is little that is ideal or transcendent in their dreams, they have no religious vision of a new Jerusalem nor any political vision of an earthly Utopia; they are truly children of Nature and the love and happiness and beauty of which they dream is in terms of this world, and particularly of the natural world, here and now; their paradise is the continuation in unchanging fullness of joys they have experienced partially and momentarily in this life. But Nature is not God; she may lead to God and she is a source of loveliness and solace for human beings but she is also harsh and ugly, and Synge's figures in staking all on her are bound to lose in the end.

Alan Price. Synge and the Anglo-Irish Drama
(London, Methuen, 1961), pp. 216–17

Synge had no pretensions as a philosopher. He was a humorous pessimist. His plots seem slight—a pair of tinkers who try to get married, and fail; an old woman who loses her sons at sea; a peasant's wife who runs off with a tramp; two old people who are cured of blindness, and dislike it; a lad who claims to have killed his father, and finds he has not; an elderly king who sees his betrothed elope with a youth, and brings them both to their deaths. Even Synge's characters, though vividly alive, do not leave the stage to inhabit our imaginations as eternal types, like Antigone, Hamlet, Falstaff, or Rebecca West. They simply possess vitality, and are true to their own selves; as their author was to his. Perhaps Synge's greatest achievements were that he found a new corner of the world to write of; took the trouble to know thoroughly what he wrote of; and worded his writing in a style both new and bewitching. Indeed I do not know any dramatist whose success depends quite so pre-eminently on the magic of his style. It is fifty years since I first heard the language of Synge in a paper read by a master to a literary society at school. It was instant intoxication. And from that day to this, its enchantment has never failed or staled.

Synge may be narrow; he may be minor. But there are certain minor writers—such as Sappho, or Beddoes—who remain, none the less, unique. There are certain combinations of qualities to be found in them alone. If you miss such writers, you will go to your grave having missed something, a certain kind of savour, that you will find nowhere else. So it is a pity to go through life without ever tasting Synge, who so admirably deserved his name—that name which the melodious voice of an ancestor had won, according to the story, from Henry Tudor four centuries before.

F. L. Lucas. *The Drama of Chekhov, Synge, Yeats, and Pirandello* (London, Cassell, 1963), pp. 236–37

Synge's vision, a view of the world presented with consistency in *The Aran Islands* and in the plays, was one which makes his work particularly congenial to the modern reader. He insisted upon a realistic assessment of man's life and the struggle which he felt it to be in the face of an alien universe and a vigorously beautiful but nonetheless indifferent nature. As Synge saw it, man's difficulties in such a universe were multiplied by his insistent attempt to impose his own rigid codes of behavior upon the world. This judgment is the source of the unique fusion in Synge's plays of the primitive world, the world of nature, and a social commentary that drama has ordinarily relegated to an urban, mechanized world. The primitive and the natural provide a meaningful structure for understanding the intensely basic nature of the conflicts and the lies which man has imposed upon himself.

Synge's attempt to revitalize the language of drama, to find a living idiom which could become a part of the dramatic experience, prefigured an unending concern of modern poetic dramatists. Although the solution he reached—a dramatic approximation of the vitality of peasant speech—is not realistically available to dramatists in all cultures, Synge demonstrated what can be done when the language once again is set into operation as a total part of the dramatic whole. The use of rhetoric in *The Playboy of the Western World* as a part of the whole statement of the play provides an example of the part language can play in fully realized drama.

Donna Gerstenberger. *John Millington Synge* (New York, Twayne, 1964), p. 136

John Millington Synge, poet and playwright, the youngest son of a conventional, middle-class Protestant family living in the Dublin suburbs, a rationalist, anticlerical descendant of Anglican bishops, was a writer who gave up Paris for the hills of Wicklow and the bogs of Mayo, preferring the conversation and friendship of tramps and tinkers to the company on the Left Bank.

Although Yeats and Lady Gregory are rightly regarded as the centerpieces of the Irish theatrical renaissance, it was Synge far more than either of these who gave the movement its national quality, and left to the world the type of play that has since become the prototype of Irish folk drama. Yet he managed to get the entire Abbey Theatre Company arrested in Philadelphia, and is still viciously denounced as anti-Irish by most of the grimmer Gaelic enthusiasts.

There are other paradoxical aspects to this strange, sociable hermit—this glum-faced humorist—the associate of a generation of intellectuals, who nevertheless was neither an intellectual nor a nationalist himself. He was a storm-tossed genius, but not a frustrated one. Whether he realized the extent of the international fame that was to be his is something that it is impossible to say: but he certainly gave no signs of caring about it. He was a writer of love passages of enormous lyrical beauty who was never much of a hit with the women he wanted to marry. He was a celebrity about whom the general public, until recently, knew very little—thanks to the disapproving attitude of his family toward its principal claim to distinction.

> Denis Johnston. *John Millington Synge* (New York,
> Columbia University Press, 1966), p. 3

When we turn from the quarrels they have evoked to [Synge's] works themselves, we find that they are essentially personal rather than social. Synge's plays are, in fact, more expressive than has been generally supposed of certain questions concerning the nature and function of art prevalent both in Synge's day and in ours. Yeats told Synge to go to Aran to "express a life that has never found expression," but in reality Synge expressed not so much the life of the Irish peasant as his own feelings about the relationship of art to existence and of the artist to the society around him. . . .

The ending of his preface to *The Playboy of the Western World* suggests Synge's attitude towards his material. . . . Synge has here let slip the truth, that Irish life is material for "those of us who wish to write." That wish is Synge's central impulse. More than anything else, he desired to create an image of beauty that would stand against the sense of the absoluteness of death that rarely seems to have been far from his mind. Just as the "springtime of local life" is threatened by the encroachments of a vulgar urban civilization, so in Synge's plays, the beauty that he longs for is subject to destruction by the forces of life and time unless it is metamorphosed into the eternal beauty of art. It is one of the minor ironies of literary history that despite Yeats' injunction to Synge to express the life of Aran, Synge in actuality expressed through his concern for art as a response to the pain and transience of life something much closer than perhaps either of them consciously realized to the central concerns of Yeats himself.

Arthur Ganz. *MD*. May, 1967, pp. 57–58

Freed of the Yeatsian vision, let us look at reality through Synge's eyes. It must be sought in a "comprehensive and natural form," he tells us in his preface to *The Playboy of the Western World*. In Ireland there are still places where this reality is superb and wild, and therefore joyous—even to the point of the Rabelaisian. But always, for it to remain valid, this joy must be rooted in its natural form, must, in fact, flow from the imagination of the people. When one is true to the folk imagination, it follows that one will be true to their mode of expression. The richer the imagination, the richer and more copious the language. And always, for the artist to remain true to his subject, the delicate balance must be perceived and tested, the tension between form and spirit preserved. The artist must never become so carried away with a wild joyousness that he loses sight of the form which contains it. "The strong things of life are needed in poetry also," he warns us, "to show that what is exalted or tender is not made by feeble blood." The Rabelaisian may even incorporate the brutal. Nor can there be true affirmation without testing all verities. In wit, as Oscar Wilde has taught us, forcing the verities to walk a tightrope leads to paradox. In drama, Synge shows us it leads to irony, both in choice of subject and technique.

For art which has its roots in "the clay and worms," yet seeks after what is "superb and wild in reality," implies the very conflict that provokes the ironical vision. This conflict between the ordinary and the ideal, the bitter and the sweet, reason and the imagination, reality and fantasy, Synge saw as basic both to life and to nature. The conflict takes two forms in his plays—externally in nature, and internally in the heart and mind of man. In external nature there is the continual struggle between the beauty and joy of life and youth and the ugliness and sorrow of old age and death. In the soul of man this struggle is reflected in his eternal conflict between the illusion and the reality, and his constant efforts to reconcile the two. Nature to man symbolizes power, wildness, and a dreadful joy; the "common, week-day kind of" life man has built around him symbolizes ugliness, boredom, decay, and eventually an unhappy death. By choosing to dramatize the life of the Aran Islanders, the vagrants of Wicklow, the countryfolk of Mayo and Kerry, Synge was tearing away the veils of sophistication one finds in town life, and dealing with reality in its more elemental form. Humanity, art and nature are inextricably bound in the conflict between the real and the ideal. We can examine this basic conflict first as Synge represents it in the power of external nature, second in the lives and emotions of his characters, third in the most elaborate effect this conflict had on his people—the creation of the myth.

Ann Saddlemyer. *J. M. Synge and Modern Comedy*
(Dublin, Dolmen, 1968), pp. 12–14

An innovator in the theatre, [Synge] based his innovations upon a strong belief in the significance of traditional elements in Irish culture, and upon his observation of the richness that came into being when old and new ways of life existed alongside each other. He was a highly conscious and deliberate writer, who took everything he wrote through numerous drafts, paying attention to every smallest detail. He was thrifty in that he threw very little away that might conceivably serve for future use; notes made in his twenties were pressed into service for works written in his middle thirties. Though he developed considerably over the years, the obsessions of his youth still operated during his maturity, and his earliest and latest writings have much in common; his vision is a unity from first to last. His influence upon later Irish and other writers has been immeasurable. The work of Sean O'Casey, George Fitzmaurice, Jack Yeats, Samuel Beckett and a host of lesser writers owes an inestimable debt to Synge's discoveries. Perhaps one of his greatest debtors, however, was W. B. Yeats, to whom he himself owed so much, for it was Synge's poetry that taught Yeats to move ahead to his greatest work as a lyric poet, and was directly responsible for the shift in Yeats' style that occurred in the years 1908–10.

Synge does not fit easily into any of the pigeon-holes allotted him by his critics. Long regarded with Lady Gregory as the originator of a school of naturalistic peasant drama, he was, in fact, less concerned with naturalism than almost all his followers. Believed to be a simple, though eloquent, recorder of peasant life, he was, in truth, intent upon the creation of universal myth from particular experience. Dismissed for years as a poet of no importance, he wrote poems of an originality and strength far greater than those of many more lauded writers. His true qualities have been obscured from us by many accidents of history. Too many critics have, like Daniel Corkery, viewed his work only in relation to the nationalist movement of his time and to the theatrical revival of the Irish Renaissance. When these limitations upon one's vision are removed, it becomes clear that, while J. M. Synge was indeed passionately concerned with what was essentially Irish, and emotionally involved in working for the cultural renaissance of his country, his work is, in any serious sense of the word, international, for he tackled fundamental crises of the human spirit, and, in his shanachie plays especially, did not limit but extended the territory of twentieth-century drama.

Robin Skelton. *The Writings of J. M. Synge*
(Indianapolis, Bobbs-Merrill, 1971), pp. 172–73

The position of Synge . . . within the Irish Tradition is a special one; he cannot be simply accommodated within the early Abbey Theatre and left there. From one point of view he accepted the idea of the early movement and exhausted its possibilities. From another point of view be brought to that ideal a complex sensibility which modified radically the implied romanticism of a drama "of the noble and the beggarman." And I believe this sensibility can be understood by way of reference to that first rejected play, which Synge, incidentally, continued to nurse with a personal attachment even after its rejection. He exhausts the early ideal in several ways. Firstly, his plays unite, often within the one theatrical image, the aristocratic and the humble, imposing an heroic mould on common life, as in *Riders to the Sea*, and a peasant mould on heroic myth, as in *Deirdre of the Sorrows*. Above all, perhaps, he solved more successfully than anyone else in the early days the stated ambition to revive poetry in the theatre. His theatrical language is a highly stylised, artificial medium, combining the poetic and demotic, some of the properties of formal poetry with a particular kind of relationship to a rooted, vernacular, spoken speech. And lastly, the truth of Synge's dramatic action, the truth of his dramatic language is a poetic truth, not a social truth as in Ibsen or Shaw. The important thing, which his critics at all times have failed to appreciate, is not the way in which his plays imitate life in the West of Ireland as he observed it. The important thing is the way in which the plays conform to a shaping imagination, the way in which they serve a personal, poetic idea of what a work of art should be.

But a great deal of energy has already been expended down the years analysing the way in which Synge the playwright was conditioned by his part in the Irish Dramatic Movement and by his immersion in the rich folk culture of Ireland. It is time that we began to assess what Synge himself brought to the drama from outside. I have already tried to suggest the source of Synge's radical, subversive spirit and its kinship to the modernist drama outside Ireland. . . .

Where . . . does Synge get his models in stage-craft? Not, I believe, from Lady Gregory or Yeats, whose dramatic skills at this point are rudimentary. Nor indeed from contemporary European models, although I think the influence of modernist drama on Synge, while oblique, is important. Synge looks back into the past for his models, to sixteenth- and seventeenth-century drama. As an artist he is technically conservative while one of the very distinctions of modernism in the theatre has been its progressive search for new forms to match the radical social programme of the dramatists themselves. This, it seems to me, is the important distinction between Synge and his contemporaries of equal stature in the theatre outside Ireland.

Thomas Kilroy. Mosaic. 5, 1, 1971, pp. 14–15

The usual theory among historians of the Irish dramatic movement is that Synge was viewed by his contemporaries as a realist and that his influence impelled the dramatic movement away from the direction Yeats had charted for it towards realism. Thus it was Synge and not Yeats who was responsible for Lennox Robinson, Brinsley MacNamara, Sean O'Casey, Paul Vincent Carroll and Brendan Behan. Yeats and Lady Gregory talked about the folk, and yet the Abbey Theatre produced only one folk dramatist—George Fitzmaurice—whom it then proceeded to ignore. Earlier critics claimed that Fitzmaurice was a disciple of Synge, but it would have been more accurate to have described him as a casualty of Synge's influence. After Synge, it seemed, realism counted.

Synge, of course, wrote one play—*In the Shadow of the Glen*—which romanticized an authentic folktale. But the audience were unable to recognise the fact that the play *was* based on a folktale and insisted upon seeing it as a realistic treatment of loveless marriage among the country people. No wonder Synge was puzzled by the violent reaction his work received. His unfortunate statement in the preface to *The Playboy of the Western World* about lying with his ear to a crack in the floor listening to the servant girls talking in the kitchen of a County Wicklow house and his defense of the authenticity of the language of that play not only made things worse but diverted attention from his real purpose.

Synge, as we know now, was not a realist. His vision was unique, personal, poetic, romantic. His view of Irish rural life was, in its own way, just as romantic as Yeats's. Yeats wrote nonsense about the peasant being the key to the collective unconscious of the race. Synge indulged in no such fantasies, but he nevertheless tended to idealize Irish rural life. He could, for example, convince himself that tramps were all artists or that when he listened to Pat Dirane reciting an ancient Gaelic poem he could hear the intonation of the original voice of the ancient poet. These are of course more acceptable myths, but myths nevertheless.

David H. Greene. In Maurice Harmon, ed.,
J. M. Synge: Centenary Papers 1971
(Dublin, Dolmen, 1972), pp. 194–95

What is this reality which is the root of all poetry, and which we must have in the theatre? For Synge, apparently, the life of human passion, of the senses and of the earth. In his own poetry, as in his plays, the natural world is present to the senses or the imagination at every moment. It is the wildness, not the beauty, of nature he admires, and if nature is related to man it is by the needs of living. The modern literature of towns, he reminds us, has moved away from the profound and common interests of life. It is part of our debt to Synge that he brings us back these interests, not least that he brings us back to the reality of the body. Physical action in his plays is energetic, and this delight in the body is strengthened at every moment by the sensuous pressure of the dialogue.

This has important consequences. For while it is an axiom of naturalistic (representational) drama that characters are to be taken as real, the dramatist's conviction of their reality rarely includes more than the mind. Hence character is commonly defined by intelligence, profession, habits, interests, tastes; more crudely, as in O'Casey, by tricks of speech. In Synge there is almost nothing of this. Since his concern is the whole person (including the body) his conception of character is dynamic. Like every dramatist, he gives his characters strength by opposing one to another, but the opposition, as in Pegeen's quarrel with the Widow Quin, is of energies rather than traits of personality. Synge is interested in Pegeen as a woman, not just in what makes her different from other women, because he is interested in the total reality of his characters.

This reality is defined by a vivid awareness through their senses of the world about them. It is defined also by their awareness of each other: for speech of such vitality, in its freedom from self-regard, implies appreciation of the reality of others. Where a firmer outline is required, Synge works for it not by providing his character with a profession to be exploited in clichés or allusions, but by a genuine objectivity.

> Ronald Gaskell. *Drama and Reality: The European Theatre since Ibsen* (London, Routledge & Kegan Paul, 1972), pp. 99–100

John Millington Synge's own personal drama—the drama of his career and death—is, for many, the creation of W. B. Yeats. Yeats witnessed, shared in, and half believed he had half created this drama. With his genius for seeing polarities, Yeats shaped in his mind's eye the portrait of a quiet, unassuming, enigmatic and lonely artist, much like his fisherman, whose journey to the rocky heart of his inspiration took him where no vulgar crowd would have the hardiness to follow, to the well springs of the Greek dramatic vision. His senses of Synge's story, as expressed in his poetry, has tended to obliterate the truth which it so genuinely resembles. Yeats, with great analytical acumen, as well as with imaginative sympathy, saw in Synge a type of the heroic self-creator, a romantic ideal affirmed at least as early in the romantic movement as Keats's speculative thought about the relationship between the making of poems and the making of souls. What Yeats made of Synge's story was certainly largely determined by the romantic heritage he brought to it.

But Yeats was also thoroughly aware—he could hardly help being—of Synge's independence. Unfortunately, most of Synge's critics have simply accepted the Romantic Synge acclaimed by Yeats, and have ignored Yeats's perception of Synge's central place in the shift of romantic strategy that produced a very modern kind of art. To Yeats and to James Joyce, Synge's work was a major clue to a new kind of art and thus to a new kind of moral vision.

What was most exciting in Synge's career was his success in recovering the dynamics of a genuinely dramatic art, resonant rather than imitative, and authentic without being neurotic. Yeats locates its central thrust when he speaks of the relationship between its hard and virile bitterness and its healthy, self-transcendent joy. Synge's sensibility was a richly cultivated one, and he could draw on the art of the past—Greek drama, Irish saga, Irish folklore, Shakespearian drama—with a complexity of intelligence that baffles. Mythic, parodic, romantic—no single perspective dominates. Synge's is the sort of drama which Francis Fergusson, in discussing the Elizabethan dramatic image, characterized as many-faceted. Synge's gift is catalytic rather than static, and his dramatic image, like Shakespeare's, is frequently mock-ritualistic, sometimes in so serious a way that irony disappears momentarily into ritual again. The action of his drama sets a variety of perspectives into play and absorbs them into the dramatic image.

C. S. Faulk. *SHR*. Summer, 1974, pp. 431–32

When it comes to assessing the stature of Synge, the importance of the Irish background has tended to narrow down the dimensions of his work. The six plays do not bulk very large, and the overall impression is of a strictly limited and consistent body which can be conveniently labelled Irish peasant drama. We should no longer have to fight the old fight over whether Synge's main purpose was the realistic representation of peasant life. But his methods and techniques are similar throughout the six plays, and, as we have seen, he is weakest in those areas where he is not directly concerned with the realities of rural Ireland. Synge's critics were right—he was uninventive, although their charges of plagiarism were without foundation. His imagination worked always from what he knew, and any form of life in his plays which was invented rather than observed looks insubstantial or unconvincing.

For many readers all this adds up to a writer of limited significance, the interpreter of one specific place and time. By his setting and style he is removed from the main tradition of English literature; within his special field, it may be allowed that he is accomplished, but an artist who cannot transcend the circumstances of his art is not of major importance. These are difficult arguments to counter. It has been the object of this book to try to show that within the very definite limits of his work, it was yet possible for Synge to achieve plays of outstanding merit which can bear comparison with the best the twentieth century has to offer. The narrow dimensions of Synge's world did not preclude complexity; the foundations in a circumscribed reality which he required did not make imaginative profundity impossible. If he stands as an "original," an awkward figure to fit into any hierarchy or chart of greatness, his anomalous position should not lead us to place him lower than he deserves.

Nicholas Grene. *Synge: A Critical Study of the Plays* (Totowa, N.J., Rowman and Littlefield, 1975), pp. 185–86

In the Shadow of the Glen and *Riders to the Sea* made it clear that in Synge Irish drama had found a new master; *The Well of the Saints,* his first three-act play to be produced at the Abbey, solidified his reputation. Again there were complaints from the nationalists who claimed, rightly, that the action of the play was based on a foreign source and that, therefore, the play could not possibly be Irish. But its characters and its setting are thoroughly Irish, as is its theme, that illusion is often more satisfactory than reality. That theme, one which runs through all his later plays, finds its great expression, though, in *The Playboy of the Western World,* a play which would be a comedy if it were not so close to tragedy, a tragedy if it were not a comedy.

It was his masterpiece, but it was simply too much for most of his audience. Irish nationalists were infuriated by the portrayal of brutal peasants who condoned violence and murder and were vulgar, crude, and small-minded. In three acts of realistic fantasy, Synge more or less destroyed a century of myth about the peasantry of the west of Ireland, myth which had held that their sufferings had made them into quintessential Irishmen, a "saving remnant" which had to be honored for its patience, fortitude, and piety. The myth was based on the modern urban belief that country people who live close to the natural world are somehow made holy by it; in Ireland, the myth had been encouraged by Catholic piety and the nationalist theory of the innate superiority of spiritual Ireland to materialistic England. In fact, centuries of ignorance and oppression had left much of the Irish peasantry degraded, superstitious, and violent. Synge himself also idealized peasant Ireland, but the peasants he loved were the traditionally oppressed: tinkers, tramps, and the poor. In these real people, rather than the imaginary mystics of the Celtic twilight or the plaster saints of Irish nationalism, he found his myth of the Irish soul—passionate, hard, unforgiving, and wild. . . .

For all the glory of its language, *The Playboy* is a strange play. In one sense, it is a Dionysiac comedy in which anything goes, a fulfillment of Synge's desire to create what is "superb and wild" in reality. In another, it is a satire on the traditional lawlessness of Ireland and a satire, too, on its patterns of courtship and marriage. It is more than a little a tragedy in which the hero, Christy, discovers his identity and his "fate," but only by leaving Pegeen, the archetype of the strong woman of so much Irish drama, bereft of all comfort.

Richard Fallis. *The Irish Renaissance* (Syracuse, N.Y., Syracuse University Press, 1977), pp. 105–6, 108

[Synge] imagined a future when some young man would appear and "teach Ireland again that she is part of Europe." He would sweep away what was narrow and parochial in the "credo of mouthing gibberish," but with "the pity that is due to the poor stammerers who mean so well though they are stripping the nakedness of Ireland in the face of her own sons." It is tempting to fill in the features of this young man who was to teach Ireland that she was part of Europe; for in the world of art two indeed have appeared who might be thought of as fulfilling Synge's prophecy: both certainly have affinities with him as a playwright. Joyce was the first: he carried the torch for Ibsen at a time when it seemed that Ireland might be in danger of missing that great European experience and his one play, *Exiles,* was a delicately Irish flavoured exploration in modes derived from Ibsen and Chekhov. Synge's early unproduced play, *When the Moon Has Set,* most unusually for him, also looks towards Ibsen in many ways; in its contemporary middle-class setting, the strand of plain contemporary usage in its language, its cosmopolitan, intellectually torn hero, restlessly returned from Paris, like Richard Rowan [in *Exiles*] and Ibsen's Oswald [in *Ghosts*], to a narrow provincial society which he has to come to terms with. It becomes very Ibsenite in its combative ending, with Eileen stripping off her nun's habit and asserting her right to the "joy of life" with Colum; perhaps, as some have thought, Ibsen was in Synge's mind when he wondered whether the play might not have some stage success "with a certain kind of very modern audience."

Beyond Joyce, however, steps Beckett, and it is to that further off figure that Synge especially reaches out. Synge's career remarkably anticipates Beckett's: he moved from Ireland to Paris, studied French, used French methods on Irish material, almost became a Frenchman, so his mother said when his hair was affected by his illness and he took to wearing a black wig and a soft hat in French style. Their drama is still closer: Beckett's masterful handling of loneliness is shadowed in Synge's theatre of bareness and austerity where, as Yeats pointed out, time runs slowly and there is little outer movement to distract attention from the powerful fantasies of the violently imaginative, comical, afflicted beings at the centre, who amuse and appal and impose on us with enormous élan and strength of personality their interior drama.

Synge picked up from the French, from the symbolists, from Maeterlinck, and then let his imagination loose on a rich Irish material which he made in the process European. His "Irish" method has inspired Yeats, O'Casey and now Beckett, through whom it has become familiar far beyond Europe. . . . Despite all that is of the nineteenth century in his style and technique, Synge is in a way one of the most modern of the moderns. He claims that place by the use he makes of his sardonic humour and by his subtle handling of the self-conscious theatricality that seems so natural to his characters, but in the end persuades us it represents a mysterious, universal process of the human mind, the endless self-creation of "men who are dark a long while and thinking over queer thoughts in their heads."

Katharine Worth. *The Irish Drama of Europe from Yeats to Beckett* (Atlantic Highlands, N.J., Humanities Press, 1978), pp. 138–39

The use of a famous legend as the basis for a modern play is fraught with dangers and constrictions. The plot will be so well known as to deny all possibilities of excitement or surprise. This problem is particularly acute when the play deals with a prophecy of ultimate tragedy. . . . When a famous legend [of Deirdre], which ends in a predicted massacre, has already been dramatised by two eminent writers [George Russell and W. B. Yeats], there must surely be little scope for invention or experiment. When the sense of foreknowledge is pervasive in the plot, there can be little room for resistance against fate. Insofar as there are artistic possibilities with such a plot, they will be lyrical rather than dramatic. In the work [*Deirdre of the Sorrows*] of a dramatic genius like Synge, however, this foreknowledge is turned into a virtue, since it encourages a critical attitude in the audience towards the production. The interest now lies not so much in what is done, as in how it is done—in the author's personal interpretation of the action. Here Synge's triumph is complete. Where other versions of the tale had emphasised the betrayal and death of the lovers as the final disaster, Synge, more subtly, locates the real tragedy in the death of their love. His play gains power from suspense rather than surprise. Since both audience and protagonists know the inevitable outcome, all interest centres on the brave attempts of the lovers to snatch some happiness despite the tragedy to come. In dramatising this clash between the free will of the lovers and the forces of necessity, Synge adds a new and exciting dimension to the legend. The tragedy of their foretold death at the end seems of minor importance in comparison with the disaster of their lost love. . . .

For the translators and versifiers of the nineteenth century, the Deirdre legend had been the occasion for Tennysonian pastiche. To Russell, the tale had presented itself as a mystic reverie and to Yeats as a symbolic problem. For Synge alone, it had all the dimensions of a distinctly human crisis. Where dramatists like Yeats and Russell had to rely on collated English versions of the legend, Synge drew his inspiration directly from a Gaelic source, *Oidhe Chloinne Uisnigh* [the fate of the children of Uisneach], and indirectly from his study of the evolution of the legend. This directness of approach is one reason why his play is more faithful to the legend itself and, finally, more exciting as drama.

Declan Kiberd. *Synge and the Irish Language* (Totowa, N.J., Rowman and Littlefield, 1979), pp. 193, 195

Each of Synge's first three plays involves some specific reflection of what he realized through his experiences on the [Aran] islands. In *In the Shadow of the Glen* Synge intentionally varies the plot of a story he heard on the islands, so as to draw his audience into a familiar stereotype. But having done this, he then shatters the stereotype and throws his audience into the confusion that results when our expectations, our perceptual sets, are frustrated. The result is to put his audience through a perceptual and intellectual shock analogous to what Synge himself had undergone upon reading Darwin or upon imbibing the milieu of the islands.

In *Riders to the Sea,* Synge tries to present as veridically as possible the quality of life he felt on the islands. His aim was to be faithful to the tone and mood, to the affective realities, of that world. But as the reaction to the play shows, most critics have been unable to respond to that world without attempting to pigeonhole the play in terms of genre or of world view. The result is a body of critical discussion largely irrelevant to the play, and another illustration of the authority of received categories of thought.

The Tinker's Wedding focuses directly upon "cultural relativism" by depicting a contrast between the world view of the tinkers and that of the priest. The theme we are tracing enters the play primarily in the invasion of young Mary Byrne's world by an abstraction from the other society; through Mary's superficial aspiration to marriage, Synge explores the folly and frustration of trying to fit one's experience into a social or intellectual frame unnatural to it. The marriage ritual is as procrustean to her experience as the marriage ring is to her finger.

In *The Well of the Saints* and *The Playboy of the Western World,* Synge moves into a new phase of his response to his experiences on the islands, one characterized by pursuing certain philosophical issues raised by these themes, especially the problem of the relationship between our ideas, or dreams, or hopes, and "reality."

Weldon Thornton. *J. M. Synge and the Western Mind* (New York, Barnes & Noble, 1979), p. 156

WESKER, ARNOLD (1932–   )

Arnold Wesker is one of the latest of these young playwrights [social realists] to arrive on the English stage. In June and July of this year his trilogy [*Chicken Soup with Barley, Roots,* and *I'm Talking about Jerusalem*] was performed at the Belgrade Theatre, Coventry, and, now, three months later these three plays are published in one volume. . . . Wesker is clearly drawing heavily in these plays on his personal life—Ronnie, for instance, carries to a large degree the unity of the plays as a character and as a chorus—but the point that Wesker wishes to emphasize at the outset is the intimacy of his involvement with the life and people who, as a dramatist, he is committed to exhibit. His attitude is not imposed upon the plays with distance and detachment but is allowed to evolve; to emerge gradually and painfully through the actual development of the play itself so that—in a sense—Wesker and his audience carry the burden of the dramatic experience together and find its coherence as an artistic statement simultaneously. The trilogy is an exploration in dramatic terms and through it, eventually and with great honesty, Wesker defines his attitude—however inconclusively—towards his background, himself and the society to which he belongs. He is an idealist whose passionate concern is to regenerate people and society and, perhaps, only those who want to change society care desperately enough for society—or they would never bother to try. Certainly, Ronnie, the idealist, moves through the trilogy from disillusionment to disillusionment but he emerges in the end, his ideals only slightly impaired, with a firmer grasp of life's exigencies and a more deliberate and purposeful sense of urgency. Perhaps, however, Wesker's chief virtues as a dramatist stem from two main sources; firstly, from the way in which his passionate concern for individuals transforms what otherwise might have been puppet figures into people of life and substance about whom we are too intensely concerned; and, secondly, from the severe and often terrifying honesty with which he pursues his theme, without compromise or favour, without permitting his ideals to subvert his material or his politics to tempt him to easy or clear-cut solutions. . . .

Wesker's plays are full of incident and dramatic interest, however domestic. His world is one of the family, an intimate group bound by affection and experience; moving through social changes and being changed by them. He is sometimes clumsy with inexperience, unable quite to handle the sheer wealth that his themes throw up; his characters are not altogether clearly conceived or fully projected and his dramatic situations are often over-contrived to the point where the theatrical machinery creaks. He has not yet learnt to handle direct conflict and his trilogy has a certain ingrown quality the potential of which is not entirely brought out in dramatic terms. But to say that he is promising would be insulting; the trilogy represents a real achievement. Wesker and his contemporaries have taken the initiative in drama, and the life of theatre might well compensate us for the death of, say, the novel as an art form.

A. R. Jones. *CQ*. Winter, 1960, pp. 367–70

Preposterously high and absurdly low assessments have been made of the three plays by Arnold Wesker somewhat grandiloquently labelled the "Wesker Trilogy"—*Chicken Soup with Barley, Roots,* and *I'm Talking about*

Jerusalem. . . . Exacerbated by the solemn hosannas of his more chuckle-headed fans (and also, no doubt, by his own earnest proclamations) Mr. Wesker's enemies dismiss him as a mere brand-name oversold by the theatrical Left. Why, they ask indignantly, should they pay homage to a writer who has not yet learned to construct a piece; who takes three acts to get to the point of a play, and three plays to tell a story; who fills the stage with boring, sordid, lower-class people talking continually about Socialism; who has a disgusting preoccupation with incontinence (in two of these plays Mr. Wesker presents semi-paralysed men unable to control their bowels)? On the other side, Mr. Wesker's idolaters seem to be mesmerized by the sheer arithmetic of his work, as if three plays must be better than one. With awe-struck reverence they point out that no one else *under thirty* has written a *trilogy,* an argument which only a sterile, youth-worshipping age like ours could be asked to take seriously as a sufficient reason for admiration. With no less irrelevance they invite us to kneel before the trilogy because it is a unique exposition of the political dilemmas of our time. . . .

On the credit side, first of all, Arnold Wesker has—at his best—a refreshingly accurate ear for what ordinary people say and how they say it. In the English theatrical context, moreover, their language is almost exotically unusual, for it is the idiom of Norfolk farm labourers (in *Roots*) and East End Jews (in the other two plays . . .). This freshness of language, rubbing the familiarity off everyday talk and feeling, helps the dramatist to camouflage the staleness of the fourth-wall naturalism within whose forms he works. Socially, his plays are important because they introduce members of the "working class"—and, in particular, the *rural* working class—as human beings with rights of their own on the stage, instead of as comic silhouettes and stereotypes. . . . *Roots* may be considered as a milestone in the modern English drama, on linguistic and sociological grounds alone. What is more important, however, is Wesker's attitude towards his characters: a burning moral concern, fuelled by compassion and forgiveness, blazing up in a flare of theatrical life force. This author labours to show the love between people, especially people in a family; to affirm their essential individual value, as members of mankind, and to remind the audience that they belong to it, too. As a dramatist, he has the courage of his inexperience. He is not afraid of looking sentimental in trying to illustrate kindness and generosity or of looking "pi" in his attempt to dramatize ideas, and at his best his characters project a stirring emotional power which helps to make good theatre *and* good life. He is a major dramatist in the making, with one play [*Roots*] of lasting value already to his credit.

Richard Findlater. *TC*. Sept., 1960, pp. 234, 236

It is safe to say that Mr. Wesker's plays are superior to anything by Mssrs. Auden, Spender, and Isherwood in that genre in the nineteen-thirties. And it would be difficult to point to much in the Fifties (with the single exception of Mr. John Whiting's plays) or in the preceding era of the verse-play (with the exception of [Eliot's] *Murder in the Cathedral*), that is conclusively better than *The Kitchen, Roots,* and *I'm Talking about Jerusalem.* Mr. Wesker's achievement is certainly relevant also to the assessment of Orwell's work. The objectivity with which Mr. Wesker is able to observe the English working class, and turn his observations into art, reveals Orwell's limitations the more clearly. But it is not only intelligent and honest observation that counts in documentary writing, as I have argued; it is also a question of commitment, of ideological orientation. And in this respect, Mr. Wesker's understanding both of the English working class and of Socialism must seem far more mature and more considered than Orwell's (there are no doubt biographical reasons for this: Mr. Wesker's starting position as the child of Jewish immigrants, born within a tradition of Socialist political activity and political thought, was perhaps more favourable than Orwell's as an Eton Colleger. Mr. Wesker had the advantage of being a partial outsider in class-divided English society.

Mr. Wesker's achievement has a bearing, too, on the question of the dichotomy of the "social" and the "psychological" we found in some of Mr. Angus Wilson's short stories, and in *Death of a Salesman.* Mr. Wesker was brought up, even more than Mr. Wilson and Mr. Arthur Miller, in the school of Marxism: but not in that of Freud. In this, he was surely very fortunate. Mr. Wesker's psychology is drawn directly from life: he does not look through the prism of an essentially unverifiable depth-analysis. Yet is Mr. Wesker's psychology so much less subtle than Mr. Wilson's or Mr. Arthur Miller's? Is it inadequate to explain the phenomena of everyday existence? Mr. Wesker is not, of course, primarily interested in man-as-an-individual in his plays; his subject is man-in-society. But the individual psychology he uses in his plays, is nevertheless, entirely adequate to his theme. One consequence of Mr. Wesker's achievement, then, may prove to be the disappearance of that dichotomy between Marxist and Freudian analysis that has bedevilled a great deal of Left-wing writing in the past three decades. And in this Mr. Wesker, and others of his generation, will be returning, I think, to the mainstream of tradition.

John Mander. *The Writer and Commitment*
(London, Secker & Warburg, 1961), pp. 209–10

"Then where do we look for our new vision?" The question is proposed . . . by Ronnie at the end of *I'm Talking about Jerusalem,* the last play in Arnold Wesker's trilogy. In *Chicken Soup with Barley, Roots,* and *Jerusalem* Wesker chronicles the struggles of the Kahn family to live the good Communist life. . . . What this trilogy says is not that Communism is false but that even the "truth" of Communism, if it were to obtain, would not automatically make a man free or whole. If visions don't work, the failure is a human failure, don't blame life: "Free agents, Sammy boy." This strikes me as an adult acknowledgment, and it largely accounts for the resonance of the trilogy which persists after one has forgotten Ronnie's remarks about the Labour Party and Sir Winston's Sunday paintings. The play is concerned with man's own resources when the dream and the ball are over. Ronnie is trying to write a socialist novel, but Wesker has written a sturdy trilogy which should ring bells for anyone, Harold Macmillan included. Even Tories try to build Jerusalem, some kind of Jerusalem. Wesker's trilogy is a humane imitation of an action; it has the same kind of force as that splendid moment in *The Entertainer* by John Osborne when Archie Rice, explaining his own failure, invokes the memory of a great negress, in a bar, standing up and singing and defining her entire being in the song. These are not cheery-beery affirmations, slogans painted on a humanist bandwagon; they are precise formulations, acts in a human scene.

Denis Donoghue. HudR. Spring, 1961, pp. 96–97

Together, Wesker's plays are a statement of the vitality of belief. To continue to care for ideals in the face of contradictions and betrayals assures one of life. His ardor and his certainty are something to be cherished in the contemporary theatre, if only to balance our too heavy diet of despair and doubt. But too much enthusiasm has its dangers as well. It leads Wesker to bubble over with too much to say at once. He enters too readily into his characters to prompt them with his words. Not only does he make himself into one of the characters (Ronnie), but he can be seen darting among the others to cue them. Employing the familiar form of nineteenth-century realism, Wesker is admittedly a didactic writer. Furthermore, he is incapable of that detachment of the artist from the "live reality" which is so much a part of the dehumanization of contemporary theater; he is much too earnest in his beliefs and too eager to share his point of view to be lured into the amusing and puzzling excursions of the avant-garde. His didacticism demands clarity and the direct approach. But he does not sacrifice the drama to the idea. The Kahn family argue eternally about Socialism, but they argue as characters that are round and full and not merely as ciphers parroting political slogans. Wesker's command of language, his lyricism, is already accomplished. With his gift for a language of feeling and with his understanding of character he can become even more than what the enthusiasms of the moment portend.

Henry Goodman. DramaS. Oct., 1961, p. 222

Wesker, it is evident, tries to get free from illusions: the illusion of a simple life in the countryside, the illusion of political hope, the illusion of permanence in any human situation. His plays tell us frankly of the squalid conditions under which people may live. They emphasise the sickness of old age, the pity (hard to tolerate) given to a weakness that grows with the years, the sudden swings between possessiveness and repudiation within a human tie. But against this background of mutability and precariousness, there is in Wesker's writing a recurrent insistence on the need, in the teeth of evidence, to affirm the notion of human brotherhood and the demand for affection that humanity makes upon us. This is strikingly conveyed in *The Kitchen,* a short play which is at first view the purest documentary. It is indeed a picture of a quite possible world that is given to us, doubtless a near-replica of what could be found behind the scenes in many a popular restaurant. The play has the strength that comes from being rooted in the actual. But it is soon obvious that Wesker's kitchen and his workers are intended to have a symbolic function. Realistically enough, they represent different groups of the world's people: they are Italian, German, Irish, Cypriot, Jewish, as well as gentile English. Their problem of living together is the world's problem: this becomes for a moment explicit when the Cypriot porter Dimitrios calls the crowd in the kitchen "the United Nations." But the basis of the play is not political. It is concerned with the human being's need for comfort and relaxation with others, a mode of existence that the sweat and bustle, the noise and elbowing of the kitchen will not allow. Peter goes berserk as an instinctive protest against the impossibility of coming near his inexpressible dream. The play has more sustained force than Wesker has since achieved. Its general avoidance of the explicit statement preserves it from the danger of seeming to offer a commonplace "message." Its speed and apparent casualness of its incidents save us from demanding a stronger individuality in the characters. The people of the kitchen remain people we have glimpsed: they keep the secrets that each individual always partially hides beneath the uniform of his type.

Clifford Leech. In John Russell Brown and Bernard
Harris, eds., *Contemporary Theatre* (London,
Edward Arnold, 1962), p. 20

Sending up the Air Force may mean different things at different times—in war and in peace for instance. Also at different theatres. Because we have just had Mr. [Henry] Livings's worm's eye view of an RAF station at the Arts Theatre, some people in last night's audience assumed that Mr. Wesker was on the same tack and went on tittering at scenes of square bashing which, like most things Mr. Wesker writes, were in fact intensely earnest, and about as far from Mr. Livings's Fred Carno army jokes as could well be imagined. Not that the play [*Chips with Everything*] has not its funny moments; the raid on a coke dump is a beautifully timed dumbshow and there is good natural reporting of the talk to be heard in any hut or NAAFI. But Mr. Wesker's airmen are the truest I have seen on any stage and make

Mr. Rattigan's *Ross* melodramatic and Mr. Livings's like comic postcards compared to documentary film. . . .

I find the first half of the play irritating, but I think what I rejected was the audience's facile assumption that this was simply a not very amusing exposé of the way recruits are broken in. What Wesker was saying came over eventually with great conviction. All the same, I believe we should have had less stamping and a more explicit characterisation from an earlier point in time but I incline to think that as a whole, this is Wesker's best play, moving away from the particular and autobiographical towards a larger study of the disillusion which betrays the nonconformist.

Philip Hope-Wallace. Guardian. April 28, 1962, p. 5

Wesker's special talent . . . lies not in his attacks on a hierarchical society that may be as tough as he thinks but is certainly a lot more devious. Still less does it lie in his William Morris-style detestation of mass culture, which makes him want to replace Elvis Presley with fourteenth-century songs of peasant revolt. Appropriately, when one such song is performed in *Chips* as a gesture of defiance toward the officers, it makes an exciting bit of movement but the words are totally lost.

Wesker's gift, in fact, is for the side of the theater that has most to do with dance. One of the best moments in *Roots* comes when the farm girl does an awkward little dance in an attempt to show her mother what she feels on hearing Mendelssohn's Fourth Symphony. In *The Kitchen* the exasperated cooks and waitresses build up to a sort of lunch-hour ballet. His other plays, even at their crudest, are full of strong stage pictures. In *Chips* one of the best scenes . . . is the wordless, nimble raid on the coal supply; another is the incompetent Smiler's running on one spot as he tries to flee from his tormentors. The drill movements too are dances of a kind; the play is punctuated with moments of song and collective movement. As an experience in the theater, the play that *Chips* has most in common with, flaws and all, is not some inspirational Soviet work of uplift; it is *West Side Story*.

John Rosselli. Reporter. Sept. 13, 1962, p. 52

To appreciate Wesker as a playwright, it's only necessary to remember that his commitment to Socialism is a product of family background. Compared with the commitment of a Brecht, Miller, or Sartre, it is a sheltered position in time and place; but it has led Wesker to the heart of a problem which is occupying the full attention of greater minds than his. The context is the affluent society of the mid-century capitalist Western world and the problem is in the end moral and/or social. How is the underprivileged mass to become fully human? Wesker's solution, that of an artist rather than a moralist or propagandist, is roughly on the lines of E. M. Forster's "only connect." He believes that it can be done by education and the arts. This positive aspect of his drama distinguishes Wesker from other new-wave playwrights and from many other Socialists. It accounts for the inner coherence which controls his dramatic writing; but, in so far as the wiring system along which the benevolence travels is of Socialist pattern, commitment is at times a source of weakness.

Regarded strictly as a dramatist, as an audience would regard him without reference to his personal background, social significance, "message" or mission, Wesker's most notable qualities are emotional maturity and his command of action in depth. The first means that he never condescends to his characters, the second that what happens on stage is always more interesting in performance than we would be likely to guess from quotation. In much "literary" drama the reverse is true in both cases and causes a quick dismissal to the shelf, whereas *Roots* was immediately successful with provincial audiences. The contact is usually made without resorting to verbal artifice or strenuous theatrical effects. Under the surface of dialogue which, like O'Neill's, is often limp and colourless on the page, there comes into focus a network of relationships more significant than the interplay in the foreground, which can be written off as a quarrel between cooks or the gushing quotation of a half-educated young man's ideas, accurate but uninspiring. The inner framework, on the contrary, contains social and political issues, held together dramatically by the playwright's urgent concern for them and by his conviction that they affect the homely characters in front.

Laurence Kitchin. In William A. Armstrong, ed., Experimental Drama (London, G. Bell and Sons, 1963), pp. 171–72

Some twenty odd years ago Clifford Odets wrote *Awake and Sing!,* a play about Jewish family life in the Bronx. The play had a success in its day, though it was never very good, and then faded out. A production of *Awake and Sing!* in the United States nowadays would be as anachronistic as a May Day parade down Fifth Avenue. Not so in England. Inspired by the hopeful, before-the-fact announcements of the critics that England is experiencing a dramatic renaissance under the second Elizabeth to rival the one under the first, Arnold Wesker has written a trilogy that does for the Jews of London's East End what *Awake and Sing!* did for the Jews of the Bronx.

Wesker's trilogy is an extremely curious piece of work. Partly, I suspect, because Wesker is the first English playwright to announce anything as impressive as a trilogy of connected plays, and partly because Wesker himself has done a great deal of self-conscious talking about the "seriousness" of his art, it has had a distinct *succès d'estime* in England. The English look upon the Wesker trilogy as their answer to [O'Neill's] *Mourning Becomes Electra:* Englishmen can write epics about crumbling families too. Wesker, then, was extremely shrewd when he announced that he intended to write a trilogy. He was shrewd because (i) the series of plays is not a trilogy (the second play, *Roots,* is, strictly speaking, not connected to the other two plays at all); (ii) it assured the production of the last two plays once the first was produced; and (iii) the designation of "trilogy" gave the work an appearance of profundity, just as Galsworthy had given *his* scenes eavesdropped from family life an appearance of profundity 52 years earlier by calling them a "saga."

George E. Wellwarth. *The Theater of Protest and Paradox* (New York, New York University Press, 1964), p. 234

Wesker is willing to move onto the battlefield for his ideas. He may not be a prophet, but he is not bothered that some accuse him of donning the mantle of a prophet. Perhaps to Americans—who are more affluent than their neighbors, who have lived through their own Depression, who have been cynical about politicians—Wesker is "old-fashioned." But old fashions have a habit of becoming once again new fashions. The world is restless and in constant flux. There is more to art than concentrating and focusing on love affairs and sexual conflicts. The world is large and man's activities are many. Wesker has broadened horizons and always has remembered to create plays that have social passion. Now his dramas are being performed all over the world. Obviously Wesker's work is not narrow in its interests or parochial, even when he is depicting a Jewish family in London, or an inarticulate girl seeking to express herself among her own people living on a farm in Norfolk; or the rise and corruption of a Labour leader, or the lack of communication between a pair of lovers.

Harold U. Ribalow. *Arnold Wesker* (New York, Twayne, 1965), p. 121

If many in England see [Wesker] as a symptom of Britain's malaise since Suez and a result of the intensified class hatred and narrowed educational opportunities in England after eleven years of uninterrupted Conservative Party power before Labour's latest and rather teetering victory, still others find him only a curious political anachronism. Whatever the limitations of Wesker's plays—their political ignorance and naïveté, their sense of being mired in outmoded doctrinal bogs of the thirties, their deficiencies of imagination and craft—the popularity of the plays with both the anti-Establishment Left and an even wider "West End" audience in Britain is a significant cultural and political fact. Wesker's present popularity, however controversial, is a symptom of an important attitude in Britain, particularly among the militant younger intellectuals of the British Left, some of whom have been the driving forces of such social and political groupings as the Aldermaston marchers, SANE, and Wesker's own Centre 42 for a "people's culture." And Wesker, whatever his shortcomings as a playwright and his importance as a socio-political touchstone, if he breaks out of the bonds of autobiography, lays away the megaphone of his muddled dogma and blatant political proselytizing, and perhaps succeeds in fusing his realistic and impressionistic impulses—in short, if he matures—may yet turn out to be one of the significant dramatists of the English-speaking stage.

Abraham Rothberg. SWR. Autumn, 1967, p. 378

The enormous time-span and the frequent time-changes [in *Their Very Own and Golden City*] (whether seen as forward or back) inevitably make for a sequence of loosely-linked episodes. The last quarter of the play is described by the author as a "continuous scene," which in fact means only that the scenes become even shorter and the advance into the future more rapid. This possibly is intended to suggest that time appears to pass more quickly as a man grows older, but more likely Wesker gave so much space to Andy's early days that the building of the City had to be compressed. The pattern of the decline of a man morally paralleling the rise of his tangible achievements is a good one, but this contrast enters only in the second half, leaving the first part on Andy's youth awkwardly detached.

Nevertheless, Wesker has attempted a highly ambitious work, in content and form. The man who moved from the accomplished use of three conventional acts in *Chicken Soup* to the four balanced phases of *The Four Seasons,* with its subtle changes in pace and tension, could no doubt have repeated mastery of structures like these. Instead he adventurously tries something different, and in the London production, [Simon] Trussler reported, "the potentially bitty action fell together into a final shape that can only be described as epic."

The mention of "epic" suggests Brecht, and *Golden City* and *Chips with Everything* are probably influenced by the form of plays like *Galileo* and *Mother Courage*. Some scenes in *Chips*—bayonet-drill, stealing coke, the party—are amongst Wesker's finest theatrical effects, but the uncertainty of style and multiplicity of themes limit the total achievement.

The strengths of the trilogy included a strong social conscience, concern with the nature of life in England in his lifetime, and effective studies of ordinary people (including Wesker himself and several members of his family). In these three later plays he no longer needs to draw on relatives for characters, and his own experiences come into wider perspective. *Chips* examines how his air force years helped form Wesker, especially the public man, while *The Four Seasons* examines an important aspect of Wesker the private man. His own experiences and idealism, and a scrutiny of public events that have affected his generation, are all in *Golden City*. In *Golden City*, in addition, he is for the first time analysing, albeit clumsily, one of his present problems rather than a past one. The seriousness and the choice of big issues is admirable; perhaps all these pieces are preparatory to political plays about Britain in the sixties and seventies. Though I judge only *The Four Seasons* to be successful of these three plays, they show Wesker striving to extend his range, moving through structural experiments to greater self-knowledge and new linguistic attainment.

Malcolm Page. *MD*. Dec., 1968, pp. 324–25

The most pervasive and unifying concern that runs through all Wesker's plays and draws in most of the other themes could hardly be more basic—the search for systematic sense in life, for an interpretation that is at least workably inclusive yet also life-affirming. The lack of this, though scarcely articulated, bewilders the cooks in *The Kitchen,* caught in their enervating routine and groping in unresponsive isolation for an alternative. Ronnie's search for it, as embodied in his political philosophy, is, it seems, close to being abandoned by the end of the Trilogy: for him, it is irreconcilable socially with what he experiences as an individual—whilst for Dave and Ada it fails to offer even the personal salvation it maybe promises Beatie Bryant. And Beatie's problem has been precisely a rootlessness that denies her not so much her rural inheritance as a means of grasping, ingesting, co-ordinating and communicating *all* experience. A fallen, sterile substitute of a system subjugates the airmen of *Chips with Everything* in their faith-sustained, hierarchical world; and in *The Four Seasons* Adam and Beatrice fail to live with and for each other because they have failed to live with and for anybody else. Finally, and most fully, the search for a unifying order infuses the patchwork and fragmentation themes of *Their Very Own and Golden City* and *The Friends*.

What does seem to have changed is the emphasis: in the earlier plays the central characters are baffled and dismayed by the inordinate muddle of society, so meekly accepted by its members, whilst, after the transitional *Chips,* the protagonists are aware not only of the confusion that surrounds them in their sense of community, but of the dislocation and unpredictability within themselves. To have sought to cope with such a theme as this within even so tentatively naturalistic a framework as *The Friends* was to invite ridicule and rebuke—just as the Trilogy, once its polemical appeal begins to wane, may seem only overweeningly ambitious, and presumptive in its ambition, alike to the enemies of its ideas and to friends who sincerely doubt the usefulness or the possibility of such a wide-ranging investigation as Wesker's work actually attempts. It is, of course, much more acceptable in the present theatrical climate to reduce a sense of anguish to formal, laughable or intractable absurdity, and it takes a brave mind to lay itself bare in a manner less allusively, more explicitly revealing. But because Wesker is seeking to reconcile individual anguish with social anger, the lonely lover with the golden city—

and because, as *The Friends* confirms, he believes that such reconciliation is possible—he will probably continue to write plays which, self-consistent without being self-satisfied, continue his exploration from its original starting point, wherever that may lead, instead of distorting his talents into the latest modish mould.

Glenda Leeming and Simon Trussler. *The Plays of Arnold Wesker: An Assessment* (London, Gollancz, 1971), pp. 191–93

Arnold Wesker calls his new play [*The Old Ones*] a comedy, which, on the face of it, is a hopeful sign. Comedy implies a sense of proportion, flexibility of method, and a readiness to take life on the wing: qualities which one would have been grateful to find in his other plays, and whose value he recognizes in this. In *The Friends,* Wesker wrote a didactic requiem for a generation which had lost its capacity to teach: in this equally despair-haunted sequel he moves appropriately into comedy, a form that springs from the sense of human defeat.

Like his earliest plays, *The Old Ones* is about a family of London Jews, with the difference (as the title underlines) that its emphasis shifts from middle-age to the frontiers of senility. No matter. Most of them are battling on as strenuously as the Kahns in *Chicken Soup with Barley.* Manny, the eupeptic old tailor, is still waging quotation duels with his nihilistic brother Boomy, each left hook from Voltaire being met with a body blow from Buber. Lonely Teressa struggles on with the translation she has been at for 15 years. Dotty old Millie hangs on to her little nest, showering the floor with £5 notes and ringing up sister Gerda to inquire irritably after her three dead brothers.

There are also youngsters on the scene whose presence begins to make this catalogue, and also the play, I fear, somewhat unwieldy.

Heaven knows how autobiographical it may be, but it marks no development in Wesker's powers of selection. To present a Jewish family in full cry, every passionate member ignoring what the others are saying, a large cast is doubtless necessary. But why overload the audience's strained attention with irrelevant information? The cousins Rosa and Martin meet and commiserate with each other over their broken marriages: nothing is heard of those marriages again. Manny opens the play by torturing Gerda with despairing nocturnal cries; then he goes on to represent all that is most positive and hopeful in the play. . . .

Why pick on trivial details in a piece concerned with the profound issues of our time? Because, yet again, Wesker is too obsessed with those issues to pay more than spasmodic regard to the people he has chosen to discuss them. And the word is discuss. *The Old Ones* contains only one consistent line of action: the building and decoration of a *succoh* (a kind of harvest festival arbour) which brings the contentious family together in display of joyous orthodoxy in the final scene.

Wesker has often achieved his most theatrical effects by demonstrating a physical task, but this time he has stretched a task to the whole length of a play and treated it as if it were a plot. The result is lacking in forward drive, and incapable of carrying the weight of additional material that accompanies it. Some of the writing is very touching . . . . But when the tom-toms of Weskerian doctrine start throbbing it is another matter. . . .

Irving Wardle. The Times (London). Aug. 9, 1972, p. 10

The Journalists is both one of Wesker's most disciplined plays and one of his most relaxed. Certain points may be underlined too heavily; for example, towards the end we get too many repetitions of the point about the danger inherent in a newspaper's selective attention to detail. But there is a good deal of compensating comedy and vitality.

The organic movement of the play grows up around the newspaper's movement towards the moment when, at about six o'clock on Saturday evening, the printing presses start to roll. Toward the end of the week, there is an inevitable frenzy of last-minute activity as decisions are made about the allocation of front-page space. The physical bustle may be very different from that of cooks and waitresses in a busy restaurant, but more than in any other play since *The Kitchen,* Wesker cashes in on the theatrical possibilities of large-scale corporate activity reaching a climax of intensity; and he shows the same talent for dramatizing it.

Halfway through the final act he calls for a film projection of the turning presses, and as they start we hear the full blast of their noise. The volume of this has to be taken down for the dialogue which is to follow, but the hurried movements of the messengers, the speed with which decisions have to be taken, the changing rhythm of the characters' speech patterns, and the rhythm of the sequence of short scenes all contribute to the climacteric accelerando. As in *The Kitchen,* the full potential of the play can be realized only with the help of a director capable of disciplining his actors into an intricate choreography of physical actions; but *The Journalists* is much more complex than *The Kitchen,* more carefully structured, with a more calculated interdependence of dialogue and movement.

Since the over-ambitious *Their Very Own and Golden City,* each of Wesker's plays had been less ambitious than its predecessor, but with no compensating consolidation of technical *savoir faire.* Now, suddenly, he has bounded ahead to write an extremely ambitious play in which his technique matches up to the demands he makes on it.

Ronald Hayman. Arnold Wesker (New York,
Frederick Ungar, 1973), pp. 122–23

WILDE, OSCAR (1854–1900)

It is somewhat surprising to find Mr. Oscar Wilde, who does not usually model himself on Mr. Henry Arthur Jones, giving his latest play a five-chambered title like *The Case of Rebellious Susan*. So I suggest with some confidence that *The Importance of Being Earnest* dates from a period long anterior to *Susan*. However it may have been retouched immediately before its production, it must certainly have been written before *Lady Windermere's Fan*. I do not suppose it to be Mr. Wilde's first play: he is too susceptible to fine art to have begun otherwise than with a strenuous imitation of a great dramatic poem, Greek or Shakespearian; but it was perhaps the first which he designed for practical commercial use at the West End theatres. The evidence of this is abundant. The play has a plot—a gross anachronism; there is a scene between the two girls in the second act quite in the literary style of Mr. Gilbert, and almost inhuman enough to have been conceived by him; the humour is adulterated by stock mechanical fun to an extent that absolutely scandalizes one in a play with such an author's name to it; and the punning title and several of the more farcical passages recall the epoch of the late H. J. Byron. The whole has been varnished, and here and there veneered, by the author of *A Woman of No Importance*, but the general effect is that of a farcical comedy of the seventies, unplayed during that period because it was too clever and too decent, and brought up to date as far as possible by Mr. Wilde in his now completely formed style. Such is the impression left by the play on me. But I find other critics, equally entitled to respect, declaring that *The Importance of Being Earnest* is a strained effort of Mr. Wilde's at ultra-modernity, and that it could never have been written but for the opening up of entirely new paths in drama last year by *Arms and the Man*. At which I confess to a chuckle.

I cannot say that I greatly cared for *The Importance of Being Earnest*. It amused me, of course; but unless comedy touches me as well as amuses me, it leaves me with a sense of having wasted my evening. I go to the theatre to be moved to laughter, not to be tickled or bustled into it; and that is why, though I laugh as much as anybody at a farcical comedy, I am out of spirits before the end of the second act, and out of temper before the end of the third, my miserable mechanical laughter intensifying these symptoms at every outburst. If the public ever becomes intelligent enough to know when it is really enjoying itself and when it is not, there will be an end of farcical comedy. Now in *The Importance of Being Earnest* there is a good deal of this rib-tickling; for instance, the lies, the deceptions, the cross purposes, the sham mourning, the christening of the two grown-up men, the muffin eating, and so forth. These could only have been raised from the farcical plane by making them occur to characters who had, like Don Quixote, convinced us of their reality and obtained some hold on our sympathy.

But that unfortunate moment of Gilbertism breaks our belief in the humanity of the play.

George Bernard Shaw. *SR* (London).
Feb. 23, 1895, pp. 249–50

Mr. [Walter] Pater once said that Mr. Oscar Wilde wrote like an excellent talker, and the criticism goes to the root. All of *A Woman of No Importance* which might have been spoken by its author, the famous paradoxes, the rapid sketches of men and women of society, the mockery of most things under heaven, are delightful; while, on the other hand, the things which are too deliberate in their development, or too vehement and elaborate for a talker's inspiration, such as the plot, and the more tragic and emotional characters, do not rise above the general level of the stage. The witty or grotesque persons who flit about the hero and heroine, Lord Illingworth, Mrs. Allonby, Canon Daubeny, Lady Stutfield, and Mr. Kelvil, all, in fact, who can be characterised by a sentence or a paragraph, are real men and women; and the most immoral among them have enough of the morality of self-control and self-possession to be pleasant and inspiriting memories. There is something of heroism in being always master enough of oneself to be witty; and therefore the public of to-day feels with Lord Illingworth and Mrs. Allonby much as the public of yesterday felt, in a certain sense, with that traditional villain of melodrama who never laid aside his cigarette and his sardonic smile. The traditional villain had self-control. Lord Illingworth and Mrs. Allonby have self-control and intellect; and to have these things is to have wisdom, whether you obey it or not. "The soul is born old, but grows young. That is the comedy of life. And the body is born young and grows old. That is life's tragedy." Women "worship successes," and "are the laurels to hide their baldness." "Children begin by loving their parents. After a time they judge them. Rarely if ever do they forgive them." And many another epigram, too well known to quote, rings out like the voice of Lear's fool over a mad age. And yet one puts the book down with disappointment. Despite its qualities, it is not a work of art, it has no central fire, it is not dramatic in any ancient sense of the word. The reason is that the tragic and emotional people, the people who are important to the story, Mrs. Arbuthnot, Gerald Arbuthnot, and Hester Worsley, are conventions of the stage. They win our hearts with no visible virtue, and though intended to be charming and good and natural, are really either heady and undistinguished, or morbid with what Mr. Stevenson has called "the impure passion of remorse." The truth is, that whenever Mr. Wilde gets beyond those inspirations of an excellent talker which served him so well in *The Decay of Lying* and in the best parts of [*The Picture of*] *Dorian Gray*, he falls back upon the popular conventions, the spectres and shadows of the stage.

W. B. Yeats. *BkmL*. March, 1895, p. 182

[Wilde's] work was distinct from that of most other playwrights in that he was a man who had achieved success outside the theatre. He was not a mere maker of plays. Taking up dramaturgy when he was no longer a young man, taking it up as a kind of afterthought, he brought to it a knowledge of the world which the life-long playwright seldom possesses. But this was only one point in his advantage. He came as thinker, a weaver of ideas, and as a wit, and as the master of literary style. It was, I think, in respect of literary style that his plays were most remarkable. In his books this style was perhaps rather too facile, too rhetorical in its grace. Walter Pater, in one of his few book-reviews, said that in Mr. Wilde's work there was always "the quality of the good talker." This seems to me a very acute criticism. Mr. Wilde's writing suffered by too close a likeness to the flow of speech. But it was this very likeness that gave him in dramatic dialogue as great an advantage over more careful and finer literary stylists as he had over ordinary playwrights with no pretence to style. The dialogue in his plays struck the right mean between literary style and ordinary talk. It was at once beautiful and natural, as dialogue should always be. With this and other advantages, he brought to dramaturgy as keen a sense for the theatre as was possessed by any of his rivals, except Mr. Pinero. Theatrical construction, sense of theatrical effects, were his by instinct. I notice that one of the newspapers says that his plays were "devoid of consideration as drama," and suggests that he had little or no talent for construction. Such criticism as this merely shows that what Ben Jonson called "the dull ass's hoof" must have its backward fling. In point of fact, Mr. Wilde's instinct for construction was so strong as to be a disadvantage. The very ease of his manipulation tempted him to trickiness, tempted him to accept current conventions which, if he had had to puzzle things out laboriously and haltingly, he would surely have discarded, finding for himself a simpler and more honest technique. His three serious comedies were marred by staginess. In *An Ideal Husband* the staginess was most apparent, least so in *A Woman of No Importance*. In the latter play, Mr. Wilde allowed the psychological idea to work itself out almost unmolested, and the play was, in my opinion, by far the most truly dramatic of his plays. It was along these lines that we, in the early 'nineties, hoped Mr. Wilde would ultimately work. But, even if he had confined his genius to the glorification of conventional drama, we should have had much reason to be grateful to him. His conventional comedies were as superior to the conventional comedies of other men as was *The Importance of Being Earnest* to the everyday farces whose scheme was so frankly accepted in it. At the moment of Mr. Wilde's downfall, it was natural that the public sentiment should be one of repulsion. But later, when he was released from prison, they remembered that he had at least suffered the full penalty. And now that he is dead, they will realise also, fully, what was for them involved in his downfall, how lamentable the loss to dramatic literature.

Max Beerbohm. SR (London). Dec. 8, 1900, p. 720

The difficulty about Wilde as a playwright was that he never quite got through the imitative phase. *The Importance of Being Earnest* is the nearest approach to absolute originality that he attained. In that play, for the first time, he seemed to be tearing himself away from tradition and to be evolving a dramatic form of his own. Unhappily it was the last play he was to write, and so the promise in it was never fulfilled. Had his career not been cut short at this moment, it is possible that this might have proved the starting-point of a whole series of "Trivial Comedies for Serious People," and that thenceforward Wilde would have definitely discarded the machine-made construction of the Scribe-Sardou theatre which had held him too long, and begun to use the drama as an artist should, for the expression of his own personality, not the manufacture of clever *pastiches*. It would then have become possible to take him seriously as a dramatist. For, paradoxical as it may sound in the case of so merry and light-hearted a play, *The Importance of Being Earnest* is artistically the most serious work that Wilde produced for the theatre. Not only is it by far the most brilliant of his plays considered as literature. It is also the most sincere. With all its absurdity, its psychology is truer, its criticism of life subtler and more profound than that of the other plays. And even in its technique it shows, in certain details, a breaking away from the conventional well-made play of the 'seventies and 'eighties in favour of the looser construction and more naturalistic methods of the newer school. [1908]

St. John Hankin. In Dramatic Works (London,
Martin Secker, 1912), Vol. III, pp. 185–86

Once . . . Wilde's own nature, with all its limitations, worked clearly in delight of itself, and achieved what is in its own province a perfect work of art. *The Importance of Being Earnest* is not really a comedy of manners in the sense of being primarily a criticism of the follies into which a society is betrayed by its conventions, and a tearing off of the masks. Nor is it primarily a comedy of wit, sure and sustained as the wit is. Attempts have been made to derive the play in some measure from the Restoration masters, but without much conviction, and while the manner employed by Wilde has clearly influenced some later writers, notably St. John Hankin, *The Importance of Being Earnest* really forms a class in English drama by itself. It is in mere simplicity that one says that it seems to be the only one of Wilde's works that really has its roots in passion. Every device of gaiety and even seeming nonsense is employed to keep the passion far back out of sight, and, if it were otherwise, the play would not be the masterpiece it is. But the passion is there. That is to say that the play is directly an expression of that part of Wilde's own experience which was least uncontaminated and in which he could take most delight. And this meant that all his great gifts as a craftsman were for once employed in work where, with insincerity almost as the theme, there was more sincerity than in anything else he did.

John Drinkwater. Introduction to *The Complete Works of Oscar Wilde* (Garden City, N.Y., Doubleday, Page, 1923), pp. xi–xii

There is no term which so perfectly expresses the tone of Wilde's comedies as *nonchalance*. The astounding thing is that, in his sincere effort to amuse the public, he best succeeded with the public by holding it up to scorn and ridicule with the lightest satire. "If we are to deliver a philosophy," says Mr. [G. K.] Chesterton, in speaking of contemporary life, "it must be in the manner of the late Mr. [James McNeill] Whistler and the *ridentum dicere verum*. If our heart is to be aimed at, it must be with the rapier of [Robert Louis] Stevenson, which runs through without either pain or puncture." If our brain is to be aroused, he might have added, it must be with the paradox and epigram of Oscar Wilde. Horace Walpole once said that the world is a comedy for the man of thought, a tragedy for the man of feeling. He forgot to say that it is a farce for the man of wit. It was Wilde's creed that ironic imitation of the contrasts, absurdities, and inconsistencies of life, its fads and fancies, its quips and cranks, its follies and foibles, give far more pleasure and amusement than faithful portraiture of the dignity of life, its seriousness and profundity, its tragedy, pit, and terror. His comedies are marked, not by consistency in the characters, continuity of purpose, or unity of action, but only by persistence of the satiric vein and prevalence of the comic mood. Like Flaubert, Wilde gloried in demoralizing the public, and he denied with his every breath Sidney Lanier's dictum that art has no enemy so unrelenting as cleverness. His whole literary career was one long, defiant challenge to Zola's pronunciamento: *l'homme de génie n'a jamais d'esprit.*

Archibald Henderson. *European Dramatists* (New York, D. Appleton, 1926), pp. 311–12

Insensitivity to slight and delicate things is insensitivity *tout court*. That is what Wilde meant when he declared that the man who despises superficiality is himself superficial. His best play is connected with this idea. As its title confesses, it is about *earnestness*, that is, Victorian solemnity, that kind of false seriousness which means priggishness, hypocrisy, and lack of irony. Wilde proclaims that earnestness is less praiseworthy than the ironic attitude to life which is regarded as superficial. His own art, and the comic spirit which Congreve embodied and which Meredith had described, were thereby vindicated. Wilde calls *The Importance of Being Earnest* "a trivial comedy for serious people" meaning, in the first place, a comedy which will be thought negligible by the earnest and, in the second, a *comedy of surface* for connoisseurs. The latter will perceive that Wilde is as much of a moralist as Bernard Shaw but that, instead of presenting the problems of modern society directly, he flits around them, teasing them, declining to grapple with them. His wit is no searchlight into the darkness of modern life. It is a flickering, a coruscation, intermittently revealing the upper class of England in a harsh bizarre light. This upper class could feel about Shaw that at least he took them seriously, no one more so. But the outrageous Oscar (whom they took care to get rid of as they had got rid of Byron) refused to see the importance of being earnest.

One does not find Wilde's satire embedded in plot and character as in traditional high comedy. It is a running accompaniment to the play, and this fact, far from indicating immaturity, is the making of a new sort of comedy. The plot is one of those Gilbertian absurdities of lost infants and recovered brothers which can only be thought of to be laughed at. Yet the dialogue which sustains the plot, or is sustained by it, is an unbroken stream of comment on all the themes of life which the plot is so far from broaching. Perhaps *comment* is too flat and downright a conception. Wildean "comment" is a pseudo-irresponsible jabbing at all the great problems, and we would be justified in removing the prefix "pseudo" if the Wildean satire, for all its naughtiness, had not a cumulative effect and a paradoxical one. Flippancies repeated, developed, and so to say, elaborated almost into a system amount to something in the end—and thereby cease to be flippant. What begins as a prank ends as a criticism of life. What begins as intellectual high-kicking ends as intellectual sharp-shooting.

Eric Bentley. *The Playwright as Thinker*
(New York, Reynal & Hitchcock, 1946), pp. 172–74

In *The Importance of Being Earnest* . . . the tedium is concentrated in the second act, where two young ladies are rude to each other over tea and cake, and two young gentlemen follow them being selfish about the muffins. The joke of gluttony and the joke of rudeness (which are really the same one, for heartlessness is the basic pleasantry) have been exhausted in the first act: nothing can be said by the muffin that has not already been said by the cucumber sandwich. The thin little joke that remains, the importance of the name Ernest for matrimony, is in its visible aspects insufficiently entertaining. That the joke about the name Ernest is doubtless a private one makes it less endurable to the audience, which is pointedly left out of the fun. To the bisexual man, it was perhaps deliciously comic that a man should have one name, the tamest in English, for his wife and female relations, and another for his male friends, for trips and "lost" week ends; but Wilde was a prude—he went to law to clear his character—and the antisocial jibe dwindles on the stage to a refined and incomprehensible titter.

Yet, in spite of the exhausting triviality of the second act, *The Importance of Being Earnest* is Wilde's most original play. It has the character of a ferocious idyl. Here, for the first time, the subject of Wilde's comedy coincides with its climate; there is no more pretense of emotion. The unwed mother, his stock "serious" heroine, here becomes a stock joke—"Shall there be a different standard for women than for men?" cries Mr. Jack Worthing, flinging himself on the governess, Miss Prism, who had checked him accidentally in a valise at a railroad station twenty-five years before. In *The Importance of Being Earnest* the title is a *blague,* and virtue disappears from the Wilde stage, as though jerked off by one of those hooks that were used in the old days of vaudeville to remove an unsuccessful performer. Depravity is the hero and the only character, the people on the stage embodying various shades of it. It is deepest dyed in the pastoral region of respectability and innocence. The London *roué* is artless simplicity itself beside the dreadnought society dowager, and she, in her turn, is out-brazened by her debutante daughter, and she by the country miss, and she by her spectacled governess, till finally the village rector with his clerical clothes, his vow of celibacy, and his sermon on manna, adjustable to all occasions, slithers noiselessly into the rose garden, specious as the Serpent Himself. [1947]

Mary McCarthy. *Sights and Spectacles* (New York, Farrar, Straus and Cudahy, 1956), pp. 107–8

Though the characters of Wilde's farce [*The Importance of Being Earnest*] are all of the same species, its plot is at times too heavily contrived, especially in the last act: the sudden revelation of Miss Prism's past solves too conveniently the problem of the hero's origin, and too many of the embarrassing lies of the play are too neatly resolved into truth. Such reliance on the whimsies of chance weakens the satire of a comedy of manners; its plot should seem to grow more directly out of the follies of its characters, mirroring the irrationality of an absurd society of human beings responsible for their own predicaments rather than the irresponsible tricks of a contemptibly frivolous destiny.

In spite of the polished brilliance of its paradoxical dialogue and the sure pace of its surprising action, *The Importance of Being Earnest* thus never transcends, as a work of art, the incomplete or the trivial. Its tone is that of satire, but of a satire which, for lack of a moral point of view, has lost its sting and degenerated into the almost approving banter of a P. G. Wodehouse. Satire, whether in the comedy of manners or any other genre of satirical literature, must be founded on more than a dandy's mere tastes and opinions; from some sounder moral philosophy, it must derive a necessary bitterness without which the satirist remains ineffectual while the manners of his comedies, not yet structurally integrated, seem superimposed as mere ornament on an arbitrary plot of farce.

Edouard Roditi. Oscar Wilde (Norfolk, Conn.,
New Directions, 1947), pp. 138–39

The peak of Wilde's dramatic achievement, and the one piece of writing in which he came nearest to artistic perfection, was *The Importance of Being Earnest,* of which the critic A. B. Walkley said, with justice: "It is of nonsense all compact, and better nonsense, I think, our stage has not seen." *The Importance of Being Earnest* is indeed unique in English dramatic literature; so far as it has any ancestors, they are to be found in those last and most whimsical of Restoration wits, Congreve and Vanbrugh, but even *Love for Love,* with all its passages of equally stimulating nonsense, has a sufficiently rational basis to place it in a quite different category.

Sometimes his influence was bad, as when his decorative style, which even in his own hands was not always successful, tempted younger writers to abandon simplicity for a pointless elaboration. But more often it was a liberating one, opening literary forms and ways of thought to new ideas and techniques.

Undoubtedly he was the greatest influence in restoring genuine comedy to the English stage. Shaw was almost as much influenced by him as by Ibsen, and had Wilde lived and continued to write for the theatre, there is no doubt that Shaw's prestige would never have reached its present magnitude. It was Wilde's reintroduction of the comedy of wit and satire that opened the minds of theatrical audiences to the kind of social drama which Shaw produced, but even more effectively it detached the stage from melodrama and brought comedy back to its genuine function of an ironical or satirical commentary on life.

In *Salome* Wilde introduced to the English public that type of poetic drama which Maeterlinck was already popularising in France, and this play, rejected by English religious prejudice, became the occasion for [Max] Reinhardt on the Continent to introduce the new stage techniques which started a whole series of revolutionary alterations in the theatrical art.

George Woodcock. The Paradox of Oscar Wilde
(New York, Macmillan, 1950), pp. 242–43

After the fiasco over *Salome* there was nothing for it but a return to the vein that had proved itself so rewarding, and Wilde's second serio-comedy, *A Woman of No Importance,* was produced in February 1893 by [Herbert Beerbohm] Tree, who played Lord Illingworth. With the same kind of setting, the same kind of scintillating dialogue and a theme appealing to the same range of emotions, it was sufficiently like its predecessor [*Lady Win-*

dermere's Fan] to score a similar success; but in some ways it represents a step backwards. Firstly, in construction. The conversation of the minor characters is less carefully dovetailed into the action than in *Lady Windermere's Fan*. It is said that Wilde wrote the first act, which consists entirely of delightful conversation with scarcely any bearing on the plot, as a defiant answer to some critic's objection that the brilliant chatter in *Lady Windermere's Fan* did nothing to advance the action. The second act carries on in much the same way until the dramatic entrance of Mrs. Arbuthnot, with which the play finally begins to move; and even after that the main function of Lord Illingworth's talk with Gerald about life in general seems to be to give Wilde a chance of working off some favourite epigrams.

Secondly, in moral atmosphere, *Lady Windermere's Fan* seems to be informed with a valuable idea, that of the obtuseness of most moral judgments and the harsh inadequacy of the conventional code, especially as administered by "good" women, which is driven home not only by the mixture of good and bad in Mrs. Erlynne but also by the moral evolution of Lady Windermere: indeed, if sub-titles had been in fashion, we might well have had *Lady Windermere's Fan; or, The Education of a Prig*. In *A Woman of No Importance,* on the other hand, priggery, in the person of Hester Worsley, goes entirely unchastened, and the drama is a contest between unshaded black and white. Lord Illingworth, who starts as a second Henry Wooton, manages to introduce a little natural grey when he seizes on the selfish element in Mrs. Arbuthnot's possessive love of Gerald; but it is quite washed away in her tirade on the ewe-lamb theme, and in the end Illingworth himself degenerates into the complete villain of melodrama. The play finished with the rout of Gilded Vice, while the Victim of his Passion is left in full possession of the field, and, in the author's plain intention, of the sympathies of the audience. The resulting impression is one of acquiescence in the conventional code, which the victors, Mrs. Arbuthnot and Hester, both firmly uphold all through, joined with the fullest exploitation of its pathetic possibilities. There is something almost suggestive of dual personality in the combination of such a drama with the conversation of the minor characters, which alongside of the expected wit has at times a new and delightful inconsequence that makes the bold bad epigrams of Lord Illingworth and Mrs. Allonby seem almost heavy in comparison.

Alan Harris. Adelphi. Second Quarter, 1954, pp. 229–31

It is usually said that Oscar Wilde's society comedies have foolish plots and brilliant dialogue, and as far as it goes this critical commonplace is true. *Lady Windermere's Fan, A Woman of No Importance,* and *An Ideal Husband* do in fact have foolish plots and brilliant dialogue. But the foolishness of these plots does not prevent them from expressing Wilde's personal and artistic positions, while the brilliance of this dialogue has often obscured both its value and its meaning. These are the things that I wish to demonstrate here.

This dichotomy between plot and dialogue which mars the society comedies does not appear in Wilde's masterpiece, *The Importance of Being Earnest*. But to achieve the unity of *The Importance* Wilde had to suppress half his nature. That suppression constitutes a kind of deception, for we are given only a part of Wilde's reaction to his world. If we wish to understand fully what Wilde put into *The Importance*, we must also understand what he left out.

But however useful the society comedies are as an explication of *The Importance*, their real significance lies in themselves. Each of these plays contains two worlds, not only contrasting but conflicting. One is the world of the sentimental plots, where ladies with mysterious pasts make passionate speeches and the fates of empires hang on intercepted letters and stolen bracelets. This is the world I will call Philistine. Opposed to it is the dandiacal world, where witty elegants lounge about tossing off Wildean epigrams and rarely condescend to notice, much less take part in, the impassioned actions going on about them. The tension between these two worlds gives to the society comedies their peculiar flavor, their strength, and unfortunately their weakness.

Arthur Ganz. *MD*. May, 1960, p. 16

What is it . . . which distinguishes *Earnest* from *Charley's Aunt*?

The difference, ultimately, is the same as that which distinguishes Shakespeare and Jonson from countless less successful dramatists, the use of language. But whereas their language was a means to an end, and their end conforms fairly directly with [Samuel] Johnson's definition of the function of literature—"to enable readers better to enjoy life or better to endure it," Wilde was concerned with the linguistic artifact itself, with a kind of poetry which Auden has described as "a verbal earthly paradise, a timeless world of pure play, which gives us delight because of its contrast to our historical existence with all its insoluble problems and inescapable suffering." To think of Wilde's art as merely "escapist" is to oversimplify the position. What he gives us is a completely realized idyll, offering itself as something irrevocably *other* than life, not a wish-fulfillment of life as it might be lived. Consequently, to think of Wilde's idyll in terms of "aspiration" or "rejection" is as idle as the notion of "accepting" or "rejecting" Keats's *Ode on a Grecian Urn*, or the urn itself, or Mozart's *Marriage of Figaro*. "Truth in art is the unity of a thing with itself," and the truth in Wilde's dictum can be falsified by art too self-consciously pursued, as well as by life. *Salome*, Wilde's last produced play, is a monument to art, not art itself; it is as entangled with an aesthetic commentary on life as *A Woman of No Importance* is with a moral one. *Earnest* is the dramatic expression of a precise aesthetic ideology, where Art is seen as the supreme ordering and perfection of life. In such a play the plot can never be our sort of plot, and so, in Wilde, it is a farce; the characters can never be human, and so, in Wilde, they are pure and simple; the language has to be our language, but if it is the language of paradox it can continually contradict us. Such a play can contain oblique criticism of life, but it will never be a direct imitation of life, since that would imply an intrinsic value in life superior to that of art. Even at its most topical *The Importance of Being Earnest* avoids the didactic and the narrowly satirical, and remains resolutely faithful to its aesthetic aim. It was a success which Wilde achieved only once, and we can feel reasonably certain that the sudden ending of his dramatic career did not deprive us of any better play.

Ian Gregor. SewR. Spring, 1966, pp. 520–21

In the comedies, the duality between what the characters show on the surface and what they really are inside produces conflict and moral disequilibrium, leading to disillusionment and a more intense awareness of reality. In *An Ideal Husband,* we are not satisfied with the promotion of Sir Robert Chiltern after having known his youthful malfeasance. On the whole, we are uneasy about the happy endings of the comedies. Orthodoxy, though accepted, is seriously undermined. We feel uneasy about the moral position arrived at in the dénouement, which directly contrasts with the sympathies revealed in the dialogue; the intrigue tends to negate the happy outcome. Some readers have the impression that in the complication of the intrigues, the constant reference to tainted life and the need for purity is almost pathological. But few object to the "serious" people who exaggerate and twist ideas, who play with sentiments; to the immoralists who attack bombast with jolly ripostes which savagely disabuse the moralists.

What sustains the tension and lucidity of the comedies is mainly the paradoxical formulation of dramatic speech. The habit of conformity, the blind adherence to organization and authority, to Wilde, springs from the lack of imaginative sympathy. Absence of imagination prevents men from recognizing that life is fluid and forever changing. In paradox Wilde found the appropriate medium for the sense of life as dynamic. For what he wanted to do above all was to dramatize the conflict of ideas in which truth emerges gradually, by selection and omission and emphasis. The paradox exaggerates under the semblance of logical deduction; it stresses a half-truth which is more fecund than the platitude. Its pattern is simple: A implies B; A is not B but C—thus frustrating our normal expectations of a syllogism. The paradox breaks categories and common-sense opinion in an experimental fashion. Conventional values are upset, new aspects of actuality disclosed, truths arrived at by a provisional "lie" usually expressed in a formula with a piquant epigrammatic turn.

Epifanio San Juan, Jr. *The Art of Oscar Wilde* (Princeton, N.J., Princeton University Press, 1967), pp. 200–201

Although Wilde's social philosophy is as socialistically egalitarian as Shaw's, we get less a theory of social living than a vision of it. His world is polarized between dandy and philistine. He found the types too antipathetic for reconciliation or inner change, ruling out the more complex meshing of vitalist and truly vital character in Shaw. Wilde's image of the affected, ostentatious, and rebellious dandy helps him objectify his feelings and rationalize his art, personifying his aim as a "mask with a manner." On the surface, his resentment is directed at the ascendent bourgeois insistence on realism in art, marriage in sex, incorruptible dullness in politics, conformity in behavior. He supports the creation of a socialistic state which would extend the opportunities for creative individuality from a favored few to the many, freed from the necessities of toil. Yet he never suppresses his sense that uninhibited, transcendent kinds of innovation inevitably arouse the malevolence and envy of society as Nietzsche had warned, fusing them into a punishing mob. He may try to persuade us, like Shaw and O'Casey, that the absurdities of contemporary society can never be mitigated by purifying the individual, only by reshaping the social structure. But even though "what begins as a prank ends as a criticism of life," Eric Bentley concludes, Wilde's dandies remain too rigid and self-sufficient to support any consistent evolutionary drive. In his "pseudo-irresponsible jabbing" at the inconsistencies of an ostensibly Christian culture, attacks he laces with Biblical allusions, he seems more malcontent than rebel. As a social critic, he fills his plays with probing sorties against society, marriage, religion, money, and art; his theorizings are ameliorative, paradoxical, and liberating. But in the depths, he revolts against the fixing of identity (and thus destiny) by anatomy, conditioning, and societal repressions. He longs to withdraw to self-sufficient, idyllic refuges cut off from reality altogether. Thus his existential strivings appear subjective, romantic, and pessimistic.

Emil Roy. *British Drama since Shaw* (Carbondale, Ill., Southern Illinois University Press, 1972), pp. 23–24

The relation of the plays to [*The Picture of*] *Dorian Gray* is that of a cannibal tribe to its sacrificial king. Bits and pieces of the novel's dialogue keep turning up in one or other of the plays—in all of them except *Salome*. That play, according to Wilde, was constructed along the lines of a ballad—an observation made while he was in the process of writing [*The Ballad of*] *Reading Gaol*—the recurring phrases, like the recurring motifs in a piece of music, being "the artistic equivalent of the refrains of the old ballads." But it is important to note that the same principle of composition also operates in the comedies, and in none more obviously or more successfully than in *The Importance of Being Earnest*. For the true origin of all romantic drama was for Wilde the ballad, and he found the predecessors of Shakespeare and the early English dramatists not among "the tragic writers of the Greek or Latin stage, from Aeschylus to Seneca, but [among] the ballad-writers of the Border."

Wilde's estimate of his own place in the history of English drama is a fair reflection on the quality of at least one of his comedies, however debatable may be the claim made for his other dramatic work: "I would say that my unique position was that I had taken the Drama, the most objective form known to art, and made it as personal a form of expression as the Lyric or the Sonnet, while enriching the characterization of the stage, and enlarging—at any rate in the case of *Salome*—its artistic horizon."

Kevin Sullivan. *Oscar Wilde* (New York,
Columbia University Press, 1972), p. 21

The two most prominent words in the play [*The Importance of Being Earnest*] are *nonsense* and *serious,* or their synonyms. This is entirely appropriate, since the play itself is a reduction of all seriousness to the level of nonsense. In it, Wilde pauses for a space, takes a hard look at his career to date, and has a good, long laugh at himself. The play is absolutely devoid of sober content, and any attempt to find serious meaning in it must of necessity fall wide of the mark.

To say that the play has no serious meaning, however, is not to say that it has no meaning at all. Its very message, paradoxically, lies in its lack of seriousness, for here Oscar Wilde has a hearty laugh at his own expense. The target of the fun is Wilde's work up to this time. "Lord Arthur Savile's Crime," *The Picture of Dorian Gray, Salome, A Woman of No Importance,* even *An Ideal Husband*—Wilde singles out these works and, one by one, destroys their intellectual content, reducing them to the level of harmlessness and absurdity. Quite earnestly, he informs us that every serious thought he has had to date is nonsense—and very laughable nonsense at that.

The Importance of Being Earnest is essentially a private joke, though the source of its great popularity is Wilde's ability to translate the joke into public terms. By achieving and maintaining a perfect balance between the public and the private, Wilde managed to write one of the most brilliant comic masterpieces of the nineteenth century.

Christopher S. Nassaar. *Into the Demon Universe:
A Literary Exploration of Oscar Wilde* (New Haven, Conn.,
Yale University Press, 1974), pp. 129–30

[*The Importance of Being Earnest*], it seems to me, is more successful than most Restoration comedies because it is more pure—more purely absurd, if you like. The process of distorting actuality for expressive purposes is carried out more thoroughly, and the play's moral and aesthetic integrity is better maintained. In the dialogue alone, there is a more consistent heightening, amounting to a transfiguration of everyday conversation. The trouble with many Restoration comedies is that they express values only half-believed in by the audience for which they were intended. The characters praise aristocratic recklessness and sneer at commerce, yet the original courtly audience was committed to, and dependent on, commerce for at least a large part of its wealth. As a result, because of a secret uncertainty in the playwrights, there is often a confusion between symbolic action and action seriously recommended to the audience for imitation. We are presented with hyperbolic actions and sentiments, which we find not entirely convincing and perhaps a shade hysterical. There is the standard paradox of Restoration comedy, for instance: all moralists are hypocrites; only libertines can see the truth and maintain a fundamental decency. The confusion carried over into real life. Many of the court wits and gallants tried to live out such paradoxes, not always with happy results. Wilde too tried to live out his own paradoxes, with decidedly unhappy results, but in his greatest play artifice and advice do not get mixed up. "I don't quite like women who are interested in philanthropic work," says Cecily. "I think it is so forward of them." This is funnier, and more percipient, than jokes about hypocritical Puritan tradesmen. Wilde's symbol for sensual vitality and obedience to impulse is itself more wisely chosen than that of the Restoration playwrights: instead of using sexual behavior, he uses eating, something much more easily distanced. Contrary to what [Mary] McCarthy says, *The Importance of Being Earnest* rarely slips over into recommending attitudes that are morally repellent—relative to Restoration comedy, at any rate. You have to stand a long way off from the play to be able to think so. It is difficult to get indignant with the characters.

David Parker. *MLQ*. June, 1974, pp. 174–75

Wilde's dramatic work has an asset of tremendous value, that of appealing to the common man. . . . Wilde himself . . . boasted that he had taken the plot of *A Woman of No Importance* from the *Family Herald*; Ibsen was in the habit of cutting paragraphs from newspapers which appeared likely to supply material for his plays, and Henry James continually jotted down anecdotes, pieces of gossip and similarly intriguing items from newspapers, the point being that it is what the writer does with the subject that ultimately counts rather than the intrinsic value of the material itself. In using a situation from a family newspaper of wide and popular appeal Wilde showed his grasp of popular sentiment; and without this basis in everyday life, sentimental or adolescent, Wilde would not have achieved his place in the history of drama. Had a sufficient amount of hard cash been offered, he could no doubt have dramatised the telephone directory, but his concern was never with technique but with ideas and emotions—the two rarely being so apart in life as some writers seem to believe. Wilde's critical sense shows itself in his awareness of the society about which he was writing, realising that its interest lay in its very superficiality. He saw that there was much more on the surface of society than is generally supposed to meet the eye, perceiving that other writers had strayed in trying to give their society characters a depth which such people did not possess in real life. His plots had the exact degree of sardonic flippancy for the balance of comic and dramatic effect, so that while they could not be described as cynical or criticised as blatantly unrealistic they were satirical to a point sensed if not openly recognised by his audiences.

When Shaw wrote of Wilde and the "new manner" he was indicating the substitution of verbal humour for the knock-about farcical antics of the old school of dramatists. He should have included Wilde's attitude to plot and, what is of even greater importance, his sense of language, for Wilde's dramatic genius is almost exclusively verbal. Eric Bentley says of his dialogue, which is both the blood and skeleton of his plays, that it is "an unbroken stream of comment on all the themes of life which the plot is so far from broaching." Unlike many dramatists he did not write a basic play which he later embellished with witticisms (although he did make additions at various stages) but from first to last engaged his creative intellect on the theme so that, in effect, every joke, every epigram, almost every line of dialogue adds to the accumulative and total drama. If his plays do not add up to a criticism of life they are certainly a criticism of the society of the day and of the continual preoccupations of the English social mind with class, prestige, and money.

Alan Bird. The Plays of Oscar Wilde
(London, Vision, 1977), pp. 208–10

Usually discussed as technique, these prentice pieces [*Vera; or, The Nihilists* and *The Duchess of Padua*] are by no means so lacking in intellectual content as is generally supposed. As the beginnings of Wilde the dramatist they would command a certain attention. As the beginnings of Wilde the self-dramatising egotist they command rather more. With *Salomé* they comprise the greater part of his Romantic drama, and the strident internal conflicts expressed in them, though temporarily gagged by irony or muffled by mythopoeic distances in the narrative and critical endeavours of the 1880s, broke out again in *Salomé*, where, in their Romantic form at least, they were silenced once and for all.

They have also some claim to artistic originality, of conception if not of execution. It may be coincidence that neither contains more than one female character, or perhaps Wilde despaired of writing anything worthy of

Henry Irving and concentrated on capturing a leading actress instead. (Later, with greater self-confidence and, perhaps, more pressing financial problems, he did offer *The Duchess of Padua* to Irving, to no effect.) However, this was the decade when the "woman as hero" emerged in the novel and the drama, and Wilde's three romantic female leads are convincing specimens of this class. Family tradition was conceivably a factor in this. The heroic female sublimely active in a male world may have been stimulated by [his mother] Lady Wilde's example. The details of her career as Speranza, champion of Irish nationalism, must have constituted Wilde's earliest and vividest exposure to professional mythopoeia, a blueprint for literary treatment of Romantic anarchism. . . . Whatever prompted Wilde's choice of the woman hero, he evidently found in Vera, Beatrice, and Salomé figures expressive of that Romantic conflict which occurs when the exceptional personality, as it must, seeks self-perfection in despite of law and duty. . . .

In 1887, two tragedies the wiser, Wilde played with self-fulfilment in "Lord Arthur Savile's Crime." In the lyrical dramas, he developed something resembling a personal myth, similar in shape to that Victorian favourite, Perseus and Andromeda. The ego is the distressed maiden; duty or restraint the rock to which she is fastened; disobedience or rebellion the ravening monster which guards her or threatens her destruction; while the individual will, expressed through anarchic courage, is the saving heroic force. Once more, however, Wilde transforms familiar picture into critical paradox. The hero delivers the captive not so that she can flee the monster, but so that she can embrace it without embarrassment. Rebellion and self-expression become virtually synonymous. Capitulation to the *status quo* means a despicable betrayal of self. Naturally, Wilde ensures that the *status quo* never appeals. In this single point his Romantic and critical works agree.

Rodney Shewan. *Oscar Wilde: Art and Egotism*
(London, Macmillan, 1977), pp. 130–32

Wilde . . . challenged one of the most basic conventions of nineteenth-century plotting: rewarding virtue and condemning vice. Each of these plays [*Lady Windermere's Fan, A Woman of No Importance,* and *An Ideal Husband*] makes it apparent that the distinction between good and bad is almost impossible to draw. No one becomes "ideal," because, as Wilde reminds us, no one can be ideal. If Mrs. Erlynne is moved to rescue her daughter, she is still capable of lying to Lord Augustus. If Mrs. Arbuthnot feels repentance for her sin, she is nonetheless something of a hysteric and a nag who wants to keep her son all to herself. And when Lord Goring asks Sir Robert Chiltern if he has suffered much regret for what he has done, Sir Robert has the candor to say "No." Each of these characters is mixed. And in all cases, Wilde lets them have their own way. Mrs. Erlynne gets her man, Mrs. Arbuthnot frustrates Gerald's plea that she marry his father, and Sir Robert gets a seat in the Cabinet. Even Wilde's most disagreeable characters manage to get off scot-free. Lord Illingworth glides off to another party. And if Mrs. Cheveley's stock manipulation has been thwarted, she is nonetheless still at large, spared the exposure as a thief that a more conventional plot would surely have brought about.

If these plays are not completely successful, it is because of the very conflict which makes them so interesting. On the one hand we have the world of language—the world of intelligence and art; on the other hand, we have the world of orthodox moral opinion. Juxtaposed against the epigrams of a Lord Illingworth, we have the passionate propriety of a Hester Worsley. It is incredible that they can exist in the same play: It is as if one had crossed William Congreve with Jonathan Edwards—the combination does not work. Wilde is at his best when he can sustain the illusion of one world or another, be it the almost pure comedy of manners of the opening scenes of both *Lady Windermere's Fan* and *A Woman of No Importance*, or the fine drama of *An Ideal Husband*. But in each play the illusion is allowed to break as Wilde shifts from one level to another. As a result, we tend to enjoy these plays in part but not in whole.

Robert Keith Miller. Oscar Wilde (New York,
Frederick Ungar, 1982), pp. 70–71

YEATS, WILLIAM BUTLER (1865–1939)

Beauty seems always something remote from the stress of common life. Though it may exist in such life, it can be conceived only as at a distance. The greater the distance, the clearlier can it be conceived. And it is for this reason that Maeterlinck billets his figures on some castle that never existed or perhaps existed "nowhere once." And it is for that reason, also, Mr. Yeats has laid his play [*The Countess Cathleen*] "in Ireland, and in old times." It was inevitable that Mr. Yeats should choose Ireland as the scene, even had he known that Irishmen would be so foolish as to treat the play as a contribution to history. But, so far as his play is concerned, I see no essential reason why the scene should have been laid anywhere really on the map. Perhaps that is because I am not an Irishman? To an Irishman, perhaps, Mr. Yeats' play may seem steeped in national character. To me it seems merely a beautiful poem about some men and women.

Rather, I should have said a play about a woman. The Countess Cathleen learns that her peasants are selling to two demons their souls for bread. That she may save them, she sells all that she has, and distributes the gold.

But that sacrifice is not enough. The hunger is still in the land, and still the demons are driving their bargains. At last, the Countess Cathleen gives the demons her own soul to redeem the rest. She dies. Comes an angel, telling the peasants that their lady is

>   passing to the floor of peace
> And Mary of the seven times wounded heart
> Has kissed her lips, and the long blessed hair
> Has fallen on her face; the Light of Lights
> Looks always on the motive, not the deed,
> The Shadow of Shadows on the deed alone.

Logically, this conclusion of the play cannot be defended. It is also, I think, a mistake in drama. A sacrifice that turns out to be no sacrifice at all loses most of its pathos, and the beauty of the Countess Cathleen's action is inevitably cheapened for us by the knowledge that she was saved its consequence. Even in a commercial theatre it is no longer necessary for the dramatist to invent at all costs a "happy ending." That Mr. Yeats has invented one for *The Countess Cathleen* seems to me a matter of deep irony. However, it is the only fault I find with him. For the rest, he has written a poem of exquisite and moving beauty. I do not suggest that he is a dramatist in the sense in which Maeterlinck is a dramatist. He is so far a dramatist that he can tell things simply and clearly in dramatic form. But he is, pre-eminently, a poet; and for him words, and the ordering of words, are always the chief care and delight. His verses, more than the verses of any other modern poet, seem made to be chanted; and it is, I fancy, this peculiar vocal quality of his work, rather than any keen sense of drama, that has drawn him into writing for the stage.

Max Beerbohm. SR (London). May 13, 1899, p. 587

Mr. Yeats makes no technical alterations in the English poetic drama. He takes a few of the accepted variations of the heroic line whereby the effect of monotony may be broken up, and tries to create a blank verse on that basis, using the strict line occasionally as the old men used the broken line to heighten the effect or to give balance.

A more definite and satisfactory contribution to the art he practises is to be noticed in his introduction into his plays of fays and fairies and the whole vague choir of an impalpable demonology. He concerns himself thus with certain aspects of human thought, which, though exclusively Irish in his treatment of them, are yet of universal interest. It may surely seem strange to a later critic of our age that a dramatist of these days could write plays like *The Land of Heart's Desire* or *The Countess Cathleen* with their mediaeval mysticism and eerie superstitions now so alien to the language in which they are expressed. For whom, one is inclined to ask, is such a play as *The Land of Heart's Desire* written? It tells of a fay, or a "good person," entering the house of some peasants who are sitting talking to the priest. The fay persuades the father to put the crucifix into another room out of sight and takes away the soul of a girl who is present. One is aware, of course, that there is still a widespread belief in fairies and all such mysterious spirits in Ireland, but such a belief in them as is indicated in this play seems obscurantist and rather affected.

If it is the object of the Irish National Theatre to re-awaken the national spirit, it seems hardly a likely way to encourage it by coddling its pretty superstitions. One does not argue about the existence of fairies and such creatures. When one has no personal experience, one says simply they may or may not be, but to present them merely in a picturesque way without any regard to the opposition of modern science seems a lazy method of revitalising a nation weakened in its self-belief. I fancy there is more of the true spirit of nationalism in Mr. Shaw's satirical contrast of English and Irish ideals in *John Bull's Other Island* than in most of Mr. Yeats' dramas. Even *Cathleen Ni Houlihan* draws its force out of a memory.

Edward Storer. *BR*. March, 1914, pp. 418–19

It is customary to deplore the loss to Irish poetry which has resulted from the absorption of Yeats by the theatre. It should not, however, be forgotten that this interest in drama did not come to him as a later phase. His first published work, which appeared in *The Dublin University Review* in 1885, was *The Island of Statues: An Arcadian Faery Tale in Two Acts,* followed in 1886 by *Mosada, a Dramatic Poem,* both of which indicate a certain leaning towards the dramatic form of writing. Neither was written, of course, with a view of being produced upon the stage, but, though subsequent practical experience has given the author some command of the technique of the theatre, those early poems are not so widely removed from the later plays as might be imagined. The dramatic element being usually subordinate to the poetic, the young poet is still plainly visible in the more experienced playwright. The development of Yeats as a dramatist is intimately connected with the development of the Irish National Theatre, but it is hardly correct to say that the latter is responsible for the former. The rise of the Dramatic Movement in 1899 coincided with the culmination of his lyric efforts in *The Wind among the Reeds,* but . . . the relative inactivity which ensued may be attributed to another cause. The creation of a national theatre did not so completely absorb the lyricist as is usually asserted. If Yeats devoted himself with such intensity of purpose to the work of the theatre it was because he felt that there he would find opportunities to develop, rather than in the direction he had hitherto exclusively followed.

The Dramatic Movement was the occasion, not the cause, of the second phase of Yeats's evolution. The dramatic instinct was in him from the beginning. [1916]

Ernest Boyd. *Ireland's Literary Renaissance*
(New York, Barnes & Noble, 1968), pp. 145–46

On the whole, though Mr. Yeats has enriched the theatre of our time with much that is beautiful, it cannot be maintained that he is entirely at home on the stage. Two or three of his plays are dramatic in the ordinary meaning of the word, but all the others depend upon something which is strictly not necessary to the theatre. In few of his plays is there any action, and in one only is there any attempt made at individual characterisation. Of course, Mr. Yeats has stated that characterisation is the attribute of comedy only, and comedy he has resigned to others. He has made few experiments in form, but in the verse treatment of his subject-matter he has been a pioneer in the modern theatre. He is not the greatest of the symbolists, in fact it is doubtful if he be a profound thinker at all. Surfaces and emotions have attracted him more than logic and thought, and always he has held that reality is in the mind only. No one will ever remember the names of his characters after they leave the theatre, they will not go home with audiences as [Ibsen's] Nora Helmer goes with them, or [Synge's] Christy Mahon, but audiences will want to read the plays when they have seen them so that the beauty of their lyrical content may be enjoyed more fully and more frequently. In every sense he is the poet in the theatre rather than the poet-dramatist, and it is remarkable that he has no successor in the Abbey Theatre. The verse plays of younger poets have been rejected and have been left for little theatres in England to put upon their stages. So Mr. Yeats stands alone as the only poet-dramatist of the Irish theatre, not so much because he is the only one as because the work of the others has never been produced. That his contribution to the modern theatre has been remarkable will be admitted, but it cannot be contended that he is a great dramatist.

Andrew E. Malone. *The Irish Drama* (New York,
Charles Scribner's Sons, 1929), pp. 145–46

The poetic plays of Yeats, those of his three phases, all spring from a lyrical impulse. That impulse never leaps beyond one act, and these one-act plays have all the attributes in content and in style of a lyric poem. They are sparse in substance and economical in speech, from his earlier wistfulness of loveliness to his later wispiness of power; for subject, there always appears the same conflict of spirit or intellect. In these plays majesty descends on threadbare speech; we gaze upon the sinewy thigh; through his invigoration, poetry on the stage again becomes sovereign. He had dreamed of a poetic stage, as I have said, with himself as main occupant; and that is what he has achieved. The influence of his distinguished work, particularly the influence of his earlier lyric work is seen in subsequent English and Scottish verse plays. Watch for it in [John] Masefield, in [Gordon] Bottomley, in [John] Drinkwater—not to mention Fiona Macleod. Yet, curiously, his influence on Irish poets produced no subsequent verse plays in the Abbey Theatre. "The Irish movement began with Yeats and will end with Yeats," said George Moore. Is it possible that Moore prophesied correctly, at least concerning the production of Irish poetic plays? We will not admit it.

> F. R. Higgins. In Lennox Robinson, ed., *The Irish Theatre* (London, Macmillan, 1939), pp. 85–86

During the early days of the Irish Theatre [Yeats] worked hard at production, producing not only his own plays, but, with Lady Gregory, the other plays in the repertory. Ten years later, when he made me Manager and Producer of the Theatre, his only reason for doing so (I had no technical qualifications) was that I had written a promising play or two, and a dramatist should know his instrument. Consciously or unconsciously he knew that he himself had learned his instrument in those years of producing, and he was not putting a beginner to school. By the time I came to the Theatre, in 1910, the days of his great verse-plays were over, but I made the first production in Ireland of *The Player Queen,* some of the Plays for Dancers, *The Words upon the Window-Pane, The King of the Great Clock Tower* and *The Resurrection,* and his two translations from Sophocles. With the exception of the first play, which was produced during his absence in England, while not actually producing them, he took an active part in their rehearsal. Strange to say, he had not many, perhaps had not any, theories about the speaking of verse. He hated any affectation of speech; chanting or crooning would drive him frantic; his ideal verse-speaker should have a rich and varied voice and the sense of acting that evokes those qualities. These things come only from constant practice in verse-speaking, practice which makes verse come as naturally from the lips of the player as does prose. If he never got in Dublin the theatre of poetry he had dreamed of, it was not for the want of a few very good verse-speakers—I instance Frank Fay and Sara Allgood—and others who were potentially good; the theatre of his dream failed because the Irish theatre took a different, a realistic path. But that theatre had been founded to be a National Theatre, a mouthpiece for the young writers of Ireland; he had never intended it to be his particular plaything, and when the young writers turned away from poetry, he more and more as the years passed allowed his own work to be put on one side. Lady Gregory might plead, I might plead, it was of little use. He had an artist's pride; he knew he could only rely on an audience which would be polite but indifferent to his work, which would count the moments until the curtain fell on *Deirdre* and rose again on some peasant comedy or some tragedy dealing with an event very close to their own life. Later on, he was to make his own theatre for his peers. [1940]

Lennox Robinson. In Stephen Gwynn, ed., *William Butler Yeats: Essays in Tribute* (Port Washington, N.Y., Kennikat, 1965), pp. 72–75

In Yeats three things work together which in creative writers had for a long time been antagonistic: spiritual, dramatic, and poetic values. He had a life to express, he was a poet, and he had an acute sense of the power of dramatic form. His plays, therefore, which have so distinct an originality that they might seem to call for a judgement only on their intrinsic value, have in fact a wider historical significance as well. For the continuity of drama and its connection with the main stream of poetic writing his work is much more important than that of either Synge or the "realists."

In technique he asserts in a new way the virtue of convention and formality, exploring to the full the expressiveness of design in speech, movement, stage-setting and music. But his formal patterns are always appropriate; they are an extension of the convention of verse itself and fulfil the same function of enhancing expression, of making explicit the poet's theme and subject. . . .

In subject-matter Yeats broke new ground in attempting to adjust drama to the vital trends of artistic effort, which were towards the exploring of more and more complex and subtle mental worlds. He indicated that the content and expressiveness of the form could in fact be extended in a new direction. That he had emotion and vision of the kind that suit lyric poetry was under the circumstances more help than hindrance, because it freed him from the slavery of preconceptions. The picture of moral relations that we find in most drama was not his subject; so from the start he could search unhampered for the dramatic form of what was his subject. To have been more "dramatic" in the conventional sense would have done less for drama.

Ronald Peacock. *The Poet in the Theatre* (New York, Harcourt, Brace, 1946), pp. 125–26

The five plays which date from 1903 to 1910 are filled with [Yeats's] sense of guilt at having separated himself from "the normal active man." The first of these, *On Baile's Strand,* was written on the theme of father against son which was close to Yeats's heart as it was to Matthew Arnold's. Yeats had handled the theme before in a short verse narrative, but into his new treatment he put "heart-mysteries," as he admitted near the end of his life. Though the armed combat is between Cuchulain and the stranger who will not give his name, the real struggle is between the warrior Cuchulain, instinctively loving and hating, and the crafty king Conchubar who forces Cuchulain to slay unwittingly his own son. Cuchulain's tragic fate, like

Yeats's own, is caused by his listening to the voice of apparent reason; instead of following his impulse to make friends with the unknown warrior, he allows Conchubar to persuade him that the cry of his heart is witchcraft, and discovers too late the identity of his opponent. Yeats never explained this meaning of the play, said in fact that he had forgotten what his symbols meant except that the fool and blind man, who constitute a kind of chorus to the main action, are the shadows of Cuchulain and Conchubar. Thus he divided himself into four parts: the warrior and his opposite, the fool; the wise man and his opposite, the helpless blind man; and put all his raging bitterness into blind man and fool who steal the bread from the ovens while Cuchulain, overcome with grief at what he has done, battles madly with the waves.

Richard Ellmann. Yeats: The Man and the Masks
(New York, Macmillan, 1948), pp. 166–67

While Bernard Shaw could base his kind of drama on the sort of performance in which the post-Ibsen actor excelled, a performance marked by a clear grasp of psychology and idea, by urbanity and pace, by colloquial tone and realistic facial expression—in a word, by prose excellence—Yeats's whole theory and practice were devised in revulsion from the whole Ibsenite-Shavian movement. He proposed two alternatives. The first was to cut below it. Beneath the surface of middle-class civilization there still lurked, in Ireland at least, a peasant culture possessing a living speech and not yet wholly robbed of simple human responses. Not feeling competent to tap this vein himself, Yeats pushed Lady Gregory and J. M. Synge into doing so. For him, the second alternative: to rise above "the play about modern educated people," a drama confined to "the life of the drawing-room," in a drama of symbol and myth. He asked for a theater that was everything the naturalistic theater was not—something "remote, spiritual and ideal," he wrote as a young man. "Distinguished, indirect, symbolic," was his later characterization. Throughout his career he believed in "a drama of energy, of extravagance, of phantasy, of musical and noble speech." It was to be a theater to liberate the mind, a theater in which one would feel no uneasiness when the final curtain falls, a theater in which all would be caught in "one lofty emotion," an "emotion of multitude."

Yeats was asking for something neither the Abbey Theatre nor any existing theater could provide. Even if there had been a public, there were no actors for it. The acting profession is not divided into radically different schools of practice. A particular style dominates the whole profession for a good many years; then under the impetus of a new major force in the theater—usually a playwright—a new style breaks through and in turn becomes the only one. Now, Yeats began to write for the theater at a time when such a new style—that of naturalism—was in the first flush of energy. If he could not make use of it—many anti-naturalistic playwrights did—he could not easily make use of the modern theater. After all, much as W. G. Fay acted in Yeats, his favorite modern playwright was J. M. Barrie!

Being a poet, Yeats was not frightened by the prospect of isolation. He simply declared: "I want, not a theatre, but the theatre's antiself." And: "I want . . . an unpopular theatre." Since by this time—the time of the First World War—he had been thoroughly schooled in theater practice, isolation would do him no harm, if he could stand it; the older Ibsen was almost as isolated. Indeed, isolation meant to Yeats the freedom to work with the dramatic techniques he had acquired unhampered by the thousand bothersome circumstances of every actual theater. Cut loose from the box office, as well as from Stanislavskyan actors, he could range as widely as he chose. Even as far afield as Japan. [1948]

Eric Bentley. *In Search of Theater* (New York,
Alfred A. Knopf, 1953), pp. 321–22

In W. B. Yeats the Irish drama had not only a founder, an acute business man and a courageous fighter, but something without which these would have been barren, a visionary poet . . . Whether or not he was primarily a dramatist matters little; many of the Elizabethans were not, but they produced one of the greatest surviving bodies of drama. He was, or made himself, enough of a dramatist for his purpose; he apprenticed himself to stage technique, and his belief in the theatre as the vehicle of poetry was strong enough for him to work with endless patience at the expression of his vision in dramatic form. His plays, even the earliest, are not lyric or narrative poetry loosely attached to a dramatic form; no more are they the drama of the library only, as were perforce those of the English poets of the nineteenth century. The union, however new to his century, was integral, not incidental.

In his early plays, *The Land of Heart's Desire, The Countess Cathleen* and *The Shadowy Waters,* he communicated his experience of certain aspects of beauty. Neither then nor at any other time did he allow influences which were not part of his artistic experience to affect his poetry or his drama. This is not, of course, to say that he did not accept all aesthetic experience that offered itself, even to the exploration of some of the stranger territories of metaphysical speculation, as in *Where There Is Nothing* at the beginning of his career or *The Words upon the Window-Pane* some thirty years later. But, strict as was his discipline in such matters as theatrical technique, he never allowed even the technique of the theatre so to interfere at the moment of conception as to modify the resulting material and its inevitable choice of form. This, though it did not always make for theatrical effectiveness (it did not, clearly, in *The Shadowy Waters*), made, in the long run, for something of far deeper value, the habit of and a testimony to that

artistic integrity which is at once a severe, positive discipline and the inseparable companion of great poetry. In the next phase of his dramatic writing,
in *The Hour-Glass, The Unicorn from the Stars* and *The King's Threshold*,
thought and sensation deepened and clarified and both drew closer together,
just as, in the heroic plays of the same period, *On Baile's Strand, Deirdre*
and *The Green Helmet*, there was a simpler presentation, the implications
lying deep beneath the surface of the words. This is still more noticeable in
the five *Plays for Dancers*, where there was a plain confronting of mystery
stripped of all unnecessary substance, narrative or dramatic, and most noticeable of all in the latest plays, *The Resurrection, The Words upon the
Window-Pane* and *Purgatory*.

Una Ellis Fermor. *The Irish Dramatic Movement,* 2nd ed.
(London, Methuen, 1954), pp. 91–92

Yeats was introduced to the Japanese Nō by Ezra Pound, who was translating excerpts with the help of Ernest Fenellosa. He saw the relation to his
own work, and of course admired the plays as the work of dedicated artists
done for a class of cultivated warrior-aristocrats—this was for Yeats the true
heroic situation for poetry, life being all action and courtesy, poetry all
contemplation and style. . . .

Every aspect of the technique and presentation of Nō must have struck
Yeats as certain proof of the soundness of his own theory of drama, which
in itself stems from the Romantic Image. Above all these were dance-plays,
and so antithetical to the realism that was, in Yeats's view, draining the
force of the theatre, so hostile indeed to the whole mimetic tradition of the
West, that the players went masked. The Nō answered, better than Wagner
or any merely synaesthetic experiment, the prayer of a Symbolist poet for a
fitting theatre—Mallarmé had desired a Symbolist drama but was put off by
the prospect of irrelevant *expressions* in the actors' faces—and though they
came too late to coincide with Yeats's earlier mood of heroic vision they
provided him with a drama-medium in which he at last fully found himself
as a poet for the theatre. . . . His actors would have the blank, inward
faces of the wooden Japanese masks; they would not necessarily even speak
their own lines. Musicians would frame the action, and comment in song.
All would be inexplicit, suggestive, but faultless in design; and often the
climax of the play would be a dance like Salome's. There would be no
separable meaning; the verses would be spoken as the dance was danced,
and would dispense with that kind of expression that points "meaning."

Frank Kermode. *Romantic Image*
(London, Routledge & Kegan Paul, 1957), pp. 78–80

The Death of Cuchulain is the most majestically designed and the most
perfect of the five [Cuchulain] plays. Yeats has moved a long way from the

altogether more obscurely rendered antinomies of *On Baile's Strand*. In the last play he contrived more explicitly than ever before, and with a bold disregard for the timider realisms which it is not absurd to compare with the methods of Shakespeare's last plays, the acting out of the ironies attendant upon the hero's nature and fate. This is done by the characteristic Yeatsian method, which has operated in all the plays, of building up episode against episode and character against character so that the antitheses they form permit the ironic inference to be drawn, or culminate in a moment of revealingly double-natured action: the heroic decision that is also a mistaking *(On Baile's Strand, The Death of Cuchulain)*, the love or courage whose expression in action unties the knot one way only to tighten it in another *(The Only Jealousy [of Emer], At the Hawk's Well)*. Yeats's strategy for putting the mythological hero on to the modern stage was cautious and full of ironic reserve in this series of plays. This saved his subject from the Pre-Raphaelite and rhapsodic air that dates the earlier Abbey plays, and from other perishable simplicities, Ossianic or patriotic. But he is never mean or malicious to his hero, and did not permit his audiences to look upon him with a levelling or a rancorous eye or "pull established honour down."

Peter Ure. *Yeats the Playwright*
(London, Routledge & Kegan Paul, 1963), pp. 82–83

The plays take up the primary questions posed by *A Vision:* how do we account for the perpetual vigor of the imagination, and how should we react in the presence of an obsolete poetic tradition? In *The Player Queen,* we are counseled to cast the old tradition aside, without regret, and accept whatever bizarre inspiration the new dispensation may provide. The Dance Plays insist on the mutual subjugation of poet and Muse, and the mixed nature of all art. The "religious plays," *Calvary* and *The Resurrection,* show that the symbols which are the vehicles of inspiration lose their validity with time, and must be discarded in favor of a new revelation, which is generally the direct opposite of the preceding gospel. In the purgatorial plays, Yeats is concerned with the process whereby experience is "abstracted" from its context in life and made suitable for art; and finally, in the Cuchulain plays, Yeats shows us the conflicting claims laid by life and Muse upon the artist.

Helen Hennessy Vendler. *Yeats's "Vision" and the Later Plays* (Cambridge, Mass., Harvard University Press, 1963), p. 254

It is noteworthy that three of these "dramas of perception," three middle and late plays which are quite different from each other in form and which cover the most significant periods of Yeats's dramatic development, have as their common subject the essential Francesca-Paolo-Dante situation. *The Dreaming of the Bones* is one of the plays for dancers with which Yeats experimented after studying the Noh drama of Japan—the very antiself of circumstantial realism. *The Words upon the Window-Pane,* in which the spirit of Swift interrupts a seance, uses realistic set, characters, and method. However, Yeats has picked the one occasion on which realism must testify against its own completeness or sufficiency as truth. *Purgatory* is a third sort of drama, showing a realism simplified, stylized, reduced to barest essentials, so that the play becomes symbolical without being cut off from the recognizable world. It successfully fuses elements of the two previous forms. . . .

That these plays, with some of the Noh plays which he studied, show a marked similarity in subject is only an instance of the general similarity among Yeats's plays. His favorite action of recognition often appears as the recognition of some sort of supernatural manifestation. This action is often given a twist, the recognition being not only of the manifestation but of the witness's own nature or circumstance. To see the ghost is often to live over, but symbolically, simultaneously, in full knowledge of their fateful meaning, one's moment of greatest passion or suffering. The external manifestation parallels and dramatizes an internal recognition.

Yeats's entire dramatic production reveals this remarkable consistency in subject preference. Some sort of vision of the supernatural is important in almost every play.

David R. Clark. *W. B. Yeats and the Theatre of Desolate Reality* (Dublin, Dolmen, 1965), pp. 23–24

It is perhaps indicative of their failure to offer a serious presentation of the supernatural that *The Land of Heart's Desire, The Countess Cathleen,* and even *On Baile's Strand* are so easily accepted into the traditional repertory. If *Purgatory* is also accepted, I think that must be laid to the fact that the play looks a little like [Beckett's] *Waiting for Godot,* that is, seems to fit into the new fashion.

The question then is this: Do the last plays, understood as serious embodiments of spiritual reality, have any place in the tradition of plays that deserve a stage, or are they brilliant closet dramas at best, despite Yeats's intention? One easy answer is to "interpret" these plays in some way so that they do become psychological after all. Another such answer, a better one, is to invoke the "willing suspension of disbelief," to say, in substance, that in their own terms the plays are valid, as *The Divine Comedy* is valid for non-Catholics or unmedieval Catholics.

The first answer will not do; the second is somewhat evasive and fails to do justice to what I have called Yeats's philosophical seriousness as a playwright. For Yeats demands belief, if not in his system, then in the reality the system names and orders. Just how much belief he demanded is indicated by the requirements for staging his dance plays: better than fair actors, unremitting adherence to the convention, and an audience that comes with no expectation of daily reality or some noble form of it. Yeats saw to it, in short, that his last words in the drama would not be easily domesticated to the modern stage. And naturally enough the reaction from those not willing to make concessions to so stubborn an eccentric has been indifference, baffled irritation, or patronizing dismissal. It is one thing to admit the "theatre of the absurd" into the repertory; it is quite another to admit what looks very odd but lays claim to being just the opposite. Yeats is perhaps *too* clear to misinterpret on this score. So he can be safely left to the bravery of college theatres which may not be quite so devoted to fashion and so much the victims of box office. Or the plays can be studied in class as literature, an adjunct to the poems but less important than some of the secondary texts used.

Yeats understood the consequences of his position but was willing to take the risks. He never expected, at least in our era, that he would be regarded as another in a long line of tragic playwrights of the western tradition and that his last plays would be familiar to a wide audience, so perhaps any justification of these plays as part of the great tradition is beside the point.

Leonard E. Nathan. *The Tragic Drama of William Butler Yeats: Figures in a Dance* (New York, Columbia University Press, 1965), pp. 252–53

One must always remember that the later plays of Yeats, no matter how closely they are related to the theories of *A Vision . . .* were not written for an audience of adepts in those theories. The Old Man who acts as prologue in *The Death of Cuchulain* may demand an audience of no more than a hundred, but he does not require even these select few to have read *A Vision:* ". . . they must know the old [Irish] epics and Mr. Yeats's plays about them: such people, however poor, have libraries of their own."

Nor were these plays written merely to be read; the whole tone of the stage directions ought to be enough to convince us on this point. Except at the very beginning of his career, in works like *Mosada* and *The Island of Statues* which he soon rejected, Yeats did not write closet dramas, intended to be read rather than performed. On the contrary, having written as yet only two plays that he felt to be "stageworthy," he overcame enormous obstacles—political and economic as well as artistic—in order to found a theater that would perform his plays to his satisfaction, and incidentally the plays of others. The Abbey Theatre, however much it may have grown away from Yeats, is first of all the monument of a poet who despised closet drama and who went on writing plays for its stage all his life. *Purgatory,* written the year before he died, was not a Noh play for the drawing room but a piece of blood-and-thunder for the Abbey stage on which it appeared as soon as written. It should be obvious, though to some academic critics it is not, that when Yeats called a work of his a play, he meant it to be played—and knew enough, from long experience and hard labor in the theater, to make it playable. Forty-five years, remember! Nobody can do anything, even write academic criticism, for forty-five years without learning something about it.

Vivian Mercier. *MD*. Sept., 1965, pp. 162–63

It is clear, when one thinks of the Cuchulain plays as a cycle, that *At the Hawk's Well* and *The Only Jealousy of Emer* are the most successful; feeling and form are indistinguishable. Everything comes together—theme, gesture, rhythm, dance. If form means achieved content, as modern critics say, these plays are formal satisfactions. *On Baile's Strand,* beautiful as it is and drawn from the same sources of feeling, has an air of existing at one remove from Yeats's deepest concerns, and the reason must be a defect of form. The play gives an impression of being a made thing, if well-made; it does not move to its own tune. In *The Death of Cuchulain* the dance form has not survived at all: like nearly everything else at this late stage—Symbolism, mask, role-playing—the form exists so that it may be abused, and most of the feeling is in the abuse. The play is remarkably powerful, as many of Yeats's last poems are, but its feeling spills out on all sides: we love it for the recklessness with which it turns against itself. A theater in which the Noh, Nietzsche, Mallarmé, and Yeats would find themselves simultaneously acknowledged would be a monster. Yeats did not devise such a thing; it may always have been a chimera. One or another personality must predominate. In that respect the most fortunate dominance was the Noh, because it enabled Yeats to "climb to his proper dark" out of the conventional theater. Mallarmé qualifies Yeats's theater, gives it a nuance of feeling not otherwise possible; Nietzsche brought turbulence, inciting Yeats to release his own.

Denis Donoghue. *William Butler Yeats*
(New York, Viking, 1971), p. 118

From the very beginning of the Irish dramatic movement there had been disagreement about the kinds of plays that should be written. To name the chief authors who contributed in the early days of excitement to the founding of a new dramatic literature is to list talents so individualistic and so widely varying in temperament and technique that the wonder is how they could have collaborated as closely as they did. Douglas Hyde, Edward Martyn, George Moore, AE, Yeats himself, Lady Gregory, and then Synge—they are a fascinating group. But even before Synge's death in 1909 it was unfortunately evident that Yeats was to have no competitor for his kind of poetic drama. Nor in fact did Synge or the sometimes underestimated Lady Gregory have real followers either. Only in Synge's work, perhaps, were the two streams of mythological fantasy and contemporary reality success-fully combined in a way to ensure permanent interest. In Yeats's plays, which already show constant experimentation and change not only from one play to the next but even in different versions of the same play, a singular devotion to *both* poetry and theater produced a splendid variety of drama unified by the belief that the revelations of poetic truth provide the most strikingly dramatic instances of how reality enters life. Yeats deliberately avoided everything the drama he disliked emphasized: the effect of casual conversation arising out of homely situation, interesting little touches of personal eccentricity to "humanize" character, all the critical perplexities any ordinary person might have to face. But he never left out of account the pressure of that usually invisible and inaudible world operating on principles beyond the scope and control of restless, time-bound men but not to be disregarded by them. According to their ability to respond to the challenge, this force might destroy or liberate, or sometimes do both at once. Cuchulain in *On Baile's Strand* is the kind of hero who disrupts established order for the sake of a greater order to which he instinctively belongs. For Yeats, whose curiosity about occult knowledge and ardent desire to master its imagery were life-long pursuits, the writing of such plays was neither insincere nor soul-destroying. For most other writers it might well have been.

John Rees Moore. *Masks of Love and Death: Yeats as Dramatist* (Ithaca, N.Y., Cornell University Press, 1971), pp. 30–31

Among the great modern Irish dramatists, W. B. Yeats may be the most enigmatic—at once open and concealed, both simple and complex. His poetic preeminence is undisputed, at least among writers in English. Yet his plays have dropped from the repertory of the Abbey and may even be unproduceable today. The considerable authority of his accomplishment in the drama is undeniable, though, for his sensitive and perceptive peers. For all the social and ideological conservatism of his plays, their peculiar vibrancy and spontaneity reflects Yeats's enormous resources of imagination. Despite his leadership of nationalist agitations, his aristocratic prejudices, and his refusal to accompany many of his artistic countrymen to exile, Yeats is an extremely ambivalent artist. His works, for all their elitist tendencies, remain almost embarrassingly rooted in the sweat and mire of desperate human struggle.

Superficially, J. M. Synge seems Yeats's closest associate in his revival of revitalized Irish poetic theatre. Both reject a theatre of protest, ideology, and persuasion, an approach Yeats took only fleetingly in his early *The Countess Cathleen* (1892) and *Cathleen Ni Houlihan* (1902). If their countrymen are to be saved, it will come not through the reform or destruction of institutions, but through a rebirth of humane sensitivity. Both are absorbed by the artless, "poetic" speech patterns of an untutored peasantry, free of stultified, materialistic reflexes. And although both attempted, for a time, to reveal the temper of their nation through realistic treatments of folkloric incidents often in remote, unblemished settings, both involuntarily overcame the narrow theoretical limitations they imposed on their art.

Still, for all their resemblances Yeats is even further removed from Synge than Shaw is from Ibsen. Rather than letting his stories spread outward toward other stories without, however, losing their roots in psychological states of mind as Synge and O'Casey did, Yeats deliberately used mythic patterns in the mode of Eliot and Joyce; he pulled them in or brought them down to earth in concrete, modern meanings. Synge's awareness of evil exists side by side with a very strong sense of personal identity. His fury at inhumanity is mollified by his personal warmth and social optimism. But for Yeats, the personality is split apart and acknowledged to be so. He is harrowed by a sense of inner pulsations between fixed, dangerously inadequate and unstable poles. Synge's concretely sensuous language both links and distances his characters' passion and contemplation. Yeats's personae, like Pirandello's, are created and seen to be masklike, stripped down to their abstract humanity. Bereft of a self in its health and complexity to mitigate their sense of panic and emptiness, they see no refuge from unceasing inner conflict in their blinding rationality.

Emil Roy. British Drama since Shaw (Carbondale, Ill., Southern Illinois University Press, 1972), pp. 36–37

The dream of establishing in Ireland a ritual theatre like that of Aeschylus and Sophocles, which came to dominate Yeats' imagination, had its roots in the somewhat older dream of establishing on Irish soil rites like those of Eleusis and Samothrace.

The ancient Celtic saga materials were as important to Yeats' theatre work as they were to his work on the Irish Mystical Order. When Alfred Nutt offered to supply Yeats with translations of the old Gaelic epics if he would undertake to pick the best versions and put his English upon them, he declined. Lady Gregory took up the project, making or finding the translations herself. The result was her *Cuchulain of Muirthemne,* the book which Yeats used as the basis for his Cuchulain plays. In the Cuchulain plays, which Yeats wrote between the years 1902 and 1939, we can trace the growth of Yeats' power to adapt certain of the ideas which had their origins in the work on the Celtic rituals to the requirements of theatrical presentation.

In *On Baile's Strand,* the first written of the Cuchulain plays, Yeats took Shakespeare as his model. The early version of the play owes something to the technique of *King Lear* but the resemblance is superficial. After much revision of the play, Yeats, who regularly attended and wrote about the Shakespeare productions at Stratford-on-Avon, seems to have penetrated to the heart of Shakespeare's techniques. In the final version of *On Baile's Strand,* Yeats uses the fool in a way which closely parallels Shakespeare's treatment of the fool in *Lear,* that most symbolic of Shakespeare's plays. In *The Green Helmet,* Yeats experimented boldly in an effort to capture the peculiar tone of the Irish sagas themselves. He adapts imagery, stagecraft and theme to a *genre* he calls "heroic farce."

Reg Skene. The Cuchulain Plays of W. B. Yeats
(New York, Columbia University Press, 1974), p. 13

Yeats's quest for a means to bring "personal utterance" into the theatre led him through perhaps the widest range of experiment of any major dramatist in the history of the theatre. . . . I believe it is a mistake to view Yeats's development as a continuous evolution towards a definitive dramatic form. No one play or series of plays at any given time can adequately reveal the many-sided greatness of Yeats. Taken as a whole, Yeats's work ranges from the epic sweep of *The Countess Cathleen* to the taut Beckettian introspection of *Purgatory*; from the exquisitely poetical *The Shadowy Waters* to the total theatricality of *Fighting the Waves* and *The King of the Great Clock Tower* in which words were intended to be lost in "patterns of sound as the name of God is lost in Arabian arabesques." In almost every instance, the form of an individual play is an organic reflection of its content. Yet there is an astonishing consistency of purpose and coherence of thought to the entire body of Yeats's dramatic work. While some of his plays are undoubtedly more successful than others, at his best Yeats was not merely a poet in the theatre but a poetic dramatist who combined the arts of literature and the theatre so as to create effective and profoundly significant drama.

The development of Yeats the dramatist cannot be separated from the development of Yeats the poet; nor can the development of Yeats the poet be separated from the society in which he lived or the theatre in which he first practised. During the short period of time in which Yeats specifically wrote plays for the Abbey Theatre, he learned his trade as a dramatist. One may ask whether *The Hour-Glass* is theatrically as successful as *Purgatory,* but without question its revisions prepared the way for the success of his later plays. It is also probable that the revisions of *The Hour-Glass* encouraged Yeats to explore again the theatrical possibilities of ritual through the dramaturgical form of the dance plays.

Through his involvement with the Abbey Theatre, Yeats developed not merely dramaturgical skills and innovative theatrical ideas but a much deeper awareness of himself as a man and artist. Out of his personal struggles and disappointments at the early Abbey Yeats evolved his conception of tragedy with its profound implications for the conduct of life. From his practical work as a dramatist Yeats discovered that it was only as a poet that he was able to express the full metaphysical and spiritual implications of his tragic vision of life.

James W. Flannery. *W. B. Yeats and
the Idea of a Theatre* (New Haven, Conn.,
Yale University Press, 1976), pp. 314–16

The basic question for the criticism of Yeats's plays is now, "In what context are they best examined?" The answer is quite plainly—the context which has hitherto been ignored: that of the one-act play. . . . What he did was to invent the modern Irish tradition of the one-act play; he sustained it by constant experiment in his own work; he nurtured it by encouraging his fellow-writers to write one-act plays; he exalted it by giving the one-act theatre the best dramatic verse to be written since the seventeenth century. . . .

Yeats used the short play to make various experiments in dramatic form crucial to his art in such works as *The Shadowy Waters, The Land of Heart's Desire, At the Hawk's Well, The Player Queen,* and *The Resurrection.* He explored the life and death of the hero in his cycle of plays about the Celtic warrior-god Cuchulain. The theme of the quest for the absolute he dramatised in *The Shadowy Waters* and *At the Hawk's Well.* Related to this concern is the religious theme in *The Countess Cathleen, The Hour-Glass, Calvary, The Cat and the Moon, The Resurrection,* and *The Herne's Egg.* He widened his scope yet further with his passionate treatment of politics in *Cathleen Ni Houlihan, The Dreaming of the Bones,* and *The Death of Cuchulain.* His thematic range is greater yet: he gave us masterly treatments of love in *Deirdre, The Only Jealousy of Emer, A Full Moon in March, The Words upon the Window-Pane,* and *Purgatory.* Such is their richness and suggestiveness that they can, of course, be discussed under several headings. *Purgatory,* for instance, explores the consequences of an ill-fated love-match, but it is also an exploration of the soul's relationship to necessity and free-will, besides being a grim political statement about Ireland. Yet the central action of the play is the murder of a youth by his own father. All this Yeats could cram into a short one-act play. There is an analogy for this rich use of the miniature in Yeats's poetry. It is the sonnet "Leda and the Swan." We can trace the development of the after-piece and curtain-raiser towards the serious one-acter through Yeats's career: for instance we may analyse the use of the form in its nineteenth-century guise of curtain-raiser in *The Land of Heart's Desire,* and then trace the political themes in *Cathleen Ni Houlihan,* an after-piece, and in *The Dreaming of the Bones* and *The Death of Cuchulain,* a group of plays which conveniently reveals the fertility of Yeats's one-act technique.

Andrew Parkin. *The Dramatic Imagination
of W. B. Yeats* (New York, Barnes & Noble,
1978), pp. 55–56

There is no need, really, for the rather widespread feeling that [Yeats's] plays cannot be appreciated without a great deal of special knowledge. In a teasing phrase Yeats once spoke of different levels of meaning in his work, for the Boy and for the Sage. This could be taken as endorsement of the esoteric view of his drama, but it does not have to be, for in a way it is true of all drama of any richness; we receive from it according to the mental store we bring to it. In that sense, certainly, Yeats's plays call for preparedness, but he writes in the first place, as all good playwrights do, for the Boy, for the open imagination, responsive to what is *there*, not daunted by surprise, but eager for it, wanting the experience, not the explanation of it. I want to take up that Boy's viewpoint, not arbitrarily shutting out knowledge when it would be natural to bring it in, but equally not feeling the need to bring it in nor to continually test my own responses on other critical interpretations, but rather to register my view of the plays in a context of the theatre of Beckett, Maeterlinck, O'Casey, as part of a great modern repertoire.

"Modern" may seem an odd word for the "antiquated romantic stuff" as the Old Man [in *The Death of Cuchulain*] sardonically calls it, out of which Yeats made his plays. How can anything be modern that is always looking backwards to Irish history and ancient legends, and if it takes the present for its theme, as in *The Dreaming of the Bones,* does so only to show it being invaded by a ghostly past? But it is not in the Irishness or in the ritual shaping of old legend and mythology that the heart of the drama lies, or so I am suggesting. All that is the "stuff." What Yeats fashioned from it is something different, a self-delighting theatrical process which continually reminds us of its theatricality, and in doing so subtly implies an analogy with the inner processes of the mind itself. It is a drama of the interior, which may use names like Cuchulain rather than Ygraine or Estragon, but has the same sense of timelessness as the plays of Maeterlinck and Beckett, and like theirs can be grasped intuitively, without benefit of book.

Katharine Worth. *The Irish Drama of Europe from
Yeats to Beckett* (Atlantic Highlands, N.J.,
Humanities Press, 1978), pp. 158–59

Yeats's use of verse in his plays should alert us to the fact that he is creating drama, that is, literature *and* theater. . . . Yeats's plays, indeed, connect the theater with resources of language and stage technique from which it had all but severed itself in his time; he seeks to attain in them the richness of language and technique of the ancient Greek, or the Elizabethan, or the Japanese stage. . . . It is the naturalistic play and not the poetic drama, Yeats would claim, which is eccentric in its relation to the golden ages of European and world drama. To exclude verse, dance, mask, and music from the theater is to rule out realms of expression and ways of feeling that were, and still can be, among the very richest aspects of drama.

So it is with Yeats's use of Irish mythology and his own mythology, set forth in *A Vision*. The use of myth, insofar as myth tends to universalize human experience, gives drama one of its greatest and most ancient strengths. Yeats's plays are, by and large, successful in their use of myth, so that one can argue that their action, characters, and setting tend to be archetypal, not merely Irish or Yeatsian. This is not to say that Yeats expects his audience to *identify* with the patterning of human experience embodied in a particular Irish myth; on the contrary, he usually employs various distancing techniques that result in his audience being *confronted* with myth. . . .

Though Irish myth and history are very important in any consideration of Yeats's work, they are important not because of their intrinsic value, but because they give Yeats, so often, a subject that is perfectly suited to the kind of symbolic, ritualistic drama he wanted to create. The element of ritual, the sense that drama has a religious significance in the way that it recreates myth and history, is, again, an important aspect of Yeats's plays, and one which, while it goes back to the origins of the drama, is virtually absent from modern drama. . . . The rare exceptions to Yeats's successful use of mythology do not indicate that Yeats is writing for a coterie, or that his drama is, in any real way, esoteric.

As for the brevity of most of Yeats's plays—it is, first of all, the nature of symbolic drama to be brief. Realistic drama requires a certain length because everything must be explained and accounted for, whereas symbolic drama operates in a different, archetypal realm, one to which details of time, place, and motivation are largely irrelevant. Moreover, when brevity is a concomitant, as it almost invariably is in Yeats, of such striking intensity and concentration, then brevity is not to be considered, necessarily, as a shortcoming.

Anthony Bradley. *William Butler Yeats* (New York, Frederick Ungar, 1979), pp. 243–45

GERMAN, AUSTRIAN, AND SWISS DRAMATISTS

FRIEDHELM RICKERT, EDITOR

BRECHT, BERTOLT (1898–1956)

On the theater posters Brecht gave his play [*Drums in the Night*] the alternate title *Anna, the Soldier's Fiancée*. The author's purpose in exaggerating this tired banality (an old device) was obviously to render harmless blunt criticism of the *plot's* banality. He had no need to do this. True, it is the same old story of the soldier, believed to be dead, who returns during the revolution just in time to confound his fiancée during her engagement party. And yet nothing is intrinsically banal, and the way the writer handles the situation does not make it so.

Brecht's dialogue is driven by a thrilling and soaring energy. Despite the visible influence of Strindberg, Wedekind, and Georg Kaiser, it strikes its own note—a raw scream from a blood-drenched throat. His rude, caricaturing hatred of the philistine is not cold like Sternheim's, and his redemptions are not calculated like those of Georg Kaiser.

This wretched soldier who has been expelled from the ranks of the living, this creature who has been mud-covered and withered by four years in the trenches and in African captivity is truly felt and given credible form. The way he stammers and gropes, very slowly rediscovering the thoughts and words for his feelings; the way his soul gradually awakens from its numbness; the way he stands there in dirty clothes, yearning and pure amid the elegantly dressed war profiteers—all this is experienced and honestly written.

The first two acts, with their impetuous theatrical tempo, could almost have been written by an unusually gifted naturalist of the 1880s. It is not until later that the expressionistic style acts as a brake on the play's theatrical power. The third and fourth scenes are completely dominated by con-

334

versation, and there is still too much talk in the fifth. It is lyrical, ecstatic, vulgar, and satirical—at times with a strong tone of original savagery—but it is still talk.

The dramatic movement comes to a halt. After the horrible disillusioning exchange with the fiancée, which forms the strong close of the second act, the returned soldier is supposed to slip into a nihilistic, revolutionary mood in the following scenes. But the talk takes up too much time for the small step forward on the dramatic road. The third act, too, must be more stringently compressed if the significant new turn in the hero's life, which it presents, is to be theatrically effective.

Julius Bab. Hannoversches Tageblatt. Dec. 23, 1922†

In the Jungle of Cities is Bertolt Brecht's third and richest drama. A police report from Chicago's Chinatown becomes a vision, and melodramatic material is transformed into an apocalyptic parable. Brecht does not "interpret" a criminal incident, which is what "observing" and psychologizing writers would have done. Nor does he seek to heighten the exciting aspects in the style of sensationalistic dramatists. . . .

Brecht creates an atmosphere in which shocking, inexplicable events must occur. With the very first words he establishes a third world in which the struggle between people on another plane, "suspended in the air," unfolds. The spectator can either accept or reject the author's assumptions. Either he feels the suggestive power of the language, or he remains totally indifferent to the entire drama. He either senses the current passing between the characters, or he finds everything "obscure."

The sequence of events embodies one of the boldest creative visions: the struggle between the Malayan lumber dealer, Shlink, and the lending-library clerk, George Garga, is fought with exchanged weapons. The destroyer, the Malayan, is motivated by self-renunciation and love; the defender, the white man, by hate and indignation. The characters flow into one another. They sink into and rise up out of the foul, flickering atmosphere of the "jungle" (Chicago's Chinatown). They exchange social positions in the jungle's dim light; they tear each other apart and seek relationships to one another. But the closer their circles approach, the further apart they move. Not even in hatred do Shlink and Garga come together.

Herbert Ihering. Berliner Börsen-Courier. May 12, 1923†

The hero of these fourteen scenes [of *Baal*] is a mixture—half self-portrait of the author, half the object on which Brecht takes out his hatred of his own impoverished soul and actions. The hero is viewed from two angles, and one understands the conflict in the spectator confronted by this character and its author. The man who created this figure was born with a poetic vision, but his soul is wretched, banal, and empty. Those spectators who applaud

(perhaps) see the poet, the bits of human yearning that live in him. . . .
Those who boo (perhaps) see the man behind the total portrait—his poverty
of soul and the fact that he is himself only too well aware of it. . . .

Thus, the conflict in Brecht becomes the conflict in the audience. The
attention of the audience is held at times by the freezing child in the aged
landscape—a child who feels he belongs among the last of those who can
still see the plain outside, a child who knows what abandonment is and
weeps, whose words occasionally well up from the depth of the soul where
life shapes them. But the man whom this child becomes prevents this sympathetic attention from taking root. He is divided and irresolute. He vehemently rejects the world, but both accepts and rejects himself. Like a pen-
dulum he swings hopelessly between naked self-knowledge and self-
aggrandizement, self-denial and self-apology.

The author has some insight into the world, and small as it may be, it
is genuine. But it is dominated by a mind and will unable to deal with the
two obligations set by life. The dramatist is basically ashamed of his own
work (not its value). Were Brecht capable of coming to grips with essentials, he would draw the same conclusion from his life and understanding
that Rimbaud did from his—and he would stop writing.

Paul Fechter. Deutsche Allgemeine Zeitung. Feb. 19, 1926†

The subtitle of Brecht's comedy [A Man's a Man] is The Transformation of
the Porter, Galy Gay, in the Military Barracks at Kilkoa. That sounds quite
robust and altogether manly. Many a man in the prewar period changed
himself from an individual with a soul into a man with a number in the
military barracks, from Potsdam to Paris. . . .

Brecht shudders with horror. No, it is not something he would want to
happen to him. He himself is not just a ''man''; neither is he an impersonal,
nameless figure. After all, he expanded the name Bert into the more imposing two-syllable Bertolt. Bertolt is more than a typical example of the male
sex and of the mechanical. Everyone certainly has an impersonal streak of
''Baal'' within himself, and the political right-winger has his streaks of
Mars and Moloch.

Still, there is the self. . . . Here I come to a stop because that is where
Brecht stops, too. Brecht wants to destroy the self and replace it by mechanized man—and he knows of no more appropriate symbol for the latter than
the uniform. The equation, mass man = the military! is obvious. The number immediately becomes militaristic, and who wants to be a soldier . . . ?
Brecht will avoid that. ''A Man's a Man!''—that sounds ominous. But how
much of this motto is meant earnestly? For Brecht's play is called neither
farce nor satire, but an altogether inoffensive ''comedy.'' . . . The spectator shakes his individual head.

Bernhard Diebold. Frankfurter Zeitung. Sept. 27, 1926†

The writer Bertolt Brecht . . . is more interested in the work than the finished result; more in the problem than the solution; more in the road than the goal. It is his habit to re-write his work interminably, twenty or thirty times, and then once again for each unimportant provincial production. He is not interested in a work being complete. Repeatedly, even if it has been published ten times, the final version turns out to be only the penultimate one; he is the despair of publishers and theatre directors. . . .

Bertolt Brecht strives for classicality, that is to say strict reality. But the lack of external credibility makes him appear romantic, and all of his works have a certain appearance of the fragmentary.

He shies away neither from crudity nor from extreme realism. He is an odd mixture of tenderness and ruthlessness; of clumsiness and elegance; of crankiness and logic; of wild cries and sensitive musicality. He repels many people, but anyone who has once understood his tones finds it hard to drop him. He is disagreeable and charming, a very bad writer and a great poet, and among the younger Germans undoubtedly the one showing the clearest signs of genius. [1928]

Lion Feuchtwanger. In Hubert Witt, ed., *Brecht—As
They Knew Him* (Berlin, Seven Seas, 1974), pp. 19–20

[*The Mother*] serves as the example in support of the idea of the inevitability and necessity of Communism. Programmatic intention: the spectator "is to be forced to make decisions." But the situation is such that the decisions are being made on the stage, and it is left to the spectator to accept them or not.

Without fail, the effect achieved is that those spectators who are in complete agreement with the opinion propagated from the stage are won over to an opinion that is already firmly established in their minds. They are being convinced of the conviction they hold and carried away to a profession of the belief to which they are sworn. . . .

Decisive conclusions are drawn through music; practical applications, likewise, are mostly sung. Here Brecht's art of simple, strong formulations holds good; radii of circles of thought, they take the shortest linguistic road, which, in its straightness, is more beautiful than the most poetic detour around the periphery. Together with the story that he is told, the spectator is also provided with the moral—ready for use—of the story, the former, outlined as simply and broadly as possible, being only the base for the latter. It remains questionable whether the indirect method—to present events, facts, and experiences, and to present them in such an impressive way that the spectator himself cannot fail to draw the right conclusions from what he sees—is not a more effective method.

In theory, Brecht rejects a theater addressing itself to the emotions of the spectator; but he does not spurn the succor of music which, because it cannot help it, does nothing but stir up emotions. What do its obstinate drumming, its threatening, its wailing, its lashing, and its promising have to do with reason, which, as far as its theory goes, is all that matters for epic theater? It presents the spectator with information and knowledge in a deliberately cool manner, but not, however, without making it warm for him through piano, trumpet, trombone, and percussion. [1932]

> Alfred Polgar. In Günther Rühle, ed., *Theater für die Republik* (Frankfurt, Fischer, 1967), p. 1106†

The Russian writer Ossip Brick noted very cleverly that Brecht's works are always court cases, in which Brecht proves himself to have litigation-mania, and shows himself a skilful and cunning casuist. He is without compare when he conducts his case against bourgeois logic, on condition that the legal argument is based upon the precise foundation of bourgeois jurisprudence. In such a case he is unbeatable. So-called "beauty," so-called "truth," so-called "justice" and "honesty" and "progress," and all these other fine-sounding words so beloved by liberal aesthetes; all these phrases he drives into a corner, into a blind alley, rubs their noses in the horrors of the social system which produced them. He takes down the trousers of the solid citizens, and they can do nothing but howl, hit out in all directions, and slander Brecht, who has forced them to look at themselves in all their rapacious and stupid abominableness. . . .

I know of nothing that Brecht dislikes more than hokum. Whether sentimental hokum or pseudo-heroic hokum, Brecht always sees to it that the philistines and cowards preen themselves, and that the murderous knaves weep real tears. . . .

In what does Brecht's strength lie? In his invincible aversion to hypocrites, villains, the sanctimonious, the respectable cowards, the egotists however they may express their egotism, either in greedy accumulation or humanitarian self-sacrifice. And particularly his disgusted derision for the modern guerrillas—the fascists. [1934]

> Sergei Tretyakov. In Hubert Witt, ed., *Brecht—As They Knew Him* (East Berlin, Seven Seas, 1974), pp. 74–75, 78

Only political drama can be the proper concern of theatre in emigration. Most of the plays which attracted a political audience ten or fifteen years ago have since been overtaken by events. The theatre of emigration must start again at the beginning; not just its stage, but also its plays must be built anew.

It was a sense of this historical situation which united the audience at the Paris première of parts of a new drama cycle by Brecht. The audience was recognizing itself for the first time as a dramatic audience. Taking account of this new audience and this new situation of the theatre, Brecht introduces a new dramatic form. He is an expert in fresh starts. . . .

Terror [i.e., *Fear*] *and Misery of the Third Reich* is a cycle formed of twenty-seven one-act plays constructed according to the precepts of traditional dramaturgy. Sometimes the dramatic element blazes out like a magnesium flare at the end of an apparently idyllic development. (Those who come in at the kitchen door are the Winter Aid [*Winterhilfe:* a spurious charity campaign mounted by the Nazi Party to ingratiate itself with the workers] people with a sack of potatoes for the little household; those who walk out are storm troopers leading between them the daughter of the family, whom they have arrested.) Other parts of the cycle have fully developed dramatic plots (e. g., in *The Chalk Cross* a worker tricks a storm trooper into revealing one of the methods which the Gestapo's accomplices use in fighting the underground). Sometimes it is the tension of a contradiction in social relations which, almost without transposition, is revealed dramatically on the stage. (Two prisoners taking exercise in the prison-yard under the eyes of the warder whisper among themselves; both are bakers; one is in gaol because he did not put any bran in his bread, the other was arrested a year later because he did.) . . .

The cycle represents for the theatre of German emigration a political and artistic opportunity which palpably demonstrates, for the first time, the necessity for that theatre. The two elements, political and artistic, here merge into one. [1938]

Walter Benjamin. Understanding Brecht (London,
New Left Books, 1977), pp. 37, 39–40

The theme of *The Good Woman of Sezuan* is not, and is not meant to be, hard to grasp. Clarity is the first requisite of didacticism. The surprising thing is the way Brecht makes his lessons into works of art. Obviously there were many ways of bungling the treatment of the Sezuan story. It could lose force through being too quaint and charming. It could fall short of art if the allegory were too earnest and ponderous or if the propaganda were too eager and importunate. Brecht manages to escape these pitfalls, and the result is something entirely new in didactic theater. Although the message is firm and sharp, it is not coaxed into us by pathos or thrown at us in anger. It is worked out by craftsmanship, that is, by Epic procedure and Brechtian characterization. The dialogue, delicate but not quaint, strong but not heavy, poetic but not decorative, is diversified with songs such as only the poet Brecht could write, using a manner which has ripened down the years since his *Beggar's Opera*. The mock naïveté, the speeches to the audience, the witty exchanges, the Chinese conventions, go to make a rich texture and a rapid tempo. The big scenes in the grand manner—such as the wedding (which never takes place) of Shen Te and the final trial scene—give the piece a dignity and a spaciousness that Brecht has perhaps only once before achieved—in his biographical play *Galileo*.

Eric Bentley. *The Playwright as Thinker* (New York, Reynal and Hitchcock, 1946), pp. 265–66

The fascination that Brecht constantly exerts I ascribe above all to the fact that here one sees a life that is genuinely ruled by thought (whereas our thinking is usually only a retrospective self-justification: it does not steer, but is dragged behind). Confronting an outstanding talent—which Brecht incidentally is, the greatest indeed in the German language at this moment—one can of course take refuge in admiration; one bows the knee like an acolyte before the altar, and the thing is done: one can go on. But confronting an attitude, a way of life, that is not enough. . . . Brecht, perhaps like all other people who live independently, is not at all interested in approval; on the contrary, he is waiting for challenge, is merciless when the challenge is unworthy and bored when it does not come at all. . . . Brecht has no desire to lecture, but finds himself in the position of a man who, wanting to talk about poetry, ends, in order to avoid mere chat, in having to give a lesson in elementary grammar. . . . But basically, I believe, Brecht is happy when he does not have to catechize. . . .

His attitude—and with Brecht it really is an attitude covering all aspects of life—consists in the daily application of those philosophical conclusions that reveal our social system as outmoded and its perpetuation by force as despicable, so that this system can only be seen as an obstacle, not as a standard to measure things by. Brecht's concern is with the future; an outlook that inevitably contains an element of restriction, the intermittent danger of a rigidity which admits no modification. It is no accident that, even in his dealings with actors, Brecht strives so tirelessly to achieve something loose and relaxed; these qualities are indeed always present to a high degree in his poetical work. Loose and relaxed: a staggering requirement in the context of a life such as Brecht leads, a life devoted to a world that as yet nowhere exists, that is visible only in his own behavior, that is a living contradiction, unrelenting and never, throughout his long years of toil as an outsider, crushed. Christians act in relation to the life beyond, Brecht to the life here below. That is one of the differences between him and the priests, whom, because of his differing goal, he loves to mock; yet he is not so very unlike them: the doctrine of ends justifying the means has identical features even when the ends are opposed. There can also be Jesuits of the life here below. . . . [1948]

Max Frisch. *Sketchbook 1946–1949* (New York, Harcourt Brace Jovanovich, 1977), pp. 200–201

In his postscript to the opera [*The Rise and Fall of the City of*] *Mahagonny*, first performed in 1930, Brecht fires his first volley, in the form of a comparative catalogue, against the concept of the tragic in Aristotle, who postulates an eternal human essence conflicting with fate. . . .

A little bit further on, in the same postscript to *Mahagonny*, Brecht dismisses Wagner the way he did with Aristotle, drawing up a brief catalogue of the foundations for an epic opera. . . .

Although Brecht claims that *Mahagonny* is nothing but an opera, and even a "culinary" opera at that, like any fashionable opera, the attack has nevertheless been launched against opera as simple "digestive" amusement and profitable business, against its facility, its reassuring bathos, its bad taste. . . .

Each of the various elements that compose the opera retains its own characteristic value and independence. Thus it is the job of the music to express something that the text itself does not convey. With Brecht, this principle applies in general to all incidental music, which is always present in and essential to his plays. Its task is no longer, as it traditionally was, to "pave the way" for the text, to create a mood—in short, to operate as a magic, hypnotic agent; rather, it plays its distinct role in the entire ensemble. . . . Music *signifies* in this context something apart from the text, something unusual that is added to the text without blending with it, just as in a painting a splash of green throws into relief a vibrant red, thus enriching the whole composition although preserving its own distinct character.

The many projections of photographic material, a device straight out of the technique cherished by [Erwin] Piscator, likewise have a function of their own. They serve to remind the spectator of the actual reality of the world outside at a moment when, on the stage, there unfolds a transposed action that may appear either as similar or contrary or linked by yet another subtle relationship to the actuality thus recalled.

For it is not a question of explicitly expounding a moral lesson. "There is a moral lesson to be learned," says Brecht, "but it is to be deduced from the manifest actions of the characters."

Geneviève Serreau. Bertolt Brecht (Paris,
L'Arche, 1955), pp. 39, 41–45†

In certain respects, Brecht is one of us. The richness and originality of his work should not keep the French from rediscovering in them ancient traditions of their own which have been buried by the romantic, bourgeois nineteenth century. . . .

I think Brecht was hardly influenced at all by our major playwrights, or by the Greek tragedians who were their models. His plays evoke Elizabethan drama more than tragedies. And yet what he does have in common with our classical dramatists and those of antiquity is that he has at his disposal a collective ideology, a method, a faith. As they do, he puts man back into the world, that is, in truth. Thus, the relationship between the true and the illusory is reversed: as it does in the classical dramatists' works, the event represented in Brecht's works itself proclaims its *absence*—it took place some other time or even never existed—and reality fades into pure appearance; but this sham shows us the true laws governing human behavior. Yes, truth exists for Brecht as it did for Sophocles and Racine: not as something the playwright must *speak,* but as what he must *show.* And this proud undertaking of showing men to men without making use of the dubious charms of desire or terror is unquestionably what we call classicism. . . .

Brecht does not put any heroes or martyrs on stage. . . . The reason for this is that Brecht does not believe in individual salvation. Society has to be completely changed, and the playwright's function is still that "purgation" Aristotle spoke of. He shows us what we are—both victims and accomplices. That is why Brecht's plays move us. But our emotion is very singular. It is a perpetual uneasiness. . . . And this uneasiness Brecht's plays arouse in us throws light on the uneasiness we live through. In our time "purgation" has a different name: raising the level of consciousness. But wasn't that calm and strict uneasiness which *Bajazet* or *Phèdre* provoked during the seventeenth century in the soul of the spectator who suddenly discovered the inflexible law of human passions also—in a different time and social and ideological context—a raising of the level of consciousness? It's for these reasons that Brecht's theater, this Shakespearean theater of revolutionary negation, seems to me to also be—without the author's ever having planned it—like an extraordinary attempt to link the twentieth century to the classical tradition. [1957]

Jean-Paul Sartre. In Michel Contat and Michel Rybalka,
eds., *Selected Prose* (Evanston, Ill., Northwestern
University Press, 1974), Vol. II, pp. 225–28

It is not possible to dignify Brecht as a dramatist, because he did not in the accepted sense put new worlds before us. Indeed, he only uses the drama to demonstrate first his nihilism, then his Marxism. What little reality he is able to use in this process remains limited and shallow. A metaphysical, truly moral reality does not exist for him. The world of nature hardly exists for him at all. A social world does exist for him, but it can be affirmed only to the extent to which it is communist.

We must do justice, then, to his convictions. Brecht was a nihilist first, a Marxist second. . . .

Accordingly, it is a mistake in staging Brecht's plays to worry about the dramatist and to perform his pieces as dramatic creations. To do so means to make Brecht into something that he is not and to conceal what he in fact is. And this—what he in fact is—ought to be stressed. . . . We have before us a Marxist hack of German origin; we see in him neither a pure poet, nor a great dramatist, nor a new German author of classic stature.

Otto Mann. *B. B.: Maß oder Mythos?* (Heidelberg, Rothe, 1958), pp. 115—17†

The weakness of the man Galileo [in *Galileo*] is inseparably linked to the social structure—much more so than in the case of Mother Courage [in *Mother Courage*]. Her blindness, as revealed by Brecht, consists in her participation as an individual in something that destroys her; he therefore calls on us to reject such blind participation and to make the personal decision to work collectively at changing the world. Through the drama of Galileo (a drama that, as he remarks, "is not a tragedy") and the explanation of this drama by Galileo himself, Brecht invites us not to reject Galileo but to become aware of the significance of his "crime" for his time, for science, and also for our own time. He calls into question not so much Galileo himself as the rupture that occurred between him and science—one would even have to say: between the intellectuals and the people; he shows us how it came about; he makes us understand it so that we of today can consider its consequences—consequences from which we still suffer.

Although he stands in the center of the work (the role is one of the longest Brecht ever wrote), Galileo is less important than his drama, this "beginning of a new age," whose greatness and misery become Brecht's subject. . . .

The center of gravity in Brecht's work changes: it shifts from the central character, and the blindness of this person vis-à-vis the world, to the world itself—a world in the process of change. . . . Brecht now stresses the progressive transformation of history through men and their actions. These actions, however, must be properly understood in order to be carried on or to be corrected. Knowledge and action thus enter more than ever into a close alliance: the theater—art—becomes the privileged place in which their mediation takes place.

Bernard Dort. *Lecture de Brecht* (Paris, Éditions du Seuil, 1960), pp. 176–77†

Brecht's readiness to sink his own personality in the work of his predecessors and contemporaries, to use the whole storehouse of past literature as so much material for his own handiwork, was in accordance with his views about the nature of poetry itself and the poet's function in society. Here, too, he rejected the mystical, romantic view of the poet as the vessel of divinely inspired intuitions, called upon to fulfill and express his unique personality. To him the poet was a craftsman serving the community and relying on his reason and acquired skill, a man among men, not a being set apart by virtue of some special quality or power. That is why Brecht was ready to accept the advice of numerous collaborators, whom he conscientiously named when his works were published. As he did not consider the work of art divinely inspired, he never hesitated to alter, and often debase, his own work, according to the circumstances of the moment. . . .

Within his own sphere of craftsmanship, however, Brecht never suffered from undue humility. . . . But his arrogance remained confined to the sphere in which he regarded himself as a craftsman, an expert. It never led him to regard the poet as a higher being. [1960]

Martin Esslin. *Brecht: The Man and His Work*
(Garden City, N.Y., Doubleday, 1961), pp. 117–18

Brecht's work once more advanced the claim—though from a viewpoint that was not, and did not mean to be, that of bourgeois society—that the theater must fulfill a committed, educational, socially reforming task. It must do more than occupy an audience for an evening. It must, by what it presents and how it presents it, bring about new insights and significant social action. The problem of *intention* in Diderot's *Paradox about the Actor* is thus posed in an altogether new sense. What is now at stake is no longer only the intention of a master craftsman who, even when portraying extreme passions, remains in control of his means and technique. What is now at stake is a theater that is to render social relationships intelligible and, in performing, to influence the consciousness of the audience. The audience, to be sure, is of a new kind, with a new social function.

This concept of the drama, however, called for a new and adequate *theatrical and stage style*. It was not enough merely to turn away from the culinary theater: this drama required the pursuit of new dramaturgical means and staging techniques.

Hans Mayer. *Bertolt Brecht und die Tradition*
(Pfulligen, Neske, 1961), pp. 116–17

The plot of both Shakespeare's comedy [*Measure for Measure*] and Brecht's play [*The Roundheads and the Peakheads*] are very similar; but at the same time a completely different syndrome of ideas is implied within the framework of two such similar fables. Shakespeare, the humanist of the era of the Renaissance, composed a passionate hymn to universally significant, lofty passions and moral concepts—love, honor, justice. He glorifies love as a feeling organically inherent to the nature of man, unconquerable, selfless, and free; he glorifies the honor of women, to which force or compulsion to love is the vilest outrage; he glorifies justice, by which retribution is rendered in full measure to any hypocrite or violator, however high a social position he may occupy, according to the enormity of the crime he has committed.

Keeping the plot outline of Shakespeare's comedy almost intact, Brecht parodies all of its elements. Impure and self-seeking love unites Nana with de Guzman—blackmail on one hand, material calculation on the other. Isabella does not turn to a priest for advice but to the owner of a brothel. Not the loving, abandoned wife goes to the rendezvous in place of Isabella, but a prostitute whom she hires . . . and so on. And all these parodied situations taken together emphasize and strengthen Brecht's ideologically tinged message, the red thread woven through the entire play. Brecht refuses to recognize universal meaning free of class distinctions in the feelings or moral categories advertised in bourgeois society. . . .

Brecht's parody has nothing in common with the narrow conception of parody as mere "literary imitation." His parody has gone far beyond the limits of purely literary arguments and conflicts of various artistic tastes and style, and its purpose is not at all to debunk this or that classic work. If Brecht in some way parodies Shakespeare, Goethe, or Schiller, it is by no means with the intention of discrediting or disparaging these writers. . . .

Brecht tended to borrow subjects so often and, moreover, parody them because he found this a profitable and very flexible way to stimulate the revolutionary awareness of the masses. Forcing the spectator by means of parody to reconsider critically the common concepts which he has learned in school, Brecht leads him "*via* literature" to a critical re-examination of the bases of bourgeois morality and ideology.

> I. Fradkin. In Peter Demetz, ed., *Brecht* (Englewood
> Cliffs, N.J., Prentice-Hall, 1962), pp. 100–102

The persistency of the self-and-others within the characters of Brecht is presumably a lingering echo of his earlier expressionism. Central to an expressionist drama is a concern with the relation of the self to an external reality which is frequently a subjective statement (the "terrifying semireality about an imaginary creation" of which Strindberg speaks in reference to his own drama). On the expressionist's stage, the hero (who is frequently the author himself) peoples the stage reality with the tangible creatures of his hallucinations (one of the first manifestoes of German expressionism stated: "The real image of the world is within us."). Baal was such a hero; when Brecht rejected him, he rejected the temptation of anarchic self-indulgence in favor of criticism disciplined by dogma. But the fragmentation of the expressionist hero into figures other than his own remained a constructive element of his later drama.

Whether or not Brecht was conscious of this heredity, he was soon aware that any dramatic statement of illusion and reality through the human presence on stage defies rational analysis and jeopardizes the principles of a theater meant to resist—through analysis—absorption into what Brecht saw as a favorite German Valhalla, the hazy land of generalities "incorporeal and abstract.'' It is presumably for this reason that his people generally evidence little feeling for their own nonideological problems. Whatever they may have to say about themselves of their relationship to others is less the expression of formless and intimate feelings than the crisp outline of a sociopolitical commentary, the value of which—in terms of historical cogency—reflects the degree of their maturity on this sociopolitical stage. The fundamental detachment on Brecht's stage is that of the human actor *impersonating* a character that consciously evinces the symptoms of a human being. [1962]

David I. Grossvogel. *The Blasphemers* (Ithaca, N.Y., Cornell University Press, 1965), pp. 23–24

Is the epic theater perhaps a ''moral institution''? Brecht himself asked this question, quoting a speech young Schiller had delivered in 1784 . . . and published later under the title *The Theater as a Moral Institution*. Schiller, the popularizer of Kant and educator of the German middle classes, had always been a thorn in Brecht's side. . . . And yet, although Schiller's drama appeared to him as the epitome of ''culinary'' stagecraft, he could not completely detach his epic theater from the ethics of Schiller's dramaturgy. . . .

If Brecht wanted the underprivileged and ''damaged'' to profit from his plays, then he was coming dangerously close to Schiller's precept that the stage is ''to teach us to wield greater justice towards the miserable and to judge them with increased clemency. Only when we fathom the depth of their oppression are we allowed to adjudicate upon them.'' If the paradigms in Brecht's didactic plays are meant to establish a healthy balance between the society of the future and their rulers, then he could have found the idea of this kind of *Lehrstück* anticipated by Schiller. . . .

In the final analysis Schiller, too, persuaded his spectators to come to a decision. This decision, with which he concludes his essay, is ''to be human.'' Deeply convinced of man's inhumanity, Brecht harangued his audiences through his Alienation Effects, urging them to *become* human. It is this dynamic that distinguishes the epic theater from Schiller's drama. Inasmuch as this dynamic shows man to be ''on trial'' and ''in the process'' of becoming, Brecht's epic theater is a legitimate offspring of the expressionist revolution of the 1920s and of European theatrical history in general. Since his aesthetic theory is a mechanism, both of offense and defense, it may well be recognized for what it is: the intellectual mimicry behind which a creative mind hid from outward persecution and inward doubts.

This creation at times leaves its ''epicality'' behind to grow into theater, great theater, pure and simple.

Heinz Politzer. *MLQ*. June, 1962, pp. 112–14

Brecht wrote *Baal,* perhaps the most poetic play Expressionism produced, as a parody and refutation of the romantic concept of the poet's martyrdom in the philistine world. Like the Dadaists of the same period, the twenty-year-old, guitar-strumming, ex-medical orderly whom war had shocked into "coolness" and nihilism, could not stomach the naïve dreams of grandeur and the lachrymose self-pity of many Expressionists. His intent was to show the truth of a contemporary poet's existence, stripped of sentimentality and pseudo-romantic claptrap. . . .

Brecht's *Baal* strikes one as disturbingly up-to-date. Baal, a "beatnik" of genius, a link between Rimbaud and Genet, transforms twentieth-century despair into poetry. Baal rejects society not because he believes in a new ideal but because he is bored and revolted. In his boredom, which is his revolt, only one thing can inspire him—physical experience. While the rich publisher offers success and security, Baal only notices the fine body of the publisher's wife. He knows no inhibitions and propositions her in front of her husband, with the result that he will sleep with the wife and lose the husband's support forever. With his "cool," blunt proposition, Baal sweeps all values aside. . . . Brecht's Baal cannot be understood. His is a directness and immediacy which make civilization impossible.

We must not misinterpret Baal's motives as simply honesty or Rabelaisian *joie de vivre.* There is a cruel complexity, a tragic sadness about him, which makes his unending string of debaucheries not an expression of thirst for life but a challenge to and a confirmation of the absurdity of life. Baal toasts in one everlasting carousal and orgy his knowledge that life is feeding on life, and God forgets his rotting creation. Sex is the means by which Baal expresses his revolt against and his enactment of the purposelessness of a universe in which nothing lasts. Not Rabelais's Pantagruel but Camus's "stranger" is his brother.

Baal is a return to nature, not as Rousseau and the Romantics had conceived it, but as Darwinism taught modern man to see it. Baal's sky is filled with vultures that wait to eat him, unless he manages to eat them first. And yet this sky is beautiful and loved by Baal.

Walter H. Sokel. In Walter H. Sokel, ed., *German
Expressionist Drama* (Garden City, N.Y., Doubleday,
1963), pp. xxvi–xxviii

The only meaningful punishment that a poet can suffer, short of death, is, of course, the sudden loss of what throughout human history has appeared a divine gift. To Brecht the loss came rather late. It came, finally, after he had settled down in East Berlin, where he could see, day after day, what it meant to the people to live under a Communist regime. . . . For seven years Brecht lived and worked in peace under the eyes—in fact, under the protection—of Western observers but now in infinitely closer contact with a totalitarian state than he had ever been in his life before, and seeing the sufferings of his own people with his own eyes. And the consequence was that not a single play and not a single great poem was produced. . . .

His punishment caught up with him. Now reality overwhelmed him to the point where he could no longer be its voice; he had succeeded in being in the thick of it—and had proved that this is no good place for a poet to be.

This is what the case of Bertolt Brecht is likely to teach us, and what we ought to take into consideration when we judge him today, as we must, and pay him our respect for all that we owe him. The poet's relation to reality is indeed what Goethe said it was: they cannot bear the same burden of responsibility as ordinary mortals; they need a measure of remoteness, and yet would not be worth their salt if they were not forever tempted to exchange this remoteness for being just like everybody else. On this attempt Brecht staked his life and his art as few poets have ever done; it led him into triumph and disaster.

It is the poet's task to coin the words we live by, and surely no one is going to live by the words Brecht wrote in praise of Stalin. . . . The worst that can happen to a poet is that he should cease to be a poet, and that is what happened to Brecht in the last years of his life.

Hannah Arendt. NY. Nov. 5, 1966, pp. 69–70, 72, 75, 121

Brecht was involved, whatever else he committed himself to, in an examination of human depravity anywhere while trying to find sufficient decency somewhere to make life minimally tolerable. In this he was like Freud, who started as a physician of the sick and awful in the individual and became a moralist concerned with man. One or two of Brecht's plays may even be read as schematically Freudian. *The Good Woman of Setzuan,* for example, is very much a morality play about the schizoid balance involved in survival: idealism vs. accommodation, good vs. evil. The moving action involves a split: "the injunction to be good and yet to live. . . . I could not do it." This is the theme: how to be good in the world, yet good to oneself: how to be both moralist and egoist, how to satisfy both self and conscience, both ego and superego.

Setting in Brecht is unrealistic or irrelevant; his China is not any real China, the stockyards are not Chicago. He was concerned with allegorical landscapes, with jungles, which loom as ideas. No matter how specific a situation, Brecht transcended it. *Mother Courage* takes place, "fantastically" of course, over a panorama of time and space: it is an "epic" of a mother, her attempts to survive and protect her family not in the context of any specific war but in that of war in general, and, by extension, in the context of all catastrophe. She improvises endlessly, working with whatever of the human residuum she finds at hand, keeping her identity in disaster. . . . She survives by the constant study of how one survives, salvaging identity through studying and exercising identity.

Morris Freedman. *The Moral Impulse* (Carbondale, Ill., Southern Illinois University Press, 1967), pp. 99–100

Brecht's first contact with the Chinese theater was apparently through a free adaptation of the fourteenth-century text, *The Chalk Circle,* made by the Viennese poet and sinologist Klabund in 1924 for Max Reinhardt. The work exhibits few of the peculiarities of Chinese production and is quite Westernized in its use of decor and prose speech. Nor does Klabund point out any symbolic gestures. As a contemporary of Brecht, Klabund could, however, have acquainted the German poet with other important phases of perform ance in Chinese theater. Or Brecht may well have read some of the books or articles published by then; that he was interested in Chinese thought is clear from certain of his poems. He understood Chinese theater as a blend ing of the didactic with the artistic. . . .

The Caucasian Chalk Circle is a model of epic theater and the epitome of Brechtian technical virtuosity, with its mingling of prose, verse, chorus, and song; its cool objectivity given by the device of using the Story Teller to describe much of the action as it occurs; the use of masks for those characters who are least human, unchangeable; the suggestivity of decor which may enter and disappear as needed. All these facets of *The Caucasian Chalk Circle* also remind us that the play was inspired by a translation, however loose, of an ancient Chinese play.

What is particularly interesting in this text, however, is the immense role that mime plays. Brecht rarely states that a character is to move or to walk in a certain fashion, but his manner of movement is established quite clearly in one of two ways: by the characterization of the person through his speech or through the Story Teller's description. Time and again one comes upon scenes that suggest a very specific type of highly stylized movement. This symphony of stylized movement . . . begins when the Story Teller takes his place onstage; his gestures tell us that he has told the story many times, and it is he who gives the signal for the scenes to begin, with an appropriate gesture.

Leonard Cabell Pronko. *Theater East and West* (Berkeley, University of California Press, 1967), pp. 56, 62

On a formal level, *A Man's a Man* is an episodic illustration by parable in which Brecht is already utilizing much that will become staple in his later epic theater. Actors step out of character to underline the illustrative nature of the proceedings; moody lyrics make us conscious of universal truths to which all the sound and fury of the moment will have to conform; commentary focuses on the illustration pattern's critical implications; and each scene, though it provides a building block to an interlocking pattern, contributes its share of self-explanatory tragicomic observations on such matters as military values, the importance of personality, the power of money, etc. As he will later on, Brecht loads his scenes with broad social satire, deflating left and right what he smells as fake. . . .

The Brecht who will mix comic and tragic effects in order to demonstrate that what seems comic is laden with tragic implications, is already present in *A Man's a Man*. So is the Brecht who will teach by grotesque example that man is his own worst enemy. *A Man's a Man* has all the ambivalence of the plays which we identify most fully with Brecht's concept of epic theater, suggesting on the one hand a cynic who observes the human menagerie with a detached hopeless smile, on the other, a humanitarian who cannot shirk his emotional involvement. It even suggests that most glaring paradox about the later Brecht—his failure to confront the tragic implications of his deepest convictions.

Max Spalter. *Brecht's Tradition* (Baltimore,
Johns Hopkins University Press, 1967), p. 174

In the early poems and plays Brecht explores the human consciousness, attempting to define itself in terms of that which is outside of itself. In *Baal*'s metaphysics, Brecht reaches the conclusion that man is the victim of Nature. In the final scene, Baal commits himself to this devouring Nature, but with a pathetic regret that he is dying alone.

With *In the Jungle of Cities* Brecht perceives the human consciousness attempting to define itself in terms of a relationship with another human being; and, in the acute sufferings of the protagonist as he experiences a tragic recognition, Brecht seems to conclude that man is unable to reach communication with another human soul even in the intimate proximity of a sexual relationship. Communion with another human being is the dream; the reality is exploitation and consumption as the other becomes either an object for sexual use or a devouring agent itself.

Within *In the Jungle of Cities* Shlink attempts to assert his will. Brecht regards his encounter with Garga as motiveless, and critics interpret the action as an *acte gratuit*. In rational terms, surely, this encounter is inexplicable; and yet, as Baal must exploit and consume other human beings because that is human action, so Shlink must reach out and consume. However, Shlink attempts, through his own will, to reach out and experience another human being. In his attempt to realize, in his own consciousness, a sense of another person as more than an object, he can only initiate a sexual relationship in which he uses the other person. He can extend himself toward another only by imposing his own identity upon him and assuming the other's identity. Even this sensual exchange of identities is fruitless and unsatisfying, and succumbing to the natural law of consumption, Shlink dies, used and assimilated by Garga who has learned that exploitation is the only course in this hostile and inexplicable world. Garga accepts the natural law of consumption, submitting to Nature. Brecht's own response to human suffering informs these plays and poems, and that anguished isolation is more painful as its compassion seems futile. These plays are intimations of an event which becomes the essential action for Brecht: the vain struggle of a human consciousness to exert its own will in a hostile world. That struggle becomes, in Brecht's dramatic disguises, the submission of the individual will to some energy which exists apart from it.

Charles R. Lyons. Bertolt Brecht (Carbondale, Ill.,
Southern Illinois University Press, 1968), pp. 42–43

Modern morality plays from Brieux to Brecht must inevitably suffer from some of the pains of propaganda. Whether by devices of emotional persuasion on the one hand or disguise by exaggeration or other comic method on the other, we are given a necessarily limited view. . . .

Bertolt Brecht's indefatigable pursuit, in both his playwriting and his directing, of an effect of estrangement or "alienation" could be argued as a cover for his teaching, a lifelong attempt to avoid the responsibility of the greatest drama, which uses the theatrical medium to explore reality in communion with its audience. As a playwright he has no doubt been overrated, because his impulse to treat the sentimentality of his subjects with the comic eye of the estranger produced a series of plays having the rough edge which appealed to a cynical generation. . . .

Brecht's notion of epic theatre, therefore, is far from being that of the heroic tradition which the word may suggest; rather, it describes a pantomime which only incidentally narrates a story, while all the apparatus of chorus and narrator, song and music, placards and titles, guides us to the cool, reflective kind of attention we should pay to its meaning.

Brecht was anxious that his technique should suppress the natural wish of the audience to identify itself with a serious character, without the need for comic distortion. Identification would prevent the audience from thinking. The suffering of the character was to move the spectator, but he was to remain free to laugh about those who weep on stage, and weep about those who laugh. Yet this theory was constantly in conflict with his practice, for Brecht was fighting against the irrepressible impulse toward shared feeling. . . . In the drama of Bertolt Brecht, all efforts to promote a cold and rational response while at the same time presenting an intensely human drama produced an inevitably tragicomic response, and theory became gratuitous.

In sum, the contrapuntal structure of his drama encouraged both repugnance for Macheath the thief and parody of capitalism, and affection for Macheath the philanderer defying the law; it encouraged both repugnance for Galileo the social coward and affection for Galileo the man. Alienation as a production method, like comic "relief" in Shakespearian tragedy, served to strengthen rather than to weaken any incipient emotionality in such equivocations and it increased such ironic tensions as the play possessed. As well as being an object lesson, Courage can be a comedy or a tragedy queen; she is each of these.

J. L. Styan. *The Dark Comedy,* 2nd ed. (Cambridge, Cambridge University Press, 1968), pp. 166–67, 169, 175

After Brecht's death, his name quickly became world famous. . . . It was primarily *Mother Courage* and, in the second place, *Galileo* that established and sustained his fame. They are considered *the* classic dramas of our time.

Fame, and especially world fame, is almost always based on misunderstanding, but rarely so tragically as in this instance. These two plays, seen today from our present point in history, deny everything that Brecht had worked for all his life in his dramatic experiments. *Mother Courage* is a thoroughly conservative, sweeping, magnificently composed bourgeois drama—the work of a theatrical genius. In German literature it is close to Gerhart Hauptmann's dramas. *Galileo* has been interpreted in all kinds of ideological terms—as have many of Brecht's works—especially its ending with its long, dramatically unintegrated dialogues. This does not change the fact that *Galileo,* too, is a "modern classic" in a conservative, bourgeois sense. *Mother Courage* and *Galileo* are great plays—I would say, the greatest German plays since Gerhart Hauptmann. They were written during exile in the Western countries; their structure, apart from some ideological curlicues perhaps added at a later date, shows how far Brecht, at that time, had departed from his ideology.

Willy Haas. *Bert Brecht* (New York, Frederick Ungar, 1970), pp. 106–7

Brecht's entire literary work is concerned with the problem of the struggle between subconscious impulse and conscious control. He made increasingly strenuous efforts at calculated, active self-control and tried to become wholly rational and impersonal. Ostentatiously he rejected all sentiment and emotion. But his sensitive nature required a stronger and more positive discipline than he could provide for himself. This he found in communism. It rejected the existing world in its cruelty and absurdities; it provided a technique of self-control, rational thought, and discipline. It claimed to be entirely scientific.

Despite his pacifism, or rather anti-militarism, Brecht believed in the use of force. If man can be transformed by violent methods into something evil, he can also be made into something better by the practices of the communist social engineers. Communism, or rather his own brand of it, provided the focus around which he could integrate the forces that pulled his split personality in many directions.

In his plays he pictures the predicament of man and the irony of human conditions as seen by James Joyce, Kafka, and the French existentialists. The world is evil; virtue brings no reward. Human nature is pretty much the same; the poor are mean and the rich are ruthless and cruel. War is the natural state of man. There is no justice. . . . Life continues only because mothers doggedly and irrationally persist in rearing their young. It is a world sullied by evil. The place of fate is taken by the inscrutable workings of the social order, which molds the lives of characters. But this is only half the picture. On the positive side there is the hope of communism.

Curiously enough, however, Brecht in his plays presents the negative side with greater skill, conviction and color. One is reminded of Milton's *Paradise Lost,* Goethe's *Faust,* and Dante's *Inferno.* The new, unfolding world is merely postulated, assumed, taken for granted.

Theodore Huebner. *The Literature of East Germany*
(New York, Frederick Ungar, 1970), pp. 57–58

While it is true that the Brechtian hero is almost inevitably defeated by the interaction between his own cunning and the social forces which shape his fate, it is the essence of these social forces rather than that of the individual that is shown to be at fault. As Galileo puts it, it is the nation that needs heroes (and thus forces men to turn coward to save their skin) that is unhappy, just as it is the war that forces Mother Courage to employ cunning to preserve her means of eking out an existence yet see her children perish, and as it is the combined misery and greed of the oppressed that brings Shen-te to invent an alter ego who ruthlessly subverts her good intentions. These are all social institutions which are, at least theoretically speaking, subject to change. And yet they are institutions before which the individual appears to be powerless, for a single voice raised against the monolithic mechanism of mass society is unheard; a single life laid down before the juggernaut of bourgeois conformity is easily snuffed out without effect, without attracting more than momentary notice. In short, as long as society reacts as a mass, as long as the individual surrenders his being to gain security at the cost of his identity, society cannot change. Brecht's mature works make one painfully aware of the human weakness of the individual; as Shen-Te puts it, the human being is simply inadequate to be good, absolutely good, in times like these. And yet, in making us aware of our weakness when confronted by an impassive mass culture, he also makes us aware of our individuality, however tenuous it may be, and of our guilt in silently watching injustice, the while paying lip service to justice.

Julian H. Wulbern. *Brecht and Ionesco: Commitment in
Context* (Urbana, University of Illinois
Press, 1971), pp. 218–19

With too narrow a focus on Brecht, it is easy to see him as the one bright spot in utter darkness and to imagine him as he himself imagined himself—the Messiah come to save the modern theater. If Brecht was in fact a Messiah, we must in the interest of both fairness and historical accuracy remember that he had a host of John the Baptists preparing the way for him. In the closing years of the nineteenth century and the early years of the twentieth many people (now almost forgotten) worked out theatrical innovations that later became associated with Brecht's name. The more we learn of this period, the clearer it becomes that many of the things we have previously assumed were originated by Brecht are in fact either borrowings from other avant-garde artists of the period or are revivals of such musty forms as the medieval or the Jesuit theater or of exotic forms such as the various types of classical oriental theater. Seen in this light, Brecht's unbridled attacks on German theater in particular and international theater in general are simply an echo of something that the avant-garde had been shouting for years. The crucial difference historically is one of manner rather than matter; when Brecht shouted, he shouted in such a way that he could not be ignored.

John Fuegi. *The Essential Brecht* (Los Angeles,
Hennessey & Ingalls, 1972), p. 11

[T. S.] Eliot ignores or depreciates the human body and the physical world. Brecht takes every opportunity to stress the simplest needs and sensations of the body (hunger, cold, sexuality, fatigue) and the resistance of the physical world. For the life of man, as Brecht sees it, is social, that is, economic; and the basis of economics is biology. *The Threepenny Opera* announces the priorities that will govern all his later work: "eats first, morals after." Not because morals are a luxury, but because our freedom to lead a decent life varies with the strength of economic pressures which we have to meet in order to live at all.

This realism of Brecht's, though it gives his plays their bedrock of conviction, would be nothing without his delight in the humour and resilience of men. Like Synge he has a grasp not just of the world of the peasant—what we can touch and smell and taste—but of emotions uncorrupted by sentiment or habit. Unlike Synge, he sees the life of action as essentially political; for the world, in Brecht's view, must be changed before men can lead lives worthy of a human being.

This is the clue to that belief in narrative which runs through all his experiments in the theatre. A strong narrative line on the stage makes the point that man belongs inescapably to history. By showing events as they happen it lets us see that they might have happened otherwise if men had acted differently; and in doing this, reminds us that men can always change their world. At the same time, as in Shakespeare, the episodic structure of narrative, since it leaves the dramatist free to turn from the general's tent to the cook's, admits ironic juxtapositions that expose the significance of events.

Ronald Gaskell. *Drama and Reality* (London, Routledge & Kegan Paul, 1972), p. 139

The songs as autonomous structural units within Brecht's plays—distinctly set off "sideshow acts," as it were—represent the epitome of the principle of "each scene for itself," the focal point for Brecht's concept of paratactic dramatic structure, of the structure of a play as a series of loosely connected, autonomous units. . . . Brecht's "musical addresses to the public" often serve, in their form as independent units of presentation and through the person of the actor as singer, as a "confidant of the playwright," to mediate the author's moral thesis to his audience. Making the songs distinct "acts" in themselves is accomplished not only by the actor in his presentation. . . . The songs are to be accompanied by song titles (quite in the manner of the musical presentation of the *Bänkelsang* [popular ballad], the title of the ballad being printed on the picture sheet), the music itself being an autonomous element of the presentation and serving as a commentary on rather than an accompaniment to the text (a contrast between music and text which . . . was frequently the case with the *Bänkellieder*).

Sammy K. McLean. *The "Bänkelsang" and the Work of Bertolt Brecht* (The Hague, Mouton, 1972), p. 192

From the first Johanna [in *Saint Joan of the Stockyards*] is unequal to the task she has chosen, to "convert" the world by her own good will. Brecht demonstrates with great clarity, yet with sympathy, the inadequacy of her concepts and the inadequacy of her ability to "learn." Johanna's insight arrives too late, when her "good will" has already been exploited by Mauler and his class in their own best interests. Like the historical St. Joan, her fate is to be used by others; her goodness lacks the discrimination of the good cause, the knowledge which is required to place it at the service of the "good collective." Thus her aims are not realized in the results of her actions; instead of "improving" the world by the "help" which she brings, she merely plays into the hands of the unjust order which rules, by providing an ornament for the ideological "Überbau" [superstructure] which this order uses to conceal the anarchy by which it lives. Mauler is an expert in the fabrication of such false motives—he renders Johanna not merely harmless, but actually useful to the cause which she in fact opposes, the continuing triumph of the capitalists. The dangers of "Hilfe" [help] and the omnipresence of "Gewalt" [force] which had been schematically presented in *The Didactic Play of Baden* are here clothed in a "real action" which makes their significance clear. On this level it becomes apparent that there is a very real political problem involved, a problem with which many German Communists were preoccupied in these years: the building of a united Socialist front against the National Socialists, a union of "gute Menschen" [good people] against the Fascist menace. For the social democrats such an alliance remained to the last suspect, for the same reasons that Johanna gives for her failure to carry out the commission with which she is entrusted: "I am going away. Nothing good can come of violence. I do not belong to them. . . ."

The play reads like an attempt to refute these arguments, to demonstrate the necessity of a united front against "Gewalt," even if it is necessary to resort to "Gewalt" oneself.

John Milfull. *From Baal to Keuner* (Bern, Lang, 1974), p. 115

Brecht represents a radical departure from the writer's relationship to tradition as it had been known since Romanticism. He was contemptuous of "original creativity." In his view, the notion of plagiarism was an outgrowth of bourgeois property concepts that arose in the late Middle Ages. Half in jest, but with considerable accuracy, he observed that every period of literary greatness was based more or less on its plagiarism. He lamented the fact that he had not yet accomplished anything significant in this area. Why, he asked, would anyone who knows the value of a striking expression try to improve on it when he can simply appropriate it? But he boldly announced that he intended to re-establish plagiarism in its "ancient inherent rights" by restoring it to social acceptability. . . . Brecht succeeded in his intentions better than almost any single twentieth-century writer, with the possible exception of Joyce, and Kipling helped him do it.

The mental intimacy that drew Brecht to a poet whose name had become synonymous with British imperialism waxed and waned at varying points in his life, but it remained one of the few literary friendships that endured until the end of his life. Brecht recognized in Kipling a kindred spirit, and he expressed his sense of congeniality in many ways. . . . Rudyard Kipling's writings had fallen into the hands of one of the most unscrupulous and brilliant sovereign imaginations in twentieth-century literature. The results would have surprised Kipling himself.

James K. Lyon. *Bertolt Brecht and Rudyard Kipling* (The Hague, Mouton, 1975), pp. 2–3

Brecht's lifelong efforts to evolve a consistently new approach to the theatre seem to have created the erroneous impression that he was therefore a contemptuous arch-enemy of the classics, especially of German classical plays. But it is wrong to see Brecht as the gratuitous literary firebrand and revolutionary iconoclast of the popular image; a feature of his work, from the first to the last plays and theoretical writings, is his concern with a literary tradition; many of his own dramas are stimulated by existing models or are counterpoints to them. Brecht's quarrel is seldom with his literary ancestors (Shakespeare, *Urfaust,* [Schiller's] *Die Räuber* are frequently cited as admirable past models of playwriting technique and involvement outside literature), but he does not spare his scorn for the traditional ways of performing the classics and makes virulent attacks on the misappropriation of past drama by society. An early move in his career to counter the hallowed lifeless approach to the classics was Brecht and Feuchtwanger's adaptation of Marlowe's *Edward II,* on which Brecht later commented that it was an attempt to break away from the ossified Shakespeare of the German stage. . . . Brecht had of course to contend with the particularly German notion of the theatre as a place of serious moral edification. Formal attire for the audience and generous subsidy by public authority are only two aspects of this quasi-religious character of the theatre in Germany; and religion requires ritual, which is paralleled on the stage by norms of production that are stultifying in their rigidity. . . .

Never content with solely negative criticism, Brecht sought to define the true greatness of the dramatic heritage that was so frequently obscured by unimaginative convention: he saw it as "human greatness," not something detached and superficial, and he complained that the tradition handed down from the court theatres had diverged more and more from this human greatness, while formalistic experiments had only made matters worse. . . .

Brecht was not only inimical to the reverential type of production but altogether sceptical of the whole approach to literary ranking and the allocation of the title "genius." . . . In his view a heaven studded with stars of the first rank only was not a heaven, and though Goethe offered things that Lenz did not have, the converse was also true.

Arrigo Subiotto. Bertolt Brecht's Adaptations for the
Berliner Ensemble (London, Modern Humanities
Research Association, 1975), pp. 1–2

Throughout his life Brecht was deeply interested in things Chinese. He followed political events in revolutionary China with keen interest but also delighted in the achievements of her ancient culture and civilization. Mixing old and new wisdom, China taught him many useful things. First and foremost, China was for Brecht a focusing point of social problems generally, including those besetting modern Europe, and provided proof that they can be solved. . . . Secondly, China helped Brecht to come to terms with his role as modern European poet, teacher, political thinker, and exile. Thirdly, the achievements of China, both ancient and revolutionary, showed Brecht that the essence of Marxist thinking is not new and revolutionary at all, but that it is as old as human civilization itself. Finally, Chinese culture—or whatever Brecht knew about it—seemed to offer something that Marxism was lacking. Ancient Chinese philosophers provided him with guidelines for the practice of Marxist ideology in daily life and suggested ways to Brecht in which the truth could be spread more successfully. . . .

In the twenties and early thirties, when in Berlin, Brecht made a serious effort to study Chinese philosophers, including Lao-tse, Confucius, Chuang-tse and, above all, Mo-tze, a contemporary of Confucius and the first Chinese philosopher who espoused views that strongly resemble modern socialist thought. . . .

Brecht's serious study of Chinese philosophy coincides with his study of Marxism, which he began in the late twenties. . . . This is more than a mere coincidence, for Brecht was no longer merely interested in the exotic quality that—for a westerner—surrounds anything Chinese. Rather he was now looking for something to fill gaps which Marx and Engels had left in their social philosophy. These gaps included matters relating to human psychology, to practical questions about how to earn a living, what to do when in love, how to avoid dangers, and other mundane matters which had escaped the attention of Marx and Engels. Above all, Brecht wanted to find ways that helped him spread the truth that he felt Marx and Engels had found. Chinese literature and philosophy helped him to mix the old wisdom of China with what he regarded as the new wisdom of Marx.

Renata Berg-Pan. *GQ*. March, 1975, pp. 204, 206–7

Brecht was, one suspects, not a man of great physical courage. His courage of the mind, in going on asserting the necessity for each man to decide for himself, is all the more remarkable: it could have led to torments that for him would have been completely unbearable.

His best answer was Schweyk [in *Schweyk in the Second World War*], and it is still the best answer for many who live today under a regime that will not brook real opposition in the slightest degree. Schweyk runs the risk of unspeakable pain, if his light-hearted opposition ever encounters more than stupid obedience to orders from the higher-ups. In Brecht's play the risk is never allowed to incur its probable consequences, any more than it is in Hašek's original version. That is as it should be, in a play or novel—to pursue grimly every possibility of retribution would be to destroy the possibility of even imagining opposition. But ultimately, we have to recognize that the forces opposing Brecht, on both sides of the political coin, were so powerful that only a Schweykian, satirical compromise was really effective, or rather useful as a means of still keeping one's head up. It is condescending, and almost, though not quite, pointless, for people living in a parliamentary democracy where dissidence does not inevitably involve retribution from the State, to reprove the kind of adaptive tactics which Schweyk uses: it took more than Schweyk to defeat Hitler, and may take more still to modify the totalitarian régimes of today. Yet among Brecht's plays are some which will always remain as a potential challenge, even if only by virtue of appearing to require personal decisions. At their best, they do more than that. Mother Courage, Azdak, and even Baal, have a resilience and an individuality inimical to any societal regime, and if one wants to point to what matters most, politically, in Brecht's achievement as a dramatist, one could do worse, in the present state of the world, than to point to them, all three.

Ronald Gray. *Brecht the Dramatist* (Cambridge, Cambridge University Press, 1976), pp. 180–81

The Measures Taken by far surpasses the previous didactic plays in its austerity and ideological severity. Brecht's most doctrinal play, it expresses his first frank and unreserved profession of communism, and his only attempt to present the extreme sacrifice required by the class struggle. Its purpose is "to teach politically correct behavior by showing politically incorrect behavior." . . .

Perhaps never before nor after has a play by Brecht caused so much discussion, particularly in leftist circles. The discussions have not ended; even today the play remains what it was from the beginning—uncomfortable for both the left and the right. . . .

For Brecht, *The Measures Taken* was the most significant of his *Lehrstücke* [didactic play]. As late as 1953 he noted that he had plans for a play about Hans Garbe, an East German worker-hero who had set new production norms. It was "to be written in the style of *The Measures Taken* or *The Mother.*" And when Manfred Wekwerth asked him to name a play for the theater of the future, Brecht answered unhesitatingly, *"The Measures Taken."*

At the same time (1929 and 1930) that Brecht was working on *The Measures Taken,* he also wrote another, much less doctrinal, didactic play: *The Exception and the Rule,* in collaboration with Ernst Burri and Elisabeth Hauptmann, with music by Paul Dessau. The play is centered around the ironic fact that a good deed, if it occurs, must necessarily be misunderstood in a society where the bad deed is the rule. . . .

Brecht's *Lehrstücke* have often been compared with medieval morality plays, religious plays in the service of the Protestant or Catholic cause, and oratorios. And, indeed, the didactic play was frequently used during the seventeenth century by the Counter Reformation in Germany, particularly by the Jesuit order to illustrate and teach their doctrine. The primary purpose of the religious or morality play was to teach correct behavior and to spread the gospel. With communism being a kind of secularized gospel, it comes as no surprise that Brecht resorted to this dramatic form.

Diversified as they are in subject matter, Brecht's *Lehrstücke* are characterized by a certain rigidity and uniformity of purpose. They are also good examples of his progressive concept of epic and dialectic theater as well as of his newly found creed, Marxism-Leninism.

Karl H. Schoeps. *Bertolt Brecht* (New York,
Frederick Ungar, 1977), pp. 175, 180, 181–82, 184

Depending on their respective persuasions, critics have been disposed to interpret *The Good Woman of Setzuan* as a statement about the impossibility of ethical behavior in a venal world or, alternatively, as an overt critique of capitalism, an illustration that virtue cannot be practiced until an inhuman economic system has been superseded. However, the play can also be viewed as a very different kind of indictment: an indictment of an absolute value system and of individuals who persist in adhering to an immutable morality. In short, it is possible to argue that in [this play] the emphasis is on the inadequacy of the moral rather than the social system. [It] need not be read as a play about goodness. On the contrary, there are cogent reasons for considering it a Brechtian model illustrating the fallacy of an absolute concept of goodness. The closing scene of the play, in demonstrating an irresolvable conflict between Shen Te's moral aspirations and her material survival can be read as a prima facie case: she cannot begin to solve her problems until she eliminates her double standard. She must adopt an ethical position which she can acknowledge publicly. . . .

The distinction is a simple shift in emphasis. Heretofore, in Europe and the United States, [*The Good Woman of Setzuan*] has been perceived as a parable about virtue. Shen Te's dilemmas have been analyzed as inevitable and tragic. Critics have focused on her suffering, comparing her to Christian martyrs and even Christ himself or relegating her to the role of the noble prostitute.

I am suggesting that the play is a parable about the adherence to an unrealistic standard of virtue. Such a shift in critical point of view significantly alters the implications of the play, leading to a reevaluation of the heroine's behavior and character.

Janet K. Swaffar. *UDR*. Spring, 1979, p. 65

Azdak's character [in *The Caucasian Chalk Circle*] is coherent but cannot be reduced to one unifying principle. He is a recognizable human being whose motives can be identified and for whom certain actions could be ruled out of character. He is dominated by his desire for pleasure, his commitment for revolutionary justice, and his tendency to do and say the unexpected. His character is less heterogeneous than the contrasting incidents of his story might suggest: sparing his enemy is a manifestation of his love, as are his fear of death, enjoyment of food and drink, moderate greed, and sensuality. Being a judge coordinates the different aspects of his personality. Compulsively merciful as he is, he distinguishes himself more by protecting the good than by punishing the wicked. His subtle intelligence, his sympathies, his need for bribes, and his predilection for shock tactics combine to inspire him as he twists the laws. If his judicial career is consistent on the whole, in the separate scenes he neglects one of his goals while pursuing the others. He is aware that his impulse to hide the Grand Duke conflicts with his principles, and he reproaches himself afterwards. Otherwise he does not suffer from the contradictions within himself. His malpractice verdict is based on profit and paradox rather than justice, and he shows more eagerness to convict Ludowika and take the horse than to acquit the servant. At the end he is one-sided in the opposite manner: he is primarily the cunning champion of the poor, despite his dislike of taking risks. . . .

Because Azdak is so complicated, he serves as a good example, a warning, and a provocation. He shares the Brechtian cardinal virtues of vitality and friendliness. Placing individual need and social usefulness above the statutes, as Azdak does, is fundamental for Brecht's version of Marxism. . . . At the same time the coincidences to which Azdak owes his position make him a warning that justice cannot be guaranteed by the actions of an extraordinary individual but only by a revolutionary society, as in the prolog. . . . Both his anti-social tendencies and his mixed character are provocative. His sensuality and his scorn for honesty and order are reminiscent of the outcasts with whom Brecht challenged the audiences of his earlier works.

Linda Hill. *GerSR*. Oct., 1979, pp. 328–29

Bertolt Brecht was, however, not only a passive observer of the struggle of the revolutionary worker's movement and a sympathizing reporter. He also wanted, in his own way, to take part in this movement. During the last years of the Weimar Republic, he attempted, with his learning plays, to support the development of class consciousness and disciplined struggle. He addressed himself directly to the workers' choruses and amateur theater groups. For all practical purposes he had given up on a bourgeoisie that had celebrated his *Threepenny Opera* without comprehending that it was applauding its own cynicism. It was not until the exile period, when he was forced to address an audience that was indeed antifascist but still not completely proletarian (to the extent that he had an audience at all), that his pieces were intended to bring convincing arguments to a bourgeois public. This view is supported by the fact that these pieces were great successes in the postwar period—especially in the Federal Republic and for West German bourgeois intellectual audiences who made up a considerable part of the audience for productions by the Berlin Ensemble in East Berlin. . . . But Brecht did not want such an audience to enjoy, in a self-assured and sentimental manner, its own moods in the theater. He wanted the audience to learn, to comprehend that only through a revolutionary alteration of society can the incongruities be overcome, the incongruities under which we still suffer. Usually, in the theater, this effect was not achieved. The liveliness of the characters, the richness of the language, the sophisticated dramaturgy, and the brilliance of the actors made it possible to react to these pieces as culinary art—even though the playwright denounced such a stance very loudly. All of his theatrical provocations were enjoyed by a satiated postwar public simply as additional spice.

Iring Fetscher. In Betty Nance and Hubert Heinen, eds.,
Bertolt Brecht: Political Theory and Literary Practice
(Athens, Ga., University of Georgia Press, 1980), pp. 12–13

Brecht plays are still doing splendidly at the box office, and often last year's productions are held over for the new season.

Should we conclude that all is well with Brecht on the German stage? The answer we'd get from the theatre workers and critics alike is a resounding "No." Beginning in the late 1960s reservations were voiced about Brecht's theatre and about its validity for the contemporary stage and society. During the 1970s these voices have been proliferating. Nearly all the leading directors in today's German theatre seem to refrain from doing his plays; the important playwrights have distanced themselves from his theory and dramaturgy, in the mode of their writing and often in published statements as well; and most of the prominent critics tend to deprecate Brecht productions or pay no attention to them at all. . . .

Most of the younger directors don't deny that they owe a lot to Brecht and probably learned more from his work than from anyone else's in their own development. Yet, Ernst Wendt's reply when asked by the critic Guenther Ruehle why Brecht's plays don't present a challenge anymore is representative. Wendt, the chief-dramaturg and a highly successful director at Munich's Kammerspiele, named two areas the directors of his generation are deeply involved in and stimulated by at the present: one being the fascination with the socio-psychological "inner space" which poses the task of tracing the innermost motivations of man; the other being the urge to define themselves in terms of German history and classical German literature and to arrive at a self-understanding in terms of historical arguments. Wendt concluded that Brecht doesn't offer insights or information for either the psychological or the historical complex of their questions.

Carl Weber. *TDR*. March, 1980, p. 117

DÜRRENMATT, FRIEDRICH (1921–   )

It has often been asked why Switzerland has no pre-eminent dramatists, and widely differing answers have been given. There is much to be said for one such thesis; Switzerland, it says, is steeped in security. The country was spared from the last two wars, and even before their outbreak it had enjoyed a prolonged period of peace. Consequently the disturbing forces that might go to make a great dramatist are lacking. . . .

The young dramatist Friedrich Dürrenmatt has attempted to bring contemporary events onto the stage . . . impelled by the agonies of his own soul. His play *It Is Written* was hissed off the stage at its first performance, but nevertheless became the centre of prolonged and general discussion. A second work of his, *The Blind Man,* is soon to be played in Zürich. . . . Although he is certainly without the mature judgment of the artist, his talent is worthy of attention. His relentless honesty cuts right to the heart of the problem, and he is a born fighter—and that, in Switzerland, is something very rare. It cannot be decided to-day whether or not he has been called to create a new Swiss Drama, but he may certainly be cited to show that Switzerland, the island of peace, does not lead to lethargy and stagnation, but, on the contrary, awakens keen interest for all the problems of the day.

A. Munke Schütz. GL&L. April, 1948, pp. 231–33

The work of two dramatists, Max Frisch and Friedrich Dürrenmatt, is very largely conditioned by the war and the post-war period; yet at the same time these poets have in view an idea which, standing above politics, serves to bind the nations together, and before which the actual tensions existing between the different peoples forfeit their ultimate justification. In this connection Frisch's tragedy *When the War Was Over,* and Dürrenmatt's *Romulus the Great* must be mentioned. It is interesting to observe how Frisch seeks the possibility of an understanding between persons of different nationalities by means which are outside the scope of normal dramatic method . . . whilst in Dürrenmatt's comedy it is precisely the power of speech which, as the expression of all that is human, reaches its full significance. . . . It is an epicurean, generous, wise and infinitely superior emperor, the last of his line, who convinces us by his brilliant oratory that all pretensions to power and all measures backed by force are, at bottom, mere laughable and childish games, which serve only to mask the self-deception of an immature humanity. The revelation of falsity comes about, not by violent action, but by considered inactivity, and the use of the right word in the right place. It is, perhaps, on the plane of comedy where the present-day dramatist can find the ground most suited to the dramatic treatment of nations at war, and of those who suffer through warfare. For to encompass all this in one single tragedy would demand a faith on the part of his audience, which no contemporary dramatist can count upon. . . . He has either, like Frisch, to content himself with the portrayal of a few pregnant scenes, which lead to no definitive solution, or else, like Dürrenmatt, to use the means of comedy, in order to expound the relativity of the horror which he is portraying.

Maria Bindschedler. *GL&L*. Jan., 1951, pp. 123–24

What in the end is the tragic sense of Dürrenmatt's comedy and who are its heroes, if any? If unmasking is a basic function of comedy, then Dürrenmatt fulfills it in every instance. One basic trait is common to all his characters up to but excluding *The Visit of the Old Lady,* namely immutability. They are what they are, and for better or worse they remain what they are, unbroken by life or by death. Therein lies also their tragedy, for most of them cannot conceive that their cause may be wrong or selfish or sought in their own image. Their *hubris* is their downfall. They do not pass the "Bewährungsprobe" (the test). They do not hesitate, in humility or Promethean vanity, to presume on the will of God or to sit in judgment over their fellow men, be it in the Münster of the Anabaptists, or the Germany of the Thirty Years' War, or dying Rome, or the present age, or Biblical times. They are the self-styled heroes and saviors and martyrs who come back again and again, as the resurrected Saint-Claude and Mississippi [in *The Marriage of Mr. Mississippi*] sing at the end of their play. As the ancient Bishop in *It Is Written* knows, they try to fly before they learn walking, and their very deeds, whatever their motivation, are the traps of a guilt that they are neither aware of nor understand, but which brings about their punishment.

But then there are the Jobs of faith like the blind Duke, and the Quixotes like Übelohe. They are not heroes, they are the courageous. And there is Ill [in *The Visit of the Old Lady*], who literally grows as a character as he gradually begins to comprehend his guilt and to accept the necessity of punishment. . . . And thus the tragic comedy of a scapegoat—that bears minute resemblance to the *agnus*—assumes aspects of a religious play.

We have saved for the last that wonderful beggar, Akki [in *An Angel Comes to Babylon*]. Better than the blind Duke [in *The Blind Man*] or Übelohe [in *The Marriage of Mr. Mississippi*] he represents Dürrenmatt's true hero—the nonhero. He is the little fellow, who knows that he cannot win against the mighty and principled. He knows he must survive. For, unless the unheroic Akki survive, there will be no happiness, no beauty, no poetry, no refuge for Divine grace, only grim pursuit of duty, and sooner or later the great heroes will have finished off each other and the world. This fear of extinction keeps Akki and Kurubi and the world, and us, running.

Adolf D. Klarmann. *TDR*. May, 1960, pp. 102–4

The Swiss consider Dürrenmatt an *enfant terrible* among their writers. His literary style is somewhat reminiscent of Frank Wedekind's, with whom he shares the grotesque and scurrilous in his vision as well as the passions of a moralist. This trend becomes more noticeable with each new play. Unlike

Wedekind, Dürrenmatt makes full use of the possibilities of the epic theater. Also his humor is much more genuine than that of Wedekind, who is usually too aggressive to provide for laughs. But Dürrenmatt's type of humor does not necessarily please the audience. He uses it to attack the listeners. His so-called comedies are anything but that; particularly in *The Visit,* the laughs soon freeze on the spectators' faces. His language shows plasticity and strength. In intensity it excels anything that the present-day German-language drama has to offer. . . .

In 1959, Dürrenmatt with Paul Burkhard as his collaborator wrote a musical play. It was the first attempt by Burkhard to produce such an ambitious work. These two most prominent Swiss, the one in music, the other in the field of drama, had set themselves the goal of producing a Swiss national opera in *Frank V, Opera of a Private Bank.* Before it was finished, Dürrenmatt made this characteristic statement about it: "It is a very angry and very wild play. It will be a kind of Shakespearean royal tragedy, projected into the bank atmosphere. . . . It is a tragic story with a great number of funny things in it." [May, 1961]

F. E. Coenen. In Carl Hammer, Jr., ed., *Studies in German Literature* (Baton Rouge, Louisiana State University Press, 1963), pp. 124–25, 127

Dürrenmatt, like Shaw, achieves dramatic interest and tension largely by means of a conflict of ideas, and he shares with Shaw the rare talent of giving each side powerful arguments which counterbalance each other, thus masking his own viewpoint. This "allowing the Devil to have some of the good tunes" is by no means the sole reason for difficulty in deciding where Dürrenmatt's sympathies lie. Such difficulty arises in no small measure from the clash between an earnest belief and a flippant, comic mode of expression, or between a ludicrous faith and an earnest, unbending statement of it, between horrific subject-matter and humorous or at least dispassionate treatment. In short we are puzzled by (apparent) discrepancies between content and presentation. The resultant frivolity is apt to disturb the serious-minded who take it for granted that a faith which is held in earnest requires a befitting dignity of statement as inevitably as Sunday demands one's best suit. This clash between content and presentation may be described as "grotesque" and such grotesqueness produces an astringent flavour which constitutes one of the main attractions of Dürrenmatt's style of writing.

Peter Johnson. *GL&L.* July, 1962, p. 264

[Dürrenmatt's] first literary works were symbolic prose, and in 1946 he had his first play performed. Since then he has been an unceasingly active writer: he has written novels and plays, has given the radio play decisive impulses, and has stimulated even the cinema with his subjects or his direct participation. His infrequent theoretical works, above all the slim volume *Problems of the Theater* and the lecture on Schiller, are highly noteworthy as well. . . .

His work is inconceivable without the Christian paradox. No book has influenced him more strongly than the Bible, and no idea has pursued him more than the relationship between justice and grace.

Dürrenmatt rests absolutely on the fundamental principle that man as a mortal and knowing creature is "condemned to death." But he takes up this ordinary, hackneyed expression in its fullest sense: "condemned" presupposes a judge and an executioner. This basic idea in Dürrenmatt—man under judgment—is reflected in the aesthetic sphere. When, after *The Blind Man,* Dürrenmatt turned decisively to comedy, he did it on the basis that contemporary man no longer deserves tragedy. . . . It is obvious that such a moral, indeed metaphysical, justification of the comic must leave traditional comedy far behind. No single one of Dürrenmatt's works ends cheerfully.

Elisabeth Brock-Sulzer. Monat. May, 1963, pp. 56–58†

The force of the written word in a production of *The Marriage of Mr. Mississippi* had to come to the fore, and this could only be accomplished by reassessing the staging of the play. The stage is a tribunal; like Brecht and Schiller, Dürrenmatt wants the audience engaged; he does not write plays to entertain. He is protesting and criticizing, and he does not want the audience to forget what it has seen and heard. In addition, he is also experimenting by exploring new possibilities of the theater, seeking new limits, and revising and rewriting when necessary. Dürrenmatt once referred to the theater as an instrument with which he was continuously trying to become better acquainted. He insists that he is not interested in the theater as a field for theories, philosophical points of view, and statements. He is trying to solve practical problems. . . . Actual experimentation on the stage is necessary to test the relationships between the parts and the whole. When the right balance between the text and the stage realization has been attained, the result will be a fusion into a harmonious whole, a whole which is not only visible, audible, and comprehensible, but which at the same time has about it a sense of immediacy.

Leland R. Phelps. MD. Sept., 1965, pp. 159–60

The dichotomy between the world (viz. the stage) and the behavior of men (viz. the actors) reveals an incongruousness that is conveyed repeatedly in the set designs contrasted with the plot of the drama. Dürrenmatt, the son of a Calvinistic preacher, crystallizes with the aid of the visual paradox the message that grandiose human endeavors, even the most laudable of righteous crusades, are often absurd illusions when measured honestly against reality. A man without humility is more apt to be blinded or limited by his intelligence than enlightened by it; that is, he may become a sort of Don Quixote, "not a man out of his senses, but a man in whom the imagination and the pure reason are so powerful as to make him disregard the evidence of senses when it opposes their conclusions." In every one of his plays Dürrenmatt singles out men as major characters in whom principles or plans overrule reason and whose well-intending actions, although inwardly logical and consistent, are seen to be self-contradictory when pushed to the extreme.

The irony that grows out of Dürrenmatt's visual-verbal dichotomy is twofold: first we *see* cities and empires *(It Is Written, An Angel Comes to Babylon)*, castles *(The Blind Man)*, people *(The Visit)*, and civilizations *(Romulus, The Physicists)* decimated by the very people who in word and deed are trying to save them, and secondly we learn how men distort the evidence of reality to do what they need to in order to feel great and noble. And it is only through his total use of the theater that Dürrenmatt is able to present his concepts of contradiction with real force. . . . And by juxtaposing words and images in a forceful manner on stage, Dürrenmatt succeeds in expressing ultimately by means of precise craftmanship a philosophy that logically escapes definition, one that is paradoxical.

Edward Diller. Symposium. Fall, 1966, pp. 204–5

Dürrenmatt's originality becomes even more unmistakable in the confrontation with his greatest rival, Brecht. It is true that both oppose the entertaining play cooked according to recipe and absolute art. Both assign to the theater the task of clarifying and interpreting our contemporary situation. But the difference between them is revealed in the effect each seeks to produce. Brecht wants to infuse the public with a feeling of detachment; Dürrenmatt strives for a direct response. The playwright's art consists in provoking the audience to thought immediately after the performance: "A thoughtful public transcends itself."

Theatrical means shape dramatic ends. Brecht appeals to the members of a social class, Dürrenmatt to individuals. Brecht's plays are intended to be challenges to change the world, Dürrenmatt's are a summons to the individual to rethink the world in relation to himself. This is the crucial point of their difference. Dürrenmatt's plays concretely demonstrate the impossibility of changing the world in the figures of revolutionaries who have failed. For him, there is no history in Brecht's sense. The present situation for him is the result of a necessary and natural process. . . .

He believes this modern world, recognized by us as our destiny, should be resisted, not accepted.

Karl Pestalozzi. In Otto Mann and Wolfgang Rothe, eds.,
Deutsche Literatur im 20. Jahrhundert (Bern, Francke,
1967), Vol. II, pp. 400–401†

The critical responses to this multi-leveled play [*The Visit*] vary from the trivially superficial to the excessively erudite. It is a tribute to the inner wealth of *The Visit* that it can appeal to so many different viewers and supply the grounds for such disparate interpretations. One common view is that the play is basically a religious drama. Ill's acceptance of his guilt and punishment, and his insistence that the community must also face its guilt, is the point of departure for a consideration of the religious aspects of the play. Ill's path through suffering to the attainment of serenity in the expectation of death is not only the central action but also the characteristic pattern of a religious drama with obvious parallels to Christian salvation. It was possible for one critic to state: "*The Visit* is a modern presentation of the Passion story, not only in part or in grotesque or nihilistic distortion, but in the full sense of the word." It is true that the Biblical echoes and parallels are numerous, if sought for, but they are not obtrusive and belong to the texture of the play as one of several formative elements. The psychological, economic, and sociological levels of the play are equally important in an analysis which attempts to reduce . . . to its constituent parts its finely woven fabric. There is no single, simple message or moral in *The Visit,* but rather a powerful action with a wide range of suggestibility.

Murray B. Peppard. *Friedrich Dürrenmatt* (New York, Twayne, 1969), pp. 61–62

Dürrenmatt takes up again in *The Marriage of Mr. Mississippi* something of the grotesqueness of *It Is Written,* though in this instance he is more firmly determined to interpret it in a spirit of comedy. . . .

It has been pointed out that Mississippi, Saint-Claude, and Bodo von Übelohe may represent faith, hope, and charity. These three main characters are united in their search for an absolute, in their desire to change the world and in their dissatisfaction with the policy of preserving the existing situation which is manifested in the figure of the minister Diego. Thus they are united by a gleam of what is regarded by others as fanaticism and folly, and hold together, symbolically at least, like the Anabaptists in the face of the traditional forces of Church and Empire, or like the Duke when confronted by Negro da Ponte [in *The Blind Man*]. Bodo von Übelohe resembles Knipperdollinck, the Duke, and Romulus when he strips himself, or is stripped, of his riches until, possessing nothing, he embodies the ideal of poverty and powerlessness. Knipperdollinck and the Duke, in holding fast to rigid attitudes, are tragic martyrs; Romulus and Übelohe have no illusions about themselves, are willing to be regarded as clowns, and thus (from Dürrenmatt's point of view as apparently implied in these plays) can speak for ideals of wisdom and love.

H. M. Waidson. In Alex Natan, ed., *Swiss Men of Letters* (London, Oswald Wolff, 1970), p. 268

Dürrenmatt himself often points out Aristophanes and Nestroy as prime influences on his work; but one would certainly venture to say that he has also read his Kafka quite thoroughly. . . .

Unlike Kafka . . . Dürrenmatt never studied the law. His interests, outside literature itself, lie in the areas of philosophy and art. Nevertheless, his obsession with justice and his frequent use of legal machinery indicate that he, too, shares Kafka's feeling that man's life is a state of being on trial, for a guilt which he may be unaware of, but which, nonetheless, must exist. . . .

Ultimately his concern with the problem of justice is simply the artist's way of expressing the crisis of his time. The problem of justice looms large in all his works but . . . Dürrenmatt often works with scathing humor. There is the parody of justice in *It Is Written,* the acid caricature of the *Staatsanwalt* [state prosecutor] in *The Marriage of Mr. Mississippi,* the grotesque apotheosis of Claire Zachanassian in *The Visit,* voluntary exile to the madhouse as the ultimate *reductio ad absurdum* of the *Physicists'* attempt to restore justice in a world gone mad. . . .

Dürrenmatt makes it . . . clear that what looks like innocence can be at best an accidental circumstance, beneath which the basic sinfulness of man is bound to reveal itself. When Traps asks his hosts, at the outset of the trial game [in *Traps*], what crime he is supposed to have committed, the gentlemen just laugh, and he is assured that "a crime always turns up." In *The Double* also the man who protests against his death sentence is told "we are all deserving of death," an assertion borne out later in the play. The all-pervasive nature of human guilt makes crime an interchangeable commodity. . . . The man Pedro may be innocent of the crime committed by his double Diego; but this innocence is only accidental. "You would have killed, if you had been tempted," he is told by Diego, and in fact, he subsequently does kill, not only once, but twice, thus bearing out the justice of the mysterious high court which had condemned him from the beginning. Again, the basic situation of Kafka's *The Trial* is repeated; it is not necessary to have actually committed a crime in order to be called to trial. . . .

Dürrenmatt's trials also end with the acceptance of full responsibility on the part of the accused, and the concomitant demand for punishment to restore justice. . . . [However,] Dürrenmatt's cynical attitude towards modern life becomes apparent in the ironic ending of both plays. Traps' catharsis turns out to have been no more than alcoholic stupor; Pedro's high court, an empty hall, where a somewhat damaged statue of Justice stands on a lopsided old table. "And are we to be satisfied with that?" asks the director of the play; "We have to be satisfied with that," is the poet's laconic reply. Dürrenmatt here makes perfectly clear . . . the total dichotomy between human jurisprudence and absolute justice, the impossibility of justice in the modern world.

Renate Usmiani. Mosaic. Summer, 1970, pp. 166–68, 170–73

In the notes to his adaptation Dürrenmatt announces that *King John* is a political play "showing the machinery of politics and how its agreements and accidents are brought about." It is a game played out among the murderers, not the victims, but its relevance for us is proved by the kind of problem we face: "I do not deny it is a nasty play but it is borne out by our times." At first sight it may appear that Dürrenmatt's intention was to bring up to date the content of *King John,* the first of Shakespeare's plays to introduce a sombre political theme into his work. The contemporary interest is avowedly present, but the significance of Dürrenmatt's version lies almost entirely in its structural divergence from Shakespeare, not in the similarity of material used. Indeed, Dürrenmatt's formal innovations are primary and so deeply embedded in the play that they actually alter its content. . . .

Shakespeare notoriously handled the facts about King John in cavalier fashion . . . and Dürrenmatt too juggles with events and dates to suit his rather different purpose—to create a parable. But the great discrepancy in the impact of these two plays is not to be sought in their varying factual distortions; it ensues from Dürrenmatt's determination not to allow political thinking to dominate dramaturgical thinking. Although he does have opinions about politics—and forceful, well-argued ones at that—his primary aim is aesthetic; he is intent on creating a viable theatrical experience. . . .

The Life and Death of King John, woven of incident and language in Shakespeare's particular vision, is recast by Dürrenmatt into a "Komödie der Politik" that puts the doers and the done-to on the stage of history and tells in its grotesque structures of the frustration and futility of ideals and the sensuality of living.

Arrigo Subiotto. In R. W. Last, ed., <i>Affinities: Essays in
German and English Literature</i> (London, Oswald Wolff,
1971), pp. 139–40, 152

For Dürrenmatt *Wirklichkeit* is a broad term encompassing the ultimate reality of man's existence, whether it be called "God," "the essence of being," or simply "the way it really is," as opposed to what man *thinks* life is or what he wants it to be.

Dürrenmatt has repeatedly stated that this "reality" can never be directly known and certainly not controlled. . . . In the early dramas, including *It Is Written,* this elusive "reality" was simply called "God." Decisively influenced by both Kierkegaard and Karl Barth, Dürrenmatt demonstrated in these openly religious plays that man could not come to know God directly, although God is the decisive reality with which man has to deal. . . . But the playwright came to see that presenting this Christian paradox on the stage to a modern secular audience was well-nigh impossible. . . .

In giving up religious drama, Dürrenmatt by no means gave up his view of ultimate "reality." In his new plays, now called "comedies," he continued to demonstrate that even the wisest of men could not grasp the ultimate reality of existence. But the shift of emphasis is expressed in a shift of language: the annihilating blow is no longer attributed to a transcendent "God" but to a more immanent *Wirklichkeit* or—since it is increasingly the outward manifestation of this "reality"—*Zufall* [chance], expressing itself on the horizontal plane of history. . . . That the concept of "reality" has replaced—if not totally, at least to a large degree—the concept of God, becomes clear when one compares the effect of "God" in the earlier plays and "reality" in the later on the hero or central character. In both cases ultimate reality destroys the hero's thoughts and plans and casts him into despair, but after a recognition and stock-taking, a humble attitude of courage emerges, not only in the bishop or the blind duke of the religious plays, but also in Romulus and Übelohe of the comedies. The basic characteristic of Dürrenmatt's "courageous man" in both cases is that he does not capitulate to the absurdity that looms up in the void left by his inability to make sense of "reality." His acceptance of life involves a courageous leap of affirmation.

Margareta N. Deschner. GQ. March, 1971, pp. 231–32

It is probable that Dürrenmatt still has much to offer. What he has achieved up to now, however, would be enough for us to consider him among the more important dramatists of German (and world) literature. Besides obvious genius, Dürrenmatt possesses the characteristics that distinguished Shaw: a sharp critical intelligence and the honesty to think through a problem logically and uncompromisingly (even when the end is despair). Dürrenmatt has the background of a great humanist. He also has a vital and indestructible sense of humor, which encompasses everything from crude puns to grotesque absurdities, and includes satire as well as the most polished parody.

Dürrenmatt is convinced of the absurdity of human existence; isolated man stands powerless, facing the void. The human race is digging its own grave because of its senseless worship of technology. Even if Dürrenmatt, with his hard logic, is far from being a devout Christian, many of his works are like sermons. . . . They ask us to distrust slogans and shibboleths and any kind of political leadership.

Armin Arnold. Friedrich Dürrenmatt
(New York, Frederick Ungar, 1972), p. 100

The conflict in *It Is Written* between a Don Quixote of morality (Knipperdollinck) and a Don Quixote of amorality (Bockelson), left unresolved, is reexplored in Dürrenmatt's second play, *The Blind Man*, in which the historical has all but yielded to the allegorical. There is the mere suggestion of a historical basis for the events in the play, The Thirty Years War, while the fore-ground is occupied by symbolic figures of the proportions of Satan and Job. The fact that *The Blind Man* is a reworking of the Job theme has frequently been acknowledged. The man of moral temper, like Job called upon to affirm his belief in a just God and a just creation, is in the paradoxical metaphoric language of Dürrenmatt a blind man. A confrontation between good and evil takes place in the soul of this protagonist, a philosopher-king without a king-dom—actually a duke in devastated Germany, a man of conscience and good will. His adversary, Negro da Ponte, named with Dürrenmatt's usual sub-tlety, represents the powers of darkness and evil. Da Ponte, champion of an amoral materialism, makes it clear that Dürrenmatt is concerned with a de-bate on ethics in the form of a play: "The curtain rises," he says, "and you see nothing else but a human being, the (sole) content of my play."

The peace of mind, the inner assurance of the duke, is at stake in a struggle between belief and disbelief. Is his faith in the goodness of God and of life dependent on an illusion so patent that only a blind man could harbor it? A stranger, da Ponte, whose ruthlessness is based on his amoral character and lack of responsibility, appears—as will become the custom in Dürrenmatt's plays—and the attempt at disillusionment begins. . . .

Winner in . . . minor philosophical skirmishes, the duke has only an ambiguous kind of success in his struggle against the abstract amoral force represented by da Ponte. Dürrenmatt lets the devil have the last word in his play, even though the tempter has to quit the scene and allow the duke to keep his blind faith. . . . Dürrenmatt has written a problem play, to which a solution, such as that provided by the advocates of the new morality based on the principle of love, is still lacking, although at times it seems that the answer is imminent.

> Kurt J. Fickert. *To Heaven and Back: The New Morality
> in the Plays of Friedrich Dürrenmatt* (Lexington,
> University Press of Kentucky, 1972), pp. 20–22

A central theme [of *The Meteor*], the unmasking of literature, which consti-tutes a self-judgment on the part of Schwitter, is taken up again and brought to a conclusion only in the last part of the play. The occasion is a dialogue between Schwitter and the toilet attendant Nomsen. . . . In the description of her business career—the toilet attendant owns, after all, "two villas in the English quarter and a commercial building downtown"— . . . in her life entirely devoted to money-making, Schwitter now sees his own career mirrored. The literary profession loses its last luster as Schwitter compares it to the professional rise of the former madam Nomsen, now a toilet atten-dant. Schwitter declares: "I find you extremely likable. . . . I envy you. Your business was prostitution, mine merely literature. I wrote only to make money. . . . I invented stories, and nothing else. . . . In retrospect, Mrs.

Nomsen, I may state with some pride: Commercially and morally I was more or less your equal.''

With that Schwitter has carried out the liquidation of any higher meaning of his literary work. There is a straight progression from his burning of his manuscripts at the beginning to this confession toward the end of the play. And when his cynical son . . . tells him at the end, ''You have gone out of fashion . . . your plays are forgotten. The world wants hard facts, not invented stories; documents, not legends; instruction, not entertainment. The writer must be committed, or else he is superfluous . . . ,'' this pronouncement of Schwitter's literary death completely misses its mark; for Schwitter is already finished with literature.

One can perhaps also see in this last quote a reflection of the author Dürrenmatt regarding his own position as a writer in the present-day literary scene. For Schwitter's son touches upon a dilemma of personal concern to Dürrenmatt, who, in comparison with the documentary theater of Heinar Kipphardt, Peter Weiss, or even Rolf Hochhuth, appears somewhat antiquated. As Dürrenmatt presents it through Schwitter's point of view, however, such changes are but phases of fashion and as irrelevant as his own writing. . . . Literature itself cannot withstand the scrutiny of self-criticism. . . . At the same time the author calls into question his own ability to find the truth.

Manfred Durzak. Dürrenmatt, Frisch, Weiss (Stuttgart,
Reclam, 1972), pp. 133–34†

With *The Physicists* a phase of attraction in [Dürrenmatt's] relationship to Brecht was followed again by one of repulsion. This is indicated by the very form of the play. Basically, Dürrenmatt's theater shows only a slight tendency toward the scenic revue technique of the Epic Theater. Neither in *Romulus* nor in *The Visit* do parts become autonomous. In *The Physicists*, though, the action plainly forms such a close-knit unity—through the observance of the so called three unities, for example, and strictly applied principles of connection—that the author has even been called an ''Aristotelian.'' More decisive than such contrasts to the ''non-Aristotelian'' Brecht are the differences in the treatment of the same theme. As in *Galileo*, it is the problematic nature of modern science that is up for discussion. Brecht emphasized . . . the immense social effect of scientific discoveries and therefore attributed a high degree of responsibility to the individual. He understood science as a great social force. Dürrenmatt pursues this thought to its logical conclusion, with a consistency that results almost in its inversion. The social repercussions of any discoveries in the nuclear sciences are so immense that it is the duty of the scientific genius ''to remain unrecognized,'' that is, to isolate himself from society.

Walter Hinck. Das moderne Drama in Deutschland
(Göttingen, Vandenhoeck & Ruprecht, 1973), pp. 190–91†

In a time when so much that's written for the theatre seems tentative and small, self-conscious and undramatically reflective, the plays of the Swiss playwright Friedrich Dürrenmatt, by comparison, are marked with the grandeur of an almost Jacobean excess. When we enter his fantastic world there can be no doubting that we have come into a realm where the impossible has become probable. Like those writers whom he most admires—Aristophanes, Wycherley, Nestroy, and Thornton Wilder—Dürrenmatt is the master of the dramatic conceit. He invents a bizarre and improbable situation and exploits it for all it is worth, and then some.

However, just beneath the apparently absurd lunacy of the surface conceit we discover a stern moral vision which shapes all that he writes. Like Ibsen, only with a somewhat better sense of humor, Dürrenmatt has a Lutheran conscience much like that of a Protestant pastor who has defrocked himself because he has lost his belief in the possibility of a salvation. He is a stern judge of the world, but his harshest judgments are directed against himself. Like a cynical Shaw, we sense he is ever ready to turn the stage into a pulpit from which to preach about the evils of a world turned sour. But until *The Physicists* he has always stopped short just in time. His troubled agnosticism would reassert itself at the final moment, and with awkward protestations that his sermon would be of little use, he returns to the theatricality with which he began, once more ironic and aloof.

With *The Physicists,* Dürrenmatt seems to be entering a new stage in his development as a playwright. His fantastic imagination and his unrivaled powers of invention are still very much present, but they seem to be completely under control for the first time. This play has a concentration which all of his earlier plays except *The Visit* have lacked. In his important essay, *Problems of the Theatre,* Dürrenmatt bemoans the fact that the modern dramatist is incapable of achieving that tightness of form which characterizes the classical Greek theatre. *The Physicists* indicates that Dürrenmatt can, and we only hope that his achievement will persuade other playwrights that theatrical richness and a rigorously controlled form need not be considered mutually exclusive or incompatible in the contemporary theatre.

Robert W. Corrigan. *The Theatre in Search of a Fix*
(New York, Delacorte, 1973), pp. 247–48, 252

God crosses the stage in august form in [Hugo von] Hofmannsthal's *World Theater* and in pathetic form in [Ernst] Barlach's *The Deluge.* In Dürrenmatt's theater [*An Angel Comes to Babylon*] God is absent from this world; his divinity appears in certain characters in the human comedy, one of whom [Kurrubi] he himself has created. The human drama is not directed, nor is there any attempt to direct it. History and reliance on precedent are senseless. The world has its own independent forces, those of character and role. God has provided the setting, but man must put on the play.

At the end of the play it is evident that men have created a farce. Nebukadnezar cannot produce the kind of drama he desires. In anger he turns away from his attempts to compromise with God, commanding the hangman to take the girl [Kurrubi] into the desert and bury her. He will try to create a social utopia with a tower in its center, with which he hopes to challenge God. Significantly, his creation will be a social and material one that runs counter to God's artistic act in creating Kurrubi. Akki, the actor, God's creative representative in this world, that is, God's theater, flees into the wilderness, alienated from society. But even in his flight his words show an appreciation for the creative possibilities of this stage in contrast to Nebukadnezar's rigid formulas for society and the angel's wonder at the mere setting: "And I love an earth which still exists; an earth of beggars, unique in its happiness, and unique in its dangers, colorful and wild, wonderful in all its possibilities; an earth which I conquer again and again, maddened by its beauty, entranced by its face, ever oppressed and never defeated."

The poets are free after having eaten and drunk their fill. They remain a passive creative force that retains the ideal. The idiot is the ultimate heir to the state. His grinning performance walking a tightrope across the stage suggests the precarious future of society in which the role of king will be played without real contact with the stage world. . . . Akki marches toward a vision of the earth he loves, one "full of new persecutions, but full, too, of new promises, and full of the songs of a new morning." Renewing his commitment to life, he will play another role.

Ernest L. Weiser. Monatshefte. Winter, 1976, pp. 392–93

A high degree of *Problemträchtigkeit*, density of problems, is usually taken as a merit in modern literary research. Judged by this criterion Dürrenmatt is a remarkable artist. He belongs to a German and central European stage tradition in which the various modifications of theatricalism have been more strongly emphasized than realism. . . .

Growing from the aftermath of World War II, Dürrenmatt's work ran parallel with absurdism, yet kept within the limits of grotesque tragicomedy. He is a leading representative of this genre in both practice and theory. Admitting that chance and senselessness have a role in life, Dürrenmatt refuses to base his whole vision of the world and concept of art on absurdity. In the 1960's he turned toward politics, yet remained faithful to his belief in his task as a detector of conflicts, not as a solver of problems. He believes neither in the ultimate absurdity of life, nor in easy changes to be achieved through political action. He is comparable with Frisch in his readiness to construct stage models and to take social attitudes, though not along the lines of party politics. Dürrenmatt's place in the total pattern of postwar drama is in the middle, outside the fields of absurdism and the epic theater. He is, of course, something more than a central European court jester. He is an author *sui generis*. There is no pen like his in the wide world of literature.

Timo Tiusanen. *Dürrenmatt: A Study in Plays, Prose, Theory* (Princeton, N.J., Princeton University Press, 1977), pp. 437–39

The sequence of Dürrenmatt's heroes is a procession of foolhardy moralists who act under the delusion that they can, through violence or self-sacrifice, save the world, and who perish in the face of a world that is by definition amoral.

In *Portrait of a Planet* there no longer are any such heroes, merely shabby caricatures of them, like the failed revolutionary who has been consigned to a lunatic asylum . . . or a grotesque little group of female missionaries trying to convert cannibals to pork. . . . *Portrait of a Planet* builds up, from a multiplicity of small scenes, the picture of a world, no less, that is without fixed values or a fixed perspective.

Portrait of a Planet offers a shorthand version, a distillation of the "whole" world in a 90-minute scenic kaleidoscope—capitalism, colonialism, racism, socialism, terrorism, cannibalism, poverty, drugs, aircraft hijacking, moon landing, Vietnam war, apartheid, communes and promiscuity, consumer fetishism, conceptual art, concentration camps and everything the casual newspaper or magazine reader might recognize as a "topical issue" comes up in this play. . . .

Of course, this survey of the world has not been done for its own sake; there is a grand "idea" behind it; Dürrenmatt shows us our planet in the final seconds before its end. . . . The huge flash of the exploding sun becomes the flashbulb of a cosmic camera which takes a final portrait of the world: hence *Portrait of a Planet*. A final general audit. . . .

Dürrenmatt . . . draws the final surprising conclusion that his view of the world in this play, in spite of its patent references to here and now, and to topical matters, is, and can only be, a-historical. The earth can only be portrayed eschatologically, in the present. Its disorder can only be demonstrated radically if it is wrenched from its history and its future, if history is no longer accepted as an excuse, nor the future as a ground for hope. . . .

The play is intended to show us the writing on the wall, and it is the first play in twenty years that he does not call a comedy.

Urs Jenny. *Dürrenmatt: A Study of His Plays* (London, Methuen, 1978), pp. 154–58

Unlike Romulus [in *Romulus the Great*], Mississippi, and Übelohe [in *The Marriage of Mr. Mississippi*], Cop [in *The Conformer*] is not an idealist; he is not convinced that a higher principle, such as justice, can be realized in the modern world. On the contrary, Cop is certain that his actions will have no effect whatever on the course of events. . . . What he hopes to achieve is merely . . . a momentary disruption of the corrupt workings of a corrupt society. Yet Cop's concept of justice, as modest as it sounds, is problematic, for the steps he takes to achieve it—the murders of Mac, Bill, Boss, and Jack, among others—are themselves criminal acts. . . . Unlike *Romulus the Great* and *The Visit, The Conformer* does not culminate in an apotheosis of justice. . . .

Cop is primarily concerned not with justice, but with self. . . . *The Conformer* attests to a subtle shift of emphasis in Dürrenmatt's approach to the problem of the individual in the modern world. The point of reference has moved from a supra-personal dimension to the self, the Christian and humanistic ideals present in Dürrenmatt's earlier works being replaced by a view of the self as absolute. . . .

The Conformer reflects the author's current interest in Kierkegaard; Cop is Dürrenmatt's version of Kierkegaard's ironic hero, the individual who, in Dürrenmatt's words, dares to take the step "into absolute subjectivity." Yet Cop's position is far less convincing than that of many of Dürrenmatt's earlier heroes. . . . Cop's self-oriented outlook is a much more sobering and, indeed, pessimistic one: a kind of ethical solipsism as a desperate last resort. Where the isolated self was originally regarded as a state to be overcome through the recognition of a higher, supra-personal dimension, it is now accepted as an immutable fact of life. Indeed, it has been elevated to something of an ideal. In a world which is incorrigibly corrupt, where all reforms are senseless, and where there is no longer any belief in a higher order, the self is all that remains, both existentially and aesthetically.

Joseph A. Federico. *GR*. Fall, 1979, p. 150

FRISCH, MAX (1911–   )

One of the outstanding representatives of modern German drama whose reputation as a playwright is becoming increasingly widespread is Max Frisch, a native of Zürich. . . . We may somewhat discount Frisch's Swiss citizenship as a factor in his career as a writer, since none of his works has its setting in Switzerland. It has, on the other hand, no doubt proved an advantage by giving him, in contrast to young authors in Germany, the opportunity of observing and keeping in touch with the trends of literature in the West. An architect by profession, Frisch began his experiments in playwriting during the war. . . .

I have used the term "experiment" deliberately, not to imply that Frisch concerns himself principally with technical devices, but rather to indicate that he attempts in each of his plays to find *the* form of expression that will affect the reader or spectator most deeply. He is aware that the present-day author who does have something to say can fail utterly to reach his public when he uses conventional dramatic forms. What Max Frisch has to say is not new; his message is the eternal one of truth and humanity. Precisely because he is imbued with great seriousness of purpose, he has resorted to surrealistic, expressionistic, and other such techniques to express his ideas. . . .

His plays are amazingly rich in surprising and stimulating aspects in the treatment of subject material. However, the very diversity of his "experiments" makes it apparent that Frisch is still groping for a new type of drama of which he does not seem to have a clear idea. . . . Although it remains to be seen whether Frisch will succeed in overcoming his weaknesses in the future, we must acknowledge him as one of the outstanding— if not the greatest—young German playwright of the present day.

Walter E. Glaettli. *GQ*. Nov., 1952, pp. 248–49, 254

Since the 1940s, Frisch's works—the plays, the novels, and his journal— have aroused an ever-growing interest that soon extended beyond the borders of his native Switzerland. As with other Swiss writers . . . it actually was abroad that the significance of his work was recognized in all its aspects. . . .

Frisch's first plays kept close to the reality of the war and the immediate postwar situation. In 1945 no German was able to talk about it the way he did, but many Germans felt it should be expressed that way. The Schauspielhaus in Zurich—during the war a refuge for German actors and directors—was the first to produce his play *Now They Are Singing Again*, in 1945. The play shows both his fervent ethical concern and his poetic imagination. . . . There is, artistically speaking, the dexterous interpenetration of dream and reality, the broadness of scope, and the bold freedom in handling the dramatic material; the human interest focuses on the burning issues of a reality where men find themselves caught in the machinery of war. A certain lack of stagecraft—which Frisch is the first to admit—is perfectly offset by an ingenious idea of his: the presence, on stage, of the dead of the war, the airmen as well as the victims of their raids, together forming a strange community, singing, breaking bread, drinking wine. Here, as in several other plays of Frisch, the spectator is captivated by the poetic qualities and the forcefulness of the text rather than by a perfect mastery of the technical aspects of stagecraft—a mastery Frisch does not attain until . . . *Biedermann and the Firebugs* and *The Great Wrath of Philipp Hotz*.

Greta Rau. *Preuves*. Aug., 1958, pp. 44–45†

Instead of being lulled with illusions, the audience [at *Biedermann and the Firebugs*] has to be awakened to a consciousness of reality. This idea, coming from Brecht and Thornton Wilder, also applies to Max Frisch.

That is why Biedermann asks the audience across the footlights: "And you, what would you have done in my place?" But usually Frisch prefers to create an unreal atmosphere that isolates the scene from the outside world and brings out its exemplary significance. He juggles time and space; the dead and the living exist side by side. If in his early plays he was dependent on Hofmannsthal, he has subsequently turned more and more away from lyricism. He opts . . . for farce, undoubtedly convinced, like Musil and Dürrenmatt, that tragedy in its traditional form is no longer suited to our time.

Should Max Frisch be reproached for putting marionettes on stage, ideas somehow or other disguised to resemble human beings? Certain critics do not hesitate to take him to task for it. . . . Similar reproaches have been directed against Brecht, Camus, and Sartre. Yet none of Frisch's plays is as close to a theorem as is Brecht's *The Measures Taken;* first, because the author of *Biedermann and the Firebugs* refuses to be dogmatic, limiting himself instead to calling [certain attitudes] into question; second, because Frisch the man cannot be separated from Frisch the writer. Frisch, calling attention to the taste of our time for all that remains unfinished and sketchy, perceives here a similarity with romanticism: and is there not, in him, too, a romantic whom he has difficulty keeping under control? As despairing as man's solitude and the absurdity of the world may be, Frisch does not yield to the temptation of nihilism, does not shut himself up in negation. Those sudden fits of anger, the rage to destroy, which come over [Philipp] Hotz and over the prosecutor in *Count Öderland,* are the mark not of cynics but of impassioned souls.

Marius Cauvin. *EG.* Jan.–Mar., 1960, pp. 62–63†

Frisch has, to be sure, a most lively sense of the underlying grotesque humor in a situation and a caustic irony, but he remains in the last analysis within the human universe, the realm of human fate, of the individual, suffering, concrete person, torn by his inner conflicts. He is a kind of existentialist writer who, however, is concerned with goals of self-realization, responsibility, and authentic individual being, "the continents of one's own soul, girt round with mystery, the adventurous quest for veracity." He is a writer in whose works the "arena is always the human soul," the soul of this human creature who suffers from his finiteness and mortality, his transitoriness and his thirst for love, who at the same time lives in the midst of an eternal leave-taking and is again and again cheated by life of the best.

Frisch, at any rate, in the midst of the sparkling dramatic inventiveness and mastery of stage technique which give him his vitality in the theater, produces a more human effect than Dürrenmatt, whose propensity for the infernal often conjures up in the theater visions of inhuman monstrosity. . . . Frisch's works are the expression of a kind of more or less humanistic existentialism.

Peter Seidmann. *BA*. Spring, 1960, p. 114

Biedermann and the Firebugs is more than just a very telling piece of political satire. The political satire is certainly there: Biedermann's situation . . . is based on the situation of President Beneš of Czechoslovakia, who took the Communists into his government although he knew that they were bent on destroying the country's independence. It is also the situation of the German intellectuals who thought that Hitler did not mean what he said when he spoke of war and conquest, and so allowed him to start a world conflagration. And it is also, in a sense, the situation of the world in the age of the hydrogen bomb, when the attics of the world's major powers are stored with very highly inflammable and explosive material. But beyond this purely political aspect, Frisch's play describes the state of mind of the family in Ionesco's *The Bald Soprano* and *Jacques*—the dead world of routine and empty bonhomie, where the destruction of values has reached a point where the bewildered individual can no longer distinguish between the things that ought to be preserved and those that should be destroyed. The fire brigade is ready, but there is no one left who can recognize the incendiaries as dangerous, and so the measures taken to prevent the fire are bound to fail. What is more, in a world of dead routine, of unceasing consumption and production, the destruction of a civilization will be felt merely as a beneficial way of clearing the ground for a new building boom—so that production and consumption can continue.

Martin Esslin. *The Theatre of the Absurd* (Garden City,
N.Y., Doubleday, 1961), p. 193

In [Frisch's] *Don Juan* [*; or, The Love of Geometry*], the pieces of the legend play a role which every reader of Camus' *The Stranger* will recognize. Frisch's reluctant lover is a cousin to Shaw's John Tanner [in *Man and Superman*] and to Mirabell in Fletcher's *Wild-Goose Chase;* but a cousin who has waded the swamps of Existentialism. For him, life is only a series of sensations. Like Camus' Meursault, he rejects *patterns* and *deeper meanings,* though he does so with patrician dash. Not only religion, but "eternal" love, honor, friendship, obligations, fidelity—all these are *Schwindel,* humbug. . . .

But Don Juan is not simply another Meursault. He has a desire. He desires to make human life imitate the exactness, limpidity, dependability of the cosmos. And if not this, he desires to be rid of human concerns altogether in order to contemplate the geometry of the physical world, where "what is valid today is valid tomorrow, and valid when I no longer breathe, without me and without you." But this world is denied to him, because he is a man; it is not a world meant for mankind. He ends his days in the Castle of Imperfection, subject to the "morass of our moods," loving against his will a woman who loves him but who never comes to dinner on time (a charming symbol), and even begetting, of all useless objects, an heir. Sex is the inescapable irrationality. But Don Juan must make himself as comfortable in the shoddy human world as is humanly possible. He remains comically suspended between rebellion and submission, or at the center of a triangle formed by anger, love, and despair.

Solemnity would have undone this play. But like Figaro, Frisch laughs at the world lest he must weep over it. His argument always moves from pathos to a somewhat clinical amusement, from moments of philosophical insistence to unrepentant farce.

Oscar Mandel. In Oscar Mandel, ed., *The Theatre of Don Juan*
(Lincoln, University of Nebraska Press, 1963), pp. 696–97

Frisch reveals himself as a traditionalist. The trend in the contemporary drama—and this includes also Frisch's countryman and rival, Friedrich Dürrenmatt—is to treat characters impersonally. With the principal "experimental dramatists" (Beckett, Ionesco, Adamov, etc.) this impersonal treatment is motivated by the conviction that in modern society individuality has been castrated. These writers see modern man as a sort of blind, groping creature playing a perpetual play of blind man's buff. Dürrenmatt treats modern man in the same way, but he assumes the Olympian position. He is an aged and very wise lecturer indulgently explaining the foibles of mankind. Frisch is none of these things. He is a human being like everybody else. It is a status that he never forgets and never rejects. He is *involved*. His characters are human beings, and we understand them through recognition, through a sort of intuitive Bergsonian identification. They are not the bloodless specimens split open on the dissecting table that Dürrenmatt and the experimentalists provide for us. Frisch's characters are fully rounded psychological beings. His themes—the psychological impossibility of human self-sufficiency and the inability of men to learn by experience—are presented in a personal manner, sometimes to the extent of becoming personal pleas. Frisch's two best plays, *The Chinese Wall* and *Biedermann and the Firebugs,* are consciously foredoomed pleas for a better world. The irony implicit in them no longer sounds like the scornful laughter of the gods we hear in Dürrenmatt; it sounds like the self-reproaching wailing of the damned.

George E. Wellwarth. *The Theater of Protest and Paradox*
(New York, New York University Press, 1964), p. 183

As for *Andorra,* no contemporary playwright since Brecht has succeeded, as Frisch has succeeded in this play, in raising a topical, wide-ranging issue like that of anti-Semitism to the level of a fully integrated complex of human beings, involved in a kind of archetypal conflict which pertains to twentieth-century social life. Avoiding hollow expressionism and shadowy allegory, the setting is convincingly drawn and the characters have the hallmark of types which could be Andorrans as well as whatever other nationality one could think of. The plight of the cowed school-master, that of his ex-mistress, that of his sacrificial daughter, and above all, that of his son Andri, who assumes his fate in a way similar to that with which Christ assumed his regal crown of thorns, is the kind of moving and chastening experience which one encounters in tragedy. . . .

In as far as this play is Brechtian, it is a spectacle depicting a social structure and its effects, upon some of the individuals which compose it, but without any attempt at psychological depth or sustained verisimilitude. Some of the characters are simply used as appearances of social manifestations exhibited on the stage, and the acting must needs partake of this surface presentation of the characters, which is a kind of pure phenomenalism without any involvement or identification with them. . . .

The spectator is not asked to take sides as when confronted with the crude emotionalism of [Hochhuth's] *The Representative* [i.e., *The Deputy*]; he is asked, or rather to be more precise, he is oriented by the structure of this kind of Brechtian play toward assessing, through his own consciousness, the interplay of individual and social forces, so as to derive from it enlightenment and an incentive to action. All in all, *Andorra* seems to me one of the important plays of our time and certainly a remarkable achievement.

Joseph Chiari. *Landmarks of Contemporary Drama*
(London, Jenkins, 1965), pp. 184–87

How does Frisch portray Don Juan [in *Don Juan; or, The Love of Geometry*]? He is not the hero of Cordoba in the sense that Don Gonzales imagines. True, he measured the Moorish battlements, but, as is explained later in the play, it was from afar and by geometric calculations, not by exposing himself to the dangers of possible capture. Far from perishing in the flames of hell, Frisch's Don Juan cleverly calculates the whole scene as a hoax. Most important, he is not the famed seducer, as is commonly imagined, but an intellectual in love not with women but with geometry. He is not, as Frisch clarifies in his notes, torn from one love affair to the next out of desire; rather his unfaithfulness arises from the fear of losing his freedom and surrendering his identity to the numbing effects of love. He is actually indifferent to sex and prefers, when in a bordello, to play chess. He is bored by women. . . .

Don Juan believes that there can be no romantic love, since life consists of a series of sensations and love is just one of these sensations. So he tries to ignore the existence of love altogether. He is primarily an intellectual in respect to love and shows his ability to separate what is real from illusion. . . .

The study of geometry is Don Juan's way to absolute values. Unlike Mozart's Don Giovanni, described by E. T. A. Hoffmann as striving for the absolute through sensual experience, through possible experience of the ideal woman, Frisch's Don Juan says that the search for knowledge through the exercise of reason is man's only worthwhile pursuit. . . .

Thus Don Juan's *hybris* in this modern version of the legend is not that he defies or shatters a moral universe with his flagrant immorality or that he stands against the world and against God with his crimes and licentiousness, causing God to punish him, but rather that both the crimes and the order they attack are illusions. Don Juan's real flaw is that he believes too absolutely in the sufficiency of the self and the capabilities of reason.

Peter Gontrum. CLS. 2, 2, 1965, pp. 118–20

Although Max Frisch's work, viewed as a whole, is characterized by its diversity, one important theme emerges with insistent frequency in all his major productions. This theme may be defined as the conflict between "Ordnung" [order] and "das wirkliche Leben" [true life]. The concept of "das wirkliche Leben" signifies for Frisch a state of being in which man is able to realize his true self, to attain, that is, to the full and harmonious evolution of all aspects of his personality in order that he may develop into a thoroughly integrated human being. "Ordnung," on the other hand, implies all those forces in modern civilization, and particularly in middle-class society, which, in Frisch's view, hinder such a development by imposing upon the individual a restrictive and artificial pattern of behaviour leading to the suppression of his essential humanity.

In his early work Frisch is concerned simply to state the nature of the conflict and to analyse its consequences rather than to attempt to resolve it, though each time he adopts a somewhat different approach. . . .

In *Count Öderland* the concept of "Ordnung" takes on a wider significance than in Frisch's earlier works in that it is no longer identified simply with bourgeois values but with civilization itself. As the Innenminister is ironically made to point out in one of the closing scenes of the play, the modern democratic state, precisely because of its concern to safeguard man's freedom and individuality, only succeeds in destroying them. . . .

The axe which the Staatsanwalt takes into his hands is a symbol of his revolt against all those arbitrary forces in the modern state which demand the suppression of his true vital self. Yet in spite of his revolutionary methods he achieves nothing. . . . Ironically the very rebels whom he would lead to freedom compel him in the end to assume sole power within the state and to become himself the defender of "Ordnung" and the upholder of all that he had once sought to destroy.

D. Barlow. *GL&L*. Oct., 1965, pp. 52, 57

Frisch, even at his most grotesque, deals with the profoundest questions confronting humanity, particularly as they relate to the people of today. Just after the Second World War, Frisch was hotly concerned with the problems of the country neighboring his own, Germany, whose people speak the language in which he writes. Plays such as *Now They Are Singing Again* and *As the War Came to an End* displayed various aspects of recent German activity; *The Chinese Wall* concerned itself with the future of mankind seen against the terms of its past, while *Count Öderland* again dealt with contemporary anxieties, in this case again examining power, here contrasted with *bovaryste* dullness. The last of these is in part existential because it involves a choice, and Frisch in his plays is as acutely concerned with exploring present-day problems as any of the French existentialists are. Technically he is often more experimental than they are: there is the Zürich-café and Brecht background, and the influence of plays by Thornton Wilder, particularly *Our Town* and *The Skin of Our Teeth,* is often discernible. Frisch has, however, assimilated his influences usefully, and has a distinctly forcible personality of his own in the theater.

Harry T. Moore. *Twentieth-Century German Literature* (New York, Basic Books, 1967), pp. 144–45

The first of Frisch's *Zeitstücke* [*Now They Are Singing Again*] made its point without the use of historical dates or local color. It was neither based on an actual experience nor tied to a recognizable geographical setting. Most importantly, the characters—notably in the realm of the dead—spoke and understood one and the same universal language. As a Requiem intended for all human beings, irrespective of their color, creed, race, or nationality, it had to forgo the usual barriers and conflicts. *As the War Came to an End,* on the other hand, is a *Zeitstück* in the literal sense of the word. Written between December, 1947, and August, 1948, it was first performed on January 8, 1949, at the Zürich *Schauspielhaus*. Its plot originated from an authentic anecdote told to the author during his visit to Berlin in November, 1947. . . .

By writing *As the War Came to an End,* Frisch sought to discourage two views regarding the German, collective or individual, guilt then current among his Swiss compatriots; first the convenient retreat into the realm of German classical literature, "where the affinity to the German mind is conceived of as harmless," and, secondly, the blind compassion "which offers no less dubious a solution by resolutely forgetting, and thus betraying the victims of yesterday." Frisch disagreed with Churchill who, in 1949, had proposed to let the past take care of itself. He wanted to deal with the present without losing its immediate antecedents out of sight. As the heroine, Agnes, states in the third act (subsequently removed) of the play, "It is impossible to live in the same house with a criminal without turning against him. It is impossible, or we share his guilt."

Ulrich Weisstein. *Max Frisch* (New York,
Twayne, 1967), pp. 109–10

Max Frisch's *The Fire Raisers* [*Biedermann and the Firebugs*], which was first produced in 1958, is an ingenious ironic fable: what he himself describes as a "morality without a moral." The phrase is the key to an analysis, for this is a deliberately representative action, intended to connect with a generation of political violence in Europe, and yet what is represented, both in the action and in the dramatized attitudes to it, is an ironic detachment from reality: a kind of negative universality. . . .

The tone, here, is decisive. It is the laconic, self-evident, resigned tone of a generation which has seen the fire raisers, not in the theatre but in history. As such it connects, to contemporary audiences: a history into a fable, a fable into a tone. . . .

The laconic tone is that of a world which has "seen it all," but explains only by multiplying allusions and analogies, from the metaphysical to the political, at once conscious and half-made. Not only the fire, but the reasons for it, have been seen and heard before: the tone rests on an exhaustion beyond both; an exhaustion which as in so much post-war European drama is expressed as irony.

In its essential structure of feeling, *The Fire Raisers* is then at once representative and opportunist, and its essential conventions correspond to this: an engaging surface realism in an absurd action; a critical chorus, an internal self-consciousness, which rests not on critical explanation but on making every possible point and letting them all interact. It is the dramatic method of Brecht adapted to a quite different consciousness, which is in the end not critical but paradoxically reassuring: that characteristic contemporary distancing which says in the end "stupid man." At the same time, because this is a real structure of feeling, and not just an idiosyncrasy, the play has an energy, a theatrical brilliance, which makes it a major example of this dramatic kind. Saying "shut the door, we have seen it before," it replays history as farce, to let us see it again, "experimentally," in a safe theatre.

Raymond Williams. *Drama from Ibsen to Brecht*
(New York, Oxford University Press, 1969), pp. 308–12

For Frisch *Kultur* has always been identifiable with the manner in which a civilization solves "the problem of its social order." . . . Thus he deplores those of the intelligentsia who recoil from social or political involvement out of a peculiar fear that concern for the body politic is unaesthetic or anti-intellectual, who, indeed, attempt to use *Kultur* as an escape from the responsibilities of down-to-earth existence. In Frisch's view the abstention from action is a vote cast in favor of the forces in power. The Dr. Phil., exemplifying in the drama [*Biedermann and the Firebugs*] the academician's unwillingness to take direct action on current social problems, reappears in the *Nachspiel* [afterpiece] in the form of a *Meerkatze* [long-tailed monkey] as the Devil's servant. Try as he might, man as a recipient of *Kultur* cannot escape his tie to humanity. Likewise the creative artist is first and foremost a human being and accountable for all his socio-political actions. . . .

Frisch, the writer, thus finds himself in a dilemma. On the one hand he is catering to the bourgeois "Kulturmenschen" by providing yet more material which could be and surely has been misused as an escape from social involvement. On the other hand he still hopes to point out the danger of self-destruction to those who complacently consider themselves "cultured" and yet ignore the social wrongs they are responsible for. The evident rise in Frisch's cynicism during the years in which *Biedermann and the Firebugs* achieved its final form can only be the result of a pessimistic conviction that the author as reformer has failed to move an intransigent and socially unconcerned public and has thereby been reduced to a state of utter frustration.

John T. Brewer. *GR*. March, 1971, pp. 127–28

In dramatic action *Biography* [*: A Game*] is literally a stage play: "The theater makes possible what reality does not allow for: to make changes, to begin once more, to experiment, to try out another biography." The play's structure is derived from the common theatrical practice of rehearsals. Scenic representations alternate with discussions. In this setting the protagonist plays the part of the principal actor who carries out the rehearsing. . . .

Having a complete view of his life and aiming at specific revisions, he takes it for granted that they can be realized. The procedure he has in mind resembles the one practiced by a conventional dramatist. Focusing on the end to be reached, the latter so constructs an action that it flawlessly leads up to that end. Through the protagonist's failure to achieve his stated goal, Frisch—among other things—unmasks the deceptive character of the conventional drama. Its course of action, so he suggests, is devised in an order contrary to life: backward instead of forward, and the inevitable outcome portrayed is but a product of the dramatist's rational planning. By contrast, Frisch illustrates that a course of life is an actualization in time and, hence, historical in character. Creating a fictional situation in which time has been suspended as far as external events are concerned, and depicting a man unable to change these events, he demonstrates that the factor resisting modification is lodged in the protagonist himself. The ideal conditions provided for Kürmann throw into relief the hidden dimension of his life history, i.e., the irreversible nature of his inner development.

Brigitte L. Bradley. GQ. March, 1971, pp. 212, 216

Frisch labeled this play [The Chinese Wall] a "farce," but it would be wrong to interpret this designation in the sense of the medieval farce. It may be that this carousel-like presentation of slices of world history was thought of by Frisch as being only a farce. It encompasses everything in the way of scenic and technical means to shape a whole world passing in review, to make the truth Frisch has discovered even clearer. When we consider this profusion of scenes and stage devices, which, when effectively presented, carry the audience along, it is "total" theater that makes its appearance. Masks, pantomime, choreography—all are present. Indeed at times masquerades are such independent elements that one might almost think the play could be presented as théâtre de mime.

The symbolism of The Chinese Wall has been interpreted as expressing a final entreaty, warning mankind of the consequences of a possible atomic war. It is a magnificent allegory in which all laws of time and space are suspended in order to project the ideas of the omniscient dramatist who, in this play, becomes almost a visionary. . . .

Frisch's attitudes and the manner in which they are presented, the highly effective theatrical qualities of the play, and the unusual and vivid combinations that Frisch presents on the stage are all very impressive. But The Chinese Wall is a pessimistic work. Freedom is only in the realm of the spirit; for, in the real world, the possessors of power end up by doing the same things over and over again. Everything remains as it was before, and nothing beyond debunking has happened. It is only a grandiose demonstration of what was fated to happen, ironically emphasized when Hwang Ti himself places a golden chain around the neck of Today's Man, the representative of the intellect. The intellect as decoration but not as an agent that controls power—this appears to be its position now and forever. . . . Frisch does not want to arouse hopes that might in the end turn out to be deceptive. And it may be that his pessimism has more to offer than a comforting optimism, which would leave people to their emotional and intellectual inertia.

Carol Petersen. Max Frisch (New York,
Frederick Ungar, 1972), pp. 37–39

The traditional Don Juan play focused upon Don Juan the Seducer and Blasphemer, but in the progressive historical development of this tradition there unavoidably occurred a falling away of the human presence of the actor from the Don Juan role: the Don Juan character progressively assumed an objectivized status which was devoid of the human. Frisch's technique in his own *Don Juan* has been to capitalize upon this alienation of the human from the Don Juan character. Through the symbolic portrayal on the stage of this historical development within the Don Juan tradition, Frisch accomplishes on one level an archeology and deconstruction, while on another level he reinvests Don Juan with a human presence. But this reinvestment takes place not on the level of Don Juan the character but upon Don Juan the actor who has been cast in this theatrical role by tradition. Frisch's play is, strictly speaking then, not a Don Juan play, but rather a play about Western man's interaction with the Don Juan tradition in theatre. Certainly within today's critical perspective, Frisch's analysis of the interaction of man with an institution which man has created for his own self-understanding is a timely attempt to revitalize a theatrical tradition by means of the very historico-critical powers which effected its demise.

Robert J. Matthews. MLN. Oct., 1972, p. 752

To look at Frisch from the perspective of tragedy is to locate some central elements in his moral and aesthetic style. For him, a repeated source of wrongdoing is what we might call the simplified melodramatic consciousness—the sense of evil as the property of other individuals and other classes; it is a theme that often lies beneath farce and fantasy, jest and riddle. It is there in the panoramic allegory *The Chinese Wall*. It is the overt substance of *When the War Was Over* [*As the War Came to an End*] and *Andorra;* behind the nationalistic antagonisms of Germans and Russians in the one, and anti-Semitism in the other, Frisch discovers the self-congratulatory parochialism of all class feelings, be they those of country or of race. He observes different modes of melodramatic life: a healthy man may have to fight others to survive, and a sick man may express the absolutism of self by destroying others (as in [*Biedermann and the*] *Firebugs*). Most men drift into melodrama and find comfort in it. This observation, urbane or bitter in different plays, is central in Frisch.

He is always aware, then, of the tragic alternatives, though in his view man does not readily choose them. Frisch's own detachment inhibits the passionate imaging of tragic emotion which would give it preeminence in a drama; more than once we have to say that though a given plot could develop tragically it is not what he is after. However, the tragic possibility is rarely absent. Even in *The Chinese Wall* Columbus tells Don Juan that there is still "the continent of your own soul!" to be explored—a major strand in the tragic theme. [*Biedermann and the*] *Firebugs* inveighs against applying the term "Fate" to one's "mistakes," that is, evading the tragic view. In *Biography* [*: A Game*] Kürmann's belief in "choice" gives him a tragic potential. Agnes in *When the War Was Over* [*As the War Came to an End*], the Teacher in *Andorra,* and Don Juan [in *Don Juan; or, The Love of Geometry*] all have something of the sense of guilt which belongs to the tragic rather than the melodramatic style. For the Teacher it is central; in the others Frisch sees it as an emotional episode rather than an ultimate motive. It is as if he were observing their lack of range and thus anticipating disaster rather than moral discovery. His treatment of guilt is most ironic in [*Biedermann and the*] *Firebugs,* in which Biedermann's guilt is the door not to clear-sightedness but to a fatal vulnerability.

Robert B. Heilman. *The Iceman, the Arsonist, and the Troubled Agent: Tragedy and Melodrama on the Modern Stage* (Seattle, University of Washington Press, 1973), pp. 209–10

Frisch's first drama, *Santa Cruz,* is characterized by an interjection of dream and memory into the fictional reality of plot and person, which affects the structure of place as well. It manifests itself in a duality of place, with which Frisch seeks to portray and reconcile the worlds of "objective" and "subjective" reality within the drama. The action, after an opening scene in an inn, alternates between the winter setting of a snowbound castle belonging to the *Rittmeister* (acts 1, 3, 5) and a town and boat in the warm and summery south seas (acts 2, 4). The first setting, the objective location of the play, is offset by the second, a subjective realm evoked by the minstrel's words and succoured by the dreams and memories of the characters. The format and content of the play demand that equal credulity be granted to each setting and action, and figures move freely between the two, creating a projected unity which is substantiated by the final scene in which the two realms merge in the world of "objective" reality, the consequences of the world of yearning, memory, and fantasy having been fully integrated and accepted into the action at the castle.

The attempt to reconcile these two worlds, which is a thematic concern of the work as well, achieves more than conciliation. The integration which the final scene represents, through the unification of the disparate realities which it effected, colours the entire work, and, as a result, the work as a whole is "subjectivized." The play seems to hover, severed from place considerations—its ultimate location in Frisch's words being the human soul.

Gertrud Bauer Pickar. *Seminar.* June, 1973, p. 135

It is fascinating and depressing at the same time to discover that a play arising from the political atmosphere of 1946, and pointing back into history, can be so in line with the concerns of our time. The threat of the bomb still makes us cower, and we feel chagrined by our inability to overcome human nature: the ambitions of selfish rulers, the indifference and vanity of the ruled, and their uncanny knack of repeating past mistakes time and again. *The Chinese Wall* is a mirror to history and an appeal to break out of its invariant cycle. For the mistakes of the past that lead to local disasters will now lead to total destruction: "A single mood by him who sits now on the throne . . . and everything is lost." But can society be transformed, and is the individual willing to adjust? That is the question posed by the play. *The Chinese Wall* does not offer a clear-cut solution, nor should it. . . .

In the middle of the whole commotion stands the Heutige [contemporary] who wants to show the truth. But whatever he does, whether he exposes or conceals his knowledge or convictions, whether he timidly hesitates or moves forward bravely, he finds that he can convert neither emperor nor people—he cannot change the world. In the end, he is exposed as inconsequential, powerless. He is not heroic in the scenes where he fears the emperor's dagger or lights a cigarette and shrugs his shoulders when stronger measures are called for. But he realizes his shortcomings ("Maybe I am a coward, otherwise I would see what I have to do") and he learns to say what he has to say. Yet he achieves nothing; he becomes another mute, the one figure described by Mee Lan as the only human being in this crazy ghost story. . . .

His play, *The Chinese Wall,* has not changed the world, but it does ask the right questions. It is on a sceptical note that the play ends. But despite all weakness of mankind, despite all the aberrations that we saw enacted, the outlook is not altogether hopeless. The last sentences of the play testify to the presence of love and persisting trust in humanity.

Marie Wagner. MD. Sept., 1973, pp. 149, 154–55

In accepting the image of seducer and murderer, Frisch's protagonist [in *Don Juan; or, The Love of Geometry*], a man of abstract, intellectual tastes, accepts a form of existence which is repulsive to him. To understand the play, we must understand why he accepts this image and the Don Juan existence that accompanies it. . . .

Clearly, Frisch takes Don Juan's crimes seriously and finds that, even in a world characterized by an absence of absolutes, the transgressions of human beings against one another are meaningful. Indeed, it is not that Don Juan is forced into his actions, but that his actions represent an unwillingness to take responsibility for himself, to take direction of his life. The pervasive trait that Frisch's Don Juan exhibits throughout the first four acts of the play is the desire to lose his subjectivity, to become objectified (absolutized) in one way or another. What he fears is the ambiguity of consciousness, the possibilities and choices that consciousness raises.

Juan's devotion to geometry is an expression of his desire to objectify himself. A mathematics of necessity, of immutable axioms, its chief value for Juan is that it obviates subjectivity itself. For he cannot change its rules and cannot be responsible for them, and, as he says, they will be as valid tomorrow as they are today, even after he is no longer alive. This love of absolutes is a caricature of a basic trait of all Don Juans—the desire to avoid ambiguity, to have an absolute "being." As Frisch points out in the Notes, each Don Juan "thirsts after the Absolute and senses that he will never find it." This "thirst" is implicit in Don Juan's perennial excessiveness, his need to exceed the limits of human (and "divine") law; it is explicit in his compulsive challenge to the Statue. Behind the sensuousness, the "erotic genius" of Don Juan, is abstraction, the desire to be abstracted out of the ambiguity and complexity of ordinary human consciousness.

Peter Ruppert. Monatshefte. Fall, 1975, p. 238

In his "Schillerpreis-Rede" [Schiller Prize Speech] (1965), Max Frisch describes reality as a "Summe von Zufällen" [a sum of coincidences] in which every individual decision is merely the "Gebärde eines Gesteuerten, der nicht weiss, was ihn steuert" [the gesture of one controlled who does not know what controls him]. . . .

The view of the individual as the hapless victim of powerful manipulatory forces beyond his control is a common one in much postwar literature. In the plays of Frisch, Dürrenmatt, and Handke, this idea is often mirrored in the image of the hero as actor, role-player, or even marionette. Thus, Frisch's preoccupation with the "Bildnis" [image] idea reflects his own conviction, "daß jedes Ich, das sich ausspricht, eine Rolle ist" [that every self speaking out is a role]. Most of his heroes are actors in a script dictated by society or by their own shortcomings, the play depicting the individuals in various stages of the search for the "true" self. None of Frisch's heroes, however, is entirely successful. Indeed, Frisch's own outlook seems to become increasingly fatalistic. In *Andorra* (1961), Andri abandons his attempts to discover his true identity and finally accepts his role as real. Even Kürmann (*Biography*, 1967), who is given the opportunity to alter his biography at will, is unable to change any essential aspects of his behavior.

Joseph A. Federico. GL&L. Jan., 1979, p. 166

It is important to see, however, that *Triptych* functions not just as a reflection of themes long familiar in Frisch's *oeuvre,* but also as a comment on literary production itself. Hence one of the persistent guises of "Wiederholung" [repetition] in the play is the device of overt or covert quotation—a phenomenon which could lead to a misunderstanding of Frisch's purpose. For despite the apparent pessimistic reflection of literary activity, which is the concomitant feature of the negative portrayal of lives characterized by missed opportunities and failed personal relationships, this triptych can be seen on the contrary as an unmistakable "Warntafel" [warning]. For the pale, indeed fading, reflection of the people in the "Bilder" [images] themselves enables the reader/spectator to see something of his own self reflected back at him. The formal brilliance of this play, it can be said, raises the banality of its theme to the level of art. Rejecting the wit and polish of traditional theatrical essays set in Hades, Frisch aims at the demystification of death and shows how what he calls "das Tödliche" [the deadly] in all its subtle and unexpected manifestations is more to be feared than death itself. For death is a necessary end which properly grasped gives shape and meaning to life, whereas "das Tödliche" is at work insidiously at every stage of life, poised to corrupt every relationship at any time—and always with the cooperation of the principals.

Thus *Triptych* can be "read" not as the statement of a weary pessimist, but as the warning of a very much alive moralist.

Michael Butler. GL&L. Oct., 1979, pp. 72–73

Frisch's campaign against the theater of fate and against the ambiguity of the Brechtian parable guides him toward a new dramaturgy which . . . he calls "eine Dramaturgie des Unglaubens; eine Dramatik der Permutation" [a dramaturgy of disbelief; a dramaturgy of permutation].

The author's first position deals with our coercion in accepting our experiences as a chain of causalities: Everyone invents his own story which he assumes to be his biography. According to Frisch's theory we can live out life only if we lift our experiences into our consciousness in the form of stories and thereby accepting them as the only incidents that could have possibly happened to us. On the other hand, says Frisch, one and the same incident could be the origin of a hundred different experiences. Thus an experience is an idea, not the result of an incident. Obviously there is no other way to demonstrate an experience than to tell a story about it. This means that our experience invents its own cause. The past is a fiction that does not admit being fictitious. Thus: any narrating self plays a role and any self is therefore an invention.

These considerations are the origin of Frisch's theatrical experiment with his new concept of a "dramaturgy of permutation." What is not possible in real life is possible in art, on the stage: to return to the incidents in one's life and to rehearse a variety of possible experiences resulting from them until one finds the life story that fits. The only incident which does not allow any varieties is death. Therefore the sense of such a "game" is to rehearse the possible manners of behavior of a self in view of the one incident which does not allow any variations.

Rolf Kieser. In Edward R. Haymes, ed.,
Theatrum Mundi: Essays on German Drama
and German Literature, Houston German
Studies 2 (Munich, Fink, 1980), pp. 192–93

HACKS, PETER (1928–   )

Even after two years of rewriting and changing, Peter Hacks's *Worries and Power*, a play dutifully placed in the milieu of a "socialized" coal mine engaged in the struggle for reaching the plan norms, offers insights into and analyses of the complexities of social and economic factors in interplay with simple human elements too honestly confused in order to teach the desired lesson.

Hacks is a disciple of Brecht, under whom he studied problems of historical drama for several years at the East Berlin Theater am Schiffbauerdamm; hence an extremely clever technique of applied dialectics in Hacks's play, achieved in Brechtian fashion by subtle strokes of *Verfremdung* [alienation] in language and setting. This, too, is didactic theater, but not of the immediate kind envisaged by the propagandists of the political regime; the attitude is necessarily ironic rather than pathetic, appealing through its ambiguities very much in the manner postulated by Brecht.

Kurt Opitz. BA. Winter, 1964, p. 23

Peter Hacks is an inventive, promising playwright. . . . His literary productivity is determined by his being extremely well-read—a fact that also explains his main shortcoming to date. He first tried his hand at historical subjects, such as *The Chapbook of Duke Ernest; or, The Hero and His Retinue, Inauguration of the Indic Age, The Battle at Lobositz,* and *The Miller of Sanssouci.* His adaptations—*Peace,* after Aristophanes; *Beautiful Helen,* an operetta for actors after Offenbach; and *Polly; or, The Battle at Bluewater Creek,* after Gay—turned out to be especially successful—at the same time showing the peculiarities of his talent most distinctly. Those plays in which the subject matter of a liberal education alone is not sufficient, but in which one would have also needed the basis of one's own experience, such as *Worries and Power* and *Moritz Tassow,* suffer, above all, from their "contrived" plots. Peter Hacks is a writer of comedies—thus an exceedingly rare phenomenon in the German literature of the theater. This must always be kept in mind when evaluating his writing . . . in order to understand the almost inevitable difficulties that arise for him from our country's lack of tradition in this genre. . . .

Peter Hacks's striving for a modern form, suitable for the theater, for effectiveness on the stage, and for an artistic contrast of the theater to the novel, film, and television certainly represents a significant experiment in the development of the theater; and, taking Brecht's concept of the "epic theater" as the point of departure, one might speak in Hacks's case of "feuilletonistic theater."

Hermann Kähler. Gegenwart auf der Bühne (East Berlin,
Henschel, 1966), pp. 21–22, 24†

Peter Hacks's earliest work, *The Chapbook of Duke Ernest,* which is now receiving its first stage production, is almost fifteen years old. . . .

Hacks's first drama is . . . an application of certain theatrical means to a well-known subject matter: *The Chapbook of Duke Ernest.* . . . The characters from the Christmas tale and those of the well-known story of the good old knight join together and bustle about in colorful scenes to show how the great live at the expense of the small, how virtues are only phrases used as a screen behind which Hacks reveals selfish economic motives. The Middle Ages and their grand words are denounced so that we may see that today's pretenses and grand words are no different. In his pedantic desire to criticize and correct, Hacks follows the *Volksbuch* step by step; no episode is omitted, since it is a question of using it to show that things are contrary to what they seem. . . . This negative procedure makes the drama both witty and thin-blooded. The action depends on the loose thread of the critical juxtaposition. . . . Since Hacks is merely giving an old theme an acidly critical content, the *Chapbook* runs the risk of gaily dissolving into thin air on the stage.

Hellmuth Karasek. Zeit. May 30, 1967, p. 19†

The heart of the problem presented in [Hacks's] *Beautiful Helen* is class conflict. Three social classes are present in the drama, gods, warrior-heroes, and the lower classes. On one level these three classes are to be understood literally, as in Homer, where the same three categories exist, gods, heroes, and others. The ruling class of warriors is above the people, but below the gods, who may be thought of as the various forces to which the rulers are subject. . . .

More often, however, the three classes in the drama represent the three classes of men in the traditional Marxian system; Hacks's gods play the role of the distant rulers, the slaves and *Volk* are the equally distant proletariat, and the Greek heroes, upon whom the action is centered, are the bourgeoisie. . . . The "upper-class" gods are concerned only with power and prestige within their own ranks. By virtue of their birth they automatically have an overabundance of the things for which the middle class must constantly struggle, especially wealth and sex, and to which the lower class can never aspire. . . .

The trouble, which began at the top of the social ladder in the form of a quarrel among three goddesses, results in numerous difficulties for the middle class, but—and this is presented by implication only—ultimately the burden of war will fall upon the common man.

We are never told what is wrong, but the message is impossible to miss. Hacks, thematically following his mentor Brecht, presents a capitalistic society in all its pretentious splendour, splendour which is shown to have no more substance than the emperor's new clothes of the fairy tale.

Hacks, in *Beautiful Helen,* is more humorous than Brecht, and the humour is often more slapstick than subtle. Elements of Brecht's technique of alienation, however, are noticeable. . . . The viewer or reader of *Beautiful Helen* may laugh more heartily than with Brecht, but as with Brecht he is required to think as he laughs, and when he thinks only one conclusion is possible.

Jerry Glenn. Seminar. Spring, 1969, pp. 12–15

Hacks's first plays, with which he had already made a name for himself in the 1950s, are hardly more than exercises in the revision of history à la Brecht. . . .

Then, in the 1960s, Hacks turned away from the somewhat mechanical exercises in turning history upside down and applied himself to contemporary themes. In the topical drama *Worries and Power* he treats the politics of production. . . . But Hacks's attempt to get at the factory problem was rejected by the Party as being basically false in its conception, and the play was taken off the stage.

Hacks's second play dealing with the socialist present, *Moritz Tassow,* likewise incurred the displeasure of the Party and was therefore also taken out of the repertory. . . .

Since then Hacks has exclusively applied himself to satirical fairy tales and to adapting classical writers to the contemporary scene, both of them tendencies that have many adherents in the West although they are not understood here in their Eastern trimming. The concept of "contemporization" actually refers to an approximation of present conditions, whereas that of "alienation" implies some remoteness; but they both have the same aim. Both render a familiar subject in such a manner that critical applications with regard to our present situation are made possible. [1971]

Marjorie L. Hoover. In Wolfgang Paulsen, ed., Revolte und
Experiment (Heidelberg, Stiehm, 1972), pp. 84–86

The general historical optimism, the dutiful mandate of historical materialism in its present ex-cathedra narrow-mindedness, permits, when it comes to writing, discreet nuances but not the representation of destructive forces within the socialist society. The author must fall back upon prefabricated antagonisms, namely upon those outside his society. The result is strange. Whatever impresses the GDR bureaucracy as explosive, so critical toward the new social order that it is forbidden—. . . Hacks's *Worries and Power*—seems flat, aggressively political, strange, and undramatic to the Western observer. In *Worries and Power* especially nothing can be found any longer of all that formerly had caused people to speak highly of Hacks; the characters appear to be undifferentiated, without contours, the language is artificial and contrived, the metaphors are ineffectual. Describing the activities of a generator attendant, Party official, or foreman in a briquette factory is not sufficient for characterizing a human being, for creating a character for the stage. And the stylized speech, applied to dissension within the Party and debates about matters of production, is reduced to ridicule. The arranged reality—Hacks depicts, after all, the reaction of German glass-workers to the Hungarian uprising in 1956—becomes in art not just a half-truth but a complete lie.

> Fritz J. Raddatz. In Manfred Durzak, ed., *Die deutsche Literatur der Gegenwart* (Stuttgart, Reclam, 1971), p. 363†

Hacks's early plays—*Inauguration of the Indic Age, The Chapbook of Duke Ernest, The Battle at Lobositz,* and *The Miller of Sanssouci*—doubtlessly give evidence of the vital impulses Hacks received from Brecht. But they also show significant divergences from the dramatic and theatrical practices of Brecht. In Hacks's plays the political principle became more important: not only to see history as a mere background for demonstrating present-day prob-lems but also to connect the poetic interpretation of historic events with clear standards for the present-day behavior of his contemporaries. Hacks's assim-ilation of Brecht is closely interwoven with his study of Marxism. . . .

There are two motifs that stand out: the repeated criticism of an overly exalted heroism, and the unmasking of the philistine behavior of the petite bourgeoisie in history. . . .

A specific variant of the first can be found in *The Chapbook of Duke Ernest,* where the heroism of the alleged folk hero is presented as a "func-tion of the social position." The subtitle, "The Hero and His Retinue," hints at the fact that this heroism is based not on personal qualifications but on the achievements of the duke's bondsmen. . . .

Likewise, in *The Miller of Sanssouci,* Hacks attacks a legend. Follow-ing an idea of Brecht's, Hacks has the miller fight for his mill on direct orders from the king. The monarch needs the dispute to restore his image as a just ruler by a "lawful" decision. Hacks's concern, however, does not end with the revision of the legend alone. Still more noteworthy is his crit-icism of the conduct of the miller, who shows himself to be a petit bourgeois subject—consistently oriented toward philistine, materialistic expediency—deceiving himself with the fiction of his steadfastness and thereby ending up as the dupe in the long run.

These plays were undoubtedly intended as contributions toward coming to terms with the most recent history. Both the emphasis on the constraints on human actions and the destruction of false and harmful illusions were to make possible a critical insight into the widespread self-deception in coming to terms with the past.

> Rolf Röhmer. In Hans Jürgen Geerdts, ed., *Literatur der DDR* (Stuttgart, Kröner, 1972), pp. 456–57†

However little doubt there can be that Hacks is well disposed toward the GDR . . . it is equally clear that he is no strict "socialist realist": his realism, his intelligence, and his tastes obviously prevent him from producing on the stage those undifferentiated workers, farmers, and optimistic plots that Party and union officials expect from him. That got him into trouble again with his *Moritz Tassow:* after only a few performances the play had to be taken off the stage.

What does a dramatist do whose plays dealing with contemporary issues are not performed? He looks for old subjects and plays and "reorients" them. As Hacks learned from Brecht both sarcasm, which has an especially cutting edge when seemingly formulated with guileless naïveté, and the construction of models, which are correct in themselves but entirely sealed off against reality, so also he learned the technique of "reorienting" from Brecht: the moral of some well-known subject matter or play is turned upside down—thus, for instance, the anecdote of the miller of Sanssouci, as presented by Hacks, does not prove that Prussia was a state of justice but rather an especially insidious state of injustice. Often this procedure also allows for making advantageous use of the dramatic qualities of the source material to boot.

Georg Hensel. *Theater der Zeitgenossen* (Frankfurt,
Ullstein, 1972), pp. 166–67†

[Hacks's] *Moritz Tassow* tells the story of a "poetic" swineherd who, in 1945, after the defeat of fascism, casts off his pretended deaf-muteness and leads the inhabitants of a Mecklenburg village to establish a commune. In so doing, he comes into conflict with the pragmatic policy of gradual progress, as suggested by the veteran Communist Mattukat. . . . The moderate Mattukat wants only agrarian reform. And the cleverness of the play lies in the fact that the utopian (almost anarchical) free man does not emerge as a vision of the future at the end of the play, but is established as a reality, as the present, at the beginning of the play. Mattukat, Tassow's antagonist, pragmatically working at mastering the present, gives up in the end, showing himself to be broken by the past. And at the very end—Tassow quits with optimistic resignation and becomes a poet—the play magically conjures up the "new man": Blasche, the unproductive, unpractical, philistine ideologist. It is only in the light of this ending that the play reveals its full meaning.

After all, the new man, being trotted out as a 1945 vision of the future, actually corresponds to the spectator's present reality. This new contemporary man, then, is he unproductive and petit bourgeois, is he a pretense and a camouflage of existing conditions rather than a person to end them, is he an ideological scheme without any real identity? And Tassow (the dialectical structure of the comedy suggests this conclusion), is he the truly utopian form of the new man after all, only slyly disguised in the garb of the past and, of course, not entirely free of flaws either? In that case, however, wouldn't Tassow's antagonist Mattukat function not only as the antithesis of Tassow but also of Blasche? Wouldn't the solution have to be sought not in Mattukat's reverting to Blasche, but in an anticipation of Tassow, or (to state it according to the sequence in the play), not in an anticipation of Blasche, but in a reversion to Tassow? . . .

Hacks, in his *Moritz Tassow,* presents these questions as unresolved, but not as unresolvable: after all, his play is a comedy.

> Volker Canaris. In Benno von Wiese, ed., *Deutsche Dichter der*
> *Gegenwart* (Berlin, Schmidt, 1973), pp. 597–98†

Peter Hacks . . . is among the most significant dramatists now living in the GDR. He became known to a wider public—he had already written two radio plays—with his Columbus drama, *Inauguration of the Indic Age.*

The "Indic age" is the age of capitalism—and Hacks uses Columbus to review it. Columbus needs wealthy sponsors to finance his undertaking; but the judicious and intelligent men are poor, the men of learning are haughty and ignorant, and the rulers are stupid. Columbus learns that "science enlightens only him who wants to be enlightened."

Hacks has written a play about the bondage of science; it is only free enough to be able to lead the way from feudalism to capitalism—and it is granted even this freedom only reluctantly. Eventually the Spanish minister of police provides Columbus with the necessary money—"the man of genius has to be commercialized"—giving gold for ships in exchange for ships full of gold. Queen Isabella—human when not confined by the observance of etiquette—hopes that Columbus's discovery will save her in the eyes of history.

Columbus has a vision, revealing that he knows the consequences of his discovery—he foresees misunderstandings due to linguistic inadequacies, and robbery and murder of the Indians; he hears himself say: "It is . . . not in our power to get along with them in a friendly way." . . .

Hacks's play ends before the actual discovery of "India"; the vision has anticipated what will happen—an artistic master stroke. Hacks proved with this early play that he knew the theater, its effects and the impressions produced by them, that he was a Marxist, that he had learned from Brecht. . . . His first work made it clear that he was a gifted playwright.

> Konrad Franke. In Konrad Franke, ed., *Die Literatur*
> *der Deutschen Demokratischen Republik*
> (Munich, Kindler, 1974), pp. 546–47†

Peter Hacks . . . who, in 1955, at the time of the Brecht boycott, left the FRG to live in the GDR, began as a resolute disciple of Brecht. Plays such as *The Chapbook of Duke Ernest, Inauguration of the Indic Age, The Battle at Lobositz,* and *The Miller of Sanssouci* attest to the Brechtian influence.

In these dramas history is examined from a one-sided, socialist perspective and is divested of its false glamour, which bourgeois historiography had bestowed on it. To be sure, even in these plays the underlying system of coordinates, based on the Marxist philosophy of history, produces, in a sense, a somewhat un-Marxian distortion of the specific, historical contours; the materialistic dialectic, as handled by Hacks, displays a "mechanistic" narrowness, with the author attributing to past ages and their people things less of the past than of our present time. But even if the author shows himself inclined, in these historical dramas, to put the socialist idea, abstractly and abruptly, before concrete historicity; even if, urged on by the conviction that better social conditions have been achieved in the meantime, he asserts his comedian's right to sovereign wit and social cheerfulness a bit too plainly, a bit too markedly—the literary subjectivity thus manifesting itself in these works is still strongly saturated with historically relevant polemics, with the topical need of a new, young society to rid itself of the shackles of its past.

Franz Norbert Mennemeier. *Modernes deutsches Drama*
(Munich, Fink, 1975), Vol. II, pp. 364–65†

From [an] examination of Hacks' plays, it is clear how much he owes to Brecht, at whose feet he went to sit in 1955 . . . , but there are two major differences.

The first is that although there are a few Utopian elements in Brecht like the "golden age almost of justice" under the wise judgments of Azdak, most of his plays end pessimistically: Azdak himself must flee for his own safety. . . . Hacks' plays end with almost consistent optimism. It is not that he would wish us to believe that life is a Utopia; on the contrary we are constantly reminded to examine our lives and our society to see where we fail to achieve what is so desirable. Braeker [in *The Battle of Lobositz*] may go happily on his way, the Miller [in *The Miller of Sanssouci*] may be able to continue grinding corn, but we do not forget to ask why the war or the threat to a man's livelihood was there in the first place.

Secondly, and this is in accord with the idyllic nature of the plots, there is a charm and grace about Hacks' writing which looks quite rococo beside Brecht's style. One sometimes has the impression of a Feydeau employed by the Berliner Ensemble. Indeed, in his wit and ebullient good humour Hacks will not spurn knockabout humour or simple farce. . . . We also find elements of the grotesque far beyond anything in Brecht. There is the corpse of Margaret [in *Margarete in Aix*] being given a turn on the floor during a Provençal banquet, and when one dying soldier on the battlefield of Lobositz asks another to give him his hand, the latter obliges by tossing over his severed hand.

In Hacks' attempt to return to the popular language, idyllic settings and exciting incidents of the chap-book, we recognize a highly intellectualised attempt to create the naïve.

Michael Patterson. *German Theatre Today*
(London, Pitman, 1976), pp. 55, 57–58

On closer examination it becomes apparent that Hacks's interpretation of the socialist present is indebted to the ancient myth of the lost paradise to be regained, a myth which not only can be found in Marx but which ever since Rousseau has played an important part in modern literature in general. . . . Hacks, therefore, can claim that his utopian thinking is an amalgam of the old and the new, the bourgeois myth of history and the Marxist prophecy. . . .

It goes without saying that the myth of the lost paradise to be regained can be presented neither with the neonaturalistic stylistic means of socialist realism nor with agitprop methods nor with Brecht's alienation technique nor with the avant-garde process of demolishing traditional speech. The art of the ugly, of the grotesque, and of the absurd, Hacks believes, has been buried together with capitalism. And he himself leaves no doubt about his aesthetic intentions. . . .

The beautiful utopia can, of course, be presented only through the medium of the beautiful. Hacks, therefore, does not hesitate to raise beauty, long defamed, to the throne. After a century of "dismantling the plot, dismantling character, dismantling beauty," the task of the socialist playwright is "dialectical, critical, and revolutionary restoration." The proclamation of the classical ideal of form thus must not be understood as a retrogression, as a restoration of Weimar classicism. . . .

The epoch-making significance of Hacks's dramatic theory lies in his having broken with the prevailing antipoetic poetics that has dominated Western literature ever since the appearance of the avant-garde. His comedies are tuned to a note of cheerfulness that is in pleasant contrast to the monotony of the black-on-black painting of certain contemporary authors. The image of modern literature has become richer, more complex, more meaningful because of Peter Hacks's acknowledgment of the beautiful.

William H. Rey. *Monatshefte*. Winter, 1976, pp. 398–99, 406†

Peter Hacks's uniqueness as a contemporary GDR playwright lies in his great versatility and skill as a theoretician and practitioner of the theater. In his attempt to develop three specifically "socialist" genres during the fifties and sixties, Hacks cultivated aspects of Greek or "bourgeois" traditions, such as Aristophanic comedy, Schiller's historical drama, the Viennese *Volks-*

stück [folk play], and the Brechtian *Lehrstück* [didactic play]. According to Hacks, his dramas adapt these models in a new way, and at least one level of their meaning is directed toward contemporary social problems in the GDR. . . .

[However,] there *is* a degree of abstraction from socialist "everyday" reality in Hacks's concentration on the self-realization issue in his dramas of the sixties. While . . . it is a relevant issue to the development of the socialist personality, its orientation is nevertheless more philosophical than practical. That is, this issue focuses on a future state of emancipation rather than on a realistic reflection of present social circumstances. The settings of Hacks's plays of the sixties in ancient Greece *(Peace)* or in a mythological kingdom *(Omphale)* further abstract the main character's process of self-realization from the problems of the individual in the GDR.

Judith R. Scheid. *"Enfant Terrible" of Contemporary East German Drama: Peter Hacks in His Role as Adaptor and Innovator* (Bonn, Bouvier Verlag Herbert Grundmann, 1977), pp. 171–72

Parallel to the development of man and human society is the evolution of art: from the poetry of the ancient myths, which reflect the harmonious existence of man, to prose during the period of man's alienation—prose as the characteristic literary form of capitalism—to a new age of poetry, the artistic expression of man's new state of oneness with society.

Hacks understands the new classic socialist literature—a poetic literature as opposed to the prose of the bourgeoisie—as an anticipation of the ideal third stage of man's development. . . . The timeless, poetic elements of art are at once a reminder of the former harmonious state of existence and an indication of the new state to come. They offer man an alternative to his everyday reality. The goal of art is man's realization of his intended perfection. . . . Art has, then, in Hacks' system, an educative function, one that is, however, much less direct than that of "revolutionary" art: Hacks' classic literature does not attempt to convert—or to convey information or knowledge; its purpose can indeed only be fulfilled when it makes no attempt to educate, when it is simply concerned with itself. The parallel relationship between socialist classicism and the German *Klassik,* on the one hand, and revolutionary art and the Enlightenment, on the other, is clear. . . .

The process of human development is dialectical; change comes about as the result of the interaction of opposites, i.e., as the result of conflict. Also art must deal with conflict; in Hacks' view the presentation of conflict is the very basis of literature. He assumes, moreover, that in the post-revolutionary age, since art need no longer be propagandistic, conflicts can be described with the greatest candor. Hacks, like other Marxists, holds that conflicts are basically solvable in socialist society, that, contrary to those rooted in the capitalistic system, they are non-antagonistic and will be resolved in time, as the socialist society evolves. Because conflicts in socialist society are non-antagonistic, Hacks considers the tragedy to be out-of-date. . . .

Although Hacks' outlook on the future is a positive one, he rejects any kind of false optimism or rosy coloring of the present. In contrast to other socialist writers, he refuses to give the impression in his plays that conflicts are immediately solvable.

Margy Gerber. UDR. Winter, 1978, p. 6

HANDKE, PETER (1942–   )

Ignoring the social and political problems treated by Genet and Weiss, Handke's drama [*Abusing the Audience*] . . . deals with the form of art and the difficulties of communication. It is a desperate attempt at establishing contact and mutual involvement. It is narcissistic, because rather than wanting to correct the world by inciting action on the part of others, it tries to arouse audience attention to the author. This is communication for its own sake: the unloved, misunderstood, slightly paranoid adolescent is acting up to gain attention, affection, understanding. . . .

This small-scale nihilism abolishes theater tradition for the sake of absolute, gratuitous rebellion. The gratuitousness is specious, the ulterior motive is a need for direct contact. The editorializing interludes, monologs, and songs of traditional and modern theater have flowered into an evening-long essay, a genre alien to the stage except in the forms of lectures.

Handke, in fact, has composed an aggressive lecture. The spoken word has upstaged action, plot, and characterization. A mesmerizing rhythm, inspired by beat poetry (e.g., Allen Ginsberg), is created by parataxis and anaphor: monotonous use of the same syntax over and over again and repetition of the same word at the beginning of and at other focal points of sentences within a series.

Joachim Neugroschel. AGR. Feb.–Mar., 1967, p. 28

It can be taken as a sign of Handke's naïveté that he uses negation itself as the dramatic impulse. Hence the title *Abusing* [*the Audience*], for abusing implies the transformation of the negation into an active reaction. He who abuses not only negates but also attacks. Whom or what does Handke attack? . . . As the title indicates, Handke abuses the audience, the theatergoers. He reviles them because they still have not given up the convention of watching and listening to conventional stage plays in a conventional way. And what does he offer instead? Another theater? Does he alter the basic prerequisites of the theater? Does he tear down the stage apron separating actors and audience? Does he offer new dramatic techniques? He reverses the procedure of conventional theater by having the actors describe the audience as theater connoisseurs. Handke addresses the spectators through the actors. But that is not actually anything new. Ever since Shakespeare it has been part and parcel of the tradition of conventional theater occasionally to address the audience directly, to step out of the role. What is new with Handke is that he no longer takes the trouble to invent a play to go with it. [1969]

Helmut Heissenbüttel. In Manfred Brauneck, ed.,

Das deutsche Drama vom Expressionismus bis zur

Gegenwart (Bamberg, Buchners, 1972), p. 307†

In German a speak-in is a *Sprechstück:* a piece to be spoken. The voices that speak the speak-ins should be regarded as musical instruments. The four voices of *Offending the Audience* "play ensemble," a term equally applicable to music as to acting. The voices of the male and female speaker in *Self-Accusation* "are attuned to each other, alternate with one another or speak in unison, quiet and loud, with very abrupt transitions, thus producing an acoustic order." In other words, the speak-ins are highly formal, as music must be to qualify as music, closely patterned and rigorously structured, employing repetition, variation, counterpoint and orchestration in their verbal and thematic development. Words here are used as though they were notes to create independent (non-imitative) artistic structures. The words, as Handke says, "do not point to the world but to the world within the words themselves." In that sense the speak-ins are hermetic, even monolithic, but it is precisely because they are self-contained that the speak-ins can speak to the audience. . . .

If Handke can be said to be a realistic playwright, then [it is] only in the sense that he has shorn reality of its superfluities and presents us with its essence. *Offending* demonstrates and makes us experience the essence of the dialectical relationship between illusion and reality. The confession *Self-Accusation* makes the audience-priest finally aware of its own guilt. Here essences are laid bare by means of highly formal structural procedures. That these procedures are frequently playful, ironic, and amusing is not in conflict with their overall intent, which is a more nearly scientific one. . . . Handke is the first critical scientific German playwright since Brecht.

Michael Roloff. *AGR*. April–May, 1969, pp. 12–13

From the very first, Handke was in no way radical, neither politically nor linguistically nor aesthetically. He belongs to those who, as in Bazon Brock's formulation against Adorno, have given up the "silly pathos of mental reservation against the thought-manipulating industry" and acknowledged the consumer society. Still more important: Handke is no avant-garde writer, and whoever labels him thus either betrays his ignorance of literary history or intentionally tries to cloud the issue. An avant-garde writer is someone who believes he is moving *ahead of* the social institutions and their self-image because he has discovered something aesthetically new, which at first cannot be assimilated for general consumption, and because he has introduced something futuristic into the present. Handke, however, has written nothing that, in theory or practice, goes beyond what had already been achieved in the works of Robbe-Grillet and especially in "concrete poetry"; as a matter of fact, he has retrogressed behind the latter. . . . Handke, therefore, did not extend the boundaries of what in the 1950s and 1960s was understood to be progressive literature in terms of either form or content; rather, he varied, to some extent with the skill of a virtuoso, already existing methods. At the same time, however, he maintained—as for instance in his essay "I Dwell in the Ivory Tower"—that these methods were his own, invented by himself, and that now, after *he* had used them, they could no longer be employed. Never did he refer to his close dependence upon what the Vienna Group . . . Mon, Heissenbüttel, Jandl, and others, had done fifteen years before him— and had done with far greater consistency and imagination.

Michael Buselmeier. *FH*. April, 1970, pp. 287–88†

It was said and we saw [in *Kaspar*]: Only through language does the world assume a sense of order for us; or: Man can establish order in the world through language, he can make his home in it (which, perhaps, is bound up with pain)—indeed, as far as he himself is concerned, it means that he actually acquires an identity only through language. *(Language, then, makes possible the determination of the natural order.)* But how does it follow from this that he is pervertedly taught a *false* order, a *false* identity by those who instruct him in the language? The statement advocated now—*Language violates the natural order, determining how things have to be*—by no means follows from what was initially demonstrated.

Here, finally, the spectator, especially the one who, acting according to Handke's ideas, tries to "concretize" his observations, applying them to his own situation, asks himself: Who, actually, are those indoctrinators? To whom do they correspond in my reality? What do they signify? The so-called establishment? The mass media? The supporters of capitalistic society? And Kaspar, is that probably who we are? But that does not quite agree with our reality. For the real manipulators of speech are not the same people who originally teach us language. This much is true: We actually do learn how to master, as it were, our world by means of *our* language. If, however, others control *us* by means of *their* language, then that depends on— well, what that depends on, what the connection is there, that would be really worth our attention.

But that is not what Handke calls to our attention in *Kaspar*; on the contrary: by simply equating the teachers of language with its wrongful manipulators, he obfuscates it.

Rainer Taëni. *NRs.* 81, 1, 1970, pp. 164–65†

Ever since he burst almost simultaneously onto the literary and theatrical scenes as recently as 1966, critics, producers and playgoers have been vociferous in their rival affirmation or denigration of Handke's talent. The question has never been: is he a good writer or a mediocre one? It is more absolute than that: is he a genius or a charlatan? The sort of question, in other words, that was asked at first about Beckett, Brecht, Hauptmann, Ibsen, Schiller, or Goethe, with all of whom Handke's supporters would rank him, and indeed have done so.

True to form, each of Handke's plays regularly causes an uproar in the theater in which it is first performed. . . . From the start (that is, from his first appearance in public as an author) critics and fellow authors were ruefully noting a phenomenon called "Handke-Publicity" and taking sarcastic swipes at his Beatle haircut, his effeminate features, and his championing of rock (or "Beat," to use the German word). Since launching himself, Handke's appearances at various functions have usually been stormy or, at the very least, controversial, even to the extent of his being dragged off to the police station after a brawl outside a Frankfurt rock club. Indeed his polemical, and often politically activist essays and speeches, the unconventional form of his theater pieces and his whole persona are all deliberately calculated, however sincerely meant, to achieve maximum impact on the literary and theatergoing public as well as on the multimedia publicity machine that stands ready to focus on anyone who makes a big enough noise. [1971]

Nicholas Hern. *Peter Handke* (New York, Frederick Ungar, 1972), pp. 1–2

The fact that man can be influenced is also the subject of Handke's . . . *The Ward Wants to Be Guardian.*

Dependence, lack of individuality, other-direction: this reiteration of the underlying concerns in *Kaspar* is intensified by the absence of speech. Speech is not even necessary any more to influence or to mold another person; gestures and actions will suffice for directing man's reactions, for making him into a useful robot run by remote control.

In front of a scene depicting a farm, which must be recognizable as a backdrop, are presented some in part quite trivial occurrences that are to be watched or perceived: the cutting of toenails, the filling of a tub with water from a hose. "The cat does what it does,". . ."the bottle falls to the ground and does what it does." Whatever happens on the stage is meant to be nothing more than what happens on the stage.

But there are also some occurrences that represent more than just an occurrence in itself. The ward eats an apple; the process of eating the apple is like a Happening. The ward eats a second apple, this time watched by the guardian. "The longer the guardian watches, the more slowly the apple is eaten," until finally the ward stops eating altogether and just holds the rest of the apple in his hand. Another example: the ward fetches his guardian a newspaper . . . [and] the farther away he goes from him, the more "light-hearted" and louder his steps become; when he comes back, the process is reversed.

What happens takes on two levels of meaning, becomes symbolic; man's susceptibility to influences, the dependence of one man on the other (both characters wear masks!), compulsive behavior caused by the mere presence of another person or else by the feeling of being observed. . . .

The ward attempts to break loose from this master-slave relationship but is indeed too much engrossed in it to be capable of giving expression to his own self.

Karin Kuchenbäcker. DU. Oct., 1971, pp. 12–13†

At first sight Handke is a belated representative of the Theater of the Absurd. The very fundamentals of his dramatic theory have been borrowed from it. All of the plays, including *Abusing the Audience, Prophecy,* and *Self-Accusation,* which he has had produced since 1966, are based on a kind of "questioning of language." By impartially stringing together linguistic clichés, empty phrases, and platitudes—but treating them downright seriously—he charges them, through the medium of the theater, with cryptic and to some extent parodistic references. And herein lies the only fun of his plays. One does not understand Handke's dramatic technique if one takes his products to be merely "speech plays," better suited for listening than for playing. . . . It is Handke's very forte to be extraordinarily well versed in the laws of the theater and to know how to use them. In particular, he has the theatrical instinct of an experienced boulevard author, and that is, after all, what he basically is. Handke's so-called subtle, complicated poetic theory is very simple, almost primitive.

It is based on two premises that through their direct interaction, brought about by the inner laws of the theater, result in specific effects of importance to the manipulator. First premise: Handke, the representative of "modernism," takes the theater in its simplest form, in its narrow restriction as a "peep-show". He ignores any interaction between theater and audience. Second premise: Handke assumes a modern stance, rejecting the metaphor. To present images, to act metaphorically, is for him—he chooses the word with careful deliberation—"counterrevolutionary." Since, however, any movement on the stage, even the most insignificant one, takes on a meaning simply because of its symbolic character—this as a result of the inner laws of the theater—it produces a statement, albeit an ambiguous one, even though the audience may be addressed in incoherent words and phrases only. And from this very fact Handke devises his aesthetic theory, pointing out that the more the proceedings on the stage represent an entity complete in itself, the more readily the spectator finds himself able to concretize these abstractions with regard to his own situation. This means that, because of the accretion in significance with which the inner laws of the theater endow anything that happens on the stage, the insignificant acquires a meaning, which has its origin, however, exclusively in an arbitrary, momentary, subjective frame of reference established by the spectator.

Werner Mittenzwei. *SuF*. Jan., 1971, pp. 117–18†

The fundamental assumption behind *Kaspar* is that language represents a brutalizing instrument of repression that is employed by society—through such agents as parents, teachers, journalists, and bureaucrats—to transform the free unconditioned individual into a subservient puppet of the state. . . .

Kaspar is the work of a young man, but one with undeniable gifts; in fact, compared with most of the pretentious and imitative efforts of the post-Beckett avant-garde, it has real integrity, even considerable originality. . . .

Kaspar was partially inspired by the story of Kaspar Hauser, who, having spent the first seventeen years of his life in a closet, first communicated with the outside world through a single sentence: "I want to be someone like somebody else once was." The same sentence is repeated endlessly by Handke's Kaspar—the primitive demand for social identity that begins his social conditioning. As a group of cool, anonymous speakers bombard him with instructions, model sentences, clichés, syllogisms, proverbialisms—their voices sometimes tortured by overloaded loudspeakers and squealing electronics—Kaspar develops from a wild, disordered creature, mewling at inanimate objects and pulling furniture apart, into a neat, well-regulated, domesticated, and rather lobotomized member of society. In short, the play is a Romantic's view of history and phylogeny, encapsulating the progress of the child into adulthood, the ignorant into learning, the savage into civilization, the lunatic into sanity—always at the cost of considerable shame and agony. [1973]

Robert Brustein. *The Culture Watch* (New York, Alfred A. Knopf, 1975), pp. 72–73

Irritation is again the basic stylistic principle [in *The Fools Are Dying Out*], although in this play Peter Handke for the first time fills out his characters in precise detail, down to the exact determination of their social standing. He goes still further, in the beginning, by suggesting the atmosphere of a modern comedy of manners: room with a big window, silhouette of a city, servants in dress coats, entrepreneurs in sweatsuits. The milieu is that of nouveau-riche haughtiness, with the intimacy of the gym clothes adding a gentle touch of irony. It all amounts to a revival of the spectator's "peep-show," namely to be able to have a look at "another world." . . . Handke—contradicting, by the way, the intentions behind his "speech plays"—fully and undauntedly furnishes the spectator with the illusion, hence with the traditional gift of the theater. Thus, the play *The Fools Are Dying Out* falls structurally and formally far short of his previous works, represents a hardly secret return to the old, customary theater of illusion. . . .

But Handke introduces a new subject, which sustains the play: the leading character's struggle with himself, the possibility—but also the impossibility—of a person's breaking out of his own role, of acting out of character, of being "foolish" enough . . . to show "feelings," and, being an entrepreneur, of endeavoring to treat himself to the luxury of emotions in addition to that of his material wealth. . . .

[In the end] the attempt to break out of the role of ruthless rationality proves unsuccessful; and yet, the call to, indeed the necessity of, opposition and resistance nevertheless persists: "Hardly anyone looks as if he could still act out of character." On the very verge of resignation, Peter Handke, through the figure of the contradictory entrepreneur Quitt, who refutes himself, pleads for a deregulated rationality, for a wise foolishness, for an imagination not browbeaten by advertising slogans and ethical norms of behavior—an imagination increasingly threatened.

Uwe Schulz. *Peter Handke* (Velber,
Friedrich, 1973), pp. 87–88, 103†

For Handke theater is the place where one can see what the world is really like only by being placed outside its ordinary actions and, most important, its self-definitions, which are of course our own. In this attitude he is not so very far from Ibsen, who also saw the theater as judging the world. . . .

Handke is even closer, of course, to such immediate predecessors and contemporaries as Beckett, who revealed his attitude toward the invented-ness of artistic works when he remarked of Joyce that "he is not writing about something, he is writing something," and Jerzy Grotowski, who believes that the theater ought not to attempt to resemble life because it is a means precisely of "going against" life in order to reanimate it. The strange theatrical power of all Handke's plays springs . . . from some of the same sources as Beckett's: the reduction of drama to non-contingent, non-historical elements; the setting free in this space cleared of anecdote of a primal awareness of consciousness itself; the pressure on language to dramatize itself; the involvement of the spectator in a process rather than a story. Like Beckett, too, Handke has felt the extreme difficulty of composing meaningful works out of language which is forever betraying our specific meanings, and the sentiment this gives rise to of mingled rage, despair, and crafty resolution is what animates these plays of language on exhibition.

Richard Gilman. *The Making of Modern Drama*
(New York, Farrar, Straus & Giroux, 1974), p. 277

Not since Beckett and Ionesco has a playwright provoked and bewildered his audiences as much as Peter Handke has . . . and with good cause: He is challenging our ability to know anything.

In his play *Self-Accusation* Handke attacks the various ways in which we attempt to define ourselves. In *Kaspar* the socialization of man through language is seen as an artifact of questionable value. And in *The Ride across Lake Constance* not only the theater but life itself becomes a terrible fiction. . . .

Admittedly an admirer of Wittgenstein, Handke has been influenced more directly by philosophy than any other playwright since Pirandello. But this fact shouldn't place him in the "closet dramatist" category. His actors and audiences don't have to know the wellspring of his imagination to enjoy his word-and-gesture play, the *non sequiturs,* and slapstick humor. However, the very nature of his epistemological investigation has broadened the theatrical form. In Handke's *Ride* all that is predictable in life is undetermined on the stage. What one sees becomes half-seen. The audience is forced to re-examine common everyday experiences. . . .

The origin of the title, *The Ride across Lake Constance,* comes from a German legend about a horseman who rides across Lake Constance at night through fog and snow. When he arrives at the other side of the lake his friends tell him he has traveled over ice no more than an inch thick. The horseman, suddenly realizing the danger of his ride, drops dead.

There is no better description of this work. Our life is a blind journey over thin ice. If we stop to think about it we may die of fright.

William L. Lederer. *ChiR.* 26, 2, 1974, pp. 171–72, 176

Whatever one may feel about Handke, he cannot be ignored. From the age of 24 he has repeatedly found new ways of confronting the theatre and its public and has, remarkably, remained extremely popular in the process. In the last ten years he has been the third most frequently produced contemporary German-language playwright, a considerable achievement for a young *avant-garde* author (although it is questionable whether he is as *avant-garde* as he claims, if the old guard of the German theatre are marching along beside him). There is a danger with such clever and articulate young writers that the audience is impaled on a fork: if Handke's work is admired, his talent is recognised; if not, then this is sure proof that he is a misunderstood genius like Ibsen, Brecht and Beckett before him.

Dispensing with language or using it with the purpose of undermining its own meaning necessarily leads to ambiguities. And ambiguities lead to the situation where all interpretations are valid. And where all interpretations are valid, non are. . . .

Handke's great talent lies in his ingenuity. He has hit upon some truly startling ideas and created new frames of reference. *The Ride across Lake Constance* makes one more aware of the somnambulistic rituals which form so much of daily living, just as Pinter will attune one's ears to the incoherences of everyday conversation. Unfortunately, when Handke exhausts one of his brilliant ideas, he tends to exhaust the audience in the process.

Michael Patterson. German Theatre Today
(London, Pitman, 1976), p. 32

The Ride [*across Lake Constance*] is not a modern example either of the Dada spirit of archly playful negation, or of surrealism's unconscious connections of images within a somewhat limited, because equally unconscious, range of emotion. If the play seems illogical in structure it is because logic is one of Handke's subjects; it is because he is trying to understand it rather than either embrace it or flee from it. *The Ride* is a formulation of the relationship between action and language, or, more precisely, between perception and interpretation. There is nothing of the surrealists' alternatives of cold emotional quietism or narrow frenzy in the face of outrageous imagery. *The Ride* is one of the most emotional intelligibly avant-garde plays ever written. One of its central, communicable feelings, for example, is a sense of the shame of self-consciousness, the shame that sets in from our knowledge of the difference between the self and the world. This knowledge is not only made possible by language but is synonymous with it. . . .

The play is progress to consciousness and death by consciousness. . . . The predicament is our reliance on the mind's interpretation of experience, and even more on arbitrary communal assignments of meanings to actions so that minds can work together. This insistence on the meaning of events gives our perceptions a function, gives ourselves a function of interpretation—something to do while existing—and of course makes existence possible. But it destroys our own relation to the world and to our own experiences.

Ira Hauptman. PR. 45, 3, 1978, pp. 426–27

In his review of the 1971–72 production at Lincoln Center of Handke's second full-length play, *The Ride across Lake Constance*, John Simon asks, with obvious disapproval, "When is a play not a play but a fraud? When, in fact, is any so-called work of art not a work of art but a piece of trickery, a hoax, a nonsensical game, a fraud?" With characteristic perspicacity (though somewhat hasty displeasure), Simon has posed the single most important question concerning our attitude toward Handke's drama. For it is only when we decide Handke is *not* a charlatan that we can begin to discover the underpinnings—and hence the substance—of his artistic tricks.

It is difficult to imagine a play more worthy of Simon's question than Handke's fourth speech play, *Calling for Help*. . . . This piece, shorter even than the others (only twelve minutes in production), is literally described by its title, for it consists simply of the search for the word *help* in order that the speakers may use it. . . .

The piece, however, is not merely a joke, but an ingenious demonstration of a fundamental truth about language: it has a reality of its own. . . . Handke now presents statements and words which are not intrinsically insignificant but which in the context of the speech play become "pure" language, with no relationship to phenomenal reality. Every statement is offered only as another guess in the language game the speakers are playing, and once the audience realizes the speakers are in search of a particular word, they, like the speakers, cease to consider the usual significance of the statements but view them simply as words to be rejected as unsatisfactory. . . .

Yet *Calling for Help* does not only demonstrate a linguistic principle, which might adequately have been done through a dictionary recitation. *Calling for Help*, like the other speech plays, protests the reified condition of a language that thrives—or at least exists—on staleness. Every statement or phrase in *Calling for Help* is recognizable as one of the many signs of society one repeatedly sees, accepts, and obeys without thought. The piece is a collage of advertising slogans, clichéd orders and responses, announcements, prohibitions, newspaper headlines, and moral maxims which reduce language to a weather-worn bumper sticker.

In the context of this piece, the audience does precisely what Handke hopes it will do outside the theater: it rejects as meaningless the ready-mades of mass and private communication. Only in retrospect does an audience realize the didactic intention of the piece and consider its effectiveness in dramatizing the need for new forms. The opening appeal for "mutual understanding," "deeper knowledge," and "an open heart" ironically applies to Handke's plea as readily as it does to any other: Handke is calling for a "community of men" who will reject inherited rhetoric and revitalize language and perception. He is, finally, calling for help.

June Schlueter. *The Plays and Novels of Peter Handke* (Pittsburgh, University of Pittsburgh Press, 1981), pp. 37–40

HAUPTMANN, GERHART (1862–1946)

In works such as *Before Dawn*, which have much of the ballad in them, tone is well-nigh all important, for the question of tone is synonymous with the question of truthfulness or untruthfulness. . . . Gerhart Hauptmann . . . has not only a true tone, but also true courage and true *artistic skill* to match this courage. It is foolish to assume that naturalistic coarseness is always tantamount to artlessness. On the contrary, if properly employed . . . it attests to the highest artistry. . . .

He appears to me as altogether the fulfillment of Ibsen. All I had been admiring in Ibsen for years, the "Reach into life, it is a teeming ocean," the novelty and boldness of the problems, the ingenious simplicity of the language, the talent for characterization, together with the most rigorous organization of the action and the elimination of anything not directly related to the plot itself—all of this I also found in Hauptmann. Moreover, all the things I disliked about Ibsen—the ruminating; the fidgeting; the attempt to stress the point so much that, at long last, it breaks off; the lapsing into vagueness; the speaking in oracles and riddles, riddles that no one tries to solve because they have already become boring before the answer is given—all these flaws I do *not* find in Hauptmann. He is not a realist who sporadically suffers from whimsical fits of philosophical romanticizing but a realist in good style, which is to say that from beginning to end he is always the same. [Oct. 21, 1889]

Theodor Fontane. *Sämtliche Werke* (Munich,
Hanser, 1969), Vol. II, pp. 819–20†

The Weavers was an enormous success. It certainly must be admitted that no French dramatist is capable of creating a fresco of such scope and power. When first performed by the Freie Bühne in Berlin, the play caused a great stir. Hauptmann, backed by all the young German literati, succeeded in having an Imperial ban rescinded. Here in Paris, this drama of revolt was received, contrary to my expectations, above all as an outcry of despair and misery; the deeply moved audience applauded it from beginning to end. It is the masterpiece of an evolving social theater, and [the French Socialist deputy] Jaurès, in raptures about it, sent me word that such a performance achieved more than all the political campaigns and discussions.

Furthermore, since I have a strong feeling that this is one of my last productions and that the end of my troubles is in sight, I gave it all I had left of my strength, resources, and energy; and I must say that the performance was outstanding. . . . The entire second act, with the Weavers' Song serving as a leitmotif, repeatedly resounding ominously from behind the scenes, produced an extraordinarily impressive effect. When, in the fourth act, the weavers storm the manufacturer's home, the terror generated was so intense that all the people sitting in the orchestra jumped to their feet. The last scene, in which Old Hilse is killed, fatally hit when a volley is fired, while the crowd is shrieking and yelling, was played amid general applause. [May, 1893]

André Antoine. *"Mes souvenirs" sur le Théâtre-Libre*
(Paris, Arthème Fayard, 1921), pp. 290–91†

Gerhart Hauptmann possesses two qualities rarely combined in one author. As subtle as Ibsen in the analysis of character, as frank as Zola in placing the brutality of life before us, Hauptmann nevertheless introduces into nearly every one of his dramas some *motif* so poetically conceived as at once to impress us with the fact that we have in him both a realist and an idealist. . . .

Hauptmann, like the majority of modern German playwrights, has paid his tribute to Ibsen; but it is his chief claim to distinction that, with that tribute, he bought his freedom. Relying solely on his own genius, he has become perhaps the most original creator in the dramatic world since Goethe. . . .

The same year that saw the production of this cruelly realistic play [*The Weavers*] saw the production of another drama by Hauptmann, of a wholly different character. *Colleague Crampton* is sad enough, it is true; but the pathos of it is relieved in the end. It deals with the almost complete ruin of an artist who has seen better days, but who is at war with established conservative art-elements represented by *Die Akademie*. His downfall is also hastened by certain personal irregularities, among which is a too great fondness for looking upon the wine when it is red. But there is in this drama a reaction from the extreme realism of *The Weavers*, as if Hauptmann could no longer restrain his idealistic impulse. For, side by side with sadness in *Colleague Crampton*, there is an element of poetic beauty in the touching devotion of the daughter of this man for her ruined father. Indeed, this poetic motive is the mainspring of the play; for it is through the daughter's devotion and that of a young art student who loves her, that Crampton is finally saved. . . .

It is capitally constructed, from a dramatic point of view—indeed, when acted, is one of the most effective of Hauptmann's plays—and the language is often pointedly satirical. *Die Akademie*, from the principal director down to the janitor, gets a lashing which would delight the soul of any modern artist of the Impressionist school.

Gustav Kobbé. *The Forum*. Dec., 1897, pp. 432–33, 437

Johannes [in *Lonely Lives*] is an intellectual through and through. He is a young scholar who has grown up in a university town. He lacks all bourgeois characteristics and has the manner of a well-bred young man who is accustomed to the society of decent people (such as Anna). His movements and appearance are full of youth and gentle, like those of a man who has been brought up in a family and pampered by that family and is still living under mama's wing. Johannes is a German scholar and is therefore dignified in dealing with men. When left alone with women, on the other hand, he becomes tender in a feminine manner. The scene where he cannot keep from caressing his wife even though he already loves or is beginning to love Anna illustrates this point nicely.

Now about his nerves. Don't stress [Chekhov recommends to Vsevolod Meyerhold] his nervousness to the point of allowing his neuropathological nature to obstruct or subjugate what is more important: his loneliness, the sort of loneliness that only lofty, yet healthy (in the highest sense) person-alities experience. Project a lonely man, and show his nervousness only insofar as the script indicates. Don't interpret his nervousness as an individ-ual phenomenon. Keep in mind that nowadays almost every civilized per-son, no matter how healthy he may be, never feels so irritated as when he is at home among his own family. The irritation is chronic; it has no pathos, no convulsive outbursts. It is an irritation that guests fail to notice, because its entire burden falls primarily on the people he is closest to—his mother or wife. It is an intimate, family irritation, so to speak. [Oct., 1899]

Anton Chekhov. Letters (New York, Harper & Row, 1973), p. 368

With the single exception of a few lines of verse with which *Hannele* ends, Hauptmann for his first eight years of known authorship was a prose dra-matist of the realist school. Then of a sudden (1897) he threw upon the world like a bombshell his *The Sunken Bell*.

Few things in the history of literature of such high merit and originality have been received so well as this. Those who were already of the Haupt-mann party were enthusiastic, and the anti-realists rejoiced over the author as over a sinner that repented. It was hailed as the finest German poem since Goethe's day; and some went further still and were not afraid to place it in a category near to *Faust*. What speaks well for the moderation and sound sense of Hauptmann is that he has allowed the thing to stand apart; has not immediately flooded the world with inferior copies of this master-piece. . . . Hauptmann did not, because of his success with *The Sunken Bell*, give up his old realistic drama, nor prose drama of other kinds. . . .

This work is both symbolic and allegorical. Symbolism and allegory are by no means the same thing: Symbolism may be described as mythology in being. The great achievement of the play is the creation of the beings who inhabit the mountain, from the old witchwoman (Wittichen), who, though she is a hideous being, and though she uses the folk-language of Hauptmann's folk-dramas, yet (like Caliban) speaks in blank verse, and is in truth a sort of Earth-mother, to the Faun (Waldschrat), the water-spirit (Nickelmann), and all the fairies and nymphs who dance in the moonlight, last of all up to Rautendelein, who is a transformed Undine. The very name Rautendelein is a poem. . . .

But however good was the idea of the story, and however poetical the conception of Rautendelein and her kin, that would not be enough if the technical achievement were not there. . . .

Both in his ideas and his execution (his technique), Hauptmann, in *The Sunken Bell,* shows himself a poet of a high order. But until we have from him work which in the smallest degree can compare with the incomparable lyrics of Goethe, one can hardly so much as mention the two poets side by side.

Edinburgh Review. July, 1903, pp. 172–75, 177

And Pippa Dances, the last play which Hauptmann has produced thus far, is more a puzzle than a drama. In the first act we have extreme naturalism, mingled with a few mystic traits, which in themselves are not at all incompatible with the naturalistic method. As the play goes on we get altogether into the realm of phantastic mysticism and symbolism.

The play has been interpreted as a symbolic presentation of the truth that art cannot exist without a high degree of culture, that it must perish in the contact with the primitive man, even if the latter is not hostile in his disposition towards it. The author of the play himself is reported to have given it this interpretation. But it is first of all a forced one, and it secondly gives no clue as to the significance of many traits and details contained in the play. In the case of a naturalistic drama the author could make the plea that life is complex and capricious and that we are by no means able to comprehend and account for everything. It is, however, the chief purpose of the dramatic art to interpret to us what is apparently without meaning. . . . Hauptmann has surely not solved a philosophical problem in the play under discussion, nor has an important meaning revealed itself at once to the common understanding.

Josef Wiehr. *JEGP.* 6, 4, 1906–7, pp. 574–75

[Hauptmann's] latest production, *Drayman Henschel,* [is] a dialect tragedy which has been the doleful *pièce de résistance* of the Deutsches Theater of Berlin during the last few weeks. Nothing could be gloomier and more depressing than this mournful picture of Silesian peasant life. Even Tolstoi's *The Power of Darkness,* which undoubtedly suggested the outline of character and the general trend of action in Hauptmann's drama, is, in its final effect, less oppressing and saddening. . . .

Hauptmann's consummate skill in depicting diseased states of mind has perhaps never been as strikingly illustrated as in this pathetic figure of a man who goes to ruin from sheer mental disintegration. But never, too, has there been a more striking illustration of the inevitable failure of exclusively pathological poetry. The whole drama, to speak plainly, is as intolerable as it is perfect. There is not a glimpse of the higher life in it; not a single figure which calls out our affection; not even an appeal to our sense of indignation or our righteous wrath; nothing but the cold analysis of a scientific observer. And that from the author of *The Weavers, Lonely Lives,* and *The Sunken Bell!* Indeed, the extraordinary wealth and versatility of Hauptmann's genius could not be more graphically brought to our minds than by placing *Drayman Henschel* side by side with the three dramas just mentioned.

Kuno Francke. *German Ideals of To-day* (Boston,
Houghton, Mifflin, 1907), pp. 243–44, 248–49

Gerhart Hauptmann is the dramatist of whom it may be justly said that he revolutionized the spirit of dramatic art in Germany: the last Mohican of a group of four—Ibsen, Strindberg, Tolstoy, and Hauptmann—who illumined the horizon of the nineteenth century. Of these Hauptmann, undoubtedly the most human, is also the most universal.

It is unnecessary to make comparisons between great artists: life is sufficiently complex to give each his place in the great scheme of things. If, then, I consider Hauptmann more human, it is because of his deep kinship with every stratum of life. While Ibsen deals exclusively with *one* attitude, Hauptmann embraces them all, understands all, and portrays all, because nothing human is alien to him.

Whether it be the struggle of the transition stage in *Lonely Lives,* or the conflict between the Ideal and the Real in *The Sunken Bell,* or the brutal background of poverty in *The Weavers,* Hauptmann is never as aloof as the iconoclast Ibsen, never as bitter as the soul dissector Strindberg, nor yet as set as the crusader Tolstoy. And that because of his humanity, his boundless love, his oneness with the disinherited of the earth, and his sympathies with the struggles and the travail, the hope and the despair of every human soul. That accounts for the bitter opposition which met Gerhart Hauptmann when he made his first appearance as a dramatist; but it also accounts for the love and devotion of those to whom he was a battle cry, a clarion call against all iniquity, injustice and wrong.

Emma Goldman. *The Social Significance of the Modern
Drama* (Boston, Badger, 1914), pp. 87–88

I never met Hauptmann in person, . . . but I always felt the greatest admiration for him and his works, the more so, since he was a figure of such great importance for the cultural life in Russia. I value him most as a dramatist and am less interested in his novels and novellas. The play I like best? *Drayman Henschel.* . . .

Hauptmann . . . did not only exert a highly stimulating influence upon the literary Russia of my generation, he also gave rise to an immediate Hauptmann school among our playwrights. Kosorotov and Urwanzew can be considered direct imitators of Hauptmann in their formerly popular plays. This is, however, not the decisive aspect when speaking about Hauptmann's significance for Russia; rather it is the fact that Hauptmann's plays were at that time almost as much at home in Russia as were the works of Anton Chekhov. Indeed, Hauptmann and Chekhov represent two parallel tendencies of the Russian theater of the time, both equally germane to the Russian intelligentsia of an era characterized by pessimistic disillusionment and, at the same time, a yearning for ideal values and a dream of beauty.

Maxim Gorky. In Ludwig Marcuse, ed., *Gerhart Hauptmann und sein Werk* (Berlin, Schneider, 1922), p. 107†

The fact that Prospero [in *Indipohdi*] embraces the "nothing" is not to be interpreted as signifying the author's renunciation of his faith in life. Hauptmann, though heart-sick and discouraged beyond measure by the unspeakable misery and degradation caused by the war, the unrestrained application of the philosophy of force, does not give up in despair; but still believes in the forces of life and love. . . . Hope lies not in merely cherishing and preserving the dead past, but rather in bringing forth, through love, the new, the living.

And what are the new revelations which Prospero intends to write on the tablets of bronze? May we not conclude that one of them is the principle of self-effacement, which by his last act he has indelibly inscribed upon the heart of his son? This is, of course, not a new philosophy, for it is the fundamental principle of Christ's teaching; but in recent years it was displaced, with most dire consequences, by the philosophy of the Superman, the philosophy of self-assertion.

Thus we see that Hauptmann finds salvation for the individual as well as for society as a whole not in the findings of science or the ever changing shibboleths of *Sozialpolitik* [social legislation], not in the dead creed of the church, nor in the self-assertive philosophy of the Superman—but rather in the principle of self-sacrificing human love. . . . This is the heart and essence of Hauptmann's religion, a religion not of the head, but of the heart; not of a book or unchanging creed, but of expanding life full of changes; a religion not hostile to nature; a religion which is not the tool of the oppressor and exploiter and militarist, but one of social justice, of peace and goodwill among men; a religion of light, warmth, beauty, freedom, and love, of joy and fullness of life.

Gottlob Charles Cast. In *Studies in German Literature* (Madison, University of Wisconsin Press, 1925), pp. 95–96

When they first appeared, *Drayman Henschel, Rose Bernd,* and *The Rats* were looked on as perfect specimens of a controversial new literary movement. Today they are seen in a different light: they are no longer considered experimental literature; they have become folk plays—in fact, the most powerful, the richest in audacious and compassionate humaneness ever to be created in Germany and, indeed, probably in all the world. Whatever is attempted and produced in that vein nowadays—a close look at it shows clearly that it feeds on those plays; the Bruckners and Brechts, it is to be hoped, know themselves that they are indebted to Hauptmann for their best.

His works will never disappear from our theater, not only because they are such powerful plays, but, above all, because a socially aware time to come will take up these songs of truth and legends of the people and make them its own, as spirit of its spirit and blood of its blood. Hauptmann the socialist! This title of honor will remain his forever, in his case, a title with the purest ring of kindheartedness. His is a socialism not of manifestos, of theory, of intellectual criticism, but of emotions, of a profound vision of the yearning and unredeemed beauty of the lowly—not a question of hatred, but one of love. . . . This socialism is not a program. It displays the poetic mediacy and latency that characterized Goethe. . . . It is art—which more than any political proclamation, speaks to the innermost depths of the soul. [1932]

Thomas Mann. *Gesammelte Werke* (Frankfurt,
Fischer, 1960), Vol. X, pp. 336–37†

The composition of Hauptmann's dramas has been described on several occasions as "symphonic." This is true especially of *The Weavers* and of *Florian Geyer,* but not only of them. As one reads or hears one of his plays, one is conscious that many voices and motives are in constant interplay, and that these are interwoven into a poetic fabric which is essentially vital with life. There are certain dominant moods and emotional themes, solo voices and voices in parts, in major and minor key, overtones and undertones, not always merely human, for at times nature itself, the scene or situation, seems to become vocal with demonic utterance. The dramatic friction which emanates from and surrounds the characters becomes at times the expression of other, even superhuman, forces which vibrate with magic and mystery. The human voice becomes something of an elemental tone of nature. Hauptmann uses rhythm rather than architecture in his dramatic composition. There is definitely dramatic intensity in the gesture, the silences, the lyrical moments of reverie and song which give pause and relief, as well as in the outbursts of passion and the inarticulate muttering and stammering of the voice. His use of crescendo, retard and lapse gives the dialogue an undertone of musical and at times Dionysian tempo, a rhythm which is due to the masterful handling of language, speech that is alive and has been "heard" by the poet's inner ear. Things evolve naturally in Hauptmann. With Ibsen, Hebbel, or Shaw the parrying thrusts of rational discussion or dialectic often intrude upon the purely emotional aesthetic effect. They employ dramatic architecture rather than dramatic rhythm. . . .

Unity in the composition of Hauptmann's drama, however, is the result of the poet's ability to clothe character and scene and action in a magical poetic atmosphere. This, a sort of dramatic aura, creates and is the drama. It gives to each work its unforgettable vitality, its suspense and intensity. Scenery is not background; all the elements of the stage and the drama "act" in unison. This is as evident in interiors as in outdoor scenes. . . . It has been rightly said, that Hauptmann as a dramatist, a creator, stands among his characters on the stage and does not direct from the wings or from in front. . . .

Each work reveals the nervous strain and friction which results from the interplay of human beings in a given situation and which finally leads to an eruptive climax. Character, situation, language are a unity and have a distinctly characteristic rhythm.

F. B. Wahr. *GR*. Oct., 1942, pp. 167–68, 172

It is only with the work of the young Hauptmann . . . that the naturalistic movement temporarily grew beyond the all-too-narrowly drawn literary confines of the Freie Bühne and again headed toward a great national literature. The young Hauptmann brought with him what the 1880s longingly demanded: closeness to the vibrant life of the present, the creation of people of flesh and blood who speak our language, an art close to the people, in which the important issues of the time found adequate expression. The fact that Hauptmann succeeded in achieving this to perfection in only two of his works, *The Weavers* and *The Beaver Coat*, does not in any way detract from the historic significance of his early work.

The artistic maturity of the young Hauptmann, his artistic tact for delimitation in these two works, is astonishing: on the one hand, the revolt inspired by a yearning lacking clearly defined aims (the uprising of the weavers in the 1840s); and on the other hand, the guerrilla warfare of the lower class against the obsolete and corrupt upper class. Yet such a delimitation is, in the last analysis, rooted in the conditions of his time itself, the Germany of those days; his artistic tact consisted in creating everything possible within the given framework. As soon as he tried to transcend it, he was bound to fail. *Florian Geyer:* the historical tragedy of a movement of universal significance, Germany's failure at the threshold of the transition from the Middle Ages to modern times. Yet Hauptmann did not grasp the profound historical dialectic of his subject matter. He achieved artistic greatness only in evoking local color and in presenting purely human greatness in the situation of the tragic downfall of a person aspiring to absolute purity. [1944–45]

Georg Lukács. *Schriften zur Literatursoziologie* (Neuwied, Luchterhand, 1961), pp. 460–61†

Gerhart Hauptmann's achievement is not easily summarized. In many respects he has been an awkward and, at times, even irresponsible artist whose long career has been filled with surprises and disappointments. But in the company of his more superficial and less courageous—and now generously forgotten—contemporaries, he remains, in Germany, the only genuine representative of the modern realistic drama. The spectacular aspects of his early success, *Before Dawn,* brought him instantaneous prominence. He had, once and for all, shown the dramatic possibilities of a truly "modern" conflict. But within a brief period of ten or fifteen years, he enlarged the indistinct medium of naturalistic speech and action into a variety of impressive poetic accomplishments. The influence upon him of Ibsen's, Björnson's, and Dostoevsky's religious idealism is strong at first, and compassion remains his most persistent trait.

The Weavers, a stirring account of exploited and tragically charged human beings, has proved to be Hauptmann's most straightforward work, free of the cliché and claptrap of similar propaganda plays. By the force and detachment of his own temperament he develops the naturalistic style both in comedy *(The Beaver Coat)* and in historical tragedy *(Florian Geyer)* to such perfection that the nineteenth-century epic drama seems here to attain its final fruition. Two later and equally powerful plays, *Drayman Henschel* and *Rose Bernd,* reaffirmed his skill in human portraiture; but Hauptmann had then already passed beyond the strict pattern of naturalistic doctrine, for in *Hannele* and his most widely played lyrical drama in verse, *The Sunken Bell,* he had made use of newly developed symbolic poetic devices. With *And Pippa Dances* his dramatic work reached a masterly climax; what followed in the more than fourteen plays to come was reiteration and reassertion of a singularly enterprising but never fully disciplined vitality.

It is a sign of the vigorous resources of Hauptmann's talent that, throughout his later career . . . he has displayed an astonishing range of technical accomplishments. But what has given him continued relevance among the more recent poets and dramatists is his faith in the creative value of irrational and instinctive energies. He has remained characteristically immune to the disturbing influence of Nietzsche: his strength is drawn not from the philosophers but from a deep sense of the nervous energy and delicate contour of the individual human being. [1945]

Victor Lange. *Modern German Literature: 1870–1940* (Port Washington, N.Y., Kennikat, 1967), pp. 24–26

Gerhart Hauptmann was a great man, one of the greatest—and Gerhart Hauptmann was a weak man who failed in the decisive hour of the German genius, at a moment when it became the duty of the great spiritual leaders to make their decision known. When, in 1933, darkness descended upon Germany, Hauptmann remained silent. He, the poet laureate of the Weimar Republic, symbol and representative of Social Democratic Germany, did not say a word when the hordes of barbarous fanatics conquered his fatherland, when his closest friends, those who had most faithfully served his work and his fame, disappeared into exile—if no worse fate befell them. To be sure, he was an old man at that time, a septuagenarian, from whom one could not expect the impetuosity of youth. But when has it ever been said that old age absolves one from responsibility and did he have the right to use his advanced age as an excuse, since it was, after all, this very dignity and wealth of experience associated with old age that made him the representative, the symbol of the good will of his people, as well as the respected and weighty spokesman within the chorus of European nations?

No, there is no excuse for his silence; and indeed, we would do neither him nor ourselves any favor whatsoever, if we were to attempt, by way of embellishing touches, to brighten up the distressing image presented by the aged Gerhart Hauptmann. He was no equal to the greatness of his task; he chose to remain a bystander at a loathsome spectacle from which to turn away emphatically would have been his duty, even though it is true—and it is true a thousand times—that he himself remained the same, and that no inner ties bound him to the barbarians among whom he lived.

Oskar Seidlin. *Monatshefte*. Oct., 1946, p. 332†

Although Hauptmann, particularly in the latter part of his life, contributed to every genre of literature, he will always be known first and foremost as a dramatist. It was in drama that his greatest faculty, the creation of live characters, found its fullest scope. . . . Hauptmann sees drama in all human existence; life, for him, is in its essence an unceasing strife— a strife that rends the heart of man from the first moment of his conscious existence. . . . Hence genuine drama is for Hauptmann in the first place a drama of the mind, of character, and not of action. "The more complex the plot, the less there is of character. The simpler the plot, the richer the character. . . . What you give to the plot you take away from the character."

This basic conception of drama partly explains why Hauptmann's principal characters are throughout passive. They do not act; things happen to them. Their tragedy springs not so much from an excess of action, or of passion, as from an insufficiency, an incapacity to cope with the exigencies of life. Their keynote is suffering. However, Hauptmann's intrinsic philosophy is not one of fatalism. His central theme, shaped in countless variations, is redemption through suffering. In the end, when tragedy has taken its course, the victim, though felled by the force of circumstance, emerges as the true conqueror.

Hugh F. Garten. Gerhart Hauptmann (New Haven, Conn.,
Yale University Press, 1954), pp. 12–13

The earlier plays . . . remain his finest single accomplishment, and if there have been frequent references to Ibsen and Shaw in these pages it is because he has no other rivals in modern literature in the field of realistic prose drama. . . . Hauptmann's work has breadth, a unique power of creating men and environment, and an attitude which makes it as progressive as that of his often more argumentative contemporaries. His first service to his own and succeeding generations is his ability to paint human beings from many spheres of society, from the lower classes as well as the middle, and with equal understanding and concern for both. But his second service is that, though his plays lack the intellectual quality of those of Ibsen or Shaw, he touches in his own way on just as wide a range of problems, social and economic, religious and political. And his whole attitude implies a desire for reform wherever it appears to him that the society of his day has become rigid in its ideals, careless of the lives of its individual members, or blind to the inevitability of change.

Margaret Sinden. Gerhart Hauptmann (Toronto,
University of Toronto Press, 1957), pp. 230–31

In the earliest plays the characters in their suffering had been seen in significant relation to the material things which surrounded them. Then, at least as early as Hannele, had come the careful venture, inwards to the world of fantasy of the sufferer, outwards to the spiritual environment which had informed it. The way being found for the convincing projection of this upon the stage and into the structure of novels, the impulse was never lost; perhaps it had never been entirely absent. The growing throng of little, limited human beings was augmented by angels, sprites, and chthonic creatures summoned from the lore of Hauptmann's homeland, and at times these predominate as mysterious yet homely symbols of man's affections and aspirations. But it is not just the elves and demiurges; the setting, the casing air itself became charged with meaning as extension of the lives drawn from Hauptmann's own life. . . . We are, somewhat uncannily, made aware of space and significant environment. . . . We may say that we recognise here the debt to Shakespeare, for in the mature works of Hauptmann what we may coldly call the irrational suddenly at times comes nearer to us, not through the head, but through our senses, alluring, with a hint of terror, and we know it to be the "strange intelligence" which guides the human creature without helping him and yet establishes for us a bond of understanding for his suffering, his submergence in the panic and the ecstasy of communal tumult, and his sacrifice. A very careful study, centred on Hauptmann's symbolism, has recently demonstrated the continuity and the expansion of the theme of disruptive forces of which we become aware in the poet's advancing years. . . . It is to the dire extravagances and extremes of human life that Hauptmann leads us with increasing urgency.

W. F. Mainland. In K. G. Knight and F. Norman, eds.,

Hauptmann Centenary Lectures (London, University of

London, Institute of Germanic Studies, 1964), pp. 24–25

Known in the years before 1914 as a pacifist, at variance with the Imperialist regime, there was nevertheless a resigned passivity about [Hauptmann's] literary work, together with a heavy sentimentality which permeated even some of his earlier and best plays. By comparison with Ibsen, he lacked spirit, despite the technical ability which made him internationally known. Even so, the First World War found him writing patriotic verse and defending the imperialist cause in an open letter to Romain Rolland. And during the Weimar Republic he suddenly and a little unaccountably became the grand old man of German letters. On the occasion of his sixtieth birthday in 1922, his plays were performed throughout Germany. Thomas Mann, heir-elect to him at the time, greeted him with a characteristic paradox as King of the Republic. . . .

At the centenary celebrations in 1962, the German theaters put on *The Weavers, The Beaver Coat, Rose Bernd,* and other works published in the 1890's and early 1900's. They scarcely touched the later work, although Hauptmann continued to write at prodigious length almost until his death in 1946. In his old age he had become a helpless reed, at first out of favour with the Nazis for his passivity, for his "enlightened" ideas and his reputation as a democrat and a socialist during the Republic, then suddenly welcomed back to the same kind of prominence as he had enjoyed in 1922. . . . His plays were performed again, and his books, having at first been banned, appeared once more in the bookshops. Why, nobody explained. It was a freak of fortune which the old man could scarcely appreciate. He was left to write on in blacker and blacker pessimism which reached its peak at the total destruction of Dresden, where he was living, in the bombing raids of February 1945.

Ronald Gray. *The German Tradition in Literature: 1871–1945*

(Cambridge, Cambridge University Press, 1965), pp. 88–89

The dramas comprising Hauptmann's *Atrides Tetralogy,* the final dramatic statement of this master of the theater, were composed during the grim war years of 1940–44. The first fruit of this dramatic *Spätlese* was not the opening drama *Iphigenia in Aulis,* as one might expect from the sequence in which we now read the cycle, but rather the concluding one, *Iphigenia in Delphi*. The latter was followed by the second and third dramas of the cycle, *Agamemnon's Death* and *Electra*, and only then by *Iphigenia in Aulis*. Hence the dramas did not develop "organically," in the strictest sense of the word, and the circumstances surrounding their composition, i.e., the war and the advanced age of the poet, combined to produce an occasional blurring of the dramatic focus. Yet there is one powerful unifying element in these dramas which, together with the unfolding motifs of curse and expiation, keeps the four separate plays "aus einem Guβ" [a uniform whole]: their remarkable language. . . .

By language we mean the poetic diction, the tone, imagery, the rhetorical and emotional configurations operating within the dimensions of the spoken word. If these elements can be kept consistent, yet unobtrusive, they can serve as signposts, guiding the reader—or, if the plays are performed, the listener—through a complicated dramatic landscape. . . .

It is obvious that Hauptmann, the most successful practical dramatist in the history of the German theater, took great pains to see that plot, scenery, lighting effects and symbolism insured cohesion in what his practical theater sense told him could be a diffuse dramatic undertaking. That he was able to bid the language to serve similar ends, without sacrifice of its main poetic function, is a tribute to the completeness of his art.

Donald H. Crosby. GR. Jan., 1965, pp. 5, 16

The decisive experience undergone by the hero in these plays—*Lonely Lives, Drayman Henschel, Dorothea Angermann, Rose Bernd, The Rats*—is not that of conflict in the normal dramatic sense. He does not feel himself opposed by a powerful adversary bent on his destruction. It is essential to the nature of this experience that it arises out of the dissolution of a relationship with a being long loved and trusted. In the emotional life of the hero this represents, as it were, the severing of the umbilical tie which leaves him dazed by an agonized sense of loss and absence. . . .

The ultimate experience of the hero in Hauptmann's domestic plays is that of abandonment in a world hostile to his existence. In this insight into his immediate situation he is visited by the realization that it has not been brought about by accidental causes but that it is a manifestation of an antagonism which is inescapable since it is inherent in the very conditions of human life. It is this awareness of the irreconcilable alienation of the individual which finally destroys the spiritual integrity of his being. . . .

It is essential to the dramatist's whole conception of these works that the central figure attains through suffering a deeper awareness of life. In extreme anguish of mind a profounder consciousness of the human situation comes into being. This insight may in the widest sense be termed "tragic," since it involves a moral discovery which pertains to the totality of man's existence in the world. The humble hero in these domestic dramas has, like his great forebears, "seen for an instant through its mist the sheer mountain-side of life."

Edward McInnes. *GL&L*. Oct., 1966, pp. 56–57, 59

It is Hauptmann's great achievement to again have infused the German drama, which had been stagnating since Hebbel's death, with full-blooded life and to have oriented it toward contemporary reality. With extraordinary poetic vigor and authenticity of environment he presented the social problems of his time and the frequent, often deeply moving, struggle of the wronged and degraded for their human dignity. From *Before Dawn* to *Before Sunset* he depicted the decay of bourgeois family relations, the double standard of the moral code, helplessness, alienation, the dangers threatening man's humanity. Several tragedies about the failure and the bitter isolation of the artist in a capitalistic society are but variations of these themes. Above all, however, he gave expression to the feelings of the simple people; in *The Weavers* and in *Florian Geyer* he put on stage deeply moving scenes of the masses and (as also in *Rose Bernd* and *The Rats*) suggested, through illustration and faithful reproduction, the necessity of social change.

In his best works Gerhart Hauptmann, as an advocate of humanity, resolutely attacks Junkerdom, militarism, religious fanaticism, and any kind of oppression and persecution. All his sympathies were with the loving and suffering "man in the street," whom he was able to portray masterfully and for whom he eloquently tried to enlist our compassion and understanding.

The poet, it is true, showed a strong interest in the Social Democratic movement of the 1880s and 1890s, and was open-minded about such social reforms as were advocated by the utopian Socialists; but he could not bring himself to put his trust in the proletarian power to change the world. He always saw only tortured, suffering individuals, at most masses desperately rising in revolt, but never the people, resolutely fighting with an aim in mind, to whom the future belonged. The revolutionary position, which he took only once in his work, in *The Weavers*, was later on abandoned again.

Eberhard Hilscher. *Gerhart Hauptmann* (East Berlin, Verlag der Nation, 1969), pp. 512–14†

The Coming of Peace is a much more tautly constructed and firmly circumscribed work than its immediate predecessor. The broad social problem which lay in the background of *Before Dawn* is here abandoned in favour of greater concentration on the central issues of marriage and the family, and the interior struggles of the characters. Coherent argument between people of equal intelligence has a much larger role, as it does in the following play, *Lonely Lives;* indeed, both plays illustrate the preference of the Naturalist dramatists for the middle-class, intellectual sphere, and they are, at the same time, the two of Hauptmann's plays in which the resemblance to Ibsen is most marked. *Ghosts* and *Rosmersholm* are the plays which most readily come to mind in this connection. . . . The superficial similarities between this latter play and *The Coming of Peace* are indeed considerable; the two plays share the same technique of analytical exposition, they reveal the tyranny of the past in hereditary disease, and they condemn the "lie" of modern marriage. But, despite all this, they remain characteristically different, as two plays by Hauptmann and Ibsen inevitably are different. . . . In *The Coming of Peace* Hauptman . . . gives a demonstration of determinism, the loss and exposure of man in the world as he understands it, the quality of his suffering, and considers the price it is necessary to pay to ensure survival.

John Osborne. *The Naturalist Drama in Germany*
(Manchester, England, Manchester University
Press, 1971), p. 88

For all his obsequious behavior in public, Hauptmann was not without certain insights into the moral decay of Germania. The Reich, as he knew very well, had been nourished on a diet of success ever since the collapse of France in 1870. What if this war [World War I] was lost? What, then, would happen to German honor, German loyalty, and all the other catchwords of Germanity?

His answer to this question was given in *Magnus Garbe,* a drama he completed in the fall of 1915. Although set in the sixteenth century, the action could easily be transported to the twentieth.

It is the fate of Magnus Garbe, the decent mayor of a Free City, to face the hysteria aroused by the Dominican monk Paulus Gislandus, who turns the once comfortable town into a hell in which no torture is too terrible to be tolerated, and no accusation, no matter how transparently invented, is examined before the victim is surrendered to the craven executioners. Dorothea Meulin, once a servant in the home of the parents of Garbe's wife, Felicia, is accused of witchcraft. Her breasts burned by glowing tongs, she makes an admission that sets the mob after Felicia, who is dragged off to prison while giving birth to a child. In the prison we meet Görg, the executioner's assistant, bragging of earning twenty-four florins for boiling an evildoer in oil, ten florins for a beheading, another ten florins for a hanging, and thirty florins for burning four heretics alive. In the meantime the mob is howling that Felicia must have her tongue cut off, her eyes burned out, and her body branded by hot irons. But this is not all. She is driven insane, and Garbe, forsaken by the townspeople who once hailed him as a benefactor, drops dead, paralyzed, at his wife's deathbed.

For reasons that will be apparent, *Magnus Garbe* was not performed on any stage until the fourth of February, 1956, twenty-three years after Adolf Hitler created the world that Gerhart Hauptmann anticipated.

Wayne Andrews. *Siegfried's Curse: The German Journey
from Nietzsche to Hesse* (New York,
Atheneum, 1972), p. 139

Lonely Lives is perhaps the outstanding attempt [in naturalist imaginary literature] to present the theme of the emancipated woman, embodied here in Anna Mahr, a Zürich student, in whom Johannes Vockerat finds an intellectual and spiritual companion. Vockerat, though a philosophical Darwinian, cannot overcome his piety to his religious parents and his wife, and when Anna leaves him commits suicide. The whole failure seems to be symptomatic of the German middle class. The center is not the emancipated woman (as in Ibsen) but the man who longs for a wife who can also be an intellectual companion, and whose irresolution leads him to delude himself about his feelings for Anna. Though theoretically progressive, Vockerat is not only unable to revolt against family piety, as he knows, but is also, and this he does not know, an egoistic, spoilt and tyrannical husband, very largely the cause of the timidity and ineffectiveness of his devoted wife. He is so feeble that some critics see Hauptmann's purpose as ironical, but both Anna's attitude and the views held by Hauptmann's associates suggests that he did not mean to question the genuineness of Vockerat's progressive ideals but to show the external and internal obstacles to their realization.

In this play the emancipated woman only passes, a visitor, over the stage. Later, Hauptmann succeeds in creating strong and independent female characters only when they belong to the working class and derive their strength precisely from their family feeling, not from revolt against the family—thus the women heroes of *The Beaver Coat* and *The Rats*.

Roy Pascal. *From Naturalism to Expressionism*
(New York, Basic Books, 1973), pp. 208–10

The time of the Weimar Republic saw the poet—then in his sixties—at the height of his fame. The irony of fate which had him write a peace masque shortly before the outbreak of the First World War repeated itself when, in 1932, he delivered an address at several American universities—on his second trip to this country—in commemoration of the hundredth anniversary of Goethe's death. Praising the kind of progress that Goethe had advocated, a progress brought about by "perpetual quiet reformation," he denounced in the name of Goethe all fanaticism, all subjugation of the mind, misanthropy and persecution, and urged that in an existence which makes tremendous demands upon mankind, we attempt "to live resolutely in the Whole, the Good, the True"—using Carlyle's version of this Goethe maxim. The next year, Hitler came to power. Hauptmann's position as the grand old man of German letters was unshakable—the most lavish edition of his works, in seventeen volumes, appeared for his eightieth birthday in 1942. However, life in Hitler Germany—he was too old and too much a part of his native soil to be transplanted—was stifling and painful to a man whose nature was as deeply opposed to such a regime. This is revealed in a manuscript written but kept hidden during the Nazi years. The work, called *Die Finsternisse,* laments the tragic fate of the Jews and hints at Germany's coming downfall; the biblical quotation, "Woe to him who buildeth a town with blood!" is used as the basis for the prophecy.

Hauptmann's dramatic work, various and abundant (he has written more than forty dramas), is not without consistency. The tetralogy of the last decade is not too far removed from the early plays that he wrote in the 1890's. Hauptmann has simply advanced from the immediate—although no less universal—problems of individuals and their environment to broader issues of mankind, irrespective of time and place. However, the deep compassion and feeling for humanity have remained the same. This is indeed the distinguishing mark of Hauptmann's dramatic work: social sympathy, social pity, social compassion. His social feeling is not intellectual; it is intuitive. Thanks to this elemental feeling for his fellow men, Hauptmann has remained the foremost social poet of Germany. And thanks to this deep feeling for humanity he is counted among those modern dramatists who, like Ibsen, Strindberg, and Shaw, have outlasted the changes of time and fashion.

Horst Frenz. Introduction to Gerhart Hauptmann,
Three Plays (New York, Frederick Ungar, 1977), pp. xii–xiv

Although *Drayman Henschel* superficially conforms to the naturalistic method, another literary undercurrent, one which serves to illustrate further Hauptmann's experimentation with other literary forms, emerges: surrealism. Whether or not Hauptmann consciously employed this mode, especially since surrealism did not find formal definition until a much later date, is questionable. The fact remains, however, that germs of surrealism are present in the play despite its naturalistic label. . . .

A most significant indication of surrealism rests with the protagonist himself, Wilhelm Henschel; in his very inability to contend with the problems which confront him, since his actions are apparently directed by an uncontrollable "inner" force which, ultimately, is responsible for leading him down a path of no return. This unseen but sensed power, which Ernest Alker associates with *nemesis divina,* seems to regulate not only the actions of the "hero" but those of the other characters in the play as well, by punishment of the victim through self-destruction. Although the stimuli imposed on Henschel logically appear to come from society (including Hanne), the ultimate cause would seem to lie with a supernatural power (of either subjective or objective cast) and, therefore, beyond the realm of naturalism. Superficially, Henschel's fate may be attributed to his environment and, in this respect, may be termed naturalistic; but on the other hand, because of this extrasensory factor, the strict boundaries of naturalism seem to have been breached, and we seem to have touched the penumbra of another literary form, surrealism.

Laurent Gousie. *GR*. Fall, 1978, pp. 156–57

HOCHHUTH, ROLF (1931–   )

Hochhuth's play *The Deputy* is one of the few significant contributions to mastering the past. Ruthlessly calling things by their names, it shows that history written with the blood of millions of innocents can never become out of date; it apportions to the guilty their share of guilt; it reminds all involved that they could have made their own decisions, and that in fact they did make one even by not making any.

The Deputy gives the lie to all those who claim that historical drama as drama of decision is no longer possible since decisions as such are no longer possible for man, in view of the faceless anonymity of sociopolitical measures and pressures, and given the absurd makeup of a human existence in which everything is predetermined from the outset. Such a theory, which obliterates any and all historic action, appeals to all those who today would like to evade the truth of history, the true significance of their own past actions.

This play is a historical drama in Schiller's sense. It presents, as does Schiller's drama, man as acting; and he acts as a "DEPUTY," the representative of an *Idea: free* in the fulfillment of this idea, free in his awareness of the necessity to act "categorically," that is, in an ethical manner worthy of a human being. This freedom, which everybody possesses, which everybody possessed even under the Nazi regime, must be our point of departure if we want to come to terms with our past. To disavow this freedom would amount to a disavowal of the very guilt incurred by each and every person who did not make use of this freedom to decide *against* inhumanity. . . .

Hochhuth's great achievement lies in the very fact that he goes beyond the "novelistic," the unheard-of, the uniqueness of the "particular case." His play does not aim at the "interesting," at achieving a point, at devising a plot—which characterizes the novelist, the narrative, and which could have been a dangerous temptation in this extraordinary, "particular" case. Rather it aims at making the totality of human conduct the object of its probing while writing history rather than just telling a story. Hochhuth dis-

plays the material obtained through scientific research artistically formulated; he orders, arranges it with all the means—and I do not say this
lightly—of a distinguished dramatist. [Nov. 6, 1962]

Erwin Piscator. Introduction to Rolf Hochhuth,
Der Stellvertreter (Hamburg, Rowohlt, 1963), pp. 7–11†

It is not by chance that Hochhuth's text [*The Deputy*] combines a drama
with historical notes. The question is to recognize the common denominator linking these two modes of expression: in both instances Hochhuth
assails what he once referred to as "Hegelian detachment." . . . For
that purpose it is necessary, however, that people are exposed to the suffering, that they are enabled to empathize with it and then to relate it to
the attitude of those in power. And to that end Hochhuth provides not
only for the historical judgment he deems fitting—in his "Sidelights on
History." He sees to it that the suffering plays its due part in the judging. He presents it to those who will judge as he himself perceives it.
And he therefore goes beyond any merely historical presentation, beyond
his historical sidelights—in his play itself. Here he calls upon the resources of the writer: the drama that seeks to reproduce reality, the representation of the historical situation; for it is now a matter of establishing a perspective from which history is to be viewed. . . . Thus the
drama becomes an imaginary as well as an imaginative on-the-spot investigation without which judgment should not be passed. Hochhuth counts
on the reality of suffering in order to impeach a "detached" historiography
as well as the detached coldness of those representatives of power whose
praises it sings.

For Hochhuth it is entirely a matter of bringing out the outrageous; and
that end justifies the artistic means employed. This formula, in fact, makes
things much clearer when we look more closely at the literary form of Hochhuth's *The Deputy*. Making the outrageous stand out . . . is the very principle of the drama's theatrical structure. . . . There is not a single scene
that does not aim at arousing the indignation of the reader or spectator.

Rolf C. Zimmermann. In *Der Streit um Hochhuths
"Stellvertreter"* (Basel, Basilius Press, 1963), pp. 138–39†

When the gifted German novelist and playwright Martin Walser hailed *The
Deputy* as a "legitimate offspring of the long overdue marriage of Sartre
and Brecht," he was only half right. Though *The Deputy* owes much to
Sartre's skill in casting political and philosophical polemics in highly stage-
worthy molds, it has nothing of Brecht's alienation and epic theatre or even
didactic satire. Erwin Piscator, who gave the play its first production (in
Berlin), was nearer the mark when he called it "a historic drama in the
Schillerian sense."

It is certainly true that Hochhuth has all the moral fervor of Schiller, the disciple of Kant, and that the ethical criterion of the play is a categorical imperative that will have no truck with relativist notions of comparative good or comparative evil. However, Schiller's use of the historic in drama is not Hochhuth's. Most patently in *The Maid of Orléans,* but also elsewhere, Schiller was willing to alter historical facts radically to suit his purposes, whereas Hochhuth is at great pains to include all possible historical data and limit his invention to the interstices—sometimes to the detriment of his play. . . .

What makes *The Deputy,* as Hochhuth has written it, important, however, is not so much the political revelation it may have made. Nor technical devices such as having the same actors enact several contradictory parts, to convey that in our age it is merely a matter of "military conscription. . . whether one stands on the side of the victims or the executioners." Nor in the elaborate stage directions which bitterly project certain characters into the future, describing, for example, such and such a Nazi as a solid citizen of postwar Germany. What *is* momentous is that in an age which has progressively convinced itself that its significant dramatic form is dark comedy, that, to quote Dürrenmatt, "our world has led to the Grotesque as to the atom bomb, just as the apocalyptic pictures of Hieronymus Bosch are grotesque, too"—that in this era when "the death of tragedy" has become a literary commonplace, *The Deputy* stands as a valid tragedy: not great, but good, and anything but commonplace.

John Simon. *Nation.* March 16, 1964, pp. 270, 272

Hochhuth's tendency to make the individual accountable for the failures of the institution is a heritage of his German idealism, an influence which can also be seen in the shape and substance of his play. *The Deputy* is written in the ponderous heroic style of Schiller, full of vaunting speeches, generous sacrifices, and externalized emotions angry confrontations dominate each scene, the verse pitches and rolls, and indignation keeps the tone at a high boil. As for the characters, they are larger than scale, and, therefore, not always very convincing. When the author permits himself poetic license, he can create an interesting and complex individual—the Doctor, for example, whose fatigued cynicism, experimental cruelty, and intellectual arrogance make him a figure of absolute evil, a creation worthy of Sartre or Camus. But more often, Hochhuth's characters are members of a cardboard nobility: Gerstein, for example, the compassionate German who joined the S.S., risking his own life to help the victims of Hitler, or Father Riccardo Fontana, the anguished Jesuit priest, who pinned the Jewish star to his cassock when the Pope refused to protest, and accompanied the Jews to Auschwitz. . . .

Hochhuth is limited . . . by his own apparent lack of interest in the inner workings of character. Cataloguing his personages almost exclusively according to their attitudes toward the Pope's silence, Hochhuth preserves the moral integrity of his work, but at the cost of its aesthetic weight and complexity. [1964]

Robert Brustein. *Seasons of Discontent* (New York, Simon & Schuster, 1965), pp. 205–6

[Hochhuth's] very shaky theology, coupled with the fact that the author's hand is all too evidently at work, has resulted [in *The Deputy*] in cardboard-like characters sometimes made to move in a lurid background of snippets of filmed atrocities which make the presence of these characters even more unreal and incomprehensible, except in a few striking instances. The use of filmed extracts of concentration camp horrors, in a play which is not a true representation of reality but a subjective view of events and opinions, is a deceitful way of buttressing a tendentious thesis with emotionally charged facts. It is a process which seriously lets down the ethics of art, for it aims at making use of emotions roused by the sight of horrors, if not to blame the Pope for them, at least to blunt rational processes and make acceptable the author's thesis that the Pope has failed to prevent them through coward-ice and Machiavellianism. This is an obvious lack of intellectual honesty which makes one long for the humility, profound humanity, and sense of Christian responsibility so shiningly displayed by Pastor Niemöller. . . .

If the author had been able to forget about his anti-papism, which is gratuitous and undramatic, and had concentrated his considerable dramatic powers and skill on the conflict of characters reasonably matched, he would have produced a very good play and not simply a dramatic work, often marred by melodramatic patches and hollow rhetoric used in order to ex-pound a thesis. . . . As it is, this play contains large desert stretches and much baying at the moon, which are neither pleasant nor rewarding.

Joseph Chiari. *Landmarks of Contemporary Drama* (London, Jenkins, 1965), pp. 192, 194–95

It is the personal nature of the attack which remains as the outstanding impression [of *The Deputy*]. Not the Catholic Church, not the College of Cardinals, but Eugenio Pacelli is to be held if not fully responsible, at least *mitverantwortlich* for the execution of a policy which cost six million Jewish lives. If one can shut from one's mind the historical Pius XII (and a literary evaluation of the play is otherwise not possible) the case seems far from proven. The original part of the play, the Gerstein-Fontana-Jacobson com-plex, seems to be unmotivated by the scenes which show of decisions reached in the Vatican. Hochhuth's view remains unilateral, and therefore intellectually unsatisfying, because his assumptions are so great—in partic-ular the assumption that the Pope's protest would have brought Hitler to reconsider his policies, and the complementary assumption that Hitler felt able to become so fanatic in his pursuit of the Final Solution *because* the Vatican remained silent. Future generations who will bring no more emotional associations to the play than the present-day reader brings to the historical dramas of *Egmont* or *Wilhelm Tell* must surely find it arbitrary, prejudiced, and largely lacking in persuasive power, for the dramatic Pius XII here portrayed is a caricature of a tragic villain, and Riccardo too much the impetuous adventurer-priest to be convincing in the role.

None of this is to gainsay the accuracy of Hochhuth's observations, nor does it remove his strictures upon the Pope's self-imposed silence at the fate of the Jews. But there *is* a wide gulf between historical appraisal and dramatic representation, and it is into this gulf that Hochhuth has fallen. And while we cannot deny the moral cogency of his utterances, we must deny their dramatic force.

James Trainer. *FMLS*. Jan., 1965, p. 24

It is my contention that a large part of the popular success of [*The Deputy*] is due to the fact that while articulating the German trauma [it offers] ways to by-pass a naked and final confrontation with it.

The Deputy had, of course, a mixed reception, but for reasons extraneous to this argument. It is understandable that partisans to Roman Catholicism should be upset by a play charging the politic Pius XII, already marked for canonization, with betrayal of his calling as Christian and Pope by refusing to intervene on behalf of the Jews at a time when such intervention might have saved millions, particularly when that charge is historically and substantially correct. What matters here is that quite aside from the question of its veracity such a play enables an audience to escape its own responsibility in the events depicted by transferring it to someone else, in this case even someone who should have been so much more above reproach than they themselves. . . .

Not that Hochhuth intended it this way. His concern was with historical truth. The characters in *The Deputy* are all taken directly or indirectly from real life. Much of the dialogue is based on verbatim documents. And Hochhuth does not spare his own people. In the play he demonstrates the macabre perversity of men like Eichmann, and in his copious annotations he makes it clear that Germans have *not* dealt with their past in a manner worthy of a civilized nation. Surprisingly, in spite of all this Teutonic thoroughness and exactitude, the play is alive and compelling. One never becomes aware that one is watching a meticulous reconstruction of history—except through painful personal memories. . . . Zuckmayer was highly complimentary about Hochhuth: "At last a German author who can write poetic drama— who can create people with a few sentences, . . . who can construct a play properly."

Henry Beissel. *Seminar*. Spring, 1965, pp. 59–60

Rolf Hochhuth's *The Deputy* was the first instance where the author of a historical drama felt the need to justify in detail, in a voluminous appendix to his play, any license he had taken with regard to the documented facts. . . .

Apparently Hochhuth feared being reproached for distorting the facts as a result of having betrayed the historical reality as attested by the documents at his disposal; and, all told, to respect that reality was apparently much more important for him than to strive after particular theatrical effects. . . .

It is obvious that this play is the work of a moralist. The author depicts an exemplary case of pusillanimity with the intention of inducing the individual spectator to examine his own conscience, to interrogate himself about his own degree of active or passive involvement in the massacre of millions of innocent people, and, consequently, to give some thought to the most basic social obligations of the individual in our time (and perhaps at all times). . . .

The Deputy is above all an appeal to the conscience of humanity; yet many have interpreted the play as simply an accusation against Pius XII— which, to be sure, it certainly was, too, but not exclusively—and instead of taking a good hard look at themselves, they confined themselves, each according to his own preconceived notions, to taking sides with or against Hochhuth. Only a very limited number of people have actually understood the true message of the young dramatist.

Michel Vanhelleputte. *EG*. Oct.–Dec., 1967, pp. 539–41†

The main events of *The Deputy* were carefully based on the historical materials which appear as an appendix to the published version, studded with useful quotations and footnotes. Historians as well as drama and literary critics have respected the moral argument of the play, and have been as grateful as the general reader for the lengthy historical appendix—while differing about the strength of the play's historical pretensions. The playwright's position towards his own research is ambiguous. On the one hand he has declared that "as far as possible I adhered to the facts" and "allowed my imagination free play only to the extent that I had to transform the existing raw material of history into drama. Reality was respected throughout, but much of its slag had to be removed." But he has also acknowledged that "the truth, the symbolic meaning" of the infinite number of discrepant events can only be discovered if the artist declares "war on naturalism in art" and idealizes his work "in *all* its parts." He denies having written a scholarly treatise, and proclaims the importance of intuition in his work. . . . Thus the historian's criticisms of Hochhuth's exposition of the historical events behind his play are blunted at the beginning.

But if the reality Hochhuth has undoubtedly tried to respect is partly false, then how does such misrepresentation affect "the truth, the symbolic meaning" of the whole complex of events he has treated? The answer is, very little, because a close reading reveals that the author's "symbolic meaning" is not dependent on the main events of the play, but has much to do with theology and the significance of the destruction of the Jews.

Leonidas E. Hill. *Mosaic*. Oct., 1967, p. 119

It cannot and should not be disputed that Hochhuth owes his extraordinary international success [with *The Deputy*], for which there exists no parallel in the history of German drama since 1945, to a large degree to the subject matter, the touchy problem, the sensational topic. The material did not, however, just come to him out of the blue. He chose it and worked hard at it. Other writers had not been prevented from addressing themselves to that subject for nineteen years. In every era there exist central as well as peripheral questions, and it should not be a matter of indifference to us whether a dramatist or a novelist deals with the one or the other. Thus, the choice of motives and problems a writer wants to focus on already speaks, to a certain degree, for or against him. Whoever praises the appeal of the subject matter praises at the same time the writer who chose it as his topic—provided, of course, that he is capable of creating a literary work at all. . . .

And here *The Deputy*, which raises so many problems, raises yet another—that of contemporary German literature. The very existence of this drama is tantamount to an indictment of German writers—especially those who probably would have been capable to deal artistically with similar questions in a more profound, a more mature, and a more original way than did the beginner Hochhuth, and who nevertheless did not do so because they lacked the courage or the feeling of responsibility or the perseverance.

This *Christian tragedy* and its worldwide success thus touch the pulse of our present-day German literature. And that explains perhaps why there is so much quiet and awkwardness whenever Hochhuth's name is mentioned in writers' circles.

Siegfried Melchinger. *Rolf Hochhuth* (Velber,
Friedrich, 1967), pp. 35–36†

Hochhuth had constructed his play *The Deputy* after the dramatic structure of Schiller's *Don Carlos*. . . . This time [in *Soldiers*]—this was obviously Hochhuth's intention—. . . Dr. Bell was to appear as a new . . . Marquis Posa vis-à-vis Churchill.

Then came the discovery of the Sikorski problem. Hochhuth restructured his drama. Now it has two conflicts: one that is dramatically genuine and another that is politically very meaningful but dramaturgically does not produce much more than idealistic rhetoric.

It is strange that this Schillerian Hochhuth, who has no use for Brecht, had the same thing happen to him that happened to Schiller while he was working on *Don Carlos*. The *Sturm und Drang* poet became more and more aware of the power of political necessity represented by King Philip. In a similar manner Hochhuth lost himself in the figure of Winston Churchill. Reading the drama, one sides—for naturally the dramatic technique presented here is empathetic—with Churchill, not with Dr. Bell. In this case two conflicts did not achieve a greater depth but blunted the conflict of amoral political necessity.

Therefore, the secondary plot, no matter what Hochhuth may say, has the effect of an unnecessary addition, quite apart from the dramatist's unsuccessful ventures in the realm of the polemically grotesque. The combination of an ideological drama with a superimposed satiric sketch is not Hochhuth's forte. That is as obvious in *Soldiers* as it was in *The Deputy*.

Hans Mayer. Zeit. Oct. 17, 1967, p. 12†

The Deputy is a gargantuan play. An uncut performance would last seven hours, and even in its fully printed version with Herr Hochhuth's lengthy appendix of historical documentation and commentary, it undertakes a herculean task: making the monstrously unbelievable believable. Consequently, productions of *The Deputy* must invariably reduce the play, but many have so severely chopped it that only the bare bones of its central situation remain. This is unfair to the integrity of the drama, for it makes shadowy sketches of both characters and events which are fully developed and realized in the complete text. Hochhuth's enormous tapestry has dimension, texture, subtlety, and a panoramic overview of the many ramifications of his story; as performed, *The Deputy* can all too easily be distorted into nothing more than an isolated attack on Pope Pius XII, far from the intention of the total work which sees Pacelli as ultimate symbol rather than sole perpetrator of the moral cowardice that the play condemns. Unfortunate as this distortion is (and it has caused much of the anger leveled at *The Deputy*), the blame for it ultimately rests with the playwright himself for asking the impossible from a working theatre. *The Deputy* cannot be cut without changing its meaning. . . .

Rolf Hochhuth is a gifted young dramatist, but *The Deputy,* more of a dramatic novel than a drama, defies the stage and therefore fails to meet a primary obligation of a good play. A fair evaluation of the work can result only from reading it in its entirety, and for all the agitation that productions have elicited, the stature of *The Deputy* must inevitably rest with its existence on the page rather than the stage.

Peter Bauland. The Hooded Eagle: Modern German
Drama on the New York Stage (Syracuse, N.Y., Syracuse
University Press, 1968), p. 215

The impact of Rolf Hochhuth's documentary plays spread beyond the theatre and occasioned worldwide heated political controversy. In *The Deputy* (1963) he assailed the Vatican with the accusation that Pope Pius XII had placed expediency before principle in failing to speak out against Hitler's extermination of the Jews. In *Soldiers* (1967) he implied that Winston Churchill instigated the death of General Sikorski, head of the Polish Government in exile, to appease the Russians. In attacking two giants of contemporary history, Hochhuth was not seeking publicity but raising on the highest level the question of responsibility. If lesser men plead obedience to orders, what about those who are in a position to give orders? Churchill is forced to choose between public and private morality. The Pope is caught between investments and conscience. How shall the rest of mankind act, "to what extent can the fence-sitters be guilty?" is the question both plays raise. To Hochhuth if the individual can no longer be held responsible, then we have an alibi for all guilt "and that would mean the end of all drama." . . .

If Brecht used the theatre as a courtroom in which the audience acts as jury, Hochhuth acts as judge and jury.

Allan Lewis. *The Contemporary Theatre,* rev. ed.
(New York, Crown, 1971), pp. 310–11

The question of criminality and guilt . . . has been Rolf Hochhuth's major concern in all his works. His first play, *The Deputy,* examined the complicity of Pope Pius XII in the Nazi war crimes. His second dramatic documentary, *Soldiers,* is a political indictment of Winston Churchill, who is charged with the murder of innocent civilians and the Polish General Sikorski. The indictment is not as specific as it may seem. . . . Here Churchill symbolizes national leaders and professional soldiers who conceal their lust for power under the guise of patriotism, exalted men who rationalize their neurotic and criminal acts by pleading the exigencies of war. . . .

When Hochhuth condemns Churchill and his "soldiers," he does so because he refuses to become implicated in a nation's crimes—and he advises others to do likewise. This militant stand of Hochhuth's is clearly a reaction against the present political trend in the West which he sees as a criminal recurrence of the past, in particular Germany's immediate past. In this respect, the criticism of Churchill and saturation bombing is directed mainly at America's role in the Vietnam war: Hochhuth calls upon America and other western powers to stop committing crimes in the name of democracy. Like other German playwrights such as Weiss, Grass, Kipphardt, Walser, Grass, Rolf Schneider, and Claus Hammel, Hochhuth is disturbed by American politics and especially by the repercussions they have for West Germany. In fact, the stage directions in *Soldiers* call for the same actor to play a German general and an American officer, both who lobby for a policy of *laissez faire* bombing. Hochhuth is incensed over this kind of German-American brotherhood, and the artistic concept of his documentary play dramatizes the subtle tensions involved in the making of criminal history.

Jack D. Zipes. *GL&L*. July, 1971, pp. 353–54, 356

Hochhuth's third work, *Guerrillas,* is pure fiction. It is true that the present-day situation finds its way into this utopian scheme, but characters and situation are pure invention. In this play Hochhuth describes the preparations for a coup d'état in the U.S.A., whose aim is "to overthrow the plutocratic oligarchy, the club of those one hundred and twenty families, who own more than eighty-five percent of the 'people's' wealth.'' This coup d'état, patterned after the model of the Gracchi in ancient Rome, is to be carried out by a member of the establishment. The play's hero, Senator Nicolson, is "the good spirit of America'' who, together with his urban guerrillas, risks his life to realize the ideals of the American Constitution.

Hochhuth's personal experience during a Vietnam demonstration in New York as well as his reading of Servan-Schreiber, Lundberg, and especially L. L. Matthias, to whom he dedicates the play, provide the impetus for this work. Consequently, his image of America is rather one-sided and subject to many an erroneous idea. The bad guys of the establishment are taken from the stock figures of gangster movies, and one has the feeling of dealing with a grotesque rather than with a tragedy. Furthermore, the drama lacks a gripping action. Although murder and bloodshed, rape, people dropping from windows, and underwater sabotage are everyday occurrences, they seem so superficial that one remains totally unmoved. . . .

Guerrillas is Hochhuth's weakest play. Indeed, critics have referred to it as "Polit-Burlesque'' and called Hochhuth an "author against the theater.'' Nevertheless, ever since its premiere in 1970, in Stuttgart, the play has been put on by many theaters, and often with considerable success.

Gerhard Weiss. In Benno von Wiese, ed., *Deutsche Dichter der Gegenwart* (West Berlin, Schmidt, 1973), p. 628†

Initially banned in London, but eventually produced even there, Rolf Hochhuth's *Soliders* stirred nearly as much controversy in some quarters as his earlier condemnation of Pope Pius XII in *The Deputy*. It was easy to see why—provided you were British, but more difficult otherwise.

Soliders is in many ways superior to *The Deputy* (which is far from saying it is a really good play). But, like the latter, it is unlikely ever to be discussed primarily in those terms. For better or worse, Hochhuth has a way of making "technique'' seem somewhat irrelevant. Whether or not one happens to agree with him, his concerns are a far cry from the soporific concerns of Broadway and his seriousness as an involved, even a tortured, participant in the life of his time is beyond dispute.

In *Soldiers* Hochhuth comes to grips with one of the greatest figures of our time as he confronts two of the most overriding questions of that time. The man is Winston Churchill; the questions, the morality of saturation bombing of civilian population centers and the extent to which the demands of war or other political necessities justify acts that, in the normal course of things, would be termed immoral. Both in their specifics and in extension they have as much relevance today as they did at the time *Soldiers* supposedly takes place. . . .

Hochhuth raises again the perennial question, evident in the careers of figures as diverse as Richelieu and Lenin: can there be a distinction between public and private morality, between the political and the personal act? . . . Whatever one may think of Hochhuth as a playwright, it would be impossible not to acknowledge that he has employed the theatre as an arena in which the great moral issues of our time can be raised.

Catharine Hughes. *Plays, Politics, and Polemics* (New York,
Drama Book Specialists, 1973), pp. 117, 123–24

By contrast with *The Deputy,* the language [of *Soldiers*]—prose, not verse—is happily never at variance with the subject-matter. In other respects, however, *Soldiers* has comparable weaknesses. The imputation of Churchill's connivance at the killing of Sikorski is not of central thematic importance, detracts from the main issue, and distorts the character of Churchill, just as the allegations about Pius XII damaged the earlier play. The professional playwright, with an eye on the box office, goes against the aims and intentions of the documentary dramatist. The play is more modern than *The Deputy* in its dramatic structure but is still conventional theatre in its concern for dramatic effect, particularly through the confrontation of dominant individuals: Churchill with Sikorski, for example, and, later, with Bishop Bell. The continued focus on the individual is seen also in the figure of Dorland himself, the enlightened prophet whose views are doomed to be rejected. He is fatally ill, and the play is to some extent his requiem. His cause remains a personal one, and in the final analysis the problem of the inner play remains personal to Churchill. Positioned in the highest arena of politics, he is, in fact, the main character. The framework attempts to make the central problems more general, but the historical and personal stature of Churchill stands in the way.

R. Hinton Thomas and Keith Bullivant. *Literature in*
Upheaval (Manchester, Manchester University Press,
1974), pp. 100–101

Leaving aside Dürrenmatt's grotesque satires, it is in fact hard to find a more convincing play [than *The Midwife*] written in the Federal Republic which has thought to criticise an aspect of contemporary society through the medium of comedy. . . .

The Midwife takes as its theme the substitute identities of people estranged from their true selves which they have built up artificially and which they employ language to defend with all their might. The play, then, stands foursquare in the classical comic tradition which reaches back to Molière. It pokes fun, not so much at people as such, but rather at their frantic efforts to appear more than they are in reality.

In addition to this, *The Midwife* is also concerned with a concrete social issue, the problems of the homeless in the Federal Republic, which have preoccupied Hochhuth for many years, and about which he has amassed a great deal of documentary material. . . .

The Midwife gives us an amusing and convincing picture of the false facade of social life and the inhumanity of its institutions. But no one individual is held responsible for this state of affairs: almost all the characters in the play need to conceal themselves behind the mask which their role affords them, and language is an essential constituent of this mask. The alienated "language of the monsters" reduces human problems to the level of technical issues, and this makes them seem less difficult to resolve. Anyone who has this language at his command can also indulge in the illusion of a certain measure of power, and this gives him some relief for his feelings of fear and inferiority.

So *The Midwife* does far more than bring to the surface the problems of the homeless and of other underprivileged groups: it also makes a contribution to the recognition of the real nature of the society we live in, where power resides solely in whoever has the upper hand and is intent on remaining there, because the real man behind the mask is eaten away by anxiety and insecurity.

Rainer Taëni. Rolf Hochhuth (London, Oswald Wolff,
1977), pp. 104, 106, 116

Hochhuth's *Lysistrata and NATO* follows much the same pattern as *The Midwife* in the interaction between its intent, its content, and its form. It uses comedy techniques, with a heroine as the main character, to reflect on an important contemporary problem—war. . . .

It is interesting to contrast the sexual revolt depicted in *Lysistrata* with that portrayed in Aristophanes' comedy. In the Greek play the women are very conscious of being free citizens; they are therefore aware of their responsibility for the prosperity of the *polis* as well as for their own families. Despite the unusual nature of their action their motivation is clear-cut—they simply want peace. . . . The relationships between Hochhuth's women and their husbands are far more complicated and certainly less happy. Even when the real issue of the land seems to be solved, they do not want to return home. They want to use this opportunity to show the extent to which they despise, rather than love, their partners. . . .

Lysistrata and NATO combines the same elements of deadly seriousness of purpose with ribald comedy as did *The Midwife,* but far less successfully so. Hochhuth could not rely on dialect humor as in the first comedy, and often the dialogue is reduced to a recitation of clichés. Comedy is
introduced mainly by means of verbal and visual gags. . . . The obscenity
in Aristophanes' play seems natural, whereas at times in Hochhuth's play it
is forced and therefore embarrassingly unfunny. And despite the continued
use of newspaper quotations at the beginning of each act to relate the action
to current events, Hochhuth seems to have moved farther away from the
"real" world. His island could be located anywhere, and the play resembles
a parable. . . . But the final moments of the play are somber indeed, as
the memory of Hitler is invoked.

Margaret E. Ward. *Rolf Hochhuth* (Boston, Twayne, 1977),
pp. 111, 113–14

[From] the perspective of the Sartrean existential "ethic," we can see that
Hochhuth's [*The Deputy*] does not so much condemn Pius XII and acclaim
Gerstein and Ricardo as it shows us who they are. Gerstein and Ricardo
resist and are therefore resisters while the Pope washes his hands and the
whole world recognizes Pontius Pilate. The other figures as well—the
churchmen, Nazi functionaries, and Italian soliders—are described in
lengthy stage directions, perhaps the longest in modern literature. These
directions not only describe them as they *are* in the eternal present of the
staged drama, but also as they *would be* in the "future" post-war years,
although as dramatic characters they have no "future" but exist contempo-
raneously with the dramatic event they enact. Hochhuth uses this "genre
violation" seemingly in an attempt to identify moral types and to associate
culpability with identity. Guilt is not declared from without, as the result of
a transgression of an external law. It is a state of being, lived by all those
who do not or did not feel "responsible." For, if consciousness is synonymous with conscience, then those who do not assume responsibility are less
than thinking beings; they degrade themselves to mere things. In the drama,
as in Sartre's existentialism, one is obliged to resist evil, not by commandment, but precisely because divine commandments are not forthcoming. On
a purely realistic and pragmatic level one lives in the world one makes or
allows others to make. Sartre denies God outright and founds both his existential ontology and his ethic on his atheism. Hochhuth, on the other hand,
seems merely to have lost him, but is left then with the same necessity of
founding an ethic without the aid of divine inspiration. Both treat the confrontation with Nazism as the model for the human situation in general—
i.e., the individual faced with the necessity of asserting himself responsibly
against the rigorous restrictions of an oppressive world.

E. Elaine Murdaugh. *Seminar.* Nov., 1979, pp. 288–89

HOFMANNSTHAL, HUGO VON (1874–1929)

What Hofmannsthal and Strauss have done [in *Electra*] is to take Clytemnestra and Ægisthus, and by identifying them with everything that is evil and cruel, with all that needs must hate the highest when it sees it, with hideous domination and coercion of the higher by the baser, with the murderous rage in which the lust for a lifetime of orgiastic pleasure turns on its slaves in the torture of its disappointment and the sleepless horror and misery of its neurasthenia, to so rouse in us an overwhelming flood of wrath against it and ruthless resolution to destroy it, that Electra's vengeance becomes holy to us; and we come to understand how even the gentlest of us could wield the axe of Orestes or twist our firm fingers in the black hair of Clytemnestra to drag back her head and leave her throat open to the stroke.

That was a task hardly possible to an ancient Greek, and not easy even to us. . . . And that is the task which Hofmannsthal and Strauss have achieved. Not even in the third scene of [Wagner's] *The Rhine Gold,* or in the Klingsor scenes in *Parsifal,* is there such an atmosphere of malignant and cancerous evil as we get here. And that the power with which it is done is not the power of the evil itself, but of the passion that detests and must and finally can destroy that evil, is what makes the work great, and makes us rejoice in its horror. [March 19, 1910]

George Bernard Shaw. *How to Become a Musical Critic*
(London, Hart-Davis, 1960), pp. 261–62

What is most important . . . in [Hofmannsthal's] earlier works is not their plot (always of the slightest), nor even the decorative beauty of their language (as well suited, in itself, to a volume of poems as to drama), but their constant striving after new verse-forms for the theatre. All writers of verse-drama have made use of a change of rhyme or metre in order to obtain a certain dramatic effect. Among the most familiar examples are the rhymed couplet of the Shakespearean plays, used to round off a speech or to add an air of finality at the close of a scene, and the change from verse to prose in certain passages. Hofmannsthal uses both devices freely, but in other respects he goes much further than any poet before him. His verse changes its form continually. It is like a mountain lake on an April day, sensitive to the shadow of every passing cloud and rippled afresh by every gust of wind. Perhaps it would be too much to say that his verse has a new metrical lilt for every emotion, but in many passages of the later plays even this is true. The Venetian play *The Adventurer and the Singer* shows the adaptation of rhythm to the passing mood of drama.

Ashley Dukes. *Modern Dramatists* (London,
Palmer, 1911), pp. 166–67

When Hofmannsthal turned away from the Renaissance to seek fresh inspiration in Greek antiquity, it was not entirely for the purpose of replenishing
an exhausted muse, but because he was convinced that he could bring a new
and original interpretation to this fountain-head of art and literature. . . .

But . . . we find, first, that he has fallen a victim to the error of his
predecessors in emphasizing but one phase of Greek civilization, and, second, that in his interpretation he is by no means a path-finder. It is no far
cry from Nietzsche, the critic of antiquity, to Hofmannsthal, the dramatist
of antiquity. It is Nietzsche's Dionysiac principle which has taken possession of our author body and soul, and found its fullest dramatic expression
in his version of *Electra*. . . .

When Hofmannsthal selected *Electra* as the subject for his first essay
in the field of ancient tragedy he was at once confronted with a choice
between the Apollonic and the Dionysiac principle. It is not entirely to his
credit that he has reverted to the Dionysiac conception and presented us with
a drama of orgiastic vengeance, which has little in common with our modern
thought unless it be with the intensive study of hysteria, paranoia and other
related branches of abnormal psychology. The plot is borrowed without essential change from Sophocles. . . .

If Hofmannsthal is indebted to anyone besides Sophocles, it is to Euripides. . . . In the Electra of Euripides we no longer find that peculiarly
Sophoclean union of strength and gentleness which proceeds to the execution of a righteous and just vengeance, but an undaunted, cold-blooded Lady
Macbeth, actuated by an ineffable hatred of her mother. Hofmannsthal goes
a step farther than Euripides in thus degrading human passion and bringing
it down to a lower plane. His is an Electra not only of vengeance but of
ecstatic vengeance; yielding entirely to the Dionysiac passion of revenge,
she soon loses her personality through too frequent indulgence in gruesome
memories of Agamemnon's murder and horrible visions of the vengeance to
come. From a lowly slave, hiding in the palace yard, she grows before our
eyes into a wild dancing Salome, whose exultant and ecstatic frenzy finally
breaks the bonds of endurance and casts her a broken reed at our feet.

George M. Baker. *JEGP*. July, 1913, pp. 388–91

Remarkable [*The Cavalier of the Rose*] surely is, whether you like it or not.
A stage-piece that is part *opera-buffa*, part true comedy; that is at times
delicately and truly touching, and at times uproariously farcical; that is set
to a score as intricate and sophisticated as the most ingenious of modern
musicians could make it . . . a work such as this is not met with at every
turn of the way. . . .

The libretto of Hugo von Hofmannsthal is diverting, adroit, and sala-
cious. The humor is at times finely conceived and finely rendered; at other
times it is mere ponderous Teutonic horseplay—as when that pompous and

ridiculous Silenus, the Baron Ochs auf Lerchenau, falls off the sofa upon which he has been stretched by a sword-scratch in his duel with Octavian. The libretto as a whole is a hodge-podge—a gaily inconsequential mixture of sentiment and farce, satire and horseplay. It is sadly lacking in homogeneity and rectitude, and it is far too long. But it would be a dour soul indeed who could not find pleasure in its wit, its pretty sentiment, its freshness, its cheerful audacity, its hilarious fun. And that is true of the music of Strauss, which, also, has wit, sentiment, and audacity.

Lawrence Gilman. NAR. Jan., 1914, p. 141

Hofmannsthal invites no comparison with the great Attic dramatists. His aim is different. It is to get behind those dramatists to the wild human origins of the myths with which they deal, to the fierce and primitive and noble folk that must have antedated the Greece of immortal marbles and Sophoclean choruses. And that imaginative vision he has reconstructively grasped with an energy and tenacity that no one would have suspected from the heavy fragrance of his earlier work. The verse in these Greek plays is sinewy, bare, expressive, the mood stern yet impassioned, the dramatic rhythm sweeps along like the storms that hover over the dark forests and mysterious shrines of that preclassical Hellenic world. What Hofmannsthal has most powerfully laid hold upon is the idea of fate, not as a literary convention, but as the immediate spiritual experience of an entire world. We shake with Clytemnestra under the shadow of her ineluctable doom; we flee with Ödipus from the oracle's certain prediction; we cower in the courtyard with Electra under the terror of that fated revenge. The modern poetic drama has little to show that surpasses these figures and these situations in a strange gloom and massiveness of imaginative power.

Ludwig Lewisohn. The Modern Drama (New York,
Huebsch, 1915), pp. 263–64

The dreaminess and fairytale atmosphere of Venice must prove an irresistible attraction to a poet of Hofmannsthal's temperament. On three occasions he has made use of the Queen of the Lagunes in his dramatic works. One of these, Venice Preserved, bears upon its title page the information that it was built upon the work of the same name by Thomas Otway. In the main ideas of the plot it is the same, but taken as a whole it is an entirely new, entirely different creation. A puny weakling, who only through love is carried beyond his narrow self, is driven through the accumulation of misfortune into a treacherous plot concerned with the overthrow of the government. Through cowardice and perhaps also through his love for his wife, he betrays the plot and his friends. Such is the main idea of Otway's drama and also of Hofmannsthal's. But Hoffmansthal's characters are living creatures, pulsating with life, love, hate, and friendship. The accumulation of events produces emotions in them, which, whether we sympathize or not, we too are compelled to feel. Even as *Electra* is a tragedy of hate, so Hofmannsthal's *Venice Preserved* is a tragedy of treachery, but through it all runs a sweetly beautiful refrain of friendship ideal.

Elisabeth Walter. *Poet Lore.* Sept.–Oct., 1915, pp. 647–48

The reaction against realism may be forgiven its many sins in the name of Hugo von Hofmannsthal, Austrian dramatist. With Schnitzler he has dipped his drama in the magic of Vienna—Vienna before the war stabbed her and peace left her dying of her wounds—with Schnitzler he has trapped that city's mocking grace. But his plays have a glory of colour and music, a depth of passion that Schnitzler's have not. They form, moreover, the most purely artistic drama of modern times, their courtly grace establishing them in an aristocracy of the theatre. Their art is magnificent. Their dramatic value lies as little as possible in their content. Were it not for their experiments in form they would be dramatic failures. Hofmannsthal lacks a sense of the theatre, and the power to realize character. His vision is that of the artist and the sculptor. His people, like his plays, are all colour and form; their life is at best spasmodic, suggested, not realized. This is clear from the beginning of his work. His early drama has little enough of real passion or of deep thought: it has more than uncommon distinction in its beauty of style. . . .

This beauty of form and glory of verse is the lasting value of Hofmannsthal's finest plays. It is modernity's greatest protest against the deceit practised in her name and Reality's. It is more. In *Oedipus and the Sphinx,* Hofmannsthal attempts a dramatic form that brings him into touch with the whole European movement towards change, the movement for a wider and nobler rhythm of action, character and form.

Storm Jameson. *Modern Drama in Europe* (London,
Collins, 1920), pp. 217–19

Calderón's Beggar asks for alms; Hofmannsthal's Beggar [in *The Salzburg Great Theatre of the World*] no longer asks for alms but rather spurns them; and at that point the Beggar begins to become terrifying. In Hofmannsthal's figure the frightful experience of these last years has taken shape; in a word, his Beggar is communism. King and Peasant, Rich Man and Beauty, form, along with Wisdom, who stands aloof, an altogether content society. Then he, clad in rags, a real ragamuffin in the true sense of the word, steps forward among them and threatens the kingdom, forged "round as a ring" by the powers that be, with the most dreadful grievances and accusations. He comes from the border, where he and his family had been living peacefully until the war robbed him of his wife—and the ensuing pestilence of his children, who perished one by one—and made him a poor homeless wretch, a starveling, and a vagabond. Why just him, and not his better-off neighbors who, owing to their wealth, had a horse or some other means of escape? The King refuses to take responsibility. . . .

The Beggar is anything but satisfied with the existing order; he wishes for a new "world order" and gets ready to realize his desire in a horrible way by threatening to assault the entire society with the axe he has wrested from the peasant, since none of them has an answer to the question of all questions: why did it have to be this way? . . .

If one compares the genteel language [of Calderón] with Hofmannsthal's verse, which cuts to the quick, one can begin to understand by how much the modern poet surpasses the older one in this area. To be sure, Hofmannsthal cannot give us a completely satisfying answer either, at least none that satisfies the intellect. The dramatically developed antithesis of rich and poor—one could also call it that of capitalism and socialism—leads in Hofmannsthal's play to a so-called débat. . . .

The Rich Man, who here, exactly as in real life, serves as the King's advocate, does not lack very ingenious and very judicious arguments, but the obdurate silence that the Beggar, crushed by fate, opposes to them eventually destroys them all; and even kind Wisdom finds herself at a loss here. [1922]

> Raoul Auernheimer. In Günther Rühle, ed., *Theater für*
> *die Republik* (Frankfurt, Fischer, 1967), p. 391†

My very dear Friend,

I have deliberately not participated in any literary demonstration in honour of your fiftieth birthday because I cannot escape the feeling that anything I could tell you in words would be banal in comparison with what, as the composer of your wonderful poetry, I have already said to you in music. It was your words which drew from me the finest music that I had to give: this knowledge must fill you with deep gratification. Let therefore Chrysothemis, the Marschallin, Ariadne, Zerbinetta, the Empress, and, not last, Helen—"admired much and much reproved"—join me in calling on you and thanking you for all you have dedicated to me out of your life's work, and kindled in me, and roused to life. That even our contemporaries are at last beginning to appreciate the magnitude and the beauty of the work you have been doing for me is proved by the sensational success which *Ariadne* [*on Naxos*]—poetry and music—achieved in Amsterdam. [Jan. 29, 1924]

> Richard Strauss. In *A Working Friendship: The*
> *Correspondence between Richard Strauss and Hugo von*
> *Hofmannsthal* (New York, Random House, 1961), p. 380

I do not know whether Max Mell has told you, as I had asked him to do some weeks ago in Düsseldorf, how great an impression your play *The*

Tower made on me. I am much obliged to you for having sent me a copy of it. Now one can again believe in the existence of tragedy in our time.

Perhaps I shall soon have the opportunity to discuss with you in person my misgivings concerning some aspects of the last act. . . . But infinitely more important than any objection is the fact that this work does exist and that one cannot but approve of it and of its creator. [April 11, 1926]

Martin Buber. NRs. 73, 4, 1962, p. 757†

Kingship was the innermost form of Hofmannsthal's relation to the world. His poetic creativeness was only one of the modes in which this attitude manifested itself. Kingship is the knowledge of having been placed at the center of a vast realm, burdened with every dignity and all responsibility, forever embracing the whole—the whole gamut with all its variations, from beggar to prince, the meaning of all destinies, the continuity of the great ceremony. The masks of beggar and king recur in both *The Salzburg Great Theater of the World* and *The Little Theater of the World*. From his earliest poems to *The Tower,* all of Hofmannsthal's works aspire to the ideal form of a *theatrum mundi,* a universal allegorical and symbolic poem, raising all the perplexities of existence to the order of the great timeless laws so that the eternal shines through the temporal. Here allegory does not mean a diminishing of the fullness of life, nor does the mask mean mere appearance. The opposite is true: it is only when we become aware of the role-playing nature of our existence that we gain insight into its deeper truth and meaning. [1929]

Ernst Robert Curtius. Kritische Essays zur europäischen
Literatur (Bern, Francke, 1950), p. 165†

The inability to exploit the passing moment, to taste its unique quality to the full, also forms the central problem in Hugo von Hofmannsthal's dramatic poem, *Death and the Fool,* just as a century before, the same predicament had fashioned the core of Goethe's *Faust*. Hofmannsthal . . . had written this poem when only nineteen, and its pendant, *The Death of Titian,* a year earlier! While *The Death of Titian* is the apotheosis of a life of creative vigour, the later drama is the sad weighing-up by the young dilettante Claudio of his futile existence. Strive as he will to grasp life, it remains intangible to him.

In the setting of his poem, Hofmannsthal has deliberately challenged comparison with Goethe. But while Faust is encompassed, during his opening monologue, by the apparatus of the scholar and the alchemist, Claudio is surrounded by the *objets d'art* of the dilettante. Claudio is, however, as disgruntled as his illustrious predecessor with this "lumber-room, full of tawdry rubbish''; for art, like science, can erect a barrier between its devotees and life.

Cedric Hentschel. *The Byronic Teuton* (London,
Methuen, 1940), p. 163

None of Hofmannsthal's works is more famous than *Death and the Fool,* and none is more misunderstood. It probably owes its fame to the fact that it expresses, as does no work with the exception of *The Tower,* certain tendencies of its time. In his Claudio . . . Hofmannsthal described two maladies: victimization by art and victimization by the intellect; these are the afflictions of his age. . . .

Hofmannsthal's *Death and the Fool* has been compared with [Goethe's] *Werther,* and with good reason. Both works express problems of their times in the form of personal experiences. . . . And as Goethe was identified with Werther, so Hofmannsthal, to a certain extent, was identified with Claudio, and the whole wealth of his mature works could not change this. . . .

Hofmannsthal certainly is Claudio; but he is more than that: he is Claudio's creator and judge. And it has always been overlooked that Claudio is put on trial here, and that the poet appears not only as the accused but also as the accuser. One has seen the self-portrait and listened to the soliloquy, but ignored the self-judgment.

If Hofmannsthal thus identifies with Claudio, he does so in order to disassociate himself from him. He has detached one of his possibilities, one that occasionally may have pushed itself dangerously into the foreground, given shape to it, and then executed it, as it were, in effigy. . . .

However, it is not only a de facto disassociation, as in *Werther,* resulting from the psychological process of a "universal confession," but also one explicitly brought about by a moral judgment. And in this respect Hofmannsthal differs from the neurasthenic confessions of the decadence, because he breaks loose from sterile circles of self-reflection and, with serious determination, takes notice of the moral problem.

Richard Alewyn. *Monatshefte.* Dec., 1944, pp. 409–10,
420, 422–23†

In Hofmannsthal's *The Great World Theater of Salzburg* the stage represents the universe. On its upper part the audience sees steps leading to the Master's palace. On these steps the drama begins and ends. On the lower level the allegorical figure of the World arranges, at the Master's bidding, a second stage. It is the theater of human life on which the human souls, while embodied in their roles, perform their play within the play. Thus the plot of the drama develops on the two levels of the eternal and the temporal, or, as Calderón says, on the level of truth and the level of semblance. The eternal is presented as real and lasting, the temporal as symbolic and transitory.

Time is invisibly at work as an attribute of the world. Independent of the plot, it runs out, when Death, its manifestation, fulfills his function. He as the instrument of the timeless Master of the Universe is the master of the stage who calls off the players. No reason inherent in the plot brings about the end, but it comes because everything temporal is bound to end in due time. Life itself is a metaphor, Time is relative to the timeless. Man's life is a play performed for and before the master. The temporal gains significance only in its relation to the eternal.

The two-level stage makes it possible to show man as having an origin beyond the temporal. He is called to establish a meaningful synthesis of the dualism between the temporal and the eternal. Because he thus resumed the central intention of the seventeenth-century Baroque theater, Hofmannsthal likewise had to conceive his figures within an allegorical frame. Yet he masters the Baroque form in a genuine and independent fashion. To his allegorical figures he imparts individual traits, to his plot dramatic tension. Through this his players become aware, each of them in a different way, of the significance of their playing.

The plot may be seen as developing in four parts. The first one shows the Master and his angels instructing the players in the meaning of the play and the way it is to be performed. Whereas this part is centered upon the dramatic relationship of world and man to the universe, the second part develops the life of man as a social drama. The third part is a dance of death which, as the end approaches, dramatically reverses the order of values ruling the sphere of semblance. In the last part the theater of life is cleared out and from the upper stage, the sphere of truth, the Angel announces the judgment.

Arnold Bergstraesser. *GR*. Dec., 1945, pp. 262–63

A brief analysis of dominating tendencies helps us to understand how Hofmannsthal came to use such varied methods, as lyric drama, morality play, allegory, comedy, and opera texts, the latter again highly coloured and dramatic like *Electra,* or delicately sentimental and comic like *The Cavalier of the Rose;* and a certain unity of effort begins to appear amidst the differing inspiration. All these works are essentially poetic conceptions, they rely on the collaboration of various arts, and the medium of collaboration is theatre. There is no name for this composite and elastic form that Hofmannsthal developed for his complex inspiration, and the only way to indicate it briefly would be to call it a poetry of theatre, borrowing a phrase from Cocteau. . . .

The attraction of music and dance and mime for Hofmannsthal is that they have a more intense sensuousness than words have, a more direct appeal to feeling, but at the same time touch deeper levels of life, stirring primeval fears and reverences, expressing more mysteriously the emotions of religion and a life that is unseen and unspoken. Hofmannsthal was aware of the various contributions the different arts could make, as a matter of esthetic discrimination. He felt that words generalize best; that music gives the greatest emotional intensity; whilst a single gesture of mime or dancer can express a state of mind and dramatic relations with unequalled vividness. . . . But his sense of collaboration of the arts in the theatre is more than esthetic discrimination. It is a profound sense of ritual, cult, liturgy, and festival, which have always, both in primitive and enlightened religions, used the various arts in combination to one end. The unity of his whole conception of a composite art depends on his consciousness of the ritualistic foundations of theatre, of the festivals of popular and religious life, of the theatre as the conscious stylization of the natural dramas of life lived between the human and the divine.

Ronald Peacock. *The Poet in the Theatre* (New York, Harcourt, Brace, 1946), pp. 136–37

Man has not only the right but the duty to forsake, to overcome some of his own character traits. Man owes fidelity, *die Treue,* only to his innermost nature, which he must purify more and more. Fidelity does not condemn man to stagnation; it urges him on to overcome his own limitations. Its imperious commandment proclaims: *Become who you are.*

The motto seems to call for an ultrammeled cult of the individual. In the case of Hofmannsthal, however, such an interpretation would be a grave mistake. . . . Simply the role attributed to the social element makes it sufficiently clear that the egoistic solution to moral problems, a solution springing from the resourcefulness of a person taking only his own interest into account, a solution that could be called automatic, is not a possible solution for this profound mind, this all-embracing soul, this noble heart. Hofmannsthal wants the solution, but he holds valid only that solution which he calls allometric—that which springs from the reciprocal action of the combined strength and virtue of partners in an effort. It is this kind of a solution that brings about the metamorphosis, because it alone is reconcilable with the act, the work, the sacrifice, the child. It underlies the tangle of plots in *The Woman without a Shadow;* it forms the basis for the fate of both Bacchus and Ariadne and Oedipus and Jocasta; it is proposed in *The Adventurer and the Singer,* but it is chosen by only one of the parties concerned; it is offered to Claudio who, fool that he is, does not grasp it; it is dealt with, humorously on the surface but very seriously at bottom, in *The Difficult Man.* It gives marriage its value. It perfects the individual by elevating him, by purifying him, by making him part of the world; and with regard to procreation, to the family, it assures him of his place in the infinite chain of the unending process of life. In it altruism and egoism are reconciled; it is the court of arbitration between ethics and the blind will to live. It is the guiding principle and the most beautiful fruit of this our universe in which man finds himself. It is the aspect under which Hofmannsthal conceives of, first, brotherly love of men and, second, Christian love as Jesus taught it. It is what gives the world its meaning.

A. Fuchs. *EG*. Oct.–Dec., 1948, p. 365†

Perhaps in our age a traditionalist is by necessity an experimentalist, and an experimentalist a traditionalist. Hofmannsthal's impulse, in any case, was to seek in the past what was still alive there and make it live again and live differently. He discovered forms, potentialities, opportunities in the past which to others seemed set and dead, and brought them to life as things original and new. The artificial fascinated him and drove him to discover its secret, where its life lay. He brought again into the drama the elements which the previous century, with its self-righteous cult of realism, had banished: intrigue, complication, masquerade, disguise, play; and restored them to their place and their significance. *The Difficult Man* is a sort of adaptation of Viennese comedy as it was written by Schnitzler, but raised to a level of imaginative play which Schnitzler never could have reached. No doubt Hofmannsthal's passion for reshaping things once shaped was simply an outcome of his desire to assimilate the elements of the civilization he knew. He did not want anything to be lost. . . .

Hofmannsthal experimented with forms. To say this is to say very little. A writer experiments, with language or with forms, in order to say something he wishes to say, and if he succeeds he has said something new. Yet he cannot say anything new—and this was understood by Hofmannsthal better than by any other writer of his time—without resurrecting something old. The word freshly used brings back the word as it was once freshly used, for the past is renewed whenever we renew the present. Hofmannsthal's past was the past of old Austria, and when Austria was dismembered, its dismemberment was a tragedy not only for the Austrian, but for the poet, his essential tragedy.

Edwin Muir. *TLS*. May 19, 1950, p. 308

In this comedy [*The Difficult Man*] which looks like a society piece with a plot so slender as almost to escape definition, the problem of Karl Hans Bruehl, the "difficult man," is the difficulty of communication, the doubt in its possibility: "I understand myself much less well when I speak than when I am silent"—a situation which almost prevents him, "reticent out of delicacy," from winning the woman he loves. In this, the most polished and successful of his plays, Hofmannsthal undoubtedly intended to commemorate a passing civilization. . . . In *The Difficult Man* it is the aristocratic

Viennese society with all its grace and refinement of manners, tact and taste, at the moment it vanished forever. But there is a graver, more urgent note in *The Difficult Man,* for here the author suggests, with all his affection and loyalty for a world which he knows to be doomed, the causes of its downfall; there is a parallel, more than symbolic, between the decay of society and the decay of language as a means of communication. . . . Speech as an element of social intercourse, as social action *par excellence,* has become practically meaningless since there is no agreement on premises. "Nobody knows any longer what conversation is: to give the cue to others, not to perorate oneself like a waterfall!" exclaims the host at a *soirée* in *The Difficult Man,* and we feel that he is writing *"Finis"* under a whole epoch. Here begins the Brave New World of loudspeakers, slogans and mass-propaganda.

H. A. Hammelmann. Hugo von Hofmannsthal (London,
Bowes & Bowes, 1957), pp. 28–29

The function of the theater, Hofmannsthal believed, is to show that sublime and true moment in a man's life when the motivating passion-power of his existence is expressed. To Hofmannsthal this moment is more real than any external reality. . . . He knows that in life, although the process may be slower and less apparent, man is ultimately destroyed by that very passion which gives him the power to live. It is that moment when man's motivating passion-power drives him to the conflict of life and death that must be captured in the drama.

When viewed in this way we see that Hofmannsthal's Electra is more than a depraved and wild beast. In the conflict of what she says and what she does, the playwright is able to present that which is most real in Electra: her Destiny. He dramatizes that consuming and passionate power of vengeance which destroys every attribute of Electra's womanhood, and, as the play ends, kills not only Aegisthus and Clytemnestra, but herself as well. We may complain that she is a mad woman, but she is real; and if, Hofmannsthal seems to say, we could each know our own reality, we too would be thought of as mad. Hofmannsthal's play may be filled with demons, but they are demons who reveal, at the moment they are consumed, man's destiny.

Robert W. Corrigan. MD. May, 1959, p. 20

The Tower is written in prose; but here I speak of Hofmannsthal as "the poet," for the play is essentially poetic drama. . . . The latter part, with the episodes of the Gipsy and the King of the Children, becomes so phantasmagoric that one can only imagine its representation in terms of a dream-film such as Jean Cocteau might devise. The plot is suggested by that of Calderón's *Life Is a Dream;* but Calderón's play is for Hofmannsthal hardly more than a point of departure; two plays could hardly be more different in spirit and intention than these of the Spaniard and the Austrian. Hofmannsthal was well practised in the craft of the theatre, and if *The Tower* is unplayable, we must attribute this not to failure of skill but to the fact that what the author wished here to express exceeded the limits within which the man of the theatre must work. For the surface meaning, the real or apparent reason for human behaviour which must be immediately apprehensible by the audience if a play is to hold their interest, Hofmannsthal cares less and less as the play proceeds. He seems to have loaded this play, in symbolism which perhaps has more than one level of significance, with all the burden of his feelings about the catastrophe of the Europe to which he belonged, the Europe which went down in the wreck of empires between 1914 and 1918. . . . The play expresses not only the author's suffering during those years that remained to him, but also his ultimate Christian hope.

T. S. Eliot. In Hugo von Hofmannsthal, Selected Plays
and Libretti (New York, Pantheon, 1963), pp. lxxiii–lxxiv

Everyman is a "simple" play, as it has to be to fulfil one of Hofmannsthal's purposes, that of making a direct effect on an unsophisticated peasant audience. *Everyman*, one might say, tells its familiar story of sin, repentance, and redemption by faith in terms still well known in every Christianized country. . . .

Against this, however, it should be emphasized that Hofmannsthal's mind was complex in its very nature. In *Everyman* he was trying to write in a way simple enough to be understood by the peasant and subtle enough to satisfy more sophisticated audiences and more complex demands. Even in the "simplicity" of the drama there was nothing naive or spontaneous. If, indeed, the contrived nature of this simplicity does not on the whole show through this can be regarded as a tribute to Hofmannsthal's artistic skill. . . .

In *Everyman* Hofmannsthal is preoccupied with personal human destiny and salvation. In this play's insistence on individual, personal reform and personal responsibility there lies the seed from which grows the cultural-political thought of Hofmannsthal's later years. This is the principal foundation of *The Salzburg Great Theater of the World, The Tower,* and of the prose essays.

. . . In *The Salzburg Great Theater of the World* Hofmannsthal attempted to bridge the gap between "philosophical discussion of problems and timeless symbolism" (Curtius). The extent to which Hofmannsthal was successful is as debatable in this case as in that of *Everyman*. Because, however, of its frequently austere concentration on the moral essentials the effect of *The Great Theater of the World* on an audience may be considerable, even though the play is in a theatrical sense less spectacular than *Everyman*. The problem of its ultimate success and general value probably depends on the extent to which the use of these ancient religious symbols finds an instinctive and sympathetic response in the audience. . . .

Hofmannsthal does seem to have solved the problem of satisfying simultaneously the intellectual and the common man, in a theatrical sense at least. The combination of homely idiom and clear-cut dramatic situation with sophisticated cunning in the art of linguistic suggestion and traditional overtone seems to be the chief factor in this.

> Brian Coghlan. *Hofmannsthal's Festival Dramas*
> (Cambridge, Cambridge University Press, 1964), pp. 181–82

In play after play Hofmannsthal confronts his audience with men and women who are the products of their environments, and by recreating these milieus in detail, he makes one aware of their limitations as well as their transitoriness so that one realizes, as never before in Hofmannsthal's work, to what degree people are fashioned by outside forces and against what odds their human uniqueness must be asserted. Finally, in *The Tower*, his last great work, the playwright sketches a portrait of totalitarianism with such dynamic force, with so much of its sociological and psychological background, and with such a power of atmospheric evocation that those readers and spectators, who, unlike Hofmannsthal, have actually lived through the rise of the Fascist masses and the resulting destruction of culture, are shaken by a deep shudder of recognition. Such, if anything at all, is the effect of literary realism.

Nothing, of course, would distort the truth more completely than the attempt to make a naturalist out of Hugo von Hofmannsthal. There are, after all, the symbolistic fairy tales of the later period, the bombastic or frivolous operas, and the trivial social comedies, with their propensity for sentimentality. But with the reservation which these warning signals impose, an impressive case can be made for explaining Hofmannsthal's metamorphosis in terms of a conversion to reality.

> Egon Schwarz. *WSCL*. Autumn, 1967, pp. 489–90

The theme of wealth is not new to Hofmannsthal's *Everyman*. [The original] Everyman, too, turns to Goods in his distress. But Hofmannsthal has expanded this theme to such an extent that it becomes a dominant part of the drama. [His] Everyman's self-sufficiency and egocentricity appear to result from his wealth, which has allowed him to cultivate a garden of earthly delights in which neither humanistic nor spiritual values grow. But, Everyman, who considers his wealth a means and a servant, comes to learn in his encounter with Mammon that money is a cold and powerful and heartless demon who holds Everyman firmly in his clutches. The servant has become, in fact, master over his lord.

Hofmannsthal does not mean to imply that wealth is inherently evil, nor does he make an overt criticism of the existing economic structure and distribution of wealth. Everyman, however, does seem to have been blinded by his wealth and robbed of all human kindness and charity. Everyman need not renounce his wealth. He must undergo a profound change of heart.

It is at this point that the ethic of [Hofmannsthal's] *Everyman* intersects with the religion of [the English morality play] *Everyman*. Both require of man a total conversion, a knowledge of shortcomings that in turn leads to a change of the whole person. What in [the English] *Everyman* is shown externally and in adherence to Catholic dogma is in [Hofmannsthal's] *Everyman* internalized and becomes a human reawakening.

Eugene Weber. In Edda Leisler and Gisela Prossnitz, eds.,
*Hugo von Hofmannsthals "Jedermann": Das Spiel vom
Sterben des reichen Mannes und Max Reinhardts Inszenierungen*
(Frankfurt, Fischer, 1973), p. 258

The comedy *The Difficult Man* probably represents Hofmannsthal's greatest literary achievement in the decade after the War. It deals with many of the problems with which we are familiar: nostalgia for Imperial society, the decay of language, the value of tradition. It weaves these themes into the fabric of a subtle and delightful comedy. The plot, which is minimal, depicts the erratic course of an Austrian count through the hazards of Viennese high society into the arms of the woman he loves. In time-honoured fashion love finds a way to overcome all obstacles and hesitations, and behind the eventual union of the lovers there is a delicate suggestion that their personal happiness in marriage has its due place in the proper social order. Hofmannsthal conceived the plan to write a comedy as early as 1917, impelled partly by a desire to perpetuate the memory of a society that was soon to vanish forever. His depiction of Viennese high society in *The Difficult Man* is poetically rather than historically true. Although the play is set in the winter of 1918–19, social life still flourishes, oblivious of food shortages, civil disturbances, the disintegration of the Empire, and the threat of revolution and invasion. Even the Austrian equivalent of the House of Lords continues to meet when in fact it had disappeared along with all the other Imperial institutions. The War has played a major role in the hero's personal development, but unlike the general tendency of *Heimkehrer* literature—works such as [Bertolt] Brecht's *Drums in the Night*, [Franz] Werfel's *Barbara; or, Piety* or [Joseph] Roth's *Hotel Savoy,* which deal with the situation of the returning soldier—the political and economic repercussions of the War are here ignored. The milieu presented to us is thus in one sense an idealised re-creation: nevertheless it remains instantly recognisable.

C. E. Williams. *The Broken Eagle: The Politics
of Austrian Literature from Empire to Anschluss*
(New York, Barnes and Noble, 1974), pp. 21–22

Yesterday, the first of Hofmannsthal's short lyric dramas, introduced the young writer's audience to a character type that was to continue to intrigue him until his death. Although shallow and passive, Andrea is one progenitor of a diverse series of players of the game of life. He lives "between game and feast," and devotes his time to bragging, playing, drinking, and laughing, to "what one does with men, when one is not fighting." Structured on a slight theme—of Andrea's discovery that Arlette, his girlfriend, was unfaithful to him the day before—*Yesterday* gives us little more than a brief glimpse of the game-players to come. In effect, Andrea is a weak grandfather to characters whose father is another, more powerful figure, the archetype of the life-game player, Casanova.

Hofmannsthal closely patterned the leading roles for two major dramas after material from Casanova's memoirs. One of the roles was that of Baron Weidenstamm, the mature man of the world of *The Adventurer and the Singer*. The other was Florindo, the young libertine of *Cristina's Trip Home*. (Florindo is also the protagonist of a fragmentary early version of that play, which was published independently in 1923 under the title *Florindo*.) In a letter of August 1908 to Count Harry Kessler, Hofmannsthal defined their relationships to Casanova when he asked: "Isn't Florindo just as nice a cover name for the young Casanova as Weidenstamm was for the old one?"

Several other Hofmannsthal figures also bear an unmistakable family resemblance to Casanova. Among the most obvious offspring are the Baron, from the fragmentary comedy *Sylvia in the Star*, and Jaromir, the playful young husband in *The Incorruptible Man*.

> Lowell A. Bangerter. *Hugo von Hofmannsthal* (New York,
> Frederick Ungar, 1977), pp. 63–64

Hans Karl—elegant, tactful, and genuine—is an unusual character to be the central figure in a comedy [*The Difficult Man*]. The literature of comic drama is full of difficult characters, oversensitive or discontented men . . . and unconventional women . . . , but such figures are in general presented as being in one way or another comically *wrong*. Hans Karl is to an unusual degree consistently *right*: in his mistrust of glibness and intellectual pretentiousness, his lack of both calculation and pushfulness, his sensitivity of perception, his protection of his privacy, and his weariness towards language—all the features that combine to form his characteristic "discretion." In comparison with other characters Hans Karl tends to be sympathetic: the inclination of the spectator . . . "is to regard with sympathy, perhaps in part to identify with, the main figure: Hans Karl's elegance and charm, his position and personal entanglements, his discretion and reticence." Precisely to the extent that the audience tends to identify itself with the attractiveness and sincerity of the central figure, the comic effect of the role is endangered. That the empathy of the audience militates against the full realization of a comic effect is one of the cruxes in the theory of comedy. . . .

Hofmannsthal himself was well aware of the practical problem he faced in *The Difficult Man* . . . and the implications for the performance of the piece have not escaped Hofmannsthal scholars. [Emil] Staiger even goes so far . . . as to state that it is impossible to find an actor to portray Hans Karl adequately, since there is nothing to "act"; what is needed, he argues, is for the actor to convince merely by "being," as the very nature of Hans Karl precludes the conventional conception of a theatrical "role."

W. E. Yates. *MAL.* 10, 1, 1977, pp. 12–13

KAISER, GEORG (1867–1945)

Who is the tragic hero [in *Gas*]? To be sure, the billionaire's son undergoes a catastrophic disillusionment, but, properly speaking, only the workers are tragic. As is the case with all of Kaiser's figures, the son is more a type than an individual, more a herald of ideas than a heroic agent, more a wise observer and a prophet than a champion who passionately fights for the things he proclaims. And the engineer, his protagonist, is likewise more an allegorical figure and a specter of materialism than a live materialist. But between the two opponents—between the poles of the coral and the gas—there fluctuate the people, trembling and crying out with the voices of mother, wife, son, and child in utterances full of art and artifice—yet nevertheless emotionally stirring. There is something magical about the power of words Georg Kaiser possesses. One senses the technical intelligence of the constructor, one perceives the theatrical skill in the arrangement of acts and scenes, which once again results in a brilliant symmetry; one sees the schematism of all the pawns in the strategic game of dramatic conflicts. And yet his pathos kindles our passions, the sound of his words evokes a mood appealing to the emotions, his very intellectuality stirs up longings in the heart. And thus we also find ourselves moved by these unrealistic, discoursing people; people who, in defiance of the "white terror" [the gas that kills], wield the scourge of slavery with their own hands, lashing out at themselves. . . .

The [play's] symbolism . . . elevates the current issues of the drama from their burning actuality to a profound timelessness, where nameless actors shroud their impersonal typicalness in chilly poetry. But even chilly poetry can be art. [Nov. 29, 1918]

Bernhard Diebold. In Günther Rühle, ed., *Theater für die Republik* (Frankfurt, Fischer, 1967), pp. 126–27†

Kaiser has been called a number of names at home and abroad. . . . The man may be, as [Alfred] Kerr . . . has said, half-Expressionist and half-bluffer, but he has written some things that, if as a whole they reveal the influence of Ibsen, Wedekind, and Sternheim, in turn will influence the younger generation.

Even Kaiser's "bluffs," if such they really are—for example *Europa,* a "play and dance" in five acts, or *Alkibiades Saved*—contain undoubted moments of beauty; and if no single play can be pointed to as an immaculate accomplishment, there is in the sum of his work a suggestion of a novel nuance in the contemporary drama. . . . If he is not always clear, one feels that he is actually expressing something and in his own way. Call him what you will, discover the origins of his work—and a varied, wavering line his labors trace—in whatever impulse you please, the man has intuitions of beauty in the drama. He is intense in spots, rather than complete; he is a playwright of fascinating fragments; in continuing and elaborating the "speed-technique" of Wedekind he has sacrificed the continuity to which we have long been accustomed. But not merely for the sake of covering more ground or in an impatient desire for an art of outbursts. Kaiser, in his more thorough-going pieces, seeks something of the expressional power of music. If not every word be grasped, not every idea linked to the remaining phrases in a chain of logic, little harm is done. These scenes, these people upon the stage before us are visions, emotions made visible. It is the succession of emotions, the surge of feeling, that counts.

Isaac Goldberg. The Drama of Transition (Cincinnati,
Kidd, 1922), pp. 303–4

Georg Kaiser is exclusively a dramatist of ideas, and a strenuous crusader for those ideas. But these intellectual qualities do not detract from his effectiveness or his dexterity as a dramatist; and therein he is revealed, not as a philosopher at all, but as a practical reformer in action. He perceives, with devastating clarity, the drama inherent in ideas, because ideas present themselves to him much more dramatically than ever the eternal puppet-play of life.

And in carrying out his instinctive dramatization of ideological values in the theater, Georg Kaiser has accomplished a particular goal which sets him in a place apart from his alleged school [Expressionism] and all his contemporaries. Although he is one of the first and most clever practitioners of the Expressionist dramaturgy, he has adopted an objective and scientific approach in the point where his contemporaries are most subjective and mystical. A dramatist entirely born and absorbed in his epoch, he has transposed the exact tempo of that epoch in his art. His is a mechanized universe, as cruel and stark as structural steel and as curt and matter-of-fact as the telegraph: a universe of intense compression, frigid economy, and complete materialism. Here even men have ceased to exist as individuals, but disclose themselves as abstractions symbolizing the types of their various social appearances. So, from allegory to allegory, Georg Kaiser arranges his symbolical figures and plots against the background of factory smokestacks, and, by the pure passion of his conviction, makes them live, beneath their masks, a tragedy as bitter and significant as that which Hamlet designed to accuse the guilty king.

> William A. Drake. *Contemporary European Writers*
> (New York, Day, 1928), pp. 96–97

Georg Kaiser is probably the greatest dramatic artist of our time writing in the German language. His arrangement of scenes, his dialogue, his skill in construction and development will be a pattern for many others, long after the idea-content of his plays has been exhausted. In almost two score dramas Kaiser has acquired a technique that functions as effortlessly as effectively, and often derives the highest measure of the dramatic from a minor motive. This procedure is, dramatically, highly instructive. . . .

And yet, it is never mere technique that sets Kaiser's subjects in motion . . . ; undoubtedly, Georg Kaiser is born of the spirit—he is not only spirited but also spiritual. His words are always striking (so are his titles), sparks sputter at the poles where sentence and sentence meet in dialogue, yet it is not only words' wit that makes his plays dramatic, but the antithesis of character, the wittiness of situation. And who, after *The Burghers of Calais*, after *From Morn to Midnight*, after *The Sacrifice of a Woman* and *The Fire in the Opera House* would doubt that Georg Kaiser is a poet with vision? Only, this poet is never lyric, but always dramatic.

> Victor Wittner. *ThA*. Oct., 1931, pp. 813–14

The Burghers of Calais, which can justly expect to become one of the world's classics, is based on Froissart's chronicle of the siege of Calais by the English King Edward III. . . .

The problem of the play is the voluntary assumption of ethical responsibility on the part of the individual, the affirmation of life, conceived as creative work. . . . With this principle in mind, military defense and the military code of honor are deprived of their ethical justification. . . . The work of peace, the harbor, must prevail against the futility of blood-shed. Amidst the general confusion, Eustache alone is certain of his purpose and he alone is unflinching in the transparent clarity of his conception of duty: "The deed is everything, the glory nothing."

This is the chief tenet of the New Man, the thought that vaguely struggles for recognition throughout all of Kaiser's social plays and which emerges triumphant in *The Burghers of Calais*. In this sense *Calais* becomes the crowning work of Kaiser's not only in regard to form and individual content, but also in regard to the entire stream of philosophic aim.

Moses Joseph Fruchter. *The Social Dialectic in Georg Kaiser's Dramatic Works* (Philadelphia, University of Pennsylvania, 1933), pp. 44–45

In the general tumult accompanying the conclusion of the war, there died, in exile in Switzerland, one of the most significant dramatists of our time— Georg Kaiser. . . .

Kaiser is considered one of the chief exponents of Expressionism . . . the best known example of which, in his repertoire, is *From Morn to Midnight,* the story of man's futile attempt at realizing his ideals, compressed into the events of a single day. The drama depicts such typical scenes of modern life as a sport palace, a cabaret, a bank, all symbolizing various human activities. Most of the characters are nameless abstractions or types—a bank cashier, a lady, a stout gentleman, a mask. No attempt is made to have us know his characters; their features "are apprehended in the same vivid, perfunctory way that a man in a desperate hurry at a crowded railway station, looking for somebody or something, takes in the faces of other travellers."

Kaiser's language is factual, concise, at times even brutal, his style laconic, staccato, emphasizing with telegraphic brevity the haste and tempo of the action. As in all his plays, he evinces a deep understanding of theatrical contrasts, stage effects, and dramatic tension. Always an eager student of the scenic and staging techniques of modern stage designers—particularly the stylists and constructionsts—he makes extensive use of such striking technical devices as the revolving stage, cyclorama, platforms, and masks.

Horst Frenz. *Poet Lore*. Winter, 1946, pp. 363–64

Georg Kaiser's production, viewed as a whole, shows an astounding compass and variety: it ranges from romantic—occasionally even lyrical—plays to carefully contrived dialectical pieces; from the satirical to the ecstatic; from comedy and revue to tragedy. Its material is drawn from such diverse sources as Greek legend, the Platonic Dialogues, the events of history, the problems of the modern industrial world and Kaiser's own fertile imagination. In the form of his drama there is such variety as to suggest that a resourceful talent was forever experimenting with new methods of expression, while the language, though it always retains its own distinctive note, catches the raciness of colloquial speech, argues and reasons with cool detachment or explodes in outbursts of emotion. Work follows upon work in a bewildering stream, and with a prolificness that can have few parallels; differing and often contradictory solutions are offered to the same problem, as the approach to it shifts. There appears to be no order, no underlying unity. . . .

Kaiser was the "Denkspieler" who made romantic love the theme of many of his plays; he was a social reformer who denied any wish to appear as a "benefactor of mankind," and at the same time a dreaming escapist with an uneasy social conscience: his Socrates, impelled by his reason to affirm the supreme value of life (and even to die in its defense), nevertheless "parted from life as from a long sickness."

B. J. Kenworthy. *Georg Kaiser* (Oxford,
Basil Blackwell, 1957), pp. 197–98

In most of Kaiser's plays, the call for regeneration falls on deaf ears, and the prophet is doomed to pay with his life. In one instance only does his appeal succeed in transforming society—in *Hell Road Earth*. Both in form and in content, this play can be said to present the quintessence of Expressionism. The three words of the title correspond to its three parts, each representing a stage in social and moral evolution. "Hell" stands for the present state of society, with its rigid laws based on exploitation and selfishness; "Road" depicts the awakening to a sense of moral responsibility, while "Earth" denotes the ultimate goal—the full realization of the ideal. This general evolution is set in motion by an individual case. . . . From an isolated case, the plot develops into a matter concerning each and all. The collective guilt of society is established, and everybody confesses to his share in it. . . . In the end, the ecstatic call of the prophet echoes across the sunlit plain: "The earth resounds! Your blood surges—for you are the earth!"

This drama reveals more clearly than any other the close affinity existing between the expressionist idea of spiritual rebirth and Christian concepts. It is, in essence, a morality play, restated in terms of a modern and highly intellectual mind.

Hugh F. Garten. *Modern German Drama* (London,
Methuen, 1959), pp. 158–59

The kinship between Wedekind, Sternheim, and Kaiser lies in their tendency to unmask "the essence" of social reality not by naturalistic imitation, which would still lull us in illusions, but by crass and shocking formulations. Their drama seeks to demonstrate in pure and, therefore, abstract and distorted conditions (in the experimental laboratory, as it were) the true nature of existential or social problems. . . . In his *Burghers of Calais,* probably his greatest work, Kaiser demonstrates by two highly dramatic surprise effects the true nature of heroism as pacifism and self-sacrifice. In his *Alkibiades Saved* he demonstrates by a highly ironic tour de force the true nature of the intellect as both a wound and a heroic fraud. Here the trick, Kaiser's basic dramatic form, merges with the dramatic content and idea. . . .

Nietzsche saw the historical Socrates as the initiator of Greek decadence and the pioneer of the Christian "slave revolt"; Kaiser sees in Socrates the fateful innovator who ends the age of naïve self-assurance and ushers in a self-conscious, i.e., guilt-ridden, civilization. The mind replaces the muscles. Reflection drives out spontaneity. The cripple wins out over the athlete. But Socrates' revolutionary philosophy does not result from the cripple's resentment of the strong and healthy; it results from his compassion for them. Although it was necessary, Socrates regrets his victory: "I had to invent what should have remained uninvented!!—I had to blanket the sky— and wither the earth—!!" He takes Alkibiades' guilt for overturning the sacred hermae upon himself and suffers the death penalty in his stead.

Kaiser-Socrates' intellectualism reveals itself as a protective barrier against nihilism. . . . Chilling and subversive as these new values of abstract intellect may be, they still serve as a screen between man and the devastating insight into the absurdity of the universe and human existence.

Walter H. Sokel. *The Writer in Extremis* (Stanford, Cal., Stanford University Press, 1959), pp. 108–9

[In *Gas*] Kaiser has taken several steps beyond the simple protests at the misery of underpaid workers, uninteresting factory jobs, and slums, consequent on the industrial revolution. These were familiar to the later nineteenth century, both in literature and sociological writing. In drama the humanitarian protest at social misery is well seen in Hauptmann's *The Weavers*. Kaiser's protest is not against misery of that kind, held in abhorrence as an affront to human beings. His socialized world has removed those things. He protests against the loss of human status. The shrill nostalgia of the Billionaire's son for "den Menschen" would not be so excessive if it were a case simply of suffering, for that brings human qualities and virtues into play. He fights his battle against men who have lost the knowledge of what man is. They are morally destitute because the private world is gone. A wholly public world engulfs the human one. Every person is chained to a function in a closely articulated mechanism; and when human creatures exist as no more than a function within a whole, the whole itself is not human. . . .

Here one might seek an embryonic model of what we since have called the totalitarian society. . . . The pessimism is strong; and with reason, when the end of the individual and his moral independence is involved.

Ronald Peacock. *TDR*. March, 1959, pp. 64–65

The Solider Tanaka . . . was to become one of the most imposing manifestations of Kaiser's humanistic idea of life. Here his faith in man as a human being is expressed even more powerfully than in *The Leatherheads*, for now he could forgo the gruesomeness and all the extravagances resulting from the subject matter; instead, he could fill the stage with a life that in its rudimentary simplicity remains within everybody's grasp, even though he takes us to the exotic setting of the Orient. To be sure . . . the principle of dictatorship, hostile to life, on which judgment is passed remains in the background throughout; one sees only the dark shadow it casts upon the life of the common man. The tragedy of the Japanese peasant's son Tanaka arises from the tension between his personal way of life and the "system." This means: he is not a "character" who develops. What happens is that only his understanding of the situation grows. . . .

In the course of the play, Tanaka's insight increases by leaps and bounds until it reaches the point where it must lead to action, even if his act appears to be almost utterly senseless. . . . When Tanaka is tried for insubordination—in view of this charge, the murder of his sister is of no great importance—he seems for a moment to hold his fate in his own hands, as only a hero of Schiller's would: if he asks the emperor's forgiveness, he shall be free; for then the disturbed order would be restored again. But what may appear here as freedom of choice is, after all, only an illusion, a hallucination; for Tanaka is irrevocably bound to his humanity and therefore in no position whatsoever to make a choice. A Tanaka who would have even the merest potentiality of saving himself by such an act of self-degradation would no longer be Tanaka, and his drama could not possibly have come to pass at all. For the sake of his awareness and his act, he has to accept death—indeed, he must provoke it, which does not mean, however, that his attitude is in any way tantamount to suicide.

Wolfgang Paulsen. Georg Kaiser (Tübingen,
Niemeyer, 1960), pp. 76–77†

Georg Kaiser's *From Morn to Midnight* exemplifies the staccato style, the extensive use of stream-of-consciousness monologue, the episodic structure of stations, characters throughout without personal names, and dramatization of the consciousness of the principal character in response to an initial external situation. The entire play is a symbolic presentation of abstract ideas. The protagonist is a bank cashier, in the opening scene in his cage imprisoned in a colorless life of routine. A glamorous Lady enters and by misleading circumstances is taken to be an adventuress. Stirred by her perfume and the touch of her hand in a transaction through his window, the Cashier seizes an opportunity and absconds with a large sum of money. . . . By his action he has burned his bridges. He is free, life before him. . . . [But] the only verity found is the awareness by the individual of his own isolated existence, the end of which is death. . . .

From an abstract representative of a social class, critical of an economic system which dehumanizes the individual, the Cashier has developed into the symbol of Man whose idealism is denied by the reality of experience. . . . The pessimism of the play is relieved only by a kind of exultation in the stripping away of all illusions in the staccato rhythm of the Cashier's final speech.

Kaiser's drama represents not only many of the forms but a spirit that was prominent in German expressionism. Concentration on the realities of inner experience is not necessarily a denial of or a protest against the external world, but it nevertheless is true that one of the possible effects of finding the world in which one lives extremely unsatisfactory is introversion. The Germany of the years following World War I . . . was fertile ground for the subjectivity of expressionism, with pessimism as one natural direction. Kaiser's idealistic pessimism of the conflict between human aspiration and the facts of experience was one of the dramatically more productive reactions because a binding tension was maintained between the two worlds of the mind and material reality. That Kaiser's plays are distinguished by a clarity of dramatic form is compatible with, and probably in part a result of the balance of that tension.

> Kenneth Thorpe Rowe. *A Theater in Your Head*
> (New York, Funk & Wagnalls, 1960), pp. 207, 209

Kaiser's dramatic figures lack the realness, let us say, of Hauptmann's characters, but exist all the more intensely as *moral* beings. And although Kaiser never speaks directly through his figures, and they seem to lose themselves within the issues confronting them, still they can be understood only in terms of the circumstances and ideas which also preoccupied their creator. In a unique and curious way Kaiser lived in his work as his work lived in him; the fact and fiction of his life, the clash between truth and the lie in almost every play, mingle in a fashion that challenges the most careful interpretation. . . .

It is difficult to define Kaiser's actual status at the moment. Everyone now knows he is not among the very first-rate, but not everyone agrees on the rank he belongs to below that. Perhaps that place will be found before long; the critics and scholars are already alerted, the historians are sure to rediscover him soon. Meanwhile, I predict that the theater, for which he had an instinct as great as that of any other modern German dramatist, not even excluding Brecht, will someday come to rely on him as a regular source of supply, and that the public, when it is no longer nagged for neglecting a great master, will find him as stimulating and provocative as did the audiences of two or three decades ago.

> Leroy R. Shaw. *TSLL*. Autumn, 1961, pp. 401–2, 407–8

Georg Kaiser's work is often treated as the reflection of its author's unusual personality. Such a treatment, though valid, tends to obscure the fact that his writings, in their probing of existing values, their manifestation of *Lebensangst,* their quest for regeneration, and their hope for redemption, also reflect the intellectual and spiritual concerns of his period. That his visions were not, as has been often held, the fantasies of an extreme subjectivist, but that they accurately mirrored the age, is demonstrated by the fact that representative thinkers of the period, such as Bergson, Vaihinger, and Jaspers, voiced similar concerns, arrived at similar conclusions, sought similar solutions. There seems to exist a particularly strong affinity between the ideas of Walther Rathenau and those presented in Kaiser's social tetralogy *(The Coral,* 1917; *Gas,* 1918; *Hell Road Earth,* 1919; *Gas,* Second Part, 1920), which was written at a time when the impact of Rathenau's works . . . on the intellectual life of Germany was very strong. . . .

Rathenau sees the evolution of mankind in three stages: (1) the world of the instinct; (2) the only slightly more advanced world of the rational intellect; and (3), antithetical to the first two, the realm of the soul. . . .

We shall see that (1) the world of industrial civilization as it appears in Kaiser's social tetralogy resembles Rathenau's worlds of the instinct and of the rational intellect; (2) the new realm proclaimed by the billionaire worker in *Gas II* suggests Rathenau's realm of the soul; and (3) the evolution of human society presented in the *Gas* trilogy follows the pattern of Rathenau's evolutionary ideas.

The plays of the tetralogy unfold against the background of what Rathenau has described, and condemned, as the world of mechanization. The question how the individual can escape the physical and spiritual threat posed by this world is the principal theme of the *Gas* trilogy. A different approach is explored in each of its three plays: the billionaire of *The Coral* seeks to assure his salvation by waging a primitive struggle for the survival of the fittest and, after this fails, flees into a fictitious world of his own creation; his son, in the slightly more advanced world of *Gas,* attempts to save mankind through social reform; the billionaire worker in *Gas II,* finally, calls for a spiritual rebirth independent of external conditions.

Robert Kauf. *PMLA.* June, 1962, pp. 311-12

During the period 1903–1919 Kaiser's outlook lay rooted in the Nietzschean notion of dionysiac being, with many of the plays of the period dealing with the motif *Geist Leben* in the Nietzschean sense of healthy instinct versus dialectical rationality, and having other Nietzschean features as well. In the later period, Kaiser eulogized spiritual love, but even this concept was predicated on the continued existence of the world of instinct. Throughout the later period, Kaiser's idealism seemed insecure, floating like a cockle-shell on an ocean of nihilism. After World War One Kaiser liked to conceive of himself as a tragic superman, waging singlehanded the battle for humanity and practicing the master morality. All of his later protagonists are dedicated and ruthless supermen. . . .

Whether Kaiser is to be considered a Nietzschean is a matter of definition. Certainly Nietzsche in no way detracted from his originality. On the other hand, Nietzsche very definitely influenced his thinking, choice of motifs, characterization, and perhaps even the tone of his dramas and essays.

Kaiser's relationship to Nietzsche is strikingly similar to that of other eminent German writers at the turn of the century who found themselves in a terrifying world deprived of absolute standards and ideals by means of which they might chart a meaningful course through life. . . . The basic dichotomy, *Geist* versus *Leben,* which in essence concerned him from first to last, may freely be rendered as the idealist Georg Kaiser striving to cope with Nietzschean nihilism.

Herbert W. Reichert. SP. Jan., 1964, pp. 91, 107

Kaiser's chief preoccupation [in *The Burghers of Calais*] is how to express an eternal truth—the idea—in terms acceptable to the sublunar world of change and relative values. Theoretically he proposes Man as mediator: "The idea has the categorical impetus to present itself: for that which does not become perceptible does not exist!—The idea to its revelation through man. Man becomes its creator by giving it shape—since ultimate clarity can be achieved by form alone." Practically, the difficulties are almost insuperable. That he has been successful in *The Burghers of Calais* is in no small measure due to his recognition of the skill with which Rodin concentrates in his statue the diversity of constituents of the situation into a single total, frozen gesture which is at one and the same time static and dynamic, in which the idea has become object. Here is the strongest link between Rodin and Kaiser. *The Burghers of Calais* is constructed around not one but a series of such climactic points, where a figure—Man—pauses instantaneously on the brink of action in a statuesque pose after the manner of Rodin, to fuse the world of *Werden* [becoming] and compromise with the immutable idea of *Sein* [being]. The figure himself may not always be aware of his agency, but it transmits itself through him to the reader or audience with considerable power and conviction.

R. W. Last. Seminar. Spring, 1969, pp. 43–44

Twice Amphitryon is the first of his three so-called Greek dramas, the other two being *Pygmalion* and *Bellerophon*. In these plays, Kaiser not only reverted to classical themes, but also to the traditional five-act structure and to the blank-verse form. Stylistically, the retreat of the Expressionist had ended in the safe haven of traditional forms, but Kaiser's message remains the same: the play, inspired by Molière and Kleist, is his final protest against militarism. . . .

In *Twice Amphitryon,* some of Kaiser's main themes are intertwined: first, his protest against war; second, the salvation of the world by a pure woman; and third, the promised birth of a child as the future redeemer. The curse of war destroys all that is good in man; it can only be overcome if love, as exemplified by Alkmene, rules the world. And a new world can only be created by individuals; therefore it must be started by a single man, the child.

Ernst Schürer. *Georg Kaiser* (New York, Twayne,
1971), pp. 170–71

To identify Kaiser with the Billionaire's Son [in *Gas*] is almost like identifying Goethe with Werther. Certain reservations must be made in both cases. But there is a profound and fundamental difference between these two kinds of camouflaged "confessions." The difference between Goethe's empathy and Kaiser's intellectual manipulation of figures is the difference between a romantic portrait and an abstract composition. To commit a value judgment only in favor of one or the other is to overlook the fact that they both crystallize and embody the spirit and style of two different eras. Perhaps here lie both the strength and the weaknesses—and the modernity—of much of Kaiser's work. His figures speak "a language never heard in actual life and yet remarkably expressive of the alienation, confusion, and hysteria characteristic of modern life" ([Walter] Sokel). They are types and symbols, familiar in nonrepresentational art. His settings are often designed as geometrical patterns; the severe structural symmetry of the best plays has its correlative in cubism and dodecaphonic music. One is tempted to press the analogy a bit further and suggest that the structure and the technique and the tone of such dramas is the content; the play of thoughts is more important than the thoughts themselves. . . .

And perhaps it is time . . . to name those words which *sub specie aeternitatis* may some day be called Kaiser's best plays. Accepting as axiomatic that they are constructed with great skill and cast into a language that is apposite to their thesis, and acknowledging that the characters are "figures" all presuppositions of the absolute play—we might posit one supplementary criterion, namely that they have as theatre (no longer now as texts to be studied) a significant impact and at the same time a relevance which is not just of the moment. Accordingly we suggest four plays, plays that fulfill all of the suppositions and the final criterion: *The Burghers of Calais, From Morn to Midnight, Gas,* and *Gas II.* Kaiser's progress was not all a "descent" from these Expressionist heights; we would add two more plays . . . : *The Leatherheads* and *The Soldier Tanaka.*

Karl S. Weimar. In Karl S. Weimar, ed., *Views and
Reviews of Modern German Literature* (Munich,
Delp, 1974), pp. 227–28

Since its premiere in 1917, Georg Kaiser's *The Burghers of Calais* has attracted much critical attention. The rhetorically stylized language, the rigid symmetrical pattern that informs the work, and the impressive manner in which the doctrine of the New Man is presented distinguish it from the majority of plays written during the Expressionist years. . . .

Despite its stylistic, thematic, and structural consistency, there are some rather serious questions about the drama that have seemed to many critics paradoxically unanswerable; at least no one answer seems completely satisfactory. Foremost among these is the problem of how one is to explain the curiously anticlimactic ending of the drama which somehow leaves the uncomfortable feeling that all efforts toward idealistic goals in life—that is, in life as portrayed in the drama—are in vain. . . .

To interpret the ending of *The Burghers of Calais* as optimistic is, in my opinion, naïve, especially in the face of the constant mood of scepticism, distrust, and disbelief that pervades the drama. There is, however, a strongly consoling feature about it. For Eustache there was no other way of preserving the ideal than by taking his life to assure that the sacrifice would be carried out in an appropriate fashion. In so doing, he endowed the incident with a deeper significance that removed it from the chance contingencies of pragmatic existence and elevated it to a level of an act of absolute commitment. In other words, according to Kaiser's logic: an ideal that resides in the realm of the absolute requires an absolute commitment on the part of the protagonist representing it. Eustache complied with the exigency of this compelling logic. The sentiment regarding the ideal and its practicality—within the context of human frailty and shortcomings that the end of the drama manifests—is akin to that expressed in the outcry of the Milliardärarbeiter [Billionaire Worker] in *Gas II:* ". . . Nicht von dieser Welt ist das Reich!!!!" [The kingdom is not of this world].

George C. Tunstall. *JEGP*. April, 1979, pp. 178, 192

It may not be an overstatement to conclude that the ingeniously developed varieties of isolation in *From Morn to Midnight* provide most of the essential source material for true tragicomedy. However often comic and entertaining instances may seem to outweigh the existential seriousness of the situation, we must nevertheless concur with [Georg] Lukács who implies that the overall effect of the play is primarily and hopelessly tragic, for it reveals "the petit-bourgeois helplessness and forlornness in the machinery of capitalism, the impotent revolt of the petit-bourgeois against being worn down and crushed by capitalism." . . .

In the final analysis, then, Kaiser's early play is a successful experiment in applied literary sociology. Its contribution to the development of modern drama lies in its artistic method: exclusive focus on the plight of a central character isolated in extreme solipsism enables the playwright to portray symbolically the fundamental antagonism between the individual and objective reality. Kaiser's preoccupation in *From Morn to Midnight* with the

Expressionist dramatic strategy of isolation and abstraction yields forever timely social criticism in the guise of a memorable theatrical spectacle.

Steven P. Scher. In Edward R. Haymes, ed., *Theatrum Mundi: Essays on German Drama and German Literature,* Houston German Studies 2 (Munich, Fink, 1980), p. 133

SCHNITZLER, ARTHUR (1862–1931)

The seven scenes of *Anatol* are just that—seven scenes. Although they are held together by the same atmosphere, it would be foolish and inflexible to approach the work as an organic whole. The scenes float together as if nimble chance created them; and it is only in retrospect that a rounding off, a completion, may possibly give the impression of systematic planning. In the center, a frivolous melancholiac; behind him, alongside him, in front of him, women. Only this one side of life is considered, and then merely in some of its aspects. But the way it is done is unforgettable. I know that many talented people—and not the most inferior among us—view this form of art with hesitancy, even with a shrug of the shoulders; I sensed how reluctantly and half-skeptically they applauded even the most mature work of this young master. They harbor a disdain for such a transparent, gently woven, fleeting, vanishing poetry of episodes.

But even though Schnitzler does not give weighty emphasis to things, nor present himself as a Promethean, his little scenes from life do offer food for thought. Moreover, he preserves from the constantly changing flow of life here an ironic, there a pensive portrait of the soul, such as only the hand of a true poet can snatch from the flux of time. . . . More powerful writers among the moderns have no idea of the particular nature of Schnitzler's charm and of his special graceful sensitivity. What nobody can acquire by force of will, he was given in his sleep. To be sure, there are more profound writers, but they cannot do what he does. [March 1, 1896]

Alfred Kerr. *Gesammelte Schriften* (Berlin, Fischer, 1917), Series 1, Vol. I, *Das neue Drama,* pp. 121–22†

Both your drama [*The Vast Domain*] and your letter have deeply moved me. The letter, because it was so cordial . . . the drama, because it appears to me as the work of a master, fully mature.

The characters are depicted as true individuals, round and full and original, with features and idiosyncrasies that constitute a world of their own. The subordinate characters, such as Natter, or the amusingly caricatured, such as Rhon and Serknitz, are no less memorable than the thoughtfully studied and enigmatic ones, such as Friedrich, Genia, and the one *whole* person, Erna. Nothing I could write would add to the impression the play produces, nor would it further explain anything, for all that takes place is self-explanatory.

You like to pursue the incidental drives and passions, the capers and escapades of the emotional life, and to enlarge on every offshoot that diverges from the main stock. The world, viewed in this manner, becomes mournful in a special way. I feel that to complete the picture, you should take into account the uplifting element, that which makes life bearable, something we encounter now and then—although very seldom, indeed. . . . It must be possible, for instance, for a person to trust someone; but in the world you present, a very opulent and glittering world, there is no room whatsoever for trust; all are bent on extricating themselves from their ties and inclinations. [Oct. 19, 1911]

> Georg Brandes. In Kurt Bergel, ed., *Georg Brandes und*
> *Arthur Schnitzler: Ein Briefwechsel* (Bern, Francke,
> 1956), pp. 102–3†

Arthur Schnitzler is a German classic. I know no other living German author for whom this claim could be made with equal assurance. The distinguishing feature of his works is the masterly manner in which they are executed. No one else deserves the name of master more than he does. Although his first works enjoyed the greatest initial success, they have nevertheless been utterly underestimated for twenty years. The absence of all conceit, of all affectation, of all false pathos, and of all mannerism made him appear to the servants of naturalism as an uncanny guest on Parnassus. As matters stand now, there is not a single line of Schnitzler's lifework of twenty-five years that has grown stale or has become obsolete. On the contrary, only very recently have his earliest works captivated the general public because of their artistic maturity. It is just that Schnitzler's beginnings coincided with a period in literature when even the slightest appreciation for the very best works written at the time was absent. . . . Now that the literary counterfeiting of those days has been exposed and done away with, Arthur Schnitzler stands out as the poet who, during the past twenty years, has given German literature the greatest number of consummate works. [1912]

> Frank Wedekind. *Prosa* (East Berlin, Aufbau,
> 1969), p. 254†

Love and Intrigue, the title of Schiller's famous play, might well be the rubric under which to group the dramas of the Viennese physician, Arthur Schnitzler. For all of his pieces—except the recent *Professor Bernhardi*— are concerned, in one form or another, with amorous intrigue. At his best, as in *Anatol* and *Light-o'-Love,* Schnitzler bathes his intrigue in the atmosphere of romance; and always, even where the action is stirring enough, as in *The Green Cockatoo,* it is touched with the cynical melancholy of the man of the world. . . .

Whenever, as is chiefly the case in *Anatol,* both parties to such an arrangement [philandering] are the children of wisdom, there results no more than a comedy of sentiment. For neither expects of the other enduring fidelity. In *Light-o'-Love,* however, the tragedy arises from the fact that Christine, the heroine, is different in temper from these other philanderers. Humble though she be, she cannot play the love-game so lightly.

Of Schnitzler's skill as a dramatic impressionist enough can scarcely be said. He reveals in few words whole chapters of experience. Thus, in *Light-o'-Love,* the irate husband speaks but a dozen lines, and the impending duel is but hinted at, yet the story seems complete. So, too, Christine's father, the old violinist, stands revealed as a definite character in two or three speeches. He who has suffered remorse at having kept his sister too strictly has purposely relaxed his watchfulness over his daughter, but only to further her ruin. Still another witness to the dramatist's power of compression and suggestion may be found, here and elsewhere, in the way he concludes his scenes. At such times his touch is the softest—a fleeting caress; and always he relies for effect as much upon facial expression and gesture as dialogue. . . . Schnitzler is an Austrian Sterne of the stage and the twentieth century. [1914]

Frank Wadleigh Chandler. *Aspects of Modern Drama*
(New York, Macmillan, 1918), pp. 279, 286–87

Arthur Schnitzler's warm and exquisite talent has one quality that is rare in Germany: gracefulness. It is, however, a German gracefulness, not a French one. His characters and his theater are as unobtrusive as possible. If the colorful charms and great beauty of his works are to be made an integral part of German culture, this writer, who strikes one as a little pallid, will have to be frequently reevaluated. To possess an understanding of Schnitzler is to possess culture, and to be attracted by Schnitzler is to be drawn to culture. Schnitzler's plays should be performed more often than they are.

Gerhart Hauptmann. *NRs.* 1922, p. 504†

Schnitzler's plays are, of course, as much a product of Vienna's theatrical life as they are a part of it. . . . It was during the period between 1860 and 1890, just at the time of Schnitzler's youth . . . that the conversation piece enjoyed its highest vogue at the Burgtheater . . . those French comedies of manners by Dumas *fils,* Sardou, as well as Augier and Scribe—the same plays that had also exercised such a decisive influence on Ibsen's earliest dramatic technique. . . . A continuing effect of this atmosphere of the Parisian theater can perhaps be seen in Schnitzler's fondness for making the problem of marriage, or actually that of adultery, the central subject of his longer plays.

The other principal motif of his theatrical production, however, is Viennese and unmistakably reflects that passionate partiality for theater that for a hundred and fifty or two hundred years was shared by all social classes in Vienna, from the prince down to the cabbie; in this realm of theater they all understood each other. I am speaking here of "theater" in a symbolic sense, referring to that "theater" in which all the living participate by mutually exposing themselves to each other's view, the comedy of words, gestures, and social intercourse, the insignificant and the great scenes that people perform before each other in love affairs as well as in the drawing room or in politics. . . . From all this Schnitzler assembled, through the most ingenious combinations and permutations, the motor for his longer and shorter plays; and here, in the very construction as well as in the propulsion of these small but very subtle machines, he showed himself to be more of an artist, more ingenious and sagacious, than most of the German playwrights of the last hundred years. [1922]

> Hugo von Hofmannsthal. *Gesammelte Werke in Einzelausgaben: Aufzeichnungen* (Frankfurt, Fischer, 1959), pp. 269–71†

Schnitzler does not make his characters morally responsible for their conduct; this fact finds abundant corroboration in his dramatic works. . . . The actions of his characters are, quite generally, the result of causes beyond their control. . . .

It cannot be denied that Schnitzler in his writings reveals a philosophy that is above all else that of the determinist. What his characters are and what they do depends fundamentally upon what has preceded and under what conditions they exist. Natural instincts and pathological tendencies, converging at times with fatal external influences, deprive them almost entirely of any freedom of the will. . . .

But very few of Schnitzler's characters are irredeemably perverted through their natural instincts alone. This Austrian dramatist, who is primarily occupied with the moral and emotional nature of man, has not excluded accident and chance from the chain of cause and effect. But the external, actuating forces in his works are almost invariably of a harmful nature and serve only to arouse the latent impulses and tendencies which cause the moral ruin. . . . The innate instincts and passions and the fatalistic attitude towards life before which their saner reasoning succumbs might not have assumed control had not destiny determined otherwise, for accidental circumstance and the disastrous influence of the "milieu" often prove to be the causes which arouse the latent tendencies in Schnitzler's characters and make them the mainspring of action. At such times we perceive what a weak and ineffectual thing the human will apparently is. And from Schnitzler's revelations of the inner conflicts in man, when nature contends with reason, we see how easily man's will-power is dethroned. . . .

Man is at best the creature of destiny, and rarely is it permitted him to shape his own lot in life. He may be deluded into believing that the will is able to conquer at all times, under all circumstances. The freedom of the will is a delusion, however, contrasted with the more potent influences of environment, epoch, and heredity, and particularly is the power of choice a delusion when social conventions are brought to bear upon the individual.

Selma Koehler. *JEGP*. July, 1923, pp. 408–10

That Schnitzler's highly interesting play *The Call of Life* is one of its author's earlier efforts is revealed by something more than that unnatural heightening of its colors which betrays the exuberance of an undisciplined imagination. Its very theme—the brevity of life and the sin of wasting one of its fleeting moments—is a theme which youth would choose. . . . The Schnitzler who wrote *The Call of Life* had not yet arrived at the conviction, so plainly expressed in his later plays, that existence is a game played against an antagonist who always wins and whose name is Boredom; rather was he one who did not as yet know life well enough to picture it in a manner wholly convincing but who, perhaps because of that imperfect knowledge, was able to express his passionate conviction that the bitterest of all thoughts is the thought that one may be deprived of the opportunity of knowing it. . . .

The author has nowhere actually thought his way through, and his sincerity is not of a predominantly intellectual sort. Because his conviction that the call of life is higher than the call of duty is not the reasoned conclusion of a Nietzschean philosopher but the instinctive protest of ardent youth against all that stands between him and his imperious need for experience, he is capable even of a relenting conclusion which pays the tribute of a perfunctory bow to conventional ideals of remorse and atonement; but for the same reason even his theatricalities are touched with poetic passion.

Joseph Wood Krutch. *Nation*. Oct. 28, 1925, pp. 494–95

The complicated web of human relationships, the subtle interplay of illusion and reality, which so often motivate man's actions and motions, this is the field of Schnitzler's research. He ventures to lift that thin veil covering a man's inner consciousness, to peer into the depth, to press those sensitive and often painful spots on the human heart where old wounds have scarcely healed. And from these fine-spun threads of knowledge he weaves his wistful, humorous and tragic stories. Moreover, he scarcely ever achieves his effects by harsh and glaring methods or bold and heavily-drawn outlines. His concert of human emotion sounds rather [more] like intimate and finely-played chamber music than the profoundly moving themes of a Beethoven symphony. One can listen to him with a smile on one's lips and an aching heart. The depth and subtlety of his psychological insight are such, that the unattuned ear would miss the softer tones that form as it were an undercurrent to his main theme; nor would a casual observer distinguish the finer shades of his meaning or the many suggestions scattered between the lines. His character analysis is not cold and logical as in Strindberg, nor does he discourse upon current social, ethical and moral problems in brilliant, confusing and interminable dialectics like Bernard Shaw. Schnitzler's method is less obvious, though dramatically more effective. He often takes a quite simple, even casual story; his characters are for the most part ordinary people whom one is likely to meet in daily life any moment of the day. His situations and his plots seem common enough, and yet out of this apparently unpretentious material Schnitzler succeeds in fashioning dramas which are charged with a profound and tragic meaning. He touches the most secret chords in the human soul and draws forth intensely moving melodies from the most unexpected places. The classic example of Schnitzler's art in this respect is *Light-o'-Love*.

The German stage may have produced more profound and powerful plays than this straightforward beautifully written piece, but never has there appeared anything more moving and human in the field of the drama since Goethe's *Egmont*.

I. George March. *Poet Lore*. Dec., 1928, pp. 575–76

Bernhardi's stand is emphasized by the author throughout the fourth and fifth acts of the drama [*Professor Bernhardi*]. Even after public opinion has veered in favor of the unjustly imprisoned physician, and even when upon the expiration of his sentence, he can successfully effect a revision of the judicial error, he still refuses to lift a finger in his own behalf. He refuses to be made the plaything of politicians. He is first and foremost a scientist. His profession is to cure people. Schnitzler holds this calling to be more productive of human happiness than the calling of the politician. In a final scene between Bernhardi and the Minister of Education, whom the physician visits in order to regain his forfeited medical license, Schnitzler arranges a juxtaposition of the two types: the scientist who fearlessly pursues the path of his honest convictions, and the man of public affairs who must constantly alter his views to conform with changing political constellations.

Bernhardi's stand resembles that of old Dr. Stauber, in [the novel] *The Road to the Open*. When the latter's son Berthold, outraged at unfair anti-Semitic attacks, gives up his political career in order to resume his study of bacteriology, the father heartily endorses the young man's decision. When Berthold, however, a year later accepts a nomination to the Austrian Parliament and thereby again turns his back upon medicine, his father wisely points out the futility of engaging in such activity. One cannot serve two masters. If the choice lies between science and politics, the older physician insists that it is absurd to give up the positive task of healing for the doubtful privilege of haranguing people whose minds are mostly made up in advance, or of combatting opponents who generally do not themselves believe the tenets they pretend to defend. Especially is it absurd for a Jew to interfere in his country's political squabbles. In the field of science even a Jew may hope to earn his laurels and to contribute to human welfare. In the field of politics, however, he will be made to feel at every turn that he is an unwelcome stranger, though his ancestors may have sojourned in the land close to two thousand years.

In Professor Bernhardi, Schnitzler gives profound utterance to his views on the place of the Jew in modern life. The Jewish question troubled him throughout many years. It subjected him to several unpleasant, and even dangerous, experiences. He was, no less than his hero, Bernhardi, the target for anti-Semitic attacks. Once, while on a visit to Prague, he barely escaped physical injury at the hands of "Jew-baiting" youths. To this day his name is anathema to certain sections of the central European population. Nevertheless, in his literary treatment of the Jewish question, he managed to retain his wonted philosophic calm. He pleaded the cause of no single party. He advocated no royal road to salvation. He merely brought to bear upon a very complex question the light of a kind and critical temperament. His views on the Jew in contemporary life, expressed in *The Road to the Open*, in *Professor Bernhardi*, and in *The Walk to the Pond*, are pregnant with wisdom and are well worth careful study.

Sol Liptzin. Arthur Schnitzler (New York,
Prentice-Hall, 1932), pp. 192–95

The human soul was to Schnitzler a "vast domain," which descriptive phrase he uses as the title of one of his most subtle tragic plays. He explored what was then so uncharted a land, presenting his discoveries often with melancholy and always without illusion, frankly yet tenderly, but above all seeking to find the basic motives which cause the individual to behave and suffer as he does. In other words, Schnitzler brought into modern drama the *psychological* play as Ibsen and Hauptmann created the *social* play. Like Wedekind, Schnitzler believed that the single most compelling force in the life of the individual is that of sex, so dominating him that its ecstasy and happiness are but slight compared with its pain and disillusionment. But where Wedekind savagely attacks society for allowing sex to continue as a socially destructive force, Schnitzler is absorbed in the psychological effects on individuals of their usually tragic and rarely satisfying sex experiences. . . .

The Lonely Way, perhaps his most finely wrought and most poignant play, portrays with mellow understanding and pity the ultimate tragic isolation of the individual. Here the experience of every character reveals how, in all our griefs and frustrations, in the various deaths we die, including the last and final one, we are fearfully and unreachably alone. Not even the seeming complete union of sex, the seeming complete fusion of love, can save the individual, doomed by the inner laws of his own ego, from having to meet the struggles and the shocks of life in this ultimate isolation. Whoever does not know the Schnitzler of [*The Lonely Way, Living Hours, Light-o'-Love*] is missing precious contact with the modern dramatist whose warm, tolerant understanding and insight were expressed in the most deeply felt and illuminating psychological plays before those of Eugene O'Neill.

Anita Block. *The Changing World in Plays and Theatre* (Boston,
Little, Brown, 1939), pp. 64–65

Arthur Schnitzler was both a lover and a critic of his feudal bohemia. As a member of the upper middle class, Schnitzler partook of its feasts. But as a Jew he was never permitted unreserved entry. This "distance" made possible a greater objective evaluation and analysis. Thus viewing his Vienna from the outside, he was able to reveal the scepticism and irony beneath the surface laughter. As the whole structure stood under the aegis of death, so does death hover over his characters. Their central passion is to live, but it is not the will to live on the part of youth, which has not as yet found its objective, but that of senility, which has already passed beyond it. Into the "call of life" mingles the summons of death. It is their final hour, and they would let laughter and the "sighs of wild lust" reign. They would crowd every excitement into their dance of death, telescoping eternity into a single moment, knowing that beyond it there is nothingness. Their sex yearning is a desperate attempt to overcome their apartness. And as each sex act is followed by greater loneliness (for they never surrender to each other), they whip themselves into madder sex whirls, sink into the "luscious, tangled skein of intoxicated bodies." The sex act of Schnitzler's characters, as in *Hands Around,* is a way of obliterating consciousness, a death act, not a means of creating life. Schnitzler's people enact the estrangement, doubt and instability of the old Danubian Empire on its way toward 1914, 1918, 1934 and 1938.

Harry Slochower. *No Voice Is Wholly Lost: Writers and
Thinkers in War and Peace* (New York, Creative Age Press,
1945), p. 31

[Schnitzler's] plays, though by necessity not as much seen from within as the prose pieces, often reveal in their basic technique such striking similarities to the stories that they could be rewritten as such. Quite frequently, Schnitzler indeed started an idea as a story, then recast it as a drama, or vice versa, altering and eliminating as he went along.

And there is one element which plays and stories have in common, which, as effective on the stage as in a narrative, seems to me a primary element of Schnitzler's writing. It is, in a way, an instrument of technique, used so often that one might call it a signature of the author's productions. It is not the characters—they are not the central point of interest for the author because they repeat themselves too constantly: the aging Anatols, the cuckolded but forgiving husbands, the sensitive egoists, the brutal esthetes, the dilettantes obsessed by their passion for erotic adventure, the women on the verge of awakening or of resignation. The central point is, rather, a constellation of two or a few characters, an initial relationship, almost abstract, which is then wheeled around, switched back, turned in an unexpected direction until it is almost reversed.

Richard Plant. GR. Feb., 1950, p. 17

When Schnitzler dealt with topical problems in his plays, he was usually not too successful. . . . Schnitzler was at his best when he remained within the range of his personal and professional experiences. By far his best topical play is, therefore, *Professor Bernhardi,* which deals with people and issues he knew well: doctors, clinical atmosphere, a problem of medical ethics, and the issue of anti-Semitism. The first draft made in 1899 states the plot in one sentence: "A physician expels a priest who wishes to administer the last sacrament to a dying person, because this dying person imagines himself healthy and does not suspect that he is at death's door." In the final version the patient has become a girl and the director of the clinic a Jew, surrounded by political cliques and intrigues. Thus, the issue has been sharpened, and when Dr. Bernhardi is finally sentenced to jail for "forcibly hindering a priest in the exercise of his sacred duty," it is quite clear that no scandal would ever have arisen had the physician in charge not been a Jew. Bernhardi, a man of science, refuses to be dragged into politics, however, and rejects all intercessions in his behalf. Fully vindicated, he returns to his practice.

Of all of Schnitzler's mature full-length plays, *Professor Bernhardi* is by far his best work. The issues are sharply drawn, the plot logically developed, the characters superbly vivid. With the exception of one insignificant nurse part, there are no women in this drama, and no love conflict arises. Although written somewhat *pro domo* by an author who knew what it meant to be a Jew in the academic world of Imperial Austria, the anti-Semitic issue is never unduly stressed and only underlines the main problem of medical ethics.

Claude Hill. MD. May, 1961, pp. 85–86

In the crisis of liberalism in the mid-nineties, Schnitzler turned to the problem of politics, or rather, to the psyche as manifested in politics. *The Green Cockatoo* is a brilliant satirical playlet in which the instinctual life of the characters becomes central to their fate in the French Revolution. Schnitzler took no sides for or against the French Revolution, which had lost its historical meaning for him as for so many other late nineteenth-century liberals. He merely used the Revolution as a vehicle for irony about contemporary Austrian society in its current crisis. The upper-class characters of *The Green Cockatoo* are committed to the sensuous existence: some as open sensualists, others as devotees of the theatrical art. The scene and center of the play is a cabaret-theater, where the performances aim at obliterating for the patrons the distinction between play and reality, mask and man. Merely amusing in normal times, in the revolutionary situation this game proves fatal to its devotees. The corruption of art and the art of corruption blend. Stage murder becomes real murder, real murder executed by an actor out of jealousy appears as heroic political murder, the lover-murderer becomes a hero of the irrational revolutionary mob. Too much dedication to the life of the senses has destroyed in the upper class the power to distinguish politics from play, sexual aggression from social revolution, art from reality. Irrationality reigns supreme over the whole.

Carl E. Schorske. AHR. July, 1961, pp. 937–38

Hands Around bears the sub-heading "Ten Dialogues," and one of its principal original features is the circular form. Each character appears twice in succession, each time with a different partner, maintaining an overlapping link until the last character joins hands with the first in the manner of a round dance. . . . Schnitzler has in this way achieved a closed form, obviating the indeterminate and inconclusive end which is the usual defect of the one-act cycle. Its second and more notorious originality is the central climax of each episode, the consummation of the sexual act indicated by a series of dashes (and commonly pointed on the stage by the extinguishing of the lights). It is a pattern of recurring concupiscence, and assertion of the rise, fulfilment and decline of desire, not merely as an essential element of life, but as the determining factor of much human behaviour. It is a natural history of the *libido* and a delineation of the protective covering which it assumes to achieve its end. The temptation to cynicism is obvious, but Schnitzler has resisted it; rather does he, with reticent irony, expose the pretensions and vanities, the hypocrisies and deceits of the egoistical and self-satisfied. . . . The whole is a commentary on human desire enveloped in human weakness, conceit and prevarication. What might at first sight appear to be a contribution to elegant pornography, proves to be a work of a moralist, a minor masterpiece of satire.

H. B. Garland. In Alex Natan, ed., German Men of
Letters, Vol. II (London, Oswald Wolff, 1963), p. 60

Tragicomedy was the artistic means which Schnitzler selected to work out an acceptable approach to human affairs. For the sake of humanity he advocated as perfect as possible an understanding between man and man. But, for the sake of his art, he would not carry his rationality so far as Freud did. A moralist in a minor key, Schnitzler was occasionally heard to cry out against "this hodgepodge of restraint and insolence, of cowardly jealousy and fake equanimity—of raging passion and empty voluptuousness," which he saw around himself and projected onto the stage. It is no accident that this diagnosis is made by a physician and that it occurs toward the end of a play, *The Vast Domain,* which Schnitzler specifically called a tragicomedy. . . .

The poet Arthur Schnitzler was a wise doctor. Relentlessly he diagnosed the human absurdity in the tragicomedies that fill his books. He analysed the psyche of a moribund society because he foresaw and dreaded the epidemic character of the neuroses that were bred and spread by it. But unlike his successors in the field of modern tragicomedy—from Jean Cocteau to Tennessee Williams and Samuel Beckett and beyond—he did not look down on the figures he had created. He lingered among them and suffered with them. He knew about their ultimate secret, and, knowingly, kept it.

Heinz Politzer. MLN. Oct., 1963, p. 372

Schnitzler broke once and for all with the myth of woman as a pure spirit or a simple little goose or a naïve child. The only naïveté shown by his heroines, according to the example of Beatrice [in *The Veil of Beatrice*], consists in not imposing any restraint on the impulses of their flesh. . . . Without even taking into consideration a few abnormal or unbalanced characters whom the author has drawn, one has to admit that sensuality is a decisive factor for most of his female lovers. But—and in this respect they differ greatly from the men—for the women pleasure must be accompanied by a profound harmony of the hearts. Even the prostitute in *Hands Around* begs her brutal lover, the soldier, for a token of tenderness. Much less modern than their male partners in this respect, even the most liberated or most disillusioned hold onto a certain sentimental vision of the realities of love. And there is still another slant that shows them linked to tradition: they love with abandon, so much so that they forget their own interests and foster the illusion of forming a union of perfect harmony with their beloved. . . .

For all these women, love corresponds to a need for complete surrender, which is in exact opposition to the egocentrism governing most of their lovers. . . . Apart from the pleasure, man seeks in love an exaltation of his personality, whereas woman aspires with her whole being to a total union with her partner.

Françoise Derré. L'œuvre d'Arthur Schnitzler (Paris,
Didier, 1966), pp. 378–79, 381†

Schnitzler's tendency to unmask erotic adventurousness as an inauthentic form of existence can be discerned in his earliest work. It is, for instance, present in *Light-o'-Love,* where Fritz Lobheimer misses the best because, entrapped in his unfocused way of life, he is unable to enter into a genuine relationship with Christine, the true lover, and eventually falls a victim to the revenge of a cuckolded husband. In his mature works the dominating figure is that of the *aging* adventurer in whom the aging poet's sorrow about life finds its expression. Yet it is significant that Schnitzler's criticism of adventurism becomes even more severe during this period. It constitutes the decisive element of the great settling of accounts which von Sala undertakes in *The Lonely Way* with regard to the adventurous way of life and which appears so convincing because it springs from his own experience. Here the adventurer, even if an artist, is unmasked as the great egoist who never made any sacrifice, who never truly loved. For "to love means to exist for someone else," and it is precisely this surrender to the other that remains denied to the selfish and inconstant. Hence, all those "who never belonged to anyone" also find themselves condemned to a lonesome existence. *The Lonely Way* shows even more clearly than *Light-o'-Love* the destructive effects on the adventurer who threatens or destroys the happiness of the women who love him.

William H. Rey. In Benno von Wiese, ed., *Deutsche Dichter der Moderne, 2nd enl. and rev. ed.* (West Berlin, Schmidt, 1969), p. 248†

Schnitzler brought not only linguistic sensitivity, but also a passionate awareness of language as a *problem,* to bear on the world he evoked.

In his plays, particularly in his finest comedies, he was able to reveal linguistic utterances as something of infinitely variable intention and effect. What results is a complex awareness of language, which encompasses not only what is said, but why it is said, and ultimately, what is not said, and why it is not said. Put this way, it does, I hope, become clear that Schnitzler's differentiated response to the language his characters use owes a great deal to the techniques of psychoanalytical inquiry. Whatever reservations Schnitzler may have had about the moral and philosophical presuppositions of psychoanalysis, there can be no doubt that he was alive to the sense in which language is not simply a static and intact medium of communication, but changes with the psychological situation from which it derives. . . .

One should . . . stress that, however much Schnitzler was aware of the questionable nature of human utterance, he never lapsed into total cynicism about it. He never abandoned the assertion that, deeply flawed as language might be, it was one of man's most sacred possessions, and should be used with reverence. Schnitzler would surely have agreed with Hofrat Winkler . . . : "Words are everything. We just don't have anything else."

Words may almost invariably be untrue in the context of human affairs, but man's answer can never be to abandon them. He must rather use them with as much truthfulness as he can muster.

Martin Swales. *Arthur Schnitzler* (Oxford, Clarendon, 1971), pp. 155, 179–80

For nearly twenty years now the image of Arthur Schnitzler has undergone a profound—if gradual—change. As a result, he is recognized and deservedly admired today for, among other things, his amazingly thorough knowledge of depth psychology; for the *Mehrbödigkeit,* the multiple levels of appeal in his writings, that often cause different people to acclaim a particular work of his for entirely different reasons; for the honesty with which he presents the truth as he sees it; for the genuineness of his lifelike characters; for the comprehensiveness of his topical range; for his philosophical insights; and also for his courageous social criticism. . . .

Certainly one must agree with the critics who have shown that numerous works by Schnitzler contain strong elements of social criticism. But that cognition—correct as it is—does not go far enough. It does not tell the whole story and is therefore a potential source of misunderstandings.

Actually, Schnitzler's social criticism is simultaneously and primarily an exposure of human shortcomings, of the flaws in human nature, in other words not just *Gesellschaftskritik* [social criticism] but first and foremost *Darstellung des Allzumenschlichen* [representation of the all-too-human]. . . .

There is not valid evidence of an abiding interest on the part of Schnitzler in the problems of society per se. He is neither an idealistic crusader in the tradition of fighting naturalism nor a sociopolitical reformer in the spirit of expressionistic activism. He is fundamentally and unalterably a humanist, and as such he concentrates his analytical and descriptive powers on the one legitimate object of humanism: man in his multiple manifestations. Man—not society. Only when the distinction between these two concepts is blurred or ignored can Schnitzler's *diagnostic observations* be mistaken for conventional *social criticism.*

Robert O. Weiss. *MAL.* 5, 1–2, 1972, pp. 30–31

Schnitzler modified the individual by the typical. Thus tragicomedies, with individual figures, and puppet plays, with typical figures, are found side by side in his works. The schematic is found next to the particular and determinism next to free will. Schnitzler succeeded in showing the middle ground between the two extremes in *Hands Around,* which, viewed in this way, stands at the center of his work. Here the figures are types who, nevertheless, secretly have names. Their behavior is common to all of them, yet each individual is given his own unique manner. For example, not every actress kneels in prayer the way the actress in the eighth scene does, but the typical is the exaggeration of a gesture into a pose.

What other reflective writer so seriously and zealously balanced the typical with the specific and devoted his life to the theory behind this problem without having his work suffer? Schnitzler, on the contrary, by his conscious formulation stamped his work with an unmistakable identity as his creation. No detail in Schnitzler's dramas is ever subject to chance. Details are never introduced meaninglessly for the mere pleasure of creating but always satisfy his three criteria for a work of art: unity, intensity, and continuity. Aesthetic form is in every case subject to the control of ethical consciousness. Never would Schnitzler sacrifice a truth for a catchy formulation or alter a characterization merely for the sake of a beautiful sound. Often enough he portrayed hack writers who preferred glibness to truth, but he himself refused to be dominated by his style.

Reinhard Urbach. Arthur Schnitzler (New York,
Frederick Ungar, 1973), pp. 29–30

Both Fritz's and Christine's deaths [in *Light-o'-Love*] are out of phase with the meaning of the duel and the *Liebestod*. The duel is an exercise to defend the honor of someone he no longer loves. Christine dies for a love that came too late or never existed at all. Their being out-of-phase leaves the question of their relationship unresolved. Their mutual recognition, interrupted by social forces, remains in the realm of the possible or of the subjunctive mode. This might-have-been is what gives the play its poignancy. It raises the possibility that within the German cultural tradition there was a basis for mutuality, and that inclusion was still possible between the two classes caught in the greatest political and economic tension.

Yet there is evidence within the play that Schnitzler had reservations. In order to achieve this possible solution, it was not only a matter of Fritz's overcoming his fascination with death and recognizing Christine's worth in time. Christine's character and her culture are themselves matters of suspicion. Her worth depends upon her total devotion to Fritz and on her repression of sexuality: the only proof she can give of her *Treue* [faithfulness] is her death. She seems to represent health and salvation but her actual message is that of decadence—artificiality and isolation from society with an identity which can culminate only in death. . . .

When Fritz enters Christine's room like a Prodigal Son, he finds the relics of German culture: Schubert on the stove, Schiller and Hauff in the bookcase with "das Konversationslexikon nur bis zum G . . ." [the encyclopedia only as far as G]—Goethe? Even the flowers on the table are dusty and artificial. This is not merely an amusing milieu portrait but a description of a broken and petrified German culture. This tradition was not a home to which a lost son could return nor the ground for conciliation and inclusion. . . . Schnitzler has explored the romantic tradition for a resolution to cross-cultural sexual relations and for the regeneration of an aesthetic culture fascinated with its own death.

Margaret Morse. *MAL*. 10, 2, 1977, p. 42

After a careful reading of the passages containing references to mirrors in Schnitzler's works, we are impressed by the important functions the mirrors perform. In addition to the few instances where the words *Spiegel* [mirror] and spiegeln [to mirror] are used figuratively for stylistic effects, the mirror functions in the broadest sense as a device to strengthen the characterizations by making man conscious of himself and of his role as an individual. In each case the author is more interested in the image the subject provokes in the conscious mind than he is in the external characteristics of the subject. Some of the subjects reflected in the mirror are transmitted to the observer with little or no distortion, while others undergo radical modification in the mind's eye. Strange new qualities that are not apparent in reality have been added. . . .

The device of mirror imagery offered Arthur Schnitzler a vehicle well suited to probing the deep psychological and subconscious workings of his characters' minds. Moreover, through the mirror reflection Schnitzler could bring about wrenching and explosive self-realizations within these characters. . . . In exploring the theme of human understanding, in characterizing a self-encounter or change in self-image, in exposing subconscious fears or a divided self, and in fusing the world of reality with that of illusion, Schnitzler has turned to the device of mirrors for expression. Mirror imagery presents another dimension of Schnitzler's capacity to deal with the deepest psychological motivations of his characters.

Theodor W. Alexander. *Seminar*. Sept., 1978, pp. 193–94

WEDEKIND, FRANK (1864–1918)

The tragic is certainly an integral part of the core of [Wedekind's] art; behind his sneering derision there lurks a gloomy melancholy, a genuine suffering, and through his dissolute, cynical blasphemies there always can be heard a cry of distress and despair. This art gives the impression of being hopelessly devoid of ideals only because once it, too, had set its ideals too high. In present-day German literature there is, perhaps, nothing as base, nothing that bears so much the stamp of Caliban, as the art of Frank Wedekind. And yet whoever listens intently to what it has to say will perceive, buried deep, a big child's soul, a pure *anima candida*. [1901]

Julius Hart. Quoted in Günter Seehaus, *Frank Wedekind und das Theater* (Munich, Laokoon, 1964), p. 482†

Frank Wedekind . . . is one of the most perplexing figures in modern European literature. Any attempt to classify him with one or the other of the groups of naturalists, realists, romanticists, symbolists, decadents, or whatever they may be called, is sure to fail, for traces of all these movements are found in his work, but they are so jumbled, the one with the other, that he has evolved a style and a method entirely his own, in which cynicism, scepticism, satire, grotesqueness of metaphor and capricious paradox play a large part. Nuances, delicacies, and subtleties of thought or treatment, the reader will rarely find in Wedekind.

The nearest analogue among English writers is probably George Bernard Shaw. Both take the same keen delight in "having a shy" at every conceivable accepted opinion and belief; both are clever in building up preposterous theses with artificial logic; both are fundamentally very much in earnest in their *clownerie*. Shaw's boldest situations and most daring fantasies are always dominated by a purely intellectual element and contain traces of unadulterated puritanism, which are totally lacking in Wedekind, who is more emotional and tends toward sentimentality. Perhaps it is in the latter that the root of his cynicism lies. He calls a spade a spade, always with extravagant emphasis, and dealing so much in hardware is sure to cause considerable clatter. Whether writers like Shaw and Wedekind are a symptom or a disease in modern literature is immaterial; for the present, at least, they are a force that cannot be ignored, and their genuine abilities have been recognized by friend and foe alike.

O. F. Theis. *Poet Lore*. Vacation, 1913, p. 237

There can be no doubt about it: this poet is the true tragic representative of our time. If we disregard some initial groping, then there is in all of his works hardly a scene, hardly a word that he personally does not mean to be taken in all seriousness. No dramatist, not even Kleist or Hebbel, has ever toyed less with his art. Indeed, in some instances, notably in *Dance of Death, Censorship,* and *Simson,* his creative powers are overwhelmed by his confessional fanaticism—a noble defeat. And people once were blind and superficial enough to call this man a braggart. This confessional urge is at the root of all of Wedekind's mistakes and errors, but certainly also of his representative authority. In this respect, as well as in many others, he appears to be the true brother of the great Strindberg. . . .

For too long people have been dwelling on the fantastic aspect of his characters and situations. But Wedekind is, in fact, no adventurer in matters of feeling. . . . He is, especially with regard to love, the almost inflexible adherent of an ideal. But he did not believe the temperate zone of middle-class affairs to be the suitable medium in which to reveal himself with ultimate clearness, rending his own soul apart, transforming it, and giving it creative expression of the utmost clarity. . . . His Hetman [in *Hidalla*], his

Geschwitz [in the "Lulu" plays], his Marquis [in *The Marquis of Keith*]—
they certainly do not breathe the same air in which average citizens go for
walks, sleep, and earn their money; but theirs is the tremendous force and
the persuasive power of the autobiographical, paid for dearly with the
heart's blood.

Bruno Frank. In Joachim Friedenthal, ed., *Das*
Wedekindbuch (Munich, Müller, 1914), pp. 168–70†

If someone wrote in 1900 as if it were already 1914, who would receive
him with open arms? To depict a world of fierce struggle while people still
imagine themselves to be thoroughly cultured! To interpret everything differently, more menacingly, than it was generally understood at that time; to
strip everything first of its high-flown words, then of its moral pretenses,
and finally almost of its flesh! To conjure up the death of an era in advance!
And that, moreover, on the stage, where people are so very fond of seeing
themselves lovingly portrayed in a cozy and touching life!

But that was exactly the mission of the dramatic poet Frank Wedekind. . . . In his plays he anticipated what was yet to come. The 1890s,
when he was young, actually had a gentler atmosphere; they were comparatively harmless and benevolent. His young fellow writers of the time believed in everything good . . . and hinted at the imminent solution to the
social question, at peace among men.

But no one in the whole world believed less in peace among men than
did Frank Wedekind. . . . All he saw was struggle, all he experienced was
a melee that grew more and more frenzied—both in the world around him
and in his own heart. Women intent on self-indulgence only, men bent only
on making money, every unselfish act merely a deception, any friendly feeling something to be mocked, instead of human sympathy only callous curiosity, greed for power even in the thinker, laws just good enough to make
the poor shut their dangerous mouths—but for the racketeer all the success
on earth and in heaven. All this was already written clearly in his heart when
it was still just beginning to arise in the world around him, and the entire
beginning of the century sprang in full panoply from his head when it had
hardly even begun in reality. Nowhere else can it be seen as clearly as in
his plays how much of life in those days was already war, before it became
openly so. No one predicted as inexorably as he did what such moral tendencies would lead to. [1922]

Heinrich Mann. *Sieben Jahre* (Berlin, Zsolnay,
1929), pp. 76–77†

Shame and jealousy—in Wedekind's sense, of course, unbiblical concepts—
are as little the basic idea of *Samson* as are marriage and family that of
Castle Wetterstein. . . .

The work grew out of the suffering of the creative genius; this comes closest to what could be called the principal idea, and this suffering forms the core of the work. The first indication that catches our attention comes at the end of the first act, with Samson's lament about his having been blinded. When he still had his sight, he lived merely by the reality of the factual, being a man of action endowed with brutal force, ignorant and immature. Blindness makes a person turn inward, suffering makes one mature and beautiful, memory rouses the imagination. . . .

Blindness and suffering are, of course, to be taken symbolically as creative powers, but they are not sufficiently motivated. Otherwise Samson is an elect, a child of light, a mighty hero who comes to grief in this base world, who is outwitted by a woman because he trusts her, who always looks upon himself as the cleverer one, but takes her to be more stupid than she is, who is subdued and degraded by the Philistines. The warrior's song reveals the gloomy philosophy of life held by the singer and poet. The scene that follows is deeply moving: the blind man's vision, created for his happiness alone—the others act it out and enjoy it. Samson's tragic suffering and their cynical triumph is a vivid symbol for the creative person's exclusion from real life. His despair is irresistible, overpowering. His innermost revelations must serve to amuse and entertain the mob. His suffering is turned into ridicule. How bitter that it is precisely the learned man, an authority on the Scriptures, who mocks him most.

Artur Kutscher. Frank Wedekind, Vol. III (Munich,
Müller, 1931), pp. 142–43†

As the superficial prosperity and ebullience of the new German state increased, the power of cultural criticism gained momentum and eventually developed into what must be called an apocalyptic sense of crisis without which neither the generation before nor that after the First World War can be fully understood. . . .

The acid work of the dramatist Frank Wedekind is perhaps the clearest indication of the cynical despair and scepticism with which all contemporary values were being regarded. In spite of his obvious formal shortcomings Wedekind created the boldest and most fascinating world of demoniacally dislocated bourgeois characters. His impulse is at all times antinaturalistic, and although his main theme is the horror of the brutality of sex, the manner of his prose dramas is romantic in the modern and ironic understanding of that word. At the same time, Wedekind's antierotic obsession is linked with an effective sense of the grotesque disequilibrium of middle-class society. Himself outside this world, he directs the brilliant beam of his implacable searchlight slantwise at the marginal accidents of the vast human circus. Between his dream-clear and unforgettable figures there exists no genuine communication; they are related to one another not by the conventional means of dramatic context, but by their precise and speechless function within a breathtaking histrionic act. The startling elements of his minstrelsy and the shrillness of his moralizing message reappear later . . . in Bertolt Brecht, in the epic theater of the late twenties, and, in a different medium, in the stark social caricatures of George Grosz. [1945]

Victor Lange. *Modern German Literature* (Port Washington, N.Y., Kennikat Press, 1967), pp. 69–71

If Ibsen and Strindberg represent the decline of the burgher and his morality, Wedekind invents a world in which there are no burghers and no morality. . . .

Wedekind has a satirist's draughtsmanship. But his standpoint is not reason, or common sense, the often rather stolid pragmatism of the comic writers from Aristophanes to Molière. It is religious. But like Baudelaire, Wedekind is only negatively religious. He is not a believer, and his vision is solely of evil. . . .

The distortions and involutions of Wedekind's moral system are an early objectification of the same spiritual sickness which later showed itself in surrealism after one fashion, in D. H. Lawrence and Henry Miller, and after a different fashion in Franz Kafka. In all these diverse figures there is a deep consciousness of chaos, a longing for the numinous, for that mystic and mysterious part of experience which the modern imagination has so often overlooked. Wedekind is surrealist in his shock technique, his atmosphere of nightmare, his mastery of the sexual-grotesque. In his moral stand he is Lawrentian. Unlike all these men, his imagination functioned in theatrical terms, and occasionally in tragic, or, perhaps we should say, pseudo-tragic terms.

Eric Bentley. *The Playwright as Thinker* (New York, Reynal & Hitchcock, 1946), pp. 64–66

The most outspoken Wedekind play, *Hidalla* or *Karl Hetman, the Pygmy Giant,* written in 1904, is an extremely honest and provocative drama. Wedekind, the reformer and advocate of women's rights, overshadows the rebel and accuser. The story of Karl Hetman, the idealistic sex moralist, eternally misunderstood and at the same time exploited, is the story of any idealist in the modern world. In *Hidalla,* Wedekind fights for his "new morality" between the sexes, for women as "equal sex partners," for women freed of the "feudalism of love" which, Hetman declares, "created the three abhorrent, barbaric forms of woman's life in modern society: the prostitute, ostracized and hunted like a wild beast, the spinster, condemned to be a physical and mental cripple, deprived of her right to love, and the chastity of the virgin, maintained for the purpose of a most favorable marriage."

The tragedy of the man Hetman is the center of the drama, with a strong sidelight falling on the whole world of shabby promoters and business agents, of low profiteers and perverted sensation seekers. This world reveals itself as a world of abject corruption and amorality. Here Wedekind seems to strike a pessimistic note (Karl Hetman, exploited, ridiculed, jailed and even put in a mental institution, ends as a suicide) but the true thesis of *Hidalla* lies in the fact that an honest man, a reformer and fighter, is pitilessly destroyed by society. Yet, Wedekind hints, although society tries to do this to all idealists, rebels or reformers, the triumph in the end belongs to them. Morally, at least. . . .

The theater which Frank Wedekind loved so much, for which he worked and lived a hard life of constant struggles, a life of humiliating defeats, but also of glorious victories, has long since reserved for him a high place of honor. For there are only a few who equal him, only a few who have his genius, his sincerity and his depth, his forcefulness and his humanity.

John Altman. *ThA*. March, 1951, p. 31

As an artist and thinker Wedekind has much in common with Jean-Jacques Rousseau. Just as the latter rebelled against the rationalistic hedonism of his time and thought to penetrate to what is essential, to Nature, so Wedekind sought to escape from the hypocrisy and artificiality of bourgeois society, back to a natural way of life.

He regarded unfeigned sensual pleasure as the highest aim of every spiritually and physically well-rounded human being. He attributed the tragicomic situation of bourgeois society to the fact that its hypocrisy forces people to maim and conceal their natural instincts. Anyone acknowledging the truth either by words or action is repudiated by society. The only man who can live a natural life is he who puts himself beyond the range of this society and its laws and who robs and betrays it with every means that comes to hand. According to which the true hero of this society is the unscrupulous thief and swindler, the industrial brigand in the grand style. His female counterpart is the magnificent, heartless whore, born for pleasure. Wedekind does not seek merely, like the naturalistic school, to render photographically the surface of society, but to penetrate to its interior, to present it in all its complexities and contradictions. In order to view it thus comprehensively he must find a point of vantage outside it. He finds the Archemedean point and from it turns his world this way and that, ever and again exposing its tragic and ridiculous aspects in abrupt alternation, letting them in abrupt alternation explode against and mingle with each other. With the result that in his big scenes he achieves a parallelism of situation which makes the tragic and the comic apparent simultaneously to all who have eyes to see.

Lion Feuchtwanger. In Frank Wedekind, *Five Tragedies of Sex* (London, Vision, 1952), pp. 13–14

Wedekind conceived the two parts of his "Lulu" drama as a feminine parallel, as it were, to Goethe's *Faust*. Like Goethe's hero, Lulu runs through the whole gamut of passion. She climbs the social ladder, only to topple over from its dizzy heights into the abyss of prostitution, illness, and crime. Her companion is the Countess Geschwitz who, with her sterile Lesbian infatuation with Lulu, represents something akin to Mephistopheles's principle of negation. . . . Wedekind underlined the parallel with Goethe's play by opening *Pandora's Box* with a "Prologue in the Bookshop," closely modelled on Goethe's "Prologue on the Stage" down to the doggerel rhymes à la Hans Sachs. . . .

The parallel with Goethe's *Faust* culminates in the dramatic function of the Countess Geschwitz who, telescoping, as it were, the roles of the cheated Mephistopheles and *Una poenitentium* (alias Gretchen), intercedes for the sinner Lulu in the face of death. Wedekind himself encouraged an interpretation on these lines by his own assessment of his chief characters. . . .

Wedekind's *Lulu* reaches its poetical apex in the ecstatic glorification of the "Eternal Feminine" ("Das Ewig-Weibliche" of Goethe's final Chorus Mysticus), symbolized in the figure of the naïve she-demon, the incarnation of amorality and unlimited sensuality. It is this note of hedonism which distinguishes *Lulu* from the contemporary plays of the pessimistic anti-feminist Strindberg. The philosophical and, indeed, ethical ground-bass of Wedekind's "Lulu" plays evidently passed unnoticed when the public prosecutor hurled his indictment against their author. A rehabilitation of Wedekind, as moralist, preacher and playwright, occurred only in 1905, when *Pandora's Box* received its first performance in Vienna.

H. F. Redlich. *Alban Berg: The Man and His Music*
(New York, Abelard-Schuman, 1957), pp. 166–68

Wedekind wrote his first and most important dramas in the eighteen-nineties, a period when Ibsen's and Hauptmann's Naturalism had barely been accepted on the German stage. What distinguished Wedekind's plays from Naturalism, despite their highly modern, semi-Naturalistic subject matter, was the grotesqueness of situations depicted in them and the quality of the dialogue. Wedekind applied the identical idiom of stilted phrases and caustic epigrams to all his characters from newspaper publisher to ragpicker. . . . By his peculiar idiom he created a closed world similar to the autonomous space of the Cubist or the closed universe of [Franz] Kafka and [Georg] Trakl. In contrast to Kafka and Trakl, and the Strindbergian drama, however, Wedekind built his closed world not for the purpose of visualizing existential situations, but for the purpose of exaggerating and distorting social reality. Like the figures of the Cubist, Wedekind's characters correspond to objectively existing reality, but they are seen and presented in their

essential structure rather than in their empirical surface appearance. Wedekind sees sex and drive for power and prestige as the basic conflicting forces
dominating life. He distills these forces from actual society, in which they
are hidden in layers of hypocritical convention and, with provocative glee,
exhibits their "pure essence" embodied in empirically impossible specimens.

> Walter H. Sokel. *The Writer in Extremis* (Stanford, Cal.,
> Stanford University Press, 1959), p. 61

More than once in his plays Wedekind is carried away into dramatically
dubious situations by his hatred for middle-class prudery and by his wrath
against a mendacious bourgeois morality. But there can be little doubt that
this tragedy [*Spring's Awakening*] belongs to the great plays of lasting importance because it admirably invokes the troubled spirit of young people
worried by their stirring sexuality, which they cannot master physically or
emotionally. This drama displays such a deep comprehension of the adolescent psyche as Wedekind never again was able to show. . . .

The lack of a unified style is already noticeable in this early masterpiece. Moods prevail which create their own, permanently changing style.
In the sequence of scenes, which are really only dialogues, a secret unity, a
dramatic urgency are clearly dominant. Actions and moods end together in
this vernal storm of youthful awakening. Wedekind's tragedy of childhood
has remained his only play which shows an intimate awareness of Nature.
This mood for landscape, his delicate reaction to the seasons present an
essential element in this drama of awakening eroticism, which shows the
poet a worthy descendant of [Georg] Büchner's *Wozzeck* and brings to mind
his tremendous influence on the expressionistic plays of a later period. . . .
Spring's Awakening is Wedekind's first, timid attempt to preach the revolt
of the male slaves against the "Feudalismus der Liebe" [feudalism of love].
The poet does not yet crack his whip but lets the tormented creature speak
up for himself. But the last scene already contains Wedekind's philosophy:
only he who is willing to jump over open graves will find life interesting
and rewarding.

> Alex Natan. In Alex Natan, ed., *German Men of
> Letters*, Vol. II (London, Oswald Wolff, 1963), pp. 104–5

Wedekind prided himself not only on peopling his plays with characters who
would not be at home in the living rooms of Ibsen's drama but for inventing
for these characters a strange new dialogue devoid of warm human intonation. This dialogue is so mechanical that it often strikes one as the monotonous emission of the same set of signals. Above all, the impression is of
characters mouthing what will never find a responsive ear. Everyone seems
anxious to speak at the same time, sentences crisscross haphazardly, con-

versation becomes the alternation of telegram phrases. It is dialogue designed to parallel Wedekind's depersonalization of character in the realm of language.

For all its originality, this stylized speech reflects the kind of verbal mechanism by which [Johann Michael Reinhold] Lenz (1751–1792) and [Georg] Büchner (1813–1837) represented mentalities and mental states. Their characters often spoke like puppets tied to a single emotional string and defined themselves by stereotyped speech patterns. What distinguishes Wedekind is that he condenses language to the point where it comes through as the most forceful verbal equivalent of sheer drive. His language transcends self-consciousness, and one often gets the impression of words materializing themselves like circles in water shattered by rock; everything said is wholly automatic. The effect of such dialogue volleying back and forth is of a deadening mindlessness. Wedekind need not even have put any cynical phrases into his characters' mouths; only the morally dead could speak such a soulless language; here the human being verbalizes what Wedekind believed to be his real nature.

Like Lenz, Wedekind can write monologues which comment as much on the speaker as on the absurd world in which he insists on overdramatizing himself.

Max Spalter. Brecht's Tradition (Baltimore, Johns Hopkins University Press, 1967), pp. 125–26

In his intention and method Wedekind in *Music* attempted something which . . . was to have some significant effect on the theater. He permitted his characters to take their plight in great seriousness, while almost instructing the audience to take the opposite point of view. . . . The "message" should come through clearly, he felt. . . . Wedekind's didacticism, then, employed the same method that Bertolt Brecht outlined in his notes to the opera *Rise and Fall of the City of Mahagonny*, 1929, and in other writings concerning his concept of Epic Theater. . . .

Wedekind's hinting at an "epic" estrangement of stage and spectator is echoed in the peculiar structure of the play. . . . "*Music* is not a drama, but rather a chronicle." Wedekind introduces each of the acts as if it were an event in the past tense, attaching an independent motto which anticipates all the forthcoming developments. "Under Cover of Darkness" prepares us for Klara's clandestine flight; "Behind Bars" anticipates her incarceration; "From the Frying Pan into the Fire" establishes the fact that she will return to Reissner; and "The Curse of Ridicule" introduces the final emotional outpouring of Klara.

Although Wedekind never gave any specific instructions for the use of these headlines, they seem obviously intended to work as a kind of *Moritat*, which Brecht used so effectively in, for example, *The Threepenny Opera*.

With the tension relieved, the audience can sit back and need not worry about the dramatic development, having been informed in advance. . . .

Sol Gittleman. *Frank Wedekind* (New York,
Twayne, 1969), pp. 102–3

The power of Nicolo, the king [in *King Nicolo*], synonymous in the first part of the play with sterility and narcissism, is overcome by Nicolo, the liberating fool, supported by his daughter Alma as "Hanswurst," the enemy of all rigidity. The basic structure is that of classical reversal: the descent from monarch to swineherd and the rise to real power out of lowliness; the carnival theme of the inverted world in which Nicolo becomes the fool in his own court and, in advising his successor, Pietro, becomes more the ruler than when he was monarch himself. Sheltered first by the acted role of king, then by the person of Pietro, Nicolo achieves the unity of the fool-king, the "Königsmaske," and so makes implicitly the important statement that only through the medium of the mask or the role may real truth be transmitted to and accepted by men. The attempt to state inner truth and experience directly—in the last scene—brings the danger of ridicule and madness. Only the last "mask," that of death and anonymity in the royal tomb, can extend the power of this hard-won experience meaningfully beyond himself in the person of Alma.

Hector Maclean. *Seminar*. Spring, 1969, p. 21

Since transformation in puberty is a natural process, it can hardly be in itself the occasion for tragedy. Why then was Wedekind so preoccupied with showing the perversions of puberty and what justifies his calling *Spring's Awakening* a "children's tragedy"? An answer to the first question is implicit in . . . his passion for presenting things as they really are. In choosing puberty as his subject, Wedekind was simply being more perspicacious than most colleagues about "the real forces of existence" (his own terms), more radically honest than any in exploring its effects, and on firmest ground in viewing these from the standpoint provided by nature itself. What he meant by calling the play a tragedy—clearly, the term is not being used here in the technical generic sense—follows from . . . the situation. Tragedy exists because the youngsters undergoing radical change are not provided with socially acceptable channels for their energies and the transfers normally occurring at puberty do not take place: instead of becoming part of the adult community the children are excluded or isolated from it; the things they should know are kept from them; and they lose their innocence without gaining compensatory values from the system of pieties. Perversion does exist in this world—not as manifestations of the libido, however, but as a frustration of the life-force and in the blockage of nature's purpose.

What then brings about such a "tragedy"? The power of morality, of course, or rather of an attitude toward it based on an exaggerated sense of piety and a false notion of what morality really is. . . .

One need not agree with the Masked Gentleman. . . . Yet although the Masked Gentleman may be impious, he is not amoral; he is in fact an impious moralizer, supplanting "Morality," written large and grounded in social institutions, with "morality," written small and based on the "real forces" of nature, a natural morality. Thus Wedekind points to that transvaluation of values which is the ultimate purpose of any transitional process.

Leroy R. Shaw. *The Playwright and Historical Change*
(Madison, University of Wisconsin Press, 1970), pp. 59–61

Once the question of direct influence has been eliminated, the terms of the Wedekind–Theater of the Absurd connection might be stated as follows: On the level of theatrical technique and method, the reduction of language and subsequent elevation of mimic action so frequent in the Theater of the Absurd has been tried and executed much earlier by Wedekind—and in much the same spirit: from a strikingly similar belief in the theatricality of the stage, both Wedekind and the later Absurdists tried to overcome the inadequacies of the conventional theater of their respective eras. . . . Perhaps more than any other playwright before him, Wedekind's attention to, and concern with, this element gives his plays their peculiar visual character, and points to the similarity between his dramatic philosophy and that of more contemporary figures.

As in the Theater of the Absurd, expression in terms of the grotesque is characteristic of much of Wedekind's work, but while its use can be considered functionally identical to that of the Absurdists, qualifications must be made with regard to its intensity and its inception in the more limited and provincial scope of Wedekind's concerns. A functional similarity is also apparent with regard to the tragicomic element. . . . But again, one has to take into consideration the variant philosophical bases and resulting differences in their respective Dramas. All told, Wedekind is not entirely unworthy of the references to him with respect to the Theater of the Absurdists: in the process of making the necessary clarifications, however, one becomes convinced that it is really less important to establish him as a predecessor than to stress the impressive contemporaneity and modernity of his Theater in its own right.

Robert A. Jones. *CompD*. Winter, 1970–71, p. 293

The study of Wedekind's plays reveals not only his intellectual debt to the dialectic of Nietzsche's Dionysian world. It would indicate that Wedekind took off in an original way from Nietzsche's early Dionysus in plays like *The Tenor, The Marquis of Keith,* and *The Earth Spirit.* Gerardo, Keith and Lulu reflect essentially Wedekind's initial interest in the possibility of absolute aesthetic and moral freedom. The basis of this philosophy is derived from Nietzsche's early Dionysus. *Pandora's Box,* the second of the Lulu plays, introduces a shift in Wedekind's defense of Dionysian man; pessimism and doubt replace optimism and a strong sense of personal conviction. In *Pandora's Box,* Wedekind fails to find a permanent answer to the problem of inherent tragic conflict between sensual and rational existence.

King Nicolo, Hidalla and *Castle Wetterstein* are all tragedies in which the life-affirming principles of Nietzsche's late Dionysus are altered by Wedekind to point out the nihilism and the absurdity of life itself. Contrary to Nietzsche, Wedekind interprets the eternal recurrence as a life long in pain and suffering. *Hidalla* depicts idealism as a fool's paradise. Both Nicolo and Hetman suffer the humiliation of scorned heroism. *Castle Wetterstein* denies the validity of Nietzsche's will to power as a positive Dionysian concept and confirms the relationship between that power and brutal force.

Wedekind's real importance as a tragic dramatist lies in our recognizing the unique manner in which he first used and then changed Nietzsche's Dionysus into a vehicle that verifies life as a tragic experience.

Richard Arthur Firda. MLN. Oct., 1972, p. 731

There is no question but that Lulu is a mythic persona in the archetypal mode. But is she the atavistic, antediluvian creation of the gods—Lulu, Pandora, Eva; is she the apotheosis of perfect beauty and innocent seduction—Nelli-Helen; or is she the *Zwittergestalt* [androgynous figure], essentially asexual, implied in the name Mignon? In *Earth Spirit* she is, of course, all of these, yet no one of them encompasses her entire being. Casting wide the net of archetypal reference, it would seem that one mythic setting can offer a context for all the divergent aspects of Lulu's complex nature: the myth of the sculptor-king Pygmalion and the statue imbued with life. Viewed in terms of the metamorphosis of stone to flesh, the protean personae of Lulu devolve into a specific unity in tune with numerous facets of the *Zeitgeist* [spirit of the times] at the time of her creation and in harmony with Wedekind's highly personal views on human sexuality. In such an interpretation, the artist as victim of his own created reality attains central importance. This is a dimension of the drama too often overlooked.

Wedekind's use of the mythic coupling of creator and creation is not, of course, a straightforward recasting of the classic fable related by Ovid in Book X of the *Metamorphoses,* but a carefully integrated layering of identities and dramatic stylizations in his unique and compelling manner. The outlines of the classic archetype are discernible in its essentials. . . . She remains the creation of Dr. Schön—whose name also bears heavily symbolic associations for the artist-creator. The relationship between Lulu and Schön develops in the course of the drama from the master-creation constellation to the ascendancy and triumph of the creation over the creator.

Edward P. Harris. GR. Jan., 1977, pp. 44–45

In *Simson; or, Shame and Jealousy* the figure of the strong man moves into the center of the action as Wedekind pursues further the possibilities of role reversal that had been suggested in *Franziska*. Insulted when Simson praises another woman, Delila determines on revenge. Learning the secret source of his power, she has his hair shorn while he is asleep. Weak, blinded, and in chains, Simson becomes her possession. Now their roles are completely reversed: Simson stays at home and monotonously turns a mill, while Delila ventures into the world of politics and power. Helpless and totally dependent on Delila, Simson feels uncertain of himself, jealous, and in need of love and comfort. Delila abuses him, shows him off to others, and humiliates him. Simson's blindness places him in the typical position of a woman who is lacking in knowledge and experience, thus insecure and dependent for her happiness on the man. Clearly conscious of the role exchange that has occurred in their relationship, Simson even wishes he could bear children who would depend on him and thus give him comfort in his misery.

With regard to the psychology of the sexes the drama *Simson* penetrates beyond the mental attributes of female masochism and male desire to control. . . . *Simson* discloses the revolutionary insight that "female" consciousness—"Scham und Eifersucht" [shame and jealousy]—that is, a sense of inferiority and helpless anger, are a result of woman's powerless social position. Simson, the strong man, exhibits these very same mental characteristics when forced to remain in a situation of dependency and subservience, whereas possession of power by Delila changes her consciousness as well. Yet, having come thus far, Wedekind does not draw any new implications from this remarkable observation. He continues to perceive the relationship of the sexes as a problem of control, of necessary hierarchy. If the woman assumes traditional "masculine" roles then she begins to control the relationship, while the man is forced to take on the traditional "female" role of dependence. Such a role reversal, however, is shown by Wedekind to lead to complete destruction not only of the individual, but also of society. As Simson's hair grows, he regains his strength and at the first opportunity shakes down the walls of the temple on himself and on the entire community. In the context of the play this symbolic action implies that "usurpation" by the woman of the male role leads to chaos and destruction.

Adrone B. Willeke. *Monatshefte*. Spring, 1980, pp. 34–35

WEISS, PETER (1916–1982)

Marat and Sade [in *Marat/Sade*] represent two attitudes toward the revolution. De Sade is detached, disillusioned, and unimpressed by its goal: the greatest happiness for the greatest number. While the disappointed individualist does not believe in the progress of mankind, Marat is an ardent defender of *Liberté, Egalité, Fraternité*. . . .

The dialogues between Marat, the dedicated idealist, and de Sade, the utter individualist in political and humane terms, are the real backbone of the play. However regrettably, the substance of the ideas expressed in these long talks remains far behind the impression evoked by the skillful technique and staging of the drama. On the other hand, Marat's idealistic Socialism—neither he himself nor his opponent knows that it is Socialism—is not likely to degrade the play to a drama about Communism, nor is de Sade's egotism a characteristic of just this figure; both men represent widespread attitudes. The clash between them is not restricted to the era of the French Revolution; it may as well be transferred to the present time. This is where Weiss introduces the third level of his play: in our time, also, a decision must be made in the conflict between individualism and—not Socialism nor Communism—a vague desire to embrace as much of the world as possible. Weiss has not written a reactionary drama, but it may be understood as a warning against taking sides in the struggle between a kind of unlimited pseudohumanism that draws its followers into the vortex of chaos, and utter egotism which tends toward complete isolation and sterile self-satisfaction.

Manfred Triesch. *AGR*. Aug.–Sept., 1964, pp. 9–10

[The adolescent] Peter Weiss accepts himself as a pariah, but under its noble aspect: that of the artist. And struggling against himself, against his parents, against society, he seeks his personal salvation as desperately as the dramatis personae of his *Marat/Sade*. When, during the war, his friends reproached him for his refusal to become politically involved, he protested, saying, "I see my only defensive and offensive weapon in art."

The events of that period also confirm his view that ours is a chaotic and inhuman world whose meaning remains elusive. . . . From an analogous world Kafka had created his universe of the transcendent: from behind the scenes "one" pulls the strings of a world that eludes our grasp. Peter Weiss discovered Kafka with a passion, but violently rejects any transcendence, any idealism, any desexualized world. "This world of ours," he has Sade say, "is a world of bodies, each body pulsing with a terrible power." Unlike Kafka, Weiss set out, after the war, to arrive at establishing a lucid and exact world "where all can be explained." To counter his inner disintegration, he attempted to "give life to his own life."

Now, with this in mind, the significance of his *Marat/Sade* can be better understood. Here Peter Weiss settles his accounts with a universe of carnage, solitude, and oppression he saw himself faced with; and the provocations he hurls at the spectators reflect his return to the world of the living. . . . His *Marat/Sade* is without doubt one of the most intense "books from beyond defeat," to use Sartre's expression.

Christian Bachmann. TM. July, 1965, pp. 181–82†

Weiss put madmen in *Marat/Sade* because Marat and Sade no longer pass for mad among us. We think we are to be congratulated for this openness of mind. As for Weiss, he finds it intolerable. . . .

The author of *Marat/Sade* is not a "liberal." He knows his public well, and he knows how to play with its idealism. This is only too clear in his decision to endow Coulmier, the head of the asylum, a progressive psychiatrist and an urbane Bonapartist, with all the qualities of the perfect liberal. Coulmier does not hesitate to risk the double boldness of inviting a select public to the therapeutic productions put on in his establishment and to entrust their staging to the pernicious Marquis de Sade whom he treats with a courtesy not devoid of complicity. There are, of course, times when his indignation gets the better of him: when Sade retains incendiary passages he had promised to cut. Most often these passages are the protests of the people, frustrated in their revolutionary aspirations and goals by a bourgeoisie which finds its triumph not only in Napoleon's battles but also in the theatre where it comes to watch Sade's productions. This, it strikes me, is only an additional subtlety on Weiss' part, since Coulmier, though he may be the audience's representative, is none the less judged by the same audience. For the twentieth-century audience condemns Coulmier's subservience to authority. It feels itself to be automatically superior to him, and even more liberal than he. For *we* would certainly not reprimand Sade if we had the good luck to be part of the audience watching a play written and played by the *divin marquis* in person. We would willingly give him *carte blanche*. We would never behave as ridiculously as Coulmier. Yet in passing judgment on Coulmier, aren't we putting ourselves in the dock?

Michel Beaujour. YFS. 35, 1965, pp. 116–17

Weeks before the opening [of *The Investigation* in 1965] worried critics had expressed doubt that the play could even be put on the boards. Nor did the violent attacks leveled against the author for his conversion to communist socialism leave his work untouched. Suddenly a play about the Auschwitz trial was called a subversive action against the constitution of the Federal Republic. Weiss himself compounded the nonsensical fuss by strongly criticizing the Western social order in interviews and articles. In the heat of the battle, his opponents overlooked the fact that this maverick also had criticized the realities of life in the East Bloc countries.

The Investigation is a kind of conclusion to what this playwright has written so far. For many years Peter Weiss, the emigrant living in Sweden, wrote only for his desk drawer: he had to learn to handle the German language as a literary medium, for he had been exiled early in his life. Since writing *The Shadow of the Coachman's Body* he has tried single-mindedly to clear up his ideas of reality: the reality of language in his first book; the reality of his personal existence in two autobiographical novels . . . ; the reality of fictional dialogue in *The Conversation of the Three Walkers* . . . ; the reality of history in his Marat play, and the reality of society, its situation and its background, in *The Investigation*. His works have included increasingly more substance; they have struck ever closer to the heart of our times and of our political existence. In the face of this literary development the political credo of this honest author is not at all surprising. It is probably as transitory as everything he does. He has settled on no structure, no style, and in his search for a rationally based existence and a moral code for society, he does not shrink from even the tabu areas. His works have given him a feeling of solidarity with the oppressed, solidarity which at this point is epitomized for him in the Marxian thesis. But no one, not even he himself, can tell whether this is not just a way-station. In any case, this author will certainly not stop searching and criticizing; he will remain troublesome and startling.

Roland H. Wiegenstein. AGR. Dec., 1965, pp. 33, 35

The experimental, vanguard aspect is remarkable in [*Marat/Sade*], and seems to have prompted its enthusiastic reception. Weiss had had previous experience in the medium of the drama . . . he studied Strindberg and translated two of his dramatic works into German. His *Marat,* however, includes no one dependency: from pantomime to alienation, from the play about time ([Thornton] Wilder) to that of traumatic memory, from the feverish Expressionist outcry to the Theater of the Absurd, from the medieval Dance of Death to the political revue. This spectrum proves that the author has sovereign command of the stylistic achievements of past drama, which he integrated and unified in a novel way. A find for any teacher of drama to sum up major histrionic innovations and exemplify techniques of the twentieth-century theater. . . .

This drama runs counter to a sense of the clock—the fanning of the plot into many brief scenes of divergent points of time only further handicaps the timekeeper. Piecing it into 33 scenes, Weiss minimizes the story itself—film-like fragments convey changing moods. . . . Alienation, in the manner of Brecht, also serves to invalidate chronology. . . . The intellect, here represented by Sade, stands above time. Doesn't the mind exist polychronologically? Weiss suggests this: Sade's yesterday, today, and tomorrow merge into his consciousness and its manifestation on stage.

Time is meaningless for Weiss, and accordingly he reflects our world in the French Revolution, a forerunner of our epoch in terms of change, conflict, and brutality. He stimulates the audience's concern through the underlying analogies. . . . An eminently political play unfolds—political significance unifies even its comic and absurd scenes into one explosive punch. "We need violent artistic actions again—in our saturated contented state of sleep!," Weiss wrote in 1963. . . .

In accord with this maxim, his play abounds in polemic against self-deceit, belligerence against false authorities, and revolt against any presentation of reality as ultimate.

Hans Bernhard Moeller. Symposium. Summer, 1966, pp. 165–68

All except a few lines of the text [of *The Investigation*] is taken from the testimony in the 1964 trial, in Frankfurt, of the SS men attached to the Auschwitz concentration camp in Poland. No attempt has been made to shape the testimony dramatically. . . . We are not, in this play, brought into the theater to receive essential information. The theater audiences of the great cities of the world are not in ignorance of the camps and the personal bestiality of those who ran them. If one were to want the transcript of the Frankfurt trials he would better be sent to the publication of them in book form . . . than to a rapid selection offered in a theater. . . .

Peter Weiss is one of the most interesting dramatists writing now. He works in a very curious manner, almost as if he were afraid to know what he is doing. He provides librettos, scenarios, almost, and these he flings to the world, for each country, each production to do with it as it will. To accept his work plain is to miss the whole point: he seems to want to put on the stage huge explosions of the instinctual life, instincts that have become politicized but are not merely politics, in spite of his own preoccupation with that part of our current life. The camps were reality: the trial at Frankfurt was a sort of near-reality, but *The Investigation* is a drama, a sublimation, a play . . . a play within a play. It is "The prosecution of the SS as performed by the inmates of the Auschwitz Concentration Camp." And we are the audience, the benevolent director of the asylum.

Elizabeth Hardwick. NYRB. Nov. 3, 1966, p. 5

In his second play, Weiss turns his back on the elaborate theatricalism of *Marat/Sade* for the documentary sobriety of *The Investigation*. Though much of the dialogue of this "Oratorio" in eleven songs is quoted directly from newspaper accounts of the Auschwitz trial, the production is not a living newspaper. Weiss converts the Brecht trial scene into the whole drama, but his verdict is sharper and harsher. Not for Weiss is Arthur Miller's "It is also clear that the one common denominator in all violent acts is the human being." Weiss shows us inhuman beings, and he draws barbed distinctions between tormentor and tormented. Brecht's ruling classes wear masks, but Weiss's concentration camp officials wear their actual names. Their victims are reduced to numbers; as in the camp.

The Investigation is an investigation and not an imitation of a trial, much less a re-creation of the Auschwitz brutalities, which would be unbearable on stage. At first glance, villains and victims look alike in their respectable business-suits, and it is only the gradual revelation of monstrosity that belies their common civilized appearance. . . .

At the beginning of each song-scene, a ground-plan of Auschwitz is projected, so that we always know the geography of the emotional horror. Accused and accusers sit undifferentiated on the stage, each person stepping front and center to testify. There are eighteen of the accused, and only nine accusers, but the nine actors play the parts of many, speaking above all for the dead. In Weiss's text, each of the accused is fixed in his role, but the accusers are interchangeable. In this age of human degradation, this drama is an investigation into deeds. The action does not move in a linear ascent of horror, but neither is there any relief from the horror. Starting with the simple facts about the camp, the accusers introduce acts of bestiality, official and unofficial. Denials are always of detail, for the accused never perceive how appalling is the whole.

Ruby Cohn. DramaS. Winter, 1966–67, p. 290

During the last four years a wave of documentary dramas has rocked and altered the German stage. Dead since 1933, the German drama has finally revived and awakened international interest. This is due, in great part, to the efforts of Rolf Hochhuth, Heinar Kipphardt, and Peter Weiss. These playwrights have been experimenting with a mode of dramatic presentation that capitalizes on the potency of fact and reveals historical truths to audiences. . . .

By focusing on events of recent history, Kipphardt, Hochhuth, and Weiss have given new impetus to the political theatre. They believe that the dramatist should teach, and they use the stage as a podium from which they express their political views. . . . They feel impelled to mend the circuit of political theatre that was broken in 1933. . . .

Weiss, Kipphardt, and Hochhuth are continuing the revolution in the German theatre ignited by Bertolt Brecht and Erwin Piscator some forty years ago. Brecht and Piscator developed and practiced a dramatic theory that transformed the theatre into a political arena. Within the walls of this arena, issues were debated and events were broadly portrayed. The theatre assumed a moral responsibility: to convey truth to audiences and through scientific and rational means to induce the people to assert themselves. . . .

Brecht and his writings have exercised a strong influence upon Weiss, Kipphardt, and Hochhuth. . . . Weiss's choice of the oratorio form in *The Investigation* and his emphasis on social and political obligation are related to Brecht's *The Measures Taken*. But what these dramatists have in common with Brecht is primarily a strong social conscience and the desire to effect change through drama. Like Brecht, they have a special interest in the technical aspects of their plays, and they have been developing his ideas to confront the problems of their day.

Jack D. Zipes. GR. Jan., 1967, pp. 49–50, 57, 61

Peter Weiss seems the prototype of the writer whose work is created under the influence of the circumstances of his time. The author is open to all the harshness, alienation, absurdity, cruelty, and violence that exists in this world. Hence he is vulnerable. He finally turned his openness and vulnerability into a positive asset: today he feels responsible for the world. He has given an account of how he was defeated by the world; he now attempts to maintain a position from which the world can perhaps be changed. . . .

Peter Weiss's merit is to have developed his monologue into literary works whose formal novelty and lack of definition attracted so little attention only because of the urgency of their subject matter. It worked because the characteristic dialogue with himself was not abandoned, because the urgency of the questions he asked himself was intensified, and because this conversation derived its life not from fictitious material but from factual data, arranged as collages and emotionally fused by their very urgency. . . . The step into topical history, taken with *Marat/Sade*, was decisive. The next step, that into topical actuality, from *The Investigation* to *Song of the Lusitanian Bogey*, and finally to his *Viet Nam Discourse*, is, by comparison, a gradual progression. And even the present, and for us so irksome, commitment of Peter Weiss does not constitute a break with himself, but a gradual shift. . . . Weiss has taken up his position. His partners in the dialogue are we, the citizens of the "Western" world.

Henning Rischbieter. Peter Weiss (Velber, Friedrich,
1967), pp. 15, 26†

In looking at the *Marat/Sade* as a whole, it is necessary not only to note the individual occurrences of cruelty, but to understand its whole conception of history as a cruel force. This latter side of the Theatre of Cruelty, as a *Weltanschauung*, is very much bound up with the ideas of determinism and free will symbolically presented in the play.

In a work that depicts the Marquis de Sade and the inmates of a lunatic asylum, and treats the subject of the Terror, one would be surprised not to find cruelty occurring in some form. The striking thing about the *Marat/Sade* is not the fact that cruelty is present in the play, but rather the specifically stylized ways in which it is depicted. On the whole—and this is the strength of the play—cruelty is acted out symbolically rather than being imitated more literally. Rather than actual killing and torture, the play gives suggestions of cruelty and horror. This also helps to give the forces of cruelty in the play a more all-pervading nature. . . .

But apart from the catalogue of individual ritual and symbolic cruelties, one can discern a general pattern of cruelty in the play. Not only are individuals cruel in their own ways, the real cruelty of the play is the deterministic suggestion that things may be unchangeable, that people are the victims of the forces of history. It is the cruelty of nature, depriving men of their free will, which really makes the play classical Theatre of Cruelty. . . . To a large extent the idea of determinism in the play . . . is expressed by the image of "direction." The play which Sade forces the inmates to perform is a symbol of history. Everyone in Weiss's play seems to be directed by someone else. The Asylum is under the direction of M. Coulmier and the play is under the direction of Sade. As a result, much is made of a series of parallels between being made to play a role in a play and being made, by a director or despot, to play a part in society and history. As the play is an historical play, the two ideas are telescoped into one.

John J. White. *MLR*. April, 1968, pp. 446–47

Song of the Lusitanian Bogey shows an indebtedness to the tradition of the proletarian-revolutionary theater, especially that of Erwin Piscator. In Piscator's pioneering productions, the journalistic, documentary presentation of the material was coupled with a predominantly epic development of the plot. In our time, Peter Weiss raises this tradition to a higher poetic level, appropriate for a new public, basing it on a new subject matter corresponding to a new situation. . . .

Weiss's dramatic text has incorporated various modes of expression found in the earlier dramatic forms. The discrepancies from which the theater of Piscator and also that of Meyerhold suffered because of the inferior stage of development, or else the deficiency of socialist drama—here the play and there the historical principles, here man and there the social process, here the drama and there the artistry . . . —these discrepancies are abolished in Weiss's drama, because of the homogeneity of the text and its corresponding theatrical realization. Because of its high degree of artistic perfection, above all its skillfully weighed and carefully conceived use of language, its poetic features—especially in the choral parts—and its use of the alienation technique, handled with both the superb skill of the artist and the masterful accuracy of the agitator, the play opens up for the author a broad base of political influence among the different social strata of the audience.

Brigitte Thurm. *WB*. 15, 5, 1969, pp. 1097–98†

The *Viet Nam Discourse* is divided into two parts, each consisting of eleven "phases." The first part is a dramatized account of the history of Vietnam from about 500 B.C. to 1946 A.D. The second part plays mostly in the

Western world and deals with the French and American interventions in Vietnam until the Tonkin Gulf Resolution passed by the U.S. Congress on August 7, 1964. . . .

During the first part of the drama the black [the oppressed] and white [the oppressors] figures discuss and, to a lesser extent, act out the "long-lasting war of liberation of Vietnam." . . . As more than two thousand years of Vietnamese history unfold before the spectator, he cannot help but admire the steadfastness of this people in its quest for national independence and its indomitable resilience after countless defeats. The repetitiousness of the historic events presented on the stage forces the spectator to make connections with contemporary history, to place this contemporary history in its proper perspective, and to think about facts which the mass media do not choose to present. . . .

The second part of *Viet Nam Discourse* is too static and cerebral, even for documentary drama. . . . The long discussions and declarations address themselves exclusively to the intellect, as an essay or newspaper article would. Furthermore, these discussions involve almost exclusively one side—the group dressed in white. . . . The villains are among themselves.

The second part of *Viet Nam Discourse* notwithstanding, it is fair to say that Weiss's documentary dramas are quite effective, both as dramas in the Aristotelian sense, and as instruments for the explanation of reality.

Franz P. Haberl. BA. Summer, 1969, pp. 361–62

Weiss concerns himself with present-day actualities, with living realities as he sees them—Auschwitz, Angola, Viet Nam. He has sympathy with Hochhuth's stand over "burning issues," though he does not necessarily share the latter's moral outlook. He understands Beckett's viewpoint, though again without sharing it. Equally he has an awareness of past history, and also of past traditions of literature and art and their forms: Dante, the paintings of Bosch, Strindberg, who was so influential in German Expressionism, Kafka, whose novels "resemble sequences of stage settings or the reels of fantastic films," and there are other sources of inspiration too like Hesse, Wedekind, Brecht, etc. In many ways, *particularly* in the delight in formal experimentation, Weiss has remained to the present day so closely in touch with Expressionism/Surrealism. Observable in his plays are Strindberg's dream play with its reliance on visual effects and lighting, Wedekind's aggressiveness within the framework of the circus-world and its "components of music, acrobatic theatrical ballet." And the world of Kafka is evident too. It is in this context moreover that Weiss's keen interest in the cinema should be viewed. . . . The results of these multiple influences can be seen to good effect both in his prose and in his work for the theatre.

Ian Hilton. Peter Weiss (London, Oswald Wolff,
1970), pp. 70–71

The common theme of the *Divina Commedia,* and of *The Investigation,* is bitter protest against existing human society. Dante protests because man ruins the divine plan of love and justice. . . . Weiss protests against the present form of society, for whose evils, as a Marxist, he puts the blame solely on the men who made and continue to make this society. However, it is not the common theme that is important to Weiss, but the concrete details of the *Divina Commedia,* the "associations which have become actual fact in my world."

"Association" is used in psychology for the involuntary mental connection between an object and ideas. The last quotation must be interpreted in this sense. The association between concentration camps and Dante's *Inferno* has existed since the first pictures of the camps and their few survivors were shown on newsreels. The "hell of Auschwitz" is both a myth and a euphemism. To destroy this myth by showing a model of the man-made, well organized machinery, is precisely one of the tasks which the documentary theater sets for itself. Weiss saw in Frankfurt that the association was not with Dante's grand design, with his eschatology, but instead with the concrete details. Dante's vision had concretized. The associations had become authenticated analogues. No doubt Dante's language helped Weiss in the task of "redrawing the events in . . . [his] mind," of moving from "knowing" to "understanding." Consciousness is expanded by the act of redrawing events in the mind. It follows that the associations helped Weiss in writing *The Investigation,* just as the mathematical structure was useful. In Weiss's essay on Dante the antithesis of vision versus fact occurs frequently. . . . There exist, however, not only vague parallels of torture, but specific details of Dante's phantasmagoric visions which have realized themselves as objective existence. Three examples are: first a report on entrance procedure, then an instrument of torture, and finally a sign. . . .

To these associations which link *The Investigation* to the *Divina Commedia,* one must add the personal affinity which Peter Weiss feels with Dante Alighieri. Dante, too, was driven from his native country, he was a refugee, he was condemned to death, "he sits in exile and writes."

Erika Salloch. *MD*. May, 1971, pp. 9, 11

A . . . point arises concerning a work like *The Investigation.* With its rejection of any characterization or even of any continuity of the actors' roles, with its refusal to establish any kind of relationship between the characters or allow any gesturing or any movements on the stage, does this play not refuse to be dramatic? The question was asked by Gabriel Garran when he decided to produce the work, and admitted that he really did not know, but for me at any rate, the complete absorption of the spectators seemed to give the answer a producer would like to hear. An "oratorio in 11 cantos," with solos and duets, with voices replying to voices or re-echoing them, is a new dramatic form, not classical doubtless, nor yet a *pièce bien faite,* but valid none the less as theatre. The problem for Weiss with regard to this play and others he was contemplating writing, was, as he confesses himself, how to give poetic form to the political judgment which informs a work. A document cannot be expected to make a play by itself, nor will the mere intellectual appreciation of a situation. A feeling, a mood, an attitude, an artistic awareness, must govern the work, and Weiss's "cantos," his "solos" and "duets" may well do more in this respect than the realism of [Jean] Vilar's pipe-smoking [in the French production of Heinar Kipphardt's *In the Matter of J. Robert Oppenheimer*].

Dorothy Knowles. *ML*. June, 1971, p. 85

Trotsky in Exile, Weiss' new play, seems to open a new phase in his dramaturgy. The stylistic change is the most striking. . . . This play has a theatrical framework: the old, isolated Trotsky recalls the significant moments of his life, shortly before his murder; but here, in contrast with *Marat/Sade,* there is no alienating irony. *Trotsky,* like *Viet Nam Discourse,* is based on detailed documentary material, but Trotsky and Lenin, unlike the anonymous figures in *Viet Nam,* are distinct, individualized characters. The prolonged discussions between the two leaders of the Russian Revolution do not turn them into rhetorical figures, as happened to Marat and the Marquis de Sade, because the dramatic, sometimes arbitrary, mechanism of the revolution sweeps them up and makes them clear dramatic characters. The cruelty of Trotsky's end, after a long exile, even approaches the tragic. . . .

The theme of each of these plays is a revolution, but in *Marat/Sade* we see only one event from the French Revolution, presented several times, through devices derived from Brecht's Epic Theater. In *Trotsky* we are presented with many important events of the Russian Revolution, played in accordance with the historical course of events. There are, however, almost no theatrical devices of the Epic Theater, although several characteristics of the play, including the expansiveness of time and place, make the drama epic in the Brechtian sense. . . .

Within the epic scope of presentation, the flashback technique allows Weiss to mix Trotsky's utopian hopes for the future in the often grisly events of the revolutionary past. The causes and effects, motives and results, by the transposition of time and the change of viewpoint, cross over each other. In effect the play is presented on two levels that simultaneously influence each other: on one level we watch the epic plot of the progress of the Russian Revolution, and on the other level we witness the inquiring mind of Trotsky as it seeks to penetrate to the deepest levels of the development of the revolution and to uncover their significance. In this way Weiss contends that a revolution is the result of tremendous spiritual effort and clear insight on the part of the leaders, which allows them to shape the social and political situation in accordance with a long-range plan.

Gideon Shunami. *GQ*. Nov., 1971, pp. 505, 507

Weiss makes clear that he is not attempting to re-try particular Frankfurt defendants [in *The Investigation*] but to use their evidence for wider purposes: "they lend the author only their names, which stand here as symbols." The play, subtitled "Oratorium in 11 Cantos," is obviously intended to some extent as a memorial to those who died in the death camp. That it is much more than this is indicated by the allusion to Dante's *Divine Comedy* in the structuring into cantos and in the movement down from the "Song from the Ramp" to the final "Song of the Furnaces." This, too, enhances the purpose of generalisation beyond the particular and extreme case of Auschwitz, and what emerges is a plea for critical self-examination affecting attitudes and values that may still operate in our society. . . .

The Investigation thus marks the change coming over documentary literature in Germany from the middle of the sixties, away from issues of the past to a greater concern with the present, together with a more marked political engagement. . . . This shift to a committed concept of literature is reflected in the works which Weiss published after *The Investigation—Song of the Lusitanian Bogey, Viet Nam Discourse,* and *Notes Concerning the Cultural Life in the Democratic Republic of Vietnam.* All deal with the Third World.

R. Hinton Thomas and Keith Bullivant. *Literature in Upheaval* (Manchester, England, Manchester University Press, 1974), pp. 104, 109–10

Unlike *Marat/Sade, Hölderlin* is not dialectic theater. The dialogue has no heuristic function; it merely serves as a vehicle for a prefabricated philosophy of life. The initial dialogue, implied by the antithesis of Empedocles and Hermocrates, both creations of Hölderlin, is not played out. The author is solely interested in the confirmation of "truth." He assembles selected documentary facts into a simultaneity of effects in order to achieve a political propaganda effect. At the same time he attempts to maintain aesthetic elements. Speaking of *Trotsky,* Weiss noted that his montage and selection of material was aimed at restoring "proper historical proportions." What is "proper" is determined by the author—or by the "party" to which he belongs. In this fashion his succession of pictures from the life of Hölderlin becomes a chronicle demonstrating an ideological concept. Events of Hölderlin's life, shown in the proper light, serve negatively to prove the positive value of a particular ideology. The play thus becomes confessional fiction, self-expression toward a political end. By what criteria is this end to be judged, since easily proven misstatements of verifiable facts can at any time impart a negative connotation to it? Though the appearance of reality through the use of historical names preserves the mask, the hidden message differs from the apparent one. Artistic correctness and factual correctness are in a relationship of negative tension but they simulate congruence. A clear separation of the two would at the very least have been an emphatic invitation to judge the play simply as a work of art. However, . . . once the historical names and associations have been discounted, the play is nothing but an embarrassingly rattling, involuntarily comic set of cartoons. The tendency to the grotesque and the crude superficiality are so clear that even the sickly archaisms of the writing can scarcely cloak them with compassion.

The play begins and ends with an allusion to the "tower" where Hölderlin lived out his life and which the author calls a "prison." Is it coincidental that the image of the tower recalls Peter Weiss's first play, *The Tower?* Pablo freed himself from his prison by directly overcoming his alter ego. Hölderlin's liberation comes about in a different way—it is an act of faith. The "Marxist mystery play" has taken the place of the original "existentialist drama"—a transformation already apparent in *Trotsky*. Demonstration of the "essential" is intended to provide an "insight into the essential." From this angle, *Hölderlin* is a drama of martyrdom without tragedy or conflict, rather like *Trotsky in Exile*. Marx appears as the angel of the annunciation, bringing the joyful message of the Hölderlin-Christ resurrection to the "tower." He represents, not the quest for truth, but a celebration of the truth that has been found.

The process reflected in the total chronology of Peter Weiss's work, in which the antitheses strive toward resolution and reconciliation in a postrevolutionary utopia of solidarity and identity, is another celebration of its own end.

Otto F. Best. *Peter Weiss* (New York,
Frederick Ungar, 1976), pp. 133–35

Weiss's Auschwitz oratorium [*The Investigation*] transcends the simplistic charge of communist propaganda. The dream of justice, of the dissolution of the dialectic between oppressor and oppressed, is not even intimated. Dream and nightmare occur in the same world. Awareness merely leads to the painful recognition of an incomprehensible emptiness which the poet tries to fill with words. These words shape, in spite of all reliance on documents, Weiss's vision of Auschwitz, his comprehensible explanation. However, since the dialectic of the play is part of historical time, it is subject to changes and ironies that the playwright cannot predict. In a utopia of reason and consciousness, Weiss's play, if not banned, would be considered prophetic, but at the expense of those for whom the extermination camps were primarily established—the Jews.

If we imagine a future in which Weiss's oratorium is the only document of the holocaust to survive, we become immediately aware of the limitations of documentary theater as a conveyor of facts. By emphasizing the sufferings of the political prisoners, Weiss shows the individual dignity of the believer's agony. His death, torturous as it may have been, was more likely to be remembered than the death of an unnumbered Jew. When Weiss does describe the latter death in several cantos, he does so without writing the word *Jew,* for that word remains a problem for him.

Hamida Bosmajian. *Metaphors of Evil: Contemporary German Literature and the Shadow of Nazism* (Iowa City, University of Iowa Press, 1979), p. 172

When the *dramatis personae* [of *Marat/Sade*] are presented, they are designated both by their "reality" and their role. All but Coulmier are inmates of the clinic who, for purposes of rehabilitation through art, are acting out roles in a kind of psychodrama depicting the assassination of Jean-Paul Marat. . . .

The device of madmen playing historical figures is especially effective when we consider Weiss's characters in their metafictional status. The duality of the *dramatis personae,* of which an audience responding to the metafictional character is ever aware, is indeed present here, but in this case that duality requires a complicating qualification. The character (whom we would normally view as the fictive self) is in this case an historical figure, hence every bit as real as the actor himself. On the other hand, the actor (whom we normally view as the real self) is in this case one who lives in a world of illusions—a framework of unreality which characterizes his madness. And if the duality functions, as it normally does, to remind us of the inherent duality implicit in *any* dramatic character, we are one dimension further removed, and every part of the show, even the reality of the inmates, becomes sham. . . .

Already combining and confusing illusion and reality by virtue of its being simultaneously stage and history, the event takes on additional perspective by the fact that it is fictionalized in 1808, fifteen years later than its historical occurrence. The time gap is obliquely but certainly a reference to the contemporary German situation which . . . would surely be noticed by Weiss's 1964 audience.

June Schlueter. *Metafictional Characters in Modern Drama* (New York, Columbia University Press, 1979), pp. 73–74

ZUCKMAYER, CARL (1896–1977)

[*The Merry Vineyard*] is certainly the extreme opposite of expressionism; . . . it is, for those who hold literary slogans in high esteem, really something like the triumph of naturalism. But, as a closer look will show, that does not mean that it therefore amounts to nothing more than just some trivial entertainment; it is actually something like a test of strength, a sign that the young generation is on the road to recovery. . . .

The characters of this ordinary play are anything but commonplace. They are *living human beings,* and individual man . . . is never trivial. They are human because their feet are firmly planted on the soil again, because they are surrounded by air and light, because they are defined in terms of their local region and culture. . . . *Here the return to* [man as a] *living organism has come to pass.*

Closely connected with this idea is, once more, the fact that finally, after a long time, we again have before us a play that deals with love. With love between people! Until now we actually had to deal only with declamations concerning some completely intangible general love of God or man, or (and of late much more frequently) the hideous internecine struggle of unleashed animals. Love, however, is a human process that, emanating from the most intimate sensual attraction, permeates man's entire realm, ultimately transforming his whole spiritual attitude. . . . Love demands a whole human being with all of the natural and cultural traits that are in any way related to this idea. *Individuals* are the necessary prerequisite. . . . And because Zuckmayer's comedy portrays real human beings again, there also is genuine love. . . . Man—willing again to make a definite choice and to hold on to it; an organic creature capable of love—has reappeared on the stage. [1926]

Julius Bab. *Die Chronik des deutschen Dramas* (Darmstadt,
Wissenschaftliche Buchgesellschaft, 1972), Vol. V,
pp. 359, 362–63†

Schinderhannes is the story of a robber and takes place among bandits and poor peasants, musicians and soldiers; an historical period is depicted from the viewpoint of the common people. . . .

Zuckmayer wanted to portray the life and death of the brave robber chief Johann Bückler, called Schinderhannes, his fight in the name of the little man against the law and authority of the powerful—his rise to the position of master of the Hunsrück, and, finally, his capture and public execution in Mainz. The result: dramatic intensification is possible only during the first half—as Schinderhannes victoriously roams the region, a redeemer to the poor and an enemy to the rich, as he wins Julchen Blasius, the musician's daughter, and finally as he even takes up the fight against the French armed forces. The moment this fight comes to a bad end, the possibility of an actively developing dramatic action no longer exists; the lyrical element begins to take over: the theme is the downfall of Hannes, his flight, arrest, and execution. From the middle on, the curve dips; it is then no easy task to keep things moving and to retain the spectator's interest. Zuckmayer almost overcomes this difficulty. . . . The play is splendidly put together with regard to construction, its effortless arrangement of the action, and the strength of its character drawing . . . yet at times it is marked by something like the very beautiful protraction of broadside ballads and popular minstrelsy. [Oct. 10, 1927]

Paul Fechter. In Günther Rühle, ed., *Theater für die Republik* (Frankfurt, Fischer, 1967), pp. 800–801†

The Captain of Köpenick has turned out to be Zuckmayer's best play in its effectiveness on the stage and its characterization. Through an immense number of juicy and terse little scenes, he sketches a picture of bourgeois and militaristic imperial Germany with a wit that is almost always an outgrowth of his keen sense of observation. His humor has its roots in dialect. Zuckmayer listens, observes, and then creates. A profusion of people, a profusion of roles. As far as dramatic technique is concerned, the world of these role players is divided into the story of the cobbler Wilhelm Voigt, who, while trying to obtain a permit of residency and a passport, finds himself again and again thrown into prison, and the story of a uniform that sinks so low as to end up in a secondhand goods shop in Grenadier Street. . . .

Every character is humorous in himself. What is lacking, however, is an ordering principle of spiritual values against which all that takes place is to be viewed.

That is crucial. Let there be no misunderstanding. It is a good thing that *The Captain of Köpenick* has not become a rigid drama with a purpose, that it makes the claim of "art." But art can only exist on the basis of a philosophy of life, an attitude toward the world. I do not see such an ordering principle. All right: Zuckmayer takes a look at the world, he draws a picture of it. But I am unable to see the fixed position from which he views it. He changes, he is in love with characters. He does not direct the spectator's thought to a position from which to view what is going on. Thus, one person can see the play as a military farce, a second as a moderate social indictment, a third as a satire. [March 6, 1931]

Herbert Ihering. *Von Reinhardt bis Brecht* (East Berlin, Aufbau, 1961), Vol. III, pp. 142–43†

Man has to decide, before it is too late, whether he wants to live as a free being or as a slave. This however is not enough. Nor is it enough for man to know *for what* he fights or what he is fighting *against*. Before he takes up arms man must know *why* he kills. Such is the argument set forth in Zuckmayer's *The Song in the Fiery Furnace*. . . .

Zuckmayer tells us that the drama is based upon a newspaper report in the *Basler National-Zeitung* . . . of an incident in the Savoy during the occupation of France. He raises the content of the drama on to a higher human level, above the actual happenings. The inner and outer struggles are no longer those of the present generation alone. They have always existed and always will exist until man looks again upon himself as God's creation endowed with dignity and having the freedom to choose love rather than hatred. . . . From the Prologue we see that man has stepped aside from his true position in God's creation of Nature. In very effective scenes, once before the passage of the refugees across the mountain pass, and later, when all the Maquis have died, the personifications of Wind, Frost and Mist, in highly poetical language, express their relation to man. They know him not; they do not consider him. They do not help him. Only a man can help another man, and to do so he needs the help of heaven. Man viewed cosmologically has lost his ground and stands before chaos. And man has also lost God, who is wisdom and love. So from the theological point of view man has lost his ground there too. With some diffidence it may be suggested that here, in leading man to God through man's belief in himself and through worship and adoration of God, Zuckmayer follows in a wider sense the ideas of the Roman Catholic French dramatist Marcel and the philosophy of Kierkegaard, but standing above either dogma. Above all, Zuckmayer's conclusion is that human life is sacred and finds its fulfilment in self-sacrificing love and selfless action.

G. Guder. GL&L. Oct., 1953, pp. 29–30

Zuckmayer is always the artist experiencing and shaping life and concrete reality. As a poet, as a dramatist, he is more original, more of one piece, more untroubled by reflection and program than Brecht. He finds the material and style appropriate to him in *The Merry Vineyard*. Personally and objectively he is on firm ground in this play. It emanates from the folk spirit of his native region, but it is not a narrow-minded provincial work. He writes as a literary man who had previously mastered the expressionistic style and has just discovered that his talent is primarily realistic-naturalistic, that most of all the stage needs life itself and not ideas, not disembodied souls, not fashionable mannerisms. Zuckmayer often has a better command of naturalism than the naturalists themselves, being free of their programmatic presentations or schoolboylike exercises. Hauptmann is his closest, most important model, the one he follows most successfully.

Otto Mann. In Hermann Friedmann and Otto Mann, eds.,
Deutsche Literatur im zwanzigsten Jahrhundert (Heidelberg,
Rothe, 1954), p. 375†

A word about Zuckmayer's humor. It too is inextricably bound to his general view of nature in that it is best described by the word "natural," using the adjective advisedly. Those who know *The Merry Vineyard* will agree that although the humor is based to a large extent upon sex, there is nothing in it that could possibly be termed objectionable. It is a humor of people who are close to the soil, people whose life revolves around elemental natural occurrences. It is found in *Katharina Knie,* a play about a traveling troupe of acrobats, and we can see it again in *Schinderhannes.* It is rarely intellectual and always genuine. Sarcasm plays a very minor role, but there are moments of real satire, as in *The Captain of Köpenick,* where German militarism is held up to ridicule, and where, incidentally, Zuckmayer might have been pointing out the future dangers of National Socialism. In the postwar plays, *The Devil's General, Barbara Blomberg, The Song in the Fiery Furnace* and *Ulla Winblad* [*; or, Music and Life of Carl Michael Bellman*], the atmosphere is generally reflective; although there are moments when one cannot help bursting into laughter, the tone of these plays as a whole is more subdued. The emphasis on the affirmation of life is still there, nevertheless. It is not so frequently expressed in the joyous, riotous, often raucous manner that characterizes the early plays. It pulsates more quietly but just as strongly, beneath the surface, and is more often given expression in the eventual solution of inner problems than in boisterous physical outbursts.

As a master of dramatic technique and dramatic dialogue, Zuckmayer has no equal today, and can rightfully assume Gerhart Hauptmann's mantle. That could very well be why Zuckmayer was asked to rework and complete Hauptmann's drama *Herbert Engelmann,* and it can hardly be denied, with all deference to Hauptmann, that he improved on the original.

Ian C. Loram. *GQ.* May, 1954, pp. 145–46

The Cold Light has an international cast of characters with the possibilities of conflict and tension that might naturally arise. But the conflict is not determined by national ties, and nationalism is not an issue except in the person of the English scientist Ketterick, who represents an old-fashioned type of nationalism and blind service to one's country. . . .

What the play is conjuring up in its dialogue and action is then not the historical past, nor a series of moments that changed the course of world events, but on the contrary it is bringing alive to the audience the motives for Wolter's betrayal. What is being reconstructed in dramatic form is not a turning-point in world history, but the dilemma of conscience of modern man. In *The Devil's General* and in *The Song in the Fiery Furnace* the dramatic action showed the central characters groping their way through various possibilities of avoiding decision or of making the wrong one; in *Herbert Engelmann* the crime was already given; what remained to be motivated were its causes, its nature, and the effect upon the persons involved, namely the shattering of the natural unit of trust and confidence, the family. In *The Cold Light* on the other hand it is a problem of defining the mistake itself and of finding out what is right or wrong in an uncharted region. The only guide is, as in all Zuckmayer's plays, the principle of human decency. Wolter's only criterion is the nature of his relation to those who are bound to him in trust. On the political level Zuckmayer has not tried to answer all the questions he has raised, but rather he demonstrates the effect of a "wrong" choice on the conscience of the individual concerned, and even more by the effect that the steps taken have on those who trust and love the person concerned. The final "right" choice may lead to the destruction of the hero: Engelmann, Harras, the German deserters in *The Song in the Fiery Furnace,* and Wolters. The self-destruction of the hero through moral awakening is the basis of the tragic element in Zuckmayer's post-war plays.

> Murray B. Peppard. *Monatshefte.* March, 1957, pp. 122, 124

Zuckmayer, the man of action, realizes apparently with some regret the extremely limited influence that his own craft can exert on the actual course of history. All the greater, however, and indeed without limitations, is his belief in the influence the dramatist can wield in the creation of a moral climate for our generation and succeeding ones. . . .

The cathartic effect as it extends to the audience is Zuckmayer's special concern; to him this is one of the most important functions in the drama. The dramatist, through his gift of synthesis, conjures up the healing forces of wholeness. Through creative participation in the spectacle of the drama man catches glimpses of the underlying harmony which is of God, and by such an embrace of the whole, he secures the cathartic effect or gains in some measure a realization of the soundness to be found in the ultimate total. It is dramatic creation of this wholeness that Zuckmayer sees as the supreme task of the dramatist.

Thus the dramatist becomes a healer giving men through eros an awareness of their potential wholeness. More specifically, he brings about a catharsis by giving an intimation of the incommensurable unitary force in which all dualisms and all chaos are resolved and which reveals divine essence. . . . Beauty, as an outer manifestation of eros, is the closest man can get to an actual perception of the fundamental unity.

The type of drama that results from such a view Zuckmayer designates as poetic theatre, characterized by its complex substance and by its subservience to the demands of a true *Humanität* [humanity]. This *Humanität* is to be created by the transcendental or eros force which binds all elements of existence into a deep and meaningful whole.

> Henry Glade. *Monatshefte.* April–May, 1960, pp. 166, 168

Carl Zuckmayer's latest play, *The Clock Strikes One,* marks another important stage in his works. It is an evaluation of a yet more recent present than the one found in *The Devil's General,* written in 1942–45, or in *The Cold Light,* published in 1956. The subject matter is not the Germany of the war years, nor a problem arising immediately after the war, but the Germany of the years 1953–54, more precisely man and the new problems he is encountering at this period in human history. The picture given is sufficiently broad and has a sufficient depth to be significant; being presented directly, not through a framework of symbolism, nor removed to a distant past or future, it gains in urgency.

The centre of the play is occupied by Gerhard, a youth of 18. This is the generation which at this point is entering upon adulthood. The decision it makes will shape its own future and that of the world. Yet is it capable of positive action, of shaping its own life? It has no trust in the old generation which is burdened down and crippled by the guilt of the past; it has no example of a life in which love would reveal itself as a creative force. As a result it turns to scorn and hatred and finds a bitter and cynical solace in obeying a despotic power governed by and representing these forces.

It would seem that in the life of Gerhard there can be no turning point, and yet Zuckmayer, unlike many writers of today, does not let his play end on a pessimistic note. His purpose in making an analysis of our times is to offer a solution. This solution does not come in the form of a radical change in world structure but in the form of a change taking place within the life of an individual. At that moment when Gerhard for the first time in his life is able to feel love towards another human being he renounces scorn and hatred and, moreover, comes to the realization that whatever the past, whatever the environment, whatever the vicissitudes of life, there is no reason for man to despair of leading a productive life, for he is at all times in control of his own soul, his inner being. . . .

For Gerhard personally the realization comes too late in his life for him to be able to follow his desire of starting anew; his life ends but in a new attitude. But it is not too late for those who will commence their lives in the spirit of this realization, and if they do so for them too, and even more significantly, the clock will strike one and a new day begin.

Helen Hodgson. *GL&L*. July, 1962, pp. 332–33

One of the most decisive experiences [in *The Cold Light*] is that of loneliness, of the inability to communicate, not so much as a scientist, but as a human being. . . . Zuckmayer leads his physicist out of his impersonal attachment to the world of science to a committed sense of responsibility, not only to society, but above all to himself. His confession of guilt at the end of the play signifies also a confession that he has lived too long in the rays of a cold light that emanated from outside himself and filled him with an interior coldness: "And yet one moment can be fire again, in which everything is transformed. . . ."

Zuckmayer's play might be considered a Christian melodrama (in the same sense that *Faust* is) inasmuch as the hero is snatched from certain damnation. To be sure, the scene of the struggle is moved into the inner stage of the protagonist's soul, but the religious undertones are as strong as the purely psychological overtones. It is perhaps a bit too obvious when Zuckmayer has his protagonist reveal in the second scene that he changed the spelling of his given name from Christof to Kristof to purify it of the savior-symbol. But he cannot escape his fate. In the end the hero recognizes his guilt, confesses it, and is prepared to atone for it. But the role of Northon—agent, friend, and counselor—and the theme of the protagonist's education fall into the pattern of that peculiarly German traditional attachment to the idea of *Entwicklung* [development] and guidance.

Karl S. Weimar. *MLQ*. Dec., 1966, pp. 442, 445

Schinderhannes, differing from the members of the community, an individual who follows his own law, becomes the very anti-pole of society [in *Schinderhannes*]; he is in a true sense an *Einzelgänger* [outsider] who clashes at every step with the world around him. The tension between these two poles, between outsider and society, is the motivating force of the play; the *Begegnungen* [encounters] between them form the *Stationen* [stations] along which the action moves. Both sides, however, equally belong to the one and all-embracing pattern of life; both of them are indispensable. Whilst the outcome of the conflict is beyond doubt from the beginning, the outsider is still a necessary force in the life of the community, an integral part of a divine plan. . . . Schinderhannes has a definite function to fulfill; it is only through him and his actions that the community becomes conscious of itself and of its problems. . . . Wherever the prevailing *Ordnung* [order] in society is discussed, this occurs only in connexion with the name and the actions of Schinderhannes. Only through him do people become aware of their own situation; it is his existence, and the change it has brought into the world by challenging the established order, that makes people see their usual lives in a different perspective.

The obdurate individual whose presence creates a ferment which eventually lays bare the evils and faults of society's structure fulfils his function, not in the conscious pursuit of a social ideal, but unconsciously, simply by succumbing to his own nature and to his fate. . . . The interrelation between individual and society therefore takes place at a higher level and is part of a sublime purpose; whilst the influence of socialist ideas is indisputably present in this play, there is at the same time the recognition of a universal and metaphysical force which governs the life of man and society.

E. Speidel. *MLR*. April, 1968, pp. 429–30

Zuckmayer belongs among the relatively few humorists Germany has produced. He has a depth of warmly reflective perception that never fails to hit the target. His generally well-constructed plays produce theatrical effects that ultimately silence many a critical objection. His talent as a storyteller, developed by study of the best traditions, impressively reveals an open, realistic, and humane commitment to the world. Strong imagery abounds in his poetry and epic descriptions of nature.

The sources from which Zuckmayer draws his inspiration can be found in the themes of popular art, songs, fairy tales, chronicles, and anecdotes. Such a basis in the natural and folkloristic is essentially a romantic trait and is most apparent in his poems, stories, and early plays, but it does not preclude astute observations and lifelike characterization of his countrymen as real people. There is no conflict between Zuckmayer's zest for life and his intellectual curiosity. His love for his country, while not always entirely free of sentimentality, is fully compatible with the attitude of a citizen of the world who favors friendship among nations. This attitude does not reflect a blurred view of the world, but expresses a noble faith.

In tracing the development of Zuckmayer's writing career one must simultaneously study the forces that shaped Germany's destiny. The patriotic young soldier of 1914 grew into a public-spirited citizen of the Weimar Republic; then that citizen, of Jewish descent on his mother's side, became an emigrant still unable to hate his country. All these experiences left their mark on his work. . . .

It is relatively easy to determine the historical origins of Zuckmayer's literary endeavors. It is more difficult to evaluate fairly his position and intellectual standpoint in relation to the literary currents and fashionable styles of contemporary thought.

Arnold Bauer. Carl Zuckmayer (New York,
Frederick Ungar, 1976), pp. 2–3

Zuckmayer's account of Berlin and Nazism in 1941, regardless of its revealed truths or insights, proved convincing to audiences in 1946/47, not in the least because they all saw themselves in one or more of the characters. Consequently, the popularity and general acceptance of *The Devil's General* substantiates, if nothing else, the quantitative success of the play in amassing factually accurate character-types, in being "convincing." . . .

All of these types have a common trait: they reveal the impact of social change on man's behavior. There is no suggestion of the demonic, Dionysian in Germans and German culture, as for example, in Mann's *Doktor Faustus*. No Satanic overtones appear in the ardent Nazis, as in Hochhuth's [*The*] *Deputy*. . . . As a matter of fact, through Harras that very tendency among Germans toward the metaphysical, the Faustian and demonic is ridiculed. . . .

The problem lies not in the fact that the Germans are demonic but in their seeing themselves as such. Like Brecht, Zuckmayer considers the social causes, but unlike the *Stückeschreiber* [playwright], he eschews a single, facile interpretation. The only unifying factor is the Germans' tendency to take themselves too seriously and their resultant misery. Yet Zuckmayer, by his almost too "slick" use of geographical and social types, attempts a quantitatively complete presentation of all conceivable reactions—economic, artistic, moral and otherwise—to Nazi rule and war. The main danger of such type-casting lies in the very fact that each character personifies attributes so thoroughly, so purely, that he comes close to becoming a mere abstraction of historical forces.

Roy C. Cowen. UDR. Winter, 1976, pp. 83, 86–87

[Harras in *The Devil's General*] can salvage his self-respect, and still the voice of his conscience, only by clinging to his individualism, by refusing not only to join the party but also to hide his contempt of the Nazis and their methods. Even when extreme pressure is being brought to bear upon him, he is not willing to swallow his pride in order to save his skin. . . . Nonetheless, he is fully aware of his own moral degradation. . . . Only through his own death can he attempt to atone for his way of life and achieve at least partial redemption.

In many ways, Harras is a tragic figure, although not a heroic one. In spite of the personal courage he often demonstrates, it is his essential weakness, his self-indulgence, which constitutes the tragic flaw of his character and is the cause of his destruction. Throughout the play, however, he has Zuckmayer's sympathy—and that of the audience.

Many of his traits are taken directly from his real-life prototype [Ernst Udet]: his charm, his wit, his womanizing, his drinking habits, his legendary skill as a marksman, his loyalty towards friends and subordinates, which they return, and above all his attempt at self-justification. He is at heart an incurable romantic, a sentimental individualist, a naive dreamer who only fully awakens to the terrible realities and tragic consequences of his actions when it is too late. As such, he stands in sharp contrast to the two fanatics who are his counterplayers—the rabid Nazi Schmidt-Lausitz and the idealistic zealot Oderbruch. Both are extremists, and Harras represents the man in the middle, caught in what is to him an insoluble ethical dilemma.

Herbert Lederer. In Edward R. Haymes, ed., Theatrum
Mundi: Essays on German Drama and German Literature,
Houston German Studies 2 (Munich, Fink, 1980), p. 178

In his second-to-last drama, *The Life of Horace A. W. Tabor* . . . Zuckmayer again drew on his experiences as an American resident and seized upon a genuinely and uniquely American subject: an authentic hero's rise from rags to riches and, in a significant deviation from the pattern of the success story, his sudden downfall. . . .

Despite Zuckmayer's insistence that he had not intended any evocation of the Wild West, it is fair to say that he did not entirely escape the danger of making concessions to popular European preconceptions about the United States. . . . A closer look at the text reveals, however, that *The Life of Horace A. W. Tabor* is not, by any means, simply an improved version of the early drama *Pankraz Awakens*. On the contrary, although the first act begins in the run-down golddigger town of Leadville in 1879, the playwright endeavors to de-emphasize the adventuresome and exotic elements by referring to phenomena of the modern industrial world such as environmental pollution and social problems. Only as part of the exposition, presented by means of report, dialogue, and as a play within the play, does the colorful past of the pioneer and the fight against the Indians play a role. Other conflicts, that is, primarily those between workers and their employers, dominate the present. . . .

In the final analysis it was not the playwright's aim to explore the social dimensions of an important phase of American history; rather, Zuckmayer was fascinated by the figure of Tabor, whose rapid rise and fall—despite its peculiarly American traits—seems to transcend the specific time and place of the action.

Siegfried Mews. *Carl Zuckmayer* (Boston,
Twayne, 1981), pp. 125–27

PLAYS MENTIONED

Listed here, by dramatist in order of appearance in the body of the book, are all the plays mentioned in the critical selections. Nondramatic titles have been omitted. Titles are arranged alphabetically, and are followed by the date of first performance, unless otherwise indicated. All non-English titles are listed alphabetically by literal translation, as used in the selections. After each literal translation is the title in the original language, followed by the date of first performance, given in parentheses. If a published English translation exists, the title, translator, collection in which it appears (if applicable), and place and year of publication are given. Where several translations of one play are available, the compiler has chosen the best and/or most accessible.

American

ALBEE, EDWARD

All Over (1971)
The American Dream (1961)
The Ballad of the Sad Café (1963; adaptation of novel by Carson McCullers)
Box (1968)
Counting the Ways (1977)
The Death of Bessie Smith (1960 West Berlin, 1961 New York)
A Delicate Balance (1966)
Everything in the Garden (1967; adaptation of play by Giles Cooper)
The Lady from Dubuque (1980)
Listening (1977)
Malcolm (1966; adaptation of novel by James Purdy)
Quotations from Chairman Mao Tse-tung (1968)
The Sandbox (1960)
Seascape (1975)
Tiny Alice (1964)
Who's Afraid of Virginia Woolf? (1962)
The Zoo Story (1959 West Berlin, 1960 New York)

HELLMAN, LILLIAN

Another Part of the Forest (1946)
The Autumn Garden (1951)
The Children's Hour (1934)
Days to Come (1936)
The Lark (1955; adaptation of play by Jean Anouilh)
The Little Foxes (1939)
Montserrat (1949; adaptation of play by Emmanuel Roblès)
The Searching Wind (1944)
Toys in the Attic (1960)
Watch on the Rhine (1941)

MILLER, ARTHUR

After the Fall (1964)
All My Sons (1947)
The American Clock (1980)
The Creation of the World and Other Business (1973)
The Crucible (1953)
Death of a Salesman (1949)
Incident at Vichy (1964)
The Man Who Had All the Luck (1944)
A Memory of Two Mondays (1955)
The Misfits (screenplay, 1961)
The Price (1968)
A View from the Bridge (1955)

ODETS, CLIFFORD

Awake and Sing! (1933)
The Big Knife (1949)
Clash by Night (1941)
The Country Girl (1950)
The Flowering Peach (1954)
Golden Boy (1937)
Night Music (1940)
Paradise Lost (1936)
Rocket to the Moon (1938)
Waiting for Lefty (1935)

O'NEILL, EUGENE

Ah Wilderness! (1933)
All God's Chillun Got Wings (1924)

The Ancient Mariner (1924)
Anna Christie (1921)
Bound East for Cardiff (1916)
Days without End (1934)
Desire under the Elms (1924)
The Dreamy Kid (1919)
Dynamo (1929)
The Emperor Jones (1920)
The First Man (1922)
The Fountain (1925)
The Great God Brown (1926)
The Hairy Ape (1922)
Hughie (written 1940–41, produced 1958 Stockholm, 1964 New York)
The Iceman Cometh (written 1939, produced 1946)
'Ile (1917)
In the Zone (1917)
Lazarus Laughed (1928)
Long Day's Journey into Night (written 1940–41, produced 1956)
The Long Voyage Home (1917)
Marco Millions (1928)
A Moon for the Misbegotten (written 1941–43, produced 1953 Stockholm, 1957 New York)
The Moon of the Caribbees (1918)
More Stately Mansions (written 1936–39, produced 1962 Stockholm, 1967 New York)
Mourning Becomes Electra (1931)
Strange Interlude (1928)
Thirst (1916)
A Touch of the Poet (written 1935–39, produced 1957 Stockholm, 1958 New York)

WILDER, THORNTON

The Alcestiad (1955, under the title *A Life in the Sun*)
The Angel That Troubled the Waters (collection of playlets, published 1928)
The Happy Journey from Trenton to Camden (1931)
The Long Christmas Dinner (1931)
The Matchmaker (1954)
The Merchant of Yonkers (1938)
Our Town (1938)
Pullman Car Hiawatha (published 1931)
The Skin of Our Teeth (1942)
The Trumpet Shall Sound (published 1920, produced 1926)

WILLIAMS, TENNESSEE

Baby Doll (screenplay, 1956; based on two short plays: *27 Wagons Full of Cotton*, published 1945, produced 1955, and *The Long Stay Cut Short; or, The Unsatisfactory Supper*, published 1948)

Battle of Angels (1940; early version of *Orpheus Descending*)

Camino Real (1953; revision of *Ten Blocks on the Camino Real*, unproduced)

Cat on a Hot Tin Roof (1955)

The Glass Menagerie (1944)

The Gnädiges Fräulein (see *Slapstick Tragedy*)

I Rise in Flame, Cried the Phoenix (written 1941, published 1951, produced 1959)

In the Bar of a Tokyo Hotel (1969)

Kingdom of Earth (published title of *The Seven Descents of Myrtle*, 1968; revised and shortened version produced under title *Kingdom of Earth*, 1975)

The Milk Train Doesn't Stop Here Anymore (1962)

The Night of the Iguana (1961)

Orpheus Descending (1957; reworking of *Battle of Angels*)

Out Cry (1971; revised version, 1973; earlier version entitled *The Two-Character Play*, 1967; further revision also entitled *The Two-Character Play*, 1975)

Period of Adjustment (1959)

The Red Devil Battery Sign (1975)

The Rose Tattoo (1951)

The Seven Descents of Myrtle (1968; published under title *Kingdom of Earth*)

Slapstick Tragedy (1966; two one-act plays: *The Mutilated* and *The Gnädiges Fräulein*)

Small Craft Warnings (1972)

A Streetcar Named Desire (1947)

Suddenly Last Summer (1958; produced on double bill with *Something Unspoken* under joint title *Garden District*)

Summer and Smoke (1947; revised as *Eccentricities of a Nightingale*, 1964)

Sweet Bird of Youth (1959)

Vieux Carré (1977)

British and Irish

BEHAN, BRENDAN

The Hostage (1958)

The Quare Fellow (1954)

Richard's Cork Leg (1972)

BOND, EDWARD

Bingo (1973)
Black Mass (1970)
The Bundle (1978)
Early Morning (1968)
The Fool (1975)
Lear (1971)
Narrow Road to the Deep North (1968)
Passion (1971)
The Pope's Wedding (1962)
Restoration (1981)
Saved (1965)
The Sea (1973)
The Woman (1978)
The Worlds (1981)

COWARD, NOEL

Bitter-Sweet (1929)
Blithe Spirit (1941)
Cavalcade (1931)
Conversation Piece (1934)
Design for Living (1933)
Hay Fever (1925)
I'll Leave It to You (1920)
Present Laughter (1939)
Private Lives (1930)
Quadrille (1952)
Sail Away (1961)
A Song at Twilight (part of *Suite in Three Keys*, 1966)
Suite in Three Keys (1966)
This Was a Man (1926)
Tonight at 8:30 (1935)
The Vortex (1924)
The Young Idea (1922)

ELIOT, T. S.

The Cocktail Party (1949)
The Confidential Clerk (1953)
The Elder Statesman (1958)
The Family Reunion (published 1939)
Murder in the Cathedral (1935)

The Rock (1934)
Sweeney Agonistes (published 1932)

GALSWORTHY, JOHN

The Eldest Son (1912)
Joy (1907)
Justice (1910)
The Little Dream (1911)
The Little Man (1915)
Loyalties (1922)
The Mob (1914)
The Pigeon (1912)
The Silver Box (1906)
The Skin Game (1920)
Strife (1909)
Windows (1922)

O'CASEY, SEAN

Behind the Green Curtain (1962)
The Bishop's Bonfire (1955)
Cock-a-Doodle Dandy (1949)
The Drums of Father Ned (1959)
Juno and the Paycock (1924)
Oak Leaves and Lavender (1947)
The Plough and the Stars (1926)
Purple Dust (1943)
Red Roses for Me (1943)
The Shadow of a Gunman (1923)
The Star Turns Red (1940)
The Silver Tassie (1929)
Within the Gates (1934)

OSBORNE, JOHN

A Bond Honoured (1966)
The Entertainer (1957)
Epitaph for George Dillon, with Anthony Creighton (1957)
The Hotel in Amsterdam (1968)
Inadmissible Evidence (1965)
Look Back in Anger (1956)
Luther (1961)
A Patriot for Me (1965)

Plays for England: The Blood of the Bambergs and *Under Plain Cover* (1962)
Time Present (1968)
Watch It Come Down (1975)
West of Suez (1971)
The World of Paul Slickey (1959)

PINTER, HAROLD

The Basement (television play, 1967)
Betrayal (1978)
The Birthday Party (1958)
The Caretaker (1960)
The Collection (television play, 1961)
The Dumb Waiter (1960)
The Dwarfs (radio play, 1960)
Family Voices (1981)
The Homecoming (1965)
Landscape (1969)
The Lover (television play, 1963)
No Man's Land (1975)
Old Times (1971)
The Room (1957)
Silence (1969)
A Slight Ache (radio play, 1959)
Tea Party (television play, 1965)

SHAW, BERNARD

Androcles and the Lion (1912 in German, 1913 in English)
The Apple Cart (1929)
Arms and the Man (1894)
Back to Methuselah (1922)
Buoyant Billions (1948 in German, 1949 in English)
Caesar and Cleopatra (written 1898, produced 1906)
Candida (written 1895, produced 1897)
Captain Brassbound's Conversion (1900)
The Devil's Disciple (1897)
The Doctor's Dilemma (1906)
Farfetched Fables (written 1948, produced 1950)
Getting Married (1908)
Heartbreak House (1920)
In Good King Charles's Golden Days (1939)
John Bull's Other Island (1904)
Major Barbara (1905)
Man and Superman (1905)

The Man of Destiny (1897)
The Millionairess (1936)
Misalliance (1910)
Mrs. Warren's Profession (written 1893, produced 1902)
Passion, Poison and Petrifaction; or, The Fatal Gazogene (1905)
The Philanderer (written 1893, produced 1905)
Pygmalion (1913 in German, 1914 in English)
Saint Joan (1923)
The Shewing-up of Blanco Posnet (1909)
The Simpleton of the Unexpected Isles (1935)
Why She Would Not (written 1950; incomplete)
Widowers' Houses (1892)
You Never Can Tell (1899)

STOPPARD, TOM

After Magritte (1970)
Albert's Bridge (radio play, 1967)
Artist Descending a Staircase (radio play, 1972)
Dirty Linen and *New-Found-Land* (1976)
Dogg's Hamlet, Cahoot's Macbeth (1979)
Dogg's Our Pet (1971)
Enter a Free Man (1968)
The (15 Minute) Dogg's Troupe Hamlet (1976)
Every Good Boy Deserves Favour (1977)
If You're Glad I'll Be Frank (radio play, 1966)
Jumpers (1972)
Night and Day (1978)
Professional Foul (television play, 1977)
The Real Inspector Hound (1968)
Rosencrantz and Guildenstern Are Dead (1967)
Travesties (1974)
A Walk on the Water (television play, 1963)
Where Are They Now? (radio play, 1970)

STOREY, DAVID

The Changing Room (1971)
The Contractor (1969)
Cromwell (1973)
Early Days (1980)
The Farm (1973)
Home (1970)
In Celebration (1969)

Life Class (1975)
The Restoration of Arnold Middleton (1966)

SYNGE, JOHN MILLINGTON

Deirdre of the Sorrows (1910)
In the Shadow of the Glen (1903)
The Playboy of the Western World (1907)
Riders to the Sea (1904)
The Tinker's Wedding (1909)
The Well of the Saints (1905)
When the Moon Has Set (written 1901; unproduced)

WESKER, ARNOLD

Chicken Soup with Barley (1958)
Chips with Everything (1962)
The Four Seasons (1965)
The Friends (1970)
I'm Talking about Jerusalem (1960)
The Journalists (1977)
The Kitchen (1959)
The Old Ones (1972)
Roots (1959)
Their Very Own and Golden City (1966)

WILDE, OSCAR

The Duchess of Padua (published 1883, produced in New York 1891 under the
    title *Guido Ferranti*)
An Ideal Husband (1895)
The Importance of Being Earnest (1895)
Lady Windermere's Fan (1892)
Salomé (written 1891, banned from London stage 1892, published in French
    1893, published in English 1894, produced in Paris 1896)
Vera; or, The Nihilists (1883)

YEATS, WILLIAM BUTLER
(Dates for Yeats's plays are of publication.)

At the Hawk's Well (1917)
Calvary (1920)

The Cat and the Moon (1926)
Cathleen Ni Houlihan (1902)
The Countess Cathleen (1892)
The Death of Cuchulain (1939)
Deirdre (1907)
The Dreaming of the Bones (1919)
Fighting the Waves (prose version of *The Only Jealousy of Emer;* produced
    1929, published 1934 in *Wheels and Butterflies*)
A Full Moon in March (1935)
The Green Helmet (1910)
The Herne's Egg (1938)
The Hour-Glass (1914)
The Island of Statues (1885)
The King of the Great Clock Tower (1935)
The King's Threshold (1904)
The Land of Heart's Desire (1894)
Mosada (1886)
On Baile's Strand (1904)
The Only Jealousy of Emer (1919)
The Player Queen (1922)
Purgatory (1939)
The Resurrection (1931)
The Shadowy Waters (1911)
The Unicorn from the Stars (1908)
Where There Is Nothing (1902)
The Words upon the Window-Pane (1934)

German, Austrian, and Swiss

BRECHT, BERTOLT

Baal (*Baal*, 1923): *Baal*, tr. William E. Smith and Ralph Manheim, in *Collected Plays*, Vol. 1 (New York, 1971)

The Caucasian Chalk Circle (*Der kaukasische Kreidekreis*, 1941): *The Caucasian Chalk Circle*, tr. Ralph Manheim, in *Collected Plays*, Vol. 7 (New York, 1974)

The Didactic Play of Baden (*Das Badener Lehrstück vom Einverständnis*, 1929): *The Didactic Play of Baden: On Consent*, tr. Lee Baxandall, in *Tulane Drama Review*, May 1960

Drums in the Night (*Trommeln in der Nacht*, 1922): *Drums in the Night*, tr. William E. Smith and Ralph Manheim, in *Collected Plays*, Vol. 1 (New York, 1971)

Edward II (*Das Leben Eduards des Zweiten von England*, 1924): *The Life of Edward the Second of England*, tr. William E. Smith and Ralph Manheim, in *Collected Plays*, Vol. 1 (New York, 1971)

The Exception and the Rule (*Die Ausnahme und die Regel*, written 1930, performed 1947): *The Exception and the Rule*, tr. Eric Bentley, in *The Jewish Wife, and Other Short Plays* (New York, 1965)

Fear and Misery of the Third Reich (*Furcht und Elend des Dritten Reiches*, 1945): *The Private Life of the Master Race*, tr. Eric Bentley (New York, 1944)

Galileo (*Leben des Galilei*, 1943): *Life of Galileo*, tr. Wolfgang Sauerlander and Ralph Manheim, in *Collected Plays*, Vol. 5 (New York, 1972)

The Good Woman of Setzuan (*Der gute Mensch von Sezuan*, 1943): *The Good Person of Szechwan*, tr. Ralph Manheim, in *Collected Plays*, Vol. 6 (New York, 1976)

In the Jungle of Cities (*Im Dickicht der Städte*, 1923): *In the Jungle of Cities*, tr. Gerhard Nellhaus, in *Collected Plays*, Vol. 1 (New York, 1971)

A Man's a Man (*Mann ist Mann*, 1926): *A Man's a Man*, tr. Eric Bentley, in *Seven Plays* (New York, 1961)

The Measures Taken (*Die Maßnahme*, 1930): *The Measures Taken*, tr. Eric Bentley, in *The Jewish Wife, and Other Short Plays* (New York, 1965)

The Mother (*Die Mutter*, 1932): *The Mother*, tr. Lee Baxandall (New York, 1965)

Mother Courage (*Mutter Courage und ihre Kinder*, 1941): *Mother Courage and Her Children*, tr. Ralph Manheim, in *Collected Plays*, Vol. 5 (New York, 1972)

The Rise and Fall of the City of Mahagonny (*Aufstieg und Fall der Stadt Mahagonny*, 1930): *The Rise and Fall of the City of Mahagonny*, tr. W. H. Auden and Chester Kallman (Boston, 1976)

The Roundheads and the Peakheads (*Die Rundköpfe und die Spitzköpfe*, 1936): *Roundheads and Peakheads*, tr. N. Goold-Verschoyle, in *Jungle of Cities, and Other Plays* (New York, 1966)

Saint Joan of the Stockyards (*Die heilige Johanna der Schlachthöfe*, written 1929–1931, produced 1959): *Saint Joan of the Stockyards*, tr. Frank Jones, in *Seven Plays* (New York, 1961)

Schweyk in the Second World War (*Schweik im Zweiten Weltkrieg*, written 1943, produced 1958): *Schweyk in the Second World War*, tr. Max Knight and Joseph Fabry, in *Collected Plays*, Vol. 7 (New York, 1974)

The Threepenny Opera (*Die Dreigroschenoper*, 1928): *The Threepenny Opera*, tr. Eric Bentley and Desmond I. Vesey, in *Plays*, Vol. 1 (London, 1960)

DÜRRENMATT, FRIEDRICH

An Angel Comes to Babylon (*Ein Engel kommt nach Babylon*, 1953): *An Angel Comes to Babylon*, tr. William McElwee, in *Four Plays* (New York, 1965)

The Blind Man (*Der Blinde*, 1948)

The Conformer (*Der Mitmacher*, 1973)

The Double (*Der Doppelgänger*, 1960)

Frank V, Opera of a Private Bank (*Frank der Fünfte: Oper einer Privatbank*, 1959)

It Is Written (*Es steht geschrieben*, 1947)

King John (*König Johann*, 1968)

The Marriage of Mr. Mississippi (*Die Ehe des Herrn Mississippi*, 1952): *The Marriage of Mr. Mississippi*, tr. Michael Bullock (New York, 1965)

The Meteor (*Der Meteor*, 1966): *The Meteor*, tr. James Kirkup (London, 1973)

The Physicists (*Die Physiker*, 1962): *The Physicists*, tr. James Kirkup, in *Four Plays* (New York, Grove, 1965)

Portrait of a Planet (*Portrat eines Planeten*, 1970)

Romulus the Great (*Romulus der Große*, 1949): *Romulus the Great*, tr. Gerhard Nellhaus, in *Four Plays* (New York, 1965)

Traps (*Die Panne*, 1956): *Traps*, tr. Richard and Clara Winston (New York, 1960)

The Visit of the Old Lady (*Der Besuch der alten Dame*, 1956): *The Visit*, tr. Patrick Bowles (New York, 1962)

FRISCH, MAX

Andorra (*Andorra*, 1961): *Andorra*, tr. Michael Bullock (New York, 1964)

As the War Came to an End (*Als der Krieg zu Ende war*, 1949): *When the War Was Over*, tr. James L. Rosenberg, in *Three Plays* (New York, 1967)

Biedermann and the Firebugs (*Biedermann und die Brandstifter*, 1958): *The Fire Raisers*, tr. Michael Bullock, in *Three Plays* (London, 1962)

Biography: A Game (*Biografie: Ein Spiel*, 1967): *Biography: A Game*, tr. Michael Bullock, in *Four Plays* (London, 1969)

The Chinese Wall (*Die Chinesische Mauer*, 1947; rev. version, 1955): *The Chinese Wall*, tr. James L. Rosenberg (New York, 1961)

Count Öderland (*Graf Öderland*, 1951): *Count Oederland*, tr. Michael Bullock, in *Three Plays* (London, 1962)

Don Juan; or, The Love of Geometry (*Don Juan; oder, Die Liebe zur Geometrie*, 1953): *Don Juan; or, The Love of Geometry*, tr. James L. Rosenberg, in *Three Plays* (New York, 1967)

The Great Rage of Philip Hotz (*Die grosse Wut des Philipp Hotz*, 1958): *The Great Rage of Philip Hotz*, tr. James L. Rosenberg, in *Three Plays* (New York, 1967)

Now They Are Singing Again (*Nun singen sie wieder*, 1946)

Santa Cruz (*Santa Cruz*, 1947)

Triptych (*Triptychon*, 1978): *Triptych*, tr. Geoffrey Skelton (New York, 1981)

HACKS, PETER

Amphitryon (*Amphitryon*, 1968)

The Battle of Lobositz (*Die Schlacht bei Lobositz*, 1956)

Beautiful Helen (*Die schöne Helena*, 1964)

The Chapbook of Duke Ernest; or, The Hero and His Retinue (*Das Volksbuch vom Herzog Ernst; oder, Der Held und sein Gefolge*, 1967)
Inauguration of the Indic Age (*Die Eröffnung des indischen Zeitalters*, 1955)
Margarete in Aix (*Margarete in Aix*, 1969)
The Miller of Sanssouci (*Der Müller von Sanssouci*, 1958)
Moritz Tassow (*Moritz Tassow*, 1965)
Omphale (*Omphale*, 1970)
Peace (*Der Frieden*, 1962)
Polly; or, The Battle at Bluewater Creek (*Polly; oder, Die Bataille am Blue-water-Creek*, 1965)
Worries and Power (*Die Sorgen und die Macht*, 1960)

HANDKE, PETER

Abusing the Audience (*Publikumsbeschimpfung*, 1966): *Offending the Audience*, tr. Michael Roloff, in *Kaspar, and Other Plays* (New York, 1969)
Calling for Help (*Hilferufe*, 1967): *Calling for Help*, tr. Michael Roloff, in *The Ride across Lake Constance, and Other Plays* (New York, 1976)
Kaspar (*Kaspar*, 1968): *Kaspar*, tr. Michael Roloff, in *Kaspar, and Other Plays* (New York, 1969)
The Fools Are Dying Out (*Die Unvernünftigen sterben aus*, 1974): *They Are Dying Out*, tr. Michael Roloff, in *The Ride across Lake Constance, and Other Plays* (New York, 1976)
Prophecy (*Weissagung*, 1966): *Prophecy*, tr. Michael Roloff, in *The Ride across Lake Constance, and Other Plays* (New York, 1976)
The Ride across Lake Constance (*Der Ritt über den Bodensee*, 1971): *The Ride across Lake Constance*, tr. Michael Roloff, in *The Ride across Lake Constance, and Other Plays* (New York, 1976)
Self-Accusation (*Selbstbezichtigung*, 1966): *Self-Accusation*, tr. Michael Roloff, in *Kaspar, and Other Plays* (New York, 1969)
The Ward Wants to Be Guardian (*Das Mündel will Vormund sein*, 1969): *My Foot My Tutor*, tr. Michael Roloff, in *The Ride across Lake Constance, and Other Plays* (New York, 1976)

HAUPTMANN, GERHART

And Pippa Dances (*Und Pippa tanzt*, 1906): *And Pippa Dances*, tr. Sarah Tracy Barrows, in *The Dramatic Works*, Vol. 5 (New York, 1915)
Atrides Tetralogy: Agamemnon's Death, Electra, Iphigenia in Aulis, Iphigenia in Delphi (*Agamemnons Tod*, 1947; *Elektra*, 1947; *Iphigenie in Aulis*, 1943; *Iphigenie in Delphi*, 1941)
The Beaver Coat (*Der Biberpelz*, 1893): *The Beaver Coat*, tr. Horst Frenz and Miles Waggoner, in *Three Plays* (New York, 1977)
Before Dawn (*Vor Sonnenaufgang*, 1889): *Before Daybreak*, tr. Peter Bauland (Chapel Hill, N.C., 1978)

Before Sunset (*Vor Sonnenuntergang,* 1932)

Colleague Crampton (*Kollege Crampton,* 1892): *Colleague Crampton,* tr. Roy Temple House, in *The Dramatic Works,* Vol. 3 (New York, 1914)

The Coming of Peace (*Das Friedensfest,* 1890): *The Reconciliation,* tr. Roy Temple House, in *The Dramatic Works,* Vol. 3 (New York, 1914)

Dorothea Angermann (*Dorothea Angermann,* 1926)

Drayman Henschel (*Fuhrmann Henschel,* 1898): *Drayman Henschel,* tr. Ludwig Lewisohn, in *The Dramatic Works,* Vol. 2 (New York, 1913)

Florian Geyer (*Florian Geyer,* 1896): *Florian Geyer,* tr. Bayard Quincy Morgan, in *The Dramatic Works,* Vol. 9 (New York, 1929)

Hannele (*Hannele,* 1893; as of 1896: *Hanneles Himmelfahrt*): *Hannele: A Dream Poem in Two Acts,* tr. Horst Frenz and Miles Waggoner, in *Three Plays* (New York, 1977)

Indipohdi (*Indipohdi,* 1920): *Indipohdi,* tr. Willa and Edwin Muir, in *The Dramatic Works,* Vol. 8 (New York, 1924)

Lonely Lives (*Einsame Menschen,* 1891): *Lonely Lives,* tr. Mary Morison, in *The Dramatic Works,* Vol. 3 (New York, 1914)

Magnus Garbe (*Magnus Garbe,* written 1915, published 1943)

The Rats (*Die Ratten,* 1911): *The Rats,* tr. Ludwig Lewisohn, in *The Dramatic Works,* Vol. 2 (New York, 1913)

Rose Bernd (*Rose Bernd,* 1903): *Rose Bernd,* tr. Ludwig Lewisohn, in *The Dramatic Works,* Vol. 2 (New York, 1913)

The Sunken Bell (*Die versunkene Glocke,* 1896): *The Sunken Bell,* tr. Charles H. Meltzer, in *The Dramatic Works,* Vol. 4 (New York, 1914)

The Weavers (*Die Weber,* 1892): *The Weavers,* tr. Horst Frenz and Miles Waggoner, in *Three Plays* (New York, 1977)

HOCHHUTH, ROLF

The Deputy (*Der Stellvertreter,* 1963): *The Deputy,* tr. Richard and Clara Winston (New York, 1964)

Guerrillas (*Guerillas,* 1970)

Lysistrata and NATO (*Lysistrate und die Nato,* 1974)

The Midwife (*Die Hebamme,* 1972)

Soldiers (*Soldaten: Nekrolog auf Genf,* 1967): *Soldiers: An Obituary for Geneva,* tr. Robert David MacDonald (New York, 1968)

HOFMANNSTHAL, HUGO VON

The Adventurer and the Singer (*Der Abenteurer und die Sängerin,* 1899)

Adriadne on Naxos (*Ariadne auf Naxos,* 1912): *Ariadne on Naxos,* tr. Alfred Kalisch (Berlin, 1922)

Cristina's Trip Home (*Cristinas Heimreise,* 1910): *Cristina's Journey Home,* tr. Roy Temple House (Boston, 1916)

Death and the Fool (*Der Tor und der Tod*, 1893): *Death and the Fool*, tr. Alfred Schwarz, in *Three Plays* (Detroit, 1966)

The Death of Titian (*Der Tod des Tizian*, 1892): *The Death of Titian*, tr. John Heard, Jr. (Boston, 1914)

The Difficult Man (*Der Schwierige*, 1920): *The Difficult Man*, tr. Willa Muir, in *Selected Plays and Libretti* (New York, 1963)

Electra (*Elektra*, 1903): *Electra*, tr. Alfred Schwarz, in *Three Plays* (Detroit, 1966)

Everyman (*Jedermann*, 1911): *The Play of Everyman*, tr. George Sterling and Richard Ordynski (San Francisco, 1917)

Florindo (*Florindo*, 1923)

The Incorruptible Man (*Der Unbestechliche*, 1923)

The Little Theater of the World (*Das kleine Welttheater*, 1903): *The Little Theater of the World; or, The Fortunate Ones*, tr. Michael Hamburger, in *Poems and Verse Plays* (New York, 1961)

Oedipus and the Sphinx (*Oedipus und die Sphinx*, 1906): *Oedipus and the Sphinx*, tr. Gertrude Schoenbohm, in Martin Kalich et al., eds., *Oedipus: Myth and Drama* (New York, 1968)

The Cavalier of the Rose (*Der Rosenkavalier*, 1911): *The Cavalier of the Rose*, tr. Christopher Holme, in *Selected Plays and Libretti* (New York, 1963)

The Salzburg Great Theater of the World (*Das Salzburger große Welttheater*, 1922): *The Salzburg Great Theater of the World*, tr. Vernon Watkins, in *Selected Plays and Libretti* (New York, 1963)

Silvia in the Star (*Silvia im "Stern,"* 1907)

The Tower (*Der Turm*, 1902; later versions 1923, 1925, 1927): *The Tower*, tr. Alfred Schwarz, in *Three Plays* (Detroit, 1966)

Venice Preserved (*Das gerettete Venedig*, 1905): *Venice Preserved*, tr. Elisabeth Walter (Boston, 1915)

The Woman without a Shadow (*Die Frau ohne Schatten*, 1916): *The Woman without a Shadow*, tr. anon., libretto included with recording of opera, Decca Record Co. (London, 1957)

Yesterday (*Gestern*, 1891)

KAISER, GEORG

Alkibiades Saved (*Der gerettete Alkibiades*, 1919): *Alkibiades Saved*, tr. Bayard Quincy Morgan, in Walter H. Sokel, ed., *An Anthology of German Expressionist Drama* (New York, 1963)

Bellerophon (*Bellerophon*, 1944)

The Burghers of Calais (*Die Bürger von Calais*, 1914): *The Burghers of Calais*, tr. J. M. Ritchie and Rex Last, in *Georg Kaiser: Five Plays* (London, 1971)

The Coral (*Die Koralle*, 1917): *The Coral*, tr. Winifred Katzin (New York, 1963)

Europa (*Europa*, 1915)

From Morn to Midnight (*Von morgens bis mitternachts*, 1912): *From Morn to*

Midnight, tr. Ulrich Weisstein, in O. G. and L. Brockett, eds., *Plays for the Theatre: An Anthology of World Drama* (New York, 1927)

The Fire in the Opera House (*Der Brand im Opernhaus*, 1919): *Fire in the Opera House*, tr. Winifred Katzin, in *Eight European Plays* (New York, 1927)

Gas (*Gas*, 1918): *Gas I*, tr. Hermann Scheffauer (New York, 1957)

Gas II (*Gas: Zweiter Teil*, 1919): *Gas II*, tr. Winifred Katzin (New York, 1963)

Hell Road Earth (*Hölle Weg Erde*, 1919)

The Leatherheads (*Die Lederköpfe*, 1928)

Pygmalion (*Pygmalion*, written 1944, performed 1953)

The Sacrifice of a Woman (*Das Frauenopfer*, 1918)

The Soldier Tanaka (*Der Soldat Tanaka*, 1940)

Twice Amphitryon (*Zweimal Amphitryon*, 1943)

SCHNITZLER, ARTHUR

Anatol (*Anatol*, 1893): *Anatol*, Eng. version by Harley Granville-Barker, in Eric Bentley, ed., *From the Modern Repertoire: Series Three* (Bloomington, Ind., 1956)

The Call of Life (*Der Ruf des Lebens*, 1906)

The Green Cockatoo (*Der grüne Kakadu*, 1899): *The Green Cockatoo*, tr. H. B. Samuel, in *The Green Cockatoo, and Other Plays* (Chicago, 1913)

Hands Around (*Der Reigen*, 1920): *La Ronde: Ten Dialogues*, tr. Eric Bentley, in Eric Bentley, ed., *The Modern Theatre*, Vol. 2 (Garden City, N.Y., 1955)

Light-o'-Love (*Liebelei*, 1895): *Light-o'-Love: A Drama in Three Acts*, tr. Bayard Quincy Morgan, in E. B. Watson and W. B. Pressey, eds., *Contemporary Drama: European Drama* (New York, 1932)

Living Hours (*Lebendige Stunden*, 1902): *Living Hours*, tr. Grace I. Colbron, in T. H. Dickinson, ed., *Chief Contemporary Dramatists*, 2nd series (Boston, 1921)

The Lonely Way (*Der einsame Weg*, 1904): *The Lonely Way*, tr. E. A. Bjorkman, in *Three Plays* (New York, 1915)

Professor Bernhardi (*Professor Bernhardi*, 1912): *Professor Bernhardi*, tr. Hetty Landstone (New York, 1928)

The Vast Domain (*Das weite Land*, 1911)

The Veil of Beatrice (*Der Schleier der Beatrice*, 1900)

The Walk to the Pond (*Der Gang zum Weiher*, 1931)

WEDEKIND, FRANK

Castle Wetterstein (*Schloß Wetterstein*, 1912): *Castle Wetterstein*, tr. Frances Fawcett and Stephen Spender, in *Five Tragedies of Sex* (London, 1952)

Censorship (*Die Zensur*, 1908)

Dance of Death (*Der Totentanz*, 1906; republished as *Tod und Teufel*, 1909):

Death and the Devil, tr. Carl Richard Mueller, in *The Lulu Plays* (Greenwich, Conn., 1967)

The Earth Spirit (*Der Erdgeist,* 1895): *Earth Spirit,* tr. Carl Richard Mueller, in *The Lulu Plays* (Greenwich, Conn., 1967)

Franziska (*Franziska,* 1912)

Hidalla; also known as Karl Hetmann, the Pygmy Giant (*Hidalla; oder, Sein und Haben,* 1904; republished as: *Karl Hetmann, der Zwergriese,* 1911)

King Nicolo (*So ist das Leben,* 1902; republished as *König Nicolo; oder, So ist das Leben,* 1911): *King Nicolo; or, Such Is Life,* tr. Martin Esslin, in Martin Esslin, ed., *The Genius of the German Theater* (New York, 1968)

Lulu: *See* The Earth Spirit, Pandora's Box

The Marquis of Keith (*Der Marquis von Keith,* 1901): *The Marquis of Keith,* tr. Carl Richard Mueller, in Robert W. Corrigan, ed., *Masterpieces of the Modern German Theatre* (New York, 1967)

Music (*Musik,* 1908)

Pandora's Box (*Die Büchse der Pandora,* 1904): *Pandora's Box,* tr. Carl Richard Mueller, in *The Lulu Plays* (Greenwich, Conn., 1967)

Samson: *See* Simson

Simson; or, Shame and Jealousy (*Simson oder Scham und Eifersucht,* 1914)

Spring's Awakening (*Frühlings Erwachen,* 1891): *Spring's Awakening,* tr. Eric Bentley, in Eric Bentley, ed., *The Modern Theatre,* Vol. 6 (Garden City, N.Y., 1960)

The Tenor (*Der Kammersänger,* 1899): *The Tenor,* tr. André Tridon, in John Gassner, ed., *A Treasury of the Theatre,* rev. ed., Vol. 2 (New York, 1951)

WEISS, PETER

Hölderlin (*Hölderlin,* 1971)

The Investigation (*Die Ermittlung,* 1965): *The Investigation,* tr. John Swan and Ulu Grosbard (New York, 1966)

Marat/Sade (*Die Verfolgung und Ermordung Jean Paul Marats dargestellt durch die Schauspielgruppe des Hospizes zu Charenton unter Anleitung des Herrn de Sade,* 1964): *The Persecution and Assassination of Jean-Paul Marat as Performed by the Inmates of the Asylum of Charenton under the Direction of the Marquis de Sade,* tr. Geoffrey Skelton, with verse adaptation by Adrian Mitchell (New York, 1965)

Song of the Lusitanian Bogey (*Gesang vom Lusitanischen Popanz,* 1967): *Song of the Lusitanian Bogey,* tr. Lee Baxandall, in *Two Plays by Peter Weiss* (New York, 1970)

Trotsky in Exile (*Trotzki im Exil,* 1970): *Trotsky in Exile,* tr. Geoffrey Skelton (New York, 1972)

Viet Nam Discourse (*Viet Nam Diskurs über die Vorgeschichte und den Verlauf des lang andauernden Befreiungskrieges in Viet Nam als Beispiel für die Notwendigkeit des bewaffneten Kampfes der Unterdrückten gegen ihre*

Unterdrücker sowie über die Versuche der Vereinigten Staaten von Amerika die Grundlagen der Revolution zu vernichten, 1968): *Discourse on the Progress of the Prolonged War of Liberation in Viet Nam and the Events Leading Up to It as Illustration of the Necessity for Armed Resistance against Oppression and on the Attempts of the United States of America to Destroy the Foundations of Revolution,* tr. Geoffrey Skelton, in *Two Plays by Peter Weiss* (New York, 1970)

ZUCKMAYER, CARL

Barbara Blomberg (*Barbara Blomberg,* 1949)
The Captain of Köpenick (*Der Hauptmann von Köpenick,* 1931): *The Captain of Köpenick,* tr. Carl Richard Mueller, in George E. Wellwarth, ed., *German Drama between the Wars* (New York, 1974)
The Clock Strikes One (*Die Uhr schlägt eins,* 1961)
The Cold Light (*Kaltes Licht,* 1955)
The Devil's General (*Des Teufels General,* 1946): *The Devil's General,* tr. Ingrid G. and William F. Gilbert, in H. M. Block and R. G. Shedd, eds., *Masters of Modern Drama* (New York, 1962)
Herbert Engelmann (*Herbert Engelmann,* 1952 [an adaptation of Gerhart Hauptmann's unfinished *Herbert Engelmann,* 1924])
Katharina Knie (*Katharina Knie,* 1928)
The Life of Horace A. W. Tabor (*Das Leben des Horace A. W. Tabor,* 1967)
The Merry Vineyard (*Der fröhliche Weinberg,* 1925)
Pankraz Awakens (*Pankraz erwacht,* 1925)
Schinderhannes (*Schinderhannes,* 1927)
The Song in the Fiery Furnace (*Des Gesang im Feuerofen,* 1950)
Ulla Winblad; or, Music and Life of Carl Michael Bellmann (*Ulla Winblad; oder, Musik und Leben des Carl Michael Bellmann,* 1938; 2nd version, 1953)

COPYRIGHT ACKNOWLEDGMENTS

The editors and publisher are grateful to the following individuals, literary agencies, periodicals, newspapers, and book publishers for permission to include excerpts from copyrighted material. Every effort has been made to trace and acknowledge all copyright owners. If any acknowledgment has been inadvertently omitted, the necessary correction will be made in the next printing.

JACOB H. ADLER. From *Lillian Hellman*.

AKADEMIE DER KÜNSTE, BERLIN. From Alfred Kerr, *Gesammelte Schriften*. Permission of the Alfred-Kerr Archiv (Schnitzler).

EDWARD ALBEE. From Introduction to *Three Plays by Noel Coward*.

THE AMERICAN ASSOCIATION OF TEACHERS OF GERMAN, INC. From articles by Renata Berg-Pan on Brecht; Brigitte L. Bradley on Frisch; Margarete N. Deschner on Dürrenmatt; Walter E. Glaettli on Frisch; Sol Liptzin on Schnitzler; Ian C. Loram on Zuckmayer; Gideon Shunami on Weiss in *German Quarterly*.

THE AMERICAN MERCURY. From article by George Jean Nathan on O'Neill.

JOHN ARDEN. From essay in *Sean O'Casey: A Collection of Critical Essays*.

EDWARD ARNOLD. From E. M. Forster, *Two Cheers for Democracy* (Eliot); essays by Clifford Leech on Wesker in *Contemporary Theatre*, John Russell Brown and Bernard Harris, eds.; Eric Mottram on Miller in *American Theatre*, John Russell Brown and Bernard Harris, eds.

ASSOCIATED UNIVERSITY PRESSES. From Bernard Benstock, *Sean O'Casey;* Victor L. Cahn, *Beyond Absurdity* (Stoppard); Leonard Chabrowe, *Ritual and Pathos: The Theater of O'Neill;* Richard Scharine, *The Plays of Edward Bond;* from article by Emil Roy on Albee in *Bucknell Review*.

ASSOCIATED BOOK PUBLISHERS LTD. From Tony Coult, *The Plays of Edward Bond* (pub. by Eyre, Methuen); Martin Esslin, *The Peopled Wound: The Plays of Harold Pinter*, pub. by Methuen & Co. Ltd.; Martin Esslin, *The Theatre of the Absurd*, pub. by Eyre & Spottiswood (Albee, Frisch); Hugh F. Garten, *Modern German Drama*, pub. by Methuen & Co. Ltd. (Kaiser); article by Penelope Gilliatt on Behan in *The Encore Reader*, Charles Marowitz, Tom Milne, and Owen Hale, eds.; Malcolm Hay and Philip Roberts, *Bond: A Study of His Plays*, pub. by Eyre, Methuen; Urs Jenny, *Dürrenmatt: A Study of His Plays*, pub. by Methuen & Co. Ltd.; Cedric Hentschel, *The Byronic Teuton*, pub. by Methuen & Co. Ltd. (Hofmannsthal); Margery Morgan, *The Shavian Play-*

ground, pub. by Methuen & Co. Ltd.; John Russell Taylor, *Anger and After,* pub. by Methuen & Co. Ltd. (Osborne).

ATHENEUM PUBLISHERS, INC. From Wayne Andrews, *Siegfried's Curse: The German Journey from Nietzsche to Hesse,* copyright © 1972 by Wayne Andrews (Hauptmann); Eric Bentley, *In Search of Theatre,* copyright © 1947, 1948, 1950, 1951, 1953, 1981 by Eric Bentley (O'Neill, Yeats); Eric Bentley, *What Is Theatre?* (Incorporating *The Dramatic Event*) and *Other Reviews 1944–1967,* copyright © 1954, 1966, 1968, 1982 by Eric Bentley (O'Casey, Williams). Reprinted by permission of Atheneum Publishers, Inc.

MRS. BERND BAB. From Bernd Bab, *Die Chronik des deutschen Dramas* (Zuckmayer).

D. BARLOW, ESQ. From article on Frisch in *German Life and Letters.*

BARNES & NOBLE BOOKS. From Alan Bird, *The Plays of Oscar Wilde;* Andrew Parkin, *The Dramatic Imagination of W. B. Yeats;* Weldon Thornton, *J. M. Synge and the Western Mind;* C. E. Williams, *The Broken Eagle* (Hofmannsthal).

BARRIE & JENKINS.. From Joseph Chiari, *Landmarks of Contemporary Drama* (Frisch, Hochhuth).

BASIC BOOKS, INC. From Harry T. Moore, *Twentieth-Century German Literature,* copyright © 1967 by Harry T. Moore (Frisch); Roy Pascal, *From Naturalism to Expressionism: German Literature and Society 1880–1918,* copyright © 1973 by Roy Pascal (Hauptmann).

BELL & HYMAN LIMITED. From essays by Laurence Kitchin on Wesker, Katharine J. Worth on Osborne in *Experimental Drama,* William A. Armstrong, ed.

ERNEST BENN LIMITED. From Ernest A. Boyd, *Appreciations and Depreciations* (Shaw).

ERIC BENTLEY. From *Bernard Shaw.*

CHARLES A. BERST. From *Bernard Shaw and the Art of Drama.*

C. W. E. BIGSBY. From *Edward Albee: A Collection of Critical Essays.*

MICHAEL BILLINGTON. From article on Coward in *Plays and Players.*

A. C. BLACK LTD., LONDON. From Michael Anderson, *Anger and Detachment* (Osborne); Michael Patterson, *German Theatre Today* (Hacks, Handke).

BASIL BLACKWELL PUBLISHER LTD. For generous permission to quote from several articles in *German Life and Letters.*

THE BOBBS MERRILL CO., INC. From essay by Elia Kazan on Williams in *Directors on Directing,* Toby Cole and Helen Krich Chinoy, eds.; Robin Skelton, *The Writings of J. M. Synge;* Gerald Weales, *Clifford Odets: Playwright.*

DIDIER ERUDITION. From Françoise Derré, *L'œuvre d'Arthur Schnitzler;* articles by Marius Cauvin on Frisch; A. Fuchs on Hofmannsthal; Michel Vanhelleputte on Hochhuth, in *Études germaniques.*

DENNIS DOBSON BOOKS LTD. From Harry Slochower, *No Voice Is Wholly Lost* (Schnitzler).

THE DOLMEN PRESS. From David R. Clark, *W. B. Yeats and the Theatre of Desolate Reality;* essay by David H. Greene in *J. M. Synge: Centenary Papers,* Maurice Harmon, ed.; Ann Saddlemyer, *J. M. Synge and Modern Comedy.*

DOUBLEDAY & CO., INC. From Martin Esslin, *Brecht: The Man and His Work,* copyright © 1959, 1960 by Martin Esslin; Martin Esslin, *The Theatre of the Absurd,* copyright © 1961 by Martin Esslin (Albee, Frisch); Martin Esslin, *The Peopled Wound: The Plays of Harold Pinter,* copyright © 1970 by Martin Esslin; Martin Esslin, *Reflections,* copyright © 1967, 1969 by Martin Esslin. Reprinted by permission of Doubleday & Co., Inc.

DOVER PUBLICATIONS INC. From Barrett H. Clark, *Eugene O'Neill: The Man and His Plays.*

FLORENCE W. DOWNER, EXECUTRIX. From article by Alan S. Downer on O'Neill in *Theatre Arts;* essay by Malcolm Goldstein on Odets in *American Drama and Its Critics,* Alan S. Downer, ed.

DRAMA. From articles by John Peter on Bond; John Russell Taylor on Bond.

DRAMA BOOK SPECIALISTS (PUBLISHERS). From Catharine Hughes, *Plays, Politics, and Polemics* (Hochhuth); Michael E. Rutenberg, *Edward Albee: Playwright in Protest.*

THE DRAMA REVIEW. From articles by Lee Baxandall on Albee; Jacques Barzun on O'Casey; Tom F. Driver on Miller, O'Neill; Bernard Dukore on Pinter; Barnard Hewitt on Wilder; Adolf D. Klarmann on Dürrenmatt, Charles Marowitz on Osborne; Ronald Peacock on Kaiser; Henry Popkin on Williams; Gordon Rogoff on Williams; Richard Schechner on Pinter; Carl Weber on Brecht.

DUKE UNIVERSITY PRESS. From Steven H. Gale, *Butter's Going Up: A Critical Analysis of Harold Pinter's Work,* copyright © 1977, Duke University Press; article by Homer E. Woodbridge on Coward in *South Atlantic Quarterly.*

EDUCATIONAL THEATRE JOURNAL. From articles by Robert W. Corrigan on Wilder; Helene Keyssar-Franke on Stoppard; Rita Stein on Storey; Eugene Waith on O'Neill; Gordon M. Wickstrom on Behan.

RICHARD ELLMANN. From *Yeats, the Man and the Masks.*

ENCOUNTER. From articles by John Weightman on Bond, Osborne, Pinter, Stoppard.

THE ENGLISH ASSOCIATION. From essay by J. A. Snowden on O'Casey in *Essays & Studies.*

Esquire. From article by Diana Trilling on Albee.

Essays in Criticism. From article by Norman Podhoretz on Synge.

Everett/Edwards, Inc. From Michael J. Mendelsohn, *Clifford Odets: Humane Dramatist*.

Farrar, Straus & Giroux, Inc. From Richard Gilman, *The Making of Modern Drama*, copyright © 1972, 1973, 1974 by Richard Gilman, reprinted with the permission of Farrar, Straus & Giroux, Inc. (Handke); Harry Slochower, *No Voice Is Wholly Lost*, copyright © 1945 by Harry Slochower, copyright renewed 1972 by Harry Slochower, reprinted by permission of Farrar, Straus & Giroux, Inc. (Schnitzler); John Russell Taylor, *The Rise and Fall of the Well-Made Play*, copyright © 1967 by John Russell Taylor (Coward); John Russell Taylor, *The Second Wave*, copyright © 1971 by John Russell Taylor (Stoppard, Storey); John Russell Taylor, *The Angry Theatre*, copyright © 1962, 1969 by John Russell Tayor (Osborne), reprinted with the permission of Hill & Wang (now a division of Farrar, Straus & Giroux, Inc.); excerpts adapted and abridged from *The Triple Thinkers* by Edmund Wilson, copyright © 1938, 1948 by Edmund Wilson, copyright renewed by 1956 and 1971 by Edmund Wilson and 1976 by Elena Wilson, reprinted by permission of Farrar, Straus & Giroux, Inc. (O'Neill).

Librairie Arthème Fayard. From André Antoine, *"Mes souvenirs" sur le Théâtre-Libre* (Hauptmann).

Francis Fergusson. From article on O'Neill in *The Hound & Horn*.

Wilhelm Fink Verlag. From Franz Norbert Mennemeier, *Modernes deutsches Drama* (Hacks); articles by Rolf Kieser on Frisch; Herbert Lederer on Zuckmayer; Steven P. Scher on Kaiser in *Theatrum Mundi*, Edward R. Haymes, ed.

James W. Flannery. From *W. B. Yeats and the Idea of a Theatre*.

Fontana Paperbacks. From Denis Donoghue, *William Butler Yeats*.

Forum for Modern Language Studies. From article by James Trainer on Hochhuth.

Francke Verlag. From letter of Georg Brandes in *Georg Brandes und Arthur Schnitzler: Ein Briefwechsel* (Schnitzler); Ernst Robert Curtius, *Kritische Essays zur europäischen Literatur* (Hofmannsthal); Otto Mann, *B. B.: Maß oder Mythos?* (Brecht); essays by Otto Mann on Zuckmayer and by Karl Pestalozzi on Dürrenmatt in *Deutsche Literatur im zwanzigsten Jahrhundert*, Hermann Friedmann and Otto Mann, eds.

Frankfurter Hefte. From article by Michael Buselmeier on Handke.

The Freeman. From review by Hugo von Hofmannsthal on O'Neill.

HARCOURT BRACE JOVANOVICH, INC. From essay by Hannah Arendt on Brecht in *Men in Dark Times,* originally published in *The New Yorker;* Eric Bentley, *The Playwright as Thinker,* copyright © 1946, 1974 by Eric Bentley (Brecht, Wedekind, Wilde); Max Frisch, *Sketchbook, 1946–1949,* copyright © 1950 by Suhrkamp Verlag, Frankfurt am Main, English translation copyright © 1977 by Max Frisch and Geoffrey Skelton, abridged and reprinted by permission of Harcourt Brace Jovanovich, Inc.

HARPER & ROW, PUBLISHERS, INC. From M. C. Kuner, *Thornton Wilder: The Bright and the Dark,* published by Thomas Y. Crowell, copyright © 1972 by Mildred Kuner; J. B. Priestley, *Thoughts in the Wilderness* (Shaw); H. F. Redlich, *Alban Berg: The Man and His Music,* published by Abelard-Schuman, copyright © 1957 by Harper & Row, Publishers, Inc. (Wedekind); Anton Chekhov, Letter to Vsevolod Meyerhold, Oct. 1899, in *Letters of Anton Chekhov,* translated by Michael Henry Heim, Introduction by Simon Karlinsky, copyright © 1973 by Harper & Row, Publishers, Inc. (Hauptmann).

SIR RUPERT HART-DAVIS. From Max Beerbohm, *Around Theatres* (Galsworthy); articles by Max Beerbohm on Shaw, Wilde, and Yeats in *The Saturday Review* (London).

HARVARD UNIVERSITY PRESS. From Edwin A. Engel, *The Haunted Heroes of Eugene O'Neill;* Helen Hennessy Vendler, *Yeats's "Vision" and the Later Plays.*

HAWTHORNE BOOKS, INC. From Archibald Henderson, *Bernard Shaw: Playboy and Prophet,* copyright © 1932 by D. Appleton & Co.; copyright © 1956, 1958 by Archibald Henderson.

RONALD HAYMAN. From *John Osborne; Playback* (Storey).

ROBERT B. HEILMAN. From *The Iceman, the Arsonist, and the Troubled Agent* (Frisch); article on Williams in *Southern Review.*

WILLIAM HEINEMANN LTD. From Sheridan Morley, *A Talent to Amuse* (Coward); J. B. Priestley, *Thoughts in the Wilderness* (Shaw).

HELDREF PUBLICATIONS. From articles by Horst Frenz on Kaiser; I. George March on Schnitzler; O. F. Theis on Wedekind; Elizabeth Walter on Hofmannsthal in *Poet Lore;* Hans Hoeller on Weiss in *Symposium.*

HENNESSEY & INGALLS, INC. From John Fuegi, *The Essential Brecht,* University of Southern California Studies in Comparative Literature, Volume 4, available from the publisher: Hennessey & Ingalls, Inc., 11833 Wilshire Blvd., Los Angeles, CA 90025.

HODDER & STOUGHTON LTD. From essays by W. F. Mainland in *Hauptmann Centenary Lectures,* K. G. Knight and F. Norman, eds.; by Irving Wardle in *The Genius of Shaw: A Symposium,* Michael Holroyd, ed.

HOLT, RINEHART & WINSTON, INC. From Richard Burton, *Bernard Shaw;* A. R. Fulton, *Drama and Theatre,* A. R. Fulton, ed. (Coward); John Gassner, *The-*

KINDLER VERLAG GMBH. From essay by Konrad Franke on Hacks in *Die Literatur der Deutschen Demokratischen Republik*, Konrad Franke, ed.

ALFRED KRÖNER VERLAG. From essay by Rolf Röhmer on Hacks in *Literatur der DDR*, Jürgen Geerdts, ed.

VERLAG PETER LANG. From John Milfull, *From Baal to Keuner* (Brecht).

VICTOR LANGE. From *Modern German Literature: 1870–1940* (Hauptmann, Wedekind).

LITTLE, BROWN AND COMPANY. From Anita Block, *The Changing World in Plays and Theatre* (Schnitzler); Robert Brustein, *The Theatre of Revolt* (O'Neill); Alfred Kazin, *Starting Out in the Thirties* (Odets).

DR. JAN VAN LOEWEN LTD. From Terence Rattigan's Introduction to *Theatrical Companion to Noel Coward* by Mander and Mitchenson.

LONDON MAGAZINE. From articles by Colin McInnes on Behan; John Whiting on Coward.

LONDON MANAGEMENT. From articles by Max Beerbohm on Shaw, Wilde, Yeats in *The Saturday Review* (London).

LONGMAN GROUP LIMITED. From A. C. Ward, *Bernard Shaw*.

THE STERLING LORD AGENCY, INC. From Benjamin Nelson, *Arthur Miller: Portrait of a Playwright;* Hugh Kenner, *The Invisible Poet: T. S. Eliot*.

LOUISIANA STATE UNIVERSITY PRESS. From article by C. L. Barber on Eliot in *Southern Review;* essay by F. E. Coenen on Dürrenmatt in *Studies in German Literature*, Carl Hammer, Jr., ed.

MARY MCCARTHY. From *Sights and Spectacles* (Wilder).

EDWARD MCINNES. From article on Hauptmann in *German Life and Letters*

DAVID MCKAY COMPANY, INC. From Benjamin Nelson, *Arthur Miller: Portrait of a Playwright;* Richard Dana Skinner, *Eugene O'Neill: A Poet's Quest;* Stanley Weintraub, *Journey to Heartbreak: The Crucible Years of Bernard Shaw 1914–1918*.

MACMILLAN PUBLISHERS LTD. From Bernard Bergonzi, *T. S. Eliot;* Nicholas Grene, *Synge: A Critical Study of the Plays;* essays by P. R. Higgins on Yeats in *The Irish Theatre*, Lennox Robinson, ed.; Denis Johnston in *Sean O'Casey: Modern Judgements*, Ronald Ayling, ed.; Lennox Robinson on Yeats in *Scattering Branches: Tributes to the Memory of W. B. Yeats*, Stephen Gwynn, ed.; Rodney Shewan, *Oscar Wilde: Art and Egotism;* Walter Starkie on O'Casey in *The Irish Theatre*, Lennox Robinson, ed.; Katharine Worth on Eliot in *Eliot in Perspective*, Graham Martin, ed.

MACMILLAN PUBLISHING CO., INC. From Bernard Bergonzi, *T. S. Eliot;* Herbert

LOUIS D. RUBIN. From article by Jacob Adler on Williams in *South*.

MICHAEL E. RUTENBERG. From *Edward Albee: Playwright in Protest*.

RUTGERS UNIVERSITY PRESS. From Doris Falk, *Eugene O'Neill and the Tragic Tension*, copyright © 1958 by Rutgers State University of New Jersey.

ANN SADDLEMYER. From *J. M. Synge and Modern Comedy*.

ST. MARTIN'S PRESS. From Robert Hogan, *The Experiments of Sean O'Casey;* Colbert Kearney, *The Writings of Brendan Behan*.

SATURDAY REVIEW. From articles by John Mason Brown on Hellman; Henry Hewes on Williams.

SCARECROW PRESS, INC. From Harold Cantor, *Clifford Odets: Playwright-Poet*, copyright © 1978 by Harold Cantor.

ERICH SCHMIDT VERLAG. From articles by Volker Canaris on Hacks and Gerhard Weiss on Hochhuth in *Deutsche Dichter der Gegenwart*, Benno von Wiese, ed.; William H. Rey on Schnitzler in *Deutsche Dichter der Moderne*, Benno von Wiese, ed.

VERLAG LAMBERT SCHNEIDER. From Martin Buber, *Briefwechsel aus sieben Jahrzehnten* (Hofmannsthal); Marjorie L. Hoover on Hacks in *Revolte und Experiment*, Wolfgang Paulsen, ed.

CARL E. SCHORSKE. From article on Schnitzler in *American Historical Review*.

CHARLES SCRIBNER'S SONS. From Edmund Fuller, *George Bernard Shaw;* Robert Lynd, *Old and New Masters* (Synge); Leon Schalit, *John Galsworthy: A Survey;* Anthony West's Introduction to *The Galsworthy Reader;* Stark Young, *Immortal Shadows* (Williams).

MARTIN SECKER & WARBURG LIMITED. From John Mander, *The Writer and Commitment* (Wesker).

SEMINAR. From articles by T. E. Alexander on Schnitzler; Henry Beissel on Hochhuth; Jerry Glenn on Hacks; R. W. Last on Kaiser; Hector Maclean on Wedekind; E. E. Murdaugh on Hochhuth; Gertrud Bauer Pickar on Frisch.

THE SEWANEE REVIEW. From articles by Nicola Chiaromonte on O'Neill; Francis Fergusson on Wilder; Ian Gregor on Wilde; Henry Popkin on Miller.

LEROY R. SHAW. From article on Kaiser in *Texas Studies in Literature and Language*.

SIMON & SCHUSTER, INC. From Max Beerbohm, *Around Theatres* (Galsworthy); Robert Brustein, *Seasons of Discontent* (Hochhuth); Frank Harris, *On Bernard Shaw*.

GROVER SMITH. From *T. S. Eliot's Poetry and Plays*.

Society of Authors. From Havelock Ellis, *From Marlowe to Shaw* (Shaw); article by G. B. Shaw on Wilde in *The Saturday Review* (London); G. B. Shaw, *How to Become a Music Critic*, Dan H. Laurence, ed., originally pub. by Hart-Davis, 1960 (Hofmannsthal).

Walter H. Sokel. From *German Expressionist Drama* (Brecht).

Southern Illinois University Press. From Morris Freedman, *American Drama in Social Context* (Miller); Morris Freedman, *The Moral Impulse* (Brecht); James R. Hollis, *Harold Pinter: The Poetics of Silence;* Charles R. Lyons, *Bertolt Brecht;* Anne Paolucci, *From Tension to Tonic: The Plays of Edward Albee;* Salvatore Quasimodo, *The Poet and the Politician* (Miller, Wilder, Williams); John Henry Raleigh, *The Plays of Eugene O'Neill;* Emil Roy, *British Drama since Shaw* (Wilde, Yeats); Mardi Valgemae, *Accelerated Grimace* (O'Neill); Homer E. Woodbridge, *George Bernard Shaw: Creative Artist.*

Southwest Review. From article by Abraham Rothberg, "East End, West End: Arnold Wesker," in *Southwest Review.*

The Spectator. From article by Peter Jenkins on Storey.

Stanford University Press. From Arnold Silver, *Bernard Shaw: The Darker Side;* Walter H. Sokel, *The Writer in Extremis* (Kaiser, Wedekind).

Lyle Stuart, Inc. From Sheila Huftel, *Arthur Miller: The Burning Glass;* Nancy M. Tischler, *Tennessee Williams: Rebellious Puritan.*

Arrigo Subiotto. From "Bertolt Brecht's Adaptations for the Berliner Ensemble," in *Modern Language Review.*

Helen Swediuk-Cheyne. From article on Zuckmayer (signed Helen Hodgson) in *German Life and Letters.*

Syracuse University Press. From Richard Fallis, *The Irish Renaissance,* copyright © 1977 by Syracuse University Press (Synge); Peter Bauland, *The Hooded Eagle* (Hochhuth); article by Edward Diller on Dürrenmatt in *Symposium.*

Thames and Hudson Ltd. From Robin Skelton, *The Writings of J. M. Synge.*

TQ Publications. From articles by Arthur Arnold on Bond; Martin Esslin on Bond; Peter Hall on Pinter in *Theatre Quarterly.*

Times Newspapers Ltd. From articles by Richard Ellmann on Stoppard; Edwin Muir on Hofmannsthal; Irving Wardle on Wesker.

James Trainer. From article on Hochhuth's *Der Stellvertreter* in *Forum for Modern Language Studies.*

Diana Trilling. From article on Albee, first published in *Esquire* magazine.

George C. Tunstall. From article on Kaiser in *Journal of English and Germanic Philology.*

INDEX TO CRITICS

Names of critics are cited on the pages given.